USING
WORD 5.1
FOR THE MAC
SPECIAL EDITION

MW01612463

Using Word® 5.1
for the Mac®

Special Edition

Bryan Pfaffenberger

Using Word 5.1 for the Mac, Special Edition

Copyright © 1993 by Que® Corporation.

Library of Congress Catalog No.: 92-63327

ISBN: 1-56529-143-3

96   95   94   93   4   3   2   1

Interpretation of the printing code: the rightmost double-digit number is the year of the book's printing; the rightmost single-digit number, the number of the book's printing. For example, a printing code of 93-1 shows that the first printing of the book occurred in 1993.

Screen reproductions in this book were created with Exposure Pro from Baseline Publishing, Memphis, Tennessee.

Using Word 5.1 for the Mac, Special Edition can be used with Macintosh versions 5.0 and 5.1 of Microsoft Word.

Publisher: Lloyd J. Short

Associate Publisher: Rick Ranucci

Publishing Plan Manager: Thomas H. Bennett

Book Designer: Scott Cook

Production Team: Debra Adams, Claudia Bell, Julie Brown, Jodie Cantwell, Paula Carroll, Laurie Casey, Michelle Cleary, Lisa Daughtery, Denny Hager, Phil Kitchel, Bob LaRoche, Caroline Roop, Carrie Roth, Linda Seifert, Susan Shepherd, Marcella Thompson

Dedication

For Suzanne

Title Manager

Shelley O'Hara

Product Director

Kathie-Jo Arnoff

Production Editor

Kathy Simpson

Editors

Elsa Bell
Sara Black
Jane Cramer
Lorna Gentry
Heather Northrup
Susan Pink
Sharon Spicklemire

Acquisitions Editor

Patty Brooks

Technical Editor

Kathy Wood

Formatter

Jill Stanley

Composed in ITC Garamond
and MCPdigital by Que Corporation

About the Author

Bryan Pfaffenberger

ryan Pfaffenberger is the author of several best-selling books on personal computing, including *Que's Computer User's Dictionary* and *Harvard Graphics Quick Reference* (Que). A Word and Macintosh user since 1984, Bryan teaches technical writing, computer applications, and the sociology of computing at the University of Virginia's School of Engineering and Applied Science.

Trademark Acknowledgments

Acknowledgments

Writing a 1,000-plus page book is no picnic, and many people labored with me on this much-expanded edition of *Using Word for the Mac*.

I'd like to thank Title Manager Shelley O'Hara, whose suggestions helped me make this book more readable for first-time users.

Very special thanks are due to Technical Editor Kathy Wood, who combed through this book with unusual thoroughness.

Que's professional editorial staff is without peer in this industry, and an impressive team of talented editors left no sentence unturned in an effort to ensure the highest possible quality on every page: Production Editor Kathy Simpson; Product Director Kathie-Jo Arnoff; and copy editors Elsa Bell, Sara Black, Jane Cramer, Lorna Gentry, Heather Northrup, Susan Pink, and Sharon Spicklemire.

Contents at a Glance

Appendixes

Table of Contents

I Getting Started with Word 5.1

II   Word 5.1 Fundamentals

6   Creating Text   157

8 Editing Text 207

III   Using Advanced Formatting Techniques

14   Formatting with Styles 425

16 Numbering and Sorting Lines, Lists, and Paragraphs 495

20 Positioning Text and Graphics 583

IV Creating Professional Documents

21 Dividing a Document into Sections 607

22 Organizing Documents with Outlining 619

VI Creating Office Applications

Appendixes

A Using Word 5.1 with PowerBooks 987

B Using PostScript 993

C Keyboard Shortcuts 1005

Index 1021

Introduction

Do you want to use your Macintosh as something more than an electronic typewriter? You must, because you're using a copy of Microsoft Word, one of the most powerful, elegant, and useful word processing programs ever conceived. Throughout the world, high-powered writers consider the Macintosh version of Word to be the weapon of choice when it comes to knock-down, drag-out writing deadlines—the kind about which editors say, "We want it *yesterday*." Take it from me; I've written more than 35 books, the lion's share in *my* program of choice: Microsoft Word for the Mac.

But don't think we're going to begin in the stratosphere. If you're looking for a book that can teach you the fundamentals of Word, you came to the right place. The introductory chapters of *Using Word 5.1 for the Mac,* Special Edition are designed to assist beginning users. These chapters constitute an easy, step-by-step introduction to the program that doesn't assume *any* previous knowledge of computers, Macintoshes, word processing, or Word.

But this book takes you far beyond the fundamentals. If you want to get the most out of Microsoft Word for the Mac, you're holding the key: this book is chock-full of the tips, techniques, and approaches to Word mastery that professional writers use every day. Every page was written to show you how to apply Word *productively* in business and professional environments. Whether you're using Word to write proposals or poems, novels or newsletters, this book gives you the knowledge you need to crank out beautiful, high-quality documents faster than ever before.

USING
WORD 5.1
FOR THE MAC
SPECIAL EDITION

This book's unique features—notes, tips, cautions, and a quick-review section at the end of each chapter—help you learn to apply the program to your work. Moreover, this book's design, beginning with the fundamentals and going back over them as your mastery builds, is in line with the best practices of corporate training programs. *Using Word 5.1 for the Mac,* Special Edition is the ideal tool to help you learn and apply Microsoft Word.

How This Book Is Organized

This book covers Word versions 5.0 and 5.1 for the Macintosh. Versions 5.0 and 5.1 are practically identical, save for a few new features in Version 5.1 that are clearly flagged in this book. If you're using Word 5.0, you will find complete coverage of that version of the program. If you're using Word 5.1, you will find additional coverage of all the new features for multimedia, graphics, portable computing, and more.

If you're using Word 5.0, about the only difference you will notice between your computer screen and this book's illustrations is your screen's lack of the Toolbar, a new feature of Version 5.1. You still can access all the commands available in the Toolbar, however. To use this book with Version 5.0, simply skip the sections marked with the Word 5.1 icon.

This book also highlights special Word features that become available when you use Word with Apple's System 7. These sections are marked with a System 7 icon. You still can use Word with System 6, but some features (such as Microsoft Graph) will be unavailable. In addition, the Open and Save dialog boxes will look slightly different from the ones pictured in this book.

Part I, "Getting Started with Word 5.1," helps you build a solid foundation of Word knowledge. To master Microsoft Word, you should read all these chapters in sequence.

- Chapter 1, "Reviewing Mac Basics and Installing Word 5.1," walks you through the process of installing Word on your Macintosh. This chapter provides a great deal of information that isn't in the Word manual—information that you need in order to install Word for the best possible results. Also included in this chapter is a review of Macintosh basics.

- Chapter 2, "Exploring Word 5.1," introduces the on-screen personality of Word. In this chapter, you learn how to use the various parts of the screen, how to choose commands, and how to use the mouse with Word.

- Chapter 3, "Quick Start: Creating a Business Letter," walks you through the fundamentals of using Word. You follow a keystroke-by-keystroke tutorial that emphasizes high-productivity tricks and techniques from the start.

- Chapter 4, "Understanding Word's Workplace," goes back over the Word screen in detail. You learn the many ways you can choose commands, move the insertion point, scroll the screen, and display your documents.

- Chapter 5, "Managing Documents and Files," discusses all the knowledge you need to safeguard your work. You learn how to save files at intervals you specify, find elusive files, and exchange documents with colleagues who are using other word processing programs.

Part II, "Word 5.1 Fundamentals," presents the foundations of Word mastery. Every reader should read every chapter in this section.

- Chapter 6, "Creating Text," explores every aspect of the text-creation process, including controlling line breaks, using special characters, using hyphenation, and saving your work safely.

- Chapter 7, "Creating and Importing Graphics," shows you how to make full use of the Mac's graphics capabilities. You learn how to add diagrams and drawings to your text for effects that words alone could not produce.

- Chapter 8, "Editing Text," comprehensively surveys Word text-editing techniques. You fully explore the many keyboard and menu options you have for editing your documents.

- Chapter 9, "Formatting with Fonts and Character Styles," helps you build a solid foundation of character-formatting expertise. You learn how to choose text styles, positions, fonts, font sizes, and other formatting options.

- Chapter 10, "Formatting Paragraphs," continues building the foundation of your formatting knowledge, with the emphasis on paragraph formatting. In this chapter, you learn how to align, indent, and shape paragraphs.

- Chapter 11, "Formatting Pages," concludes the foundation of your formatting knowledge by covering the basics of page design with Word.

Introduction

- Chapter 12, "Checking Spelling and Grammar," thoroughly surveys Word's extensive proofing tools, including the Grammar utility, which can find many common usage, punctuation, and grammatical errors.

- Chapter 13, "Printing Documents," shows you how to get the most out of your printer and covers Word's many printing options in detail.

Part III, "Using Advanced Formatting Techniques," expands your knowledge of Word into the frontiers of desktop publishing, newsletter design, and technical writing. Read the chapters that are relevant to your professional writing needs.

- Chapter 14, "Formatting with Styles," introduces this important, high-productivity formatting technique, which every Word user can employ. You learn how to save the effort involved in choosing dozens or even hundreds of commands by developing a few styles.

- Chapter 15, "Creating Tables," explores Word's remarkable Table command, which enables you to create tables easily, without the hassle of setting tabs. You still can set all the tabs you want, but you surely will agree, after trying the Table command, that this feature is a blessing for anyone who types tables or lists. As you master the Table command, you will cut significantly—by as much as 50 percent, in typical cases—the time you need to spend fussing with table formatting.

- Chapter 16, "Numbering and Sorting Lines, Lists, and Paragraphs," explores Word's Renumber and Sort commands. You learn how you can number and sort items automatically. You don't have to alphabetize anything in your documents manually anymore; Word can do the job almost instantly.

- Chapter 17, "Using Borders and Shading," explores Word 5's improved Borders command, which enables you to add shading as well as lines and boxes.

- Chapter 18, "Creating Newspaper Columns," teaches you how to use Word to create attractive newsletters and other multiple-column documents.

- Chapter 19, "Adding Headers, Footers, and Footnotes," comprehensively surveys these features, which you need for a wide variety of documents.

- Chapter 20, "Positioning Text and Graphics," shows you how to use Word's Frame command, which enables you to position text and graphics on the page so that text flows around them. You also learn many useful document-design techniques.

Part IV, "Creating Professional Documents," covers the information professional and technical writers need as they seek to get the most out of Word.

- Chapter 21, "Dividing a Document into Sections," explores the uses of Word's Section command, which enables you to break your document into chapters that have their own headers, footers, footnotes, and page-number formats.

- Chapter 22, "Organizing Documents with Outlining," thoroughly surveys this important Word feature, which can help you keep your document well organized and help you plan it before writing. This chapter is for anyone who writes long complex documents, such as proposals, business reports, technical documentation, or dissertations. You learn how you can develop an outline structure that parallels the headings in your document and how Word dynamically updates this outline as you restructure your document. You even learn how you can restructure your entire document by making a few quick changes in the outline. If you have ever struggled with the organization of a complex document, Word offers a better way, which is explained in this chapter.

- Chapter 23, "Using Glossaries," reveals the mysteries of Word's glossaries, which you can use to store standard passages of text (called *boilerplate*). As you quickly discover, you don't need to type the same passage of text twice when you can store and retrieve often-used passages in glossaries. You learn how you can use Word's glossaries to create a comprehensive system for responding rapidly and consistently to business inquiry letters. The glossary feature is one of the greatest productivity-boosters revealed in this book.

- Chapter 24, "Creating Charts with Microsoft Graph," fully explores Word 5.1's new Microsoft Graph add-in program, which you can access if you're running System 7. You can use this surprisingly full-featured graphics program to add a huge variety of business and analytical graphs to your Word documents. What's more, you can open these graphs for editing purposes simply by double-clicking the graph that appears in your Word document.

- Chapter 25, "Using Math and Typing Equations," surveys Word 5's Equation Editor, which enables you to create mathematical formulas without using mathematical typesetting. This technique is so easy, you will know how to use it moments after you see the Equation Editor window on-screen. This chapter also covers Word's on-screen math feature, which enables you to add columns and rows of numbers quickly.

- Chapter 26, "Adding an Index and Table of Contents," is for anyone who prepares reports, proposals, or technical documents that will be reproduced directly from Word printouts. You learn about Word's outstanding indexing features, which you can use to code terms in your document so that Word automatically compiles those terms into a professional-looking index. If you have created an outline for your document, you also can generate a table of contents for your document by issuing one command.

- Chapter 27, "Working with Long Documents," details Word's File Series command, which enables you to link separate files and print them as though the files were one document.

Part V, "Creating Collaborative and Dynamic Documents," fully explores the exciting features of Word 5.0 and 5.1 that show how we will write in the next century. As current trends indicate, documents will be team efforts—and they will not be limited to one presentation medium or to one software program.

- Chapter 28, "Writing Collaboratively with Annotations," covers Word 5.1's new Text Annotations and Voice Annotations features. Both features enhance collaborative writing, in which an author's work is reviewed by one or more collaborators. You can use these features to incorporate collaborators' comments into Word documents for later review by the author.

- Chapter 29, "Playing Movies," explores Word's amazing multimedia capabilities. You learn how you can insert a movie into your Word document so that your readers can actually see how something is done.

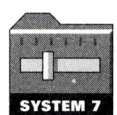

- Chapter 30, "Linking Data Dynamically," fully explores the use of Word's dynamic data-exchange capabilities under System 7, including linking, embedding, and Publish and Subscribe. If you're using System 6, this chapter still is worth reading because you can link documents with manual updating.

Part VI, "Creating Office Applications," is dedicated to the thousands of Word users who are slugging it out in offices every day. You will find plenty of information here to make your work faster and more pleasant.

■ Chapter 31, "Storing Addresses and Printing Envelopes," covers a feature that programmers would have invented long ago if they had worked clerical jobs or handled their own correspondence. This long-overdue feature makes storing addresses and printing envelopes a cinch.

■ Chapter 32, "Creating Form Letters," details the use of Word's Print Merge Helper, a feature that makes form-letter applications much easier. You learn how to create a mailing list and send form letters, taking full advantage of advanced features such as conditional merging.

■ Chapter 33, "Creating Business Forms," shows you how to unite Word's Border and Table capabilities to produce professional-looking business forms. You also learn how you can use Print Merge instructions to fill out a form on-screen and have Word calculate totals automatically.

■ Chapter 34, "Printing Mailing Labels," surveys the mysterious and irrational realm of printing mailing labels on a variety of printers. In this chapter, you learn how to print labels on a variety of Macintosh printers.

Part VII, "Customizing Word 5.1," surveys the knowledge you need to customize Word to your liking.

■ Chapter 35, "Customizing Menus and Keyboard Shortcuts," explores the program's Preferences options. You learn how to customize Word's menus and keyboards so that the commands you want are within easy reach.

■ Chapter 36, "Customizing Word's Toolbar," explores Word 5.1's new Toolbar feature and shows you how to display only the tools you want.

Three appendixes round out this book's treatment of Microsoft Word for the Macintosh.

■ Appendix A, "Using Word 5.1 with PowerBooks," explores the new 5.1 features that enhance Word's usefulness with Apple's new line of powerful notebook computers.

■ Appendix B, "Using PostScript," covers the use of this powerful, elegant page-description language in Word. Even if you don't know how to program, you will find useful information in this chapter for getting the most out of your PostScript printer.

■ Appendix C, "Keyboard Shortcuts," is a handy reference on Word's keyboard commands.

Introduction

A Word of Encouragement

If you're just getting started with Word, you may feel daunted by the program's complexity. But you will be surprised by how far you can advance by taking one step at a time. You're not a failure at personal computing if you don't understand some features right away. Remember, too, that you don't need to memorize long lists of commands and procedures. In this book, any procedure requiring more than a step or two is explained in a handy step-by-step format. Make your own index (or just dogear the pages) to highlight the procedures you think you will need to look up again, and keep this book by your computer.

Before you know it, Word will come naturally to you, even when you're using the program at its intermediate and advanced levels. As your knowledge of the program grows, you will learn how to customize Word so that it's truly an extension of your preferences and your ways of doing things.

All in all, this journey is well worth making, and it's my pleasure to be your guide.

PART

I

Getting Started with Word 5.1

Includes

Reviewing Mac Basics and Installing Word 5.1

Exploring Word 5.1

Quick Start: Creating a Business Letter

Understanding Word's Workplace

Managing Documents and Files

Reviewing Mac Basics and Installing Word 5.1

f you're reading this chapter, chances are that you have just obtained Word and you're about to install the program on your Macintosh. This chapter provides a quick overview of the installation process, including selecting a printer and installing the Word program files. The chapter also briefly reviews the basic Macintosh skills you need in order to use Word effectively.

If you already have installed Word and you're familiar with basic Macintosh skills, skip to Chapter 2, "Exploring Word 5.1."

NOTE

If you're installing Word on a PowerBook, see Appendix A for special installation instructions.

Reviewing Macintosh Skills

If you're new to the Macintosh, you should take some time to learn basic Macintosh skills. (A good way to acquire these skills is to use the lessons disk that comes with your Macintosh computer.)

USING
WORD 5.1
FOR THE MAC
SPECIAL EDITION

You should be able to perform five basic mouse procedures:

■ *Pointing.* Move the mouse pointer (an arrow) around on the screen by moving the mouse on the table.

■ *Clicking.* Point to the item you want to select and click the mouse button once. You often use clicking to select something, such as an icon or text, so that it is highlighted on-screen.

■ *Double-clicking.* Point to the item you want to select and click the mouse button twice in rapid succession. Double-clicking is more "powerful" than clicking, in that it does more than just clicking. For example, double-clicking an icon selects it and opens it all at once.

■ *Shift-clicking.* Hold down the Shift key while clicking something. You use Shift-clicking to select large amounts of text or to make more items available in menus.

■ *Dragging.* Hold down the mouse button while moving the mouse. You use dragging to move selected objects as well as to select text.

In addition, you should be able to identify and use all the standard Macintosh window features, shown in figure 1.1.

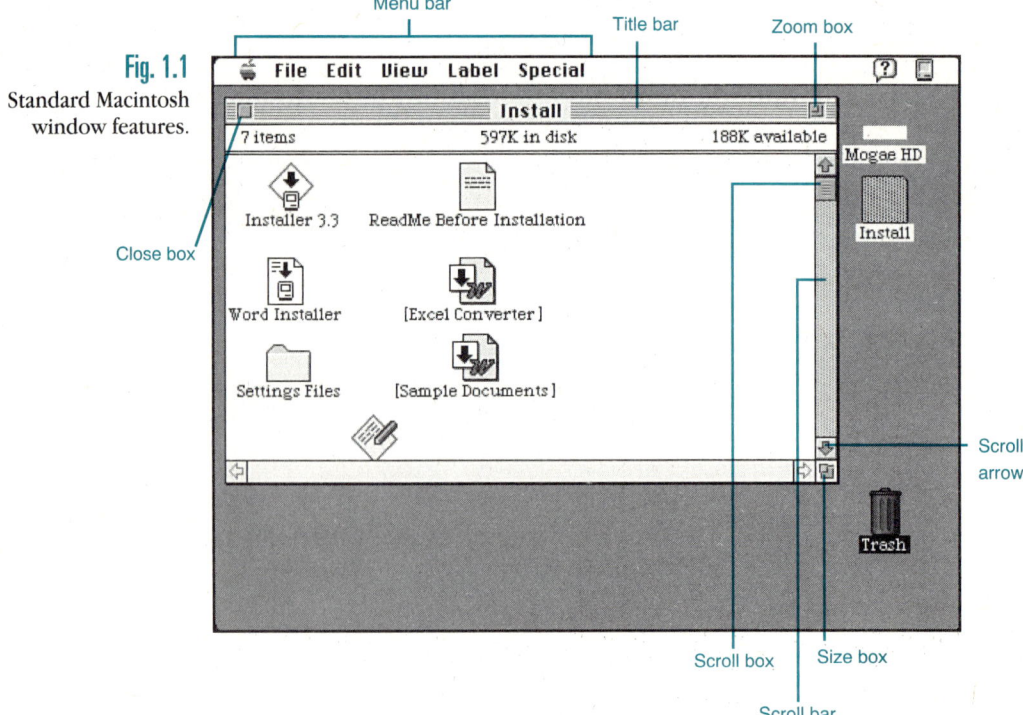

Fig. 1.1
Standard Macintosh window features.

Following is a brief overview of the standard Macintosh window features and what they do:

Menu bar. This bar shows the names of the available menus. Click a menu name to open a menu. To choose a command or option, drag down until you highlight the command or option and then release the mouse button.

Title bar. This bar shows the name of the window and indicates whether the window is active. An *active window* has a band of six lines across the title bar. An *inactive window* has a plain title bar.

Scroll arrow. Click a scroll arrow to scroll the window up or down one line at a time.

Scroll box. Drag a scroll box to scroll the window up or down. To display the beginning of a document, drag the box to the top of the scroll bar. To display the end of a document, drag the box to the bottom of the scroll bar.

Scroll bar. Click the scroll bar to scroll the window one screen at a time. If you click below the scroll box, you scroll down; if you click above the scroll box, you scroll up.

Size box. Drag the size box to change the size of a window.

Zoom box. Click the zoom box to expand the window to full size; click again to restore the window to its previous size.

Close box. Click the close box to close the window.

Good Finder skills are essential to effective use of Word. (The Finder is the Macintosh program that helps you manage your disks and files.) Make sure that you know how to perform all the Finder skills listed in the following chart:

Task	Technique
Open a disk	Insert the disk and, if necessary, double-click the disk to see the disk directory window.
Choose a command	Click the menu name and hold down the mouse button. Then drag down until you highlight the command you want and release the mouse button. The command blinks to confirm your choice.

continues

Chapter 1

Reviewing Mac Basics and Installing Word 5.1

Task	Technique
Open a folder	Double-click the folder. (You also can select the folder icon and choose Open from the File menu or press ⌘-O.)
Create a new folder	Choose New Folder from the File menu or press ⌘-N, and then type a name for the folder.
Close a folder	Click the close box. (You also can choose Close Window from the File menu or press ⌘-W.)
Activate a window	Click anywhere on an inactive window (one that doesn't have lines in its title bar).
Scroll a window	Click a scroll arrow, drag a scroll box, or click next to a scroll box.
Size a window	Click the size box and drag, while holding down the mouse button, until the window is the size you want. Then release the mouse button for the window to assume that shape.
Restore previous size	Click the zoom box.
Move a window	Drag the window's title bar.
Close a window	Click the close box. (You also can choose Close Window from the File menu or press ⌘-W.)
Start a program	Double-click the program icon.
Select more than one icon	Shift-click the icons or, if the icons are next to one another, drag the pointer outside the icons until a dotted line surrounds them.
Select text	Drag over the text to highlight it.
Eject a disk	Drag the disk icon to the Trash icon.
Discard unwanted files	Drag the file icon into the Trash icon and then choose Empty Trash from the Special menu.

Understanding Word's Requirements

To run Microsoft Word 5.1, you need a recent or upgraded Macintosh (Plus, Classic, Classic II, Macintosh II, LC, SE, SE-30, PowerBook,

Part I

Getting Started with Word 5.1

Portable, or Quadra) equipped as follows:

- Hard disk drive with at least 7.5M of free disk space

- 800K or 1.44M disk drive

- System 6 (6.0.2 through 6.0.8, with Finder 6.1 or later) or, preferably, System 7

- 1M of memory with System 6 (2M is required to use MultiFinder or the grammar checker) or 2M of memory with System 7 (3M if you want to use the Toolbar).

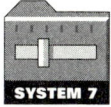

If you're running System 7, you will not get good performance unless you have installed a minimum of 4M of memory in your Macintosh. You can obtain a memory upgrade from your Macintosh dealer.

Some Word 5.1 features require the following equipment or software, which your computer may not have:

- *Microsoft Graph.* This plug-in module (PIM), a new feature of Word 5.1, requires System 7. Graph enables you to create business charts and graphs without leaving Word.

- *Voice annotations.* You can listen to voice annotations—brief recordings that are stored in an icon—on any Macintosh. To create voice annotations, you need a Mac equipped with a microphone (such as a Macintosh LC) or a sound board (such as Voice Impact).

- *Movies.* To view movies within your Word documents, you must install Apple's QuickTime Extension and System 6.0.7 or System 7. Because movies require enormous amounts of disk space, you may want to equip your Macintosh with a CD-ROM disk drive if you plan to play movies frequently. To record your own movies, you need additional digital image-processing software.

If you're still shopping for a Macintosh, heed the advice of old computer hands: There's no such thing as enough memory. Using 4M of RAM is cutting it close, especially with System 7; 5M or more will help ensure that you don't see the inconvenient Word is low on memory message. Additionally, shop for a Mac that uses the 68030 or 68040 processor, either of which enables you to use part of your hard drive as an extension of memory.

As for hard drive capacity, remember this: If you think that a 40M hard disk is enough, you will be astonished by how quickly you fill the disk. Many Macintosh users say that a minimally equipped system these days has at least an 80M hard disk.

Using Word with System 7

Word does not require System 7; the program will run under System 6. If you currently have System 6, though, you should consider upgrading your Macintosh. The following System 7 features directly benefit Word users:

- *TrueType fonts.* These scalable fonts produce excellent results on any Macintosh printer. With TrueType, you don't need a PostScript laser printer to produce beautifully printed documents.

- *Balloon Help.* System 7's Help balloons, which look like the balloons in comic strips, can help you learn Word quickly.

- *Stationery.* With System 7, you can create template documents (called *stationery documents*) that contain generic versions of documents such as letters, reports, and proposals.

- *Object Linking and Embedding (OLE).* OLE enables you to create hot links when you copy information between Word documents or between a Word document and another OLE-capable application's documents. With a hot link, any change you make in the original document is automatically reflected in the copy.

- *Improved networking.* With System 7, you can share files over a network and also use Apple's new Publish and Subscribe capabilities for exchanging information.

Installing a Printer

To use a printer with your Macintosh, you first must use the *Chooser*—an option in the Apple menu—to tell your Macintosh which printer you're using. The Chooser installs a *printer resource file*, which contains the information your Macintosh needs in order to communicate with the printer you're using.

If you haven't already installed your printer, do so now, following the instructions given in this section. When you install Word, Word will recognize your printer, and the Installer will set its document formats accordingly.

Should you forget to install your printer before installing Word, you can install your printer later. Be sure, however, to choose Page Setup from Word's File menu so that Word will record the current printer settings.

 **NOTE** If you're using a Macintosh without a printer and plan to print your documents elsewhere, you still need to choose a printer with the Chooser. Word needs the information in the printer resource file in order to format your documents correctly.

To install your printer, follow these steps:

1. Connect your printer to your Macintosh, following the instructions in your printer's manual.

2. Turn on your printer.

3. Select Chooser from the Apple menu. The Chooser dialog box appears, as shown in figure 1.2.

Fig. 1.2
Chooser dialog box.

```
┌──────────────────────────── Chooser ──────────────────────────┐
│                                                                │
│   ┌─────────────────────────────┐ ┌──────────────────────────┐│
│   │   📁            🖨            ⇧ │ │                          ││
│   │ AppleShare  AppleTalk...geWriter│ │                         ││
│   │                             │ │                          ││
│   │   🖨            &             │ │                          ││
│   │ ImageWriter  LaserWriter     │ │                          ││
│   │                             │ │                          ││
│   │                             │ └──────────────────────────┘│
│   │                             │                             │
│   │                             │  ───────────────────────────│
│   │                             ⇩ │            ○ Active         │
│   └─────────────────────────────┘   AppleTalk  ◉ Inactive      │
│                                                         7.0    │
└────────────────────────────────────────────────────────────────┘
```

Printer icon

4. Click your printer's icon. You now see additional choices on the right side of the dialog box (see fig. 1.3).

5. In the Select a Port section of the dialog box, click the icon corresponding to the port you used to connect your printer to your Macintosh (the Phone port or the Printer port).

6. If your printer requires AppleTalk (check your printer manual), click the Active radio button in the AppleTalk section.

Fig. 1.3
Chooser dialog box with
additional options.

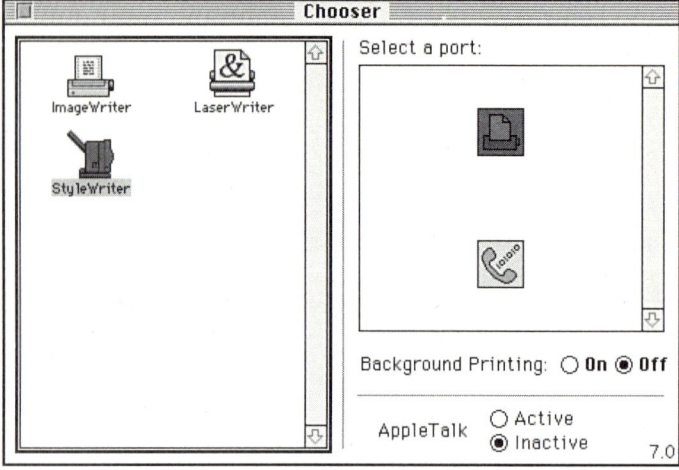

7. If you're using an Apple LaserWriter, or if you're using a
   LaserWriter or StyleWriter with System 7, choose On in the
   Background Printing section. This option enables you to keep
   working on-screen while your Macintosh prints a document.

8. To quit the Chooser, click the close box.

If you're using an ImageWriter or StyleWriter, you may want to upgrade
your printer. The printer you need depends on how you're going to use
your Macintosh. If you're a professional writer, you would be well
advised to use a high-speed laser printer—one that can crank out at least
eight pages per minute of plain text. If you want to print PostScript fonts
and graphics and to use desktop-publishing programs such as PageMaker
(Aldus Corporation), your laser printer should include PostScript
capabilities.

PostScript is a *page-description language*—a programming language that
enables your computer to send instructions to the printer. With
PostScript, you can achieve professional results in sophisticated desktop-
publishing projects. PostScript printers are expensive, however, because
they have a built-in computer that decodes the PostScript instructions.
(For more information, see Appendix B, "Using PostScript.")

If you don't plan to print PostScript fonts or graphics, you can get by
with a much less expensive non-PostScript laser printer that can use
System 7's new TrueType font technology. An example is Apple
Computer's attractively priced Personal LaserWriter LS.

You will learn more about TrueType later. For now, all you need to know is that TrueType fonts produce almost the same high quality that PostScript fonts do, but at a fraction of the cost, because the printer need not contain a computer to decode TrueType instructions. Your computer takes care of that job.

Installing Word 5.1

To install Word 5.1, you must use the Installer program that comes on the Word Install disk. You cannot simply copy the files to your Macintosh hard disk; the files on the Word disk are compressed so that the disks can be easily and inexpensively copied and distributed. Before you can use these files, the Installer program must unpack them.

You can choose one of the following installation procedures:

Easy Install. This option installs almost all the Word files—all the *plug-in modules (PIMs)* that give Word extra functions (including Speller, Text Annotation, Drop Caps, Grammar, and Microsoft Graph) and the conversion files that enable you to exchange your documents with people who use other word processing programs, such as MS-DOS and Microsoft Windows. The only files that are *not* installed are converters that enable you to read and write files to the RFT-DCA and Microsoft Works for the Macintosh file formats. If you need these converters, choose Easy Install and then run the Installer again to perform a custom installation, in which you select and install these files. Easy Install requires 10M of free space on your hard disk.

Minimal Install. Use this option only if you are low on disk space. Minimal Install installs Word and the following PIMs: Text Annotation, Find File, Picture, Spelling, Symbol, Thesaurus, Toolbar, Hyphenation, and Help. A Minimal Install requires only 3.5M of hard disk space.

PowerBook Install. For more information on this option (and instructions for installing Word on a PowerBook), see Appendix A, "Using Word 5.1 with PowerBooks."

Complete Install (no system resources). Do not choose this option unless you performed a Minimal or PowerBook installation earlier and now want to install *all* the additional files, including the PIMs and file converters.

Custom Install. This option installs only the files that you select. You should use this option only if you performed a Minimal or PowerBook installation earlier and now want to add specific PIMs or file converters.

You should choose the Easy Install option so that you can explore Word 5.1's capabilities fully. If you're low on disk space, consider removing unused applications, backing up unused data files to floppy disks, or purchasing a disk-compression program such as Disk Doubler (Salient Software). A disk-compression program compresses unused program and data files, and decompresses them automatically when you need to use them.

The Installer cannot run if other programs are running. If you are running other programs under MultiFinder or under System 7, quit them before running the Installer.

Before you install Word 5.1, move any virus-protection programs out of your System Folder to another folder and then restart your Macintosh by holding down the Shift key. The Installer will not work correctly if virus-protection programs interfere with its operation. Restarting your computer with the Shift key held down also prevents accessory programs (called *INITS*) from loading, ensuring that the Installer will not conflict with any INITS. After you install Word, you can move the virus-protection programs back to the System Folder; when you restart your computer, these programs and all your INITS will function as usual.

If you are using System 6, create a new folder called Word 5.1 and place this folder in your hard drive's top-level window.

Performing an Easy Installation

Easy Install is the option that most Word users should choose. Although Easy Install eats up 10M of disk space, it enables you to try all the Word options and features.

To install Word using the Easy Install method, follow these steps:

1. Place the Install disk in the disk drive.

2. Double-click the Word Installer icon. An introductory screen appears, reminding you to register your copy of Word.

3. Click OK. If you are installing Word for the first time, a dialog box appears, asking you to type your name and organization. (Word uses this information to identify your documents' authors in the program's Summary Info dialog boxes.)

4. Type your name in the dialog box's Name box.

5. (Optional) Press Tab to move to the Organization box, and then type your organization's name.

6. Click OK. An alert box appears, warning you to stop the installation procedure if you haven't disabled your virus-protection programs.

7. If you have disabled your virus-protection programs, or if you have no such programs installed on your Macintosh, click Continue. The Installer dialog box appears (see fig. 1.4).

Fig. 1.4
Installer dialog box.

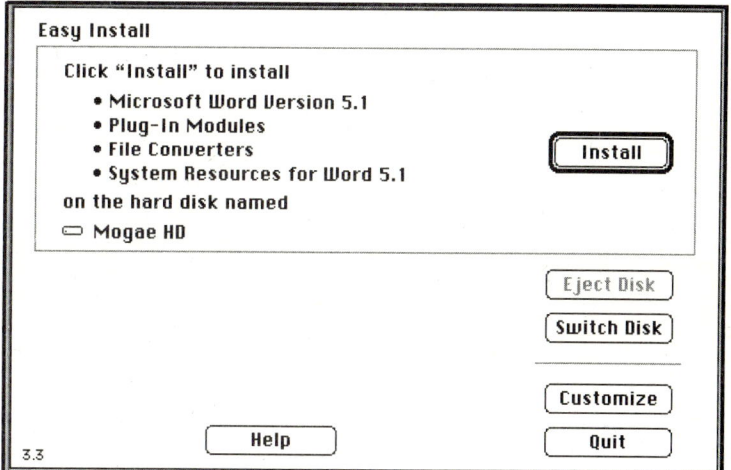

8. Click Install or press Return to start the Easy Install process. A dialog box appears, asking you to identify the folder where you want to install Word (see fig. 1.5).

Chapter 1

Reviewing Mac Basics and Installing Word 5.1

Fig. 1.5

Dialog box for identifying
the folder where you want
to install Word.

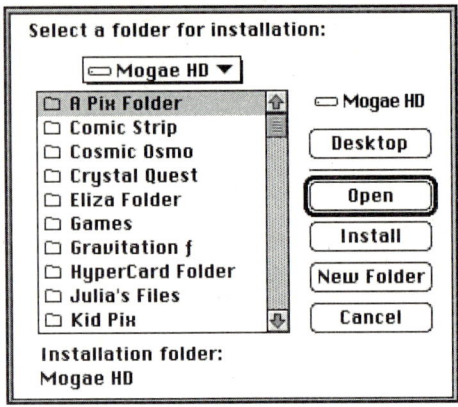

Select a folder for installation:

⌐ Mogae HD ▼

▱ **A Pix Folder**	⌐ Mogae HD
▱ Comic Strip	
▱ Cosmic Osmo	Desktop
▱ Crystal Quest	
▱ Eliza Folder	Open
▱ Games	
▱ Gravitation f	Install
▱ HyperCard Folder	
▱ Julia's Files	New Folder
▱ Kid Pix	Cancel

Installation folder:
Mogae HD

9. If you're using System 6, select the Word 5.1 folder you created before starting the Installer and then click Install.

   If you're using System 7, click the New Folder button. A dialog box appears. Type **Word 5.1**, click OK, and then click Install.

10. After you click Install, you are prompted to insert the Word disks as the Installer does its job. (When you insert the last disk, take a break: Word now must decompress all the files, which can take a few minutes.)

    When the Installer finishes, a dialog box appears, asking you which font and font size you want to use as the default.

11. Click OK to accept the default font (New York 12), or choose another font and font size and then click OK to confirm your choice.

12. After you click OK, a dialog box appears, informing you that the installation was successful. Word asks you to insert the Install disk again.

13. Click Restart to restart your Macintosh.

NOTE

You must restart your Macintosh in order to begin using Word.

Performing a Minimal Installation

If you cannot spare enough disk space for Easy Install, you may want to perform a minimal installation. Be forewarned that many of the Word options discussed in this book will not be available if you use the Minimal Install option. You can, however, add only the options you want by performing a Custom Install after the Minimal Install, as explained later.

To perform a minimal installation, follow these steps:

1. Place the Install disk in the disk drive.

2. Double-click the Installer icon. An introductory screen appears, reminding you to register your copy of Word.

3. Click OK. If you are installing Word for the first time, a dialog box appears, asking you to type your name and organization. (Word uses this information to identify your documents' authors in the program's Summary Info dialog boxes.)

4. Type your name in the Name box.

5. (Optional) Press Tab to move to the Organization box, and then type your organization's name.

6. Click OK. An alert box appears, warning you to stop the installation procedure if you haven't disabled your virus-protection programs.

7. If you have disabled your virus-protection programs, or if you have no such programs installed on your Macintosh, click Continue. The Installer dialog box appears (refer to fig. 1.4).

8. Click the Customize button. Another Installer dialog box appears, asking you to select the items you want to install (see fig. 1.6).

9. Select Minimal Install.

10. Click Install or press Return. A dialog box appears, asking you to identify the folder where you want to install Word.

11. If you're using System 6, select the Word 5.1 folder you created before starting the Installer and then click Install.

    If you're using System 7, click the New Folder button. A dialog box appears. Type **Word 5.1**, click OK, and then click Install.

Fig. 1.6

Performing a custom
installation.

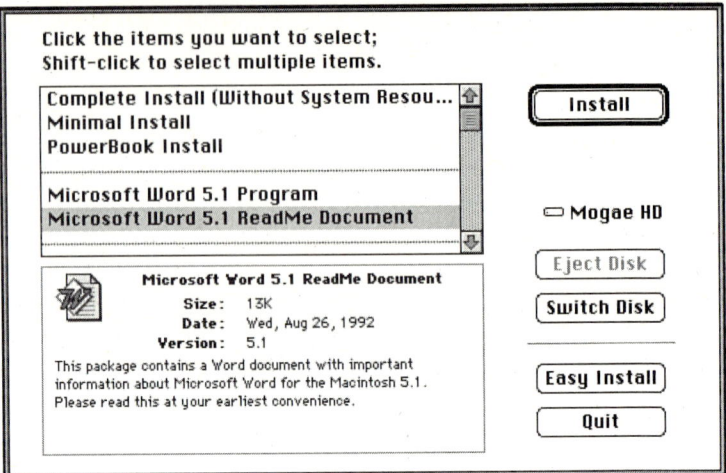

12. After you click Install, you are prompted to insert the Word disks as the Installer does its job. (When you insert the last disk, take a break: Word now must decompress all the files, which can take a few minutes.)

    When the Installer finishes, a dialog box appears, asking you which font and font size you want to use as the default.

13. Click OK to accept the default font (New York 12), or choose another font and font size and then click OK to confirm your choice.

    After you click OK, a dialog box appears, informing you that the installation was successful.

14. Click Restart to restart your Macintosh.

Performing a Custom Installation

You should perform a custom installation only after performing a minimal installation, as explained in the preceding section. The Minimal Install operation installs all the files that Word requires so that the program can run. You perform a custom installation to add PIMs, converters, and other non-necessary files.

To perform a custom installation, follow these steps:

1. Perform steps 1 through 8 in the preceding section ("Performing a Minimal Installation").

2. In the list box, select the items you want and then click Install. Another dialog box appears, asking you to identify the folder where you want to install Word (refer to fig. 1.5).

3. If you're using System 6, select the Word 5.1 folder you created before starting the Installer and then click Install.

   If you're using System 7, click the New Folder button. A dialog box appears. Type **Word 5.1**, click OK, and then click Install.

4. After you click Install, you are prompted to insert the Word disks as the Installer does its job. (When you insert the last disk, take a break: Word now must decompress all the files, which can take a few minutes.)

   When the Installer finishes, a dialog box appears, asking you which font and font size you want to use as the default.

5. Click OK to accept the default font (New York 12), or choose another font and font size and then click OK to confirm your choice.

   After you click OK, a dialog box appears, informing you that the installation was successful.

6. Click Restart to restart your Macintosh.

After performing a minimal installation, you can add PIMs or file converters as needed. To install PIMs or file converters, follow these steps:

1. Place the Install disk in the disk drive.

2. Double-click the Installer icon. An introductory screen appears, reminding you to register your copy of Word.

3. Click OK. An alert box appears, warning you to stop the installation procedure if you haven't disabled your virus-protection programs.

4. If you have disabled your virus-protection programs, or if you have no such programs installed on your Macintosh, click Continue. The Installer dialog box appears (refer to fig. 1.4).

5. Click the Customize button. Another Installer dialog box appears, asking you to select the items you want to install (refer to fig. 1.6).

6. In the list box, select the items you want and then click Install. Another dialog box appears, asking you to identify the folder where you want to install Word (refer to fig. 1.5).

7. Select the Word 5.1 folder and then click OK. You are prompted to insert the Word disks that contain the files you requested.

8. Click OK to accept the default font (New York 12), or choose another font and font size and then click OK to confirm your choice.

   After you click OK, a dialog box appears, informing you that the installation was successful.

9. Click Restart to restart your Macintosh.

2

Exploring Word 5.1

tarting Word 5.1 for the first time can be somewhat bewildering because so many things appear on-screen, but rest assured—Word is remarkably easy to use. What's more, many of the icons you see on-screen seldom come into play. After you learn a few basic concepts and skills, you will be off and running with Word. Later, you can build your knowledge step by step, and Word's many advanced features will become second nature to you.

This chapter introduces the basics of Microsoft Word. If you're new to Word, the chapter is well worth reading. If you have used previous versions of Word, you may want to skim this chapter to learn about new Word 5.1 features such as the Toolbar.

Starting Word 5.1

When you install Word, the Installer places Word in a new folder to which you give a name (such as Word 5.1). When you start Word, you can open this folder and double-click the Word icon. If you're using System 7, however, a better and faster way exists, as the following paragraphs explain.

System 7 users can access Word much more quickly by creating an alias for Microsoft Word and placing it in the Apple menu. (An *alias* is a copy of the program's icon.) You then can start Word by double-clicking its alias. Follow these steps to create the Microsoft Word alias and place it in the Apple menu:

1. Locate the Microsoft Word program icon, titled Microsoft Word, in the folder you created for Word 5.1. Click the icon once to highlight it.

2. From the File menu in the Finder, choose Make Alias.

   The Finder makes an alias of the Word program, titled Microsoft Word Alias.

Microsoft Word alias

3. Drag the Microsoft Word Alias icon to the Desktop.

4. Open the System Folder and size it so that you see the alias icon. Use the scroll bars to scroll through the window until the Apple Menu Items folder is in view.

5. Drag the alias icon to the Apple Menu Items folder.

   The Microsoft Word alias now appears in the Apple menu. To start Word, pull down the Apple menu and choose the Word alias.

NOTE

After creating a Word document, you can start Word another way. Simply double-click any Word document to start the program.

Understanding the Word Screen

When you start Word, the program automatically displays a new blank document called Untitled1. (If you create additional documents in the same Word session, Word numbers them Untitled2, Untitled3, and so on.) You also see Word's many on-screen tools. This section briefly explores the main components of the screen, shown in figure 2.1.

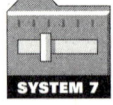

The best way to explore Word's screen is to use a nifty System 7 feature, Balloon Help. To activate Balloon Help, pull down the Help menu (represented in the menu bar as a question mark within a cartoon balloon) and choose Show Balloons. To use Balloon Help, touch any part of the screen with the mouse pointer. A help balloon appears. If you get tired of seeing the balloons, choose Hide Balloons from the Help menu.

Part I

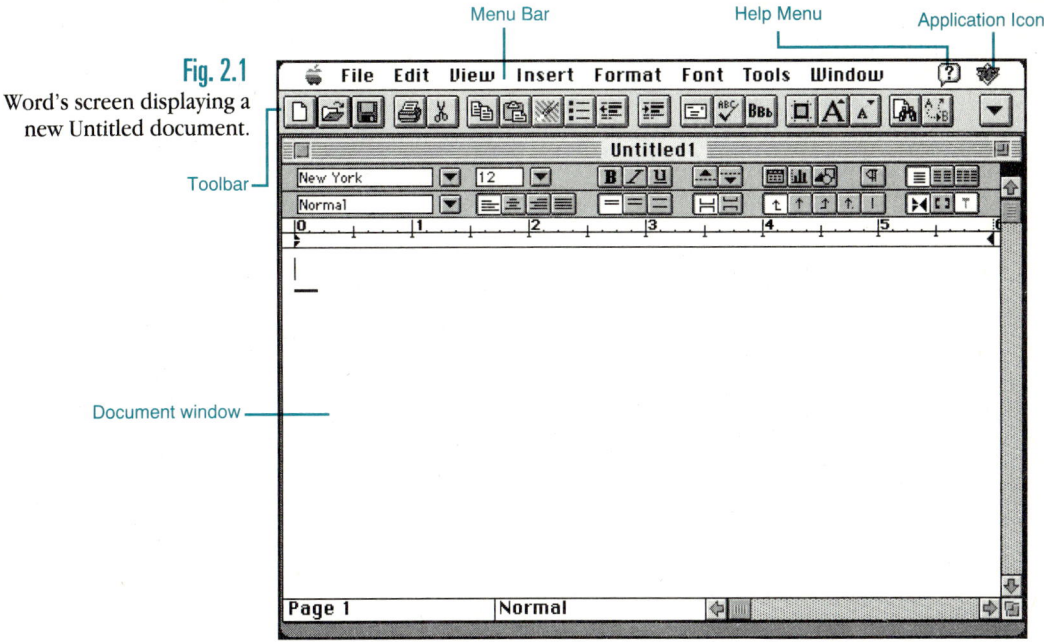

Fig. 2.1
Word's screen displaying a
new Untitled document.

The screen shown in figure 2.1 has three basic parts: the *menu bar*,
where you choose Word commands; the *Toolbar*, a new Word 5.1
feature that enables you to choose commands quickly; and the *document window*, where you create your documents. In the following
sections, you learn more about each of these parts of the screen.

Exploring Word's Menus

The menu bar at the top of the screen lists the names of Word's menus,
from which you choose commands. When you click one of the menu
names, the menu drops down, as shown in figure 2.2.

Hold the mouse button down to keep the menu down. When you
release the button, the menu disappears. To choose a command, drag
the mouse down the menu until you have highlighted the command you
want. You then release the mouse button to choose this command.

Chapter 2

Exploring Word 5.1

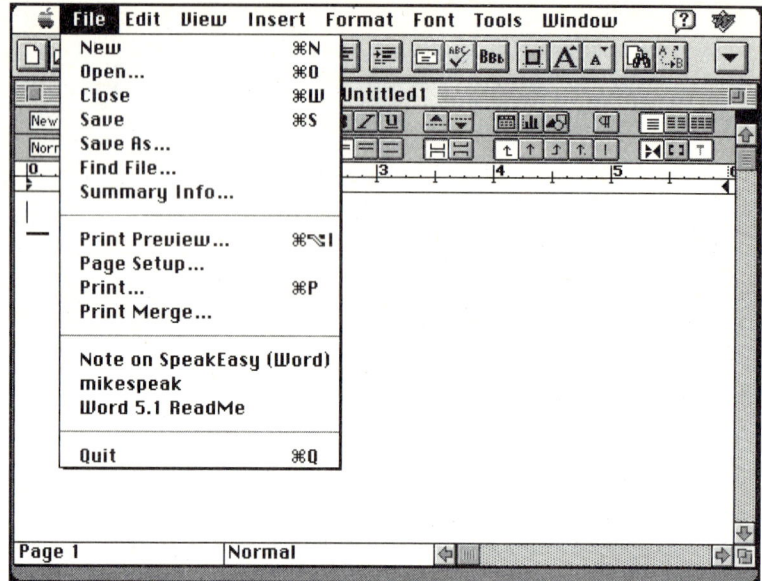

Fig. 2.2
File menu.

Following is a brief overview of Word's menus:

Apple menu (represented in the menu bar by the Apple Computer logo). Use this menu's commands to access desk accessories and the Macintosh Control Panels. Need to jot down a note to yourself? Choose Notepad. Need a calculator? Choose Calculator. You can equip your Macintosh with additional desk accessories, such as appointment calendars and telephone directories.

File menu. Use this menu's commands to create new documents, open existing ones, save work, and print. You also use this menu to quit Word.

Edit menu. Use this menu's commands to delete, copy, or move text within a document. This menu also contains commands that enable you to link your document to text in other documents.

View menu. Use this menu's commands to change the way Word displays a document on-screen. By default, you see your document in Normal view. You also can view your document as an outline (Outline view) or as it will appear when printed (Page Layout view), and you can choose View commands that turn the Toolbar and other features on or off. Still other View commands help you see text that doesn't appear in the body of the printed page, such as headers, footers, footnotes, and annotations.

Insert menu. Use this menu's commands to insert elements such as page breaks, footnotes, tables, graphics, and even movies into a document.

Format menu. Use this menu's commands to change the appearance of a document's text and page layout.

Font menu. Use this menu's commands to change text typeface and size.

Tools menu. Use this menu's commands to check your spelling and grammar, look up words in the Thesaurus, count the number of words in a document, and perform on-screen calculations. This menu also provides commands for customizing Word to your specifications.

Window menu. Use this menu's commands to open a new window in the same document or to switch to other windows. This menu also contains commands that enable you to access the help system or see the Clipboard's contents.

Help menu. If you're using System 7, the Help-menu icon (a question mark in a cartoon balloon) appears to the right of the Window menu. If you click this icon to open the Help menu, you can choose or quit Balloon Help. This menu also contains the Microsoft Word Help command. (In System 6, you access Microsoft Word Help from the Windows menu.) You learn more about the help system in the "Getting Help" section later in this chapter.

Application icon. Click this icon to switch to another application (if one is running) or to the Finder without exiting Word. You do not see this icon if you're running System 6 without MultiFinder, the version of the Finder that enables you to run more than one program at a time. If you're running MultiFinder or System 7 (which incorporates MultiFinder), you see the application icon at the extreme right end of the menu bar. In System 6 with MultiFinder, you click this icon to switch to the next application (or to the Finder, if no other application is running). In System 7, you click this icon to open the Application menu, from which you can choose additional applications or the Finder.

As you learn later in this book, you can customize Word by creating a Work menu for files, styles, and other items you use frequently. When you create this menu, it appears in the menu bar after the Window menu.

Choosing a Command

Every Word menu contains useful information in addition to the command names. The menu tells you whether the command is available, whether a dialog box appears when you choose it, and whether you can press a key as an alternative to choosing the menu command.

Examine figure 2.3, which shows the Edit menu.

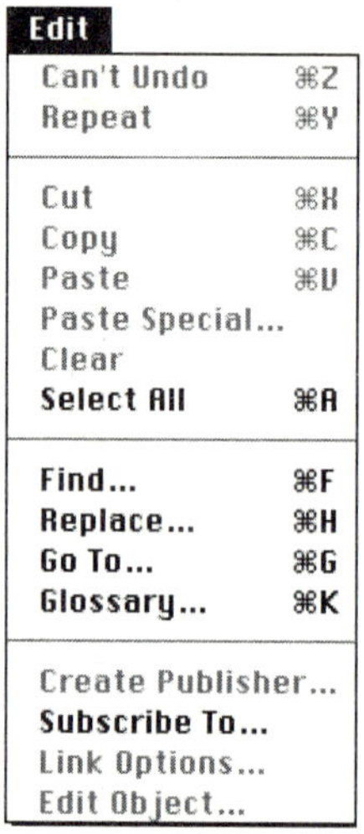

Fig. 2.3
Edit menu.

Edit	
Can't Undo	⌘Z
Repeat	⌘Y
Cut	⌘X
Copy	⌘C
Paste	⌘V
Paste Special...	
Clear	
Select All	⌘A
Find...	⌘F
Replace...	⌘H
Go To...	⌘G
Glossary...	⌘K
Create Publisher...	
Subscribe To...	
Link Options...	
Edit Object...	

Notice that some commands in the menu are *dimmed*, which means that those commands are not currently available. The Cut, Copy, and Clear commands, for example, are dimmed because nothing in the document currently is selected. After you select some text, these commands become available.

Other commands are followed by three periods (called an *ellipsis*). When you choose one of these commands, you see a dialog box that prompts you for further information.

Some commands are *toggles*, which switch an option (such as the Toolbar) on or off. When the option is on, you see a check mark next to the command name. If you choose this command, you turn the option off. The next time you pull down the menu, the check mark is gone. To turn the option on again, choose the command again.

Many commands have keyboard shortcuts, such as ⌘-F. The cloverleaf symbol stands for the Command key on your Macintosh keyboard; this key has the same cloverleaf symbol printed on it. To choose a command that has a keyboard shortcut, hold down the ⌘ key and type the appropriate letter (either uppercase or lowercase) for that command.

Part I

As the keyboard shortcuts indicate, you can choose some commands in two or more ways. For example, you can choose the New command from the File menu or press ⌘-N to create a new document. But you also can click the New tool in the Toolbar or press the F5 key (if you have an extended keyboard); both actions also create a new document.

For now, choose commands by using the menus and the Toolbar, which is discussed later in this chapter. You learn more about using Word's keyboard in Chapter 4, "Understanding Word's Workplace."

Try creating a document now. Simply start typing. If you make a mistake, press Delete (also called Backspace on some keyboards) to rub out the error. Don't press Return at the end of each line; let Word wrap the text to the next line automatically. Press Return only to start a new paragraph.

Using a Dialog Box

Dialog boxes appear for some commands. The dialog box shown in figure 2.4, for example, appears when you choose Save in a new document for the first time. This dialog box enables you to choose a location and a name for the file you want to save.

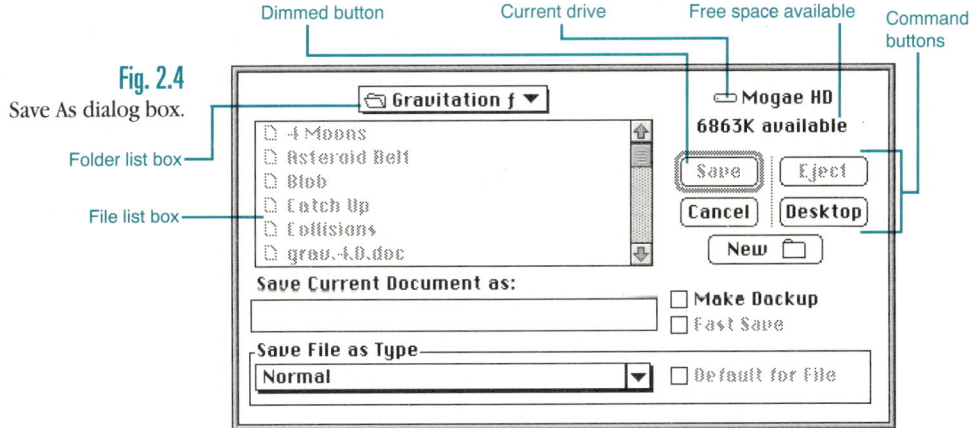

Fig. 2.4
Save As dialog box.

The Save As dialog box contains a *list box* with a scroll bar that enables you to scroll through the names of the files stored in the current folder. (These file names are dimmed, indicating that you can't use them to name your new document.) Also listed are the folders that the Installer placed in the current folder. If you want, you can open one of these folders by double-clicking the folder name.

At the top of the screen, you see a *drop-down list box* that enables you to access the folders that store the current folder. You also can access the directory for your hard disk (called something like HD40 or HD80, unless you have renamed it) and the Desktop, which helps you access other drives.

To the right of the file-name list box, you see *command buttons*. You click these buttons to carry out actions, such as performing the command with the options you have chosen in the dialog box or opening another dialog box so that you can make additional choices. In every dialog box, you can choose Cancel to return to your document.

Notice, too, that some command buttons are dimmed. In figure 2.4, the Save button is dimmed because you haven't typed a file name yet. The Eject button also is dimmed because no floppy disk is in the floppy disk drive.

When you see an outlined command button (for example, the Save button), you can choose it by clicking the button or pressing Return.

If you're using System 6, you do not see a New Folder or Desktop button in the Save As dialog box. In addition, you do not see an arrow on the folder drop-down list box, and no Desktop item appears in the folder list. To look at the files in another drive, you click the Drive button.

In the bottom right section of the dialog box, you see *check boxes*, which enable you to choose further options. Check boxes that contain an X are *activated*; check boxes that don't contain an X are *deactivated*. To activate or deactivate a check box, click it (unless it is dimmed, like Fast Save in fig. 2.4).

Below the file-name list box, you see a *text box* (Save Current Document As), where you type a name for your file.

Try typing a name for your document now. Click in the Save Current Document As text box and type **Test Document**. Notice that the Save button becomes available after you type the file name. Then choose Save (click the Save button or press Return) to confirm your choice and to save Untitled1 under the name Test Document.

After you save your document, you see the Summary Info dialog box (see fig. 2.5).

Fig. 2.5
Summary Info dialog box.

Summary Info		
Title:	Test Document	OK
Subject:		Cancel
Author:	A Word User	
Version:		
Keywords:		

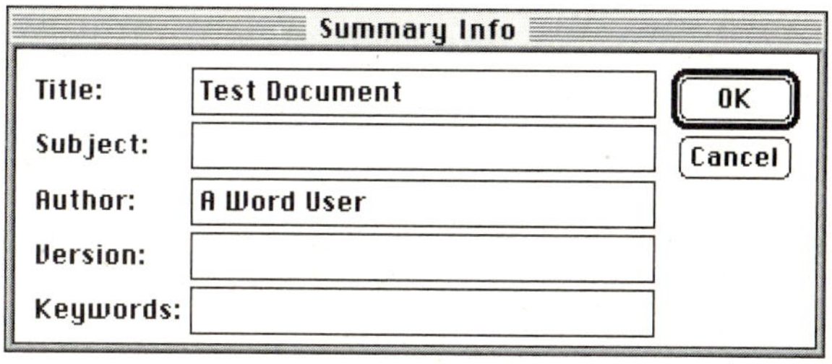

In the text boxes of this dialog box, you type information that helps you retrieve the file later. Word helps you by placing the document's title (and the user name you typed when you installed the program) in the appropriate areas. For now, choose OK (by clicking the OK button or pressing Return). Your named document appears on-screen (see fig. 2.6).

Fig. 2.6
A named document.

Document name ⎤

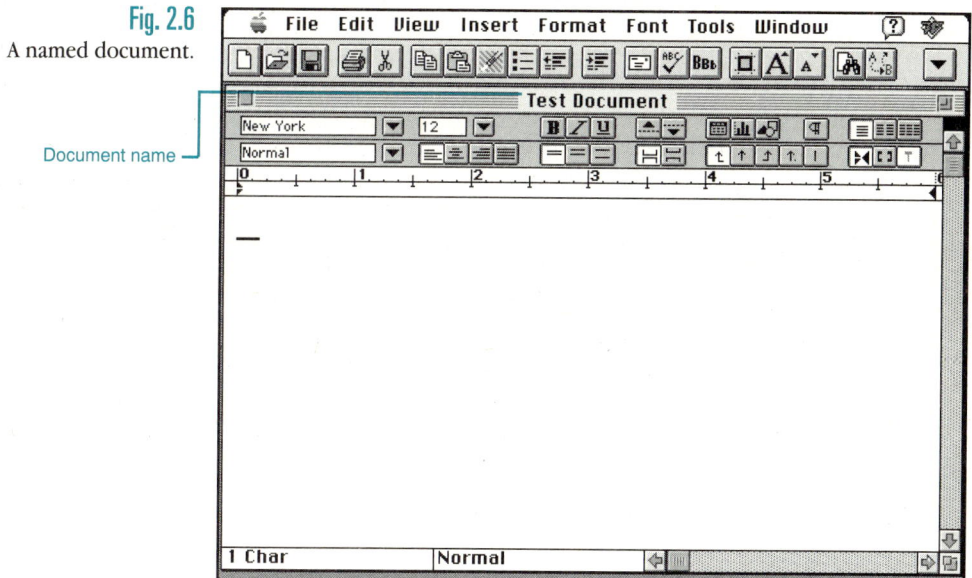

Exploring the Toolbar

The second major area of the screen, the Toolbar, contains tools that help you access frequently used commands. Many tools are displayed in the Toolbar, but this section introduces only eight fundamental tools that appear in all versions of the Toolbar. These tools provide shortcuts for many File and Edit commands.

The following table describes these tools:

Tool	Function
	Opens a new file
	Opens a file you have created and saved
	Saves a file
	Prints a document
	Removes text from a document and places a copy of this text in the Clipboard
	Copies text from a document to the Clipboard
	Moves the text that's currently stored in the Clipboard to a document
	Reverses the last command or editing action

Exploring the Document Window

Every Word document you create appears in its own full-size document window (refer to fig. 2.6). You can open more than one window at a time—a total of 23, in fact—although you seldom should open more than two or three at a time because the more documents you open, the

---

less memory is available for advanced functions. You can display a different document in each open window or two or more parts of the same document in two or more different windows. You even can split one window into two panes, revealing two parts of the same document. (For more information on managing windows, see Chapter 5, "Managing Documents and Files.")

Every Word window contains the standard Macintosh window features that you learned about in Chapter 1 and also the additional features shown in figure 2.7.

Fig. 2.7
Word document-window features.

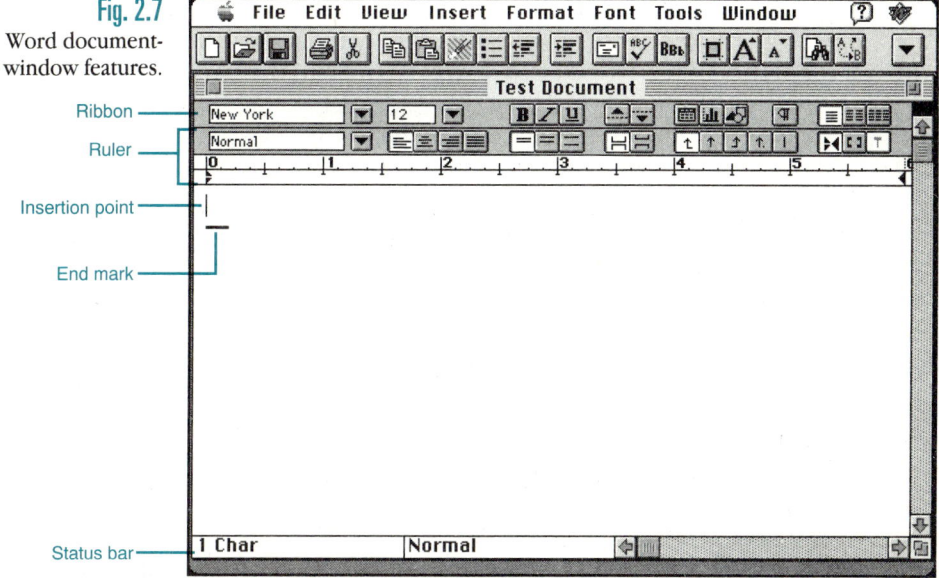

The following paragraphs describe these features in detail.

Ribbon. The ribbon gives you a quick way to choose fonts, font sizes, font styles (bold, italic, and underline), and character position (superscript and subscript). The ribbon also includes icons for more advanced operations that you learn about later in this book—for example, placing a graphic in a Picture window for editing, toggling the display of paragraph marks on and off, and choosing single- or multiple-column format.

Ruler. The ruler measures your document (with the 0 mark set at the left margin) and also provides icons that you can use for

Chapter 2
Exploring Word 5.1

formatting purposes. You can use the Ruler to set indents, paragraph alignment, line spacing, and tabs (see Chapter 10, "Formatting Paragraphs," for information on these features).

Some writers do not like the distractions of the Toolbar, ribbon, and ruler. If you agree, you can hide them easily by turning off the Toolbar, ribbon, and ruler options (View menu). (Hiding these elements creates more room on-screen for your text—a real boon on 9-inch Macintosh Classic screens.) If you choose these options again, you see the Toolbar, ribbon, and ruler again. Because you're learning the program, however, leave these features on-screen for now to learn how they function.

Insertion point. The insertion point is a blinking vertical line in the document area that shows you where text will appear when you type. When you move the mouse pointer around the document area, the pointer turns into the *I-beam pointer*, which enables you to position the insertion point precisely. (As you move the pointer around the Word screen, you may see additional shapes. You learn what these shapes indicate in the chapters to come.)

If you have used DOS applications, notice that in the Macintosh world, the insertion point always appears *between* or *after* characters. In DOS applications, the cursor (the DOS version of the insertion point) always lies *on* a character—which means that accidentally pressing Del or Backspace can wipe out a character. With the Mac, you cannot place the insertion point on a character—only before or after it.

Status bar. This bar has two boxes: the page-number area and the current-style area. The page-number area normally shows the number of the current page but also displays status messages (such as the number of characters saved) during and after your use of a command. The style area shows the name of the style that is applied to the current text. (You learn about styles in Chapter 14, "Formatting with Styles.") Your text has the Normal style by default.

End mark. The end mark is the long black underline that marks the end of your document. As you type text and press Return, you push the end mark down.

Using the Macintosh Keyboard

Computer keyboards resemble typewriter keyboards, but computer keyboards have additional keys. You learn more about these keys and what they do in Chapter 4, "Understanding Word's Workplace." For now, notice that Word's menus list keyboard shortcuts you can use instead of choosing certain commands from the menu. For example, you can use the ⌘-S shortcut to save your work. To use this shortcut, hold down the ⌘ key and type **s** (either uppercase or lowercase).

Several Macintosh keyboard layouts exist, and your keyboard might not have all the keys that the Apple extended keyboard has. For example, some keyboards lack the *function keys* (F1 through F15), the *arrow keys* (for moving the insertion point with the keyboard), and the *Delete Forward key* (a handy key that deletes the character to the right of the insertion point). If you don't have an Apple extended keyboard, don't despair—you still can use Word. In Chapter 4, you learn how to use the keys you already have to perform many of the extended keyboard's functions.

If you have used other computers for which the terms *Enter key* and *Return key* are synonymous, be aware that the Macintosh makes a distinction between the two. The Macintosh Return key is in the alphabetical keyboard, and the Macintosh Enter key is in the numeric keypad. You can press either key to start a new line or to choose the outlined button in a dialog box. For some commands, however, you must press Enter, not Return.

You already may have noticed that Word's menus contain various symbols to represent the keys you press for these shortcuts. See Chapter 4, "Understanding Word's Workplace," for a list of these symbols and their meanings.

By default, Microsoft Word displays keyboard shortcuts that use the Apple extended keyboard's function keys (F1 through F15). If you don't have an extended keyboard, you don't have to display the shortcuts that use function keys.

To restrict the shortcuts displayed in Word menus, choose Preferences from the Tools menu. When the Preferences dialog box appears, choose the View icon. Click the option called Show Function Keys on Menus so that the X disappears. Then click the close box (the square in the upper left corner of the dialog box). Thereafter, Word lists only those keyboard shortcuts that don't involve function keys.

Chapter 2

Exploring Word 5.1

Getting Help

The best computer programs include extensive on-line help systems that give you information about commands, options, and procedures. In Word, you can get help in three ways:

■ *Balloon Help.* Available only in System 7, Balloon Help explains the parts of the screen and the options that are available. To use Balloon Help, choose Show Balloons from the Help menu. As you move the mouse pointer around the screen, you see help balloons that explain the screen's various features. Balloon Help also works in dialog boxes (see fig. 2.8) and menus (see fig. 2.9).

Fig. 2.8

Balloon Help in a dialog box.

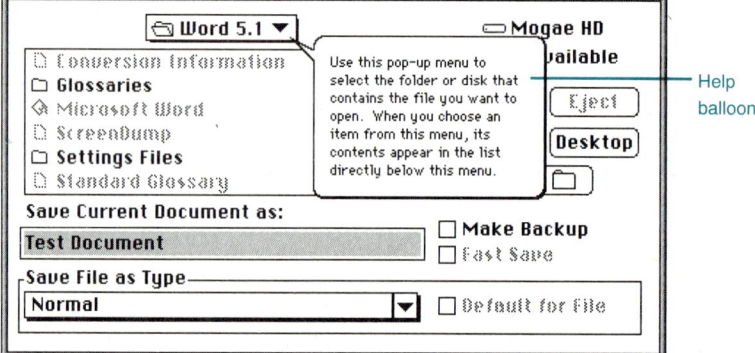

The balloons are distracting, though. After a while, you may want to turn Balloon Help off by choosing Hide Balloons from the Help menu.

■ *Context-sensitive help.* This form of help is called context-sensitive because it detects what you're doing and shows you the relevant help information. To access context-sensitive help, hold down the ⌘ key and type a slash (/) or question mark (?); the mouse pointer becomes a large question mark. Then click something—for example, a menu command, a tool in the Toolbar, or a part of the screen. You see the Help dialog box, which explains what you clicked (see fig. 2.10).

Fig. 2.9
Balloon Help in
a menu.

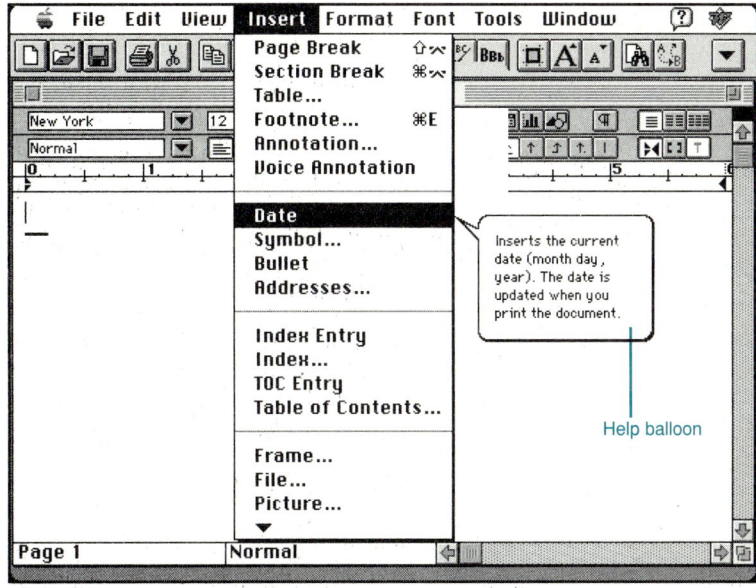

Help balloon

Fig. 2.10
Help dialog box.

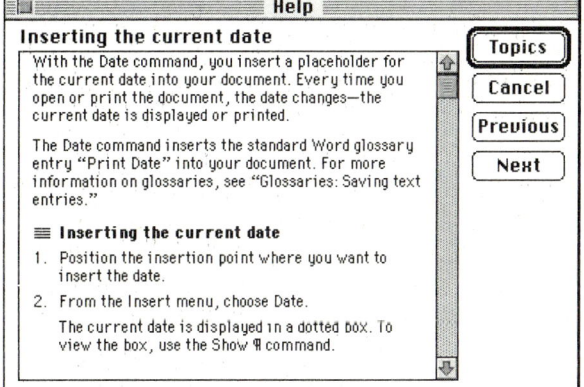

You can access context-sensitive help at any time, even if a dialog box is on-screen. If the Help dialog box contains more than one window of text, you can use the scroll bar to display the rest of the text. To close the Help dialog box, click Cancel or press Esc.

■ *Help.* You can access the help system directly by choosing Microsoft Word Help from the Help menu. Word then displays a help window in which you can choose topics (see fig. 2.11).

Fig. 2.11

Help topics.

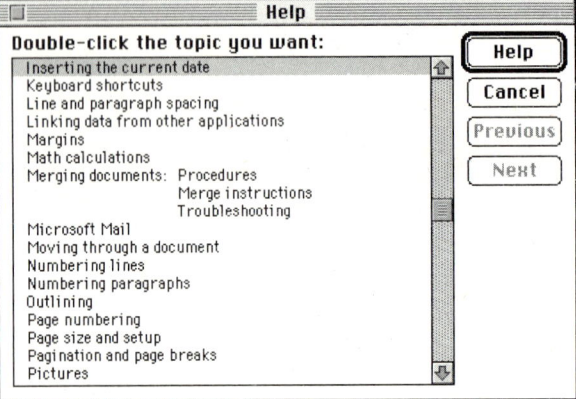

To select a topic, click the topic name to highlight it and then click the Help command button (or press Return), or double-click the topic name. When the information you want appears in the Help dialog box, the Help command button changes to Topics. To see the topic list again, choose Topics (click the button or press Return). You also can click Next to see the next help topic or Previous to see the previous one. To exit the help system, click Cancel or press Esc.

Quitting Word

In this section, you learn how to quit Word and shut down your Macintosh in an orderly way.

CAUTION

Even if you have saved all your work, don't quit Word by switching off the power to your Macintosh. You don't harm Word or your computer by switching off the power, but you do prevent Word from saving your settings and other choices you have made during the current working session. Moreover, you may forget to save a document in a window hidden behind another window on the screen. If you quit Word without turning off your Macintosh, your computer alerts you if any windows contain unsaved text.

Part I

Getting Started with Word 5.1

To first quit Word and then shut down your Macintosh, choose Quit from the File menu or use the ⌘-Q shortcut.

If any windows contain unsaved text, you see the alert box shown in figure 2.12.

Fig. 2.12
An alert box.

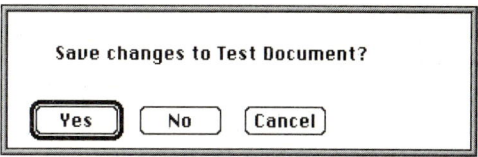

If you choose Yes (click the Yes command button or press Return), the Save As dialog box appears. If you click No, Word abandons the document. If you click Cancel, you return to Word without quitting the program.

This command has the same advantage that the Quit command does within Word: It checks to see whether you have any unsaved work in other running applications. If so, you see an alert box asking whether you want to save this work.

Quick Review

This section summarizes the most useful information in this chapter. Check "Productivity Tips" for a review of high-productivity tips and tricks—the ones that Macintosh and Word pros use every day. Review "Techniques" whenever you need a quick reminder about a specific procedure.

Productivity Tips

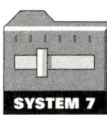

■ So that you can start Word quickly in System 7, make an alias of the Word program and place this alias in the Apple Menu Items folder (inside the System Folder). You then can start Word by choosing the Microsoft Word alias from the Apple menu.

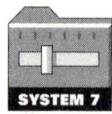

■ System 7 users can use Balloon Help to quickly find out what Toolbar tools, menu commands, and dialog-box options do.

■ In any dialog box, you can choose the outlined command button by clicking it or pressing Return. You also can close the dialog box by clicking the Cancel button or pressing Esc.

■ To get help quickly, press ⌘-? or ⌘-/ and then click a menu command or option, Toolbar icon, or screen element. A Help dialog box appears, explaining what you clicked.

■ To avoid losing unsaved work, always quit Word by choosing Quit from the File menu and then shut down your Macintosh by choosing Shut Down from the Special menu.

Techniques

Starting Word 5.1

To start Word:

1. Open the Word 5.1 folder.

2. Double-click the Microsoft Word icon.

To start Word after adding an alias to the Apple menu, choose the Microsoft Word alias from the Apple menu.

Making an Alias

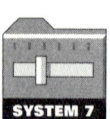

To make an alias:

1. Locate the Microsoft Word program icon in the Word 5.1 folder, and click the icon once to select it.

2. From the File menu in the Finder, choose Make Alias.

3. Open the System Folder and size it so that you can see the alias icon. Use the scroll bars to scroll the window so that you can see the Apple Menu Items folder.

4. Drag the alias icon to the Apple Menu Items folder.

Getting Help

To get help:

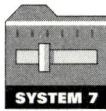

- ■ To get Balloon Help, choose Show Balloon Help from the Help menu.

- ■ To get context-sensitive help, press ⌘-? or ⌘-/ and then click a screen element.

- ■ To see help topics, choose Microsoft Word Help from the Help menu.

Quitting Word

To quit Word, choose Quit from the File menu or use the ⌘-Q shortcut.

Quick Start: Creating a Business Letter

Anyone who wants to explain the incredible success of word processing software should look no farther than the average business or professional office. In almost any business or profession, you write letters—and in some occupations, you write them daily.

Writing letters is an important job. Every time you send a first-class letter, you put yourself and your organization on the line. For this reason, preparing letters with a quality word processing program like Word is an excellent idea; Word enables you to experiment with the wording of the letter until you get it just right.

Unfortunately, most people don't take full advantage of their word processing software's capabilities. They treat the computer as if it were merely an electronic typewriter. They do so partly because they haven't taken the time to learn basic editing operations, such as performing block moves. But people also neglect these procedures because in some programs, the procedures are difficult to learn. As you will see, however, Word's advanced technology—including drag-and-drop editing—makes text editing much easier to learn (and much more convenient to use on a day-to-day basis).

This chapter teaches you all the basics of writing letters with Word by walking you through a practical writing experience. You start with a poorly written letter and alter it until it meets the professional standards of today's business environment. Along the way, you learn how to perform all the basic editing tasks that help you achieve writing excellence. What's more, you learn the tricks that experienced Word users employ to improve their writing productivity.

Envisioning the Scenario

Imagine yourself in this situation: you're the director of a small firm that specializes in training corporate employees in security techniques. You frequently use videos to show potential security problems. Last week, you spent a day training some employees of Amalgamated Precision Engineering, Inc. Everything went fine, except that the video-projector bulb blew in the final moments of the presentation. You had a backup, however, and before long you were back in action.

This week, you received a letter from Nelson T. Jones, your contact at Amalgamated Precision Engineering. In the letter, Mr. Jones thanked you for the presentation but complained about the equipment breakdown. The ball's in your court now; you have to answer the letter.

You have a problem, however: you're annoyed at Mr. Jones, and your annoyance probably will show in your letter's first draft.

Getting Started

To begin the tutorial, make sure that a blank Untitled document is on your screen (see Chapter 2, "Exploring Word 5.1," to learn how to display a new blank document). If you have another document displayed, pull down the File menu and choose the New option. You also can press F5 or click the New tool in the Toolbar (the first icon at the left end of the Toolbar).

Displaying Paragraph Marks

When you're writing and editing with Word, you may want to display paragraph marks in your document. The paragraph marks show where you pressed Return. Seeing paragraph marks is helpful for two reasons.

First, you can join paragraphs easily by deleting the marks. Second, you might accidentally delete one of the marks if they're hidden.

To display paragraph marks, click the paragraph-mark icon in the ribbon, choose Show ¶ from the View menu, or use the ⌘-J shortcut.

Centering the Return Address

The first step in entering the letter to Mr. Jones is typing your company's return address. To do this, you must set paragraph alignment to center the address at the top of the document.

To type the return address, follow these steps:

1. Click the Centered Alignment icon in the ruler or press ⌘-Shift-C. The insertion point moves to the center of the screen.

2. Type **Albemarle Valley Associates** and then press Return.

   The text you type is centered. When you press Return, Word inserts a paragraph mark. Notice that Word continues the centered format on the next line.

If you make a typing mistake, press the Delete key (also called Backspace on some keyboards) and then type the correct characters.

3. Type the rest of the return address as shown in figure 3.1, pressing Return where you see paragraph marks.

4. To leave two blank lines under the return address, press Return three times after you type the telephone number.

5. Click the Left Alignment icon in the ruler or press ⌘-Shift-P. The insertion point jumps to the left margin, but the lines that already are centered stay centered.

Keep this document on-screen. The tutorial continues throughout this chapter.

Saving the Document

Your document isn't finished. Even so, you should save your work. The work you have done so far is stored only in your Macintosh's memory

(RAM). To avoid loss of work due to a power outage, save repeatedly during your Word sessions. When you save, a copy of your document is stored safely on your Mac's hard disk.

Fig. 3.1

Typing the return address.

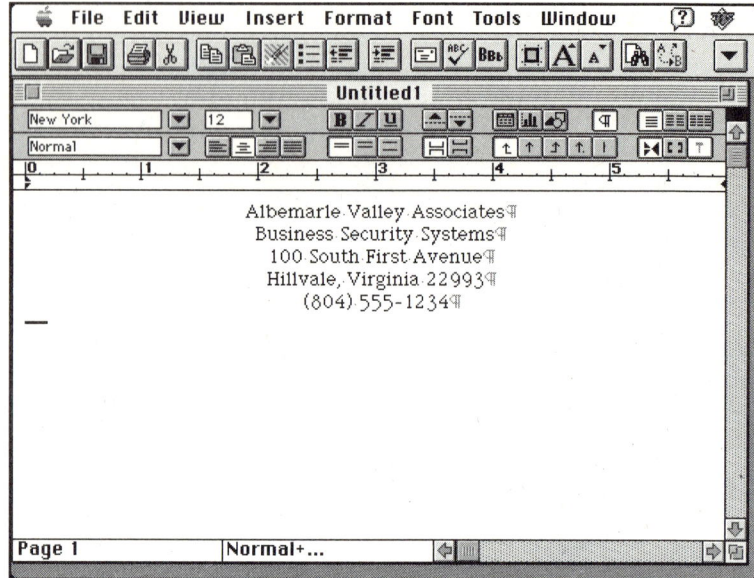

To save the document, follow these steps:

1. Choose Save from the File menu. You also can click the Save tool in the Toolbar or use the ⌘-S shortcut. The Save As dialog box appears (see Chapter 2).

2. Double-click the Sample Documents folder in the list box.

3. Type **letter** in the Save Current Document As text box and then click OK or press Return. You return to your document.

Boldfacing the Firm's Name

You have learned one kind of Word formatting: paragraph alignment (specifically, centered and flush-left alignment). Now you learn how to format characters by adding boldface type to your document. To attach emphasis to characters you already have typed, you select those characters and then choose the desired emphasis from the Format menu (or use one of the keyboard shortcuts).

Part I

To boldface the name of the firm in your letter to Mr. Jones, perform the following steps:

1. Move the mouse pointer toward the left side of the document window until the pointer changes to an arrow. When the pointer takes on this shape, you have moved the pointer to the *selection bar*, a special area of the screen that selects lines and paragraphs quickly (see fig. 3.2).

Fig. 3.2
The selection bar.

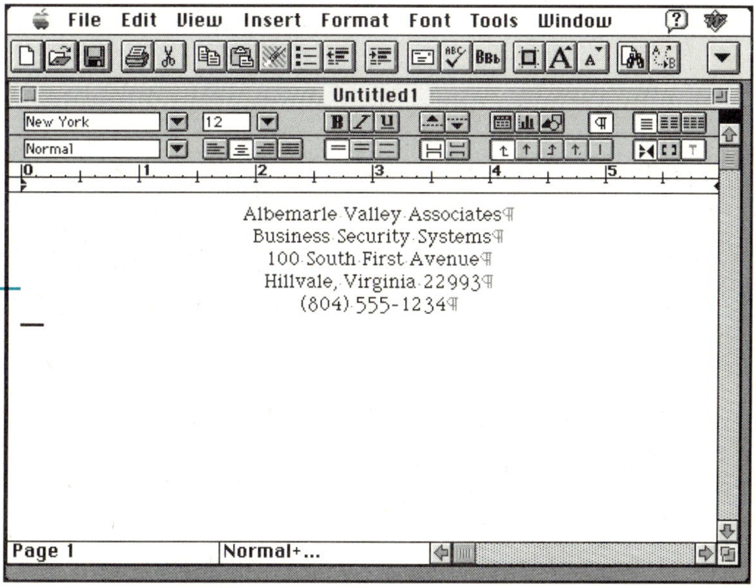

Selection bar ——

```
 File   Edit   View   Insert   Format   Font   Tools   Window
```

Albemarle Valley Associates¶
Business Security Systems¶
100 South First Avenue¶
Hillvale, Virginia 22993¶
(804) 555-1234¶

Page 1   Normal+...

2. With the pointer in the selection bar next to the top line, click to select the whole line.

3. Click the Bold icon in the ribbon, choose Bold from the Format menu, or use the ⌘-B keyboard shortcut. Word boldfaces the firm's name (see fig. 3.3).

Undoing a Change

You also should learn to use the Undo command, a basic element in your Word skills repertoire. With Undo, you can cancel the effects of many Word commands, even after you carry out those commands.

Fig. 3.3

Boldfacing the firm's name.

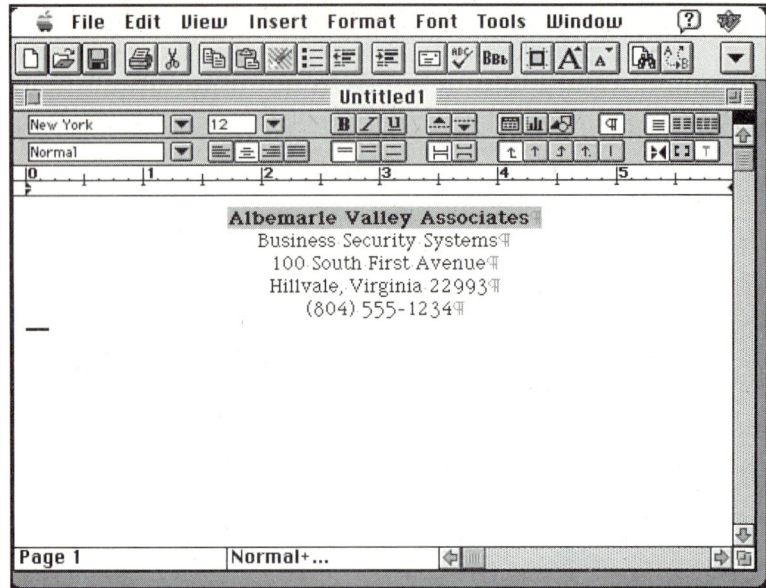

Experiment with Undo now so that you will know how to use this command to recover from a command error. To undo a change in your letter, follow these steps:

1. Highlight the name of the firm, but don't highlight the paragraph mark (see figure 3.4).

2. Choose Cut from the Edit menu, press ⌘-X, or click the Cut tool in the Toolbar. All the text disappears.

   If you ever delete text accidentally, you can restore it easily by following the next step.

3. Choose Undo Cut from the Edit menu. You also can press ⌘-Z or click the Undo tool in the Toolbar. Word instantly restores the deletion.

CAUTION

Undo will not work if you have made any other changes since the changes you want to undo took place. If you issue the wrong command, choose Undo immediately.

Fig. 3.4
Highlighting text but not
the paragraph mark.

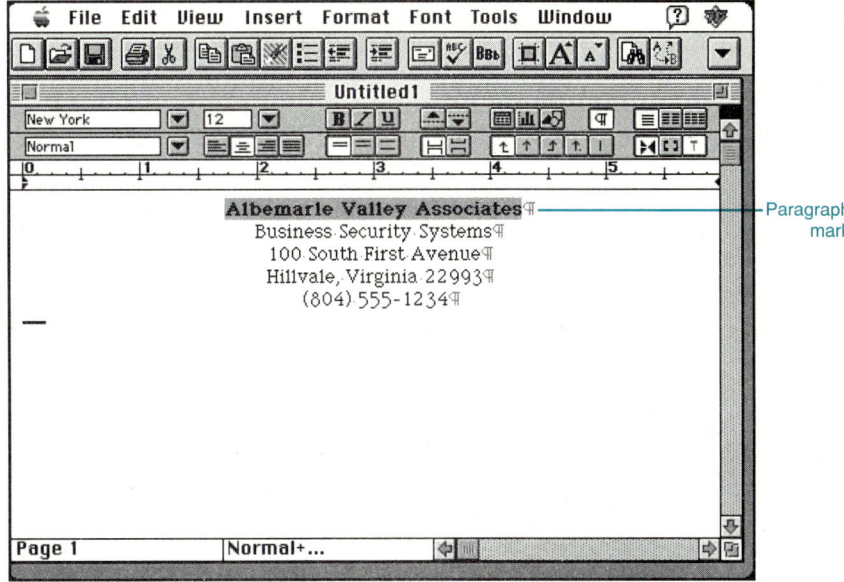

Paragraph
mark

4. Choose Redo Cut from the Edit menu. You also can press ⌘-Z or
click the Undo tool. Word removes the text again.

5. Choose Bold from the Format menu, click the Bold icon in the
ribbon, or press ⌘-B.

6. Type **Albemarle Valley Associates** again. The text you type
appears in bold.

NOTE
As you can see, Word uses the formats currently in effect when you type. Had
you pressed Return, the program would have copied these formats down to
the new line, enabling you to continue typing with these formats (centered
and bold).

Inserting the Date Automatically

You can type the current date manually, if you want, but a command can
type it for you automatically. To insert the date into your letter automatically, use the following steps:

Chapter 3

1. Place the insertion point on the flush-left paragraph mark below the return address.

2. Choose Date from the Insert menu. Word enters today's date, surrounded by dotted lines, at the insertion point (see fig. 3.5).

Fig. 3.5
Inserting the date
automatically.

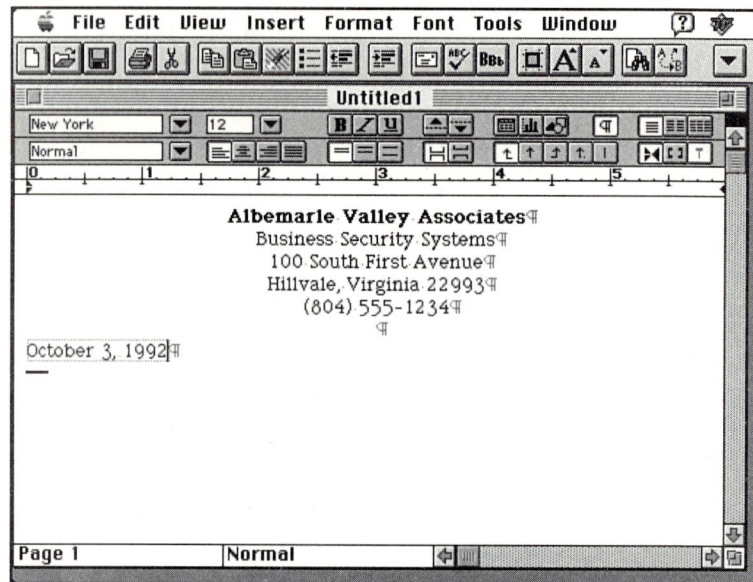

This date isn't ordinary text; a date entry always shows the current date.

The dotted lines do not print. These lines tell you that the date isn't made up of ordinary text but is generated by the Date command. If you try to select the date, you will find that it's only one character.

Typing the Correspondent's Address and Salutation

Now that you have inserted the date, follow these steps to type the correspondent's address and salutation:

1. Press Return twice to enter a blank line below the date, and then type the correspondent's address, shown in figure 3.6. Press Return after each line.

Fig. 3.6

Typing the address and
salutation.

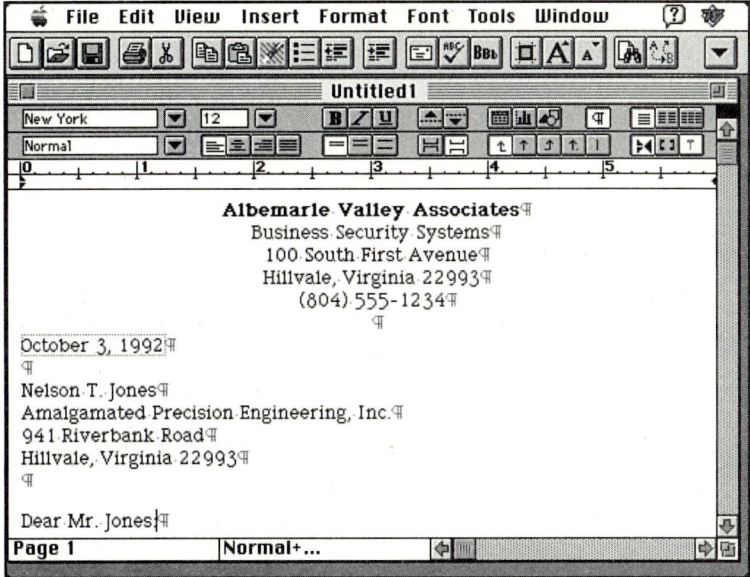

2. After you type the ZIP code, press Return twice to enter a blank line.

3. Type **Dear Mr. Jones:**, and then press Return. Word starts a new line.

4. Click the Blank Spacing icon in the ruler. After you click this icon, the paragraph mark moves down one line. The Blank Spacing icon automatically enters 12 points (one line) of blank space before each paragraph.

   You always should perform this step before typing single-spaced body-text paragraphs unless you want no blank lines separating the paragraphs. Using the Blank Spacing icon to create blank lines has many advantages, about which you will learn in subsequent chapters. For now, simply bear in mind that using the Blank Spacing icon to create blank lines before body-text paragraphs is a good habit to form.

Typing the Letter's Body

At this point, you have typed the address, date, and salutation, and the insertion point should be positioned on the second line below the salutation. You used the Blank Spacing icon to create the blank line after the salutation. Notice that no paragraph mark appears in this blank line; Word enters paragraph marks only when you press Return.

Now type the body of the letter, dreadful as it is (you're going to revise it later). If you make typing mistakes, use the Backspace or Delete key to erase the error, and then retype.

As you type, don't press Return until you start a new paragraph. Words that go past the right margin are automatically *wrapped* to the next line. When you press Return, Word enters the blank line between paragraphs automatically.

Thank you for your letter of September 30. I'm disappointed you weren't happy with the equipment failure that occurred during our recent training session.

I'm sure you understand, however, that machines do some-times fail! Really, an engineer ought to know that! We had a substitute machine and got it up and running immediately.

We have replaced the unreliable projection display system that failed during our final presentation. Now that the new computer-based overhead display systems are available, we-- and our customers--won't have to rely on those unreliable projection devices.

When you finish typing, your letter should look like the one shown in figure 3.7.

This letter is a "flame"—an ill-considered and highly emotional response. The letter focuses on the writer's feelings about the situation. To write effectively in business, a writer must learn to revise so that the focus shifts to client and customer needs. (Actually, a letter this bad probably should go straight to the trash can so that you can start with a clean slate—but that's why it's great for this tutorial. The letter needs a lot of work!)

Revising the Letter

The letter needs to be reworked. In the sections to follow, you revise this letter substantially (and, along the way, learn many fundamental Word techniques).

Fig. 3.7

First draft of a business
letter.

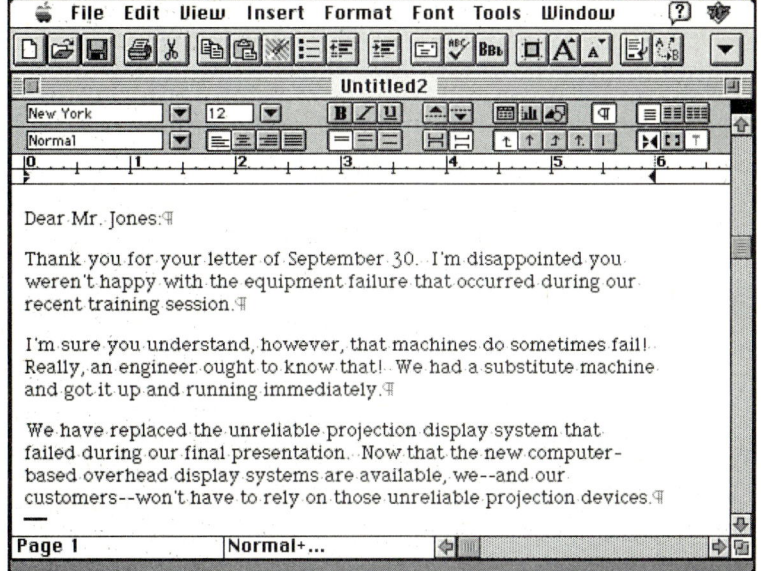

Joining Paragraphs

Your first revision involves joining the first two paragraphs to see
whether doing so improves the letter. To join two paragraphs, follow
these steps:

1. At the end of the first paragraph (the one ending with *training
   session*), select the paragraph mark by dragging over it until it
   is highlighted. If you don't see paragraph marks in your letter,
   choose Show ¶ from the View menu or click the paragraph-mark
   icon in the ribbon.

2. Press Backspace or Delete. The paragraphs are joined, as shown in
   figure 3.8. (You may need to type a space or two to separate the
   sentences you just joined.)

Deleting a Paragraph

As you inspect your letter after joining the two paragraphs, you decide
that the entire first paragraph must go. The paragraph is too negative;
besides, it violates the first principle of excellence in business com-
munication: focus on the customer, not on your own feelings and
preoccupations.

Fig. 3.8
Joined paragraphs.

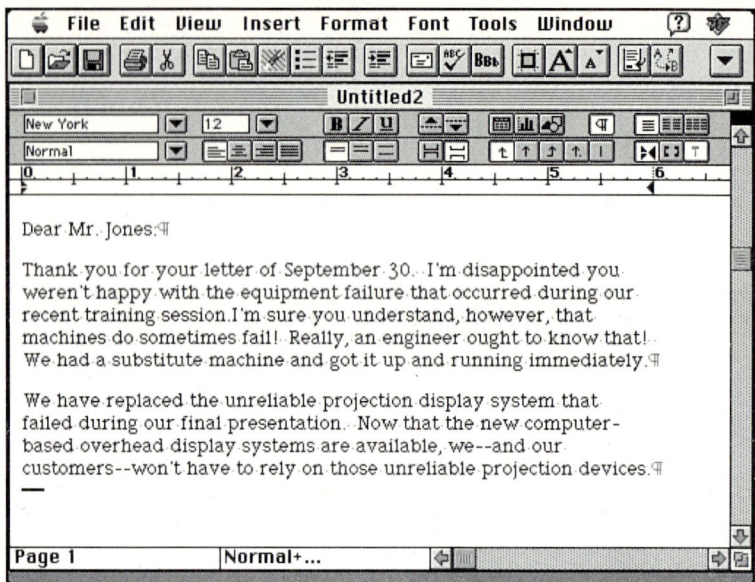

To get rid of the first paragraph, follow these steps:

1. Move the mouse pointer to the selection bar next to the letter's first paragraph.

2. When the pointer changes to an arrow, double-click the mouse button. Alternatively, triple-click in the paragraph. Either action selects the entire paragraph.

3. To delete the paragraph, choose Cut from the Edit menu, press ⌘-X, or click the Cut tool. The paragraph is deleted.

When you choose Cut, press ⌘-X, or click the Cut tool, Word removes the highlighted text from your document and places it in the *Clipboard*—a special temporary-storage area. To see what's in the Clipboard, choose Show Clipboard from the Window menu. Figure 3.9 shows the Clipboard window on-screen.

To close the Clipboard, click the Clipboard window's close box.

Fig. 3.9
Text cut to Clipboard
displayed in
Clipboard window.

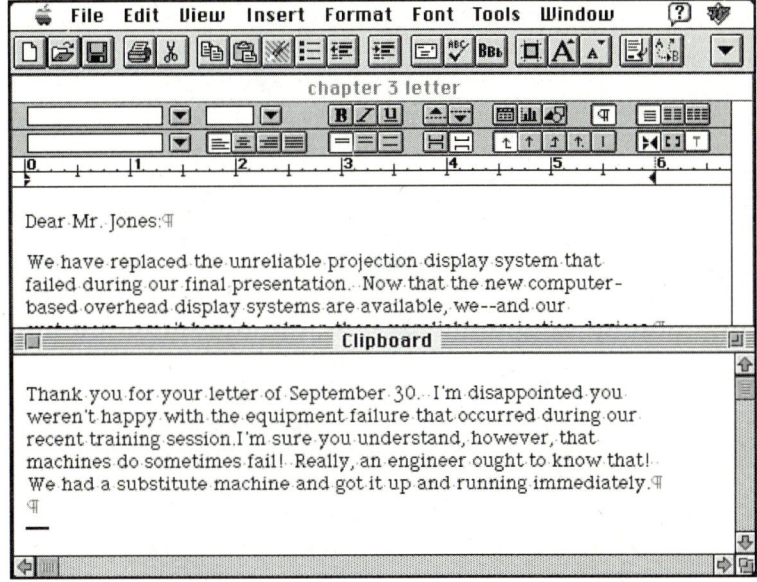

Changing the Deletion

As you consider the deletion that you just made, you realize that the first
sentence—*Thank you for your letter of September 30*—isn't all that bad.
To recover that sentence, follow these steps:

1. Choose Undo from the Edit menu, press ⌘-Z, or click the
   Undo tool. The deleted paragraph reappears in your document,
   highlighted.

2. Click anywhere in the document to cancel the highlighting.

3. Move the pointer to the beginning of the second sentence (*I'm
   disappointed*), and then drag right and down until you select all
   the way to the end of the paragraph. Don't select the trailing
   paragraph mark, though.

4. Choose Cut from the Edit menu, press ⌘-X, or click the Cut tool.

Adding More Text

To add more text to your letter, follow these steps:

1. Place the insertion point at the end of the first paragraph (*September 30*).

2. Type the following text:

   Mr. Jones, it was a pleasure serving you and your staff! Won't you consider firming up your plans for training your staff in the security techniques we detailed in our presentation? If you will give me a call or drop me a note, I'll have a proposal for you right away.

3. Press Return when you finish typing this paragraph. Your letter should look like the one shown in figure 3.10.

Fig. 3.10
Adding new text to the letter.

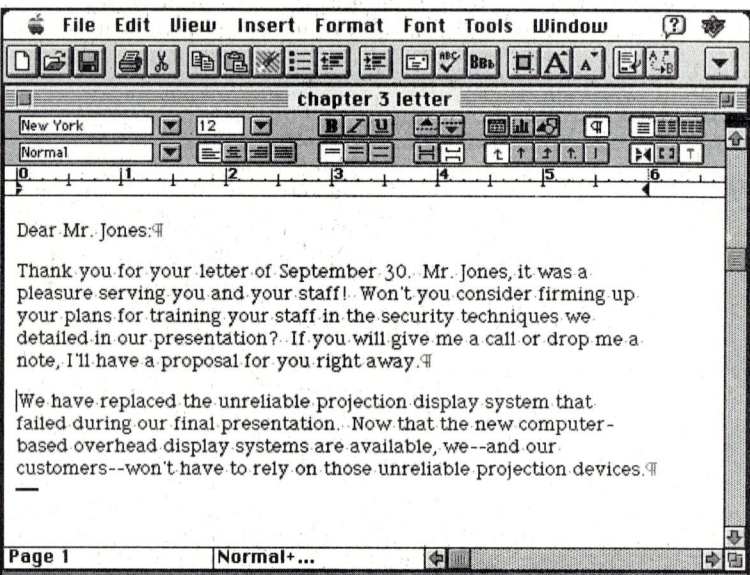

Moving Text

The letter is looking better, **but in examining what you have written, you realize that the text you just typed belongs at the end of the letter, not at the beginning.** (You remember what your business-communications

Part I

Getting Started with Word 5.1

teacher said: "End with a call for action! End on a personal note and invite a response!") You decide to move part of the first paragraph to the end of the letter.

You can move text in several different ways with Word. (See Chapter 8, "Editing Text," for a complete survey of your options.) Here, you sample a new Word 5.1 feature: *drag-and-drop editing*. Drag-and-drop editing enables you to move text by dragging a selection on-screen.

By default, drag-and-drop editing is turned off. Use the following instructions to activate drag-and-drop editing, if necessary:

1. Choose Preferences from the Tools menu. The Preference dialog box appears.

2. Activate the Drag-and-Drop Text Editing check box by clicking it so that an X appears in the check box.

3. Click the dialog box's close box. You return to your document.

To move text with drag-and-drop editing, follow these steps:

1. Place the insertion point at the end of the last paragraph and then press Return to add a blank line. A paragraph mark appears at the end of your document.

2. In the first paragraph, double-click the word *Mr.* and continue holding down the mouse button. Then drag right and down to select the rest of the text shown highlighted in figure 3.11. (Do not select the trailing paragraph mark.)

3. Release the mouse button. The selected text remains highlighted.

4. Click anywhere in the selected text and drag the mouse down. Notice that the arrow pointer appears instead of the I-beam pointer. The mouse pointer gains a gray bracket underneath the arrow, indicating that you're moving text. A gray insertion point appears near the pointer and follows it. This insertion point shows where the text will appear when you release the mouse button.

5. Place the gray insertion point before the last paragraph mark (the one at the end of the document) and release the mouse button. You have moved the text (see fig. 3.12).

Fig. 3.11
Selecting text.

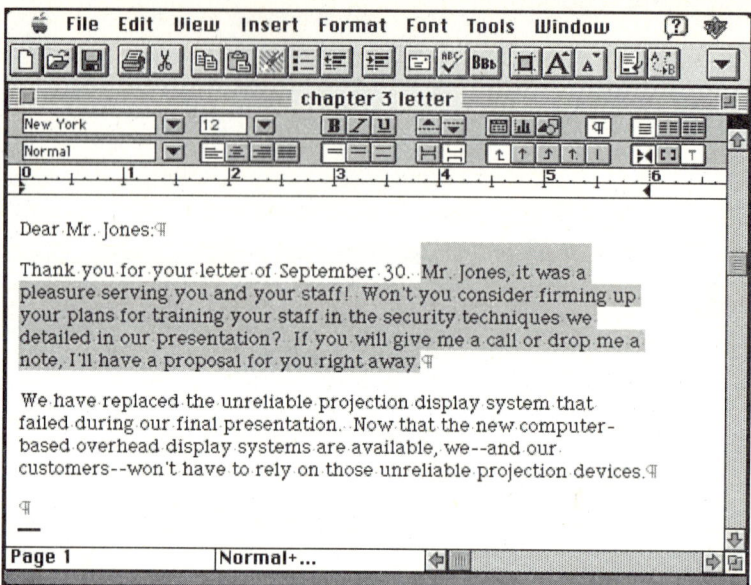

Fig. 3.12
Paragraph moved with
drag-and-drop editing.

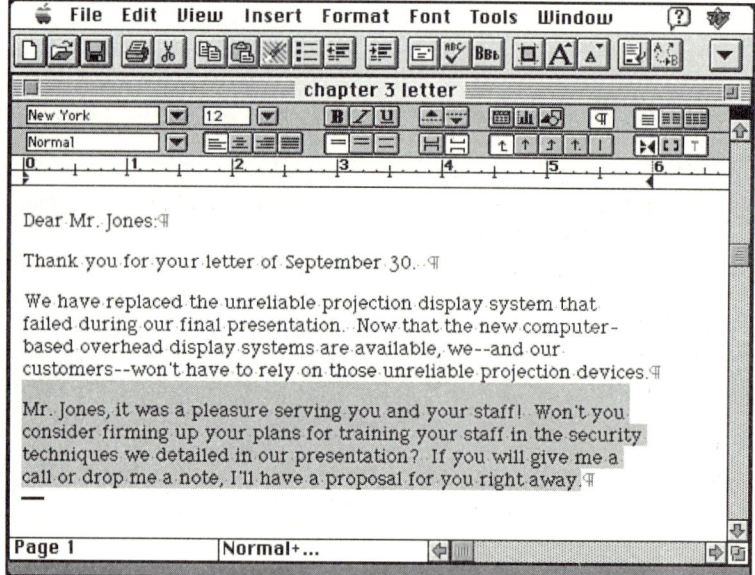

Part I

Getting Started with Word 5.1

Finishing the Letter

Now you are ready to add the closing by following these steps:

1. Place the insertion point just before the last paragraph mark and then press Return. Word enters a blank line, copying the paragraph format from the preceding paragraph. The new paragraph mark is preceded by 12 points of blank space.

 2. Click the Nest tool seven times. Word indents the paragraph 3.5 inches.

3. Type **Sincerely,** and then press Return twice.

   Because Word still is copying the current paragraph format, entering 12 points of blank space each time you press Return, you enter four lines of blank space by pressing Return twice. Word continues the 3.5-inch left indent.

4. Type **Diana B. Smith** and then press Return. Word enters another blank line—but this time, you don't want a blank line. Word continues the 3.5-inch left indent.

 5. With the insertion point positioned before the paragraph mark you just entered, click the No Blank Spacing icon in the ruler. Word moves the paragraph mark up one line.

6. Type **Corporate Training**.

You're finished. The closing of your letter should look like figure 3.13.

Previewing the Letter

In this section, you learn how to preview your letter's appearance so that you can adjust the formatting before printing. You can look at your document in four ways: Normal view, Outline view, Page Layout view, and Print Preview. (You learn more about these viewing modes in Chapter 4, "Understanding Word's Workplace.")

So far, you have been working in Normal view because your concern has been the text of the letter, not its appearance when printed. Now you are ready to use the Print Preview option to preview the formats you selected.

Fig. 3.13
The closing of the
finished letter.

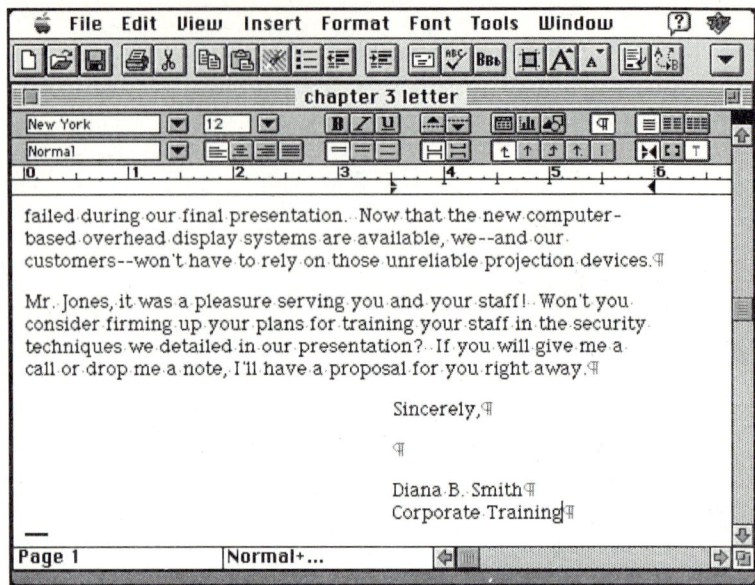

To preview your letter, choose Print Preview from the File menu or press
⌘-Option-I. The Print Preview window appears, as shown in figure 3.14.

Fig. 3.14
Print Preview of the letter.

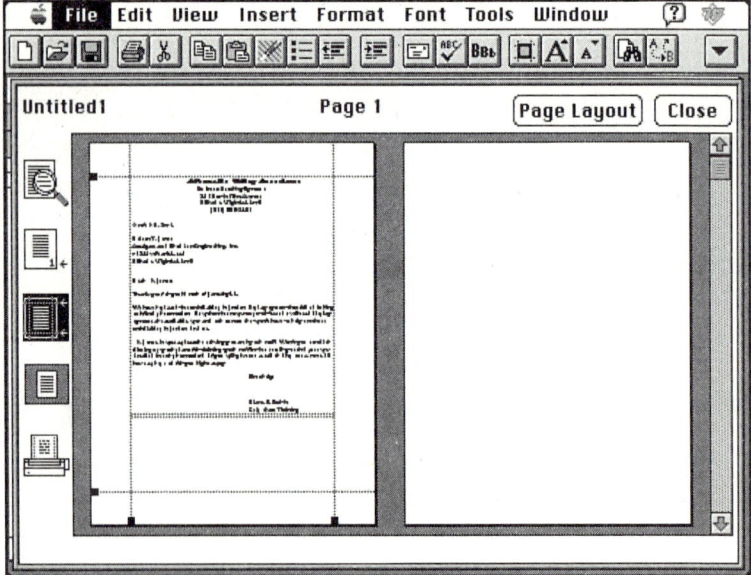

Notice how the text is laid out relative to the page as a whole. As you can see, the text is too high on the page, jammed up against the return address. To correct the problem, follow these steps:

1. Click the Close button in the Page Preview window to close that window. Your document reappears on-screen in Normal view.

2. Position the insertion point left of the date and then press Return three or four times.

3. Choose Print Preview from the File menu or press ⌘-Option-I. As you can see in figure 3.15, the letter now is balanced on the page.

Fig. 3.15
The letter balanced
on the page.

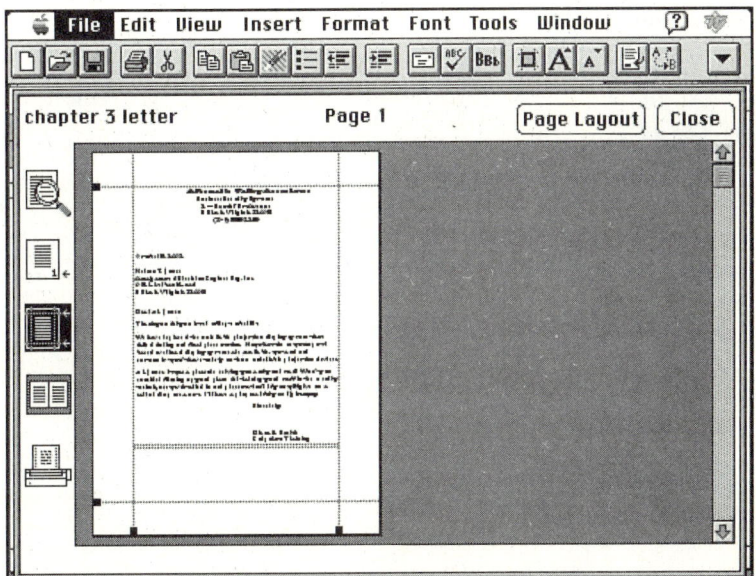

Printing the Letter

You can print the letter from within Print Preview by clicking the Printer icon, located at the bottom of the column of icons on the left side of the Print Preview window. (If you were working in Normal or Page Layout view, you would print by choosing Print from the File menu or by using the ⌘-P keyboard shortcut. You also could click the Print tool in the Toolbar.)

Chapter 3

Quick Start: Creating a Business Letter

What you see next depends on which printer you're using. Each printer has its own Print dialog box that enables you to control the printer's unique capabilities. Some features, however, appear in all Print dialog boxes. For example, you can choose the number of copies you want to print, the page range, and automatic or manual feeding. You usually can choose many other options as well, depending on the printer's capabilities. (You learn more about these options in Chapter 13, "Printing Documents.")

Figure 3.16 shows the Print dialog box for StyleWriter printers.

Fig. 3.16

Print dialog box for StyleWriter printers.

```
┌─────────────────────────────────────────────────────────────────┐
│ StyleWriter                                    7.2.2   [ Print  ] │
│                                                                   │
│ Copies:    [1    ]      Quality:   ● Best   ○ Faster  [ Cancel ]  │
│                                                                   │
│ Pages:    ● All    ○ From: [    ]   To: [     ]                   │
│                                                                   │
│ Paper:    ● Sheet Feeder   ○ Manual                              │
│                                                                   │
│ Print Pages:  ● All  ○ Odd Pages Only      ○ Even Pages Only      │
│ Section Range: From: 1      To: 1      □ Print Selection Only     │
│ □ Print Hidden Text    □ Print Next File                         │
└─────────────────────────────────────────────────────────────────┘
```

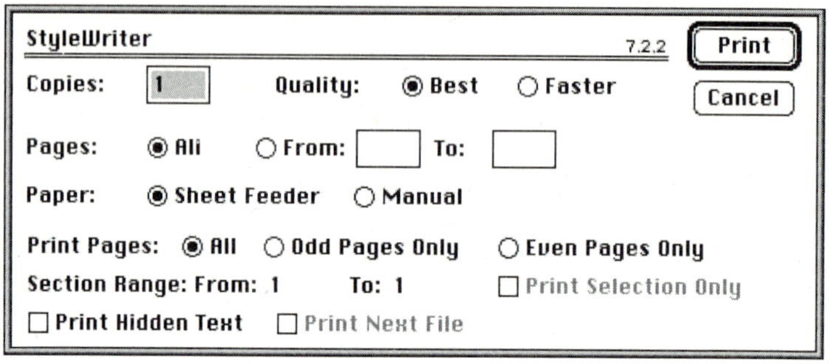

To print your letter, click Print or press Return. Figure 3.17 shows the result.

Quitting Word

Now that you have printed the letter, you are ready to save your work and quit Word.

To save your work, choose Save from the File menu, press ⌘-S, or click the Save tool.

To quit Word, choose Quit from the File menu or press ⌘-Q. If you forgot to save your letter, an alert box appears, asking whether you want to save the document you created. Click No if you want to abandon the letter. To save the letter, click Yes or press Return. (If you didn't save the document in a previous session, Word displays the Save As dialog box so that you can name the document.) If you have changed your mind about quitting Word, click Cancel or press Esc.

Fig. 3.17
Printed letter.

Albemarle Valley Associates
Business Security Systems
100 South First Avenue
Hillvale, Virginia 22993
(804) 555-1234

October 3, 1992

Nelson T. Jones
Amalgamated Precision Engineering, Inc.
941 Riverbank Road
Hillvale, Virginia 22993

Dear Mr. Jones:

Thank you for your letter of September 30.

We have replaced the unreliable projection display system
that failed during our final presentation. Now that the new
computer-based overhead display systems are available, we--
and our customers--won't have to rely on those unreliable
projection devices.

Mr. Jones, it was a pleasure serving you and your staff!
Won't you consider firming up your plans for training your
staff in the security techniques we detailed in our
presentation? If you will give me a call or drop me a note,
I'll have a proposal for you right away.

                                        Sincerely

                                        Diana B. Smith
                                        Corporate Training

CAUTION

Don't quit Word by turning off your Macintosh with Word still on-screen.
Although you will not harm Word or your computer by doing so, Word will not
save your settings, and the File menu will not contain the names of the documents you saved in the previous section. Always quit Word by choosing Quit
from the File menu or pressing ⌘-Q.

Chapter 3

Quick Start: Creating a Business Letter

Understanding Word's Workplace

n Chapter 3, you took a quick tour of Word's capabilities. In this chapter, you go back over Word's workplace—the environment in which you create your document—in more detail. You learn more about choosing commands from Word's menus and dialog boxes; managing Word's document windows; understanding the many options for viewing your document; and displaying Word's ribbon, ruler, and Toolbar.

In this chapter, you learn about the following topics:

■ *Choosing commands.* You learn all the Word techniques for choosing commands and navigating dialog boxes with the mouse or the keyboard. This section includes many shortcuts that help you work with Word more productively.

■ *Managing windows.* You learn all the fundamental window-manipulation skills. In Word, you can open up to 23 windows at a time, including some dialog boxes (such as the Find dialog box) that behave like windows. You also can split a document window so that you can view two portions of a document at a time.

■ *Viewing your document.* In Chapter 3, you learned two ways to view your document: Normal view for fast text entry and editing, and Print Preview to see how your document will look when printed. In this section, you learn all the ways you can control your view of your Word documents.

■ *Displaying the ribbon and ruler.* The ribbon and ruler—easy-to-use tools for many common formatting commands—can appear at the top of each document window. When you display the ribbon and ruler, you seldom may need to use Word's formatting dialog boxes or keyboard formatting commands. Because the ribbon and ruler take up room on the screen, this chapter teaches you how to toggle each feature on and off. (In later chapters, you learn how to format your documents with the ribbon and ruler.)

■ *Using the Toolbar.* Word 5.1's Toolbar provides a new way to access many commands quickly. In this section, you learn how to identify the tools in the Toolbar. These tools are shortcuts to menu commands that you access frequently.

Choosing Commands

Word fully conforms to Apple's standards for menus, dialog boxes, and keyboard command assignments, and chances are that you're already familiar with the basics of choosing commands. This section provides many shortcuts that can help you work more productively with Word.

This section begins with an exploration of Word's pull-down menus and dialog boxes, and concludes with an examination of Word's keyboard shortcuts for writers who prefer to keep their hands on the keys.

Using Word's Pull-Down Menus

In Chapter 3, you learned how to choose a command from the menu bar by using the mouse. When you pull down a menu, a list of commands appears (see fig. 4.1).

You see the following symbols in Word's pull-down menus:

■ *Checked options.* These options are currently in effect. If you choose one of them or another option that cancels a currently checked option, Word removes the check mark.

In the View menu, a check mark appears beside the Normal option by default, indicating that you're looking at your document in Normal view. If you choose one of the other View options, Word removes the check mark.

Fig. 4.1
Commands and options in
the View menu.

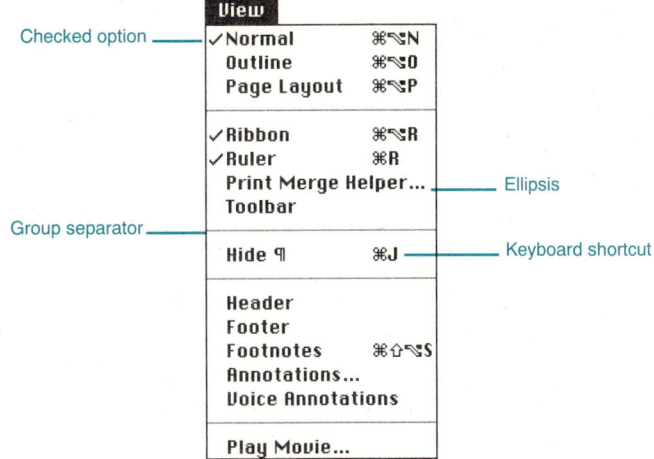

- *Group separators.* Lines divide the View menu into groups. At the top of the menu, you find three options for viewing your document: Normal, Outline, and Page Layout. Next, you find three options for displaying command information at the top of the active document window: Ribbon, Ruler, Print Merge Helper, and Toolbar.

  You will learn more about these and other command groupings elsewhere in this book. For now, notice that group separators show you which commands have similar functions.

- *Ellipses (...).* Three periods—an ellipsis—indicate that a dialog box or window will appear if you choose this command or option.

- *Keyboard shortcuts.* Many commands have keyboard shortcuts, which you can use if you would rather not take your hands away from the keyboard. (You learn more about keyboard shortcuts and how to use them later in this chapter.)

  Table 4.1 shows the keyboard-shortcut symbols you may find in Word menus.

Chapter 4
Understanding Word's Workplace

Table 4.1

Keyboard-Shortcut Symbols

Symbol	Key
⌘	Command
⌥	Option
⇧	Shift
^	Control
↵	Return
⌄	Enter
⎵	Space bar
⇥	Tab
⌫	Delete or Backspace
▦	Key in numeric keypad
⌦	Esc
⌦	Delete Forward

If you find the keyboard-shortcut symbols distracting, you can hide them. Choose Preferences from the Tools menu to open the Preferences dialog box, and then click the View icon in the left column to show the View options. Click the Show Function Keys on Menu check box until the X disappears, and then click the close box to close the Preferences dialog box.

Choosing Menu Commands with the Keyboard

Although the Macintosh pull-down menus are easy to use, many writers dislike removing their hands from the keyboard to choose commands from the menus. This section provides techniques for accessing pull-down menus by using the keyboard.

To access a pull-down menu with the keyboard, follow these steps:

1. Press ⌘-Tab. (If you prefer, you can press the period key in the numeric keypad instead.) Word highlights the menu bar, as shown in figure 4.2.

   The menu bar remains highlighted for a few seconds—long enough for you to choose a command name.

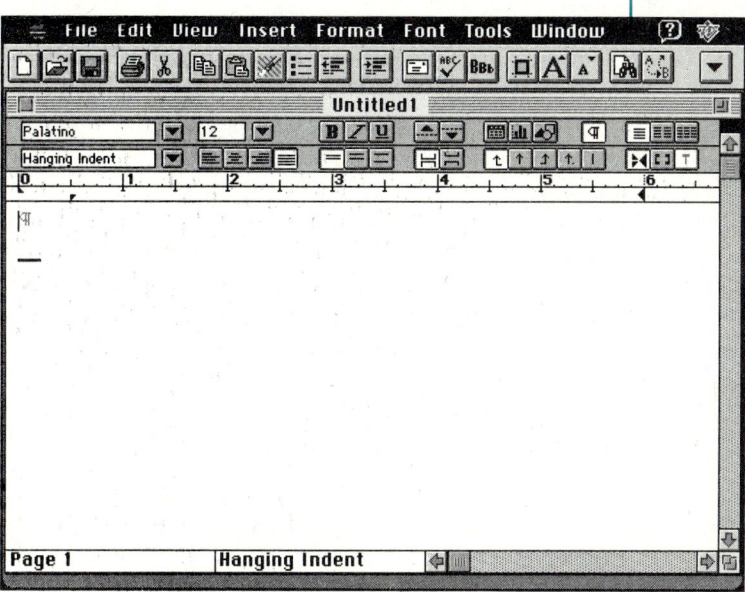

Fig. 4.2
Highlighted menu bar.

2. With the menu bar highlighted, choose the name of the menu you want to pull down. You can choose a menu name in the following ways:

■ To choose a menu using the arrow keys, press the right-arrow key to move the highlight down the menu bar to the right or the left-arrow key to move the highlight in the opposite direction. (If you go past the last command name, the highlight reappears on the left end of the menu bar.)

■ To choose a menu by letter, type the first letter of the menu's name. To choose Insert, for example, type **i**. (You can type either uppercase or lowercase.) If you want to choose the Format or Font menu, hold down the Shift key before typing **f** and keep pressing Shift-F until you highlight the name of the menu you want.

■ To choose a menu by number, type a number from 1 through 8 (according to the order in which the menu appears in the menu bar, starting with File and ending with Window). The File menu is 1, the Edit menu is 2, and so on.

Chapter 4

Understanding Word's Workplace

3. To close a menu without choosing a command, press Esc, ⌘-period (.), or Backspace.

You can use the keyboard to choose a command from a pull-down menu by following these steps:

1. Pull down a menu by pressing ⌘-Tab and then typing the first letter of the menu name.

2. Highlight the command you want in either of the following ways:

   ■ To choose a command using the arrow keys, press the down-arrow key to move the highlight down the menu or the up-arrow key to move the highlight in the opposite direction. (If you go past the last command name, the highlight reappears at the top of the menu.)

   ■ To choose a command by letter, type the first letter of the command's name. To choose Page Layout from the View menu, for example, type **p** (uppercase or lowercase). If two commands have the same first letter and you want to choose the second one, type the letter again.

T I P

If you pull down a menu and realize that you really wanted a command in another menu, you can access the correct menu quickly by using the keyboard. Simply hold down the Shift key and type the menu name's first letter. To open the Insert menu while the Format menu is open, for example, press Shift-I.

3. Press Return to choose the option you have highlighted.

Understanding Word's Dialog Boxes

Word's dialog boxes appear when the program needs more information to carry out a command. Figure 4.3 shows the Character dialog box, which appears after you choose Character in the Format menu.

Figure 4.4 shows the System 7 version of the Save As dialog box, which appears when you choose Save As in the File menu. (The System 6 version differs slightly.)

These two figures illustrate all the features you will find in Word's dialog boxes. Don't worry right now about what all the options in these dialog boxes do; your goal, for the moment, is to understand the features of these typical dialog boxes.

Fig. 4.3
Character dialog box.

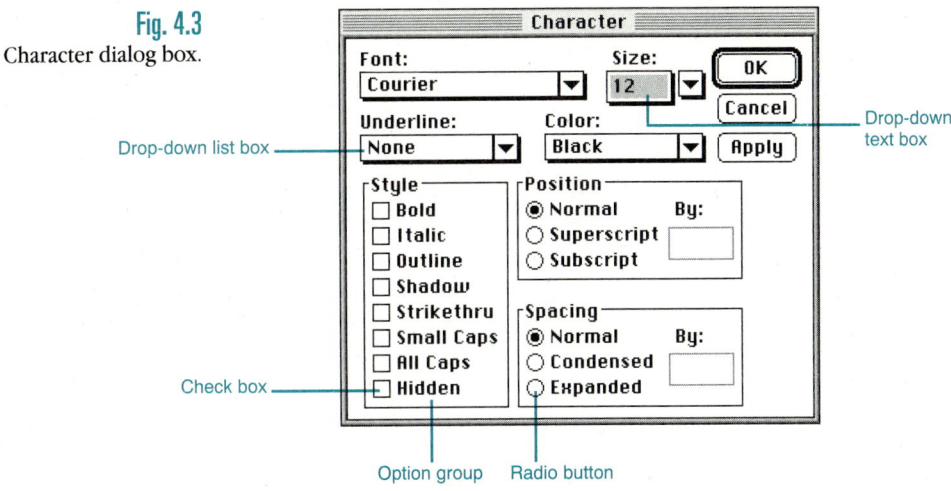

Drop-down list box

Check box

Option group   Radio button

Drop-down text box

Fig. 4.4
Save As dialog box.

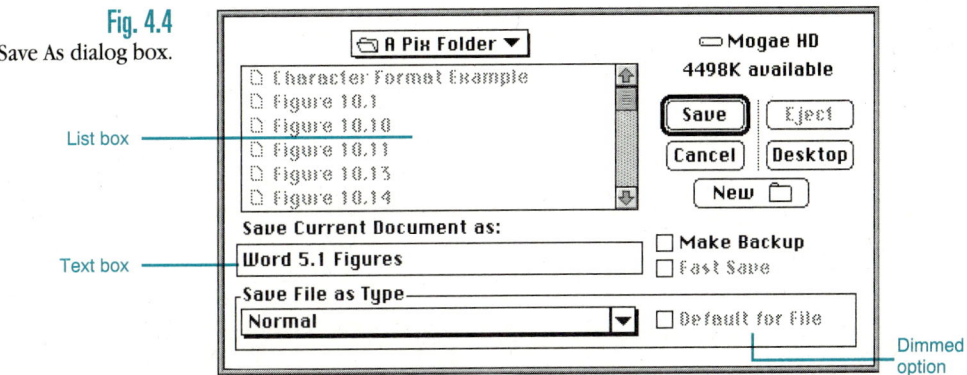

List box

Text box

Dimmed option

The following list describes the features you may find in a Word dialog box:

- *Option groups.* Related options are grouped and boxed in most dialog boxes. In the Character dialog box, for example, all the emphasis options (such as Bold and Italic) are grouped in the Style area.

To remove the default settings in an option group, click the option-group name. To remove the default character-emphasis style (Plain) in the Character dialog box, for example, click the word Style at the top of the emphasis-option group.

Chapter 4

Understanding Word's Workplace

■ *Check boxes.* Click a check box to activate the option; after you do, an X appears in the box. If you click an activated check box, the X disappears. In an option group containing several check boxes, you can choose more than one option.

■ *Radio buttons.* When you see a radio button (a small circle), you can click the button to turn the option on (a dot appears in the circle) or off (the dot disappears). These buttons are called radio buttons after the push buttons of old-fashioned car radios.

Unlike check boxes, only one option button in a group can be on at any time. When you choose one option, Word turns off the other ones in the group. In the Position area of the Character dialog box, for example, you must choose Normal, Superscript, or Subscript (because a character cannot be printed superscript and subscript at the same time).

■ *List boxes.* A list box, such as the one shown in figure 4.4, shows a list of items among which you can choose. You can use the scroll bar to scroll up and down the list. To choose an item in a list box, double-click it.

■ *Drop-down list boxes.* To reduce clutter in dialog boxes, Word uses drop-down list boxes, such as the Save File As Type list box shown in figure 4.5.

Fig. 4.5
Drop-down list box.

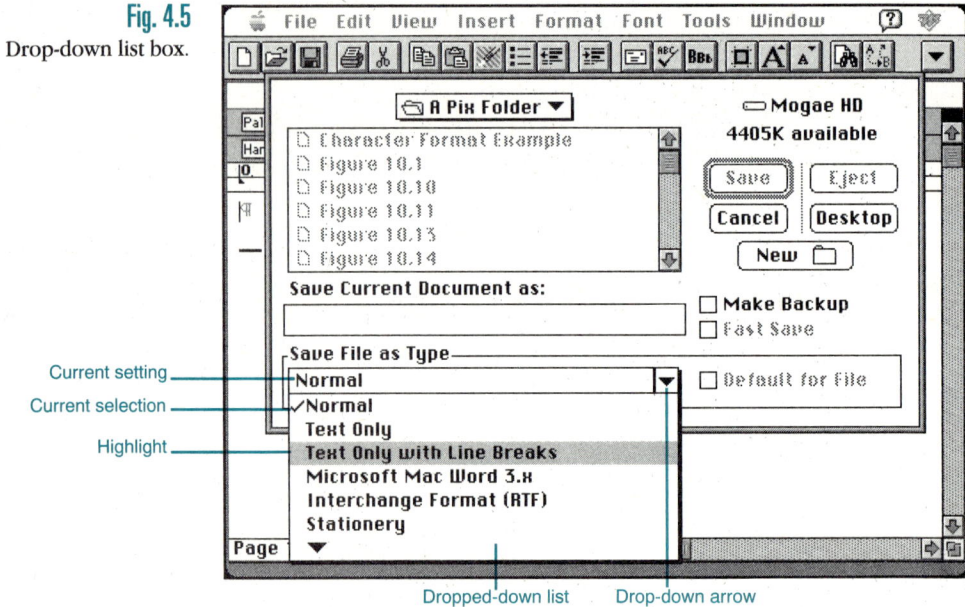

Part I

Getting Started with Word 5.1

To open a drop-down list box, click the drop-down arrow; the list appears, with a check mark indicating the currently selected option. To choose an item from the list, highlight the item you want and then release the mouse button. Your choice appears in the drop-down list box as the new current setting.

■ *Text boxes.* In a text box, you type information that Word needs, such as a file's new name. Word requires that you type information only when it can obtain the needed information in no other way.

Within a text box, standard Macintosh editing techniques apply. To delete the text, highlight the text and press Delete. If no text is highlighted, pressing Delete erases the character to the left of the insertion point.

When a text box is highlighted, start typing. Word erases the existing text from the text box, saving you the trouble of selecting and deleting that text.

■ *Drop-down text boxes.* Some drop-down list boxes also are text boxes, meaning that you can type your own option in the box instead of choosing one from the list. An example is the Size drop-down list box in the Character dialog box. You can choose a size from the list or type the size you want. If you prefer, you can treat the drop-down text box as if it were an ordinary text box and choose the option you want from the drop-down list.

■ *Dimmed options.* If you see a dimmed or grayed option, such as the Default for File option in the Save As dialog box, you cannot choose this option at present. Some dimmed options become active when you choose other options in the dialog box. If you choose an option other than Normal in the Save File As Type list box, for example, the Default for File option becomes active. You then can choose this option to make the non-Normal option the default setting for the current file.

■ *Command buttons.* Command buttons, such as the OK and Cancel buttons in the Document dialog box, carry out the choices you have made in the dialog box (see fig. 4.6).

In some dialog boxes, command buttons contain ellipses, indicating that they open second-level dialog boxes (dialog boxes within dialog boxes). The File Series button in the Document dialog box, for example, opens the File Series dialog box, which is accessible only through the Document dialog box. When you exit the File Series dialog box, you return to the Document dialog box.

Chapter 4
Understanding Word's Workplace

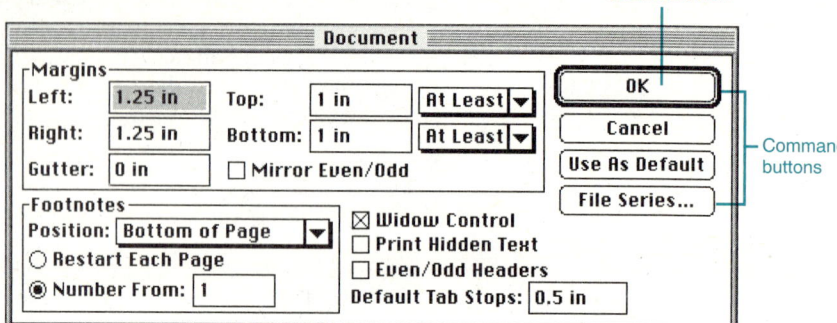

Fig. 4.6
Command buttons in the
Document dialog box.

When you see an outlined command button, such as OK in the Document dialog box, pressing Return chooses this button immediately. You can press Esc or ⌘-period (.) to choose the Cancel button immediately.

Choosing Dialog-Box Options with the Keyboard

If you like to use the keyboard, you can use the following keys to select options in dialog boxes:

- *Tab and Shift-Tab.* In dialog boxes that contain more than one text box or drop-down text box, you can press Tab to move the highlight from one text box to the next. (When you reach the last text box, pressing Tab activates the first one again.) You can press Shift-Tab to reverse the cursor's movement.

- *⌘-Tab and ⌘-Shift-Tab.* When you press ⌘-Tab, Word moves a blinking gray underline to the next option, list, text area, or button in the dialog box, as shown in figure 4.7.

Fig. 4.7
Gray underline indicating
that the Mirror Even/Odd
option is highlighted.

Option highlighted
with keyboard

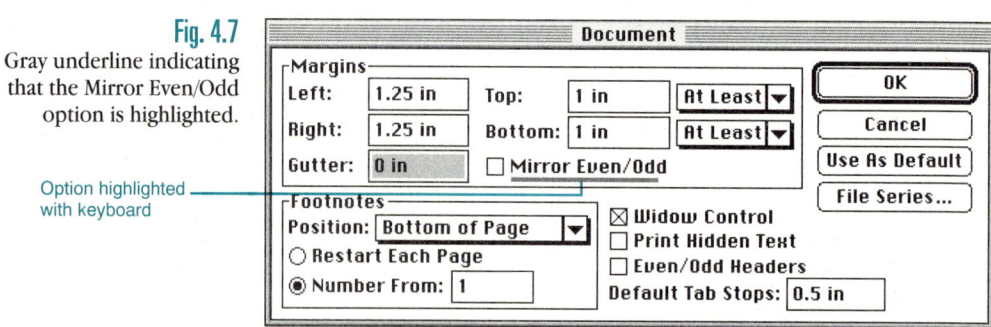

Part I

Getting Started with Word 5.1

The blinking gray underline indicates that the option is high-lighted; you must press keypad 0 (zero) or ⌘-space bar to activate the option. (The keypad 0 key is located in the numeric keypad.) Pressing ⌘-Shift-Tab moves the underline to the preceding option, list, text area, or button.

■ *⌘-space bar or keypad 0 (zero).* Press keypad 0 or ⌘-space bar to activate the selected option (the one with the blinking gray underline). If you select a drop-down list box, pressing keypad 0 or ⌘-space bar opens the list. If no blinking gray underline is visible, press ⌘-Tab to see which option currently is selected.

■ *Down arrow or up arrow.* Within a list box, you use these keys to move the highlight to the item you want. When you have selected the item, press ⌘-Tab if you want to make any additional selections within the dialog box, or press Return to select your choice immediately.

■ *⌘-down arrow or ⌘-up arrow.* These keys apply when you're working in a list of files that contain folders, such as the list box in the Open dialog box (see fig. 4.8).

Fig. 4.8
Open dialog box.

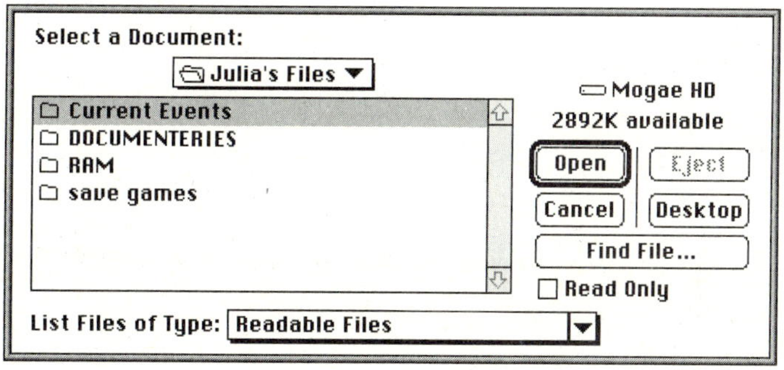

Next to the names in such a list, you see icons indicating whether the items are documents (indicated by the page icon) or folders (indicated by the folder icon). When you highlight a folder—such as the folder called Current Events in figure 4.8—you can open the folder and display its files by pressing ⌘-down arrow. After you open a folder, you can close it and return to the next folder up by pressing ⌘-up arrow.

Table 4.2 summarizes all the keys you can use in dialog boxes.

Chapter 4
Understanding Word's Workplace

Table 4.2	To perform this action	Press these keys
Keyboard Techniques for Dialog Boxes	Move to the next text box	Tab
	Move to the preceding text box	Shift-Tab
	Select the next option	⌘-Tab or keypad period (.)
	Select the preceding option	⌘-Shift-Tab or Shift-keypad period (.)
	Choose underlined option	⌘-space bar or keypad 0 (zero)
	Highlight item in list	Up or down arrow
	Choose and activate option or button	⌘-first letter of option or button
	Open folder in a files list box	⌘-down arrow
	Open next folder up in a files list box	⌘-up arrow
	Cancel choices and close dialog box	Esc
	Confirm choices and close dialog box	Return

Choosing Commands with Keyboard Shortcuts

Because Word is designed for keyboard users as well as mouse users, most mouse techniques are duplicated by one or more keyboard commands. You needn't learn both methods in order to use Word effectively. If you're planning to use the mouse, however, exploring the keyboard techniques still makes sense. When you use keyboard techniques, you don't remove your hand from the keyboard—a somewhat faster process than using the mouse.

In Word's default shortcut-key assignment, you can redefine Word's keyboard exactly the way you want. For more information on customizing Word's keyboard, see Chapter 35, "Customizing Menus and Keyboard Shortcuts."

Table 4.3 lists keyboard shortcuts for frequently used commands and dialog boxes. (For a complete list, see Appendix C, "Keyboard Shortcuts.")

Command	Keyboard shortcut
Bold (Format menu)	⌘-B or ⌘-Shift-B
Character (Format menu)	⌘-D
Close (File menu)	⌘-W
Copy (Edit menu)	⌘-C
Cut (Edit menu)	⌘-X
Find (Edit menu)	⌘-F
Go To (Edit menu)	⌘-G
Italic (Format menu)	⌘-I or ⌘-Shift-I
New (File menu)	⌘-N
Normal (View menu)	⌘-Option-N
Open (File menu)	⌘-O
Outline (View menu)	⌘-Option-O
Page Layout (View menu)	⌘-Option-P
Paragraph (Format menu)	⌘-M
Paste (Edit menu)	⌘-V
Plain Text (Format menu)	⌘-Shift-Z
Print (File menu)	⌘-P
Print Preview (File menu)	⌘-Option-I
Quit (File menu)	⌘-Q
Repeat (Edit menu)	⌘-Y
Replace (Edit menu)	⌘-H
Ribbon (View menu)	⌘-Option-R
Ruler (View menu)	⌘-R
Save (File menu)	⌘-S
Select All (Edit menu)	⌘-A
Spelling (Tools menu)	⌘-L
Underline (Format menu)	⌘-U or ⌘-Shift-U
Undo (Edit menu)	⌘-Z

Table 4.3
Keyboard Shortcuts for Frequently Accessed Commands and Dialog Boxes

Chapter 4
Understanding Word's Workplace

If your Macintosh is equipped with an extended keyboard, you can use the function keys (numbered F1 through F15) to access frequently used dialog boxes and commands. Table 4.4 lists the function keys available to users of these keyboards. (If you have an extended keyboard, you still can use the keyboard shortcuts listed in table 4.3.) In tandem with the Option and Shift keys, more function-key shortcuts are available than the ones listed in table 4.3; for a complete list, see Appendix C, "Keyboard Shortcuts."

Table 4.4
Keyboard Shortcuts for
Extended Keyboards

Command	Function-key shortcut
Bold (Format menu)	F10
Character (Format menu)	F14
Copy (Edit menu)	F3
Cut (Edit menu)	F2
Italic (Format menu)	F11
New (File menu)	F5
Open (File menu)	F6
Page Layout (View menu)	F13
Paste (Edit menu)	F4
Print (File menu)	F8
Revert to Style (Format menu)	F9
Save (File menu)	F7
Spelling (Tools menu)	F15
Underlining (Format menu)	F12
Undo (Edit menu)	F1

Choosing Commands with Hotspots

Be sure to explore Word's *hotspots*, which are areas of the screen that, when double-clicked, bring forth a dialog box. For example, you can display the Paragraph dialog box by double-clicking any of the alignment or spacing buttons in the ruler.

Part I
Getting Started with Word 5.1

Table 4.5 lists the hotspots.

Table 4.5 Hotspots	To open	Double-click
	Character dialog box	Ribbon background
	Document dialog box	Margin indicators on ruler or corners of page outside the margins (Page Layout view only)
	Footnote window	Footnote reference mark
	Go To dialog box	Page number in page-number area
	Paragraph dialog box	Alignment or spacing icons in ruler
	Section dialog box	Section mark
	Style dialog box	Style name in style-name area (in status bar)
	Tabs dialog box	Tab stop or tab icon in ruler

Undoing Commands

When a command goes awry, you can choose Undo from the Edit menu to cancel the preceding command's effects. (Alternatively, use the ⌘-Z or F1 shortcut.) You can undo the effects of most editing, formatting, and text-processing commands, including sorts and automatic numbering.

Just what Undo undoes at any time appears in the Edit menu. If you have been cutting text, for example, the Undo command reads Undo Cut (see fig. 4.9). Undo Cut restores the text you have just deleted.

CAUTION

You cannot undo all commands. If the Undo command is grayed and says Can't Undo, you're stuck with the consequences of the command you have given.

After you choose Undo, you have a chance to change your mind yet another time. To restore the effects of the command you just undid, choose the Undo command again. You will find that the name of the command has changed to Redo, followed by the name of the command or action that can be redone.

Fig. 4.9
The Undo command shows
what can be undone.

Edit	
Undo Cut	⌘Z
Repeat	⌘Y
Cut	⌘X
Copy	⌘C
Paste	⌘V
Paste Special...	
Clear	
Select All	⌘A
Find...	⌘F
Replace...	⌘H
Go To...	⌘G
Glossary...	⌘K
Create Publisher...	
Subscribe To...	
Link Options...	
Edit Object...	

CAUTION

Because Undo can erase the consequences of only the last action you undertook, be sure to use Undo immediately should a command go awry.

Repeating the Last Action

The Repeat command (⌘-Y) in the Edit menu shares one trait with Undo: the command's name changes to reflect the actions that Word can repeat. When you're typing, the Repeat command reads Repeat Typing; if you choose this command, Word inserts (at the insertion point) a copy of all the text you have typed since the last time you chose a command. (This command was called Again in earlier versions of Word.)

You can repeat an action as many times as you want, so long as you don't type any additional text or choose another command.

Learning when to use the Repeat command takes some practice. The following suggestions should help you.

Suppose that you used the word *utilize* several times in a paragraph and want to replace it with the simpler *use*. Highlight the first *utilize* in the paragraph and then type **use**. Now the Repeat command reads Repeat Typing. Without choosing any other commands or typing any additional text, highlight the next *utilize* and choose Repeat Typing from the Edit menu (or press the ⌘-Y keyboard shortcut). Word replaces the selection with the repeated text, *use*.

Or suppose that you just chose several options from one of the Format dialog boxes and want to apply those options to a second block of text. After you choose the formatting options, select the second block of text that you want to format the same way and then choose the Repeat command.

Managing Windows

Word uses standard Macintosh window features, adding some special features germane to Word's document-processing functions. In this section, you explore the features of Word's document windows. You also learn how to open windows—as many as 23 at a time, if your system is equipped with enough memory. You can open two or more documents at a time, each in its own window. You also can open two or more windows in the same document, with each window showing a separate portion of the document. You even can split a document window into two panes.

With all these windows on-screen at once, you will be glad to know that you can activate windows easily (even when you cannot see them) and that you can size, move, and close windows as you please.

Understanding Document Windows

Following is a complete description of the document windows in which you create your Word documents:

Title bar. In Word, only one window can be active at a time, even if more than one window is visible on-screen. When a window is active, you see lines in the title bar and highlighting in the scroll bars (see fig. 4.10).

When a window is inactive, the title-bar lines and scroll-bar highlighting disappear, as do other features (see fig. 4.11).

Close box. In an active window, a close box appears at the left end of the title bar. To close the window, click the close box. (If you haven't saved your work when you close a window, Word alerts you and gives you the opportunity to save.)

Fig. 4.10
Active document window.

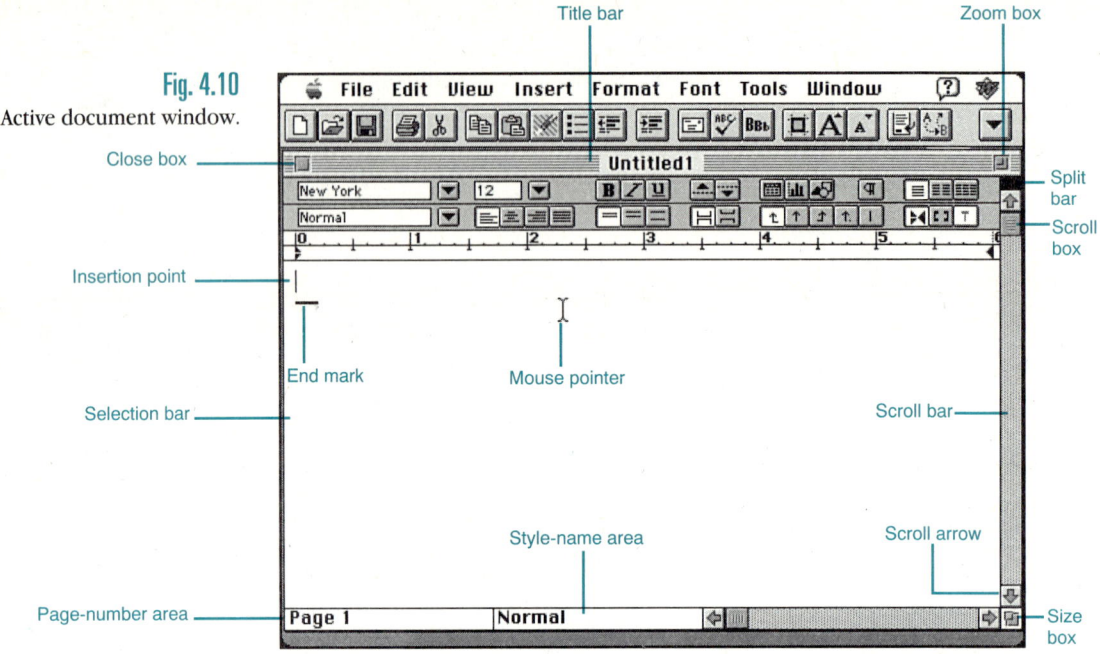

Title bar

Zoom box

Close box

Insertion point

End mark

Mouse pointer

Selection bar

Split bar

Scroll box

Scroll bar

Style-name area

Scroll arrow

Page-number area

Size box

Fig. 4.11
Inactive document window.

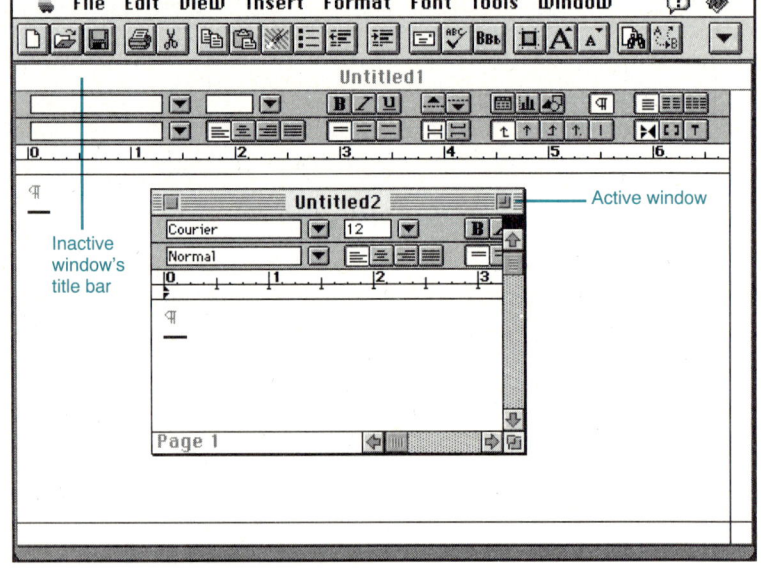

Inactive window's title bar

Active window

Zoom box. Click the zoom box to switch the window between its original size (the window's size at the beginning of your work session) and an alternative size. If you have never moved or sized the window, Word automatically sets the alternative size to approximately 50 percent of the original size. To restore the window to its original size, click the zoom box again.

Insertion point. This blinking vertical line shows where your text will appear when you start typing. If you have used an MS-DOS computer, notice that the insertion point isn't quite the same as a cursor. An MS-DOS cursor always appears *on* a character, whereas the Mac's insertion point always appears *after* a character.

Mouse pointer. This pointer shows you the current location of the mouse. In a document, clicking the mouse moves the insertion point to the mouse pointer's location. Within a document window, the mouse pointer resembles a capital letter *I*. This shape, called the *I-beam pointer*, enables you to reposition the cursor precisely between text characters, even if you're using a small font (such as 9 points or 10 points). Notice that the I-beam pointer changes shape when you move the pointer out of the document window. (You learn more about what these shape changes mean in Chapter 5, "Managing Documents and Files.")

Selection bar. If you move the mouse pointer to this area along the left side of the window, the pointer changes from an I-beam to an arrow pointing up and right. This change indicates that you can select an entire line by clicking next to the line, an entire paragraph by double-clicking next to the paragraph, or the whole document by holding down the ⌘ key and clicking.

End mark. The end mark shows the end of the document. You cannot move the insertion point or type text past the end mark.

Split bar. A black rectangle at the top of the vertical scroll bar, the split bar enables you to split the window into two panes by dragging the split bar down the scroll bar.

Scroll boxes. Drag the scroll boxes to view additional parts of your document.

Scroll bars. Clicking the vertical or horizontal scroll bar displays other parts of a document that's more than one screen long. To scroll your document down one screen, for example, click below the vertical scroll box. To scroll your document right one screen, click to the right of the horizontal scroll box.

Scroll arrows. Clicking the vertical scroll arrows scrolls your document line by line. If you click the horizontal scroll arrows, Word scrolls your document right or left in half-inch increments.

Size box. To size a window, drag the size box.

Style-name area. This area shows the name of the style that applies to the current paragraph. Until you create your own styles or apply Word's styles, you see the default style, Normal, in this area. (You learn more about styles in Chapter 9, "Formatting with Fonts and Character Styles.")

Page-number area. In this area, you see the number of the page that currently appears on-screen. Some commands, however, display other information in this area. In previous versions of Word, this area was called the *status area*, which made some sense because many commands present messages in this area.

Opening Additional Documents

Even though a document is open and displayed on-screen, you can open additional documents without closing the open document or losing your work. To open an existing document, choose Open from the File menu or use the ⌘-O keyboard shortcut. To open a new document, choose New from the File menu or press ⌘-N.

When you open a new document, Word places the new document's window on top of the first one, filling the screen. For this reason, you cannot see the first document, and you may worry that you have lost your unsaved work. Don't worry—it's still there. You can display the first document by making it active again, as explained in the "Activating Windows" section later in this chapter.

Opening Two Windows in the Same Document

A window is a "picture frame" through which you can view a document that's in Word's memory. Word enables you to open more than one window in the same document by choosing New Window from the Window menu or by using the Shift-F5 shortcut. Opening two windows in a document is useful when, for example, you want to keep one part of a document in view while you write in another.

Word gives the second window a name like the one shown in figure 4.12. (The Window menu shows all the open windows.)

Fig. 4.12
Second window in an open document.

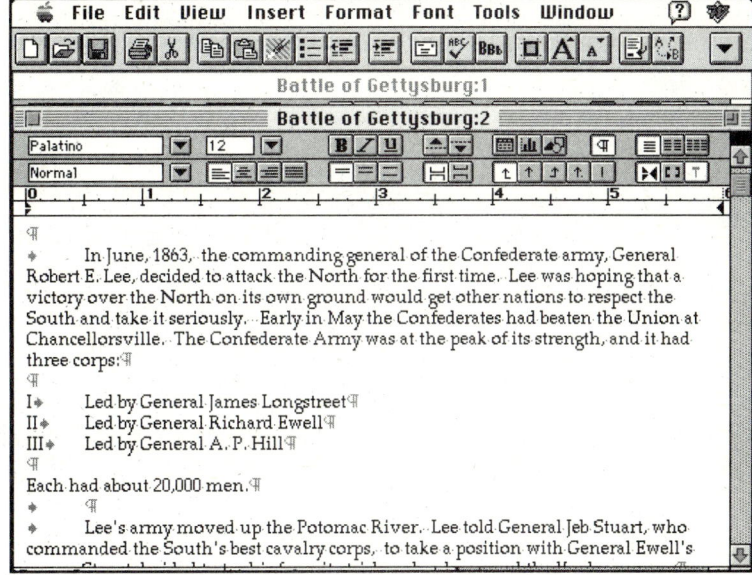

Notice that the second window serves as a second picture frame through which you can view the same document. If you make changes to this document in the window titled Battle of Gettysburg:2, for example, these changes will appear in the original window, which now is titled Battle of Gettysburg:1. You can close one of the windows in this document without any loss of your work.

When two or more windows are open in a document, you can display different parts of the document. Scrolling one window doesn't affect what's displayed in another window.

Activating Windows

Only one window can be active at a time. To activate a window, click anywhere in it; this action automatically inactivates the window that was active. If you cannot see the window you want to activate, use the Window menu, as explained in the following procedure:

1. Pull down the Window menu. Notice that a check mark appears beside the window that's currently active (see fig. 4.13).

2. Select the name of the window you want to activate.

Fig 4.13
Window menu showing
open windows.

Fig 4.13
Window menu showing
open windows.

You also can activate windows that you cannot see by pressing ⌘-
Option-W. Word activates and displays the next active window, using
the *reverse* of the sequence of windows as they're listed in the Window
menu. If the Windows menu lists Example:1, Example:2, and Example:3,
pressing ⌘-Option-W cycles through the open windows in the sequence
Example:3, Example:2, and Example:1. If you press ⌘-Option-W again,
Word displays Example:3.

Splitting a Window

As you just learned, you can open two windows in the same document.
You can achieve much the same effect by splitting a window into two
panes, as shown in figure 4.14.

Fig. 4.14
Window split into two
panes.

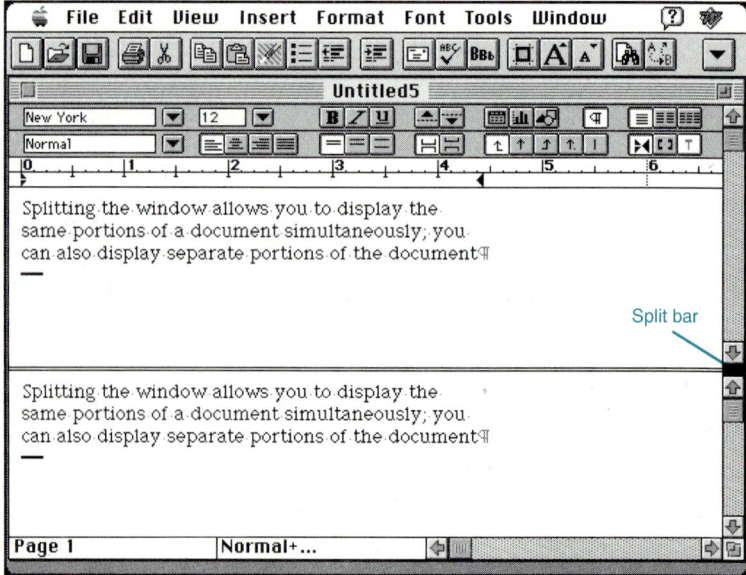

After you split a window, each pane has its own vertical scroll bar. You can view different parts of the document: scrolling one pane doesn't affect the other. You cannot, however, display two different documents in the same window. To display two different documents, you must open two separate windows.

If you want to view two portions of the same document, splitting a window is more convenient than opening two windows in the same document. You don't need to size or move the windows to get them aligned correctly, and only one title bar takes up room on the screen.

When you split the window, you can choose where you want the split to occur, or you can split the window into two equal-size panes.

To split a window and choose where you want the split to occur, follow these steps:

1. Move the mouse pointer to the split bar until the pointer shape changes (you see a white bar with up and down arrows).

2. Drag the split bar down the vertical scroll bar until you have positioned the split where you want it.

3. Release the mouse button.

Use the following nifty shortcut to split a window into two equal-size panes:

1. Move the mouse pointer to the split bar until the pointer shape changes (you see a white bar with up and down arrows).

2. Double-click the mouse. Alternatively, use the ⌘-Option-S keyboard shortcut.

After you split the window, you can adjust the location of the split in the document. Move the pointer to the split bar until the pointer shape changes (arrows pointing up and down). Drag the mouse to move the split bar.

To remove the split, double-click the split bar or press ⌘-Option-S. If you are displaying different parts of the document, the part displayed in the bottom pane will remain on-screen.

NOTE

As you will learn in the next section, you can choose any of three views of your document: Normal, Outline, and Page Layout. Each pane in a split window can have its own view.

If you want to keep the top pane on-screen after you remove the window split, drag the split bar off the bottom of the vertical scroll bar.

Sizing a Window

To quickly reduce a window to a smaller size—called the *alternative size/location*—click the zoom box or double-click the title bar. The size Word chooses for the alternative size/location depends on how many documents are open currently, how large your screen is, and other factors. (Generally, Word shrinks the document by approximately 50 percent.)

After you reduce a window's size, you can zoom it back to its original size by clicking the zoom box again or double-clicking the title bar.

Another way to change a window's size is to use the size box in the window's bottom right corner. Drag the size box in any direction to change the window's size.

After you use the size box, the size you chose for the window becomes the window's alternative size/location for the current Word session. When you click the zoom box or double-click the title bar, Word restores the window's original size. If you click the zoom box or double-click the title bar again, Word restores the size you chose when you manually resized the window.

If you want to work with two documents at one time, the following technique automatically sizes the document windows so that the screen area is split between them. Follow these steps:

1. Open the first document.

2. Click the document's zoom box. Word shrinks the document to its alternative size/location, filling the top half of the screen.

3. Open the second document.

4. Click the second document's zoom box. Word shrinks the second document to its alternative size/location, filling the bottom half of the screen.

Moving Windows

You can move a window on the Desktop by dragging the title bar. After moving the window, you can restore its original location by clicking the zoom box.

When you move a window, the new location you choose becomes the window's alternate location. Suppose that you move a window and then click the zoom box to restore its original location. If you then click the zoom box again, Word moves the window back to the location you chose earlier.

Closing Windows

Before closing a window, save your work by choosing Save or Save As from the File menu (or use the ⌘-S keyboard shortcut). Then click the window's close box, choose Close from the File menu, or use the ⌘-W keyboard shortcut.

When you close a window, Word saves its current size and location. The next time you open the document, the window opens at the saved size and location.

Exploring Word's Views

Word's View menu includes commands that toggle the program's view options on and off (see fig. 4.15).

You can choose among three View options: Normal, Outline, and Page Layout A File-menu option, Print Preview, gives you another way of viewing your document. All these options, and their uses, are discussed in the following sections.

Writing and Editing in Normal View

Word's Normal view, shown in figure 4.16, offers the fastest screen updating and is the best choice for day-to-day writing.

Fig. 4.15
View menu.

Current view

View options

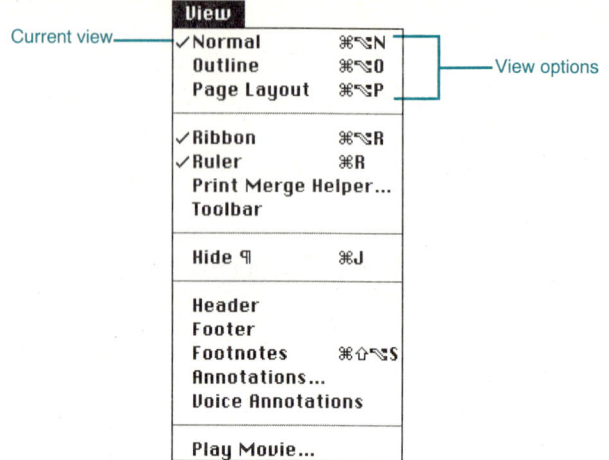

Fig. 4.16
Normal view of a document.

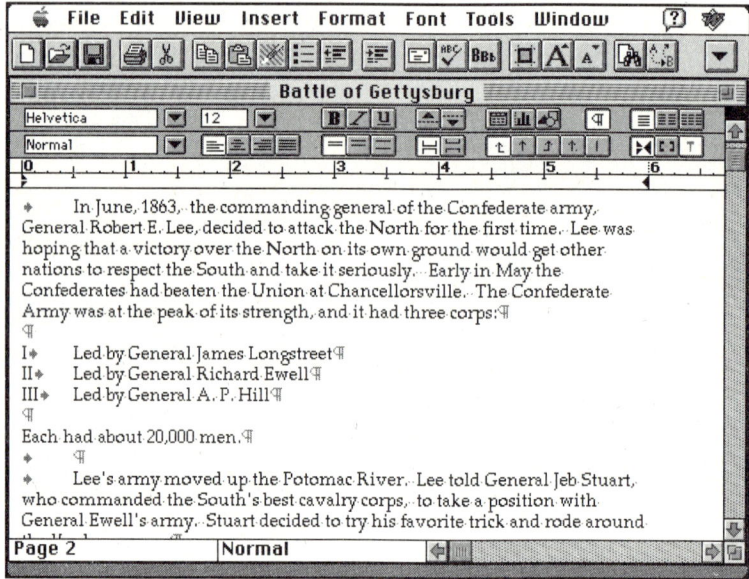

Normal is the default view. You can change the default view by choosing Preferences from the Tools menu (as explained in Chapter 35). You can see most character and paragraph formats on-screen in Normal view; you even can see graphics. Some formats, however, do not appear in Normal view the same way they will appear when printed.

In Page Layout view, you see most formats on-screen the way they will print, including the formats you don't see in Normal view. These formats include newspaper columns, headers and footers, footnotes, page numbers, and frames that you anchor to an absolute position on the page.

You still create text in these formats in Normal view. The Normal view displays text in one continuous stream, with page breaks indicated by a dotted line across the screen. When you type newspaper columns (multiple columns), you don't see the multiple-column layout on-screen; the text appears in a single narrow column.

If you fix text or graphics to an absolute position on the page, using the Frame option in the Format menu (as discussed in Chapter 20, "Positioning Text and Graphics"), that absolute position doesn't appear on-screen; instead, you see the text or graphics in line with the rest of the text. In figure 4.16, for example, the headings are shown in line with the rest of the text. Page Layout view, shown later in figure 4.18, shows you how the headings will appear when printed.

To display a document in Normal view, choose Normal from the View menu or use the ⌘-Option-N shortcut.

Working in Outline View

In Outline view, you see your document as an outline, with the text hidden from view (see fig. 4.17).

You must code your headings with Word's built-in heading styles (such as Heading 1 and Heading 2) if you want to view your headings and subheadings as outline headings. In Outline view, you can see the logical structure of your document; more important, you can restructure your document quickly by rearranging headings in the outline. You learn more about Word's Outline view in Chapter 22, "Organizing Documents with Outlining."

To view your document in Outline view, choose Outline from the View menu or press ⌘-Option-O. If you have an extended keyboard, you also can use the Shift-F13 keyboard shortcut.

Viewing the Page Layout

In Word's Page Layout view, shown in figure 4.18, you see your document on-screen as it will appear when printed.

Fig. 4.17
Outline view of a
document.

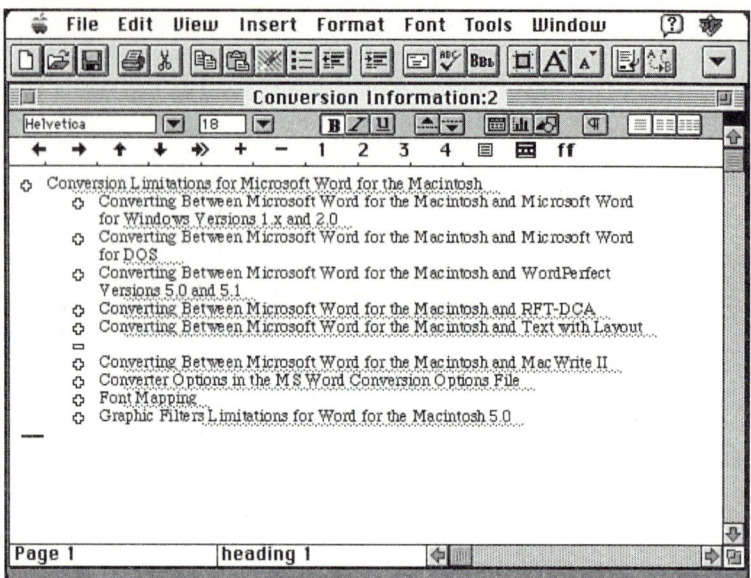

Fig. 4.18
Page Layout view.

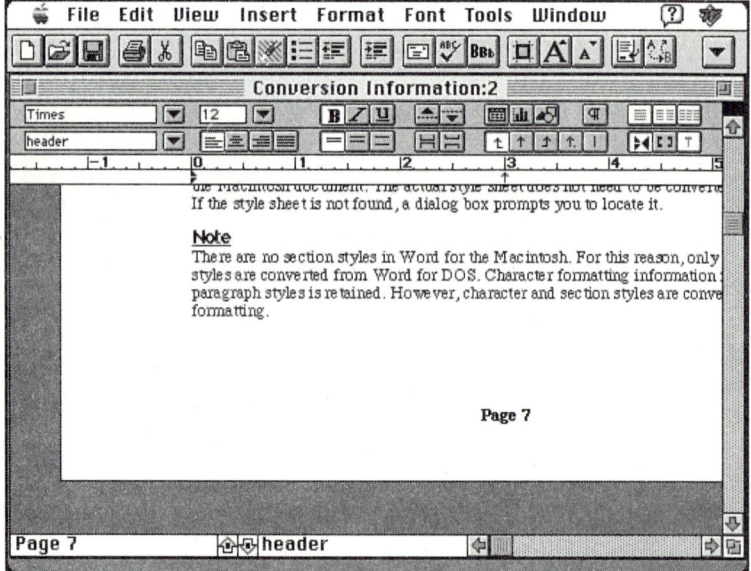

Part I

Getting Started with Word 5.1

In Page Layout view, Word displays the text in its actual size, along with any headers, footers, page numbers, newspaper columns, footnotes, and paragraphs that you have absolutely positioned on the page. You also can edit your document in this view.

Page Layout may run sluggishly on some Mac systems, such as Macintosh Pluses and old Classics, so you may want to use Page Layout view only for final previewing and cosmetic editing before printing. If you have a Mac based on the 68030 microprocessor, however, you can make Page Layout the default view for writing and editing. (For information on changing the default view, see Chapter 35, "Customizing Menus and Keyboard Shortcuts.")

To display your document in Page Layout view, choose Page Layout from the View menu or press ⌘-Option-P.

You should remember the following important points about Page Layout view:

- When you add headers, footers, and footnotes in Page Layout view, Word doesn't display a separate window, as it does in Normal view. Instead, the program moves the insertion point to the text area, where the text will actually appear when printed. Moreover, Page Layout does not allow you to create special header and footer options, such as different headers for even- and odd-numbered pages. To create these headers, you must switch to Normal view. (See Chapter 19, "Adding Headers, Footers, and Footnotes," for more information.)

- Unlike Normal view, Page Layout view enables you to directly edit headers, footers, page numbers, multiple-column text, and text that you have fixed to an absolute position on the page. To edit any of these elements, simply move the insertion point to the element and type or edit as usual.

- You can page through your document by clicking the down and up paging icons, which appear in the style area when you switch to Page Layout view. Scrolling the screen doesn't move the insertion point, however. If you want to type or edit in a page to which you have just scrolled, you must click the mouse in that page.

- If you prefer to use the keyboard to move the insertion point, notice that special direction keys become available in Page Layout view. These keys enable you to move the insertion point quickly from one text area to another. (For more information on these keys, see Chapter 8, "Editing Text.")

- In Normal view, the ruler always places the zero mark (0) at the left margin you have established for the document. In Page Layout view, the zero is positioned at the left boundary of the current text area—which might differ from the left margin if, for example, the insertion point is in the second column of a multiple-column document.

- If you choose Show ¶ from the View menu, you see gray lines that demarcate the boundaries of text areas such as columns, headings, headers, footers, footnotes, and frames (paragraphs that have been fixed to an absolute position on the page).

- If you use Word's mathematical typesetting language to create mathematical formulas, Page Layout view displays the formulas as they will appear when printed.

To view and edit your document in Page Layout view without sacrificing the speed of Normal view, divide the document window into two panes; place the insertion point in the top pane; and choose Page Layout from the View menu, leaving the bottom pane in Normal view. You then can work in the bottom pane and view the results in the top pane, where Word's beautiful Page Layout view shows you how the printed document will look.

Previewing the Printed Page

Print Preview closely resembles Page Layout view in that this view option displays all formats as they will appear when printed (see fig. 4.19).

You cannot, however, make changes to the text in Print Preview.

Why use Print Preview when Page Layout view is available? Page Layout view always shows your text full-size, but not all Mac users have a full-page display. Print Preview automatically reduces the size of the page so that one or two pages fit in whatever screen you happen to be using. Although the text becomes difficult or impossible to read on small screens, you still can see the overall page layout.

Another good reason for using Print Preview is that you can adjust many formats by dragging various elements of the page around on the screen. The following list briefly describes the formats you can adjust in Print Preview:

- *Page and column breaks.* You can adjust a bad page or column break by dragging the page-break or column-break marker. (For more information, see Chapter 11, "Formatting Pages.")

Fig. 4.19
Document displayed in
Print Preview.

Magnifier icon ———

Page Number icon ———

Boundaries icon ———

Page Display icon ———

Printer icon ———

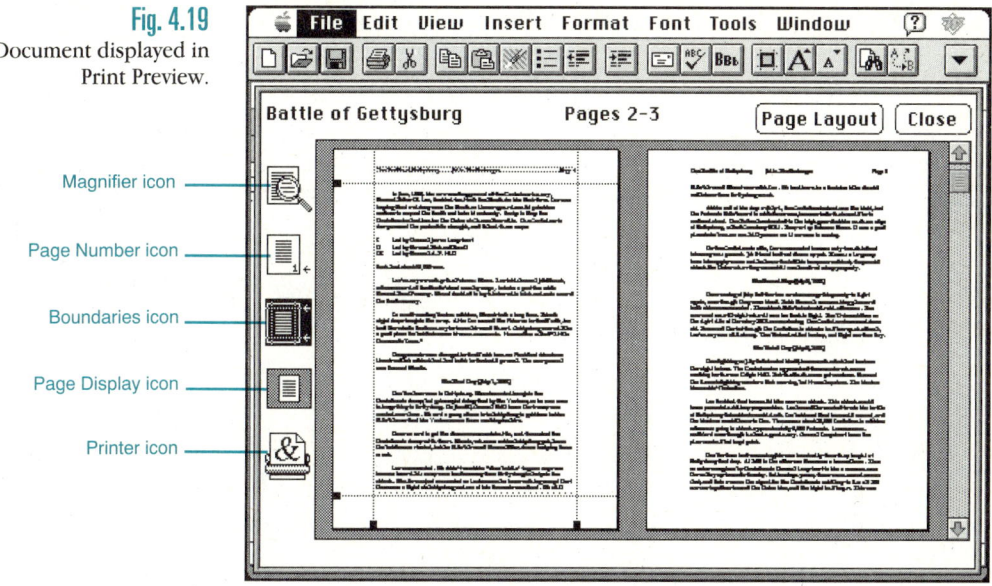

- *Margins.* Does the text look unbalanced on the screen? You can reposition the margins of your document by dragging the *handles* (the small black squares) that appear on the margins in Print Preview. (For more information, see Chapter 10, "Formatting Paragraphs.")

- *Frames.* You can format a paragraph or graphic so that it is fixed in an *absolute position* on the page, meaning that the text or graphic won't budge if you insert or delete text above it and that text will flow around it if necessary. The space set aside for this absolute position is called a *frame.* In Print Preview, you can move frames by dragging them with the mouse. (For more information, see Chapter 20, "Positioning Text and Graphics.")

- *Headers and footers.* A *header* is text that appears in the top margins of all the pages of your document (or in all the pages of a section of your document). A *footer* appears in the bottom margin. After you create headers and footers for your document, you can adjust their positions by dragging them. (For more information, see Chapter 19, "Adding Headers, Footers, and Footnotes.")

- *Page numbers.* You can adjust the position of page numbers, which you insert into the document by using Print Preview's Page Number icon or the Section dialog box. (For more information, see Chapter 11, "Formatting Pages.")

Chapter 4
Understanding Word's Workplace

To view your document in Print Preview, follow these steps:

1. In Normal or Page Layout view, display the page you want to preview.

2. Choose Print Preview from the File menu or press ⌘-Option-I. If you have an extended keyboard, you can press Option-F13.

   When you choose Print Preview from the File menu, Word automatically sizes the document so that you can see two full pages on the screen that you're using. The program also paginates the document and displays the page you were viewing when you chose the command.

While viewing your document in Print Preview, you can use the icons that appear along the left side of the screen (refer to fig. 4.19).

The following list describes the Print Preview icons:

■ *Magnifier icon.* Click this icon to turn the mouse pointer into a magnifying glass. To magnify a portion of the page, move the magnifying glass to the place you want to magnify and then click the mouse. You see a magnified view of your text (see fig. 4.20).

Fig. 4.20

Using the Magnifier icon to magnify text.

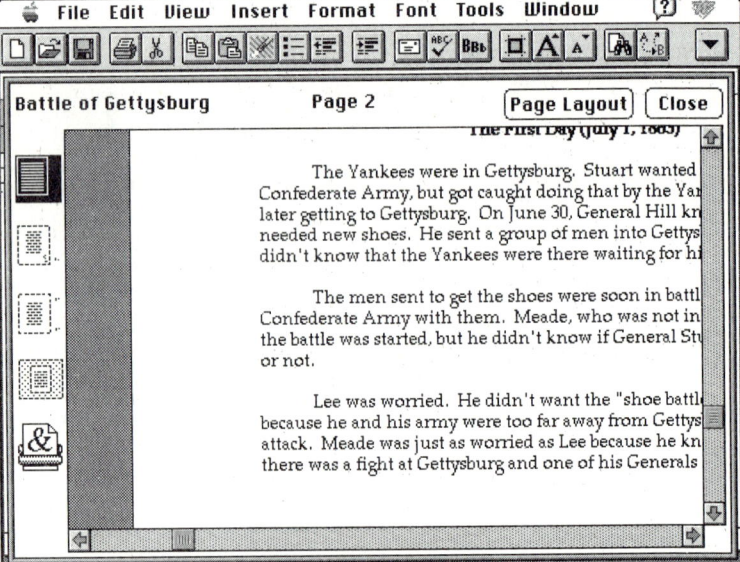

After you switch to magnified view, you can scroll the screen just as you would in the original view. To switch back to the reduced view, click the Magnifier icon again. As a shortcut, double-click the text that you want to magnify.

- *Page Number icon.* To add page numbers to a document quickly, click the Page Number icon. Word inserts a page number in the default location (1/2 inch from the top and right edge of the page). If you want to choose a different location, click the Page Number icon once. You see a page number. Drag the page number to the place on the page where you want page numbers to print, and release the mouse button. Then click outside the page to update the screen. If you want to remove page numbers that you added in this way, click the Boundaries icon to display boundaries around the page number, drag the page number off the page, and then click outside the page to update the screen.

- *Boundaries icon.* When you click the Boundaries icon, Word displays the boundaries of text areas, such as columns, headers, and footnotes. The boundaries you can adjust are shown with handles (black squares). Notice the handles shown on the left page in figure 4.19. You can drag these handles to adjust the boundaries of your document's text area. The change affects all the pages of your document, not just the one shown in Print Preview.

- *Page Display icon.* You can display two facing pages (with the even-numbered page on the left and the odd-numbered page on the right) or a single page in Print Preview. To toggle between these two options, click the Page Display icon.

- *Printer icon.* Click this icon to print your document. When you click the Printer icon, the Print dialog box appears, as it would had you chosen Print from the File menu.

You must use special keys and procedures to scroll a document in Print Preview. To display the next or preceding page, do one of the following things:

- Click the bottom or top scroll arrow.

- Click below or above the scroll box.

- Press the down-arrow or up-arrow key.

To exit Print Preview, do one of the following things:

- Click the Close command button to return to the preceding view.

- Click the Page Layout command button to return to the Page Layout view for the current page.

Chapter 4

Understanding Word's Workplace

Displaying the Ribbon, Ruler, and Toolbar

Word's ribbon, ruler, and (new in Word 5.1) Toolbar give you quick access to many commands (see fig. 4.21).

Fig. 4.21
The ribbon, ruler, and Toolbar.

Ribbon

Ruler

Toolbar

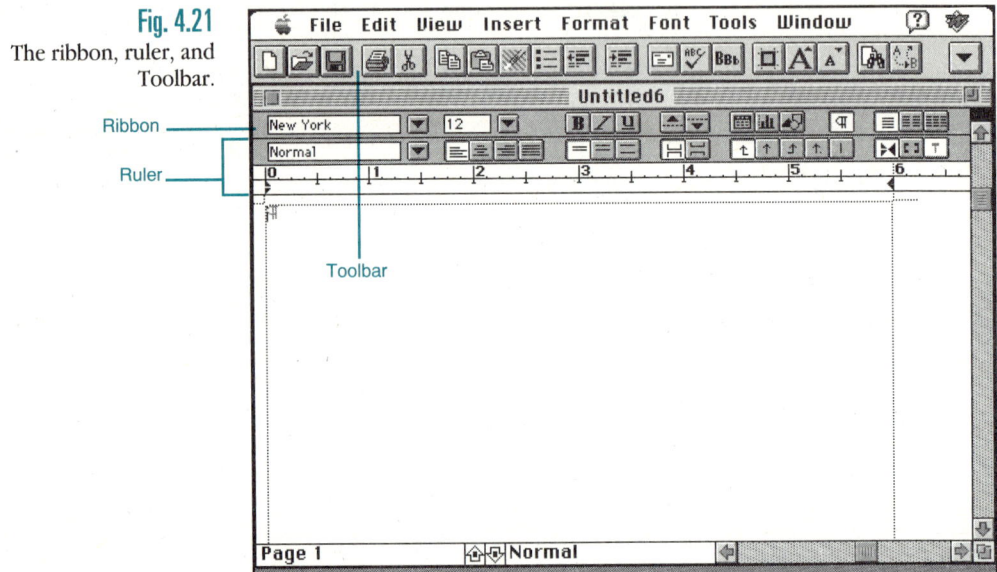

The following list briefly describes the functions of the ribbon and ruler:

■ The ribbon contains icons you can use to format text. (The term *ribbon* suggests an analogy to a typewriter; the ribbon's icons affect how your text will appear when printed.) Using the ribbon, you can choose fonts, font sizes, and emphases (bold, italic, and underline); specify superscript or subscript text; show or hide paragraph marks; and choose multiple-column layouts.

■ You use the ruler to format paragraphs. You can choose ruler icons to specify styles, alignments (such as flush left, centered, or justified), line spacing, blank lines before a paragraph, tabs, and indents.

Formatting with the ribbon and ruler are discussed later in this book. For now, you will learn only how to toggle the ribbon and ruler display off and on.

Part I

Getting Started with Word 5.1

By default, the ribbon and ruler appear at the top of every new document window. If you're using a 9- or 12-inch screen, the ribbon and ruler take up a relatively large amount of room, so you may want to toggle these features off until you need them.

If you want Word to open documents without the ribbon and ruler, you can change Word's default settings (see Chapter 35, "Customizing Menus and Keyboard Shortcuts").

To hide or display the ribbon, choose Ribbon from the View menu or press ⌘-Option-R.

To hide or display the ruler, choose Ruler from the View menu or press ⌘-R.

The following section describes the Toolbar.

Using the Toolbar

Microsoft's programmers are responsible for many innovations, including the widely imitated Toolbar, which made its first appearance in Microsoft Excel. The philosophy underlying the Toolbar is that users don't want to have to plow through several layers of menus and dialog boxes to reach commands that they use frequently. Because the Toolbar places these commands at the top of the screen, where you can access them quickly by clicking, Word now is easier to use.

Four Toolbars are provided with Word to fit the four most common Macintosh screen sizes (9 inches, 12 inches, 13 inches, and larger than 13 inches). Word chooses a Toolbar automatically. The larger your screen, the more tools you see in your Toolbar.

The following list contains the tools that appear in all Toolbars, followed by the tools' menu equivalents or keyboard equivalents (if any):

 New (File, New)

 Open (File, Open or ⌘-O)

 Save (File, Save or ⌘-S)

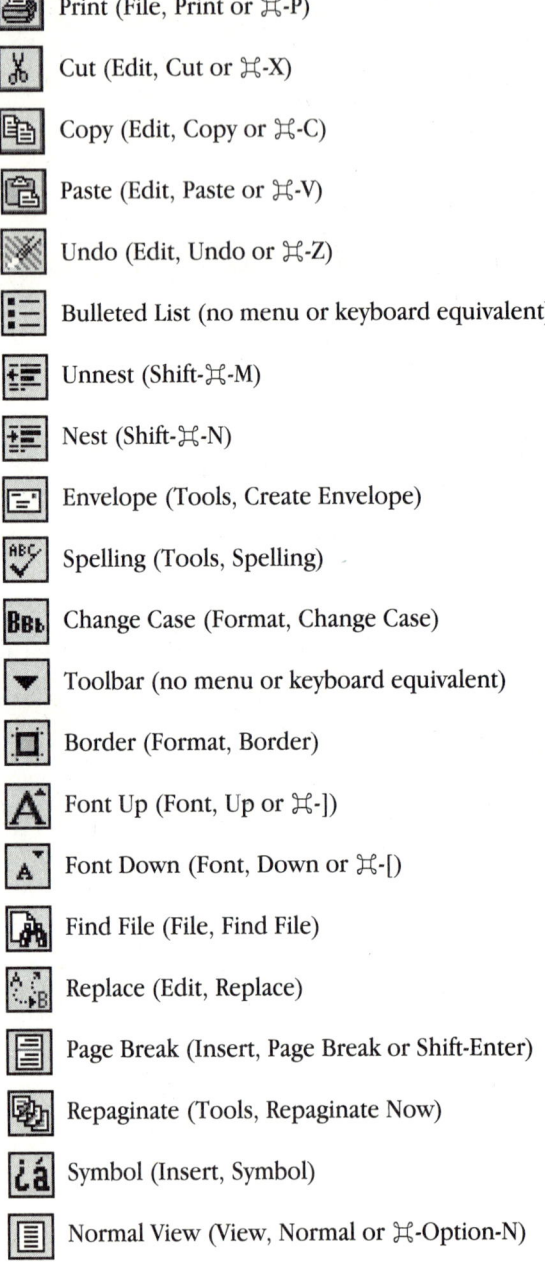

Print (File, Print or ⌘-P)

Cut (Edit, Cut or ⌘-X)

Copy (Edit, Copy or ⌘-C)

Paste (Edit, Paste or ⌘-V)

Undo (Edit, Undo or ⌘-Z)

Bulleted List (no menu or keyboard equivalent)

Unnest (Shift-⌘-M)

Nest (Shift-⌘-N)

Envelope (Tools, Create Envelope)

Spelling (Tools, Spelling)

Change Case (Format, Change Case)

Toolbar (no menu or keyboard equivalent)

Border (Format, Border)

Font Up (Font, Up or ⌘-])

Font Down (Font, Down or ⌘-[)

Find File (File, Find File)

Replace (Edit, Replace)

Page Break (Insert, Page Break or Shift-Enter)

Repaginate (Tools, Repaginate Now)

Symbol (Insert, Symbol)

Normal View (View, Normal or ⌘-Option-N)

Part I

Getting Started with Word 5.1

Page Layout View (View, Page Layout or ⌘-Option-P)

Print Preview (File, Print Preview or ⌘-Option-I)

Outline View (View, Outline or ⌘-Option-O)

Style (Format, Style or ⌘-T)

Drop Cap (Insert, Drop Cap)

Annotation (Insert, Annotation)

Help (Help, Microsoft Word Help)

For information on customizing the Toolbar and changing its on-screen position, see Chapter 36, "Customizing Word's Toolbar."

Quick Review

This section summarizes the most useful information in this chapter. Check "Productivity Tips" for a review of high-productivity tips and tricks—the ones that Macintosh and Word pros use every day. Review "Techniques" whenever you need a quick reminder about a specific procedure.

Productivity Tips

- If you're a good typist and prefer to keep your hands on the keyboard, learn how to access menus and dialog-box options with the keyboard.

- Don't bother deleting text from text boxes if you want to replace the text. When a text box is highlighted, simply start typing to delete all the existing text.

- In a dialog box, pressing Return (or Enter, in the numeric keypad) is the same as clicking the outlined command button, just as pressing Esc is the same as clicking the Cancel button.

- In a list box that contains folder names, you can open a folder and display its files by highlighting the folder and pressing ⌘-down arrow. Press ⌘-up arrow to move back up through the folder hierarchy.

- If a command has unwanted effects, you can reverse it by choosing Undo immediately—before you do any typing or choose any additional commands.

- Learn to use Word's hotspots, which bring up dialog boxes immediately.

- Familiarize yourself with the Repeat command. Use this command to enter a word or phrase repeatedly and to copy paragraph formats from one paragraph to several others.

- To work with two documents at one time, learn the procedure that automatically splits the screen area between them.

- In most Macintosh systems, write and edit in Normal view and then switch to Page Layout view for a final preview before printing. If you're using a Mac with a small (9-inch) screen, preview your document with Print Preview instead.

- If you're working with a 9- or 12-inch screen, you may prefer to hide the ribbon or ruler until you need them.

Techniques

This section provides concise summaries of all the procedures introduced in this chapter.

Choosing Commands from Menus

To access a pull-down menu with the keyboard:

1. Press ⌘-Tab or keypad period (.).

2. Use the arrow keys to choose the menu you want. Alternatively, type the menu name's first letter or a number ranging from 1 (File) to 7 (Tools).

To choose a command from a menu:

1. Press the down-arrow key until you highlight the command you want. Alternatively, type the command's first letter.

2. Press Return.

To open a menu other than the one you have just displayed:

>Hold down the Shift key and type the menu's first letter.

Choosing Options in Dialog Boxes

To move the highlight to the following text box in a dialog box:

>Press Tab.

To move the highlight to the preceding text box in a dialog box:

>Press Shift-Tab.

To select the next option, list, text area, or button in a dialog box:

>Press ⌘-Tab or keypad period (.).

To select the preceding option, list, text area, or button in a dialog box:

>Press ⌘-Shift-Tab or Shift-keypad period (.).

To activate a check box, radio button, or drop-down list box in a dialog box:

>Press ⌘-space bar or keypad 0 (zero).

To choose an item in a list box:

>Use the down- or up-arrow key to highlight the item.

To open a folder listed in a list box:

>Press ⌘-down arrow.

To close the current folder in a list box and display the files in the folder immediately below the current folder:

>Press ⌘-up arrow.

To cancel your choices in a dialog box:

>Press Esc or click the close box.

To confirm your choices and close the dialog box:

>Press Return.

Undoing a Command or an Action

To undo typing or the last command you issued:

>Choose Undo from the Edit menu (⌘-Z or F1) or click the Undo tool in the Toolbar.

Repeating a Command or an Action

To repeat typing or the last command you issued:

Choose Repeat from the Edit menu (⌘-Y).

Working with Windows

To open a window:

Choose Open from the File menu (⌘-O) to open an existing document.

or

Choose New from the File menu (⌘-N) to open a new document.

To open an additional window in a document:

Choose New Window from the Window menu.

To activate a window:

Click inside the window.

or

Choose the window's name from the Window menu.

or

Press ⌘-Option-W until you activate the window.

To split a document window:

Drag the split bar down the vertical scroll bar until you have positioned the split where you want it. Then release the mouse button.

or

Double-click the split bar (⌘-Option-S) to split the window into two equal-size panes.

To adjust the split:

Drag the split bar up or down.

To remove the split and keep the bottom pane on-screen:

Double-click the split bar.

or

Press ⌘-Option-S.

or

Drag the split bar down the vertical scroll bar until the bar disappears off the bottom of the window.

To size a window:

Drag the size box in any direction.

To toggle between the original window size and a smaller size or different location:

Click the window's zoom box.

or

Double-click the title bar.

To move a window:

Drag the title bar.

To close a window:

Click the close box.

or

Choose Close from the File menu (⌘-W).

Choosing Views

To view your document in Page Layout view:

Choose Page Layout from the View menu or press ⌘-Option-P.

To view your document in Outline view:

Choose Outline from the View menu or press ⌘-Option-O.

To restore Normal view:

Choose Normal from the View menu or press ⌘-Option-N.

To display your document in Print Preview:

Choose Print Preview from the File menu or press ⌘-Option-I.

Hiding or Displaying the Ribbon, Ruler, and Toolbar

To hide or display the ribbon:

Choose Ribbon from the View menu or press ⌘-Option-R.

To hide or display the ruler:

Choose Ruler from the View menu or press ⌘-R.

To hide or display the Toolbar:

Choose Toolbar from the View menu.

Managing Documents and Files

lthough you already have learned how to save and retrieve documents with Word, you have more to learn. Word contains many advanced features for saving and retrieving files. This chapter covers the following features:

- *Saving documents.* You learn several ways to save documents with Word, including saving your document in file formats other than Word's so that you can exchange documents with colleagues who use other software programs.

  (The term *file format* refers to the technique used to store information on disk. In general, each program uses its own unique file format, as Word does. Thanks to Word's file converters, you can save your files in the formats used by many other Macintosh, DOS, and Windows applications.)

- *Creating and using stationery documents.* In this section, you learn how to create generic or template documents, which Word stores as read-only documents. When you open these documents, Word creates a new Untitled document that you can modify. You cannot overwrite the template, so you're sure that it will be available the next time you want to use it. You also learn how stationery documents can help you manage styles more efficiently.

USING
WORD 5.1
FOR THE MAC
SPECIAL EDITION

- *Opening documents.* You can open documents created in file formats other than Word's.

- *Finding and managing files with Find File.* Word's new Find File command has impressive file-management capabilities. With this command, you can retrieve files quickly, regardless of where they're buried in your hard drive (or any other drive, including network drives). You can search for one file or a group of files according to criteria you specify (such as date of creation, document text, keywords, and author).

New to Word 5.1 is a feature that enables you to restrict the search to a single folder (and to any folders that this folder contains). After you retrieve files, you can open, copy, print, or delete them.

Saving Documents

In this section, you learn all about saving files. Even though you already have learned how to save documents, you should read this section carefully; your work with the computer is highly vulnerable to accidental data loss due to careless file management.

This section begins with a discussion of your options for changing Word's file-saving defaults. You explore the Save As dialog box. You learn why you should fill out those Summary Info dialog boxes that appear when you save a document for the first time. You also learn how to save to file formats other than Word's default, including ASCII (text) files.

Choosing Preferences for Saving Files

Take some time now to investigate the Open and Save options in the Preferences dialog box. To display these options, choose Preferences from the Tools menu to open the Preferences dialog box and then click the Open and Save icon (see fig 5.1).

Fig. 5.1
Fig. 5.1
Open and Save options
(Preferences dialog box).

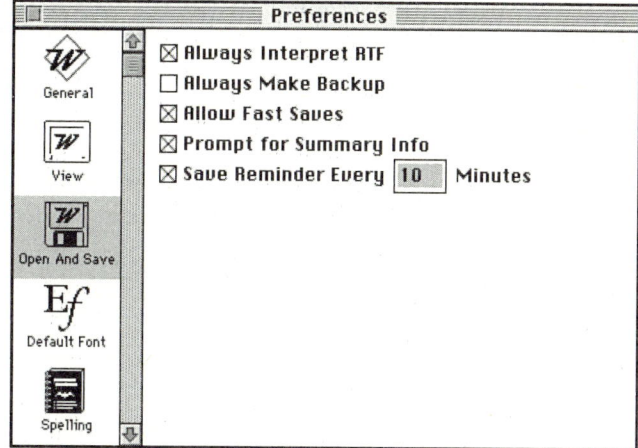

The following list describes the Open and Save options:

■ *Always Interpret RTF.* RTF stands for Rich Text Format, a Microsoft standard that enables users of different word processing programs to exchange formatted documents, even when the files are exchanged via modem or with mainframe computers. When this option is activated, Word automatically interprets RTF documents that you open. If you have deactivated the option, a dialog box appears when you open such a file, asking whether you want to interpret the RTF codes.

■ *Always Make Backup.* If you activate this option, Word automatically makes a backup copy of your document every time you save it. An important point for you to understand and remember, however, is that this copy is of the preceding version of your document, not the version that you're saving. Don't confuse this option with a well-conceived backup strategy for your documents! (You learn more about how to back up your work later in this section.)

This option consumes much disk space because it automatically keeps the preceding copy of every file you save. If you really want to keep a copy of the preceding version of a file, you can do so for only one file by choosing the Make Backup option in the Save As dialog box (explained in the following section).

■ *Allow Fast Saves.* When Word performs a normal save, the program rewrites the entire file on disk, taking into account all your changes during an editing session. For a long document, a normal save can take time—as much as a minute, or even more. When Word performs a fast save, however, it doesn't rewrite the entire document; Word simply creates a table that shows where the changes should be made. Both types of saves are safe, but fast saves consume more disk and memory space than normal saves do.

If you activate the Always Make Backup option, Word always uses normal saves (the Fast Save option will not have any effect).

■ *Prompt for Summary Info.* When this option is active, Word displays a Summary Info dialog box every time you save a new document. By all means leave this feature activated, and fill out those Summary Info boxes! Later in this chapter, you will learn why filling out the Summary Info boxes makes good sense; doing so gives Word more ways to find an elusive document stored somewhere on your disk.

■ *Save Reminder.* You should activate this option. When Save Reminder is active, Word periodically displays a dialog box that reminds you to save your work (see fig. 5.2).

Fig. 5.2
Save Now? dialog box.

When this dialog box appears, choose OK (by clicking the OK button or pressing Return) to save your work. If you don't want to save, you can postpone the reminder for 10 minutes or for another interval, or you can click Cancel. Try activating the Save Reminder option and typing **10** or **15** in the Postpone text box.

When you finish choosing options in the Preferences dialog box, click the close box to return to your document. The changes you make affect all your documents, not just the one in the active window.

Saving Your Work

You can save your work in any of four ways:

- Choose Save from the File menu.
- Press ⌘-S.
- Press F7.
- Click the Save tool.

The first time you save a document, you see the Save As dialog box, which is discussed in the following section. In subsequent saves of the same document, Word uses the settings (such as file name and location) that you chose in the Save As dialog box when you initially saved the file.

Exploring the Save As Dialog Box

Word displays the Save As dialog box when you save a document for the first time. Figure 5.3 shows the Save As dialog box that appears in the System 7 version of Word 5.1.

Current-folder list box

Current drive

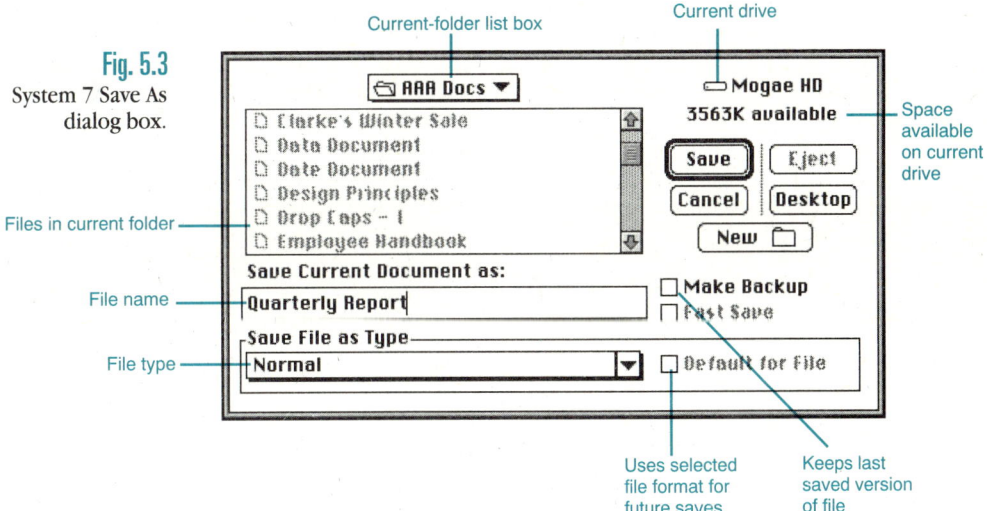

Fig. 5.3
System 7 Save As dialog box.

Files in current folder

File name

File type

Space available on current drive

Uses selected file format for future saves

Keeps last saved version of file

Chapter 5

Managing Documents and Files

If you're using System 6, your Save As dialog box differs. The following paragraphs discuss these differences.

The Desktop command button, which gives you a new way to change drives, is new in System 7. (To change drives in System 6, click the Drive button until you see the drive you want.) In System 7, you can click the Desktop button to see a list of all the disks currently mounted on your Macintosh. To open one of the disks, double-click the disk's icon in the list box. Another new feature, the New Folder command button, enables you to create and name a folder while you work in the Save As dialog box.

Why is the System 7 Desktop button an advantage? In System 6, you can view the contents of a disk only if that disk is physically inserted into the disk drive. But as you may already have noticed, you can mount more than one disk at a time. (To *mount* a disk means to place its icon on the Macintosh Desktop. A disk can remain mounted even if it's no longer in the disk drive.) For this reason, System 7's Save As dialog box enables you to choose any disk you have mounted during the current operating session.

A quick overview of the Save As dialog box's areas and features follows:

- *Current-folder list box.* A drop-down list box at the top of the dialog box shows the current folder (the System 6 version has no drop-down arrow). To drop down the list, point to the box and hold down the mouse button. You see a list of all the folders *above* the current folder in your disk's folder hierarchy.

Instead of using the current-folder list box, you also can press ⌘-up arrow to display the documents in the directory immediately above Word's.

- *Document list box.* By default, this list box shows all the documents and folders that are present in the current folder. The files shown are those that Word can read. These files are displayed so that you can see the contents of the current folder. This information helps you determine whether you are saving your file in the correct place. In addition, the display of file names reminds you of patterns or conventions you're using to name files.

- *Current-drive indicator.* This feature indicates the current drive and the amount of free space remaining.

- *Save Current Document As text box.* Use this text box to type a document name (not exceeding 31 characters, including spaces). You can use any keyboard character except one: the colon (:).

- *Command buttons.* To save the document currently highlighted in the document list box, choose the Save button by clicking it or by pressing Return.

  To switch drives in System 6, click the Drive button; to eject a disk from a disk drive, click the Eject button.

  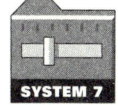

  In System 7, click the Desktop button to view all the disks mounted currently on your system; double-click the disk name to see the names of the documents it contains. Click Eject to eject the currently selected disk. You can click the New Folder button to create and name a new folder for your document.

  To exit the Save As dialog box without saving a file, click the Cancel button.

- *Make Backup check box.* Activate this check box to preserve the version of the file currently on disk—the one that *doesn't* have the changes you just made. Please note that this file is *not* a true backup copy or even a copy of the most recent version of your file. You should activate this check box only if you want to preserve previous versions of your files—but as you will learn momentarily, a much better practice is simply to save a new version of your document under a new document name.

- *Fast Save check box.* The Fast Save option enables you to choose Word's fast-save technique for storing your files on disk. Fast saves are safe and efficient if you're working with a long document, but files saved with Fast Save take up more room on your disk. Word also requires more memory to perform fast saves.

To use Fast Save, you first must activate the Allow Fast Saves option in the Preferences dialog box.

- *Save File As Type list box.* This drop-down list box controls the file format Word uses to save your file. If you want to exchange your files with colleagues who are using other software programs (or non-Macintosh computers), or if you want to send your file via modem, you need to choose a file format other than Normal. (See "Saving to Other File Formats" later in this chapter.)

■ *Default for File check box.* If you choose a file format other than Normal, you can use the Default for File check box to establish the format as the default format for the file. (Otherwise, Word reverts to the Normal file format the next time you save the file.) If you plan to transmit your file via modem, for example, choose the Text Only with Line Breaks option in the Save File as Type list box. This option saves your document as an ASCII file, which contains nothing but the standard ASCII characters.

When you open a file that has been saved as an ASCII file, make a few changes, and save it again, Word reverts to the Normal file format, which is the default format for all Word files. To avoid this problem, you should activate the Default for File check box when you're saving to a file format other than Normal.

Using the Save As Dialog Box

When you save a file, the Save As dialog box gives you the opportunity to select the storage location (disk drive and location), to keep the previously saved version of the file, to perform fast saves, and to specify the file format. The basic procedure is provided in this section; the following section provides details on saving in file formats other than Word's.

To save a document for the first time, follow these steps:

1. Choose Save from the File menu, press ⌘-S or F7, or click the Save tool. The Save As dialog box appears, with the insertion point positioned in the Save Current Document As text box.

2. If you want to save the file to a different disk, use the Drive button (System 6) or the Desktop button (System 7) to activate the appropriate drive.

3. If you want to save the file to a different folder, select that folder in the current-folder list box. (If you're using System 7, you can create and name a new folder—and make it the current folder—by clicking the New Folder button.)

4. To instruct Word to preserve the existing disk file the next time you save this document, click the Make Backup check box.

5. To activate fast saves on all subsequent saves, make sure that the Fast Save check box is activated. If this check box is dimmed, choose Preferences from the Tools menu and then activate the Allow Fast Saves option in the Preferences dialog box.

6. Type the document name in the Save Current Document As text box. You can use up to 31 characters, including spaces, using any character except the colon (:).

7. Choose the Save button by clicking it or pressing Return. Word saves the file under the name you specified.

If an existing document has been saved under the name that you typed in the Save Current Document As text box, a dialog box appears when you choose Save; this dialog box asks whether you want to replace the file. Choose No to return to the Save As dialog box, where you can type another document name, or click Yes to overwrite the existing document.

After you choose Save, the Summary Info dialog box appears. Word inserts the document name into the Title text box, and the name currently shown in the Preferences dialog box appears in the Author text box.

8. Fill out the Summary Info dialog box and choose OK. (For tips on using Summary Info boxes, see "Filling Out Summary Info" later in this chapter.) Alternatively, click Cancel to force Word to redisplay the Summary Info dialog box the next time you save.

After you save the document, Word displays the number of characters saved in the page-number area at the bottom of your document.

Resaving a File with the Save As Command

Use the Save As command to resave a file in the following situations:

- *You want to rename the document.* Choose Save As and type a new file name in the Save Current Document As text box when the Save As dialog box appears. The changes you made during the current editing session do not affect the version of the file saved under the original name. Word shows the new name in the title bar, and the next time you choose Save, Word resaves the file under the new name.

- *You want to save each version of an important document.* Suppose that you're writing an important contract or proposal, and because you're not sure that your revisions are carrying the document in the right direction, you want to keep each version on disk. Each time you save, choose Save As and specify a new document name. This procedure is much better than using the

Chapter 5

Managing Documents and Files

Make Backup option—which, as already noted, loses its usefulness when you save at periodic intervals (such as every 10 or 15 minutes).

■ *You want to save the document to a new location.* Choose Save As and choose a new folder or disk for the file. The changes you made during the current editing session do not affect the version of the file stored in the original location. The next time you choose Save, Word resaves the file to the new location.

■ *You want to activate the Make Backup option.* You can turn on the Make Backup option for any file so that Word will keep the existing copy of the document on disk, renaming it Backup of (file name). Some writers like to keep the preceding version of their document—the version that they last saved—in case they decide that they don't like the changes made during the current editing session. This option consumes a lot of disk space, however, and if you save regularly (every 10 or 15 minutes is the suggested rule), the current version of the file will not be much different from its backup version. Don't confuse this option with a true backup copy of your current file.

Use the Finder to copy valuable files to floppy disks, or (better yet) purchase a backup utility program such as DiskFit, which automatically detects all new or altered files and backs them up to floppy disks.

■ *You want to disable the Fast Save option.* If you activate the Allow Fast Saves option in the Preferences dialog box, this option is grayed the first time you save a file, but it is available afterward. (Allow Fast Save is on by default.) To choose a normal save, deactivate this option.

■ *You want to save the file to a file format other than Word's default file format.* Word's default format, Normal, saves all the formatting in your document. If you want to exchange your file with other computer users or transfer it via modem, you may want to choose a format other than Normal to save your file. Alternative formats are discussed in the following section.

If you use Save As to save an existing file but don't change the file's name or location, an alert box appears, asking you to confirm overwriting the preceding version of the file. To be on the safe side, you should *always* save a file under a new name. Many of the options you can choose in the Save As dialog box will wipe out document formats that took hours to enter. Deleting an unneeded copy of a document is much easier than reconstructing hours of work.

To use the Save As command to resave a file, follow these steps:

1. Choose Save As from the File menu or press Shift-F7. The Save As dialog box appears, with the current document name highlighted in the Save Current Document As text box.

2. To delete the current document name, begin typing the new name. To edit the name, click the insertion point in the name to cancel the highlight.

3. To disable the Fast Save option, click the Fast Save check box until the X disappears. (If the box is grayed, you first must activate Allow Fast Saves in the Preferences dialog box.)

4. If you want to save the file to another disk, click Drive (System 6) or Desktop (System 7) until you see the drive you want.

5. If you want to save the file to a folder other than the current folder, select that folder's name in the current-folder list box. (System 7 users can create, name, and activate a new folder by choosing New Folder.)

6. If you want to save the file to a format other than Word's default Normal format, choose the format in the Save File As Type box. To make this format the default for future saves, activate the Default for File check box.

7. Choose Save.

   If you typed the name of an existing document in the Save Current Document As text box, an alert box appears, asking you to confirm that you want to replace the existing file. Choose No to return to the Save As dialog box without overwriting the existing file, or click Yes to replace the file.

Saving to Other File Formats

Word normally saves your document in Normal file format, which preserves all your formatting choices. You can save the document in other formats by using the Save File As Type list box. When you pull down this list box, the options that appear depend on which file-conversion options you chose when you installed Microsoft Word.

The file formats discussed in this section are available if you used the Easy Install option when you installed Word. You can install additional file formats by using Custom Install. (For more information on installing Word, see Chapter 1, "Reviewing Mac Basics and Installing Word 5.1.")

If you have the Apple SuperDrive, which is standard equipment on new Macintoshes, you can exchange your work with a colleague who uses a DOS or Windows system. Save the file to the DOS or Windows program's file format and then use the Apple File Exchange—a utility program provided with your Macintosh System software—to write the file directly to a DOS-format 3.5-inch disk. Better yet, equip your system with Dayna Communications' DOS Mounter utility program, which enables Macintosh applications to write directly to DOS disks without going through the intermediary step of using Apple File Exchange to translate the file.

File-format options you can choose include the following:

- *Text Only.* Choose this option to transfer a Word document to another word processing program that cannot read Word's files. This option saves only the text of the file without any formatting or graphics. Line, section, and page breaks are converted to paragraph marks.

- *Text Only with Line Breaks.* Choose this option to transfer a Word document via modem; Text Only with Line Breaks creates an ASCII (plain-text) file. Like the Text Only option, this option saves only the text of the file without any formatting or graphics. Every line ends in a paragraph mark (hard return).

- *Microsoft Mac Word 3.x.* Choose this option if you want to give your document to someone who's still using Word 3, which employed a different file format.

- *Interchange Format (RTF).* This option saves your document using nothing but the standard ASCII characters; at the same time, however, Interchange Format adds codes that preserve your formatting choices. You can transmit the file via modem or give a disk to someone who uses another program, and as long as the other program can read RTF files, the formatting can be recovered.

- *Stationery.* This option, used with System 7, enables you to save a file as a *template*, which remains unmodified on disk. Suppose that you create a letterhead for your business; this document contains your return address and logo, but nothing else. If you save the document as stationery, you make sure that you never will overwrite this document accidentally. Every time you open a stationery document, Word displays a copy of the document, not the original.

- *MacWrite.* Choose this option if you want to give your document to someone who uses the original version of MacWrite.

- *MacWrite II 1.x.* Choose this option if you want to give your document to someone who uses MacWrite II, Version 1.

- *Windows Metafile.* Choose this option if you want to give your document to someone who uses Windows software that doesn't recognize any of the other file formats in this list but does recognize the Windows Metafile format (a generic document format).

- *Word for MS-DOS.* Choose this option if you want to give your document to someone who uses the DOS version of Microsoft Word.

- *Word for Windows 1.* Choose this option if you want to give your document to someone who uses the original version of Microsoft Word for Windows.

- *Word for Windows 2.0.* Choose this option if you want to give your document to someone who uses Word for Windows 2.0.

- *WordPerfect 5.0.* Choose this option if you want to give your document to someone who uses WordPerfect 5.0 for DOS.

- *WordPerfect 5.1.* Choose this option if you want to give your document to someone who uses WordPerfect 5.1 for DOS.

- *WordPerfect for the Macintosh 2.0.* Choose this option if you want to give your document to someone who uses WordPerfect for the Macintosh 2.0.

After you choose a file-format option, you can make that option the default format for the file by activating the Default for File option in the Save As dialog box. If you don't choose this option, Word reverts to Normal format if you make changes in the document and then save it. For this reason, you should activate this option if you have chosen a nonstandard format and think you might edit the document further.

Low on disk space? Switch to the Finder, open the Word Commands folder, and delete the file converters that you know you're not going to use. If you need one of these file formats in the future, you can reinstall it by using Custom Install (see Chapter 1).

Chapter 5

Managing Documents and Files

Filling Out Summary Info

An advanced feature of Word 5 is Find File, a file-retrieval command that can locate an elusive file on a huge disk in seconds. If you have ever spent precious time hunting for a file that you inadvertently saved to the wrong folder, you will agree that Find File is a boon. You can find a complete discussion of Find File in "Finding and Managing Files with Find File" later in this chapter.

To get the most out of Find File, you need to diligently fill out the Summary Info dialog box, which appears when you save a document for the first time (see fig. 5.4).

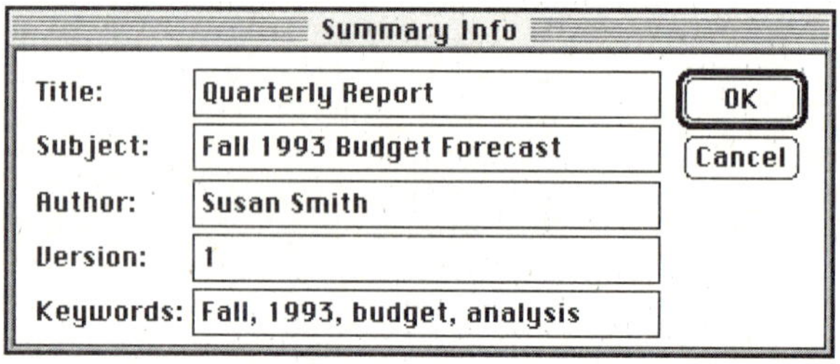

Fig. 5.4

Summary Info dialog box.

If you always fill out Summary Info, you can use Find File to retrieve files by title, subject, author, version, and keywords, in addition to the information that Finder automatically records when you save the file (the document's name, the date the document was created, and the date the document was last saved).

Following is a quick overview of the Summary Info dialog box:

- *Title.* Type the document's full title, not the abbreviated, 31-characters-maximum title that you typed in the Save As dialog box. Although the Title text box doesn't look big, it scrolls to the right as you type text. (You can enter up to 255 characters in each Summary Info text box.)

- *Subject.* In this text box, type one or more descriptors for your document. A *descriptor* is a keyword that categorizes your document so that Word can group it with others. You may want to categorize documents with descriptors like Letter, Report, Memo, Proposal, and so on. Or you may want to use descriptors that are relevant to your profession, such as Contract, Will, and Deposition (for a law firm).

- *Author.* Word automatically inserts the name currently shown in the Your Name area of the Preferences dialog box, so you can let Word do the typing for you. (The name in the Your Name area is the one you typed when you installed the program.) Sometimes, however, more than one person uses a computer. In such a case, the user can type his or her own name here.

- *Version.* If you like to keep each version of a document intact on disk, use the Save As dialog box to save each version under a different name, such as Report, New Report, and Yet Another Report. If you type the same Title text in the Summary Info dialog box every time you save the file, however, Find File can group all the versions of the file together. Use the Version text box to record the number of the version you're currently saving.

- *Keywords.* Use the Keywords text box to type one or more *identifiers*—words or phrases that uniquely identify the document you're saving. Unlike descriptors, which Word uses to group similar documents, identifiers help Word differentiate documents and conduct pinpoint searches. For example, an attorney may want to type the name of a client in the Keywords text box, along with a descriptor (such as Edward B. Smith or Trust).

If you don't want to fill out the Summary Info dialog box, simply choose OK when the dialog box appears. If you click Cancel, the Summary Info box reappears the next time you save the document.

If you didn't fill out Summary Info for a document and want to, choose Summary Info from the File menu. Word displays the Summary Info dialog box for the current document.

If you don't want Word to display the Summary Info dialog box automatically whenever you save a document for the first time, you can change Word's default Preferences setting. (You still can access a document's Summary Info dialog box by choosing Summary Info from the File menu whenever the document is open.)

To prevent Word from displaying the Summary Info dialog box automatically the first time you save a document, follow these steps:

1. Choose Preferences from the Tools menu. The Preferences dialog box appears.

2. Click the Open and Save icon. The Open and Save options appear.

Chapter 5

Managing Documents and Files

3. Turn off the Prompt for Summary Info option by clicking its check box.

4. Click the close box to close the dialog box.

Opening Files

After you create, save, and close documents, you use the Open command (File menu) to open them again for further editing or for printing.

You can open a document in any of the following ways:

■ Choose Open from the File menu.

■ Press ⌘-O.

■ Click the Open tool.

You then see the Open dialog box, which is discussed in the following section.

To open one of the last four files you saved, pull down the File menu and choose the file name from the list at the bottom of the menu.

Exploring the Open Dialog Box

When you use the Open command, Word displays the Open dialog box (see fig. 5.5).

Following is an overview of the features in this dialog box:

Current-folder list box. A drop-down list box at the top of the dialog box shows the current folder. To drop down the list, point to the box and hold down the mouse button. You see a list of all the folders above the current folder in your disk's folder hierarchy.

Document list box. This list shows the readable files in the current folder, as well as folders stored in that folder. You can open any readable document by double-clicking the document icon. To open a folder, double-click the folder icon.

Current-drive indicator. This feature indicates the name of the current drive and the amount of free space remaining.

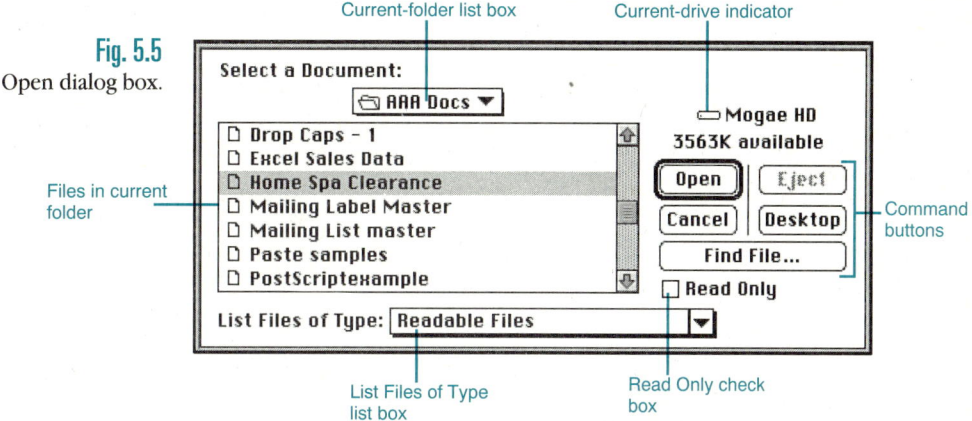

Fig. 5.5
Open dialog box.

Current-folder list box

Current-drive indicator

Select a Document:

🗁 AAA Docs ▼

Files in current folder

- ▯ Drop Caps - 1
- ▯ Excel Sales Data
- ▯ Home Spa Clearance
- ▯ Mailing Label Master
- ▯ Mailing List master
- ▯ Paste samples
- ▯ PostScriptexample

🖴 Mogae HD
3563K available

[**Open**]   [Eject]
[Cancel]   [Desktop]
[Find File...]

Command buttons

☐ Read Only

List Files of Type: [Readable Files]   [▼]

List Files of Type list box

Read Only check box

Command buttons. To open the document that currently is highlighted in the document list box, choose Open (or double-click the document name).

To switch drives in System 6, click the Drive button; to eject a disk from a disk drive, click Eject.

To switch drives in System 7, click the Desktop button to view all the disks currently mounted on your system and then double-click the disk you want. Click Eject to eject the current floppy disk.

Read Only check box. Activate this check box to open the document as a *read-only file*—one that you cannot overwrite. After the document opens, you can make changes in it. But if you then try to save the document, you see the Save As dialog box, where you must choose a new document name.

List Files of Type list box. This drop-down list box normally displays Readable Files. You can make selections in this list box to restrict the files displayed in the document list box to only those created by Word (the Word Documents option), to text files, to graphics files, and to files created by certain other word processing programs.

Find File command button. Can't locate a file by fussing manually with the document list box? Let Find File help you. (See "Finding and Managing Files with Find File" later in this chapter.)

Chapter 5

Managing Documents and Files

Using the Open Dialog Box

To open a file, you first must locate it, perhaps by using the current-folder and document list boxes. To restrict the kind of files displayed in the document list box, select Word Documents in the List Files of Type drop-down list box. When the file you want appears in the document list box, double-click the file name or highlight it and then choose Open.

Opening Files Created by Other Programs

As you learned earlier in this chapter, you can save your Word documents in formats other than Word's in order to exchange your work with colleagues who are using other word processing programs. By the same token, you can open documents created by other programs, such as MacWrite or WordPerfect for the Macintosh. If your Macintosh is equipped with a SuperDrive, you can use Apple File Exchange to translate DOS and Windows documents to your Mac's hard disk; you then can open these documents through Word.

To open files in file formats other than Word's, choose Open from the File menu or click the Open tool. When the Open dialog box appears, click the List Files of Type list box (see fig. 5.6) and select a file format in the list. Word then restricts the list of files to those that conform to the file format you selected.

Fig. 5.6
List Files of Type list box
(Open dialog box).

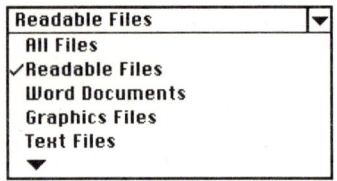

If you can't find the file you want to open, click the Find File button to search your entire hard disk or selected folders. This command can make a list of all the files on the disk or in the selected folders that have a certain file format. (Find File is discussed in detail later in this chapter.)

Creating and Using Stationery Documents

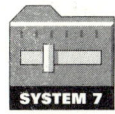

The motto "Don't reinvent the wheel" is good advice for computer users. As often as possible, you should develop new documents by opening and modifying versions called *templates*. A template is a generic version of a document (such as a letter that contains your return address and formats, but no text) that you save as a *stationery document*.

To create and use stationery documents, your Macintosh must be equipped with System 7.

Following is a list of template possibilities:

- *Letterhead.* Include your return address, a date code that enters the date at the time of printing, the complimentary closing, and other needed information.

- *Memo.* Include the memo header (including To, From, Date, and Subject) but not the memo text.

- *Résumé.* Include all the information that belongs in every résumé. Open this template and add the specifics for a particular job.

- *Periodic reports.* Include generic formats for tables, lists, and other information you must supply periodically. Also include titles, explanations, and other text that doesn't change from report to report.

- *Newsletters.* Include section formats, styles, borders, figure positions, and other layout information that doesn't change with each issue. Also include generic text, such as subscription information, editorial-staff credits, and disclaimers.

- *Price lists.* Include all the text that doesn't change (model names and numbers). Leave out the prices.

To create a template document in Word, you save an ordinary Word document using the Stationery file type. When you open a stationery document, Word places the document in a new Untitled file, ensuring that you cannot accidentally overwrite the original stationery document.

In the following sections, you learn how to create, open, and revise stationery documents.

Creating a Stationery Document

Creating a stationery document is easy. When you save the document, you choose the Stationery option in the Save File as Type list box.

To create a stationery document, follow these steps:

1. Create a generic version of a document like the one shown in figure 5.7.

Fig. 5.7
Generic version of a
letterhead document.

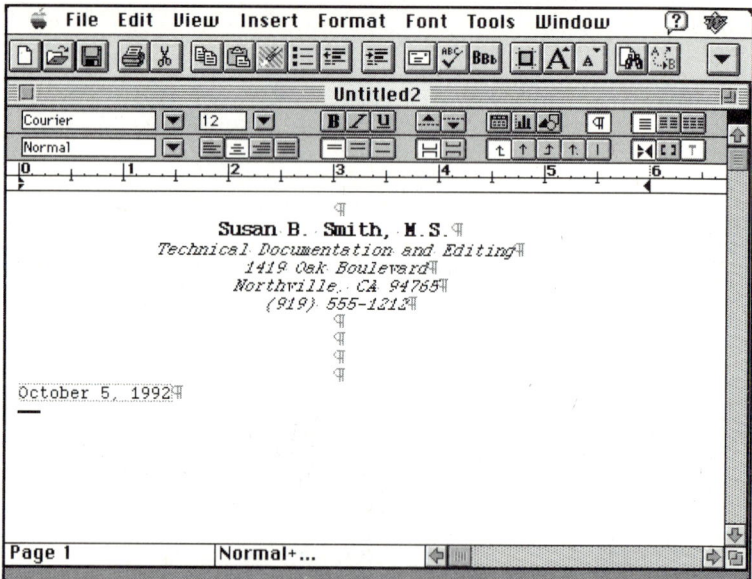

2. Choose Save from the File menu or use any of its alternatives: ⌘-S, F7, or the Save tool. The Save dialog box (similar to the Save As dialog box) appears.

   If you're using System 6, the Desktop and New Folder buttons do not appear in this dialog box.

3. In the Save File as Type list box, select the Stationery option (see fig. 5.8).

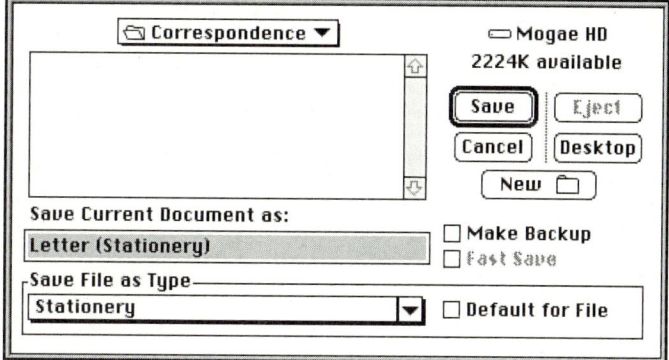

4. Type a name for the document in the Save Current Document As text box. Choose a name (such as *Letterhead Template*) that indicates that the document is a stationery document.

5. Choose Save. Word saves the file as a stationery document.

Opening a Stationery Document

After you create a stationery document, you can open it whenever you need it. Word creates a new Untitled document that you can modify.

To open a stationery document, follow these steps:

1. Choose Open from the File menu, press ⌘-O, or click the Open tool. The Open dialog box appears.

2. Select the folder that contains your stationery document.

3. If this folder contains many files that are not stationery documents, select Stationery in the List Files of Type list box. After you select Stationery, Word displays only those files that were saved with the Stationery option. Notice that the document icon is different for stationery documents.

4. Choose Open. Word opens the stationery document as a new Untitled document that you can modify and save under a different name.

Revising a Stationery Document

Stationery documents are read-only documents, meaning that Word prevents you from overwriting the file. But what happens if you need to make a change in a stationery document itself? This section describes the procedure you follow to edit a template.

To revise a stationery document, follow these steps:

1. Choose Open from the File menu, press ⌘-O, or click the Open tool. The Open dialog box appears.

2. Select the folder that contains your stationery document.

3. If this folder contains many files that are not stationery documents, select Stationery in the List Files of Type list box. After you select Stationery, Word displays only those files that were saved with the Stationery option.

4. Choose Open. Word opens the document in an Untitled file.

5. Make the changes.

6. Choose Save As from the File menu or press Shift-F7. The Save As dialog box appears.

7. In the Save File as Type list box, select Stationery.

8. In the Save Current Document As box, type the name under which you saved the stationery document.

9. Choose Save. An alert box appears, asking you to confirm that you want to replace the existing file.

10. Click Replace. Word overwrites the preceding version of the template.

    If you don't want to overwrite the stationery document, click Cancel.

If you no longer need a stationery document, you can delete it as you would delete an ordinary Word document (see "Deleting One or More Files" later in this chapter).

Finding and Managing Files with Find File

Word's Find File command (File menu) gives Macintosh users the file-management capabilities that have been standard in the DOS word processing world. Find File enables you to search an entire disk for documents based on search criteria you specify, including words you typed in the Summary Info dialog box. When Word finds a file that matches the search criteria you specify, the program displays the file name in a file list. If more than one file meets the search criteria, Word displays more than one file name.

You can sort the file list in several ways (including by date and size), and you can view information about the file, including the document text. You also can open, copy, print, or even delete all the files.

To access Find File quickly, click the Find File tool in the Toolbar.

Improving Document Retrieval

You can retrieve documents more easily if you fill out the Summary Info dialog box when you save a new file, as explained earlier in this chapter. If you fill out Summary Info, you can ask Word to perform specific searches, such as the following:

- All the files Suzy created between 11/3/92 and 11/8/92.

- All the files on the Smith contract that contain the text *Periodic payments*.

- All the files whose File Name (the File Name typed in the Summary Info text box, not the Finder file name) contains the word *Proposal*.

If you didn't fill out the Summary Info dialog box, Find File still can help you retrieve files in many ways. You can search for documents created on certain dates, for example, and for documents that contain specified text.

Find File also can search for information you typed in the Comments area of the Finder's Get Info dialog box. To use Get Info in the Finder, highlight the document's icon and choose Get Info from the Apple menu or press ⌘-I. The Get Info dialog box for the file you highlighted appears (see fig. 5.9).

Fig. 5.9
Get Info dialog box.

If you type comments about the file in the Comments area of this dialog box, Word can search for files based on that text. To close the Get Info dialog box, click the close box.

Specifying Search Criteria

To use Find File, choose the Find File command from the File menu or click the Find File tool. The Search dialog box appears (see fig. 5.10).

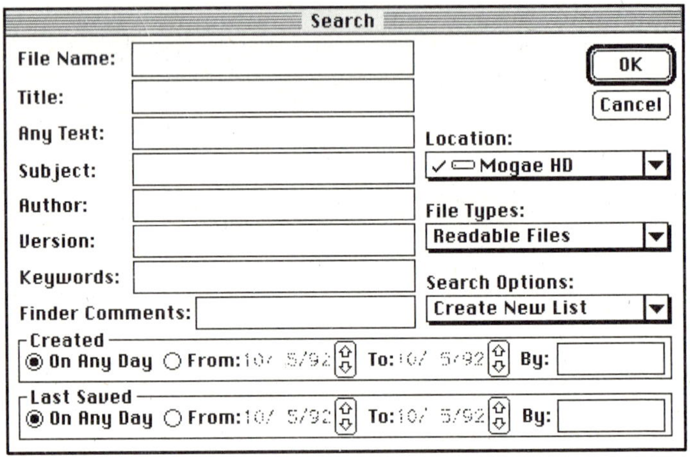

Fig. 5.10
Search dialog box.

As you learn in subsequent sections, you locate files by typing text or choosing options in this dialog box. When you choose OK, Word uses your search criteria when it searches the entire drive. When the program finds files that match the criteria you specified, a new dialog box appears, listing the files that match these criteria.

You learn more about the file list later in this chapter, in the sections titled "Viewing File Information" and "Sorting the File List." For now, look at the Search dialog box to see what kinds of search criteria you can enter, including the following:

File Name. In this text box, you type text (up to 255 characters) that matches the file name you typed in the Save Current Document As text box of the Save As dialog box. (This file name appears in the Finder.)

Title. Type text that matches the file name you typed in the File Name text box of the Summary Info dialog box.

Any Text. Find File can search the full text of your document to match the text you specify in this box—a word or phrase (up to 255 characters).

Subject. Type one or more of the descriptors you typed in the Subject text box of the Summary Info dialog box. (See "Filling Out Summary Info" earlier in this chapter for a discussion of descriptors.)

Author. If more than one person uses the computer, you can search for documents by author name. In this text box, type one of the names entered in the Author text box of the Summary Info dialog box. (By default, Word uses the name currently listed in the Your Name text box of the Preferences dialog box.)

Version. If you typed a version number in the Version text box of the Summary Info dialog box, you can search for the version by typing the number in this text box.

Keywords. Type one or more identifiers that you used in the Keywords text box of the Summary Info dialog box. (See "Filling Out Summary Info" earlier in this chapter for a discussion of identifiers.)

Finder Comments. Type the text you entered in the Comments text box of the Get Info dialog box (Finder).

Created and **Last Saved.** To search for a document by the date it was created or last saved, or to search for documents created within a range of dates, click the appropriate radio button and then click the arrows to adjust the dates. (You can type the author's name in the By text box.)

The right side of the Search dialog box contains the following drop-down list boxes:

Location. This list box enables you to specify the drive or folder you want Find File to search. When you drop down this list, you see all the folders on the current drive. If you choose a folder, Word searches only that folder (but it does search all the folders *within* the selected folder). To select a lower-level folder, double-click the folder name. If you choose a drive name, Word searches all the folders on the drive.

File Types. You use this list box to specify what kinds of files you want Find File to find. By default, Find File searches for the file type Readable Files.

Search Options. You use this list box to specify how you want Find File to build the file list. The first time you search, you use the default option, Create New List. After you perform one search, you can perform another. At that time, you can add new matches to the current list (Add Matches to List), or you can tell Word to search only the list of files retrieved by the preceding search (Search Only in List).

In the following sections, you learn how to use these options.

Using Wild Cards and the OR Operator

When you type text in the Search dialog box's text areas, you can use *wild cards*—characters that represent other characters—and an OR operator (a comma). Both kinds of characters broaden a search so that you can retrieve more documents.

You can use a question mark as a wild card, to stand for any character. If you type **Essay ?** in the File Name text box, for example, Word might retrieve Essay 1, Essay 2, and Essay 3.

In a search, an OR operator tells the program to match records that contain *either* search term you type. If you type **contracts, proposals** in the Subject text box, for example, Word retrieves all the documents that have *contracts* or *proposals* in the Subject area of their Summary Info dialog boxes. (By contrast, if you type **contracts proposals**, Word retrieves only those documents that have both words in the Subject area.) The comma—Word's OR operator—is what makes the difference.

Finding a File

When you search for a file with Find File, you have two options:

- *Pinpointing a specific file.* You can look for a file that is eluding you. You may want to see, for example, that letter in which you offered Mr. Jones a job.

- *Retrieving a group of files.* You can look for all the files that match the search criteria you specify. You may want to see, for example, *all* the letters in which you discussed job offers.

In the following sections, you learn how to carry out searches in both situations. In subsequent sections, you learn what you can do with the files after you retrieve them and display them in the file list.

Searching for One File

To pinpoint a file that you want to retrieve, you should type more than one search criterion. You also should use criteria that are unique to that document so that (ideally) File Find retrieves only the file you want.

To search for a file that meets your search criteria, follow these steps:

1. Choose Find File from the File menu or click the Find File tool. The Search dialog box appears.

2. Type your search criteria. Try to use criteria that no other file contains. The more criteria you type, the less likely Word is to retrieve files other than the one for which you're looking.

   If you know the exact file name, type that name in the File Name text box. If you used identifiers, type one or more words that exclusively identify the document in the Keywords text box. If you know that the document contains a word or phrase that's not in any other document, type this text in the Any Text box.

3. In the Location list box, select the drive or folder you want to search. To see a list of the folders within a folder, select the folder so that its name appears in the Location box and then drop down the list again. Word displays the folders within this folder and also the name of the drive. Repeat this process to see folders within these folders, and so on. To redisplay the top-level folders and the drive name, select the drive name at the top of any of the Location lists.

4. In the File Types list box, select the type of document for which you want Find File to search. You can choose one of the following options:

- *All Files.* Searches every file in the system, including program files.

- *Readable Files.* Searches only for document files.

- *Edition Files.* Finds only files saved in Apple Edition format, a format created for file exchange using System 7's Publish and Subscribe capabilities (described in Chapter 30, "Linking Data Dynamically").

- *Excel Files.* Finds only files saved in Microsoft Excel file format.

- *Word Documents.* Finds only files saved in a Microsoft Word format.

- *Graphics Files.* Finds only graphics files that conform to one of the formats that Word recognizes (paint files, EPS, PCT, and TIFF formats).

- *Text Files.* Finds only files that contain only plain ASCII text.

- *Apple File Exchange Binary.* Finds only files saved in Apple File Exchange Binary file format.

- *Stationery.* Finds only Word stationery documents.

- *MacWrite.* Finds only files saved in the original MacWrite format.

- *EPS.* Finds only graphics files saved in Encapsulated PostScript (EPS) format.

- *MacWrite II.* Finds only files saved in MacWrite II file format.

- *PICT.* Finds only graphics files saved in PICT (draw) format.

5. Choose OK. The Find File dialog box appears.

   If Word cannot find any files that match your search criteria, the Find File box contains the message No matching files found, as shown in figure 5.11.

   If Word finds a file that matches your search criteria, the file name appears in the file list, as shown in figure 5.12.

   By default, Word displays the contents of the file on the right side of the Search dialog box.

Fig. 5.11
Fig. 5.11
No matching files found
(Find File dialog box).

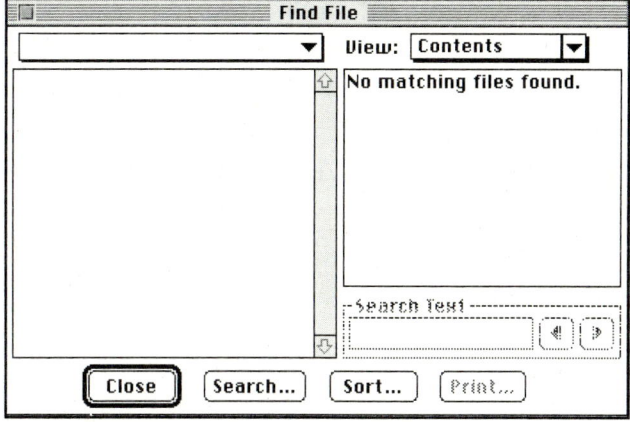

Fig. 5.12
File retrieved by pinpoint
search.

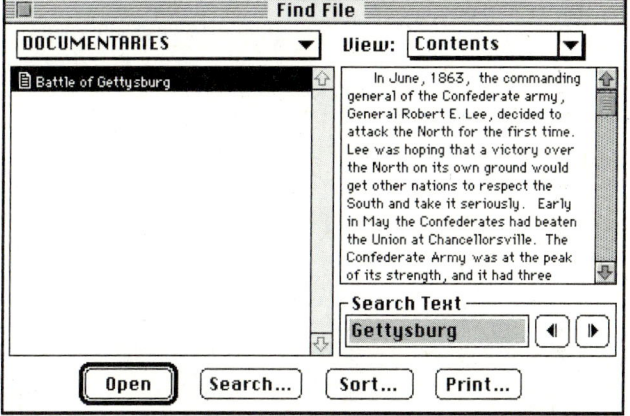

By default, Word displays the contents of the file on the right side
of the Search dialog box.

Searching for a Group of Files

To search for a group of files, you must type or choose criteria that those
files share. Avoid typing multiple criteria; the more criteria you type, the
fewer files Find File is likely to retrieve.

To search for a group of files, follow these steps:

1. Choose Find File from the File menu. The Search dialog box appears.

2. Type a criterion that the file group shares.

    To retrieve all the documents with the word *Contracts* in the Subject box, for example, type one criterion in the Subject box: **contracts**. If you type additional criteria, Find File probably will retrieve fewer files. To retrieve the contracts files created between January and May 1992, for example, type **contracts** in the Subjects box and use the Created area to specify a From date of 1/1/92 and a To date of 5/31/92. These dates are inclusive.

3. In the Location list box, select the drive you want to search.

4. In the File Types list box, select the type of document for which you want Find File to search.

5. Choose OK. The Find File dialog box appears. If Word didn't find any files that match your criteria, the Find File box contains the message `No matching files found`. If Word finds a file group, the file names appear in the file list, as shown in figure 5.13. By default, Word also displays the contents of the first file in that list.

Fig. 5.13
Group of files retrieved.

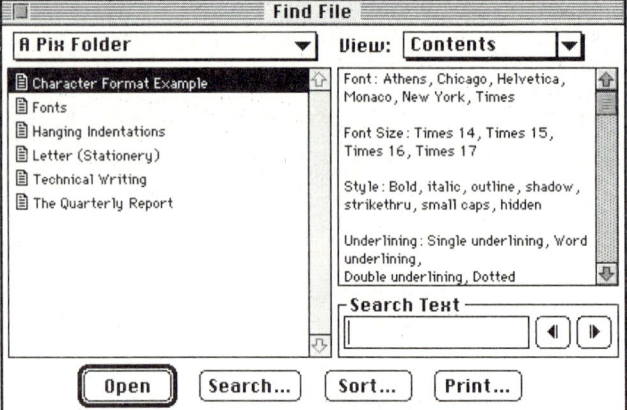

Viewing File Information

After you retrieve files, you have four options for viewing information about the files. If Word retrieved more than one file, information about the first file the program retrieved is displayed in the Find File dialog box. You can view information about other files by selecting the file about which you want to see information.

The following is an overview of the viewing options listed in the View drop-down list box:

■ *Contents.* By default, Word shows the first 12 lines of text in the first document in the file list. You can browse through the entire document or even search for specific text in this document. Type a search term or phrase (up to 255 characters) in the Search Text box and click the Forward or Backward button to initiate the search. If you typed text in the Any Text box of the Search dialog box before you started the search for files, this text automatically appears in the Search Text box of the Find File dialog box, and all occurrences of that text are highlighted in the file. Use the Forward or Backward button to display this text in context.

■ *Statistics.* Displays the author, version number, type of file, author, date of creation, date last saved, number of characters, and size (in K), as shown in figure 5.14.

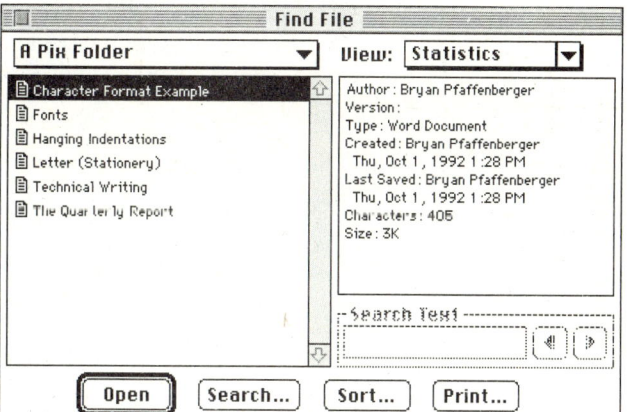

Fig. 5.14
Statistics on retrieved file (Find File).

- *Comments.* Displays the comments you typed in this document's Get Info dialog box in the Finder.

- *Summary Info.* Displays the document's Summary Info dialog box, as you typed it when you saved the document for the first time.

Sorting the File List

If you retrieve a large group of files, you may want to sort the file list in a fashion other than the default sort order (alphabetically, by file name). You can choose either of two sort orders: ascending and descending. The following list shows how your sort-order choice affects your sorting options:

- *File Name.* Sorts in alphabetical order from A to Z (ascending) or Z to A (descending).

- *File Size.* Sorts in order of file size from smallest to largest (ascending) or largest to smallest (descending).

- *File Type.* Sorts in alphabetical order of file type from All Files to WordPerfect (ascending) or WordPerfect to All Files (descending).

- *Date Created.* Sorts in chronological order: oldest file first, by date of creation (ascending), or in reverse chronological order, with the newest file first (descending).

- *Date Last Saved.* Sorts in chronological order: oldest saved file first, by date of creation (ascending), or in reverse chronological order, with the most recently saved file first (descending).

To sort the file list, follow these steps:

1. Click the Sort command button. The Sort dialog box appears (see fig. 5.15).

Fig. 5.15
Sort dialog box.

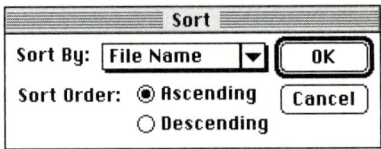

Part I

Getting Started with Word 5.1

2. Select a sorting option in the Sort By drop-down list box.

3. The Ascending radio button is selected by default. To sort in reverse order, click Descending.

4. Choose OK to sort the file list.

Managing the Retrieved Files

After carrying out a search, you can click the close box to return to your document, click the Close command button to display the Search dialog box again, or leave the Find File dialog box on-screen so that you can perform certain tasks with the retrieved files. You can carry out the following operations while the Find File dialog box is on-screen:

- *Open one or more files.* You can open the highlighted file in the file list, or you can open a group of files.

- *Print one or more files.* You can print the highlighted file, or you can print a group of files.

- *Copy one or more files to another drive.* You can copy the highlighted file, or you can copy a group of files.

- *Delete one or more files.* If you installed the Delete command, you can delete the highlighted file, or you can delete a group of files.

The following sections explain how to perform these tasks.

Opening One or More Files

To open one file, highlight the file name and then choose Open, or double-click the file name.

To open a group of files, follow these steps:

1. Select the first file you want to open.

2. Hold down the Shift key and click another file.

3. Repeat step 2 until you have selected all the files you want to open.

4. Choose Open. Word opens all the files, one to a window.

Printing One or More Files

With Find File, you can print files without opening them manually. Follow these steps:

1. Use Find File to display one or more files.

2. Select the files you want to print.

3. Click the Print command button. Word opens the first file you selected and displays the Print dialog box.

4. Choose the printing options you want and then choose OK to start printing.

5. Repeat step 4 until you have printed all the documents. Word automatically closes the documents after you print them.

Copying One or More Files

To use the Find File command to make copies of documents, follow these steps:

1. Use Find File to display one or more files.

2. Select the files you want to duplicate.

3. Choose Save As from the File menu or press Shift-F7. The Save As dialog box appears.

4. Choose a folder or drive other than the one in which you originally stored the document.

5. Choose Save.

6. To duplicate additional documents, repeat steps 4 and 5. After Word duplicates the documents, it closes them.

Deleting One or More Files

If you installed Word's Delete command, you can delete one or more files. (For information on installing the Delete command, see Chapter 35, "Menus and Keyboard Shortcuts.")

To delete one or more files, follow these steps:

1. Use Find File to display one or more files.

2. Select the files you want to delete.

3. Choose Delete from the File menu. An alert box appears, asking whether you really want to delete the files.

4. Choose OK. Word deletes the files.

5. To delete additional files, repeat steps 3 and 4.

Performing Another Search

If the initial search criteria didn't work or if you want to change these criteria for any other reason, you can perform a new search.

Word saves all your settings from the preceding search during the current operating session, even if you close the Search dialog box. When you open this dialog box again, you see your earlier settings. You can modify those settings, as explained in this section.

To perform another search, follow these steps:

1. Decide whether you want to reduce the size of the current file list, add more files to the current file list, or create a new file list. Then perform one of the following actions:

   ■ To reduce the size of the current file list, select Search Only in List in the Search Options drop-down list box.

   ■ To add more files to the current file list, select Add Matches to List in the Search Options drop-down list box.

   ■ To create a new file list, leave the Create New List option selected in the Search Options drop-down list box.

2. Change the search criteria or type additional search criteria.

   To broaden the search so that Find File retrieves more files, delete one or more of the search criteria you used, or use wild cards or the OR operator in your search criteria.

   To narrow the search so that Find File pinpoints the file you want, type search criteria that apply only to that file.

3. Choose OK. Word conducts a new search, based on your altered search criteria.

Quick Review

This section summarizes the most useful information in this chapter. Check "Productivity Tips" for a review of high-productivity tips and tricks—the ones that Macintosh and Word pros use every day. Review "Techniques" whenever you need a quick reminder about a specific procedure.

Productivity Tips

- As long as you have plenty of disk space, activate the Fast Save option. Word will save your documents in seconds.

- Use a save reminder (Preferences dialog box, Open and Save options) to make sure that you save your work every 10 to 15 minutes.

- Create templates for all the documents you frequently create, such as letters, memos, periodic reports, newsletters, and résumés. Save these templates as stationery documents.

- Use stationery documents to store authoritative versions of your document style sheets. If you need to modify a document's style, make the modification in the stationery document and then copy the stationery document's style sheet into your current document. (For more information on style sheets, see Chapter 14, "Formatting with Styles.")

- To open one of the last four files you saved, choose the file's name from Word 5.1's File menu.

- Don't waste time hunting through folder after folder to find an elusive file. Use Find File instead.

- Fill out the Summary Info dialog box whenever you save new files. This information helps you retrieve files more efficiently with Find File.

- To retrieve one file with Find File, type search criteria that apply only to that document.

- To retrieve a group of files, type a search criterion (or two criteria, at most) that the files are likely to share.

- To open more than one file in a working session, use Find File to group the files and then open them as a group.

- To print one or more files that aren't open, use Find File to display and print them.

- To copy or delete several files that aren't in the same folder, you may find Find File easier to use than the Finder.

Techniques

This section provides concise summaries of all the procedures introduced in this chapter.

Saving Documents

To save a document for the first time:

1. Choose Save from the File menu, press ⌘-S or Shift-F7, or click the Save tool. The Save As dialog box appears.

2. Use the current-folder list box to display the folder where you want to store the file. To change drives, click the Desktop button and double-click the drive name in the document list box (System 7) or click the Drive button (System 6).

3. Type the document name in the Save Current Document As text box.

4. Choose Save.

To resave your document:

Choose Save from the File menu, press ⌘-S or F7, or click the Save tool.

To resave a document under a different file name:

1. Choose Save As from the File menu, or press ⌘-S or Shift-F7. The Save As dialog box appears, with the current file name highlighted in the Save Current Document As text box.

2. To delete the current document name, begin typing the new name in the Save Current Document As box. To edit the name, click the insertion point in the name to cancel the highlighting and then make the necessary changes.

3. Choose Save.

To specify fast saves for all documents:

1. Choose Preferences from the Tools menu. The Preferences dialog box appears.

2. Click the Open and Save icon. The Open and Save options appear in the dialog box.

3. Activate the Allow Fast Saves option by clicking its check box.

4. Click the close box.

To display a save reminder at an interval you specify:

1. Choose Preferences from the Tools menu. The Preferences dialog box appears.

2. Click the Open and Save icon. The Open and Save options appear in the dialog box.

3. Activate the Save Reminder option by clicking its check box. The Save Now? dialog box appears.

4. Type an interval in the Postpone text box (suggested interval: 10 or 15 minutes).

5. Choose OK. You return to the Preferences dialog box.

6. Click the close box to close the dialog box.

To save a document in ASCII format so that you can send it via modem:

1. Choose Save As from the File menu or press Shift-F7. The Save As dialog box appears.

2. Drop down the Save File As Type list box.

3. Select Text Only with Line Breaks.

4. If you want to make this option the default format for the file, activate the Default for File check box.

5. Type a new name for the document in the Save Current Document As text box.

6. Select the folder where you want to store the document or, if you're using System 7, click the New Folder button to create a new folder for your document.

7. Choose Save.

To save your document to another program's file format so that you can exchange a file with a colleague:

1. Choose Save As from the File menu or press Shift-F7. The Save As dialog box appears.

2. Drop down the Save File As Type list box.

3. Select a file format.

4. Activate the Default for File check box.

5. Type a new name for the document in the Save Current Document As text box.

6. Select the folder where you want to store the document or, if you're using System 7, click the New Folder button to create a new folder for your document.

7. Choose Save.

To skip the Summary Info dialog box:

Choose OK in the Summary Info dialog box without filling out any of the fields.

To skip Summary Info for now, so that you can fill it out the next time you save the document:

Choose Cancel in the Summary Info dialog box without filling out any of the fields.

To prevent Word from displaying Summary Info automatically the first time you save a document:

1. Choose Preferences from the Tools menu. The Preferences dialog box appears.

2. Click the Open and Save icon. The Open and Save options appear in the dialog box.

3. Turn off the Prompt for Summary Info option by clicking its check box.

4. Click the close box.

Opening Documents

To open a document:

1. Choose Open from the File menu, press ⌘-O, or click the Open tool. The Open dialog box appears.

2. Use the current-folder and document list boxes to open the folder that contains the file.

3. Double-click the file name in the document list box. Alternatively, highlight the file name and then choose Open.

To open one of the last four documents you saved:

Choose the document's name from the File menu.

To open a document created by another program:

1. Choose Open from the File menu, press ⌘-O, or click the Open tool. The Open dialog box appears.

2. Select the file's format in the List Files of Type drop-down list box.

3. Use the current-folder and document list boxes to open the folder that contains the file.

4. Double-click the file name or highlight it and then choose Open.

Working with Stationery Documents

To create a stationery document:

1. Create a generic version of the document.

2. Choose Save As from the File menu or press Shift-F7. The Save As dialog box appears.

3. Select the Stationery option in the Save File as Type drop-down list box.

4. Type a name for the document in the Save Current Document As text box.

5. Choose Save.

To save a document as a stationery document:

1. Choose Save As from the File menu or press Shift-F7. The Save As dialog box appears.

2. Drop down the Save File As Type list box.

3. Select Stationery.

4. Activate the Default for File check box.

5. Select the folder where you want to store the document or, if you're using System 7, click the New Folder button to create a new folder for your document.

6. Choose Save.

To open a stationery document:

1. Choose Open from the File menu, press ⌘-O, or click the Open tool. The Open dialog box appears.

2. Select the folder that contains your stationery document.

3. If this folder contains many files that are not stationery documents, select Stationery in the List Files of Type drop-down list box. Word displays only stationery documents in the file list box.

4. Double-click the document name or highlight it and then choose Open.

To revise a stationery document:

1. Choose Open from the File menu or press ⌘-O. The Open dialog box appears.

2. Select the folder that contains your stationery document.

3. If this folder contains many files that are not stationery documents, select Stationery in the List Files of Type drop-down list box. Word displays only stationery documents in the file list box.

4. Select the name of the document you want and then choose Open.

5. Make the changes.

6. Choose Save As from the File menu, press ⌘-S or Shift-F7, or click the Save tool. The Save As dialog box appears.

7. Select Stationery in the Save File as Type drop-down list box.

8. In the Save Current Document As box, type the name under which you previously saved the stationery document.

9. Choose Save. An alert box appears.

10. Click Replace.

11. Choose Close from the File menu.

Finding Files

To perform a pinpoint search for one file:

1. Choose Find File from the File menu. The Search dialog box appears.

2. Type your search criteria. Try to use criteria that apply only to the file you want.

3. In the Location list box, select the drive or folder you want to search. (Repeat this step to view folders within folders.)

4. In the File Types list box, select the type of document for which you want Find File to search.

5. Choose OK. Word performs the search and displays the result in the Find File dialog box.

To find a group of files:

1. Choose Find File from the File menu. The Search dialog box appears.

2. Type a criterion that applies to all the files in the group. You can use wild cards or the OR operator (comma).

3. In the Location list box, select the drive you want to search.

4. In the File Types list box, select the type of document for which you want Find File to search.

5. Choose OK. Word performs the search and displays the result in the Find File dialog box.

To sort several files in the file list:

1. Click the Sort button in the Find File dialog box. The Sort dialog box appears.

2. Select a sorting option in the Sort By drop-down list box.

3. Ascending sort order is selected by default. To sort in reverse order, click the Descending radio button.

4. Choose OK to sort the file list.

To open a group of files with Find File:

1. Use Find File to retrieve and display the files in the Find File dialog box.

2. Select the first file you want to open.

3. Hold down the Shift key and click another file.

4. Repeat step 3 until you have selected all the files you want to open.

5. Choose Open.

To print a group of files with Find File:

1. Use Find File to retrieve and display the files in the Find File dialog box.

2. Select the first file you want to print.

3. Hold down the Shift key and click another file.

4. Repeat step 3 until you have selected all the files you want to print.

5. Choose Print from the File menu.

6. Choose the printing settings you want, and then choose the Print button.

7. Repeat step 6 until all the documents are printed.

To copy a group of files with Find File:

1. Use Find File to retrieve and display the files in the Find File dialog box.

2. Select the files you want to copy.

3. Choose Save As from the File menu or press Shift-F7. The Save As dialog box appears.

4. Choose a folder or drive other than the one in which you originally stored the document.

5. Choose Save.

6. To duplicate additional documents, repeat steps 4 and 5.

To delete one or more files:

1. Use Find File to display one or more files.

2. Select the files you want to delete.

3. Choose Delete from the File menu. An alert box appears, asking whether you really want to delete the files.

4. Choose OK. Word deletes the files.

5. To delete additional files, repeat steps 3 and 4.

To perform another search after using Find File:

1. Click the Close command button in the Find File dialog box to display the Search dialog box again.

2. Perform one of the following actions:

- ■ To reduce the size of the current file list without adding any new files, select Search Only in List in the Search Options drop-down list box.

- ■ To add more files to the current file list, select Add Matches to List in the Search Options drop-down list box.

- ■ To create a new file list, leave the Create New List option selected in the Search Options drop-down list box.

3. Change the search criteria or type additional search criteria.

4. Choose OK.

Word 5.1 Fundamentals

Includes

Creating Text

Creating and
Importing Graphics

Editing Text

Formatting with Fonts and
Character Styles

Formatting Paragraphs

Formatting Pages

Checking Spelling
and Grammar

Printing Documents

USING
WORD 5.1
FOR THE MAC
SPECIAL EDITION

Creating Text

ord is the consummate writer's tool. Even if you seldom use the program's advanced formatting capabilities, Word is well worth the money (and the time spent learning the program) for its unique combination of text-creation tools. To safeguard the text you have created, you should master saving techniques, which also are discussed in this chapter.

Following is an overview of the chapter's treatment of creating and saving text:

- *Creating text with Word.* This chapter shows you how to change the default font to one that takes full advantage of your printer's capabilities. You learn how to include special characters and symbols while you write and how to control line breaks. You learn about Word's spaces, hyphens, and the en and em dashes you need for desktop-publishing applications. This chapter also shows you how to control Word's page breaks.

- *Finding the right word with Thesaurus.* Word's Thesaurus command helps you find the words you need to express yourself clearly in your documents.

Typing Text

Typing a document with Word is simpler than working with a typewriter. You can type the text without worrying about typing past the right margin, and you can make corrections with the Delete key (Backspace) as you go. The text is not printed until you revise and proof it.

When you type your document, you can use many special features of Word. In this section, you learn when to use the Return, Tab, and Shift-Return (New Line) keys. You also learn how to choose a new default font for your document. You investigate the use of the Macintosh's many special characters, and you learn how to control line and page breaks with precision.

Moving from a Typewriter to a Word Processor

To use a word processing program like Word effectively, you need to keep the following points in mind:

- Don't press the Return or Enter key at the end of a line; Word wraps text at the right margin down to the next line. Press Return only to start a new paragraph or to end a line before it reaches the right margin.

- Always use tabs instead of the space bar to align text. To indent text to start a new paragraph, for example, press Tab instead of entering five spaces.

For desktop-publishing applications, you needn't press the space bar twice at the end of each sentence. Typeset-quality text features only one space after each period.

Inserting the Date

If you're typing a letter or report, you don't have to type today's date; Word can insert the current date for you. To insert the current date at the insertion point's location, choose Date from the Insert menu. Word inserts a date in the following format: December 21, 1992.

If you frequently type the current time in your documents, follow the procedure detailed in Chapter 35, "Customizing Menus and Keyboard Shortcuts," to add the Time command to the Insert menu.

Working with Paragraphs

In Word, a *paragraph* is any unit of text that ends with a paragraph mark. By this definition, a one-word, centered heading that ends with a paragraph mark is a paragraph. Following are a few examples of paragraphs:

A Heading¶

¶

P1X14-J   (Stock No. 14-0119)   Quantity: 112¶

¶

This paragraph is more like a traditional paragraph—a unit of meaning that develops and expresses a concept. All its sentences are unified, pertaining to one concept. Word cannot distinguish, however, between the preceding paragraphs and a "real" paragraph such as this one. The program detects only a series of characters followed by a paragraph mark.¶

The preceding examples consist of five paragraphs. Even a solitary paragraph mark is a paragraph. Keep this definition in mind, because it has many implications for formatting and other purposes. Many of Word's formatting commands act on an entire paragraph of text. The Centered alignment icon in the ruler, for example, acts on the paragraph in which the insertion point is positioned.

In this book, the word *paragraph* refers to paragraphs in Word's sense. In this chapter, you explore methods of splitting and joining paragraphs and learn how to start new lines without starting a new paragraph.

When you work with paragraphs, be sure to display the paragraph marks: choose Show ¶ from the View menu or press ⌘-J. You also can click the paragraph-mark icon in the ribbon. If the paragraph marks are displayed, you can see what you're doing when you join, split, and edit paragraphs.

Splitting Paragraphs

To split a paragraph, follow these steps:

1. Place the insertion point where you want the paragraph break to occur.

2. Press Return. Word splits the paragraph, leaving the insertion point at the beginning of the new paragraph.

You usually split paragraphs because you want to add some text to the end of the first part of the original paragraph. You can use a command to split the paragraph and leave the cursor at the end of the first part of the original paragraph, as follows:

1. Place the insertion point where you want the paragraph break to occur.

2. Press ⌘-Option-Return.

Joining Paragraphs

To join two paragraphs, follow these steps:

1. Select the paragraph mark at the end of the first paragraph.

2. Press Delete (Backspace).

3. If necessary, add one or two spaces between the joined sentences.

When you join two paragraphs that have different formats, you lose the first paragraph's formats, and the joined paragraph takes on the format of the former second paragraph. If you want the joined paragraph to have the first paragraph's format, you must choose paragraph formats again. (For more information on paragraph formatting, see Chapter 10, "Formatting Paragraphs.")

Inserting a Line Break

You can start a new line before the text reaches the right margin without starting a new paragraph by using the New Line command (Shift-Return). When you press Shift-Return, Word moves the insertion point to the beginning of the next line but does not place a paragraph mark in your document. Instead, the program places a new-line mark in your document, as shown in figure 6.1.

Fig. 6.1
New lines started with
the New Line command
(Shift-Return).

New-line mark

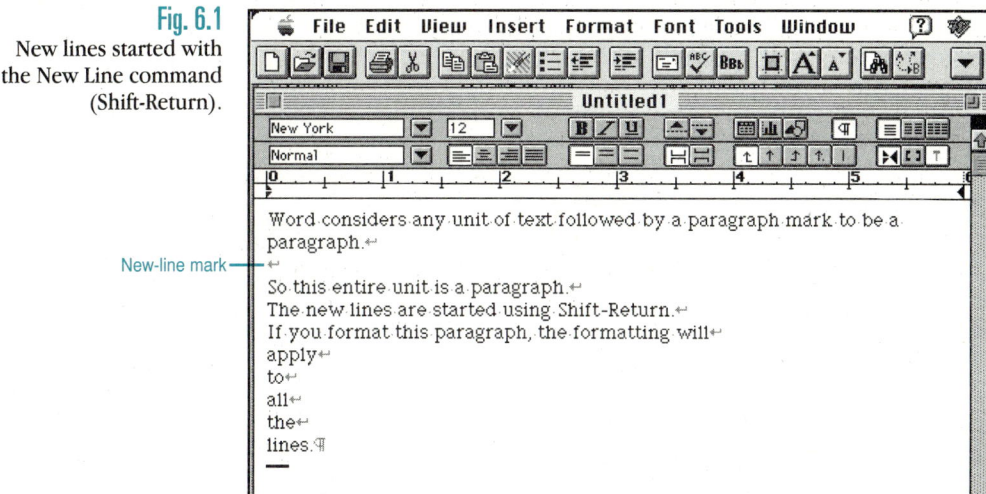

The New Line command keeps together lines that you want to treat as a unit for formatting or sorting purposes. Suppose that you type a mailing list in which names are listed last name first. If you type each name and address as a unit, with the lines separated by new-line marks except for the last line, you can use Word's Sort command (Tools menu) to alphabetize all the names and addresses. (For more information on sorting, see Chapter 16, "Numbering and Sorting Lines, Lists, and Paragraphs.")

Inserting a Blank Line

Don't space your paragraphs by pressing Return twice. This method creates problems when you use formatting options, such as the Keep with Next option in the Paragraph dialog box. (See Chapter 10 for more information on formatting paragraphs.)

 To add a blank line before a paragraph, follow these steps:

1. Place the insertion point in the paragraph.

2. Click the Blank Spacing icon in the ruler.

Using Special Characters

For anyone who uses foreign languages or technical characters in writing, the Macintosh truly is a pleasure to use. Depending on the fonts you installed, you can access many special characters by holding down Option or Shift-Option when you press a key. To see the characters available, you have three options:

- You can use the Key Caps desk accessory.
- You can use Word 5's Symbol command (Insert menu) to find and enter special characters.
- You can use Word's zero-width characters to enter accent marks.

If you create documents that include mathematical formulas, be sure to read Chapter 25, "Using Math and Typing Equations."

If you plan to use a character extensively and need to memorize its keyboard location, use Key Caps to help locate the key. If you need to insert a character and don't care where it's located on the keyboard, the Symbol command is easier to use than Key Caps. To enter an accented character, use the zero-width characters. The following sections detail each procedure.

Using the Key Caps Desk Accessory

The Key Caps desk accessory displays a keyboard map, showing which characters are available with a given font. If you installed the Key Caps desk accessory when you installed your Macintosh System software, you will find Key Caps in the Apple menu at the left end of the menu bar.

To use Key Caps, pull down the Apple menu and choose Key Caps. The Key Caps dialog box appears (see fig. 6.2). Choose a font from the Key Caps menu and then press Option to see the characters available.

Key Caps dialog box.

If you press a key on the keyboard while using Key Caps, the character you type appears in the text box. You also can click a key in the Key Caps dialog box's keyboard to make the character appear in the text box. You then can select the character in the Key Caps text box, choose Copy or Cut from the Edit menu, click the Key Caps close box, and paste the character into your Word document by choosing Paste from the Edit menu. If you prefer, you can type the character in your Word document by holding down the Option key and pressing the appropriate keyboard character. To enter a bullet (a large dot), for example, hold down the Option key and press 8 (on the keyboard, not the numeric keypad).

Your Macintosh offers many characters that you can use in desktop publishing and in conventional Word documents. Table 6.1 shows some useful characters and symbols that are available in most standard Macintosh fonts, such as Helvetica, Times Roman, Palatino, and New York.

Table 6.1
Special Characters and
Symbols

Character or symbol	Key combination
• (bullet)	Option-8
¶ (paragraph mark)	Option-7
™ (trademark symbol)	Option-2
° (degree)	Shift-Option-8
® (registered trademark)	Option-R
© (copyright symbol)	Option-G
» (European quote mark)	Option-\
« (European quote mark)	Shift-Option-\
… (ellipsis)	Option-;

Using the Symbol Command

The Symbol command (Insert menu) and the Symbol tool display a dialog box listing all the characters available for the current font (see fig. 6.3).

Fig. 6.3

Symbol dialog box.

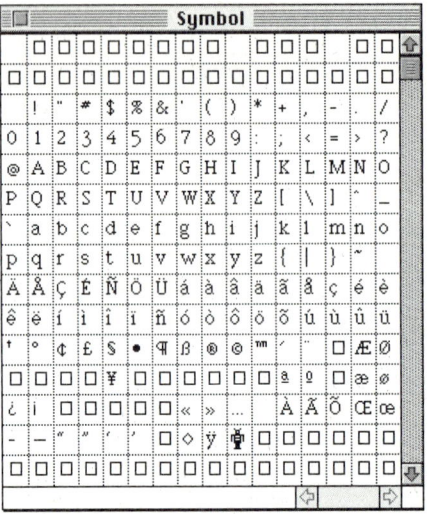

You can enter a whole series of special characters into a document quickly by clicking those characters in the Symbol dialog box. Each character you click appears in your document at the location of the insertion point.

To use the Symbol dialog box to enter special characters, follow these steps:

1. Place the insertion point where you want the special character to appear.

2. Choose the font you want to use from the Font menu.

3. Choose Symbol from the Insert menu, press ⌘-Option-Q, or click the Symbol tool. The Symbol dialog box appears.

If you forgot to choose a font before choosing the Symbol command, you still can access the Font menu.

Part II

Word 5.1 Fundamentals

4. Click the character you want to use. When you click a character, Word enters the character into your document. At the bottom of the dialog box, Word displays the decimal code (and key or key combination) for this character.

5. Click the Symbol dialog box's close box when you finish choosing characters.

Your System file probably includes fonts that offer many more special characters than normal text fonts do. Figure 6.4 shows some of the special characters available in the Symbol font, and figure 6.5 shows some of the characters available in the Zapf Dingbats font. The Cairo font offers even more graphics and symbols.

Fig. 6.4
Special characters (Symbol font).

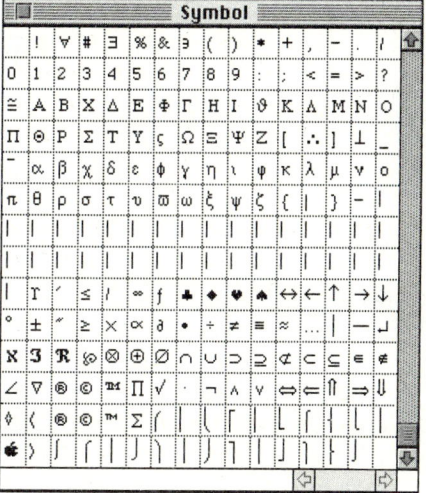

Entering Diacritical Marks

Use zero-width characters to enter diacritical marks such as accents and umlauts. A *zero-width character* is a character that, when entered, does not advance the insertion point to the next space. To enter diacritical marks, press the Option key and the key for the zero-width character together (the insertion point doesn't advance) and then press the appropriate letter key. Word enters the mark and the letter together. To enter a zero-width character by itself, press the Option key combination twice.

Chapter 6

Creating Text

Fig. 6.5
Special characters
(Zapf Dingbats font).

[Symbol character map window]

To enter an uppercase character with diacritical marks, hold down the Shift key when you type the character.

Table 6.2 lists the Macintosh zero-width characters.

Table 6.2
Zero-Width Characters

Key combination	Character
Option-`	Grave accent (`)
Option-e	Acute accent (´)
Option-i	Circumflex (^)
Option-n	Tilde (~)
Option-u	Umlaut (¨)

Using Smart Quotes

When you press the quote key on the keyboard, an application normally enters the ASCII code 34 character ("); the apostrophe key produces an ASCII code 39 character (').

ASCII code 34 (quote):	"Example"
ASCII code 39 (apostrophe):	'Example'

With Word's Smart Quotes, however, the program enters quotes and apostrophes that slant in the appropriate direction (toward the characters they precede or follow), as shown in the following examples:

Smart Quote (quote): "Example"
Smart Quote (inverted commas): 'Example'

Word automatically uses the character that slants in the correct direction. Smart Quotes aren't confused by punctuation.

Smart Quotes is turned on by default. To turn Smart Quotes off, choose Preferences from the Tools menu, click the General icon in the Preferences dialog box, and then deactivate the Smart Quotes option by clicking its check box.

You can save your document as ASCII text so that you can give your file to colleagues or co-workers who don't use Word. Turn off Smart Quotes, however, before creating such a document. When you use Smart Quotes, Word doesn't enter the ASCII code 34 and 39 characters; the program uses characters that carry the decimal codes 210, 211, 212, and 213 in most Macintosh fonts. These characters aren't part of the standard ASCII character set and display as garbage characters on the other end of the transfer.

Using Hyphens and Nonbreaking Spaces

Word offers a variety of hyphens you can use to improve your document's appearance and control how Word breaks lines. You can even use Word's Hyphenation command (Tools menu) to look up correct hyphen locations for a selected word. The following sections detail the uses of hyphens and of the Hyphenation command.

Adding Hyphens and Dashes

Following is a brief overview of the hyphens and dashes available in Word:

■ *Normal hyphen* (-). To enter a normal hyphen, press the hyphen key (-). Word breaks a line after the hyphen but not before it. The name Erskine-Brown, for example, might be broken as follows:

Erskine-
Brown

But Word never would break such a name this way:

Erskine
-Brown

■ *Em dash* (Shift-Option-hyphen). In typesetting, an *em dash* is a long dash used to indicate a break in the flow of a sentence—like this one—that's less pronounced than the break indicated by parentheses. On typewriters, people usually type two hyphens to indicate an em dash. Using two hyphens in Word, however, can cause problems. If Word needs to break the line between hyphens, it will do so. Using the em dash prevents bad line breaks; the program treats the em dash as if it were an ordinary hyphen.

■ *En dash* (Option-hyphen). The *en dash* is longer than a normal hyphen. Some style handbooks require that the en dash be used in place of all normal hyphens; others restrict use of the en dash to specialized contexts, such as compound words (for example, audio–visual). If you're preparing a document for publication in a professional context, consult the style handbook relevant to the field in which you're working to determine when to use en dashes.

■ *Nonbreaking hyphen* (⌘-tilde [~]). In a previous example, Word placed a line break within a proper hyphenated noun—a no-no in most style handbooks. To prevent Word from breaking up a hyphenated proper noun, you can use a nonbreaking hyphen. To enter a nonbreaking hyphen, press ⌘-tilde (~). The tilde is to the right of the space bar on most Macintosh keyboards. (You don't have to press Shift to type the tilde because ⌘-` works too.)

■ *Optional hyphen* (⌘-hyphen [-]). If you type an especially long word, such as *anticonstructivism*, Word might leave large gaps between words when it aligns the right margin of your document. This problem becomes acute when you're working with short line lengths (less than 3 inches) or with right-justified text. You can solve this problem by using optional hyphens in long words. The hyphen is used only when Word needs it to align the right margin.

When you choose Show ¶ from the View menu, Word displays optional hyphens and inserts special symbols indicating which hyphens you chose. These symbols, normal hyphens, em dashes, and en dashes are shown in figure 6.6.

If you choose Hide ¶, the optional hyphens disappear (except for the ones Word needs to align the right margin).

Fig. 6.6
Word's hyphens and
dashes.

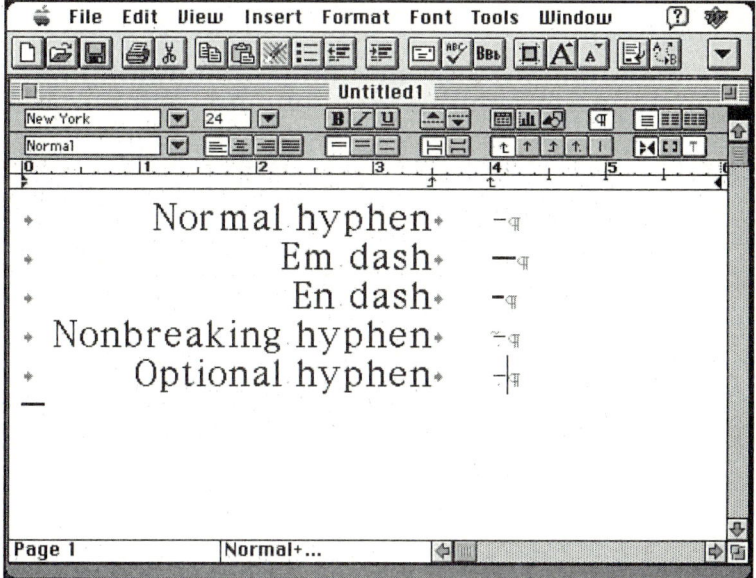

Fig. 6.6
Word's hyphens and
dashes.

Looking Up Hyphen Breaks

Word's Hyphenation command (Tools menu) inserts optional hyphens as needed throughout your document. Word inserts hyphens only into those words that need hyphens so that the right margin appears more even. You shouldn't use this feature when you write except to hyphenate an occasional long word. If you later insert or delete text, most of the optional hyphens Word inserts will not be needed, and the words that need optional hyphens will not have them.

Run automatic hyphenation as part of the proofreading process just before you print your document.

If you're not sure where to place optional hyphens in a long word, the Hyphenation command comes in handy. To look up hyphen breaks, follow these steps:

1. Type the word for which you want to look up the proper hyphenation. For example, type **dysfunctional**.

2. Highlight the word in your document.

Chapter 6
Creating Text

3. Choose Hyphenation from the Tools menu or press Shift-F15. The Hyphenation dialog box appears, displaying the word you typed in the Hyphenate text box (see fig. 6.7).

Fig. 6.7
Hyphenation dialog box.

Proposed location of
optional hyphen

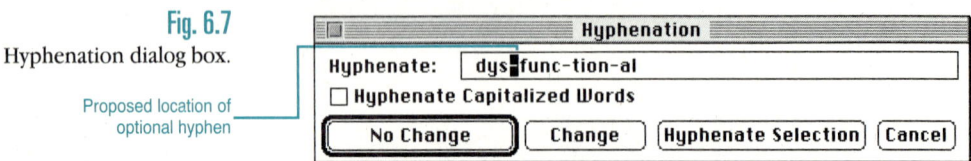

Notice that Word shows where *dysfunctional* can be hyphenated and that the program proposes to place an optional hyphen as follows: dys-functional.

4. To accept Word's suggested hyphen placement, click Change.

To insert a hyphen at one of the other locations Word identifies, click the optional hyphen in the Hyphenate text box and then click the Change button. Word inserts the optional hyphen into the word in your document and closes the Hyphenation dialog box.

Word's Hyphenation utility relies on a sophisticated hyphenation program that can hyphenate almost any English word. This program, however, is not infallible; occasionally, it inserts a hyphen in the wrong place. If you're publishing your document directly from Word printouts, be sure to proofread all word breaks carefully.

Using Nonbreaking Spaces

Some style handbooks consider breaking a line between two parts of a proper noun (such as El Capitan or Sri Lanka) to be bad form. You can prevent line breaks between words that aren't hyphenated by entering a nonbreaking space between them (⌘-space bar).

If you chose the Show ¶ option in the Edit menu (or clicked the paragraph-mark icon in the ribbon), Word displays each nonbreaking space as a tilde (~) over the tiny dot that usually appears when you press the space bar.

Inserting a Page Break

By default, Word inserts page breaks automatically as you type. This feature is called *background pagination*. (You can turn background pagination off in the Preferences dialog box, but you should have no reason to do so unless you're working with a long document.)

The page breaks that Word inserts automatically are called *soft page breaks*, which are represented in Normal view by a row of dots across the screen. The position of a soft page break isn't fixed; the program adjusts the soft page break's location as you insert or delete text. In Page Layout view, you see the effects of soft page breaks when Word paginates and displays your document.

Sometimes, however, you may want to break a page before it's filled with text (to set a title page off from the body of a document, for example). A page break you enter manually is called a *hard page break*. To enter a hard page break, choose the Insert Page Break option from the Insert menu or press the Shift-Enter keyboard shortcut. Word enters a hard page break at the location of the insertion point. You can distinguish between soft and hard page breaks on-screen because the line that marks a hard page break has twice as many dots as a soft-page-break line (see fig. 6.8).

To remove a hard page break, move the mouse pointer to the selection bar (the area at the extreme left of the document window). When the mouse pointer becomes an arrow, click the mouse to select the page break and then press Delete or Backspace. (You also can click the I-beam pointer on the page break and press Delete Forward.) You cannot delete a soft page break this way.

Unlike most other computers, the Mac assigns different functions to the Return and Enter keys. If you press Shift-Return, for example, Word inserts a line break; Word inserts a page break only if you press Shift-Enter (numeric keypad).

Create hard page breaks only when necessary (to separate one chapter from another, for example). Don't use hard page breaks to keep sentences together on a page or to prevent a widowed heading (a heading that appears at the bottom of a page, with no text underneath it). If you add or delete text later, the hard page break may produce an unattractive result, such as a page only half-filled with text. Choose paragraph formats (such as Keep With Next and Keep Lines Together) that prevent bad page breaks from occurring. For more information on these options, see Chapter 10, "Formatting Paragraphs."

Fig. 6.8
Soft and hard page breaks.

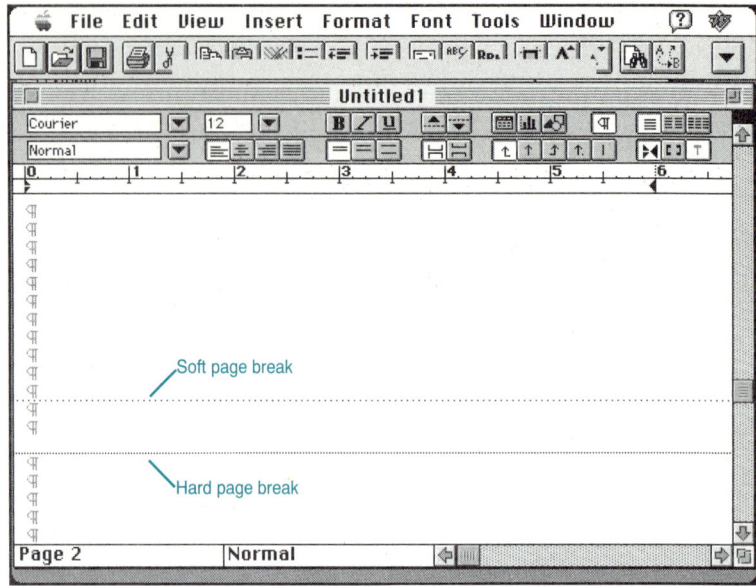

Finding the Right Word with Thesaurus

With Thesaurus, you can look up synonyms of one or more words while working in a document. You also can view antonyms (words with opposite meanings).

To look up a word in Thesaurus, follow these steps:

1. Select the word in your document for which you want to look up synonyms. If you forget to select the word before choosing Thesaurus, Word looks up synonyms for the word in which the insertion point is positioned or for the word nearest the insertion point.

2. Choose Thesaurus from the Tools menu. The Thesaurus dialog box appears (see fig. 6.9).

   In the Meanings For list box, Word displays the various shades of meaning for the selected word (*great* is used in figure 6.9), with the first meaning highlighted by default. The Synonyms list box displays synonyms for the selected word.

Fig. 6.9
Thesaurus dialog box.

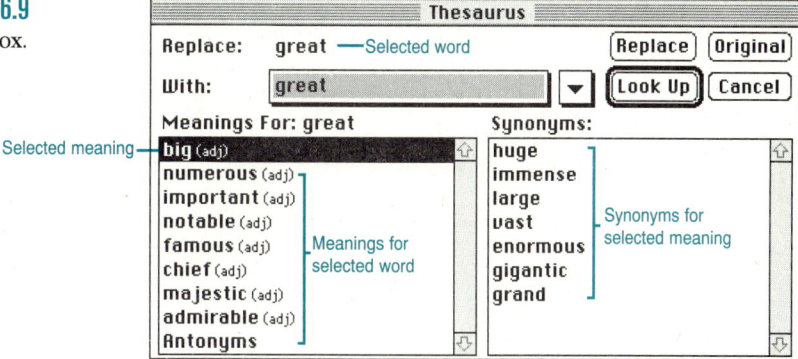

3. Select a synonym in the Synonym list box, or perform one of the following actions:

   ■ To see synonyms for another meaning of the selected word, select that meaning in the Meanings For list box. You see a new list of synonyms for that meaning.

   ■ To see synonyms of a word in the Synonyms list box, select that word and then choose Look Up.

   ■ To redisplay meanings and synonyms for a word you viewed previously, drop down the With list box and select that word in the list.

   ■ To redisplay the word you originally looked up, click Original.

   ■ To view antonyms of the word currently listed in the With box, choose Antonyms in the Meanings For list box. (Not all words have antonyms.)

4. After the word you want to use appears in the With box, click Replace. Word replaces the word you highlighted in the document with the word in the With box.

   If you don't want to use any of the words Thesaurus found, click Cancel to close the Thesaurus dialog box.

Obtaining a Word Count

Many writers must carefully adhere to length limitations, which usually are expressed in word limits. To find out how many words a document contains, follow these steps:

Chapter 6
Creating Text

1. Choose Word Count from the Tools menu or press Option-F15. The Word Count dialog box appears (see fig. 6.10).

Word Count dialog box.

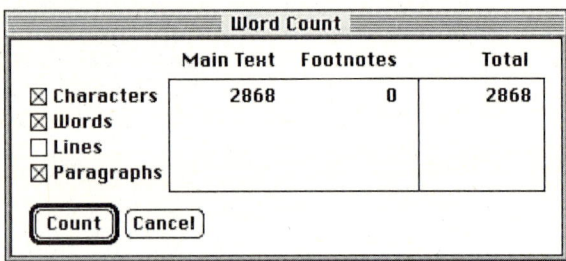

2. Activate the options you want to use. By default, Word counts characters, words, and paragraphs.

3. Choose Count. Word counts the elements you activated and displays the totals in the Word Count dialog box, as shown in figure 6.11.

Fig. 6.11
Word-count totals.

	Main Text	Footnotes	Total
☒ Characters	2868	0	2868
☒ Words	498	0	498
☐ Lines			
☒ Paragraphs	14	0	14

4. Click Cancel to close the dialog box.

Quick Review

This section summarizes the most useful information in this chapter. Check "Productivity Tips" for a review of high-productivity tips and tricks—the ones that Macintosh and Word pros use every day. Review "Techniques" whenever you need a quick reminder about a specific procedure.

Part II

Word 5.1 Fundamentals

Productivity Tips

- Press Return only at the end of a paragraph. Use tabs instead of spaces to align text. Enter blank lines by clicking the Blank Spacing icon in the ruler instead of by pressing Return.

- To sort items (such as names and addresses in a mailing list or bibliographic references), use the New Line command (Shift-Return) when you type the items and press Return only at the end of the items. Word treats the entries as a paragraph for sorting purposes.

- Choose a default font for all your documents. You always can override this choice for a particular document, and your choice probably will be better than Word's (New York).

- If you want to add special characters, use Key Caps to find and memorize the key you need to press. Use the Symbols command (Insert menu) to insert a character by clicking the mouse. Use zero-width characters to enter diacritical marks.

- Use em dashes (Shift-Option-hyphen) rather than two hyphens to keep Word from breaking a line within a dash. Use nonbreaking hyphens (⌘-tilde [~]) to keep Word from breaking a line within hyphenated proper nouns, and insert optional hyphens into long words to help Word align the right margin. If you're not sure where to put the optional hyphens, highlight the word in the document and choose Hyphenation from the Tools menu. The Hyphenation dialog box appears, showing the proper hyphenation.

- Avoid using hard page breaks, which might cause problems if you add or delete text above the page break. To prevent bad page breaks, format paragraphs with the Keep With Next and Keep Lines Together options, as explained in Chapter 10, "Formatting Paragraphs."

Techniques

This section provides concise summaries of all the procedures introduced in this chapter.

Inserting the Date

To insert the current date at the insertion point:

> Choose Date from the Insert menu.

Joining and Splitting Paragraphs

To split a paragraph:

1. Place the insertion point where you want the paragraph break to occur.

2. Press Return.

To split a paragraph and leave the cursor at the end of the first part of the original paragraph:

1. Place the insertion point where you want the paragraph break to occur.

2. Press ⌘-Option-Return.

To join two paragraphs:

1. Select the paragraph mark that divides the two paragraphs.

2. Press Delete (Backspace).

3. If necessary, add a space or two between the joined sentences.

To start a new line without starting a new paragraph:

> Press Shift-Return.

To add a blank line before a paragraph:

1. Place the insertion point in the paragraph.

2. Click the Blank Spacing icon in the ruler.

Entering Special Characters

To find out which key to press to enter a special character:

1. Choose the font you want to use from the Font menu.

2. Choose Key Caps from the Apple menu. The Key Caps dialog box appears. If necessary, press Option to see additional characters.

3. Click the close box to return to your document.

To use the Symbols command to enter special characters:

1. Choose the font you want to use from the Font menu.

2. Choose Symbol from the Insert menu or press ⌘-Option-Q. The Symbol dialog box appears.

3. Click the character or characters you want to insert.

4. Click the close box to return to your document.

To enter a diacritical mark:

1. Press Option and one of the zero-width character keys shown in Table 6.2 ("Entering Diacritical Marks").

2. Type the letter to which you want to add the diacritical mark.

To turn Smart Quotes on or off:

1. Choose Preferences from the Tools menu. The Preferences dialog box appears.

2. Click the General icon. The General options appear in the dialog box.

3. To activate the Smart Quotes option, click its check box to place an X in the box. To deactivate Smart Quotes, click the check box again to remove the X.

4. Click the close box to close the Preferences dialog box.

Using Page Breaks, Hyphens, Dashes, and Nonbreaking Spaces

The following table summarizes the keys you press to enter dashes, hyphens, and nonbreaking spaces:

Element	Key combination
Hard page break	Shift-Enter
Em dash	Shift-Option-hyphen
En dash	Option-hyphen
Nonbreaking hyphen	⌘-tilde (~) or ⌘-`
Optional hyphen	⌘-hyphen
Nonbreaking space	⌘-space bar

Chapter 6
Creating Text

To look up hyphen breaks and insert an optional hyphen into a word:

1. Select the word you want to hyphenate.

2. Choose Hyphenation from the Tools menu or press Shift-F15. The Hyphenation dialog box appears, showing the proper hyphenation.

3. If you want, click a hyphen break other than the one Word selected.

4. Click Change.

Using Thesaurus

To use Thesaurus to look up synonyms for a word:

1. Select the word in your document.

2. Choose Thesaurus from the Tools menu. The Thesaurus dialog box appears.

3. Select one of the displayed synonyms in the Synonym list box, or perform one of the following actions:

   ■ To see synonyms for another meaning of the selected word, select the new meaning in the Meanings For list box.

   ■ To see synonyms of a word in the Synonyms list box, select that word and then choose Look Up.

   ■ To redisplay meanings and synonyms for a word you previously viewed, drop down the With list box and select the word in the list.

   ■ To redisplay the word you originally looked up, click Original.

   ■ To view antonyms of the word currently listed in the With box, select Antonyms in the Meanings For list box. (Not all words have antonyms.)

4. After the word you want to use appears in the With box, click Replace. Word replaces the word you highlighted in the document with the word in the With box.

   If you don't want to use any of the words Thesaurus found, click Cancel to close the Thesaurus dialog box.

Counting Words

To count the words in a document:

1. Choose Word Count from the Tools menu or press Option-F15. The Word Count dialog box appears.

2. Activate the options you want to count (characters, words, lines, or paragraphs).

3. Choose Count. Word displays the count totals in the Word Count dialog box.

4. Click Cancel to return to your document.

Creating and Importing Graphics

S ometimes a simple diagram can convey a point more effectively than text. Word supplies the drawing tools you need to create diagrams and illustrations. These tools are in the Insert Picture window, which you access by clicking the Picture icon in the ribbon (see inside back cover).

When you click the Picture icon, you see the Picture window, which gives you many of the capabilities of drawing programs such as MacDraw. Using the Picture window, you can create illustrations such as maps, technical diagrams, flow charts, organizational charts, and interior-design sketches. You can select and size each element of a drawing (a rectangle or a line, for example) individually, even when several elements are combined. Although Word's Picture feature does not have all the tools offered by stand-alone drawing programs, this feature has sufficient tools to enable you to create and modify simple illustrations.

You also can insert an illustration created by another program into a Word document. Word can directly read most graphics files, including the bit-mapped graphics files created by paint programs such as MacPaint, the PICT files created by applications such as MacDraw and SuperPaint, and even the Encapsulated PostScript (EPS) graphics created by applications such as Aldus Freehand and Adobe Illustrator.

USING
WORD 5.1
FOR THE MAC
SPECIAL EDITION

After you create or import a graphic, you can crop or scale it. *Cropping* shows only part of the original graphic. *Scaling* resizes the graphic horizontally, vertically, or both. (As you quickly discover, you cannot resize bit-mapped graphics without introducing ugly distortions, but you can resize Picture's graphics, PICT files, and EPS graphics.)

This chapter covers the following aspects of Word's graphics capabilities:

- *Creating illustrations with the Picture window.* You learn how to use Word's Picture command to create a simple illustration.

- *Editing your illustrations.* You learn how to move, resize, and delete elements of your illustration.

- *Importing graphics.* You learn how to read many types of graphics files directly and import such files into your Word documents.

- *Cropping and scaling graphics.* You learn how to resize the graphic and reduce the portion of the graph that is visible in the graphics frame.

You also can find information pertinent to graphics in other chapters of this book. In Chapter 14, "Formatting with Styles," you learn how to create active links between Word and graphics applications that support System 7's Dynamic Data Exchange (DDE) standards. In Chapter 21, "Dividing a Document into Sections," you learn how to anchor graphics at an absolute position on the page (for example, 1.5 inches from the top margin and centered horizontally) so that text flows around and past the graphic.

Creating Illustrations in the Picture Window

Word's Picture command is available in any Word document. When you click the Picture icon in the ribbon, press Control-⌘-P, or click the Picture tool, the Insert Picture window appears, as shown in figure 7.1.

Within this window, you create an illustration by clicking one of the drawing tools and entering a shape (such as a line, arc, or oval). For each shape, you can choose a line width and color. For enclosed shapes, you also can choose a fill pattern.

Each shape you enter is an independently selectable object, which you can edit, size, move, or delete without affecting other drawing objects in the same window. New to Version 5.1 is Word's capability to *group* two or more objects so that you can select and manipulate the grouped objects as though they were only one object. (You can ungroup a grouped object later, if you want.) You learn more about grouping objects later in this chapter.

When you finish your illustration and click the close box, Word inserts the picture into your document within a *graphics frame* (see fig. 7.2).

Fig. 7.1
Insert Picture window.

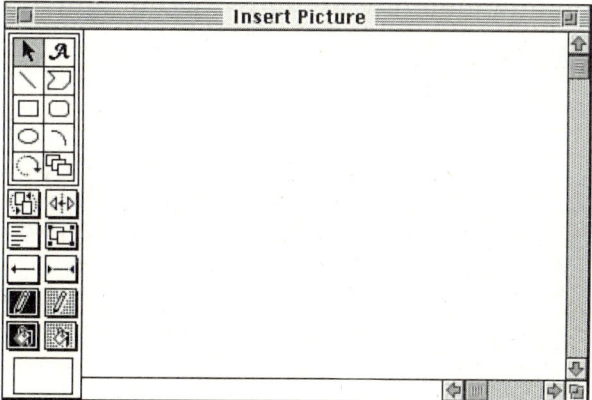

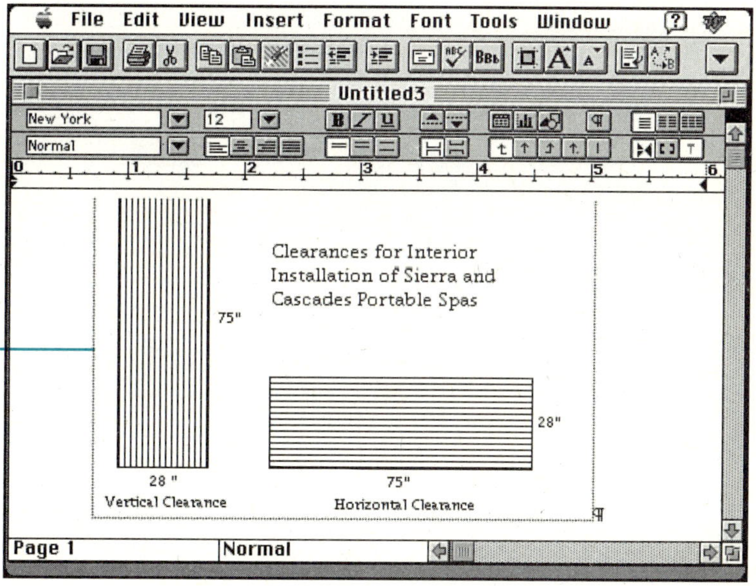

Fig. 7.2
Illustration inserted into a Word document.

Graphics frame ———

Notice the dotted lines that indicate the picture's boundary. These lines appear when you choose Show ¶ from the View menu or click the paragraph-mark icon in the ribbon.

Opening and Closing the Picture Window

You can open the Picture window in the following three ways:

- Choose Picture from the Insert menu. The Open dialog box appears, asking you to select the graphics file you want to open. Click the New Picture button.

- Click the Picture icon in the ribbon (see inside back cover).

- If you already have inserted a picture into your document, open the Picture dialog box (and display the picture for editing) by double-clicking the picture. When you open the Picture window this way, Edit Picture appears in the title bar.

To close the Picture window, choose one of these techniques:

- Click the close box.

- Choose Close from the File menu.

- Press ⌘-W.

After you close the Picture window, Word inserts the illustration into your document as a picture.

Word treats a picture as a single character. To delete a picture, select it so that you see the sizing and cropping *handles* (little black squares) around the frame and then press Backspace or Delete. A picture can be copied or moved like any other character. You also can include a picture in a glossary entry (see Chapter 23, "Using Glossaries").

Understanding the Tool Palette

The Insert Picture window's tool palette provides many graphics tools that you can use to create illustrations (see fig. 7.3).

If you are using Word 5.1, an additional tool appears in the tool palette: the Group tool. You can use this tool to group several objects so that you can select and modify these objects as though they were one object. Suppose that you want to create a corporate logo that consists of an elongated triangle superimposed on a circle. You could create the circle and then create the triangle over the circle. If you use the Group tool on both objects, you can work with the logo as a single object. If you want to work with the circle and triangle separately, you can ungroup the logo.

Fig. 7.3
The Insert Picture window's graphics tool palette.

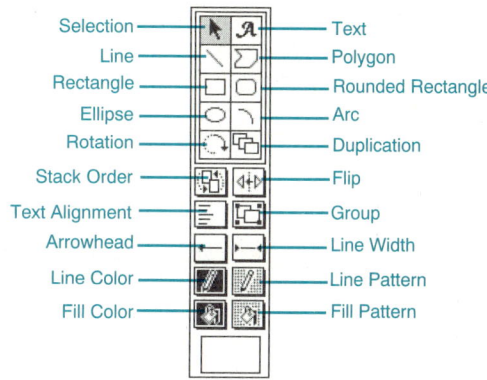

Table 7.1 provides an overview of these tools.

Table 7.1
Graphics Tools (Insert Picture Window)

Tool	Function
	The Selection tool selects one element of your illustration, such as a line, an arc, or a rectangle.
	The Line tool draws horizontal and vertical lines.
	The Rectangle tool draws rectangles and squares.
	The Ellipse tool draws ovals and circles.
	The Rotation tool rotates the selected element to the position you want.
	The Stack Order tool moves the selected element to the background or foreground.
	The Text Alignment tool opens a pop-up menu that offers the following choices: Align Left, Align Center, and Align Right.
	The Arrowhead tool opens a palette of arrowhead options. (By default, Word does not add arrowheads to lines.) You can add arrowheads at the beginning of a line, at the end of a line, or at both ends.

continues

Chapter 7
Creating and Importing Graphics

Table 7.1
Continued

Tool	Function
	The Line Color Palette tool opens a palette of line-color options. (By default, Word uses a black line.) If you have a color monitor, you can see the current line color in the box at the bottom of the tool palette.
	The Fill Color Palette tool opens a palette of fill colors. If you have a color monitor, you can see the current fill color in the box at the bottom of the tool palette.
	The Text tool creates a space for text that reaches to the right edge of the window. To create a text box, click this tool and then drag the mouse. As you drag, watch the status bar at the bottom of the Picture window to see the changing dimensions of the box you are creating.
	The Polygon tool draws irregular shapes one line (or side) at a time.
	The Rounded Rectangle tool draws rectangles and squares with rounded corners.
	The Arc tool draws arcs.
	The Duplication tool copies the selected element.
	The Flip tool opens a pop-up menu from which you can choose options that flip the selected element horizontally or vertically or that undo all flips and rotations.
	The Group tool opens a pop-up menu from which you can choose options that group two or more objects, ungroup a group, or group all the objects in the window. After you group objects, you can select and modify them as though they were one object. If you select a grouped object and click this tool, Word ungroups the object. You cannot rotate a grouped object. You first must choose Ungroup Selection from the Tools menu and then rotate each object independently.
	The Line Width tool opens a palette of line-width options. The current line width appears in the box at the bottom of the tool palette.
	The Line Pattern Palette tool opens a palette of line-pattern options. (By default, Word uses a solid pattern.) The current line pattern appears in the box at the bottom of the tool palette.

Part II

Word 5.1 Fundamentals

Tool	Function
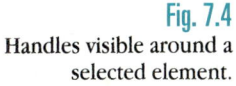	The Fill Pattern Palette tool opens a palette of fill-pattern options. (By default, Word enters no pattern.) The current fill pattern appears in the box at the bottom of the tool palette.

Drawing in the Picture Window

The Picture window is designed to help you develop simple illustrations. You can create the following elements: rectangles, squares, ovals, circles, lines, arcs, arrows, and polygons. You can choose line widths, line colors, line patterns, fill colors, and fill patterns.

To draw in the Picture window, click the appropriate tool in the tool palette, click the place in the Picture window where you want to begin drawing, and drag the mouse. As you drag, Word creates the selected element (for example, a line or a rectangle). The status bar shows you the length (or width and height) of the element. When you release the mouse, the element is selected.

As you learn later in this chapter, you use handles to resize and rotate elements (see fig. 7.4).

Fig. 7.4
Handles visible around a selected element.

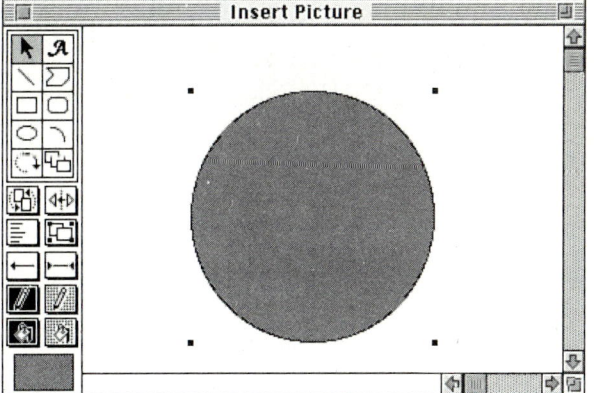

The handles are not visible after you close the Picture window, and Word does not print them.

Each element of a drawing is independent. When you select an element by clicking it, you can manipulate the element independently of other elements. The capability to select elements independently makes Word's Picture illustrations much easier to edit than graphics you create with paint programs.

A Picture window drawing has two levels—the *foreground* and the *background*—so that you can superimpose one element on another. When you create an element on top of an existing element, the existing one moves to the background, as shown in figure 7.5.

Fig. 7.5
An oval in the foreground and a rectangle in the background.

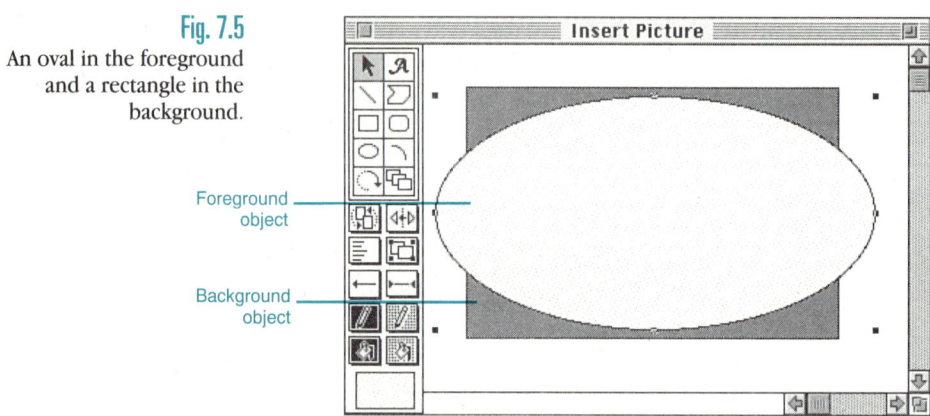

Foreground object

Background object

You can, however, use the Stack Order tool to bring the background element to the foreground, as shown in figure 7.6.

Fig. 7.6
A rectangle in the foreground and an oval in the background.

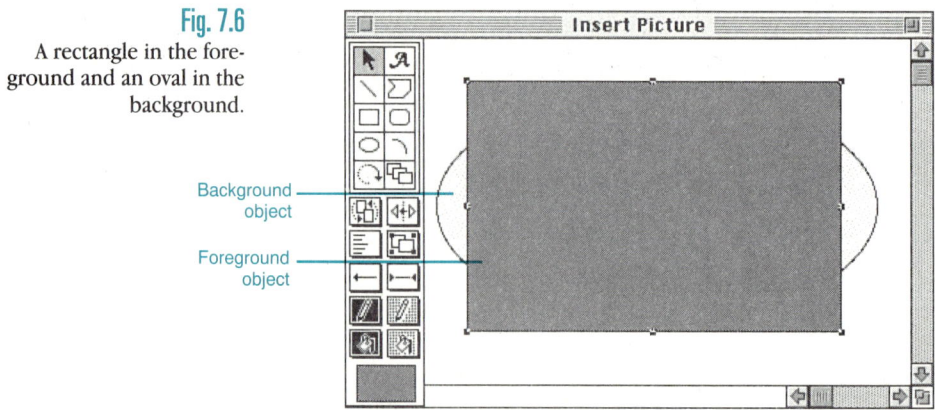

Background object

Foreground object

Part II

Word 5.1 Fundamentals

Drawing a Rectangle or an Oval

To draw a rectangle or an oval, follow these steps:

1. Click the Rectangle, Rounded Rectangle, or Ellipse tool.

2. If you want, choose one or more of the following options:

   ■ A line width from the Line Width palette

   ■ A fill color from the Fill Color palette

   ■ A fill pattern from the Fill Pattern palette

3. Click and drag to create the rectangle or the oval. As you drag, the status bar shows the element's width and height.

Drawing a Line or an Arc

To draw a line or an arc, follow these steps:

1. Click the Line tool or the Arc tool.

2. If you want, choose one or more of the following options:

   ■ A line width from the Line Width palette

   ■ An arrowhead from the Arrowhead palette

   ■ A line color from the Line Color palette

   ■ A line pattern from the Line Pattern palette

3. Click and drag to draw the line or the arc. As you drag, the status bar shows the length of the line you are drawing or the width and the height of the rectangle that describes the arc you are drawing.

To draw a square or a circle, hold down the Shift key as you draw. To draw a horizontal or vertical line, hold down the Shift key as you draw. To draw an arc that is proportional to a circle, hold down the Shift key as you draw.

Drawing a Polygon

To draw a polygon, follow these steps:

1. Click the Polygon tool.

2. If you want, choose one or more of the following options:

- A line width from the Line Width palette

- A line color from the Line Color palette

- A line pattern from the Line Pattern palette

- A fill color from the Fill Color palette

- A fill pattern from the Fill Pattern palette

You see fill colors or patterns in an object only if you create a closed shape.

3. Click and drag to draw the first leg of the polygon. You see the first side of the polygon. As you move the mouse, you see a line extending from the end of the first side to the pointer's location.

4. Move the pointer to where you want the second leg of the polygon to end, and then click the mouse. Word adds a side to the polygon.

5. After you draw the polygon, double-click anywhere. Word adds a line connecting the last point with the first one and fills the polygon with any color and pattern you have chosen.

Adding Text to an Illustration

You can add text, such as a caption or an explanatory note, to your drawing. Like other elements of an illustration, text appears in a box that you can select independently (see fig. 7.7).

Notice that the size of the box controls the text's right margin. Word wraps text automatically to keep the text in the box even if you insert text, delete text, or resize the box. You can change the size of this box, and you can move the box independently of other elements in the illustration.

You cannot use the ribbon or ruler while the Insert Picture window is on-screen. You can, however, choose fonts, type styles (such as bold or italic), and font sizes from the Font and Format menus. In addition, you can use keyboard shortcuts and choose text alignment with the Text Alignment tool in the Insert Picture window.

Fig. 7.7
Text box in an illustration.

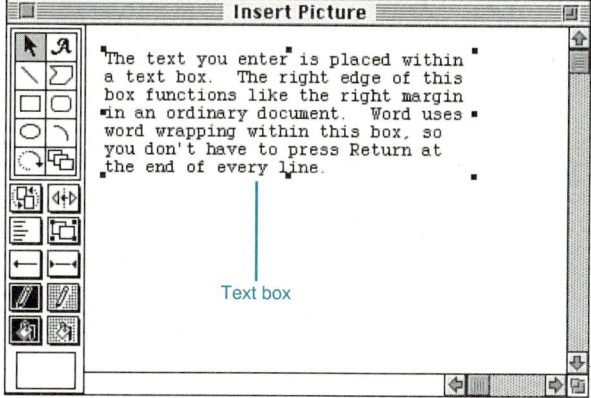

Text box

To add text to an illustration, follow these steps:

1. Click the Text tool.

2. Perform one of the following actions:

   ▪ Click in the Picture window to create a text box that extends all the way to the right edge of the window.

   ▪ Click and drag in the Picture window to create a text box that doesn't extend all the way to the right edge.

3. If you want, choose one of the following options:

   ▪ A font and font size from the Font menu

   ▪ A type style from the Format menu

   ▪ A text alignment (using the Text Alignment tool)

4. Type the text. Word extends the box as you type, wrapping any runover text down to the next line. The right edge of the text box functions like the right margin of an ordinary document. To move the right edge of the text box, click the Selection tool and drag the center handle on the right edge of the box.

5. Click outside the text box to close the text box and insert the text into your drawing.

Chapter 7
Creating and Importing Graphics

NOTE

You can assign only one font, font size, emphasis, or alignment to each text box. For example, if you try to apply an emphasis (such as boldface) to part of the text in the box, the emphasis applies to all the text in the box. If you want to use more than one font, font size, emphasis, or alignment, you must create two or more text boxes and format each box separately.

Editing Text in the Picture Window

After you create text in a text box, you can edit the text by following these steps:

1. Click the Text tool.

2. Click the text box that contains the text you want to edit. Handles appear around the text box, indicating that it is selected.

3. Edit the text as you would edit a document. You can use the Backspace key, the Delete key, and the editing commands and keyboard shortcuts in the Edit menu.

To create unusual effects, you can duplicate, flip, or rotate text in a text box. Figure 7.8 shows rotated text.

Fig. 7.8
Rotated text in a text box.

Rotated text

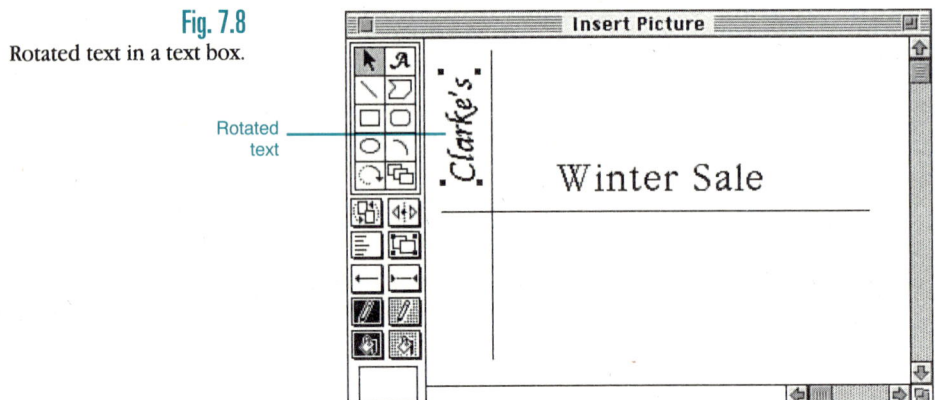

Editing an Illustration

You can edit an illustration before or after you close the Picture window. To edit an illustration you already have added to your document, double-click the graphic. The Edit Picture window appears. (This window is identical to the Insert Picture window except that Edit Picture displays an illustration you previously created.)

Because you can select each element of a drawing independently, you can alter your illustration easily by grouping, moving, resizing, flipping, rotating, restacking, or duplicating various elements. The following sections describe each of these procedures.

To preserve formatting when you copy text from your document, you must use the ⌘-Option-D keyboard shortcut, not the Copy or Cut command. If you use either of these commands to copy or cut text to the Clipboard, you lose the formatting when you paste the text into the Picture window.

Selecting and Grouping Graphics Elements

To show Word which element you want to edit, begin by selecting the element, as follows:

1. Click the Selection tool.

2. Click the element.

To select more than one element, hold down the Shift key as you select the elements, or drag a selection box around the elements you want to select. To create a selection box, click outside the objects and drag until you see a box around them. Release the mouse button to select the objects.

The Word 5.1 Group tool enables you to group elements so that you can treat them as one object. Select the elements and then click the Group tool. You see a pop-up menu of Group options. Choose Group Selection from this menu. To group all the elements in a drawing without selecting all of them individually, click the Group tool and then choose Group All from the pop-up menu.

After you group objects, you cannot change their line type or fill type. In addition, you cannot rotate grouped elements.

Moving Graphics Elements

To move a graphics element, follow these steps:

1. Select the element.

2. Click and drag the element to its new location.

Resizing Graphics Elements

When you select a graphics element, such as a rectangle or a line, handles appear. A line has two handles, one at each end; rectangles and ovals have eight handles.

To resize a graphics element, drag one of the handles. What happens when you drag depends on which handle you drag. Figure 7.9 indicates the ways in which a rectangle is resized depending on the handle you drag and on the direction in which you drag.

Fig. 7.9
Handles on a rectangle.

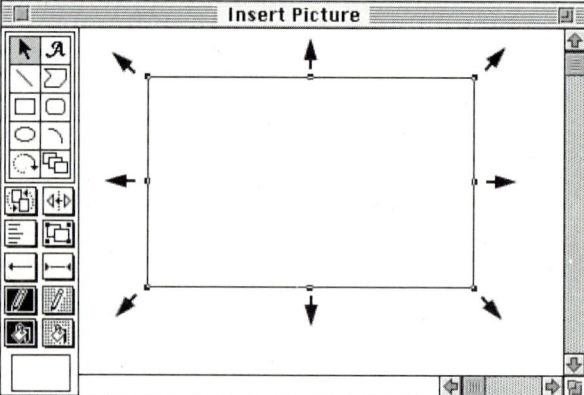

To resize a graphics element, follow these steps:

1. Select the element.

2. Drag one of the handles. As you drag, watch the status bar to see the change in size.

Flipping Graphics Elements

You can flip a graphics element vertically or horizontally. Figure 7.10 shows some of the effects possible when you duplicate graphics elements and flip them; you can create mirror-image elements in this way. (To duplicate an element, select the element and choose the Duplicate tool.)

Fig. 7.10
Horizontal and vertical flips.

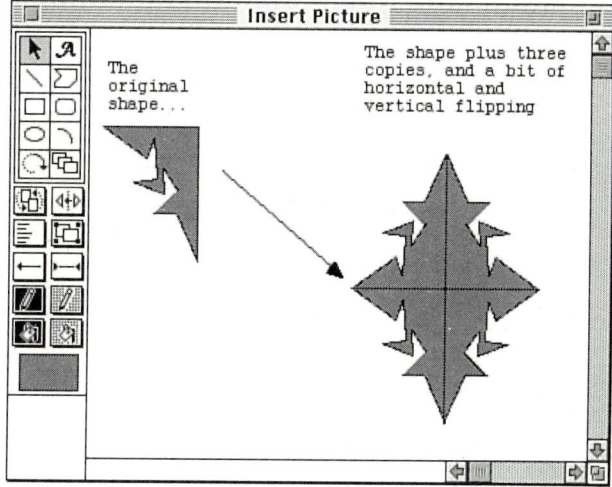

To flip a graphics element, follow these steps:

1. Select the element.

2. Click the Flip tool. A pop-up menu appears, containing three options: Flip Horizontal, Flip Vertical, and Undo All Flips and Rotations.

3. Choose Flip Horizontal or Flip Vertical.

To undo the flip, choose Undo from the Edit menu. If you have performed another action since the rotation, select the element, click the Flip tool, and then choose Undo All Flips and Rotations.

You cannot resize an element that has been rotated or flipped. To unrotate or unflip the element, click the Flip tool, choose the Undo All Flips and Rotations option, and then resize the element.

Rotating Graphics Elements

You can rotate any selected element (except grouped elements) up to 360 degrees. Figure 7.11 shows the effect of duplicating and rotating the original shape shown in figure 7.10.

Fig. 7.11
Rotated graphics elements.

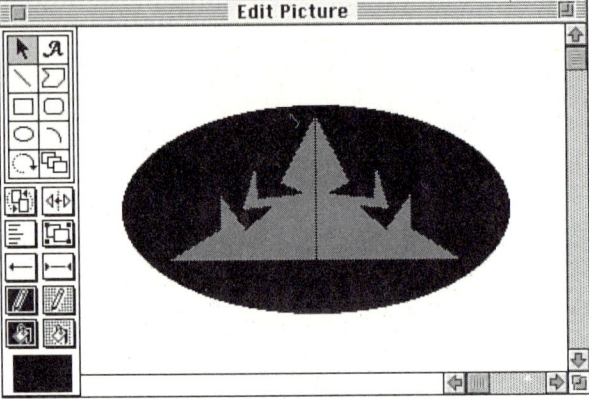

To rotate a graphics element, follow these steps:

1. Select the element.

2. Click the Rotation tool. The mouse pointer changes to a circle, indicating that you can rotate the element.

3. Drag one of the handles. As you drag, watch the status bar to see the degree of rotation.

4. Release the mouse button when you finish rotating the element.

Changing the Stacking Order of Graphics Elements

When you superimpose elements, Word stacks them on-screen in the order in which you drew them. The first element drawn is in the background; the most recently drawn element is in the foreground.

To change the stacking order, follow these steps:

1. Select the element that you want to move.

2. Click the Stack Order tool to open the pop-up menu.

3. Choose Send to Back or Bring to Front. Word moves the selected element in the direction you specified.

Duplicating Graphics Elements

The Duplication tool makes a copy of one or more selected elements and places the copy in the Picture window next to the original. You then can drag the copy to a new location.

Ungrouping Graphics Elements

If you use Word 5.1's Group tool to group elements, you can use the same tool to ungroup those elements. To ungroup graphics elements, select the group and click the Group tool. When the pop-up menu appears, choose Ungroup Selection.

Importing Graphics Files

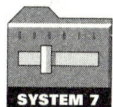

In addition to creating your own illustrations in Word, you can import graphics from other software programs in several different ways. For example, you can import graphics from another program by copying the graphic to the Clipboard and pasting the graphic into Word. You also can create a dynamic link between the other graphics program and a Word document if your System 7 graphics application supports Dynamic Data Interchange. When you create a dynamic link, changes you make in the graphics program are reflected automatically in the graphic you pasted into the Word document. (For more information on dynamic linking, see Chapter 30.)

Perhaps the most convenient way to import graphics from another program, however, is to choose the Picture command from the Insert menu. This command opens a graphics file directly. Word can read PICT, PICT2, TIFF, bit-mapped (paint), and Encapsulated PostScript (EPS) files directly, using built-in graphics file converters. When you open a graphics file, Word converts the imported graphic to Word's graphics format and places the graphic in your Word document at the insertion point.

Some graphics programs can save graphics in more than one file format. If you work with a graphics program that has this capability, save your files in a format that Word can read directly.

To open a PICT, PICT2, TIFF, paint, or EPS file directly, follow these steps:

1. Position the insertion point in your document where you want the imported graphic to appear.

2. Choose Picture from the Insert menu. The dialog box shown in figure 7.12 appears. (The dialog box in System 6 has a Drive button rather than the Desktop button.)

Fig. 7.12
Selecting a picture to open (System 7).

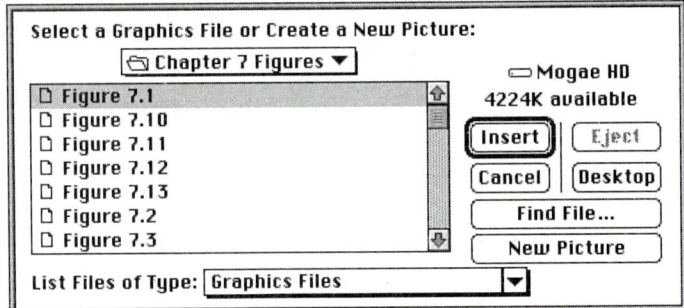

3. Select the graphics file you want to open. If you cannot find the file right away, choose Find File to search your disk.

4. Choose Insert.

If you have a PostScript laser printer, EPS graphics provide the best resolution. (EPS graphics always use the printer's maximum resolution. A PICT version of the file appears on-screen to show you what the printed file will look like.) The next-best option is to use PICT graphics, which rely on the Mac's built-in QuickDraw routines to produce sharp graphics images on non-PostScript printers.

Cropping and Scaling Graphics Elements

You can insert a graphic created by Word or by another program into a Word document and then add the graphic as a picture contained in a frame. Choose Show ¶ from the Edit menu to display the frame on-screen.

When you select the frame, three handles appear, as shown in figure 7.13.

Fig. 7.13

Handles on a selected frame.

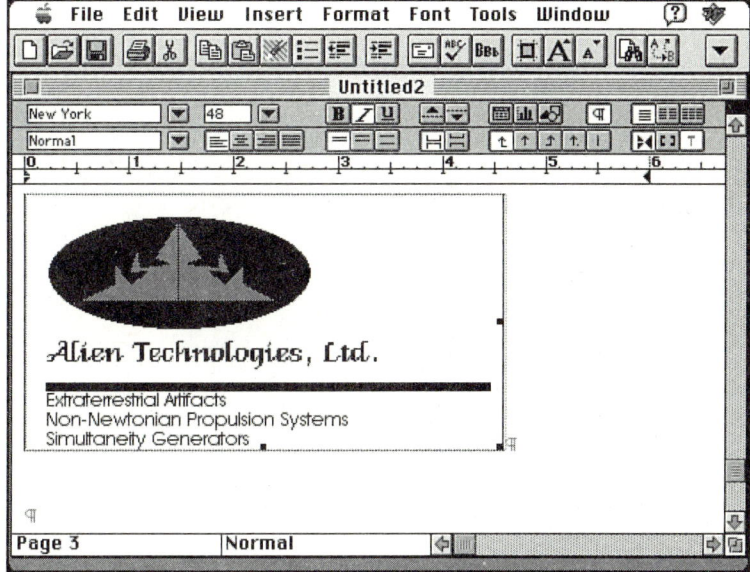

You can use these handles to crop the graphic so that part of the graphic doesn't show (see fig. 7.14).

You also can *scale* (resize) the graphic (see fig. 7.15).

Be aware that many scaled graphics print with odd distortions. Scaled paint and TIFF graphics, for example, usually produce ugly printouts. You can resize some PICT graphics successfully, however, and you always can resize EPS graphics.

To crop a graphic, follow these steps:

1. Select the graphic so that you see the handles.

2. Drag one of the handles until the part of the graphic that you want to crop out disappears from the screen.

To scale a graphic, follow these steps:

1. Select the graphic so that you see the handles.

2. Holding down the Shift key, drag one of the handles. As you scale the graphic, you see the scale percentage in the status bar.

Chapter 7

Creating and Importing Graphics

If you don't like the appearance of a scaled graphic, you can return the graphic to its original size by selecting the graphic and dragging one of the handles slightly.z The graphic snaps back to its original size.

Fig. 7.14
A cropped graphic.

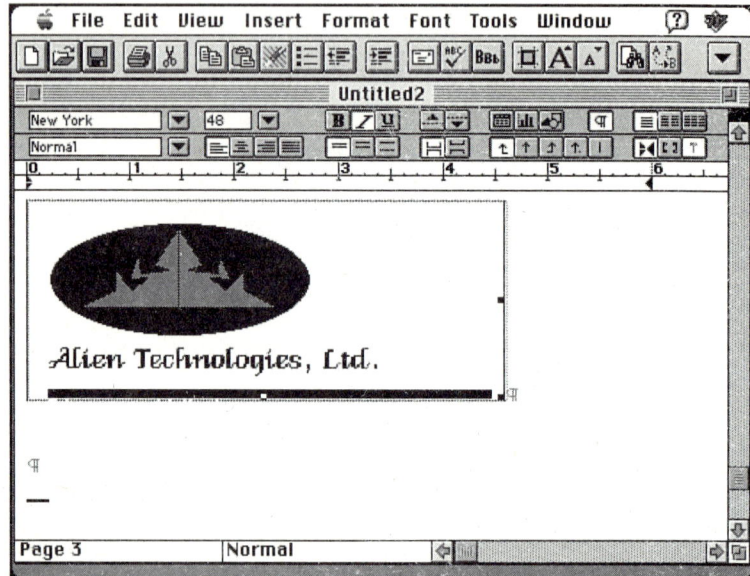

Quick Review

This section summarizes the most useful information in this chapter. Check "Productivity Tips" for a review of high-productivity tips and tricks—the ones that Macintosh and Word pros use every day. Review "Techniques" whenever you need a quick reminder about a specific procedure.

Productivity Tips

■ You do not need to switch to a graphics program to create simple illustrations. Word's Picture feature enables you to create illustrations made up of lines, rectangles, polygons, ovals, arcs, patterns, and text.

■ Take time to explore the tools in the Picture window's tool palette and to see which useful options are available.

■ Remember the Shift-key drawing tricks: hold down the Shift key after choosing the appropriate tool to draw circles, squares, and horizontal or vertical lines.

■ The Picture window provides only limited text-formatting capabilities. To ensure that text in your illustration is formatted the way you want, create and format the text in your document and then press ⌘-Option-D to cut the text to the Clipboard. When you paste the text from the Clipboard to the Picture window, Word transforms the text into a graphic, retaining all formatting.

■ Word can read PICT, PICT2, TIFF, paint, and EPS graphic files directly. To insert a file in one of these formats into a Word document, choose Word's Picture command from the Insert menu to open the graphics file.

■ Avoid scaling paint or TIFF graphics. You can scale some PICT graphics, and you can scale all EPS graphics with excellent results.

Fig. 7.15
A scaled graphic.

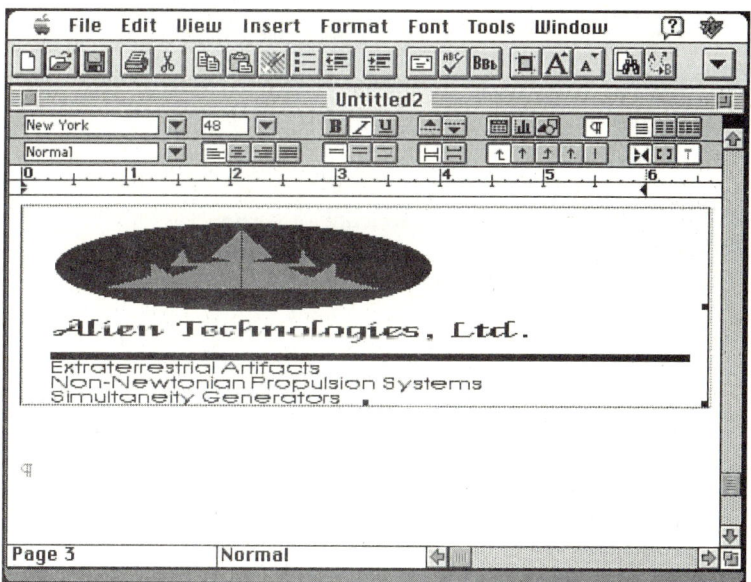

Techniques

This section provides concise summaries of all the procedures introduced in this chapter.

Opening the Picture Window

To open the Insert Picture window, choose Picture from the Insert menu or click the Picture icon in the ribbon.

Drawing Rectangles or Ovals

To draw a rectangle or an oval:

1. Click the Rectangle, Rounded Rectangle, or Ellipse tool.
2. If you want, choose one or more of the following options:
   - A line width from the Line Width palette
   - A fill color from the Fill Color palette
   - A fill pattern from the Fill Pattern palette
3. Click and drag to create the rectangle or the oval.

Drawing Lines or Arcs

To draw a line or an arc:

1. Click the Line tool or the Arc tool.
2. If you want, choose one or more of the following options:
   - A line width from the Line Width palette
   - An arrowhead from the Arrowhead palette
   - A line color from the Line Color palette
   - A line pattern from the Line Pattern palette
3. Click and drag to draw the line or the arc.

Drawing Polygons

To draw a polygon:

1. Click the Polygon tool.

2. If you want, choose one or more of the following options:

   - A line width from the Line Width palette
   - A line color from the Line Color palette
   - A line pattern from the Line Pattern palette
   - A fill color from the Fill Color palette
   - A fill pattern from the Fill Pattern palette

3. Click and drag to draw the first leg of the polygon.

4. Drag to where you want the next leg to end, and then click the mouse.

5. Repeat step 4 to create additional legs.

6. After you draw the polygon, double-click anywhere. Word adds a line connecting the last point with the first one.

Editing Text

To edit the text in a text box (Picture window):

1. Click the Text tool.

2. Click the text box that contains the text you want to edit.

3. Edit the text as you would edit a document.

Copying Text

To retain formatting when you copy text from a document to the Picture window:

1. Select the text.

2. Press ⌘-Option-D.

3. Open the Picture window.

4. Place the insertion point where you want the text to appear.

5. Choose Paste from the Edit menu or press ⌘-V.

Chapter 7

Creating and Importing Graphics

Editing Illustrations

To open the Edit Picture window:

1. In your Word document, select the graphic.

2. Perform one of the following actions:

   ▪ Choose Picture from the Insert menu.

   ▪ Click the Picture icon in the ribbon.

3. Edit your drawing.

4. Click the close box to save your changes and return to your document.

Selecting Graphics

To select a graphics element:

1. Click the Selection tool.

2. Click the element.

To select more than one element, hold down the Shift key as you select individual elements or drag a selection box around the elements you want to select.

Grouping Objects

To group two or more objects:

1. Select the objects.

2. Click the Group tool to open the pop-up Group menu, and then choose Group Selection.

To group all the objects in the window:

   Click the Group tool to open the pop-up Group menu, and then choose Group All.

To ungroup objects:

1. Select the grouped object.

2. Click the Group tool to open the pop-up Group menu, and then choose Ungroup Selection.

Moving Graphics

To move a graphics element:

1. Select the element.

2. Click within the element and drag the element to the new location.

Resizing Graphics

To resize a graphics element:

1. Select the element.

2. Drag one of the handles.

Flipping Graphics

To flip a graphics element:

1. Select the element.

2. Click the Flip tool. A pop-up menu appears.

3. Choose Flip Horizontal or Flip Vertical.

To unflip a graphics element:

1. Select the element.

2. Click the Flip tool. A pop-up menu appears.

3. Choose Undo All Flips and Rotations.

Rotating Graphics

To rotate a graphics element:

1. Select the element.

2. Click the Rotation tool.

3. Drag one of the handles.

4. Release the mouse button after you finish rotating the element.

Changing the Stacking Order of Graphics

To change the stacking order of graphics elements:

1. Select the element you want to move.

2. Click the Stack Order tool to open the pop-up menu, and then choose Send To Back or Bring To Front.

Duplicating Elements

To duplicate one or more elements:

1. Select the element or elements.

2. Click the Duplicate tool.

3. Drag the copy to its new location.

Importing Graphics

To open a PICT, PICT2, TIFF, paint, or EPS file directly:

1. Position the insertion point where you want the graphic to appear.

2. Choose Picture from the Insert menu. An Open dialog box appears.

3. Select the graphics file you want to open.

4. Choose Insert.

Cropping Graphics

To crop a graphic:

1. Select the graphic so that you see the handles.

2. Drag one of the handles until the part of the graphic that you want to crop out disappears.

Scaling Graphics

To scale a graphics element:

1. Select the graphic so that you see the handles.

2. Holding down the Shift key, drag one of the handles.

Editing Text

Because good writing involves revision, Word's many options for reshaping words are a writer's tool par excellence. This chapter explores the following editing capabilities:

■ *Opening documents.* The first step in editing is retrieving existing documents. In this chapter, you explore all the ways you can retrieve documents created by Word 5.1 and other programs.

■ *Inserting files.* You can place one document into another so that the text of the inserted file appears at the insertion point.

■ *Moving the insertion point and scrolling.* As you edit a document, you need to move around quickly and efficiently—especially in long documents. This chapter includes an extensive discussion of techniques for moving the insertion point and scrolling the screen.

■ *Finding text.* The Find command (Edit menu) enables you to locate a word or phrase in your document quickly. You can search for specific occurrences of a word, phrase, character, or paragraph format. You can find all text with a specific format. You also can search for styles, special characters, graphics, and footnotes. In this chapter, you learn how to use Find to search for text. In subsequent chapters, you learn how to search for formats and styles.

■ *Replacing text.* The Replace command (Edit menu) enables you to substitute one word or phrase for another word or phrase throughout your document. In addition, you can replace formats.

USING
WORD 5.1
FOR THE MAC
SPECIAL EDITION

For example, you can change a word from boldface to italic throughout your document. In this chapter, you learn how to use Replace to search for and replace text. The many uses of the Replace command for finding and replacing formats are discussed extensively in subsequent chapters on character, paragraph, and style formatting.

■ *Selecting text.* Text selection, which is fully covered in this chapter, is basic to editing and formatting. Few Word users explore the options for selecting fixed units of text—words, lines, sentences, and paragraphs.

■ *Deleting text.* The better your understanding of what happens when you delete text, the less likely you are to delete text accidentally. In the section on deleting text, you learn deletion techniques that enable you to recover accidentally deleted text.

■ *Copying and moving text.* This chapter also broadens your knowledge of copying and moving techniques. You learn why moving text without copying to the Clipboard sometimes is preferable to the Clipboard technique. If you have System 7, you can use the Paste Link command, which enables you to create a link between one Word document and text pasted in another Word document so that Word automatically updates the target document whenever the source document is updated.

Opening Documents

When you start Word, you see a blank document, called Untitled1, in a document window. You can create a new document simply by typing in this window, or (as you have already learned) you can create a new document at any time by choosing New from the File menu. (You also can press ⌘-N or click the New tool.) Each new document has an Untitled number (for example, Untitled2 or Untitled3). In this section, you learn how to retrieve an existing document for revision.

Starting Word and Opening a Document at the Same Time

When you want to work with an existing document, you can save time by opening Word at the same time you open the document. Follow these steps:

1. In the Finder, open the folder or disk that contains the Word document you want to open.

2. Double-click the document's icon. Word starts and displays the document.

One advantage of opening a document this way is that you have no Untitled1 document to close; the only document on-screen is the one you want to edit.

To move the insertion point to the place in the document where you stopped editing during an earlier work session, use the Go Back command (⌘-Option-Z).

Opening a Document in Word

After starting Word, you use the Open command (File menu) to find and open existing documents. You also can press ⌘-O or click the Open tool.

In Chapter 5, "Managing Documents and Files," you learned how to open documents and how to use the Find File command to search disks and folders for files you cannot find manually. This section provides additional information on opening Word documents for editing.

Opening a Word Document

Follow these steps to open an existing Word file:

1. Choose Open from the File menu, press ⌘-O, or (if you're using Word 5.1) click the Open tool. The Open dialog box appears (see fig. 8.1).

Current-folder list box

Fig. 8.1
Open dialog box
(System 7).

Document list box

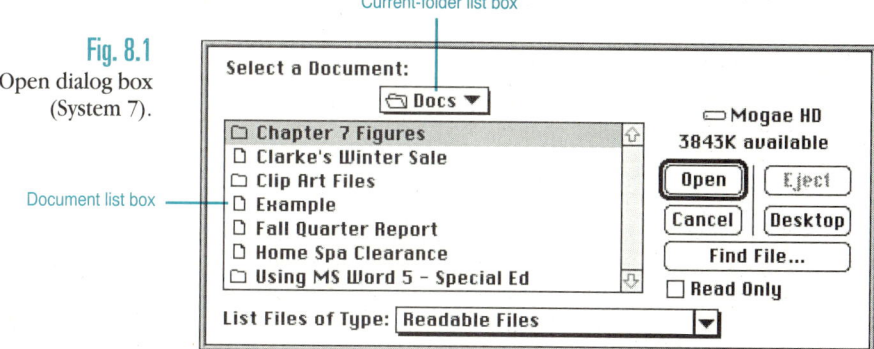

2. If the document you want to open is not in the current drive, insert the disk that contains the document and (System 6) click the Drive button to switch to the drive that contains the disk or (System 7) click the Desktop button and then double-click the drive that contains the disk.

3. If the document you want to open does not appear in the document list box, try searching other folders, as follows:

   ▪ To open a folder above the current folder, drop down the current-folder list box and then select the name of the folder you want.

   ▪ To open a folder below the current folder, select the folder name in the document list box.

4. If you still cannot find the file in the document list box, use the Find File command (see Chapter 5, "Managing Documents and Files").

5. When the document list box displays the document you want to open, double-click the document's name. Alternatively, use the arrow keys to highlight the document's name and then press Return.

If you want to reduce the number of files displayed in the document list box, select the Word Documents option in the List Files of Type drop-down list box.

If you are using System 7, take advantage of the Finder's improved capability to search the document list box. Type the first letter of the file you want to find. The Finder moves the highlight to the next file that begins with the letter you typed. If you type q, for example, the Finder highlights the next file that begins with Q or q. If a file name beginning with that character doesn't exist, Word searches to the next available file.

Opening Recently Edited Documents

The File menu lists the last four documents you opened and saved, whether in this session or in previous sessions. You can reopen any recently edited document quickly by choosing the document's name from the File menu.

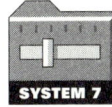

If you open a document that already is open, Word opens a second document for that file.

Opening Stationery Documents

In Chapter 5, you learned that System 7 users can save documents as *stationery* documents. A stationery document becomes a read-only file by default; you can open a stationery file, but Word opens the file as an Untitled document, leaving the original file intact. You can save this Untitled file without affecting the stationery document. For this reason, you can use stationery documents to store templates of documents you use frequently, such as letters, memos, and quarterly reports.

To open a stationery document, follow these steps:

1. Choose Open from the File menu. You also can press ⌘-O or click the Open tool. The Open dialog box appears.

2. Select Stationery in the List Files of Type drop-down list box.

3. Use the current-folder and document list boxes to locate the stationery document that you want to open.

4. Double-click the name of the document you want to open. Alternatively, use the arrow keys to highlight the document's name and then press Return.

Opening Documents Created by Other Programs

When you install Word, you have the option of installing file-conversion utilities that enable Word to read a variety of documents created by other Mac programs and by IBM-PC programs, including WordPerfect, MacWrite, Microsoft Works, and Microsoft Word for Windows. In addition, Word can open text files (ASCII), files saved with RTF (Rich Text Format) formatting instructions, files saved in the Apple File Exchange Binary format, and even graphics files. This section explains how to open a document that has been saved in a format other than Word's.

To open a non-Word document, follow these steps:

1. Choose Open from the File menu (you also can press ⌘-O or click the Open tool). The Open dialog box appears.

2. In the List Files of Type drop-down list box, select the format of the document you want to open. (If you're not sure which format to use, select All Files.)

3. Use the current-folder and document list boxes to locate the document you want to open.

4. Double-click the name of the document you want to open. Alternatively, use the arrow keys to highlight the document's name and then press Return.

Inserting Files

To insert a file into an on-screen document, use the Insert File and Insert Picture commands. This section explains the Insert File command. Chapter 7, "Creating and Importing Graphics," gives a detailed description of the Insert Picture command.

You can use the Insert File command in several ways:

■ To put together a long document, you can create the sections in separate Word documents and then use Insert File to merge the sections into one document for printing.

■ You can add a copy of a mailing list, price list, or bibliography to a letter or report you're writing.

■ You can incorporate a copy of a previous report into the report you currently are writing.

To insert a file into a document, follow these steps:

1. Place the insertion point in the document where you want the file to appear.

2. Choose File from the Insert menu. The Select a File to Insert dialog box, which closely resembles the Open dialog box, appears (see fig. 8.2).

3. Highlight the file you want to open. (If necessary, use the current-folder list box to open other folders.)

4. Choose Open. Word inserts the file into your document at the insertion point's location.

Fig. 8.2
Select a File to Insert
dialog box.

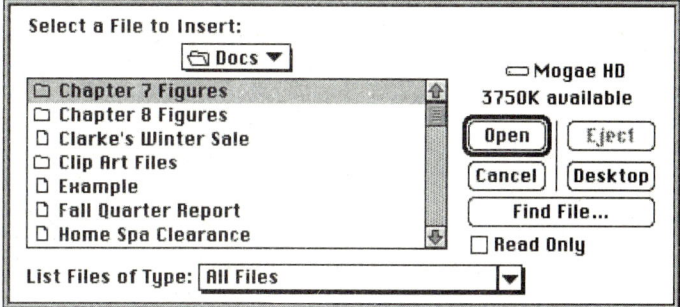

Moving around a Document

This section gives you complete information about how to move the insertion point and scroll the screen, using both keyboard and mouse techniques.

As you type, Word moves the insertion point to show where the program is placing the characters you are typing. In Normal view, Word automatically scrolls the screen when you reach the end of the window.

A quick way to move the insertion point is to use the Find command to locate a word, a phrase, or a special character (such as an end-of-line mark) in your document. The Find command is discussed in "Searching for Text" later in this chapter.

Understanding Scrolling

The simplest way to move the insertion point is to move the mouse pointer to a new location in the window and then click the mouse button. If you want to move the insertion point to a location not visible in the window, scroll the screen.

To understand what happens when you scroll the screen, you need to differentiate between moving the insertion point and scrolling. When you *move* the insertion point, you change the place where Word places characters when you type. When you *scroll* by using the scroll bars, scroll boxes, or scroll arrows, you change the position of the window on the document, as though you were moving a picture frame over a long strip of paper. The insertion point stays put when you scroll.

You can use keyboard commands to move the insertion point *and* scroll the screen. For example, if you press the Page Down key on a Macintosh extended keyboard, Word scrolls down one screen and positions the insertion point at the top of the screen.

Mouse scrolling techniques, however, do *not* move the insertion point as you scroll. This fact can cause problems if you don't know what is happening. Suppose that you are writing on page 19 and realize that you want to edit something on page 11. You scroll to page 11, click the insertion point there, and do some editing. Then you scroll back to page 19 and start typing, only to discover that because you left the insertion point on page 11, Word has scrolled back to page 11 and is entering the characters you are typing on that page instead of page 19. To resume working on page 19, you must click the insertion point on that page.

After you use the mouse to scroll the screen with the scroll bars, boxes, or arrows, remember to click the insertion point in the new location. Otherwise, the screen jumps back to the insertion point's current location when you start typing.

The scroll boxes show the current window's position in the document. (The top of the vertical scroll bar is the beginning of the document, and the bottom is the end.) You can move to another position in your document by dragging the vertical scroll box. How far you scroll with a one-inch drag depends on the length of your document. In a one-page document, for example, a one-inch drag might scroll the screen only a few lines, whereas in a 500-page document, a one-inch drag could scroll through 100 pages.

You also can use the vertical scroll box to move to a specific page. As you drag the scroll box up or down, keep your eye on the page-number area in the status bar. Even if Word updates the screen slowly, the program updates the page number quickly, so you can tell at a glance where you have positioned the scroll box. To scroll to page 15 of a long document, for example, drag the scroll box until you see Page 15 in the page-number area and then release the mouse button. (This technique doesn't work, however, if you have disabled the Background Repagination option in the Preferences dialog box.)

Moving with the Mouse and the Keyboard

Table 8.1 lists all the mouse techniques for scrolling, and Table 8.2 lists the keyboard techniques you can use to move the insertion point. Even

if you prefer to use the mouse, investigate the keyboard techniques—
you may find several that are particularly useful.

 If your Macintosh keyboard has a numeric keypad, you also can use the keypad
to move through a document. The Macintosh keypad is identical to the cursor-
movement keypad of IBM PC keyboards in that the direction keys are arranged in
a cross (8 = up, 2 = down, 4 = left, and 6 = right). As Table 8.2 shows, the keypad offers several ways to move the insertion point that are not available on the
keyboard.

Table 8.1
Mouse Scrolling
Techniques

Direction	Technique
Up line by line	Click the up vertical scroll arrow once
Down line by line	Click the down vertical scroll arrow once
Left one-half inch	Click the left vertical scroll arrow once
Right one-half inch	Click the right vertical scroll arrow once
Up one screen	Click the vertical scroll bar above the scroll box
Down one screen	Click the vertical scroll bar below the scroll box
Left one screen	Click the horizontal scroll bar left of the scroll box
Right one screen	Click the horizontal scroll bar right of the scroll box
Beginning of document	Drag the vertical scroll box to the top of the vertical scroll bar
End of document	Drag the vertical scroll box to the bottom of the vertical scroll bar

Table 8.2
Keyboard Techniques for
Moving the Insertion Point

Direction	Keyboard	Keypad
Up one line	Up arrow	Keypad 8
Down one line	Down arrow	Keypad 2
Left one character	Left arrow	Keypad 4
Right one character	Right arrow	Keypad 6
Left one word	⌘-left arrow	⌘-keypad 4
Right one word	⌘-right arrow	⌘-keypad 6

continues

Chapter 8
Editing Text

Table 8.2
Continued

Direction	Keyboard	Keypad
Beginning of line		Keypad 7
End of line		Keypad 1
Preceding sentence		⌘-keypad 7
Following sentence		⌘-keypad 1
Preceding paragraph	⌘-up arrow	⌘-keypad 8
Following paragraph	⌘-down arrow	⌘-keypad 2
Top of window	Home*	⌘-keypad 5
Bottom of window	End*	
One screen up	Page Up*	Keypad 9
One screen down	Page Down*	Keypad 3
Preceding page	⌘-Page Up*	
Following page	⌘-Page Down*	
Beginning of document	⌘-Home*	⌘-keypad 9
End of document	⌘-End*	⌘-keypad 3

* Extended keyboard only

In Page Layout view, you also can scroll by clicking the Page Up and Page Down icons at the bottom of the window (see fig. 8.3).

If Word enters a number into your document when you use the numeric keypad for moving the insertion point, look for a Num Lock message in the page-number area. If you see that message, press Clear to free the keypad for insertion-point movement.

Be careful not to wipe out your selection when you use the numeric keypad for insertion-point movement. Such a disaster can happen if you select some text for formatting and scroll up to look at an earlier passage before completing the formatting; pressing the Clear key toggles the keypad to number-entry mode. When you use keypad 9 to scroll up, Word enters a 9 instead. You now have typed over a selection, so the selection disappears. You can correct this problem by immediately choosing Undo from the Edit menu, but if you type additional text or choose a different command, the selection is irretrievably lost.

Part II
Word 5.1 Fundamentals

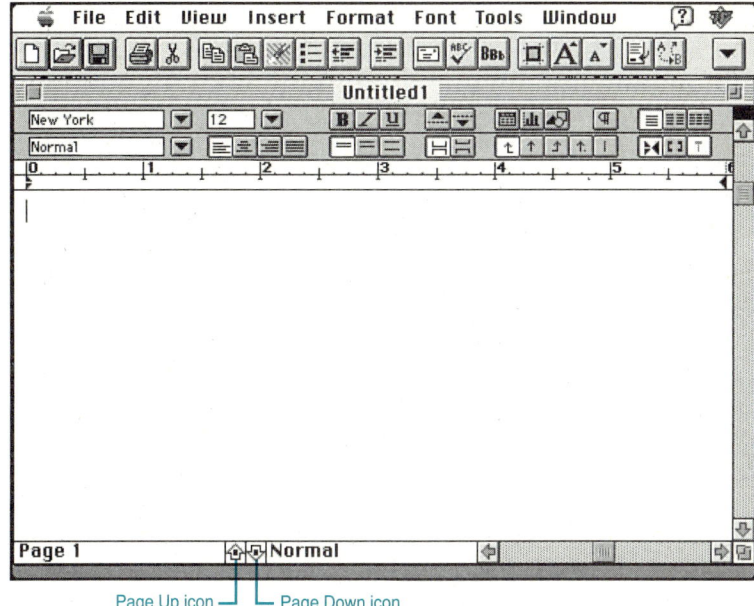

Fig. 8.3
Page Up and Page Down
icons in Page Layout view.

Page Up icon — └ Page Down icon

Word users have discovered ways around this hazard. One favorite method is to reprogram the keyboard (as explained in Chapter 35, "Customizing Menus and Keyboard Shortcuts") so that the Clear key performs some other function. Reprogramming the keys reduces the chance of accidentally toggling into number-entry mode. If reprogramming the keyboard sounds scary, take heart—it's easy. Chapter 35 details the procedure keystroke by keystroke.

Table 8.2 suggests another excellent reason for reprogramming the keyboard if you use a Classic keyboard, which has a numeric keypad but no function keys. A Classic keyboard has no keypad equivalent for ⌘-Page Up (scroll to top of preceding page) and ⌘-Page Down (scroll to top of next page); both key combinations require the extended keyboard. You can reprogram keypad 9 and keypad 3 so that they duplicate the functions of ⌘-Page Up and ⌘-Page Down. You still can scroll up or down one screen quickly by clicking above or below the vertical scroll box. Keypad 9 and keypad 3 will work the way they used to in Normal view. Page scrolling is available only in Page Layout view, where it's most handy.

Chapter 8

Editing Text

In a long document, scrolling line by line or screen by screen is tedious and slow. Use the Go To and Go Back commands, described in the following sections, to move through the document quickly. These commands move the insertion point in large steps through the text or to the precise location you specify.

Scrolling to a Specific Page

As long as the Background Repagination option is turned on, Word paginates your document as you type and edit. (Background Repagination, which is in the Preferences dialog box, is activated by default, and you should leave it that way.) Because pagination occurs automatically, the page numbers Word displays in the status bar are accurate (although the program may need a few seconds to update the page numbers as you scroll through your document). You can use the Go To command in the Utilities menu to move rapidly to a page number you specify.

To move the insertion point to the top of a specific page, follow these steps:

1. Choose Go To from the Edit menu or press ⌘-G. The Go To dialog box appears (see fig. 8.4).

Fig. 8.4
Go To dialog box.

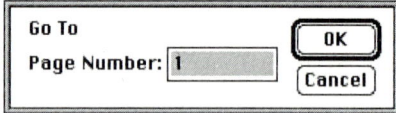

2. In the text box, type the number of the page to which you want to move the insertion point.

3. Choose OK.

If you have turned off the Background Repagination option in the Preferences dialog box, choose Repaginate Now from the Tools menu before choosing the Go To command.

Going Back to Previous Edits

As you type and edit, Word stores the last three locations where you inserted or deleted text. (Even if you exit Word, the program keeps this list of locations.) To move the insertion point to these locations quickly, choose the Go Back command from the Edit menu or press ⌘-Option-Z. The first time you issue this command, you return to the most recent location. If you issue the command again, Word moves the insertion point to the second recorded location, and so on. At the fourth Go Back command, Word returns the insertion point to the starting location.

The Go Back command's name isn't quite accurate. For example, if the insertion point's preceding location is farther along in the file, the insertion point moves forward. If the last text editing or deletion location is off the screen, Word scrolls the screen automatically.

You can use Go Back to increase your writing and editing productivity. Suppose that as you type a sentence on page 9, you realize that you need to correct something on page 6. You can scroll to page 6, edit the text there, and then issue the Go Back command to return to the exact place where you stopped typing on page 9. Suppose also that you switch off your Macintosh whenever you quit writing for the day. When you open the document again the next day, you can use the Go Back command to move the insertion point to the exact place where you stopped the day before.

Searching for Text

If you're looking for a specific passage of text, don't strain your eyes scrolling through your document: use the Find command (Edit menu) to locate text quickly. This command opens the Find dialog box, shown in figure 8.5.

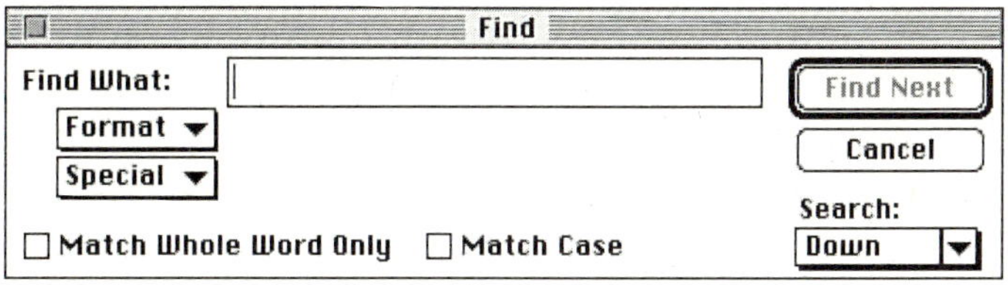

Fig. 8.5
Find dialog box.

The following paragraphs describe this dialog box in detail.

Chapter 8
Editing Text

NOTE

The Find File command displays the Find File dialog box, not the Find dialog box.

Find What. In the Find What text box, you type the character, word, or phrase for which you want to search. You can type up to 255 characters (including spaces and any Mac or Word special characters). As explained later in this section, you also can use wild cards.

NOTE

When you perform a search with Find, the text you type in the Find dialog box remains (even after you close the dialog box) for the rest of the operating session or until you type new search text.

Format. Use the Format drop-down list box when you want Word to search for text that has a certain format. Word limits the search to the characters in the Find What text box that have the formats you selected. For example, if you select Bold in the Format list box and type **Yosemite** in the Find What text box, Word finds only those instances of the search word formatted in boldface.

Special. To search for any of Word's special characters (such as paragraph marks or end-of-line marks), you can select these characters in the Special drop-down list box. The Special list box contains a variety of special characters and features, including tabs, hard page breaks, nonbreaking spaces, optional hyphens, footnotes, graphics, white space, and formula characters. (If you know the codes for these characters, you still can type them in the Find What text box; using the Special list box is optional.)

Match Whole Word Only (default: off). To restrict the search to whole words, activate this check box. If you type **report** in the Find What box and turn on the Match Whole Word Only option, for example, Word finds *report* but not *reporting, reports*, or *reported*.

Match Case (default: off). By default, Word's searches are not case-sensitive, meaning that the search program ignores uppercase and lowercase. For example, if you type **WORD** in the Find What text box, the program finds *Word, word, WORD*, or any other combination of uppercase and lowercase letters.

Search (default: down). The Search drop-down list box enables you to specify the direction of the search—Up, Down, or All (search the entire document). If you select text before choosing Find, however, the program searches only the selected text.

Command buttons. Choose Find Next to start the search. Click Cancel at any time to stop the search and return to your document.

Performing a Search

The best way to understand Find is to use the command. Open a document that contains at least a few paragraphs of text and position the insertion point at the beginning of the document. Then follow these steps:

1. Choose Find from the Utilities menu or press ⌘-F. The Find dialog box appears.

2. In the Find What text box, type the text you want to find.

You can type a maximum of 255 characters in the Find What text box. The search for a long entry takes longer but is more accurate. If you type **report**, for example, Word finds the next occurrence of the characters you typed, even if they're embedded in a word (such as *reporting* or *reported*). If you type **Quarterly Report 1 of 1992**, however, Word matches precisely—and only—what you specify.

3. To perform a case-sensitive search, activate the Match Case option.

4. To perform a whole-word search, activate the Match Whole Word Only option.

5. If necessary, select the correct search direction in the Search drop-down list box. By default, Word searches down unless you selected text before choosing Find, in which case Word searches only in the selection.

6. Choose Find Next. If Word finds a match, the Find dialog box stays on-screen, highlighting the match in your document. Click Cancel to close the dialog box or choose Find Next again to repeat the search.

If the Find dialog box covers what Word finds in your document, click the dialog box and drag it out of the way.

You can repeat the search as many times as you want. If Word doesn't find a match, an alert box appears, asking whether you want to continue the search from the beginning of the document (or from the end, if you're searching up). Choose OK to continue; click Cancel to end the search. If you choose OK and Word finds no match, another alert box informs you that Find did not find the text you specified.

If Word cannot find the text you're searching for, try the following troubleshooting tips:

- Check the text you typed in the Find What box for a spelling or typing mistake. Correct any errors you find and then choose the Find Next button again.

- If you typed a long phrase, perhaps some word in the phrase does not match what is in the document. Type a shorter version of the phrase, using only words that you know are correct.

- Deactivate the Match Whole Word Only and Match Case options.

- Clear any formats that you searched for during an earlier Find operation. To clear earlier format choices, drop down the Format list box and select Clear.

- Cancel all selected text in your document before searching; otherwise, Word will search only the selected text.

Finding Text with Wild Cards

In a card game, a wild card—such as the joker—can stand for any other card. In a computer search, a *wild-card character* stands for any character. You can use a wild-card character when you search with the Find command (or with the Replace command, which is discussed later in this chapter).

Word has an expanded repertoire of wild-card codes, as shown in Table 8.3. As in previous versions, you can use the question-mark wild card to search for any characters. In versions 5.0 and 5.1, you also can search for numbers (0 through 9), letters (*A–Z* or *a–z*), or mathematical typesetting formulas.

Table 8.3	Wild-card character	Matches
Word's Wild-Card Characters	?	Any character
	^#	Any number
	^*	Any letter (*A–Z* or *a–z*)
	^\	Any formula character

Suppose that you want to search for all the passages that mention the date of a letter you wrote sometime toward the end of May; you don't remember which day. If you type **May ^#^#** in the Find What text box, Word matches any day in May, from May 1 through May 31.

Because the question-mark and caret characters can be used as wild cards, you must take a special step to search for these characters in your document by typing a caret (^) before the question-mark or caret character. If you want to find every sentence in your document that ends in a question mark, for example, type **^?** in the Find What text box. Alternatively, instead of typing this code (or the **^^** code, which searches for a caret), you can simply select Question Mark or Caret in the Special drop-down list box. Table 8.4 lists the options in this list box.

Table 8.4	To search with this wild card	Choose this option
Special List-Box Options for Wild-Card Searches	? (any character)	Any Character
	^# (any number)	Unspecified Digit
	^* (any letter)	Unspecified Letter
	^\ (formula character)	Formula Character
	^ (any number of spaces)	White Space

Using Advanced Search Capabilities

Word enters special characters in your document when you press certain keys, as shown in the following list:

Chapter 8
Editing Text

Press this	To enter this
Return or Enter	paragraph mark
Shift-Return	end-of-line mark
Shift-Enter	hard page break
⌘-Enter	section mark
space bar	space mark
Tab	tab mark
⌘-tilde (~)	nonbreaking hyphen
⌘-hyphen	optional hyphen
Option-space bar	nonbreaking space

You can use the Find command to search for most of these characters in your document. Searching for these characters is useful in many situations, such as the following:

- You want to find the places where you pressed the space bar twice rather than once at the end of a sentence so that you can close the extra space.

- You want to find the places where you pressed Tab at the beginning of a paragraph so that you can replace the Tab keystrokes with automatic first-line indentation.

- You want to find the beginning of the next section. (A *section* is a division of your document that you create for formatting. Sections are discussed in Chapter 21, "Dividing a Document into Sections.")

Searching for Word's special characters closely resembles searching with wild cards. You can select these characters in the Special drop-down list box or type the appropriate codes in the Find What text box.

Table 8.5 lists these codes.

Table 8.5
Searching for Word's
Special Characters

To find this	Type this
Tab mark	^t
End-of-line mark	^n
Paragraph mark	^p

To find this	Type this
Hard page break	^d
Nonbreaking space	^s
Optional hyphen	^-

You can use Find to search for special characters. The special-character codes are most useful, however, when you use the Replace command (discussed later in this chapter) to substitute one character for another throughout your document. Suppose that you pressed Return twice at the end of each paragraph but later decide to add space between paragraphs by using the Blank Spacing icon in the ribbon. Instead of removing the blank lines from your document manually, you can use Replace to search for two paragraph marks (^p^p) and replace them with one (^p).

Another useful Word feature enables you to use number codes to search for document features such as footnotes and graphics. These codes are the ASCII codes of the characters Word uses to indicate these document elements. As long as you precede the code with a caret, you can search for any ASCII character by using its decimal code. You can select the codes in the Special drop-down list box or type them in the Find What text box.

Table 8.6 lists these codes.

Table 8.6
Searching for Document
Elements with ASCII Codes

To find this	Type this
Footnote	^5
Graphic	^1
Section mark	^12
Optional hyphen	^30
Space (ordinary)	^32

You also can search for white space. In a Word search, the term *white space* refers to any special character that produces white space on-screen—for example, spaces, nonbreaking spaces, paragraph marks, tab marks, end-of-line marks, section marks, and hard page breaks. When you search for white space, Word finds and highlights the next white space of any kind. If more than one special character produces the white space (for example, a paragraph mark followed by a tab mark), Word selects all the characters.

You can search for more than one special character at a time. To search for places in your document where you pressed the Tab key followed by a space, for example, type ^t^32 in the Find What text box.

Selecting Text

A basic rule for using Word is that editing and formatting commands affect the text you have selected. If no text is selected, the commands have no effect.

You already have learned some text-selection techniques. In this section, you expand your knowledge of Word's text-selection commands by exploring all possible ways to highlight text on-screen. Learning the commands that select a word, a line, a sentence, a paragraph, or even the entire document in one step can save you time and increase your Word productivity.

You can select text in the following three ways:

■ *Fixed units of text*. You can select fixed units of text: words, lines, sentences, paragraphs, and even the entire document. The selection commands, which are easy to learn and to use, are useful for performing editing and formatting operations on one unit of text (such as a word or a paragraph) at a time.

■ *Variable units of text*. When you select variable amounts of text, you show Word where the selection begins and ends. Such a selection could include part of a word, two sentences and part of a third, or any other unit of text that you want to highlight.

■ *Columns*. You can select any rectangular area on the screen. For example, if you were looking at this document on a Word screen, you could select the three squares in the left margin of this paragraph and the preceding two paragraphs without selecting any text. You then could change the font or size or delete the squares.

This section explains these three selection techniques in detail. Before you read further, notice that some of the selection techniques you are about to explore use the *selection bar* (see fig. 8.6), a narrow column of white space running down the left side of every document window between the text and the window border. (In Page Layout view, the selection bar runs to the left of the text boundary.)

Fig. 8.6
The selection bar.

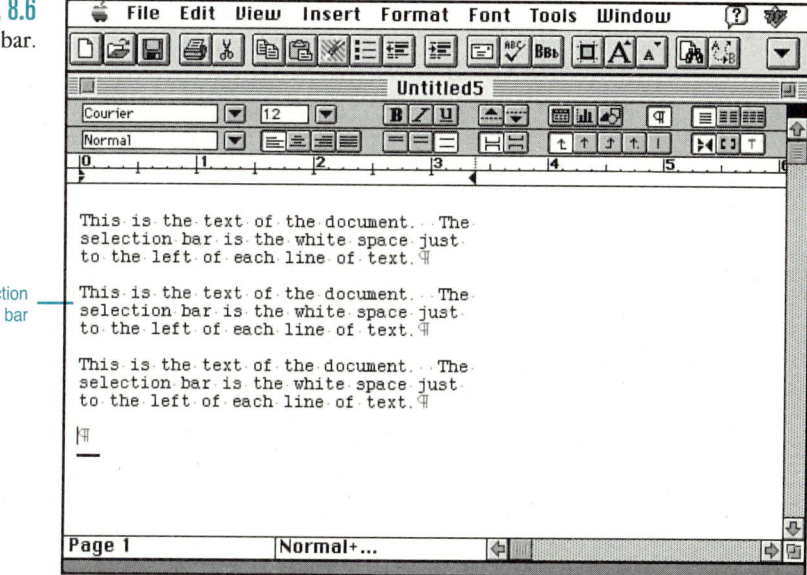

Selection bar

When you move the mouse pointer over the selection bar, the I-beam pointer changes shape, becoming an arrow pointing up, tilted slightly to the right.

Remember that you can cancel any selection simply by clicking the insertion point outside the selection or by pressing an arrow key.

Selecting Fixed Units of Text

Table 8.7 lists the techniques you use to select fixed units of text.

Table 8.7
Selecting Fixed Units of Text with the Mouse

To select this	Do this
A word	Double-click the word to select the word and its trailing space
A line	Move the pointer to the selection bar and click

continues

	To select this	Do this
Table 8.7 Continued	A sentence	Press ⌘ and click the sentence to select the sentence and its trailing space
	A paragraph	Move the pointer to the selection bar and double-click, or triple-click anywhere in the paragraph
	A graphic	Click inside the graphic
	Entire document	Move the pointer to the selection bar, hold down the ⌘ key, and click

You can extend a fixed-unit selection easily by holding down the Shift key and dragging the mouse. If you initially selected a word, the selection expands word by word. If you initially selected a sentence, the selection expands sentence by sentence.

Selecting Variable Units of Text

You can use mouse and keyboard techniques to select variable units of text. To select variable units of text with the mouse, follow these steps:

1. Click at the beginning of the block of text that you want to select.

2. Hold down the mouse button and move the mouse away from the first character you selected. (If you move the mouse to the top or bottom of the window, Word scrolls the screen line by line until you move the pointer away from the window border or release the mouse button.)

3. When the text you want to select is highlighted, release the mouse button.

If you are selecting several pages of text, however, the Shift-click technique is easier and faster than the dragging technique. To use the Shift-click method of text selection, follow these steps:

1. Click where you want the selection to start.

2. If necessary, scroll the screen, using the scroll bars, scroll boxes, or scroll arrows.

3. Hold down the Shift key and click the last character you want to select.

To use the keyboard to select a block of text, follow these steps:

1. Hold the Shift key and use the arrow keys or their keypad equivalents to expand the highlight.

2. When you finish expanding the highlight, release the Shift and arrow keys.

To select a block of text ending with a character you specify, follow these steps:

1. Place the insertion point where you want the selection to begin.

2. Press Option-⌘-H or press the minus key in the keypad. The message Extend to appears in the status bar. (To cancel the command, press Esc.)

3. Type the character to which you want to extend the selection. Word extends the selection to the next occurrence of this character.

This technique is limited in use because you can type only one character and Word selects up to the next occurrence of the character, which may not be very far if the character is a common one (such as *a* or *e*). You can extend the selection, however, by holding down the Shift key and pressing an arrow key to expand the highlight.

After you select text, you can extend or contract the selection by following these steps:

1. Hold down the Shift key.

2. Drag the mouse or use the arrow keys to expand or contract the selection.

Selecting Columns (Rectangular Areas)

To select a column of text, hold down the Option key and drag the mouse to highlight a rectangular area on-screen, beginning at the insertion point's location and extending down without highlighting the entire line (see fig. 8.7).

Fig. 8.7
Column selection.

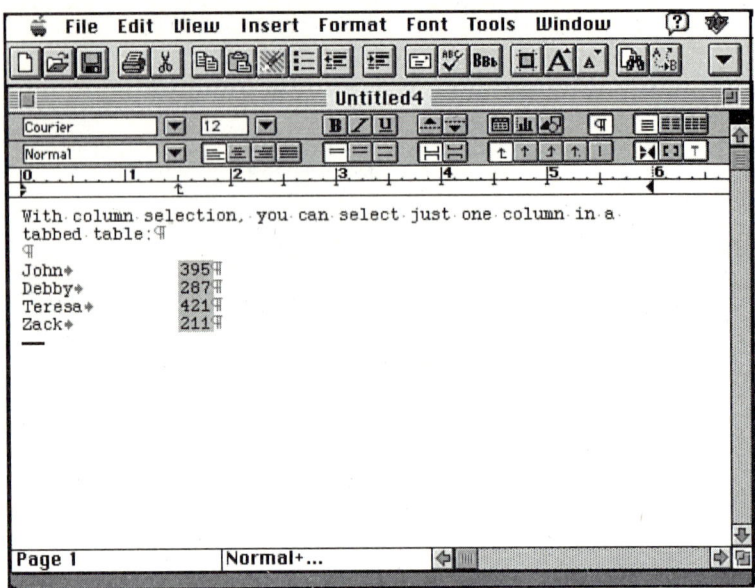

This selection technique, which frequently is used to select columns of text or numbers in a tabbed table, is called *column selection*. (Chapter 18, "Creating Newspaper Columns," covers uses for column selection.)

If the column selection didn't work right the first time and you have let go of the mouse button, you still can make adjustments. Simply press the Shift key and move the mouse to adjust the selection.

Deleting Text

The simplest—and probably the most frequently used—deletion technique is pressing Delete (labeled Backspace on some keyboards). If no text is selected, Delete erases the character to the left of the insertion point. If you have selected text, Delete removes the selection.

If you hold down the Delete key, Word deletes left and up unless it encounters the paragraph mark of a paragraph with different formatting. This feature prevents accidental deletion of paragraph formats. (Word "stores" paragraph formats in paragraph marks. When you delete the mark, you also delete the format.) When you delete backward into a paragraph mark, Word beeps to signal that you cannot delete any further.

What about deleting the character to the right of the insertion point? On the Classic keyboard and the Apple keyboard, no obvious key is provided for this purpose. You use the mouse to position the insertion point to the right of the character you want to delete and then press Delete—a laborious process at best. You can press ⌘-Option-F to delete the character to the right of the insertion point. If you are using an Apple extended keyboard, you can press Delete Forward to perform this action. (Delete Forward is the key with an X enclosed in a right-facing arrow.)

If you do not have an Apple extended keyboard, read Chapter 35, "Customizing Menu and Keyboard Shortcuts," to find out how to reprogram the Clear key so that it deletes the character to the right of the insertion point. Reprogramming this key saves you time and effort.

If you are editing an important document, you should know how to recover an ill-considered deletion. When you delete text by pressing the Delete key, typing over a selection, or choosing the Clear option from the Edit menu, the text is not routed to the Clipboard. The text is removed permanently, unless you recover it immediately in one of the following ways:

■ Choose Undo from the Edit menu

■ Press ⌘-Z

■ Click the Undo tool

To recover deleted text, you must issue the Undo command immediately after you perform the deletion. As soon as you type additional text or choose another command, the deleted text is wiped out forever.

Undo and Paste restore deletions differently. When you restore a deletion with Undo, Word puts the text back in its original location with its original formatting. When you restore a deletion with Paste, however, Word places the text at the current location of the insertion point, and you may lose the original formatting of the cut text unless you included a trailing paragraph mark in the cut.

Using the Cut command (Edit menu) to delete text to the Clipboard gives you a better chance of recovering text that you deleted accidentally. If you cut the text to the Clipboard, you have two options for recovering the text:

- Choose Undo immediately. Word returns the cut text to its original location.

- If you have performed some other action or chosen a command since you cut the text, return the insertion point to the location at which you cut the text and then use the Paste command.

Table 8.8 lists the keyboard commands you can use to delete text.

Table 8.8
Keyboard Commands for
Deleting Text

To delete this	Press this
Preceding character	Delete or Backspace
Following character	⌘-Option-F or Delete
Preceding word	⌘-Option-Delete or ⌘-Option-Backspace
Following word	⌘-Option-G

Copying and Moving Text

Almost all Macintosh programs, including Word, enable you to use the Clipboard when you copy and move text (as you did in Chapter 3, "Quick Start: Creating a Business Letter"). To copy and move text, follow these steps:

1. Select the text.

2. Choose Copy (⌘-C) or Cut (⌘-X) from the Edit menu, or click the Copy or Cut tool in the Toolbar. Word copies or cuts the selected text to the Clipboard.

3. Move the insertion point to the place where you want to move the selected text.

4. Choose Paste (⌘-V) from the Edit menu or click the Paste tool in the Toolbar. Word pastes the copied or cut text from the Clipboard into your document at the insertion point.

Copying through the Macintosh's built-in Clipboard has many advantages. One advantage is that all Macintosh programs can use the Clipboard, so text that you have copied or cut to the Clipboard can be inserted into other documents, including documents created by programs other than Word. If you cut text to the Clipboard and exit Word, the text remains in the Clipboard, ready to be pasted anywhere you choose.

If you cut or copy a large block of text to the Clipboard and exit Word, a dialog box asks whether you want to save the Clipboard. If you don't need the text anymore, click No. If you are transferring the text to another application, choose Yes. To return to Word to reconsider the question, click Cancel.

Despite its advantages, however, the Clipboard does not provide the easiest or safest way to copy or move text within a Word document. The Clipboard holds only one unit of text at a time. If you copy or cut additional text to the Clipboard, the new text wipes out the old text without any warning. Losing work is all too easy when you move text with the Clipboard.

Suppose that in a major reorganization of your document, you cut a big block of text to the Clipboard so that you can move the copy elsewhere. As you scroll to the new location, you notice—and stop to correct—an error in another area of text. In correcting the error, however, you cut more text to the Clipboard, wiping out the huge chunk that you wanted to move. When you arrive at the new location and use the Paste command, you will be in for a surprise.

You can avoid this pitfall in the following two ways:

■ *Use Outline view to rearrange large blocks of text.* This procedure is explained in Chapter 22, "Organizing Documents with Outlining."

■ *Use keyboard copying and moving techniques that bypass the Clipboard.* These techniques, which are explained in the following sections, work in only one Word document, however. To copy or move text from one document to another, you must use the Clipboard technique.

Copying Text without Using the Clipboard

The following technique works only when you copy text from one location to another within the same document. To copy text from one document to another, you must use the Clipboard.

To copy text without using the Clipboard, follow these steps:

1. Select the text that you want to copy.

2. Press ⌘-Option-C. The message Copy to appears in the status bar, and the insertion point becomes a dotted vertical line.

3. Click the insertion point where you want the copied text to appear. Because the command is incomplete until you press Return, you can adjust the location of the insertion point as often as you want. (To cancel the command, press Esc.)

4. Press Return to copy the text.

Copying Text with Drag-and-Drop Editing

Drag-and-drop editing (introduced in Chapter 3) probably will become your favorite copying technique. To make sure that you have activated drag-and-drop editing, follow these steps:

1. Choose Preferences from the Tools menu. The Preferences dialog box appears.

2. Click the General icon. The General options appear in the dialog box.

3. If necessary, click the Enable Drag-and-Drop Editing check box.

4. Click the close box to close the Preferences dialog box.

To copy text with drag-and-drop editing, follow these steps:

1. Select the text, leaving the mouse pointer on the selection.

2. Hold down the ⌘ key and the mouse button. A dotted box appears under the pointer, indicating that Word is prepared to copy the text.

3. Drag the pointer to where you want the text to appear, and then release the mouse button.

T I P

If you place the text in the wrong place, use the Undo command to return the text to its original location.

Moving Text without Using the Clipboard

The following technique works only when you move text from one location to another within the same document. To move text from one document to another, you must use the Clipboard.

To move text without using the Clipboard, follow these steps:

1. Select the text that you want to move.

2. Press ⌘-Option-X. The message Move to appears in the status bar, and the insertion point becomes a dotted vertical line.

3. Click the insertion point at the place where you want the moved text to appear.

4. Press Return to move the text.

Moving Text with Drag-and-Drop Editing

The easiest way to move text is to use drag-and-drop editing. If necessary, activate the Enable Drag-and-Drop Editing check box in the Preferences dialog box (Tools menu).

To move text with drag-and-drop editing, follow these steps:

1. Select the text, leaving the mouse pointer on the selection.

2. Hold down the mouse button. A small dotted box appears under the pointer.

3. Click the insertion point at the place where you want the moved text to appear and then release the mouse button.

Replacing Text

Word's Replace command enables you to automate certain editing tasks, such as replacing one word with another throughout your document.

Chapter 8

Editing Text

Replace is similar to Find, in that the command locates text, special characters, or formats in your document. If you use Replace rather than Find, however, you can find *and* specify a replacement for text, special characters, or formats.

Using the Replace Command

The following list shows you some of the ways that you can use Replace:

- *Replace one word or phrase with another throughout your document.* Suppose that your company, Small-Scale Enterprises, is acquired by Big Conglomerate, Inc., and you get a memo informing you that the name "Small-Scale Enterprises" is never to be used again. You can use the Replace command to replace "Small-Scale Enterprises" with "Big Conglomerate, Inc." in all your documents.

- *Replace an extraneous word or phrase with nothing.* If you suspect that you have overused a nonessential word, such as *really*, *very*, or *significant*, you can perform a Replace operation that removes the word from your document without replacement and closes the space.

- *Substitute one special character for another.* Suppose that you need to transmit by modem a document in which you have used tabs extensively. Tabs, however, give the receiving computer fits. You can use the Replace command to replace each tab with five spaces.

- *Search for and replace a format or style.* This capability is one of the most useful new features of Word. You can search for italic formatting throughout your document and change it to underlining, for example, or you can search for flush-left paragraph formatting and change it to justified.

- *Search for a word or phrase you typed in a particular format and replace only the format.* Suppose that you typed your company name in boldface in some places but not in others. For consistency, you decide to remove the boldface formatting. You can search for your company name and replace the formatting with standard text.

When you choose Replace from the Edit menu, you see the Replace dialog box (see fig. 8.8). You can also click Word 5.1's new Replace tool to display this dialog box.

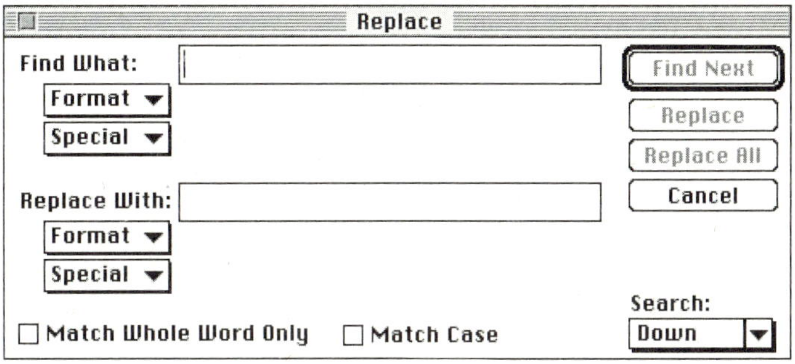

Fig. 8.8

Replace dialog box.

The following paragraphs describe the features of the Replace dialog box.

Find What. In this text box, you type the character, word, or phrase you want Word to find. You can type up to 255 characters (including spaces and special Word or Macintosh characters), and you can use wild cards.

Replace With. In this text box, you type the character, word, or phrase you want Word to substitute for the text in the Find What text box. You also can replace the search text with the following special characters: tab mark (^{t}), end-of-line mark (^{n}), paragraph mark (^{p}), hard page break (^{d}), nonbreaking space (^{s}), and optional hyphen ($^-$). This field does not accept wild cards.

Format. Word can search for and replace formats (character formats, paragraph formats, and styles). You use the Format drop-down list box under Find What to specify the format for which you want to search, and you use the Format drop-down list box under Replace With to specify the format you want to substitute. You can search for bold text, for example, and replace the boldface with italic. You do not need to use the Find What and Replace With boxes for a format search; Word searches for and replaces any text that has the specified format. This important feature is discussed in more detail in the chapters on character and paragraph formatting (chapters 9 and 10).

Special. Use the Special drop-down list boxes to place special characters (such as tab marks or end-of-line marks) in the Find What and Replace With text boxes. If you place a tab-mark code (^{t}) in the Find What box and a paragraph-mark code (^{p}) in the Replace With box, for example, Word replaces tab marks with paragraph marks.

Chapter 8

Editing Text

Match Whole Word Only (default: off). To restrict the search to whole words, click this check box. If you type **report** in the Find What box with Match Whole Word Only turned on, for example, Word finds *report* but not *reporting, reports,* or *reported*.

Match Case (default: off). By default, Word's searches are not case-sensitive; the program ignores uppercase and lowercase as it searches. If you type **WORD** in the Find What text box, for example, the program finds *Word, word, WORD,* or any other combination of uppercase and lowercase letters.

Search (default: Down). The Search drop-down list box enables you to specify the direction of the search—Up, Down, or All (search the entire document). If you select text before choosing Replace, however, the program searches and replaces only the selected text.

Command buttons. Choose Find Next to find the next occurrence of the search text. You then can click Replace to make one substitution or choose Find Next again to skip to the next occurrence. To replace all occurrences of the search text without confirmation, click Replace All. Click Cancel at any time to stop replacing.

To replace the search text with more than 255 characters of replacement text or with a graphic, copy the text or graphic to the Clipboard before choosing Replace. Then type ^c in the Replace With text box or select Clipboard Contents from the Special drop-down list box in the Replace With area.

Performing a Replace Operation

In this section, you learn how to replace a word, phrase, or special character throughout your document. In subsequent chapters, you learn more about replacing formats.

Before you choose Replace, think carefully about whether you want to replace with or without confirmation. When you replace with confirmation, Word shows each proposed replacement within its context and enables you to make the replacement or skip to the next occurrence of the search text. The Replace All command button tells Word to perform all the replacements without asking you to confirm each of them. Confirming each replacement of a word or a special character that appears dozens or hundreds of times in your document can be tedious.

Replacing without confirmation, however, can be hazardous: if you are not careful, Word may perform the replacement in inappropriate places.

Suppose that you have decided to remove the word *very* from your document. You set up Replace to find *very* and replace that word with nothing; then you click Replace All. Word dutifully removes the whole-word occurrences of the search text—and also removes *very* from all occurrences of the word *every*. As a result, a phrase such as *Every so often* now reads *E so often*. Word's spelling checker doesn't catch this mistake, because the spelling checker ignores single letters. To avert this problem and other replacement problems, follow these suggestions:

- *Activate the Match Whole Word Only option if you are changing a word.* The use of this option would have prevented Word from removing *very* from *every* in the preceding example.

- *Always begin a Replace operation with confirmation.* After you see how Word is performing the replacement, and if you are convinced that the Replace dialog-box settings are accurate, you can click Replace All to perform the rest of the replacements without confirmation.

With these cautions in mind, you're ready to try some techniques for replacing text. Use a document you don't need, or copy an existing document to a new file to create a practice document.

Like the Find dialog box, the Replace dialog box retains the settings from the preceding Find or Replace operation in the current operating session. Clear the old settings before you perform a new Replace operation. When you start typing in the Find What text box, Word deletes the old text but does not automatically remove previous format-search information. You must clear any format information before proceeding. To clear all formats, drop down the Format list box under Find What and select Clear.

To replace a word or phrase with confirmation, follow these steps:

1. Choose Replace from the Edit menu, press ⌘-H, or click the Replace tool. The Replace dialog box appears.

2. In the Find What text box, type the word or phrase you want Word to find. You can type up to 255 characters. (When the typed characters fill the text box, the box scrolls to make more room.)

3. In the Replace With text box, type the word or phrase you want Word to substitute. You can type up to 255 characters in this box, too.

4. To perform a case-sensitive search, activate the Match Case option.

5. To perform a whole-word search, activate the Match Whole Word Only option.

6. If necessary, select the correct search direction in the Search drop-down list box. By default, Word searches down unless you selected text before choosing Replace, in which case Word searches only the selected text.

7. Choose Find Next to initiate the search.

   If Word finds a match, the match is highlighted in your document. Click Replace to make the substitution and move on to the next occurrence of the search text, or click Cancel to stop the replacement operation. Word continues to find matches until no more matches are found or until you click Cancel.

   If Word cannot find a match or more matches, an alert box appears, asking whether you want to continue the search from the beginning of the document (or from the end, if you are searching up). Choose OK or click Cancel. If you choose OK and Word still doesn't find a match, another alert box appears to inform you that Word has reached the end of the document without finding the text you specified.

Quick Review

This section summarizes the most useful information in this chapter. Check "Productivity Tips" for a review of high-productivity tips and tricks—the ones that Macintosh and Word pros use every day. Review "Techniques" whenever you need a quick reminder about a specific procedure.

Productivity Tips

- To work with an existing document in your Word session, start the program by double-clicking the document icon.

- Within Word, open a recently edited document by choosing the document's name from the File menu.

Part II

Word 5.1 Fundamentals

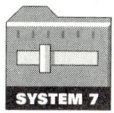

■ System 7 users can search for a specific file in a long list of files in the Open dialog box by typing the first letter of the file name.

■ To reduce the number of documents Word displays in the Open dialog box, select Word Documents in the List Files of Type drop-down list box.

■ If you see numbers on-screen when you use the keypad to move the insertion point, press Clear to toggle Num Lock mode off.

■ Don't scroll line by line or screen by screen through a long document when you try to locate text. If you know the page number, use Go To; otherwise, use Find.

■ To quickly move the insertion point to the place where you last edited a document, press ⌘-Option-Z immediately after you open the document.

■ Practice using Go Back to return to the location of previous edits.

■ Master the techniques for selecting fixed units of text: words, lines, sentences, and paragraphs. You save time by having Word locate the beginning and end of the selection. To extend the selection by the unit you originally selected (for example, sentence by sentence or paragraph by paragraph), hold down the Shift key and move the mouse.

■ To select a large block of text with the mouse, click the insertion point at the beginning of the text you want to select and then use the scroll bar, boxes, or arrows to scroll to the end of the selection. Hold down the Shift key and click where you want the selection to end.

■ To replace selected text with something else, type over the selection.

■ To improve your chances of recovering an accidental deletion, use the Cut command (Edit menu) to delete selected text. You can restore text deleted this way by issuing the Undo or Paste command.

■ For maximum protection against accidental loss while moving text, learn how to bypass the Clipboard.

■ Use the Replace command with caution. Before carrying out a Replace operation without confirmation, try the operation with confirmation a few times.

Techniques

This section provides concise summaries of all the procedures introduced in this chapter.

Opening Documents

To start Word and open an existing document at the same time:

1. In the Finder, open the folder or disk that contains the Word document you want to open.

2. Double-click the document's icon.

To open an existing Word document within Word:

1. Choose Open from the File menu, press ⌘-O, or click the Open tool. The Open dialog box appears.

2. To reduce the number of files displayed in the document list box, select Word Documents in the List Files of Type drop-down list box.

3. Use the current-folder and document list boxes to locate the document you want to open.

4. When the document list box displays the document you want to open, double-click the document's name. Alternatively, use the arrow keys to highlight the document's name and then press Return.

To open a recently edited document:

Choose the document's name from the File menu.

To open a stationery document:

1. Choose Open from the File menu, press ⌘-O, or click the Open tool. The Open dialog box appears.

2. Select Word Documents in the List Files of Type drop-down list box.

3. Use the current-folder and document list boxes to locate the document you want to open.

4. When the document list box displays the document you want to open, double-click the document's name. Alternatively, use the arrow keys to highlight the document's name and then press Return.

To open a non-Word document:

1. Choose Open from the File menu, press ⌘-O, or click the Open tool. The Open dialog box appears.

2. In the List Files of Type drop-down list box, select the format of the document you want to open.

3. Use the current-folder and document list boxes to locate the document you want to open.

4. When the document list box displays the document you want to open, double-click the document's name. Alternatively, use the arrow keys to highlight the document's name and then press Return.

Inserting a File

To insert a Word file into another document:

1. Choose File from the Insert menu. The Select a File to Insert dialog box appears.

2. To reduce the number of files displayed in the document list box, select Word Documents in the List Files of Type drop-down list box.

3. Use the current-folder and document list boxes to locate the document you want to open.

4. When the document list box displays the document you want to open, double-click the document's name. Alternatively, use the arrow keys to highlight the document's name and then press Return.

Using Go To

To move the insertion point to the beginning of a specific page:

1. Choose Go To from the Edit menu or press ⌘-G. The Go To dialog box appears.

2. In the text box, type the number of the page to which you want to move the insertion point.

3. Choose OK.

Finding Text

To search for a word or phrase:

1. Position the insertion point where you want the search to begin.

2. Choose Find from the Utilities menu or press ⌘-F. The Find dialog box appears.

3. In the Find What text box, type the text you want Word to find.

4. To perform a case-sensitive search, activate the Match Case option.

5. To perform a whole-word search, activate the Match Whole Word Only option.

6. If necessary, select the correct search direction in the Search drop-down list box.

7. Choose Find Next.

To find and replace special characters, use the following codes or select the appropriate options in the Special list box:

To search for this	Use this code
Any character	?
Caret	^^
End-of-line mark	^n
Footnote	^5
Graphic	^1
Hard page break	^d
Formula character	^\
Nonbreaking space	^s
Optional hyphen	^-
Nonbreaking hyphen	^~
Paragraph mark	^p
Question mark	^?
Section mark	^12
Space	^32
Tab mark	^t
Unspecified digit	^#
Unspecified letter	^*

Selecting Text

To select a word and its trailing space:

> Double-click the word.

To select a line:

> Move the pointer to the selection bar at the left of the line and click.

To select a sentence:

> Press ⌘ and click the sentence to select the sentence and its trailing space.

To select a paragraph:

> Move the pointer to the selection bar at the left of the paragraph and double-click, or triple-click anywhere in the paragraph.

To select a graphic:

> Click inside the graphic.

To select the entire document:

> Move the pointer to the selection bar, hold down the ⌘ key, and click.

To select a block by dragging:

1. Click at the beginning of the block of text you want to select.

2. Hold down the mouse button and move the mouse away from the first character you selected.

3. After you have highlighted the text you want, release the mouse button.

To select a block with the keyboard:

1. Hold down the Shift key and use the arrow keys or their keypad equivalents to highlight the text.

2. Release the Shift and arrow or keypad keys.

To select a block by Shift-clicking:

1. Click where you want the selection to start.

2. If necessary, scroll the screen, using the scroll bars, boxes, or arrows.

3. Hold down the Shift key and click the last character you want to select.

To select a block ending in a specific character:

1. Place the insertion point where you want the selection to begin.

2. Press Option-⌘-H or press the minus key in the keypad. The message Extend to appears in the status bar. (To cancel the command, press Esc.)

3. Type the character with which you want to end the selection.

To extend the selection:

1. Hold down the Shift key.

2. Drag the mouse or press an arrow key to expand or contract the selection.

To select a column (rectangular area):

Hold down the Option key and select by dragging.

Deleting Text

To delete selected text, use one of the following techniques:

■ Press Delete, choose Clear from the Edit menu, or type over the selection to remove the text without cutting to the Clipboard.

■ Choose Cut from the Edit menu, press ⌘-X, or click the Cut tool to store the deletion in the Clipboard.

Copying Text

To copy text through the Clipboard:

1. Select the text.

2. Choose Copy from the Edit menu, press ⌘-C, or click the Copy tool.

3. Click the insertion point where you want the copied text to appear.

4. Choose Paste from the Edit menu, press ⌘-V, or click the Paste tool.

To copy text or graphics in a Word document, bypassing the Clipboard:

1. Select the text or graphic you want to copy.

2. Press ⌘-Option-C.

3. Click the insertion point where you want to place the copied text or graphic.

4. Press Return.

To copy text with drag-and-drop editing:

1. Select the text, leaving the pointer on the selection.

2. Hold down the ⌘ key and the mouse button.

3. Drag the pointer to the place where you want the text to be copied.

4. Release the mouse button.

Moving Text

To move text through the Clipboard:

1. Select the text.

2. Choose Cut from the Edit menu, press ⌘-X, or click the Cut tool.

3. Move the insertion point to where you want the text to appear.

4. Choose Paste from the Edit menu, press ⌘-V, or click the Paste tool.

To move text without the Clipboard:

1. Select the text you want to move.

2. Press ⌘-Option-X.

3. Click the insertion point where you want the text to appear.

4. Press Return.

To move text with drag-and-drop editing:

1. Select the text, leaving the mouse pointer on the selection.

2. Hold down the mouse button.

3. Move the pointer to the place you want the text to appear.

4. Release the mouse button.

Replacing Text

To replace a word or phrase throughout your document:

1. Choose Replace from the Edit menu, press ⌘-H, or click the Replace tool. The Replace dialog box appears.

2. In the Find What text box, type the word or phrase you want Word to find.

3. In the Replace With text box, type the word or phrase you want Word to substitute.

4. If necessary, select the correct search direction in the Search drop-down list box.

5. Choose Find Next to initiate the search.

6. Click one of the following command buttons:

   ■ Replace to perform the replacement

   ■ Replace All to replace all additional occurrences of the search text without confirmation

   ■ Find Next to skip this occurrence and confirm the next replacement

   ■ Cancel to return to your document

Formatting with Fonts and Character Styles

Word formatting falls into four broad categories, or *domains*: character, paragraph, section, and document formats. Character formats, the subject of this chapter, affect the appearance of the characters you type in Word documents.

Word's default character font is 12-point New York. (A *point* is a printer's measurement. An inch contains 72 points, so Word's standard font size is one-sixth-inch high.) You can alter characters as often as you like, choosing other fonts and other font sizes, styles, position, spacing, and case.

After you choose character formats, you can repeat and copy them elsewhere in your document. You also can search for and replace character formats throughout your document.

This chapter provides an in-depth treatment of Word character formatting and introduces Word's distinctive method of document formatting. This chapter discusses the following topics:

- *Designing effective documents.* The first step in mastering document formatting is understanding the fundamentals of document design, as explained in this section.

- *Formatting with Word: an overview.* You learn how Word distinguishes among character, paragraph, section, and document formats.

- *Understanding formatting options.* You learn what options are available and how to access each option.

- *Choosing fonts and font sizes.* This section explains how to choose fonts and font sizes for your document.

- *Choosing character styles.* In this section, you learn how to choose character styles, such as boldface and italic.

- *Choosing character position.* This section provides complete guidance on using technical or mathematical superscript or subscript characters.

- *Choosing spacing (kerning).* For attractive effects, you can add additional space between characters, as this section explains. The section also explains techniques for "squeezing" a word into a narrow space.

- *Choosing case.* Rather than retype, you can use the Change Case command to change the case (capitalization) of a selected word or block of text.

- *Finding and replacing character formats.* This section details how to use the Replace command to replace one character format with another throughout your document—a genuine time-saver if you must, for example, replace underlining with italics throughout a long manuscript.

- *Repeating and copying character formats.* In this section, you learn important shortcut techniques for repeating character-formatting commands and copying them elsewhere in your document.

New to Word in Version 5.1 is the Drop Caps command, which enables you to add a large initial letter to a paragraph. This option is discussed in Chapter 20, "Positioning Text and Graphics."

Understanding Document Design

In *The Psychology of Everyday Things* (New York: Basic Books, 1988), Donald A. Norman lists two basic attributes of good design:

1. *A design should be visible.* Good design elements are obvious; you don't have to hunt for them.

2. *A design should be intuitive.* In an effective design, the relationship of one element to the others is natural and logical, so that the viewer grasps the relationship without thinking about it.

All the major principles of good design follow from Norman's two points. Consider the following principles:

- Use display type to call attention to headings. In typography, the term *display type* refers to the *typeface* (a distinctive design, such as Helvetica or Avant Garde) chosen for headings and titles.

  Many designers use *sans-serif typefaces* such as Helvetica for display type. A sans-serif typeface lacks the little finishing lines at the ends of the strokes in a letter. The use of a sans-serif typeface for display type helps the reader distinguish the headings from the document's text, or *body type*. Body type usually is smaller and printed in a *serif typeface*, such as Times Roman or New York. (Serif typefaces have finishing strokes on each letter.)

- Use font sizes and emphases logically to show the relationships of headings. First-level headings, for example, can be centered, boldfaced, or printed in a larger point size to make them obvious and to indicate their importance. Second-level and third-level headings, by contrast, can be smaller and less conspicuous.

- Use white space effectively. Break up text on the page by using lists with bullets or numbers. Scientific studies of document readability show that people remember details better if those details are listed and set apart from the body text.

- Strive for simplicity and consistency to keep your design visible and intuitively logical. Your design choices should guide readers through the document. The simpler and more consistent your design choices and usage are, the easier the reader's task is. Try to restrict your design to two typefaces: one for display type and one for body type. Use emphases (such as boldface and italic) sparingly.

Good design involves more than choosing beautiful typefaces and arranging text elements pleasingly. Above all, good design is a matter of choosing design elements that communicate effectively and naturally with your readers. Remember, however, that you can break any design rule if doing so improves the document's capability to communicate.

Microsoft Word for the Macintosh is a superb environment for interactive document design. The Mac's treasure trove of typefaces, which you can expand to your heart's content, is at your fingertips; and even if you have only a modest laser printer, you can use Word to produce output that is indistinguishable, to the untrained eye, from the output of professional typesetting machines. You can use paragraph formats (such as indentations, alignments, and blank lines) to break up text on the page and to clarify logical relationships among elements. Because you see your formatting choices on-screen before you print, you can easily judge the design's effectiveness.

Before you create an elaborate design for a document, however, remember that many publishers, government and private agencies, professional associations, and colleges impose strict style guidelines and may reject your document on the basis of style alone. If you plan to submit a document for publication or review, contact the organization to which you plan to submit the document and ask for a copy of the style guidelines.

Formatting with Word: An Overview

To design an effective document with Word, you must understand the Word approach to formatting. You learn in the following sections that Word divides formats into four domains and that you can format while you type or after you type. You also find a brief explanation of Word's font and font-size options and an overview of Word's character-formatting options.

Understanding the Four Formatting Domains

Word enables you to apply four different types of formats to your documents: *character*, *paragraph*, *section*, and *document* formats. The following sections provide an overview of the four formatting domains.

Character Formats

The smallest unit of formatting in Word is character formatting. Character formats include the following:

- *Font* (typeface design)
- *Font size* (in printer's points)
- *Style* (emphases such as boldface, outlining, italic, and underlining)
- *Position* (superscript or subscript)
- *Spacing* (compressed or expanded)

- *Case* (all uppercase, all lowercase, first letter of word capitalized, or first letter of sentence capitalized)

- *Hidden text* (text that does not display or print)

You can format as many characters as you choose, from one character to all the characters in the document.

Paragraph Formats

In Word, a paragraph is any block of text between two paragraph marks (or from the beginning of a document to its first paragraph mark). A paragraph can be a single word or a single character. Paragraph formats—such as indents, line spacing, tabs, and borders—can apply to an entire paragraph or to all paragraphs you have selected. Chapter 10, "Formatting Paragraphs," discusses paragraph formats in detail.

Section Formats

Section formats are page-style formats that can vary within a document. These formats include page numbers, columns, line numbers, headers, and footers. For single-section documents, section formats apply to the entire document. If you divide your document into sections by pressing ⌘-Enter, however, you can use multiple section formats in a document. Section breaks are useful for creating documents with separate chapters.

Document Formats

Document formats are page-style formats that apply to the entire document. These formats include margins, footnote position, and default tab width. Chapter 11, "Formatting Pages," examines section and document formatting in detail.

Understanding When To Format

Word enables you to format your document at two different times:

- *Before you start typing.* As you type, Word enters the formats and text simultaneously. To stop formats, choose commands that cancel character formatting (the Plain Text option in the Font menu or ⌘-Shift-Z) or paragraph formatting (⌘-Shift-P).

■ *After you type.* When you format this way, you select text and apply a formatting command to the selected text.

One advantage of formatting before you type is that you don't have to select the text before formatting. The disadvantage is that you must think about formatting ("What command do I want?") while you are thinking about other writing concerns ("What tense am I using? Is that a dangling modifier? What the heck am I trying to say?"). If you have trouble writing, you may want to format the document after you write it.

Writing may be easier for you, however, when you can see on-screen how the printed text will look. In technical writing, for example, document elements such as instructions are easier to write (and edit) when you set them off from the rest of the text.

Unless you're a beginning writer, document-design theory suggests a good reason to format as you type. Character and paragraph formats aren't simply variations of the way ink is stamped, sprayed, or fused onto the page—formats have meaning. Font choices, list formats, fixed-width characters, and other formats signal something to the reader about a document's nature and significance. Is the document formal or informal? Personal or impersonal? Conservative or trendy? Solemn or serendipitous? As you become more conscious of the meaning of formats, you see that Word gives you two ways to communicate your message: through the meaning of the text you type and through the signals you send with your formatting choices.

Understanding Font and Font-Size Choices

Your font and font-size options in Word depend on which fonts you have installed in your Mac's System file. In System 6 and earlier Mac systems, you install fonts by using Font/DA Mover, a utility program that comes with your Mac's System software. In System 7, you install fonts simply by dragging them to the System Folder, and you can see which fonts you have installed by double-clicking the System file.

To use your Mac's fonts effectively with Word, you need to understand some terminology. In the Macintosh world, the term *font* refers to the distinctive design of a set of characters. Each font has its own name, such as Helvetica, Times Roman, or Palatino. The term *font size* refers to the height of the tallest characters, measured from the baseline. As explained earlier, font size is measured in *printer's points* (72 per inch). By default,

Word prints a standard six lines of 12-point type per vertical inch on the page.

In the following sections, you explore additional important information about your Mac's fonts and how Word uses them. You learn the distinction between bit-mapped and scalable fonts and how this distinction affects the appearance of fonts on-screen and in your printed documents. You also learn the difference between proportionally spaced and monospace fonts.

Bit-Mapped and Scalable Fonts

Your Macintosh can use two kinds of fonts: *bit-mapped* fonts and *scalable* fonts.

A bit-mapped font (also called a *fixed-size font*) forms characters with hundreds of tiny dots. Bit-mapped fonts reside in a file that contains a complete set of characters for a given font size (such as New York 12). For most fonts, the Mac offers a variety of frequently used sizes, such as 10, 12, 14, 18, and 24. Your Macintosh can display a bit-mapped font quickly, but the font may not look good on-screen in a size other than the sizes installed in your System file. If you choose a font size that's not available in the System file, your Macintosh must try to scale the font.

The bit-mapped Venice font, for example, is supported by a file for only one font size (14 points). If you choose another size, the font looks inferior on-screen and not much better on paper.

Scalable fonts (also called *outline* fonts) generate characters of any size (within the Mac's range of 4 to 16,238 points), using a mathematical formula. For this reason, you can choose any font size for a scalable font and produce a good-looking screen image. The scalable New York font, for example, looks good in any size.

Scalable fonts have a disadvantage, however; because the Macintosh must calculate the appearance of each character, scalable fonts display more slowly on-screen than bit-mapped fonts do.

Figure 9.1 illustrates the difference between bit-mapped and scalable fonts.

The Font menu enables you to see at a glance which bit-mapped font sizes display well on your screen. The Font menu shows, for example, the 14-point font size with outline characters (see fig. 9.2).

Fig. 9.1
Bit-mapped and
scalable fonts.

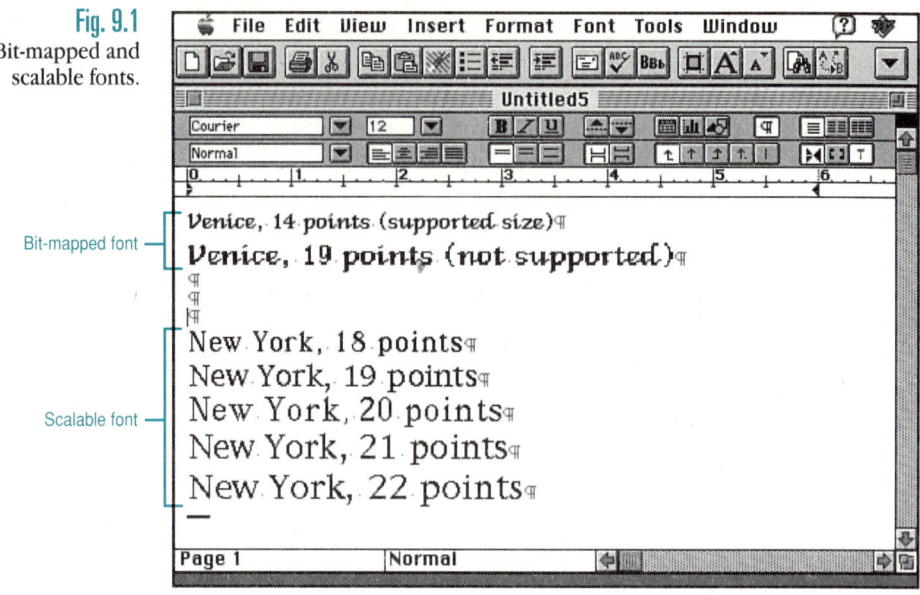

Bit-mapped font

Scalable font

Fig. 9.2
Outlined font size
(Courier 14) in
the Font menu.

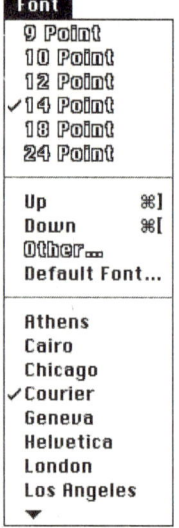

This font size is fully supported by a bit-mapped font in your Mac's
System file, so it looks good on-screen. The Font menu shows all

Part II

Word 5.1 Fundamentals

supported font sizes in outline characters. If you choose a font size that is *not* outlined in the Font menu, the font will be jagged or even illegible on your Mac's screen.

In the Mac world, the two most commonly used scalable fonts are the Adobe Type Manager (ATM) and—with the arrival of System 7—TrueType fonts.

Adobe Type Manager, available from Adobe Systems, is an add-on Macintosh utility program that manages Adobe's PostScript fonts and enables you to print these fonts even on a non-PostScript printer. When your Mac runs ATM, the ATM-compatible PostScript fonts installed in your System file look good on-screen in any font size. In addition, these fonts and font sizes look good when printed, even on a low-end printer such as an ImageWriter or StyleWriter. Adobe Type Manager, however, works only with fonts that are sold by Adobe or that are compatible with Adobe's Type 1 font specifications.

The TrueType software, developed by Apple, is built into System 7; you don't have to run an add-on utility program to take advantage of TrueType fonts. Like ATM fonts, TrueType fonts look good on-screen and on paper no matter which font size you choose. When you installed System 7, you installed the following TrueType fonts in your System file: Chicago, Courier, Geneva, Helvetica, Monaco, New York, Symbol, and Times. Additional TrueType fonts are available from font-design firms such as Letraset. If a TrueType font is installed in your System Folder, the Font menu uses outline characters to display all the font-size options for that font—an indication that you can expect good results when you print your document.

You easily can discover which fonts are installed in your System file. In the Finder, double-click the System file in the System Folder. A window opens, listing the fonts. You can distinguish TrueType fonts from bit-mapped fonts in the list, because TrueType fonts are listed without any font size. Double-click the font's icon to see an on-screen display of the font in three font sizes.

If all these options confuse you, find out whether your Macintosh is equipped with a PostScript-compatible laser printer such as the LaserWriter NT; if so, buy a copy of Adobe Type Manager. ATM comes with scalable screen fonts corresponding to the PostScript fonts built into your laser printer. If you don't have a PostScript printer, you can stick with TrueType fonts, which don't require you to purchase ATM.

For more information on using PostScript with Word, see Appendix B.

Even if you use TrueType fonts, leave the bit-mapped fonts in your System file. Bit-mapped fonts display faster than scalable fonts do (the time difference is significant on slower machines such as the LC or Classic). Also, your Macintosh automatically uses a bit-mapped font if a font for the size you have chosen is present in the System file. Macintosh uses TrueType fonts only if a bit-mapped font is not available in the size you have chosen.

Fixed-Width vs. Proportionally Spaced Fonts

The characters in a fixed-width font (such as Monaco and Courier) always occupy the same width, whether the character is narrow (*l*) or wide (*w*). Characters produced by fixed-width fonts look like typewritten characters—not surprisingly, considering that typewriters produce fixed-width type. Courier is a common choice for business correspondence and memos because the typewriter-like appearance of its characters suggests that the document was typed especially for the recipient.

In proportionally spaced fonts (such as Chicago, Geneva, and New York), wide characters take up more space than narrow characters do. The result looks professional but also looks impersonal and typeset. Readers often react to such type the way they react to a printed book: they assume that the text has been scrutinized, edited, and proofread. As a result, proportionally spaced type (especially when printed on a laser printer) carries all the authority—and the responsibility for accurate reporting and good judgment—of a printed document.

Choose proportionally spaced fonts when you want your document to carry weight. Remember, however, that the reader may assume that the document was prepared for many people to read. For this reason, proportionally spaced type may be the wrong choice for a personal message.

Figure 9.3 shows the difference between a fixed-width font and a proportionally spaced font.

Part II
Word 5.1 Fundamentals

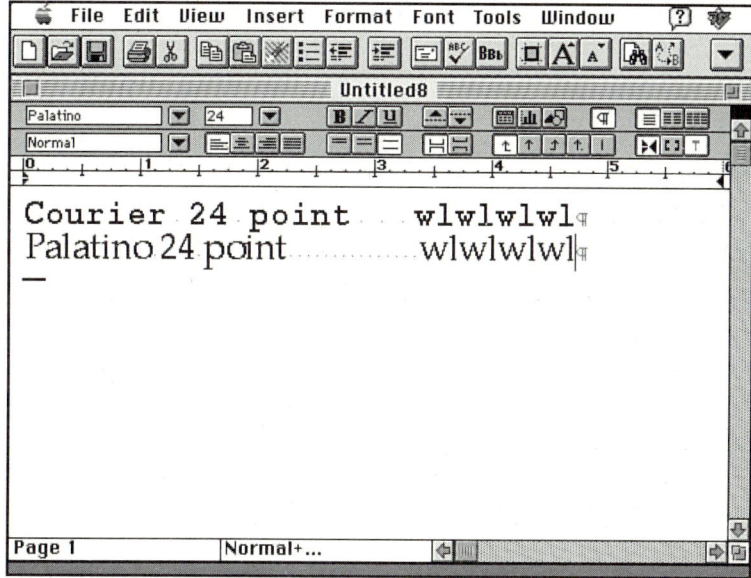

Fig. 9.3
Fixed-width and proportionally spaced fonts.

Understanding Character-Formatting Options

Now that you know the fundamentals of Word's formatting capabilities and some basic terminology, you are ready to survey the range of character-formatting options. Word enables you to vary the following format attributes of any character you can display on-screen:

Font (default: New York). The font is the type design of the characters you enter. Word uses all the fonts that are available in your System Folder.

Font size (default: 12 points). Size is the height of a font, measured in printer's points (72 per inch).

Color (default: black). If you have a color monitor, you can display characters in six colors: blue, cyan, green, magenta, red, and yellow.

Style (default: plain text). Choose emphases such as boldface, italic, outlined characters, shadow characters, and strikethrough characters. Style choices include *hidden text*, which doesn't show on-screen or in print, and *small caps*, a format in which lowercase letters are represented in print by small uppercase letters.

Chapter 9
Formatting with Fonts and Character Styles

Underlining (default: single underline). You can choose among four kinds of underlines: single underline, word-only underline, double underline, and dotted underline.

Position (default: Normal). You can position characters above the text baseline (*superscript*) or below the text baseline (*subscript*) at a height that you specify. By default, Word superscripts or subscripts by three points.

Spacing (default: Normal). You can adjust the space between characters. The Expanded option widens the space; the Condensed option narrows the space. The Expanded and Condensed options are in the Spacing options group of the Character dialog box, which is described later in this chapter.

Case. You have the following case options: uppercase, lowercase, first letter of each word capitalized (*title case*), first word of each sentence capitalized (*sentence case*), and *toggle case*.

Figure 9.4 illustrates Word's character-formatting options.

Fig. 9.4
Examples of character-formatting options.

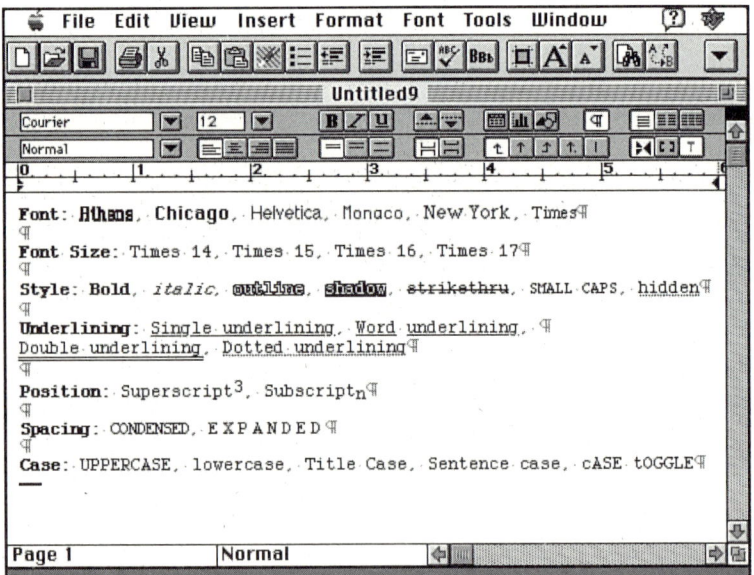

Understanding Character-Formatting Commands

As you probably have noticed, Word often provides more than one way to perform an action. You can apply many character formats in any of six ways.

You may be confused by the different character-formatting options. The following paragraphs discuss Word's six techniques for character formatting and give you tips on selecting the best technique for a given situation.

Ribbon. In the ribbon, you can choose fonts, font sizes, the most commonly used emphases (bold, italic, and underlining), and superscript or subscript. (Also available in the ribbon are tools for inserting tables, graphs, and pictures; for showing or hiding paragraphs; and for choosing multiple-column formats.) To choose a format, click the appropriate icon or make a selection in the appropriate drop-down list box (see fig. 9.5).

Fig. 9.5
Ribbon character-formatting icons.

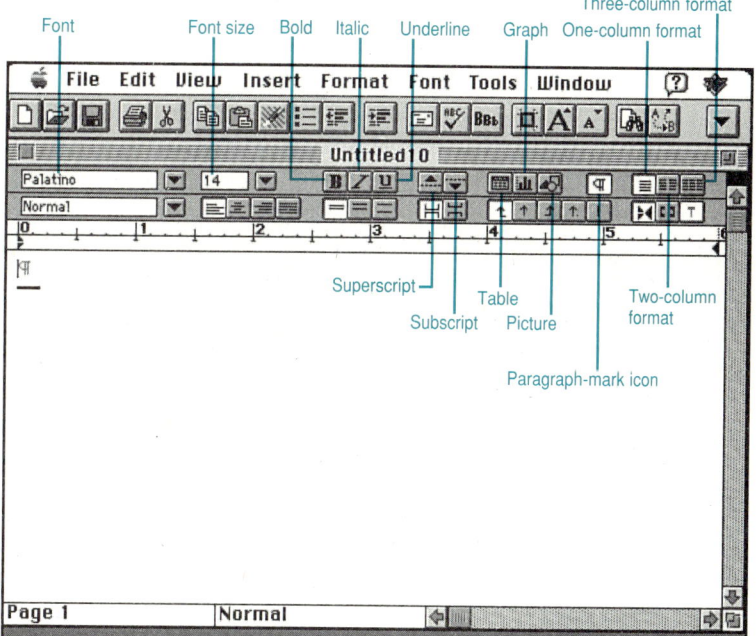

If you don't see the ribbon on-screen, choose Ribbon from the View menu or use the ⌘-Option-R keyboard shortcut.

The ribbon is a great way to choose character formats—*unless* you have a Classic or SE machine with a nine-inch monitor. You may find that the ribbon takes up too much screen space on those machines.

Format menu. You can use the Format menu, shown in figure 9.6, to choose commonly used emphases (bold, italic, and underline) and (with the Plain Text option) to cancel emphasis choices.

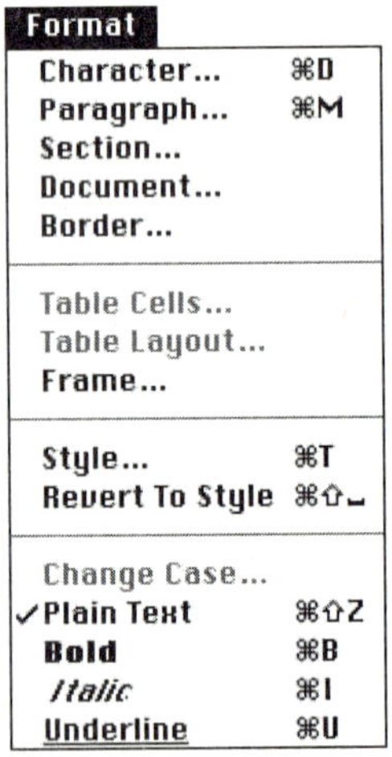

Fig. 9.6

Format menu.

Format	
Character...	⌘D
Paragraph...	⌘M
Section...	
Document...	
Border...	
Table Cells...	
Table Layout...	
Frame...	
Style...	⌘T
Revert To Style	⌘⇧⌐
Change Case...	
✓Plain Text	⌘⇧Z
Bold	⌘B
Italic	⌘I
Underline	⌘U

Although the Format menu gives mouse users a quick way to choose emphases, the keyboard shortcuts are quicker.

Font menu. From the Font menu, you can choose common font sizes (such as 9, 10, 12, 14, 18, and 24 points), and you can raise or lower the font size a point at a time by choosing the Up or Down option (new to Word). The Font menu also displays all the fonts installed in your Mac's System file. If you are not using the ribbon, the Font menu is a good way to choose fonts.

Character dialog box. The Character dialog box (which appears when you choose Character from the Format menu or press ⌘-D) is the slowest character-formatting method. You can use this dialog box, however, to choose color and spacing formats that are not available elsewhere (see fig. 9.7).

To display the Character dialog box quickly, double-click the ribbon background.

Fig. 9.7
Character dialog box.

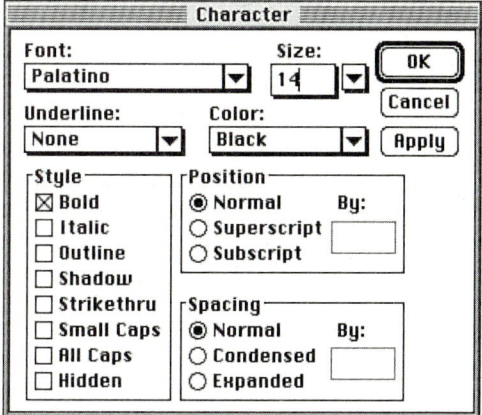

The Character dialog box also has a unique capability: you can use the Apply button to see what a format looks like (if your screen is large enough to display the formatted text behind the dialog box, which remains on-screen). If you don't like what you see, you can click Cancel without permanently affecting the text.

Shortcut keys. If you prefer to use the keyboard rather than the mouse, you can use keyboard shortcuts to enter many character formats. This chapter discusses these shortcuts and summarizes them in the Quick Review section.

Most Word formatting shortcut keys involve the ⌘-Shift key combination. Pressing ⌘-Shift-H, for example, applies the small-caps format. But to apply the most frequently used formats—bold, italic, and underline—you need not press the Shift key; simply press ⌘-B, ⌘-I, and ⌘-U, respectively.

Toolbar. From the Toolbar, you can enlarge or reduce font sizes.

The ribbon and the Character dialog box always show the formats in effect at the insertion point. To see the current formats, position the insertion point where you want to begin typing and glance at the ribbon

Chapter 9
Formatting with Fonts and Character Styles

or display the Character dialog box. If you select text that has two or more choices within the same format type, such as a few words in bold and more in italic, Word grays the ribbon and blanks the Character dialog box, enabling you to choose new formats that override all the formats in the selection.

You now know all the ways to choose character formats in Word. The remainder of this chapter discusses the formats individually, starting with fonts and font sizes.

Choosing Fonts and Font Sizes

In this section, you learn how to change the default font and font size for all your documents and how to change fonts within a specific document.

CAUTION

If you like using the Geneva or New York font, be sure to turn off the Font Substitution option in the Page Setup dialog box (choose Page Setup from the File menu). If this option is activated, your Macintosh may try to translate these fonts to Helvetica or Times printer fonts, and on many printers, the spacing and alignment will be uneven. After you deactivate the Font Substitution option, try printing again. If the results still are not satisfactory, reformat your document with the Helvetica font instead of Geneva or with Times instead of New York.

Changing the Default Font and Font Size

By default, Word uses the 12-point New York font in all new documents. The program returns to this font when you cancel other fonts or font sizes you have chosen. Suppose that you choose Helvetica 14 for a heading. You then type the heading and press ⌘-Shift-space bar or choose Revert to Style from the Format menu to cancel your font choice. Word reinstates the 12-point New York default.

Choosing the correct default font for your documents is important. If you use your Macintosh primarily for business correspondence and memos, you may want to choose Helvetica 12 to give your letters a clean, modern look. If you write business reports or articles, you may prefer to choose Times instead.

Figure 9.8 shows the fonts commonly installed in a System file for use with a PostScript laser printer. If you use an ImageWriter, StyleWriter, or Hewlett-Packard DeskWriter, you must individually install Avant Garde, Bookman, Helvetica Narrow, Palatino, and Zapf Chancery.

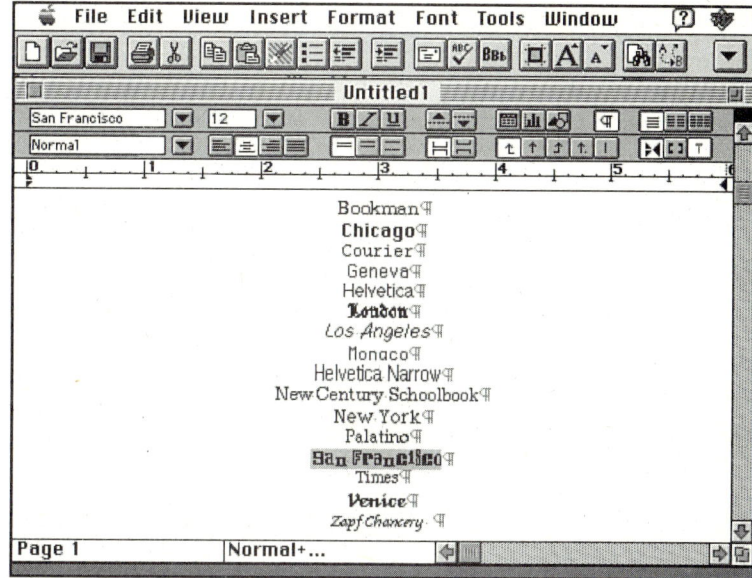

Fig. 9.8
Typical font options for a
PostScript laser printer.

To change the default font, follow these steps:

1. Choose Default Font from the Font menu. The Default Font Preferences dialog box appears.

2. Select the font you want in the Default Font list box.

3. Select the font size you want in the Default Size list box.

4. Click the close box to confirm your choices and return to your document.

After you learn how to define and apply styles, as explained in Chapter 14, you can establish default fonts for stationery documents (introduced in Chapter 5, "Managing Documents and Files").

A *stationery document* is a generic version of a document, such as a letter that includes your letterhead, return address, today's date, and your signature but no text or salutation. You can create and save stationery documents so that they include everything you need to develop a document quickly, including a special default font and font size. For example, you can create a business-letter stationery document that uses Helvetica 12 as the default font and a report stationery document that uses Times Roman 10 as the default font.

Chapter 9
Formatting with Fonts and Character Styles

Changing Fonts

Changing fonts and font sizes in your document, either before you type or after you type, is simple. You can choose fonts and font sizes in many different ways. Try them all to determine which technique is most convenient for you.

Word 5.1's Toolbar provides two tools, Font Up and Font Down, that you can use to change font sizes quickly. Both tools change the font size by one point per click.

Changing Fonts Before You Type

When you change a font or font size before you type, you "reprogram" the insertion point so that Word enters characters in the font you have chosen.

The ribbon's font and font-size list boxes always show the current font and font size. If you glance at the ribbon before typing text, you can see which font and size Word is using.

To change the font before you type, follow these steps:

1. Click the insertion point where you want to begin the new font.

2. Use one of the following techniques to choose a font:

   - Choose the font from the drop-down list box in the ribbon.

   - Choose the font from the Font menu.

   - Choose Character from the Format menu or press ⌘-D to open the Character dialog box. Select the font in the Font list box and then choose OK to confirm your choice.

   - Use the ⌘-Shift-E keyboard shortcut. When the message Font appears in the status bar, type the name of the font you want to use and then press Return.

3. Type the text.

4. To discontinue using the font, use any of the preceding techniques to choose a new font or font size or to restore the preceding font or font size.

In Word, your font and font-size choices are independent. Suppose that you choose Helvetica 14, type a heading, choose Times from the Font menu, and keep typing. Word enters the text in Times 14. To change both the size and the font, you must make two choices: font and font size.

Your font or font-size choice remains in effect until you choose a new font or font size, press ⌘-Shift-space bar, choose Revert to Style from the Format menu, or click the insertion point within text that has a different font or font size.

Until you create and define your own styles, your text appears in Word's default Normal style. When you choose Revert to Style, Word enters the formats that Microsoft assigned to this style in Word's default style sheet. (You learn more about styles, style sheets, and style-sheet formatting in Chapter 14, "Formatting with Styles.")

You can use the Revert to Style command or the ⌘-Shift-space bar shortcut to switch off your font or font-size choices. Remember, however, that this command restores all the default formats in Word's Normal style: plain (nonemphasized) text, flush-left paragraph alignment, single-line spacing, and New York 12 font.

To change the font size before you type, follow these steps:

1. Click the insertion point where you want to start typing.

2. Use one of the following techniques to choose the font size:

   ■ Drop down the point-size list box in the ribbon and select the point size you want, or type the size in the adjacent text box.

   ■ Choose a point size from the Font menu.

   ■ To increase the point size by one point, choose Up from the Font menu or press ⌘-]. A message appears in the page-number area, confirming the point size you have chosen.

   ■ To increase the point size to the next-larger point size shown in the Font menu, use the ⌘-Shift-> keyboard shortcut.

   ■ To decrease the point size by one point, choose Down from the Font menu or press ⌘-[. A message appears in the page-number area, confirming the point size you have chosen.

   ■ To decrease the point size by the next-smaller point size shown in the Font menu, use the ⌘-Shift-< keyboard shortcut.

- To increase or decrease the point size by one point, click the Font Up or Font Down tool.

- Choose Character or Other from the Format menu or press ⌘-D to open the Character dialog box. Then select the point size in the Size list and choose OK to confirm your choice.

3. When you finish typing in the font size you have chosen, use any of the preceding techniques to choose a new font size or to restore the preceding font size.

When you are using nonscalable (bit-mapped) fonts, choose point sizes from the Font menu. Only the Font menu displays installed point sizes in outline characters. Other techniques for choosing point sizes do not indicate whether the font size you have chosen is installed in the System file. If you are using Adobe Type Manager or TrueType fonts, however, the Font menu offers no advantages over other methods of choosing point sizes; these systems display all the point sizes in outline characters.

Changing Fonts After You Type

Some writers prefer to choose fonts and font sizes after they type the document text. To accomplish this type of formatting in Word, you select the text you want to format and then choose the font or font size.

To change the font or font size after you type, follow these steps:

1. Select the text.

2. Choose a font or font size from the ribbon, the Font menu, or the Character dialog box. Alternatively, press ⌘-Shift-E, type the name of the font, and then press Return.

To change the font or font size for the entire document, follow these steps:

1. Select the entire document in one of the following ways:

   - Move the mouse pointer to the selection bar, hold down the ⌘ key, and click.

   - Choose Select All from the Edit menu.

   - Use the ⌘-A keyboard shortcut.

2. Change the font size by choosing a font or font size from the ribbon, the Font menu, or the Character dialog box. Alternatively, press ⌘-Shift-E, type the name of the font, and then press Return.

Restoring the Default Font and Font Size

To change the font or font-size choices you have made, select the text, choose the font or size you prefer, and then press ⌘-Shift-space bar. Alternatively, choose Revert to Style from the Format menu to restore the default font and font size.

To restore the default font and font size throughout your document, select the entire document by ⌘-clicking in the selection bar, by choosing Select All from the Edit menu, or by pressing ⌘-A. Then press ⌘-Shift-space bar or choose Revert to Style from the Format menu to revert to the default font and font size.

Choosing Colors

If you have a color printer, you can assign colors to selected characters, and Word prints the colors you have chosen. On a color monitor, the colors appear on-screen. If you have a black-and-white monitor, Word displays all colors as black on-screen, but the colors print on a color printer.

To assign color to characters, follow these steps:

1. Place the insertion point where you want the colored text to begin or select the text to which you want to assign a color.

2. Choose Character from the Format menu or press ⌘-D. The Character dialog box appears.

3. Select a color in the Color drop-down list box.

4. Choose OK.

To remove color formatting, follow these steps:

1. Select the colored text.

2. Choose Character from the Format menu or press ⌘-D. The Character dialog box appears.

3. Select Black in the Color drop-down list box.

4. Choose OK.

With some black-and-white printers, you can choose colors that produce a dimmed effect in the printed document. Figure 9.9 shows the effect of color choices on characters printed on an Apple LaserWriter NT.

Fig. 9.9

Effect of color choices on characters printed on a black-and-white printer.

This document was printed on an Apple LaserWriter NT (black)
This document was printed on an Apple LaserWriter NT (blue)
This document was printed on an Apple LaserWriter NT (cyan)
This document was printed on an Apple LaserWriter NT (green)
This document was printed on an Apple LaserWriter NT (yellow)
This document was printed on an Apple LaserWriter NT (magenta)
This document was printed on an Apple LaserWriter NT (red)

Using Character Styles

Word uses the term *character style* (or just *style*) to refer to character emphases, such as boldface and italic, and to other character formats, such as small caps and hidden text. Word documentation also uses the term *style*, however, to refer to the named formats you create and save by using the Style option in the Format menu. (You learn about the Style option in Chapter 14, "Formatting with Styles.")

To avert confusion, this book uses the term *character style* to refer to the styles discussed in this section: bold, italic, outline characters, shadow characters, strikethrough, small caps, all caps, hidden characters, and the four underlining styles (single, word, double, and dotted).

As with fonts and font sizes, you can apply character styles in many ways. Only bold, italic, or single underline, however, are available through the ribbon or the Format menu. To choose other character styles (outline characters, shadow characters, strikethrough characters, small caps, all caps, hidden characters, word underlining, double underlining, or dotted underlining), you must use the Character dialog box or the appropriate shortcut keys.

You can add options for formats other than bold, italic, and single underlining to the Format menu. For more information on this process, see Chapter 35.

Choosing Character Styles Before You Type

When you choose a character style before you type, you "reprogram" the insertion point so that Word enters characters in the chosen character style. You can choose more than one character style at a time. If you choose bold and italic before you type, for example, Word enters characters in bold-italic characters. If you choose small caps and underlining, Word enters the characters in underlined small capital letters.

To choose character styles before you type, follow these steps:

1. Click the insertion point where you want to start typing.

2. Choose the character style you want, using one of the following techniques:

   ■ Choose the style in the ribbon. You can choose boldface, underlining, superscript, or subscript by clicking the appropriate icon.

   ■ Choose the style from the Format menu. You can choose Bold, Italic, and Underline (for single underlining) from this menu, or you can restore nonemphasized text by choosing the Plain Text option.

   ■ Choose any character style in the Character dialog box.

   ■ Choose any character style by pressing the appropriate keyboard shortcut (listed later in this section).

3. Type the text.

4. To cancel the character style you have chosen, choose the command again to toggle it off. If you used the ribbon to choose boldface, for example, click the Bold icon in the ribbon again to turn off boldfacing.

Not all character-formatting keys work as toggles. The keys for changing fonts and font sizes and for specifying subscript and superscript do not toggle these formats on and off.

Table 9.1 lists the keyboard shortcuts you can use to specify character styles.

Table 9.1			
Keyboard Shortcuts for Character Emphasis	*Emphasis*	*Keyboard shortcut*	*Keyboard shortcut with function keys*
	All caps	⌘-Shift-K	Shift-F10
	Bold	⌘-B or ⌘-Shift-B	F10
	Dotted underline	⌘-Shift-\	Option-F12
	Double underline	⌘-Shift-[	Shift-F12
	Hidden text	⌘-Shift-X	Option-F9
	Italic	⌘-I or ⌘-Shift-I	F11
	Outline	⌘-Shift-D	Shift-F11
	Shadow	⌘-Shift-W	Option-F11
	Small caps	⌘-Shift-H	Option-F10
	Strikethrough	⌘-Shift-/	
	Underline	⌘-U or ⌘-Shift-U	F12
	Word underline	⌘-Shift-]	⌘-F12

If you have an extended keyboard with function keys, notice the useful mapping of bold (F10), italic (F11), and underline (F12).

Applying Character Styles After You Type

You can apply character styles to existing text by selecting the text and then choosing the style.

To assign character styles after you type, follow these steps:

1. Select the text you want to format.

2. Choose the character style you want by using the ribbon, the Format menu, the Character dialog box, or the keyboard shortcuts listed in Table 9.1.

 Word's character styles are *additive*, which means that you can add a new character style on top of one you already have chosen. If you have formatted a heading in bold, for example, you can select the heading and add underlining or italic emphasis.

Canceling Character Styles

To remove a character format you have already applied, follow these steps:

1. Select the text.

2. Use the same character-style command again. To remove boldface, for example, click the Bold icon in the ribbon, choose Bold from the Format menu, deactivate the Bold check box in the Character dialog box, or press ⌘-Shift-B.

To cancel all the character styles you have applied in the document, choose Plain Text from the Format menu or press ⌘-Shift-Z.

Using Hidden Text

When you format characters in Hidden style, those characters do not appear on the screen (or in print) unless you want them to appear. The Hidden style option is grouped with the character-emphasis options in the Style area of the Character dialog box. Hidden style has many uses in Word, including the following:

■ Entering notes to a colleague in collaborative-writing situations.

■ Hiding special Word commands, such as the commands that mark table-of-contents and index entries (see Chapter 26, "Adding an Index and Table of Contents").

■ Hiding PostScript commands (for owners of LaserWriter or other PostScript-compatible printers who want to include PostScript programming commands in Word documents).

To format text as hidden text, select the text and then click the Hidden box in the Character dialog box or press ⌘-Shift-X. Word displays hidden text on-screen with a dotted underline.

By default, Word displays hidden text. To hide or to redisplay hidden text, follow these steps:

1. Choose Preferences from the Tools menu. The Preferences dialog box appears.

2. Click the View icon. The View options (Show, Open Documents, and Menus) appear in the dialog box (see fig. 9.10).

Fig. 9.10
View options in the
Preferences dialog box.

View icon ———

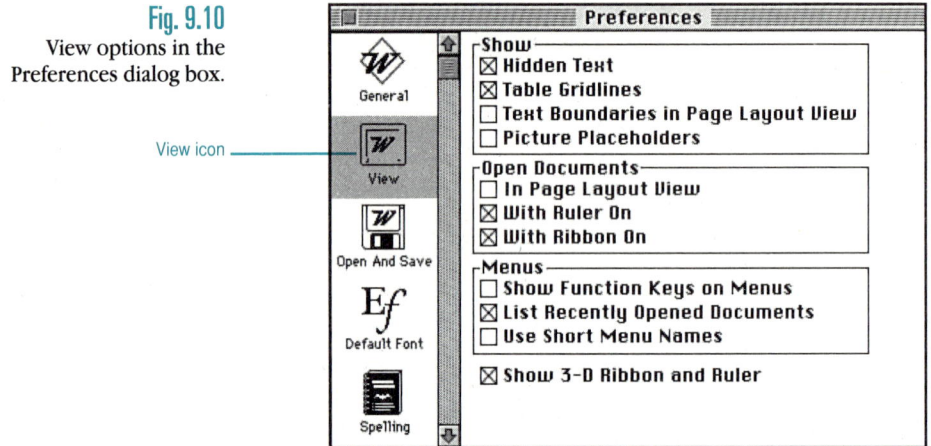

3. If you see an X in the Hidden Text check box, Word is set to display hidden text. Click the check box to remove the X if you want to deactivate this option.

4. Click the close box to confirm your choice and return to your document.

To transform hidden text into normal text, follow these steps:

1. Select the hidden text. (If the text is not visible on-screen, first activate the Hidden Text option in the Preferences dialog box.)

2. Choose Plain Text from the Format menu or press ⌘-Shift-Z.

By default, Word does not print hidden text. To print hidden text, choose Document from the Format menu to display the Document dialog box. In the Document dialog box, click the Print Hidden Text box. (Users of previous versions of Word should notice that this check box formerly was in the Print dialog box.) Even if hidden text is not visible on-screen, you can print the text by clicking the Print Hidden Text box.

Using Underlining Options

You can choose any of four underline formats:

- *Single underline* (⌘-Shift-U). All characters are underlined, including spaces.

- *Word underline* (⌘-Shift-]). Complete words and punctuation marks are underlined, but not white space (tabs and spaces).

- *Double underline* (⌘-Shift-[). A double underline appears below all words and spaces.

- *Dotted underline* (⌘-Shift-\). A dotted underline appears below all words and spaces.

To add single underlining, follow these steps:

1. Place the insertion point where you want underlining to begin when you start typing, or select the text that you want to underline.

2. Use one of the following techniques:

    - Click the Underline icon in the ribbon.

    - Choose Underline from the Format menu.

    - Use the Shift-⌘-U keyboard shortcut.

    - Choose Character from the Format menu to open the Character dialog box. Then select Single in the Underline drop-down list box and choose OK.

To add word underlining, double underlining, or dotted underlining, follow these steps:

1. Place the insertion point where you want underlining to begin when you start typing, or select the text you want to underline.

2. Choose Character from the Format menu. When the Character dialog box appears, select the underlining option you want in the Underline drop-down list box and then choose OK. Alternatively, use one of the underlining keyboard shortcuts.

To remove underlining, follow these steps:

1. Select the underlined text.

2. Do one of the following things:

   ◼ Repeat the technique you used to apply the formatting.

   ◼ Choose Plain Text from the Format menu.

   ◼ Press Shift-⌘-Z to cancel underlining and all other character formats (but not fonts or font sizes).

Using Superscript and Subscript Formatting

For technical and mathematical applications, you can raise (superscript) or lower (subscript) characters from the baseline. By default, Word raises or lowers the characters by 3 points (1/24th of an inch). If you want to type mathematical equations, however, don't bother using the subscript and superscript styles manually. See Chapter 25, "Using Math and Typing Equations," for information on an accessory program called Equation Editor that facilitates the typing of equations.

To specify superscript or subscript characters, follow these steps:

1. Position the insertion point where you want the subscript or superscript characters to appear. If you have typed the characters already, select them.

2. Do one of the following things:

   ◼ Click the Superscript or Subscript icon in the ribbon.

   ◼ Press ⌘-Shift-equals sign (=) for superscript or ⌘-Shift-hyphen (-) for subscript.

   ◼ Choose Character from the Format menu. When the Character dialog box appears, activate the Superscript or Subscript option. If you want, you also can type a measurement other than 3 points in the By text box. Then choose OK.

To cancel superscript or subscript formatting, select the characters and choose the format again in the ribbon or choose Normal in the Character dialog box's Position area.

If you plan to include footnotes or endnotes in your document, don't type the footnote reference number or superscript the number yourself. Word can do the job automatically, as you learn in Chapter 19, "Adding Headers, Footers, and Footnotes."

Using Spacing Options

The Spacing options in the Character dialog box enable you to condense or expand letters by decreasing or increasing the space after each letter. In figure 9.11, for example, Word has added 12 points to the normal space between the characters.

Fig. 9.11
Text expanded by 12 points.

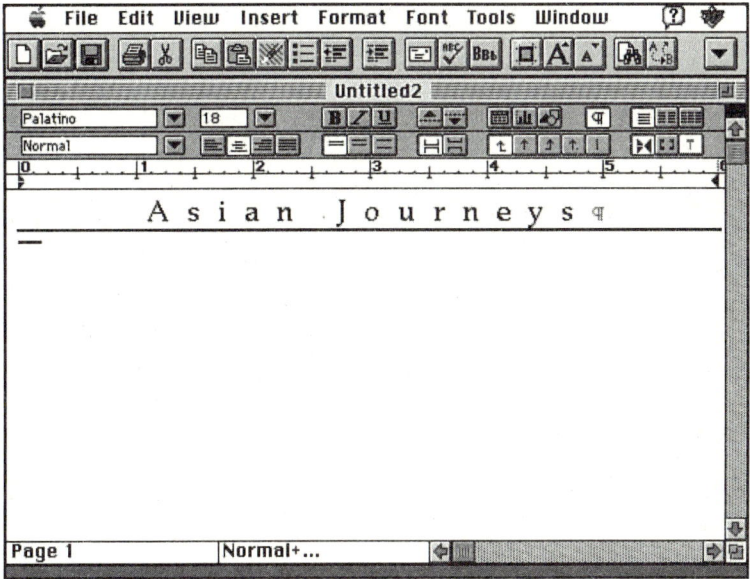

Expanded text has many uses for document design. For example, document titles gain interest and drama when expanded over a thick border.

Condensed text is useful when you must squeeze a word into a narrow space, as shown in figure 9.12. Notice that the word *Geophysical* does not fit into the narrow paragraph.

In figure 9.13, the condensed word fits.

Expanding and Condensing Text

In this section, you learn how to expand and condense text in your documents. You can use these techniques for special effects or to solve problems when a word or phrase does not fit within narrow margins.

Chapter 9

Formatting with Fonts and Character Styles

Fig. 9.12
Condensed text needed.

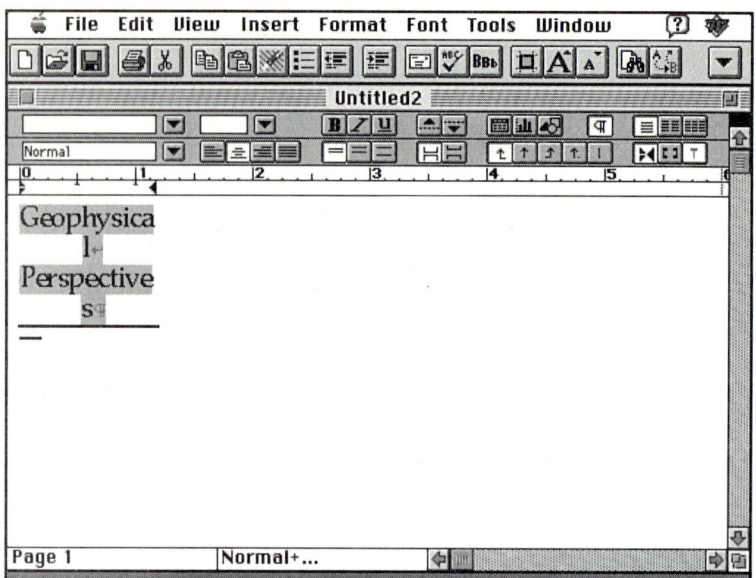

Fig. 9.13
A long word condensed
by 1.5 points.

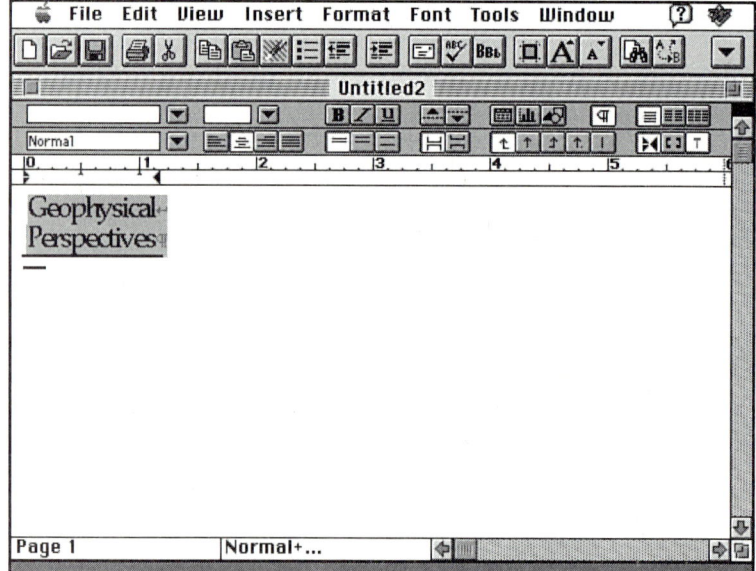

Part II

Word 5.1 Fundamentals

To expand text, follow these steps:

1. Select the text.

2. Choose Character from the Format menu or press ⌘-D. The Character dialog box appears.

3. In the Spacing area, choose Expanded. You see `1.5 pts.` in the By box, meaning that Word proposes to expand the characters by inserting an additional 1.5 points between characters.

4. To adjust the spacing by a different increment, type a measurement in the By box. You can type any number from 1.0 to 14.0 in .25-point increments (for example, 3.0, 3.25, 3.5, 3.75, and so on).

5. Choose OK.

To condense text, follow these steps:

1. Select the text.

2. Choose Character from the Format menu or press ⌘-D. The Character dialog box appears.

3. In the Spacing area, choose Condensed. You see `1.5 pts.` in the By box, meaning that Word proposes to condense the characters by taking away 1.5 points of space between characters.

4. To adjust the spacing by a different increment, type a measurement in the By box. You can type any number from 0.25 to 1.75, in 0.25-inch increments.

5. Choose OK.

To restore normal spacing, follow these steps:

1. Select the condensed or expanded text.

2. Choose Character from the Format menu or press ⌘-D. The Character dialog box appears.

3. Choose Normal in the Position area.

4. Choose OK.

Kerning Characters

Word's capability to control the spacing between characters enables you to kern a pair of characters. *Kerning* is the adjustment of spacing between specific pairs of characters to improve a document's appearance. Manual kerning is tedious, however, and kerning body text is impractical in most situations. You can improve the appearance of headings and titles, however (especially if you have chosen a large font size), by condensing certain pairs of characters that appear to be too widely spaced.

In figure 9.14, for example, too much space seems to follow the capital letters (T and W) in the title Technical Writing.

Fig. 9.14
A title before kerning.

In figure 9.15, the pairs Te and Wr have been kerned. The difference, though subtle on the screen, is apparent in the printed document.

To kern a pair of characters, follow these steps:

1. Select the characters.

2. Choose Character from the Format menu or press ⌘-D. The Character dialog box appears.

3. Choose the Condensed option in the Spacing area.

4. Choose OK.

Fig. 9.15
A title after 1.75 points
of kerning.

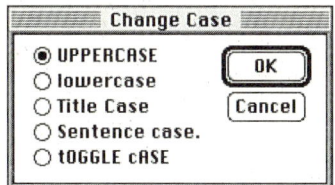

Changing Case

As you have learned, you can choose an All Caps character style in the Character dialog box. When applied to selected characters, this style changes the appearance of the characters on-screen without changing the characters themselves. If you save your document using the Text Only or Text Only with Line Breaks option in the Save As dialog box (as you might do if you plan to send your file by modem), you lose the uppercase formatting. You can avert this problem by making the appropriate settings in the Change Case dialog box (see fig. 9.16).

Fig. 9.16
Change Case dialog box.

Change Case

- ● UPPERCASE
- ○ lowercase
- ○ Title Case
- ○ Sentence case.
- ○ tOGGLE cASE

[OK]

[Cancel]

Chapter 9
Formatting with Fonts and Character Styles

You can choose the following case options:

Uppercase. The Uppercase option changes all characters to uppercase letters.

Lowercase. The Lowercase option changes all characters to lowercase letters.

Title Case. The Title Case option capitalizes the first letter of each word.

Sentence Case. The Sentence Case option capitalizes the first letter of each sentence.

Toggle Case. The Toggle Case option reverses the case pattern of the selection: uppercase characters become lowercase, and lowercase characters become uppercase. In a combination of uppercase and lowercase characters, this option reverses the case letter by letter.

To change case, follow these steps:

1. Select the text.

2. Choose Change Case from the Edit menu or click the Case tool.

3. Choose a case option.

4. Choose OK.

Because Change Case actually changes the characters, you cannot remove your case choices the way you remove character-style choices (for example, by choosing ⌘-Shift-Z). You can undo a case choice, however, by choosing Undo from the Edit menu, provided that you haven't performed any other editing or command action. Alternatively, you can choose Change Case again and choose another case-formatting option.

Searching for Character Formats

The Find command, introduced in Chapter 8, can help you locate text to which you have applied one or more character formats. (As you learn in the next chapter, you can search for paragraph formats, too.) You can search for any text that has one or more formats, including fonts and font sizes, or you can search for any word or phrase to which you have given a distinctive format.

The following examples of searches that you can perform with the Find dialog box illustrate Word's search capability:

- Find the next occurrence of the phrase `Albemarle Valley Associates` formatted in 18-point Palatino, skipping all occurrences of the phrase in other fonts and font sizes.

- Find any text formatted with small caps.

- Find any text, regardless of font, formatted in 9-point font size.

- Find any text formatted bold and italic.

To search for a character format, follow these steps:

1. Choose Find from the Edit menu or press ⌘-F. The Find dialog box appears (see fig. 9.17).

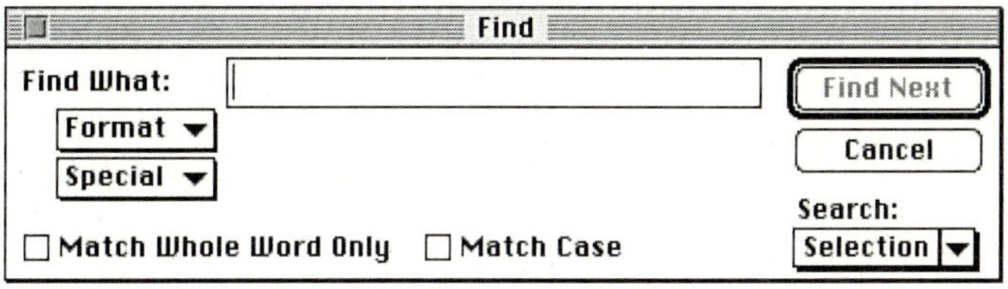

Fig. 9.17
Find dialog box.

2. Select Character in the Format drop-down list box to bring up the Character dialog box. Alternatively, you can use any of the previously discussed techniques for choosing character formats (such as keyboard shortcuts, the ribbon, the character-formatting options in the Format and Font menus, and the Character command in the Format menu).

   You also can search for more than one format. You can search, for example, for text formatted with bold, New Century Schoolbook, and 3 points of expansion.

   After you choose the formats, you see the Find dialog again. The format you chose appears below the Find What text box, as shown in figure 9.18.

3. To search for specific text that has the formats you specified in the Find dialog box, type the text in the Find What text box. To search for any text with these formats, leave the Find What box blank.

Chapter 9
Formatting with Fonts and Character Styles

Fig. 9.18
Find dialog box after
you choose Bold.

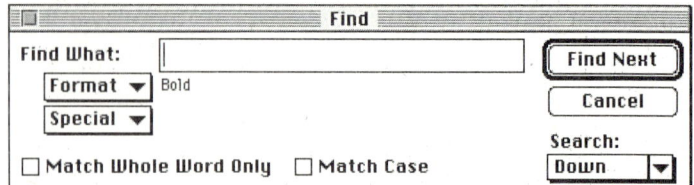

4. To change the direction of the search, select a different option in the Search drop-down list box. By default, Word searches Down (from the insertion point to the end of the document), but you can choose Up (from the insertion point to the beginning of the document) or All (to begin at the insertion point and search the entire document).

5. Choose Find Next. Word finds and highlights the next occurrence of text with the specified formats. To find further occurrences of the formats, continue to choose Find Next. To return to your document, click Cancel.

If Word cannot find any text with the formats you specified, an alert box appears, asking whether you want to extend the search from the beginning of the document (or from the end, if you're searching up). Choose Yes to extend the search or click No to cancel.

CAUTION

After you use the Find dialog box to search for a format, Word retains that format setting and any text you typed in the Find What text box for the duration of the current operating session. You must clear these settings to perform a different search. To clear text from the Find What text box, select the text and press Delete. To clear the format, pull down the Format drop-down list box and select Clear.

Replacing Character Formats

The Replace command, introduced in Chapter 8, enables you to replace one format with another throughout your document. You even can replace a group of formats (such as bold, italic, Palatino, and 14-point) with another group (such as underlined, Courier, and 12-point). These significant new capabilities are made possible by the addition of the Format drop-down list box to the Replace dialog box.

The following examples show you how this capability can save you hours of manual formatting:

- You discover that you were supposed to underline the titles of books in a huge bibliography instead of using italic formatting. You need to replace the italic with underlining.

- When you inspect a printout of your document, you find that your headings look terrible in 18-point Chicago. You decide to replace the Chicago font with 14-point Helvetica.

- You use boldface here and there throughout your document to emphasize important ideas, but when you see the printed document, you realize that the effect is overbearing. You decide to replace the boldface with plain text.

Word's Replace command (Edit menu) can perform all these tasks and more, thanks to the Format drop-down list boxes. You can replace paragraph formats and styles as well as character formats. In this section, you learn how to replace character formats; subsequent chapters detail the procedures you use to replace paragraph formats and styles.

NOTE If you frequently replace formats, consider using style formatting. Style formatting enables you to update all occurrences of text formatted in a particular style by making one change in the document style sheet. (See Chapter 14, "Formatting with Styles," for more information.)

To replace one character format with another throughout your document, follow these steps:

1. Choose Replace from the Edit menu, press ⌘-H, or click the Replace tool. The Replace dialog box appears.

2. In the Find What area, select Character in the Format drop-down list box to bring up the Character dialog box. Alternatively, you can use any of the previously discussed techniques for choosing character formats (such as keyboard shortcuts, the ribbon, the character-formatting options in the Format and Font menus, and the Character command in the Format menu).

   You also can search for more than one format. For example, you can search for text formatted with bold, New Century Schoolbook, and 3 points of expansion.

After you choose a format, you see the Replace dialog box again. The format you chose appears below the Find What text box (refer to fig. 9.18).

3. Use any of the techniques described in step 2 to select the format you want Word to substitute for the format you want to replace. The replacement format appears below the Replace With text box, as shown in figure 9.19.

Fig. 9.19
Replace dialog box with formats selected.

Replace
Find What: _____	**Find Next**
Format ▼ Bold	Replace
Special ▼	**Replace All**
Replace With: | _____	Cancel
Format ▼ Italic	
Special ▼	
☐ Match Whole Word Only ☐ Match Case	Search: Down ▼

4. To search for specific text with the format listed below the Find What text box, type the text in the Find What text box. To search for all text with that format, leave the text box blank.

5. To replace specific text that has the format listed below the Replace With text box, type the replacement text in the Replace With text box. To search for all text with that format, leave the text box blank.

6. To change the direction of the search, select a different option in the Search drop-down list box. By default, Word searches Down (from the insertion point to the end of the document), but you can choose Up (from the insertion point to the beginning of the document) or All (to begin at the insertion point and search the entire document).

7. Choose Find Next if you want to confirm each replacement before Word makes it. If you're sure that you want to perform the replacement throughout your document, click Replace All.

   If you choose Find Next, Word finds and highlights the next occurrence of the text that has the format you specified. To find further occurrences of the format, continue to choose Find Next. To return to your document, click Cancel.

If Word finds no text with the specified format, an alert box appears, asking you whether you want to extend the search from the beginning of the document (or from the end, if you're searching up). Choose Yes to extend the search or click No to cancel.

After you use the Replace dialog box to search for a format, Word retains the format setting below the Find What text box, and any text you typed in that text box, for the duration of the current operating session. (The format and text also appear in the Find dialog box.) You must clear these settings before you can begin a different search. To clear the text from the Find What text box, select the text and press Delete. To clear the format, pull down the Format list box and select Clear.

Repeating and Copying Character Formats

The formatting techniques discussed in this section can save you time. With these Word formatting capabilities, you can repeat a complex format throughout a document. This section also describes procedures for copying formats in Word documents.

Repeating Character Formats

You must repeat a character format immediately after you apply that format, as explained in the following steps:

1. Apply a character format, using any technique discussed in this chapter.

2. Select the text to which you want to apply the same format.

3. Choose Repeat from the Edit menu or use the ⌘-Y keyboard shortcut.

To repeat multiple formats (such as Palatino 18, bold, and outline), choose the formats in the Character dialog box during step 1. If you choose the formats from the ribbon or the menus, or if you use the keyboard shortcuts, Word repeats only the format you chose last.

Copying Character Formats

If you type some text or choose another command after you apply a character format, you cannot use the technique introduced in the preceding section to repeat the format. You can copy the format, however, by using the following technique.

To copy a character format, follow these steps:

1. Select a word that has the format you want to copy.

2. Press ⌘-Option-V. Word copies the formats to a temporary storage area (not to the Clipboard).

3. Select the text to which you want to copy the format. A dotted underline appears below the selection.

4. Press Return. Word applies the format to the selected text. To cancel, press ⌘-period (.) before pressing Return.

Quick Review

This section summarizes the most useful information in this chapter. Check "Productivity Tips" for a review of high-productivity tips and tricks—the ones that Macintosh and Word pros use every day. Review "Techniques" whenever you need a quick reminder about a specific procedure.

Productivity Tips

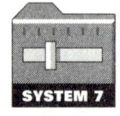

- If you format before you type, you don't have to select the text, but you do add the complexity of choosing formats to the writing process. If writing gives you trouble, format after you type.

- To maximize Word's screen updating, be sure to install in your System file bit-mapped fonts that correspond to the fonts and font sizes you commonly use.

- You can save money and get good results with TrueType fonts. You need Adobe Type Manager and PostScript fonts only if you have a PostScript printer.

- Unless you use a nine-inch Classic or SE monitor, display the ribbon and use it to choose fonts, font sizes, common emphases, and position.

- If your system isn't equipped with TrueType or PostScript fonts, you get the best printing results by choosing font sizes that appear in outline characters in the Format menu.

- Redefine the default font to one that prints well on your printer and is appropriate for most of your documents.

- Glance at the ribbon or display the Character dialog box to see which character formats currently are in effect at the insertion point.

- When you choose character formats before you type, switch the format off by repeating the command you used to apply the format.

- If you must fit a long word into a narrow space, try condensing the word, using Word's default condense setting (1.5 points).

- Rather than retype words to change case, use Word's new Change Case command.

- Use the Replace dialog box to replace formats throughout your document.

- Immediately after you apply a character format, you can repeat the format elsewhere, provided that you have not typed any characters or chosen any commands.

- To repeat a format after you have typed additional text or chosen another command, you can use the ⌘-Option-V shortcut to copy the format.

Techniques

This section provides concise summaries of all the procedures introduced in this chapter.

Changing Fonts

To change the default font for all new documents:

1. Choose Default Font from the Font menu. The Default Font Preferences dialog box appears.

2. Select the font you want in the Default Font list box.

3. Click the close box to confirm your choice and return to your document.

To change the font before you type:

1. Click the insertion point where you want to start using the font.

2. Use one of the following techniques to specify a font:

- Select the font from the drop-down list box in the ribbon.

- Choose the font from the Font menu.

- Choose Character from the Format menu or press ⌘-D to open the Character dialog box and then select the font in the Font drop-down list box. Choose OK to confirm your choice.

- Use the ⌘-Shift-E keyboard shortcut. When the message Font appears in the status bar, type the name of the font you want to use, and press Return.

3. Type the text.

4. When you finish typing with the font you have chosen, choose a new font or font size (or restore the preceding font or font size) by using any of the preceding techniques.

To change the font after you type:

1. Select the text.

2. Choose a font from the ribbon, the Font menu, or the Character dialog box. Alternatively, press ⌘-Shift-E, type the name of the font after Font in the status bar, and then press Return.

To change the font throughout the document:

1. Use one of the following techniques to select the document:

   - Move the mouse pointer to the selection bar, hold down the ⌘ key, and click.

   - Choose Select All from the Edit menu.

   - Press ⌘-A.

2. Choose a font from the ribbon, the Font menu, or the Character dialog box. Alternatively, press ⌘-Shift-E, type the name of the font, and then press Return.

Changing Font Size

To change the font size before you type:

1. Click the insertion point where you want to start typing.

2. Use one of the following techniques to choose the font size:

   - Drop down the font-size list box in the ribbon and select the point size you want, or type the size in the adjacent text box.

■ Choose a point size from the Font menu.

■ Increase the point size one point by choosing Up from the Font menu, pressing ⌘-], or clicking the Font Up tool. A message appears in the page-number area, confirming the point size you chose.

■ Increase the point size to the next-larger point size shown in the Font menu by pressing ⌘-Shift->. A message appears in the page-number area, confirming the point size you chose.

■ Decrease the point size by one point by choosing Down from the Font menu, pressing ⌘-[, or clicking the Font Down tool. A message appears in the page-number area, confirming the point size you chose.

■ Decrease the point size to the next-smaller point size shown in the Font menu by pressing ⌘-Shift-<. A message appears in the page-number area, confirming the point size you chose.

■ Choose Character or Other from the Format menu or press ⌘-D to open the Character dialog box. Select the point size in the Size drop-down list box and then choose OK to confirm your choice.

3. When you finish typing with the font size you have chosen, use any of the preceding techniques to choose a new font size or to restore the preceding font size.

To change the font size after you type:

1. Select the text.

2. Use one of the following techniques to specify a font size:

■ Drop down the font size list box in the ribbon and select a point size. Alternatively, type the size in the adjacent text box.

■ Choose a point size from the Font menu.

■ Increase the point size one point by choosing Up from the Font menu, pressing ⌘-], or clicking the Font Up tool. A message appears in the page-number area, confirming the point size you chose.

■ Increase the point size to the next-larger point size shown in the Font menu by pressing ⌘-Shift->. A message appears in the page-number area, confirming the point size you chose.

■ Decrease the point size by one point by choosing Down from the Font menu, pressing ⌘-[, or clicking the Font Down tool. A message appears in the page-number area, confirming the point size you chose.

■ Decrease the point size to the next-smaller point size shown in the Font menu by pressing ⌘-Shift-<. A message appears in the page-number area, confirming the point size you chose.

■ Choose Character or Other from the Format menu or press ⌘-D to open the Character dialog box. Select a point size in the Size drop-down list box and then choose OK to confirm your choice.

Choosing Colors

To choose colors:

1. Select the text.

2. Choose Character from the Format menu or press ⌘-D. The Character dialog box appears.

3. Select a color in the Color drop-down list box.

4. Choose OK.

Choosing and Applying Character Styles

To choose character styles before you type:

1. Click the insertion point where you want to start typing.

2. Choose a character style, using one of the following techniques:

   ■ Choose the style from the ribbon. You can choose boldface, underlining, superscript, or subscript by clicking the appropriate icon.

   ■ Choose the style from the Format menu. You can choose Bold, Italic, and Underline (for single underlining) from this menu, or you can restore nonemphasized text by choosing the Plain Text option.

   ■ Choose any character style (including shadow, outline, strikethrough, special underlining, or small caps) in the Character dialog box.

   ■ Choose any character style by pressing the keyboard shortcuts listed in Table 9.1.

3. Type the text.

4. To cancel the character style, repeat the procedure you used to select it. If you chose bold by clicking the Bold icon in the ribbon, for example, cancel boldface by clicking the Bold icon again.

To apply character styles after you type:

1. Select the text you want to format.

2. Choose a character style by using the ribbon, the Format menu, the Character dialog box, or the keyboard shortcuts listed in Table 9.1. Remember that you can add a new character style to an existing character style.

Canceling Character Styles

To remove a character format:

1. Select the text.

2. Use the same character-style command again. To remove boldface, for example, click the Bold icon in the ribbon, choose Bold from the Format menu, deactivate the Bold check box in the Character dialog box, or press ⌘-Shift-B. To cancel all the character styles you have applied in the text, choose Plain Text from the Format menu or press ⌘-Shift-Z.

Using Hidden Text

To turn on hidden-text formatting before you start typing:

1. Click the insertion point where you want to start typing.

2. Choose the hidden-text character style by choosing Character from the Format menu, activating the Hidden option in the Character dialog box, and then choosing OK. Alternatively, press ⌘-Shift-X.

3. Type the text.

4. To cancel hidden text, toggle off the character style by repeating the command.

To assign hidden-text character style after you type:

1. Select the text you want to hide.

2. Choose hidden-text character style by choosing Character from the Format menu, activating the Hidden option in the Character dialog box, and then choosing OK. Alternatively, press ⌘-Shift-X.

To prevent hidden text from being displayed on the screen or to redisplay hidden text:

1. Choose Preferences from the Tools menu. The Preferences dialog box appears.

2. Click the View icon. The View options appear in the dialog box.

3. Click the Hidden Text check box in the Show area.

4. Click the close box to confirm your choice and return to your document.

To transform hidden text into normal text:

1. Select the hidden text. (If the text is not visible on-screen, activate the Hidden Text check box in the Preferences dialog box.)

2. Choose Plain Text from the Format menu or press ⌘-Shift-Z.

To print hidden text:

1. Choose Document from the Format menu. The Document dialog box appears.

2. Activate the Print Hidden Text box in the Document dialog box.

3. Choose OK.

Choosing Underlining

To choose single underlining before you type:

1. Click the insertion point where you want to start typing.

2. Choose the underline character style, using one of the following techniques:

   ■ Click the Underline icon in the ribbon.

   ■ Choose Underline from the Format menu.

   ■ Choose Character from the Format menu or press ⌘-D to open the Character dialog box. Select Single Underline in the Underline drop-down list box and then choose OK.

   ■ Press ⌘-Shift-U.

3. Type the text.

4. To cancel the underlining, toggle it off by repeating the command you used to activate the underline character style.

To apply single underlining after you type:

1. Select the text you want to format.

2. Choose the underline character style, using one of the following techniques:

   ■ Click the Underline icon in the ribbon.

   ■ Choose Underline from the Format menu.

   ■ Choose Character from the Format menu or press ⌘-D to open the Character dialog box. Select Single Underline in the Underline drop-down list box and then choose OK.

   ■ Press ⌘-Shift-I.

To choose word, double, or dotted underlining before you type:

1. Click the insertion point where you want to start typing.

2. Choose the underlining style you want, using one of the following methods:

   ■ Choose Character from the Format menu or press ⌘-D to open the Character dialog box. Select Word Underline, Double Underline, or Dotted Underline in the Underline drop-down list box and then choose OK.

   ■ Press ⌘-Shift-] to choose word underline, ⌘-Shift-[to choose double underline, or ⌘-Shift-\ to choose dotted underline.

3. Type the text.

4. To cancel underlining, toggle it off by repeating the command you used to activate the underline character style.

To apply word, double, or dotted underlining after you type:

1. Select the text you want to format.

2. Choose the underlining style you want, using one of the following methods:

   ■ Choose Character from the Format menu or press ⌘-D to open the Character dialog box. Select Word Underline, Double Underline, or Dotted Underline in the Underline drop-down list box and then choose OK.

   ■ Press ⌘-Shift-] to choose word underline, ⌘-Shift-[to choose double underline, or ⌘-Shift-\ to choose dotted underline.

Chapter 9

Formatting with Fonts and Character Styles

Using Superscript or Subscript

To specify superscript or subscript characters:

1. Position the insertion point where you want the subscript or superscript characters to appear. If you already have typed the characters, select them.

2. Use one of the following techniques to superscript or subscript the characters:

   ■ Click the Superscript or Subscript icon in the ribbon.

   ■ Press ⌘-Shift-equals sign (=) for superscript or ⌘-Shift-hyphen (-) for subscript.

   ■ Choose Character from the Format menu or press ⌘-D to open the Character dialog box, and then activate the Superscript or Subscript option. If you want, you also can type a measurement other than 3 points in the By text box. Then choose OK.

Controlling Spacing and Kerning

To expand text:

1. Select the text.

2. Choose Character from the Format menu or press ⌘-D. The Character dialog box appears.

3. In the Spacing area, choose Expanded.

4. To adjust the spacing by an increment other than 1.5 points (the default), type a measurement in the By text box.

5. Choose OK.

To condense text:

1. Select the text.

2. Choose Character from the Format menu or press ⌘-D. The Character dialog box appears.

3. In the Spacing area, choose Condensed.

4. To adjust the spacing by an increment other than 1.5 points (the default), type a measurement in the By text box.

5. Choose OK.

To restore normal spacing:

1. Select the condensed or expanded text.

2. Choose Character from the Format menu or press ⌘-D. The Character dialog box appears.

3. Choose Normal in the Position area.

4. Choose OK.

Changing Case

To change selected text to all uppercase letters:

1. Select the text.

2. Choose Change Case from the Format menu or click the Change Case tool. The Change Case dialog box appears.

3. Choose Uppercase.

4. Choose OK.

To change selected text to all lowercase letters:

1. Select the text.

2. Choose Change Case from the Format menu or click the Change Case tool. The Change Case dialog box appears.

3. Choose Lowercase.

4. Choose OK.

To capitalize the first letter of each sentence in a selection:

1. Select the text.

2. Choose Change Case from the Format menu or click the Change Case tool. The Change Case dialog box appears.

3. Choose Sentence Case.

4. Choose OK.

To capitalize the first letter of each word in a selection:

1. Select the text.

2. Choose Change Case from the Format menu or click the Change Case tool. The Change Case dialog box appears.

3. Choose Title Case.

4. Choose OK.

To reverse the uppercase and lowercase pattern in a selection:

1. Select the text.

2. Choose Change Case from the Format menu or click the Change Case tool. The Change Case dialog box appears.

3. Choose Toggle Case.

4. Choose OK.

Searching for Character Formats

To search for a character format:

1. Choose Find from the Edit menu or press ⌘-F. The Find dialog box appears.

2. Select Character in the Format drop-down list box. The Character dialog box appears.

3. Choose one or more character formats in the Character dialog box. Alternatively, choose one or more character formats using the ribbon, the menus, or keyboard shortcuts.

4. Search for specific text with the format you specified by typing that text in the Find What text box. To search for all text with this format, leave the Find What box blank.

5. To change the direction of the search, make a selection in the Search drop-down list box.

6. Choose Find Next.

7. To end the search and return to your document, click Cancel.

Replacing Character Formats

To replace one character format with another throughout your document:

1. Choose Replace from the Edit menu or press ⌘-H. The Replace dialog box appears.

2. Choose Character from the Format box. The Character dialog box appears.

3. Choose one or more character formats in the Character dialog box. Alternatively, choose one or more character formats using the ribbon, the menus, or keyboard shortcuts.

4. Choose a replacement character format, using one of the methods explained in step 3.

5. To search for specific text with the format you specified, type the text in the Find What text box. To search for all text with that format, leave the Find What text box blank.

6. To replace specific text with the format you specified, type the replacement text in the Replace With text box. To search for all text with the format you specified, leave the Replace With text box blank.

7. To change the direction of the search, make a selection in the Search drop-down list box.

8. Choose Find Next. If you're sure that you want to perform the replacement throughout your document, click Replace All.

Repeating Character Formats

To repeat a character format:

1. Apply a character format, using any technique discussed in this chapter.

2. Select the text to which you want to apply the same format.

3. Choose Repeat from the Edit menu or press ⌘-Y.

Copying Character Formats

To copy a character format:

1. Select text that has the format you want to copy.

2. Press ⌘-Option-V.

3. Select the text to which you want to copy the format. A dotted underline appears below the selection.

4. Press Return.

CHAPTER 10

Formatting Paragraphs

Paragraph formats, the second of the four Word formatting domains, control the way Word indents and aligns text. Word paragraph formats incorporate many format elements, including line spacing, blank space before and after a paragraph, custom tabs, lines, and borders. You can vary these format elements for each new paragraph you create; therefore, Word can meet virtually all page-layout challenges.

This chapter surveys the paragraph formats most commonly used in day-to-day formatting. You find the following information in this chapter:

- *Understanding paragraph formats.* This section defines the formats that Word considers to be paragraph formats.

- *Choosing paragraph formats.* This section discusses the four techniques for choosing paragraph formats in Word and the strengths and limitations of each technique.

- *Controlling paragraph alignment.* This section comprehensively surveys Word's text-alignment options.

- *Indenting paragraphs.* In this section, you learn the many ways you can indent text from the left or right margin. You also learn how to create nested paragraphs and hanging indentations.

USING
WORD 5.1
FOR THE MAC
SPECIAL EDITION

■ *Controlling line and paragraph spacing.* This section discusses line spacing and commands that automatically add blank space before and after a paragraph.

■ *Using tabs.* This section covers all aspects of working with tabs, including changing the default tab width and creating custom tabs.

■ *Searching for paragraph formats.* In this section, you learn how to use the Find command to search a document for paragraphs that have a specific format or combination of formats.

■ *Replacing paragraph formats.* In this section, you learn how to use the Replace command to replace one paragraph format (or a combination of formats) with another throughout your document.

■ *Repeating and copying paragraph formats.* This section details the procedures for repeating or copying paragraph formats throughout your document.

Understanding Paragraph Formats

If you have used other word processing programs, you may be surprised that Word considers blank lines, borders, and tabs to be elements of paragraph formats. A paragraph format in Word is any format that applies to a single paragraph as a unit—and that format includes borders, blank lines, thick lines, shading, and custom tabs.

Because you can vary these formats from paragraph to paragraph, you have the opportunity to set up complex new formats every time you press Return to start typing a new paragraph. The format can include the usual ingredients of paragraph formatting (indents, alignment, and line spacing) and "extras" such as lines, boxes, unique tab patterns, automatically entered blank lines, and page-break controls.

This chapter shows you how to assign the following formats to any paragraph in a Word document:

Alignment (default: left). You can choose justified, left-justified, right-justified, or centered format for a paragraph.

Indents (default: none). You can indent the right margin, the left margin, and the paragraph's first line. You also can use negative values to create hanging indents.

Line spacing (default: single). You can format paragraphs for single spacing, 1 1/2-line spacing, or double spacing. You also can specify different line-spacing formats in lines or points.

Blank space (default: none). You can format a paragraph so that Word automatically inserts blank space before or after the paragraph.

Tabs (default: left, every half-inch). You can use left-justified, right-justified, centered, and decimal tabs. You also can set a vertical tab to insert a vertical line at the position you specify.

The following additional paragraph formats are covered in other chapters of this book:

Page-break control (default: none). You can choose options that force a page break before a paragraph or prevent one from following a paragraph. You also can keep all the lines in a paragraph together on one page. You learn more about page-break control in Chapter 11, "Formatting Pages."

Absolute position on the page (default: none). You can anchor a paragraph of text or a graphic (also a paragraph as far as Word is concerned) in a fixed position on the page. The special space you establish when you anchor text or graphics is called a frame. You can choose the horizontal and vertical size of the frame. If the frame is narrower than the text column, text flows around the frame automatically. You learn more about positioning text and graphics in frames in Chapter 20.

Borders (default: none). You can add lines, boxes, and shading options to your documents by using borders, as you learn in Chapter 17, "Using Borders and Shading."

For information on creating tables with Word's Table command and on creating list formats, see Chapter 15, "Creating Tables." Chapter 16 details Word's automatic line-numbering, paragraph-numbering, and sorting capabilities.

Because you can combine so many format elements to create complex paragraph formats, saving your formats for reuse makes sense. You even can save groups of paragraph formats to create a Word style. A *style* is a collection of formats you name and save as one group; subsequently, you can apply the style to a document by issuing just one command.

You can, for example, create and save a style that includes all the formats you typically use to create body-text paragraphs, such as Times Roman 12, justified alignment, 0.5-inch first-line indentation, and double line spacing. (For more information on styles, see Chapter 14, "Formatting with Styles.")

Chapter 10
Formatting Paragraphs

Reviewing Paragraph Basics

This section reviews basic information about Word paragraphs introduced in preceding chapters.

- A paragraph is a series of characters of any length followed by a paragraph mark (¶).

- A paragraph mark stores the paragraph formats you have chosen for the paragraph. If you delete the mark, you lose the formats.

- To display paragraph marks, choose Show ¶ from the Edit menu or click the paragraph-mark icon in the ribbon.

- When you press Return to start a new paragraph, Word copies the current formats to the new paragraph.

Choosing Paragraph Formats

You can use any of the following methods to choose paragraph formats:

- *Ruler.* When the ruler is displayed, you quickly can choose the most frequently accessed paragraph-formatting options: alignments, line spacing, blank lines before paragraphs, tabs, indents, and even left and right margins. The ruler always shows the formats in effect for the paragraph in which you have positioned the insertion point. When you change margins in the ruler, the change affects the entire document. But when you choose any other formatting option in the ruler, Word alters only the selected paragraph or paragraphs.

- *Paragraph dialog box.* Unlike the ruler, the Paragraph dialog box makes most paragraph-formatting options available (with the exception of alignment options). Because you must type measurements for spacing and indentation formats in the Paragraph dialog box, however, using this box requires more time than using the ruler. If you are comfortable manipulating the ruler's icons, you can limit your use of the Paragraph dialog box to those occasions when you want to assign a format that's not available in the ruler.

- *Keyboard shortcuts.* You can apply most paragraph formats by using keyboard shortcuts that (like character-formatting shortcuts) include the ⌘-Shift key combination. Most keyboard shortcuts work the same way as their ruler and Paragraph dialog-box counterparts, but some of the keyboard commands are additive in their effects. If you press ⌘-Shift-N, for example, Word indents the paragraph a half-inch; if you press the command again, Word adds another half-inch to the indentation.

■ *Toolbar.* Word 5.1's new Toolbar contains tools that enable you to create bulleted lists and nested or unnested paragraphs quickly.

Using the Ruler

Word's ruler serves two purposes: It displays the formats in the selected paragraph or paragraphs, and it provides a means of changing these formats. Like all Word formatting commands, the choices you make in the ruler affect the paragraph or paragraphs you have selected in your document.

To display the ruler (see fig. 10.1), choose Ruler from the View menu or press ⌘-R.

Fig. 10.1
The Word ruler.

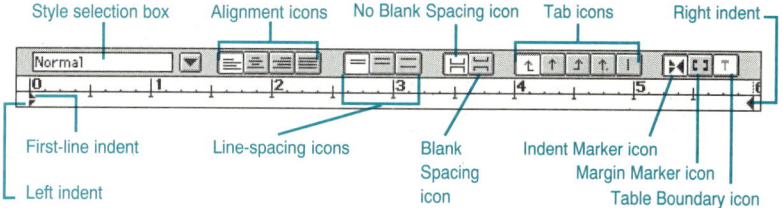

The figure shows the following features of Word's ruler:

Style selection box. This drop-down list box provides a handy way to choose styles. For more information on styles, see Chapter 14.

Alignment icons (default: left justification). Click these icons to choose left-justified, centered, right-justified, or justified alignment.

Line-spacing icons (default: single line spacing). Choose these buttons to select single spacing, 1 1/2-line spacing (18 points), or double spacing (24 points). To choose other line-spacing options, use the Paragraph dialog box (described later in this chapter).

Blank-spacing icons (default: no blank line before paragraph). Choose these icons to select no blank line before the paragraph (a closed paragraph) or 12 points (1/6 inch) of blank space before the paragraph (an open paragraph). To select other blank-spacing options, such as adding blank lines automatically after a paragraph or changing the amount of added blank space, use the Paragraph dialog box.

Chapter 10
Formatting Paragraphs

Tab icons (default: left-justified tabs). To set a tab, click one of these icons and hold down the mouse button until a tab marker emerges, and then drag the tab marker to the location in the ruler where you want to set a tab stop. You can choose left-justified, centered, right-justified, and decimal tab stops. You also can set a vertical tab, which inserts a vertical line at the position you specify; the line is the same height as the current line spacing you specified in the Paragraph dialog box.

If you prefer to type the tab's location or to add leaders to tabs, you need to use the Paragraph dialog box.

Indent Marker icon (default: indent markers displayed). This icon activates the display of indent markers in the ruler. When the indent markers are visible, you can change indents by dragging the markers. (If the markers are not visible, click the Indent Marker icon to display them.) If you prefer to set indents by typing measurements, use the Paragraph dialog box.

Indent markers. The two solid triangles stacked one atop the other at the left end of the ruler are indent markers. The top triangle is the first-line indent marker; drag this marker to control automatic first-line indents. The bottom triangle is the left-indent marker for all succeeding lines of the paragraph. The larger triangle at the right end of the ruler is the right-indent marker.

Margin Marker icon (default: margin markers not displayed). This icon hides the indent markers and displays the left and right margin markers, which look like left and right brackets. When the margin markers are visible, you can use them to change the left and right margins for the entire document. Alternatively, you can set margins (including top and bottom margins) by choosing Document from the Format menu and making the appropriate settings in the Document dialog box.

Table Boundary icon (default: grayed). This icon becomes available when you position the insertion point in a table created by the Table command (Insert menu). When this icon is available, Word displays T-shaped markers to mark the cell boundaries. You can change cell widths by dragging these markers. For more information on tables, see Chapter 15.

What you see in the ruler depends on how many paragraphs you have selected. If you have selected one paragraph, the highlighted icons show the formats in effect for that paragraph. If you click a different icon or move a marker, the formatting change you make applies to the selected paragraph.

If you have selected two or more paragraphs with the same formatting, the highlighted icons show the formats in effect for both paragraphs. If you click a different icon or move a marker, the formatting change you make applies to all selected paragraphs. Word changes only the format you specify and leaves the other formats alone.

If you have selected multiple paragraphs that have dissimilar formatting, the ruler is grayed, displaying the indents for the first selected paragraph but showing no highlighted icons. If you click a different icon or move a marker, the formatting change you make applies to all the selected paragraphs. Word changes only the format you specify and leaves the other formats alone.

Using the Paragraph Dialog Box

Choosing paragraph formats with the ruler is easy, but you cannot use it to choose all formats. To control page breaks and to specify indents and line spacing with precision, you must use the Paragraph dialog box (see fig. 10.2).

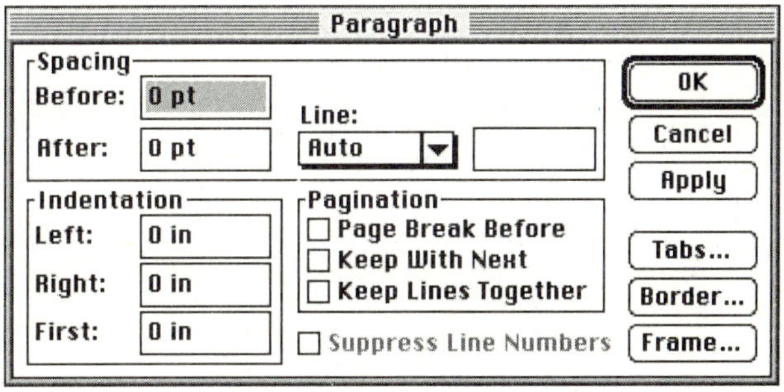

Fig. 10.2
Paragraph dialog box.

To produce the Paragraph dialog box, choose Paragraph from the Format menu or press ⌘-M.

If you work with the ruler in view, you quickly can access the Paragraph dialog box by double-clicking the right-indent marker (the triangle at the right end of the ruler). Alternatively, you can double-click a paragraph-properties mark to bring up the Paragraph dialog box. A *paragraph-properties mark*—a small black box in the selection bar—appears if you have chosen invisible formats for a paragraph, such as the Keep With Next option (discussed in Chapter 11, "Formatting Paragraphs").

Chapter 10
Formatting Paragraphs

When you choose indents and spacing in the Paragraph dialog box, you type the measurements in text boxes, using one of the measurement formats Word recognizes. The following list summarizes these formats and provides their typed abbreviations:

Inches (**in** or **"**). Inches are Word's default measurement format for horizontal formats (such as indents).

Points (**pt**). In addition to being Word's default measurement format for line and paragraph spacing, points are the default measurement for character spacing and position. Each inch contains 72 points.

Centimeters (**cm**). One centimeter equals 0.39 inch or 28.35 points.

Picas (**pi**). One pica equals 1/6 inch, 0.42 centimeter, or 12 points.

Lines (**li**). Use this format for vertical measurements only. One line equals 1/6 inch, 0.42 centimeter, or 12 points.

If you type a measurement without specifying one of the recognized abbreviations (in, ", pt, cm, pi, or li), Word assumes that you are using the default measurement format for that option: inches for indents and points for spacing.

Keep this information about measurements in mind when you type measurements in the Spacing text boxes. For example, if you type only **2** in the Line text box to specify double line spacing, you're in for a disappointment: you actually have specified 2 points of line spacing (1/36 of an inch) instead of 2 lines, because Word is using the default format (points). To specify double line spacing, you must type **24 pt**, **2 li**, or **2 pi**.

If you select two or more paragraphs that have dissimilar paragraph formats, the Paragraph dialog box shows only the format settings that those paragraphs share. You can choose additional formats for the selected paragraphs without affecting the paragraphs' current formats; you also can override the current settings. Word applies to all selected paragraphs any changes you make in the Paragraph dialog box.

Using Keyboard Shortcuts

Keyboard shortcuts are the third technique for creating paragraph formats. For adept typists, keyboard shortcuts may be the best paragraph-formatting technique. Table 10.1 lists the keyboard shortcuts for paragraph formatting.

Table 10.1	Format	Keyboard shortcut
Keyboard Shortcuts for Paragraph Formatting	Left-justified alignment	⌘-Shift-L
	Right-justified alignment	⌘-Shift-R
	Centered alignment	⌘-Shift-C
	Automatic first-line indent	⌘-Shift-F
	Indent paragraph one tab stop	⌘-Shift-N
	Remove one tab stop of indentation	⌘-Shift-M
	Hanging indentation	⌘-Shift-T
	Double line spacing	⌘-Shift-Y
	Blank line before paragraph	⌘-Shift-O
	Restore normal paragraph formats	⌘-Shift-P

When you work with fonts or font sizes other than the defaults, avoid the shortcut that restores normal paragraph formats, ⌘-Shift-P. This command restores all the default character and paragraph formats: left-justified alignment, single line spacing, and the current default font and font size.

If you want to cancel a paragraph format you have just assigned with a keyboard shortcut but want to maintain your font and font-size choices, simply use another keyboard shortcut. Suppose that you chose centered alignment by pressing ⌘-Shift-C, for example, and want to restore left-justified alignment. You can restore left-justified alignment by pressing ⌘-Shift-L.

Most of these keyboard shortcuts work the same way as their counterparts in the ruler and the Paragraph dialog box. Some of the keyboard shortcuts are additive, however, as shown in the following list:

- **⌘-Shift-N.** Every time you press this key combination, Word increases the current paragraph's left indent by 1/2 inch. To indent a paragraph 1 1/2 inches, press this key combination three times.

- **⌘-Shift-M.** Every time you press this key combination, Word subtracts 1/2 inch from the current paragraph's left indent. If a paragraph is indented 1 1/2 inches and you press this key combination twice, the indent becomes 1/2 inch.

■ ⌘-*Shift-T.* This command creates a hanging indent—a format in which the first line is flush with the left margin and the second line is indented 1/2 inch. Every time you press this key combination, Word adds 1/2 inch to the indent. If you press this key combination twice, you create a hanging indent with a 1/2-inch first-line indent and 1-inch indents for the second and subsequent lines.

You now have learned the fundamentals of choosing paragraph formats. The following sections of this chapter explain the formats in detail.

Controlling Paragraph Alignment

Word enables you to choose centered, right-justified, or justified alignment. Word's default paragraph alignment—left-justified—results in a ragged right margin. To make your documents resemble a printed book or magazine, you may be tempted to use justified alignment. Use this feature with caution, however, because Word may introduce unsightly spaces between words in an attempt to make the right margin align. Although you can resolve some spacing problems by running Word's automatic-hyphenation utility (as explained in Chapter 12, "Checking Spelling and Grammar"), left justification works best for most documents.

To change paragraph alignment before you type, follow these steps:

1. Press Return to start a new paragraph (unless you want to format the current paragraph).

2. Choose an alignment option, using the ruler or one of the keyboard shortcuts listed in Table 10.1. (If the ruler is not visible, choose Show Ruler from the Edit menu or press ⌘-R.)

3. Type the text of the new paragraph.

To change paragraph alignment after you type, follow these steps:

1. Select the text.

   To select one paragraph, position the insertion point anywhere in the paragraph. (You don't have to highlight the entire paragraph; placing the insertion point in the paragraph is sufficient to select it for paragraph-formatting purposes.)

   To select more than one paragraph, double-click the selection bar next to the first paragraph and then drag the mouse down or up until you have highlighted the desired paragraphs.

2. Choose an alignment option, using the ruler or one of the keyboard shortcuts listed in Table 10.1.

To cancel the alignment options you assigned and return to left-justified formatting, follow these steps:

1. Select the text.

2. Click the Left alignment icon in the ruler or press ⌘-Shift-L.

Indenting Paragraphs

Word can indent paragraphs four ways:

- Only the first line (first-line indentation)

- The second and subsequent lines (hanging indentation)

- All lines from the left

- All lines from the right

Using these four types of indents, you can create a variety of paragraph formats (see fig. 10.3).

Fig. 10.3
Various indented paragraphs.

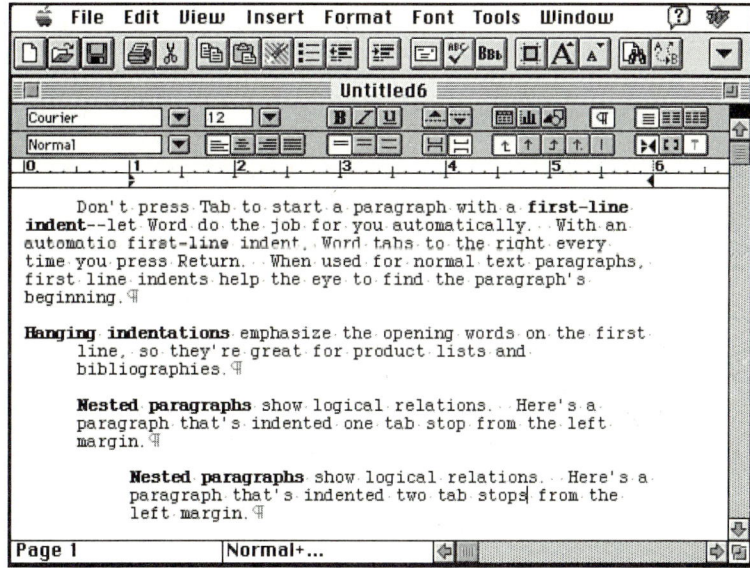

To indent paragraphs from the left, you can use keyboard shortcuts (⌘-Shift-N and ⌘-Shift-M), the ruler, Word 5.1's new Toolbar (using the Nest tool), or the Paragraph dialog box. To indent text from the right, you must use the ruler or the Paragraph dialog box.

NOTE

Indenting lines from the left or right establishes a temporary indentation style but does not change the page margins. To change the margins in your document, choose Document from the Format menu to open the Document dialog box and then type new measurements in the Left and Right Margins text boxes.

To use keyboard shortcuts to indent text from the left margin, follow these steps:

1. Select the paragraph you want to format.

2. Press ⌘-Shift-N. Word positions the left-indent and first-line markers at 1/2 inch in the ruler.

3. To increase the indentation an additional 1/2 inch, press ⌘-Shift-N again.

   To decrease the indentation by one tab stop, press ⌘-Shift-M.

VERSION 5.1

To use the Toolbar to indent text from the left margin, follow these steps:

1. Select the paragraph you want to format.

2. Click the Nest tool. Word positions the left-indent and first-line markers at 1/2 inch in the ruler.

3. To increase the indentation an additional 1/2 inch, click the Nest tool again.

   To decrease the indentation by one tab stop, click the Unnest tool.

To use the ruler to create left or right indentation, follow these steps:

1. Select the paragraph you want to format.

2. Drag the ruler's left-indent marker to the position where you want the left indentation. (The first-line indent marker moves also.)

   Drag the right-indent marker to create an indentation from the right margin.

 When you set indents with the ruler, keep your eye on the page-number area. As you drag the indent markers, Word indicates the markers' current location in the page-number area. Word moves the indent markers in 1/16-inch increments. You can set a more precise measurement by typing a different measurement in the Indentation area of the Paragraph dialog box.

To create indentations using the Paragraph dialog box, follow these steps:

1. Select the paragraph you want to format.

2. Choose Paragraph from the Format menu or press ⌘-M. The Paragraph dialog box appears.

3. In the Indentation area, type measurements in the Left and Right text boxes.

4. Choose OK.

Creating Automatic First-Line Indentations

You need not press Tab to create a first-line indentation; Word can enter one automatically. To create an automatic first-line indentation, follow these steps:

1. Select the paragraph you want to format.

2. In the ruler, drag the first-line indent marker to the place where you want the paragraph indent.

    Alternatively, type a measurement in the First text box in the Indentation area of the Paragraph dialog box or press ⌘-Shift-F. Pressing ⌘-Shift-F indents the paragraph by one default tab stop (1/2 inch, unless you have changed the default tab-width setting in the Document dialog box).

Creating Hanging Indentations

Hanging indentations are useful whenever you want to emphasize the first few words in a paragraph. Figure 10.4 shows two uses for hanging indentations: bibliographic citations and definition lists.

Fig. 10.4
Hanging indentations.

First-line indent ——

Left indent ——

```
 ⌘  File   Edit   View   Insert   Format   Font   Tools   Window        ?  ✻
┌──────────────────────────────────────────────────────────────────────────┐
│ [toolbar icons]                                                         ▼  │
├──────────────────────────────────────────────────────────────────────────┤
│                              Untitled7                                     │
├──────────────────────────────────────────────────────────────────────────┤
│ Courier       ▼  12  ▼   B / U  ▲▼  [icons]  ¶   [icons]               ⬆  │
│ Normal        ▼  [align icons]  [icons]  ↑↑↓↑↓  [icons] T                 │
├──────────────────────────────────────────────────────────────────────────┤
│ 0 . . . . . 1 . . . . 2 . . . . 3 . . . 4 . . . . 5 . . . . 6 . . .        │
│                                                                            │
│ James, Norton Xavier.  1992.  Managing Technological                       │
│      Innovation in the Organic Gardening Industry.                         │
│      Galesburg, IL:  Prairie Doldrums Press. ¶                             │
│ ¶                                                                          │
│ ¶                                                                          │
│ ¶                                                                          │
│ Celebra  →      Standard features include front bucket seats,              │
│                 rear washer/wiper, dual mirrors, full wheel                │
│                 covers, AM-FM radio with cassette, 2.0 inline              │
│                 4 engine, and high-quality carpeting¶                      │
│ ¶                                                                          │
│ Celebra XL→     All the Celebra standard features plus air                 │
│                 conditioning, power windows, power locks,                  │
│                 power sunroof, alloy wheels, cruise control,               │
│                 antilock brakes, 2.8 V6 engine, and leather                │
│                 interior¶                                                  │
│ ▬                                                                         │
│                                                                         ▼  │
├──────────────────────────────────────────────────────────────────────────┤
│ Page 1            Normal+...            ⬅▐▌                          ➡  │
└──────────────────────────────────────────────────────────────────────────┘
```

Hanging indents also are useful for creating numbered lists (with the numbers flush with the left margin).

You can use any of three techniques to create hanging indents in Word: keyboard shortcuts, the ruler, or the Paragraph dialog box. The keyboard technique is by far the easiest method.

To use keyboard shortcuts to create a hanging indent, follow these steps:

1. Select the paragraph you want to format.

2. Press ⌘-Shift-T. Word positions the first-line indent marker at 0 inches and the left-indent marker at 1/2 inch. The paragraph has a hanging indent with the first line justified left. *Turnover lines* (the second and subsequent lines) are indented one default tab stop (1/2 inch).

3. To increase the indentation an additional 1/2 inch, press ⌘-Shift-T again. To decrease the indentation 1/2 inch, press ⌘-Shift-M.

NOTE

Like the ⌘-Shift-N and ⌘-Shift-M commands, the hanging-indent shortcut (⌘-Shift-T) is additive. If you press the command again, Word indents the entire paragraph another default tab stop, positioning the first line at 1/2 inch and beginning turnover lines at 1 inch (with default 1/2 inch tab stops).

You may want to indent the turnover lines elsewhere than at the default tab stops. A hanging indent may look better, for example, with a 0.2-inch indentation rather than the 0.5-inch indentation that ⌘-Shift-T creates. In such situations, you can use the ruler to set the turnover-line indentation anywhere you want.

When you indent with the ruler, hold down the Shift key to move only one of the indent markers without affecting the other marker's position.

To use the ruler to create a hanging indent, follow these steps:

1. Select the paragraph you want to format.

2. Hold down the Shift key and drag the left-indent marker to the place where you want to position the paragraph's second and subsequent lines (the turnover lines).

3. Drag the first-line indent back to the place where you want the first line to begin.

To use the Paragraph dialog box to create a hanging indent, follow these steps:

1. Select the paragraph you want to format.

2. Choose Paragraph from the Format menu or press ⌘-M. The Paragraph dialog box appears.

3. In the Indentation area, type a negative measurement (such as **-0.5**) in the First text box and a positive measurement (such as **1.0**) in the Left text box. (In this example, you are using Word's default indent measurement—inches—and therefore need not type a measurement abbreviation.)

   When you type a negative number in the First box, you tell Word, "Start the first line to the left of the left indentation." If the left indentation is 1 inch and you type **-0.5** in the First box, Word starts the first line 1/2 inch from the left margin and the turnover lines 1 inch from the left margin.

4. Choose OK.

Using the Toolbar To Create Bulleted Lists

New to Version 5.1 of Word is the Toolbar, which contains the Bulleted List tool. If you select a series of paragraphs and click the Bulleted List tool, Word automatically formats the paragraphs as a bulleted list (see fig. 10.5).

Fig. 10.5
Bulleted list created by the Bulleted List tool.

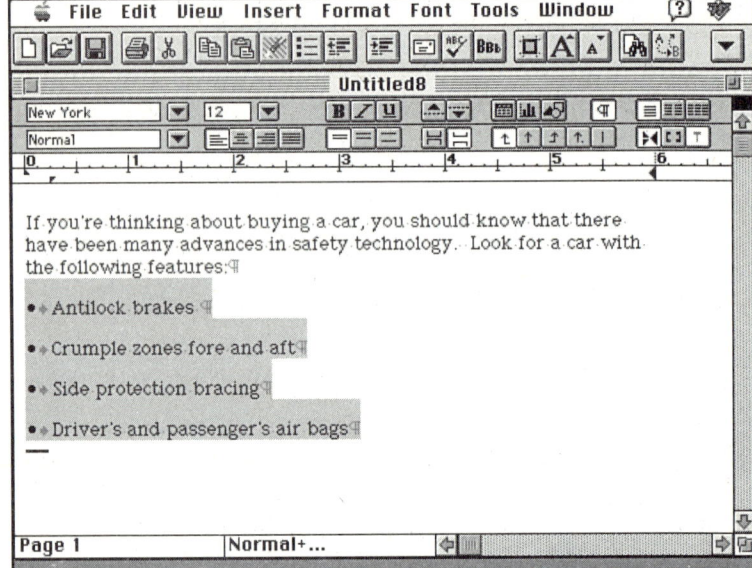

Word adds the bullets (the same bullets you get by pressing Option-8) and creates a 1/2-inch hanging indent for each paragraph. The bullets use the same font and font size as the paragraph's first character.

You can use the Bulleted List tool to add a bullet to a paragraph quickly. Position the insertion point anywhere in the paragraph and click the Bulleted List tool; Word adds the bullet and formats the paragraph with a hanging indent. You need not position the insertion point at the beginning of the paragraph; the Bulleted List tool does that job for you.

Controlling Line and Paragraph Spacing

By default, Word automatically uses single line spacing. In this format, the program automatically adjusts line spacing to make room for the largest font size you have chosen in a line. The program also adjusts automatically for superscript and subscript characters.

You can choose other line-spacing options or set up a paragraph format that adds blank space before or after a paragraph. These options are discussed in the following sections.

NOTE Word uses printer's points as the default measurement format for line spacing in the Paragraph dialog box (72 points per inch). In a 12-point font, Word prints 6 lines per inch unless you change to a larger font or use superscript or subscript formatting.

Understanding Line-Spacing Options

Word now gives you more ways to control line spacing than ever before. In previous versions, you could choose either the Auto option or a fixed-size line-spacing format. The Auto option created a single-space format that automatically adjusted for superscript, subscript, or large characters; the fixed-size option (such as 18 points or 24 points of line spacing) also adjusted automatically. As a result, you couldn't easily lock the program into fixed line spacing.

In versions 5.0 and 5.1, however, you have two more choices: the At Least option, which automatically accommodates superscript, subscript, and large characters; and the Exactly option, which doesn't adjust automatically.

Figure 10.6 shows the line-spacing options in the Paragraph dialog box.

Fig. 10.6
Line-spacing options in the Line drop-down list box.

Paragraph	
Spacing	
Before: `0 pt`	**Line:**
After: `0 pt`	`Auto ▼`
	✓Auto
Indentation	At Least
Left: `0 in`	Exactly
Right: `0 in`	☐ Keep Lines Together
First: `0 in`	☐ Suppress Line Numbers

OK · Cancel · Apply · Tabs... · Border... · Frame...

Chapter 10

Formatting Paragraphs

The following list explains these options and indicates when you would need them.

Auto. This option single-spaces lines but adjusts the line spacing to accommodate the largest font you use, as well as superscript, subscript, and graphics. Auto is the best option to use for single-spaced documents. Word uses this option when you choose the Single Line Spacing icon in the ruler.

At Least. This option spaces lines using, at minimum, the figure shown in the text box adjacent to the Line drop-down list box. If you type **18** in the text box and select At Least in the list box, Word uses 18-point line spacing. The program, however, increases the line spacing as necessary to accommodate larger fonts, superscript, subscript, or graphics. At Least is the best option to use for double-spaced documents.

Exactly. This option spaces lines according to the line-spacing measurement you type in the Spacing text boxes. Word's automatic line-spacing adjustments may give some lines more space than others and produce an uneven effect. When you choose Exactly, however, Word does not adjust the line spacing to accommodate larger fonts, subscript, or superscript, so this option assures you that every line is given the same space. (Be certain not to choose a font size larger than the line spacing you specified.)

Choose the Exactly option only if you want absolute control over line spacing. You may require such control in desktop publishing, where smooth, even page appearance (layout artists call it *color*) is important.

The easiest way to choose line-spacing and blank-line options is to click icons in the ruler, although this method of choosing line spacing has certain limitations. The following paragraphs explain the ruler's spacing icons.

Single Line Spacing. When you click this icon, Word always uses Auto line spacing, regardless of the selected font size. The program adjusts the line spacing as necessary to accommodate larger fonts, graphics, superscript, or subscript.

1.5-Line Spacing. When you click this icon, Word always uses 18-point line spacing and automatically selects the At Least option. When applied to 12-point type, 18-point line spacing creates the appearance of 1 1/2-line spacing; with 10-point type, the appearance resembles double spacing.

Double Line Spacing. When you click this icon, Word always creates 24-point line spacing and automatically selects the At Least option. Used with 12-point type, 24-point line spacing creates the appearance of double spacing. The effect is more like triple-spacing with a smaller font and resembles 1 1/2-line spacing if you are using an 18-point font.

Adjusting Line Spacing

Now that you are familiar with the line-spacing options and ruler icons, you can choose the correct line-spacing option for your document. Like other paragraph-formatting commands, the line-spacing options affect the selected paragraph or paragraphs. If you choose a line-spacing option and start typing, Word applies the format you chose to the text.

If you chose a different line-spacing option and want to change back to single spacing, click the Single Line Spacing icon in the ruler. Alternatively, choose Paragraph from the Format menu or press ⌘-M to open the Paragraph dialog box, select Auto in the Line drop-down list box, and then choose OK to confirm your choice.

To double-space your document, follow these steps:

1. Place the insertion point where you want to begin double spacing. Alternatively, select the paragraphs you want to format.

2. To double-space your document if you are using 12-point type, click the Double Line Spacing icon in the ruler.

If you are using a different font size, choose Paragraph from the Format menu or press ⌘-M to open the Paragraph dialog box. Select At Least in the Line drop-down list box. Then multiply the font size by 2 and type the result in the Line text box. Choose OK to confirm your choice. This procedure ensures true double spacing.

To use fixed line spacing that Word doesn't adjust automatically, follow these steps:

1. Place the insertion point where you want the line-spacing option to begin. Alternatively, select the paragraphs you want to format.

2. Choose Paragraph from the Format menu or press ⌘-M to open the Paragraph dialog box. Select Exactly in the Line drop-down list box. Then type the line spacing you want in the Line text box and choose OK to confirm your choice.

Adding Blank Spacing Before and After Paragraphs

One of the many formats you can assign to a paragraph is blank spacing before or after a paragraph. If you have set up a paragraph format that includes blank spacing, Word inserts the blank spacing automatically when you press Return. You also can apply blank spacing to paragraphs you already have typed.

When should you add blank space before or after a paragraph? The following list suggests some ways you can use this format.

- *Headings.* Style handbooks and guidelines typically specify precisely how much blank space should precede and follow a heading. Such guidelines may require, for example, that second-level headings be preceded by two blank lines and followed by one blank line. Use the Paragraph dialog box to specify a heading's blank spacing.

Rather than choose the blank-spacing option every time you create a new heading, copy the format from an existing heading or create a heading style, as explained in Chapter 14.

- *Single-spaced paragraphs.* Click the Blank Spacing icon in the ruler to add 12 points of blank space automatically every time you press Return.

- *Footnotes.* Add a blank line before every footnote paragraph to separate multiple footnotes. For more information on footnotes, see Chapter 19.

Do not press Return to create blank lines in your document. If you do, you cannot use the Keep With Next option to control paragraph breaks, because the next paragraph is an *empty* paragraph. An empty paragraph contains nothing but a paragraph mark. (For more information on the Keep With Next option, see Chapter 11, "Formatting Paragraphs.")

To add blank lines, use the Blank Spacing icon in the ruler or the Before and After text boxes in the Spacing area of the Paragraph dialog box. Word disregards these blank lines when it carries out the Keep With Next option. If you use the Spacing After text box and the Keep With Next option in the Paragraph dialog box to add 24 points of blank space under a heading, Word does not break a page between the heading and the next text paragraph.

Blank-spacing options affect the selected paragraphs. If you choose a blank-spacing option and start typing, Word applies the format you chose to the text.

Although you can use either the ruler or the Paragraph dialog box to add blank lines, the ruler option limits your choices. If you click the Blank Spacing icon in the ruler, for example, Word inserts 12 points of blank space before the selected paragraph. To add more or less than 12 points before the paragraph or to add any blank space after the paragraph, you must use the Paragraph dialog box.

To add 12 points of blank space before a paragraph (or before all selected paragraphs), follow these steps:

1. Place the insertion point where you want the line-spacing option to begin. Alternatively, select the paragraphs you want to format.

2. Click the Blank Spacing icon in the ruler.

To choose other blank-line-spacing options, follow these steps:

1. Place the insertion point where you want the line-spacing option to begin. Alternatively, select the paragraphs you want to format.

2. Choose Paragraph from the Format menu or press ⌘-M. The Paragraph dialog box appears.

3. In the Spacing area, type a measurement (in printer's points) in the Before text box to add blank space before the paragraphs.

4. Type a measurement (in printer's points or lines) in the After text box to add blank space after the paragraphs.

5. Choose OK.

To find out how much blank space you have allotted to a paragraph, select the paragraph by moving the pointer to the selection bar and then double-click. The resulting highlighting includes any blank line added before or after the paragraph.

Using Tabs

Word uses two kinds of tabs: default and custom. By default, every paragraph contains left-justified tab stops every 1/2 inch across the screen. You can change the default tab stops in two ways:

■ You can change the default tab width for the entire document. The new tab width you choose automatically applies to all the paragraphs in your document unless you choose custom tabs for selected paragraphs.

Chapter 10
Formatting Paragraphs

- You can set custom tabs for any paragraph, even if you reset the default tabs.

The following sections explain these procedures.

Most people set tabs when they type tables. Before typing a complex table, however, you should investigate Word's Table command, which inserts a spreadsheetlike matrix of rows and columns into your document. Typing your table data in a Table matrix is much easier than fussing with tabs. For more information on the Table command, see Chapter 15, "Creating Tables."

When you press Tab, Word doesn't enter spaces in your document; the program enters a tab character instead, as shown in figure 10.7.

Fig. 10.7
Tab characters.

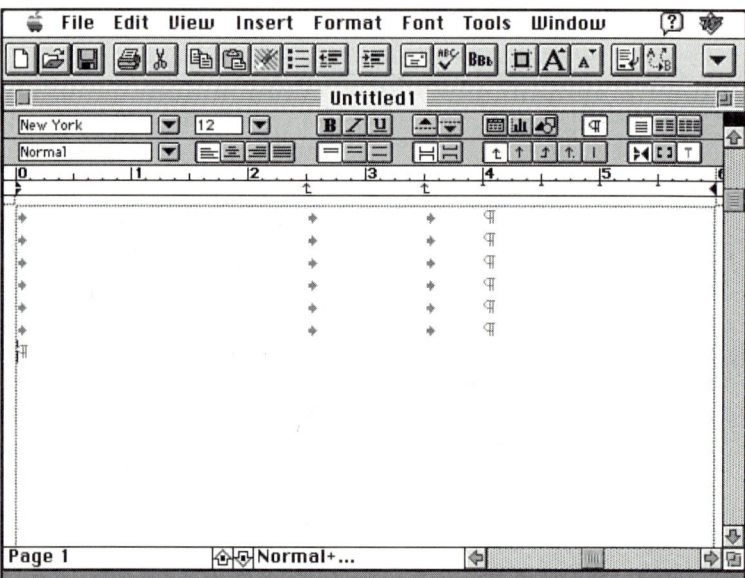

Tab characters are much like paragraph marks: you view both in the same way. To view tab characters, choose Show ¶ from the View menu or click the paragraph-mark icon in the ribbon.

Just as you can join two paragraphs by deleting a paragraph mark, you also can cause text to shift to the left by deleting a tab character. When you delete a tab character, the text after the tab character rejoins the previous text as though you never had pressed Tab.

Rather than pressing the space bar to insert spaces into your text, press Tab to indent. When you press Tab, Word enters a tab character that tells the program to advance subsequent text to the next tab stop (by default, the next half-inch or inch mark in the ruler). Word always positions the text correctly if you indent the text with the Tab key. If you try to indent with spaces, Word may fail to align the text correctly, even though the on-screen text may appear to be aligned.

Most of the Mac's fonts are proportionally spaced fonts, meaning that wide characters (such as *m* and *w*) occupy more space than do narrow characters (such as *i* and *l*). If you try to align text with spaces, character-width differences that are not obvious on-screen can cause alignment problems when you print.

Changing the Default Tabs

By default, Word places left-aligned tabs every 1/2 inch across the screen. (A left-aligned tab aligns the left edge of text at the tab stop. You learn about Word's other types of tabs in the following section.) You can change the default tab width for the current document or for all the documents you create. Some style guidelines call for tab spacings other than Word's default, so changing the default width may come in handy.

To change the default tab width for the current document, follow these steps:

1. Choose Document from the Format menu. The Document dialog box appears (see fig. 10.8).

Fig. 10.8
Document dialog box.

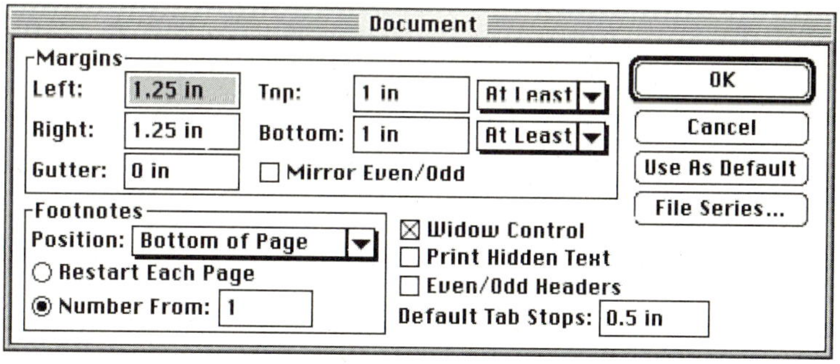

2. Type the new tab width in the Default Tab Stops text box.

3. Choose OK.

To change the default tab width for all documents, follow these steps:

1. Choose Document from the Format menu. The Document dialog box appears.

2. Type the new tab width in the Default Tab Stops text box.

3. Click the Use As Default button.

4. Choose OK.

Understanding Custom Tabs

In Word, custom tabs are paragraph formats. When you create custom tabs, the tabs you choose apply only to the selected paragraphs. As is true of any other paragraph format, however, you copy the current paragraph's tabs when you press Return to start a new paragraph.

When you set a custom tab, Word automatically cancels the default tabs that precede the custom tab in the ruler. For example, if you set a tab at the 3-inch mark, Word cancels the default tabs that would have been positioned at 0.5, 1, 1.5, 2, and 2.5 inches. Word does not delete the default tabs to the right of the custom tabs.

Why set custom tabs, when Word already has set tab stops every 1/2 inch across the screen? The following examples provide some reasons:

- Suppose that you want to align text at 3 inches and 4.5 inches. If you set custom tabs at these locations, you can press Tab once to move the insertion point to the 3-inch mark and twice to move the insertion point to the 4.5-inch mark. Without custom tabs, you must press Tab nine times to move the insertion point to the 4.5-inch mark.

- Suppose that you want to select a larger or smaller font size for a table you already have typed. If you used the default tabs in the table, changing the font size might push one of the tab characters past the next tab stop, resulting in misaligned text in the printout. If you use custom tabs, however, you have fewer tabs in your table, reducing the chance that resized text will be pushed past a tab stop.

When you set custom tabs, you can choose any of four alignment options and even can insert a vertical line. You also can have Word automatically enter leaders. Commonly used in tables of contents, *leaders* are repeated characters (such as periods or dashes) that lead up to the tab stop, filling the blank space and guiding your eyes across the page.

Figure 10.9 illustrates all four kinds of custom tabs.

Fig. 10.9
Custom tabs.

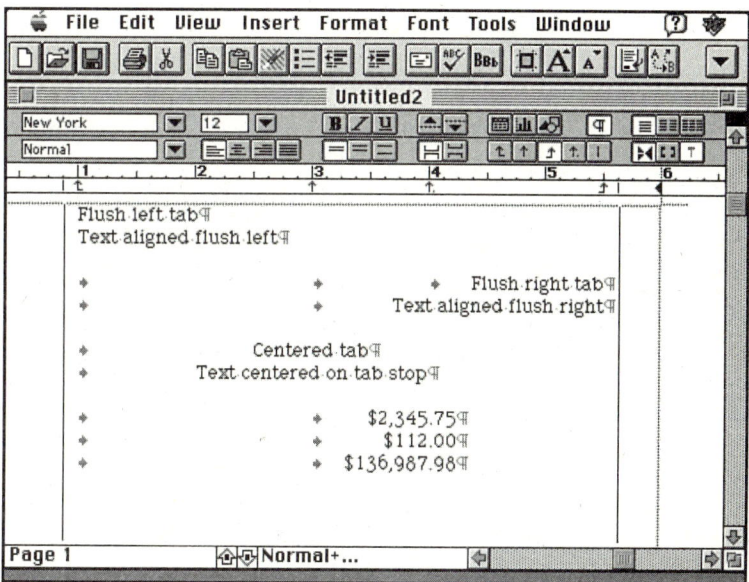

The following paragraphs describe Word's custom tabs.

Left. The text or numbers you type after pressing Tab appear to the right of the tab stop. In figure 10.9, the left tab is set at 1 inch.

Right. The text or numbers you type after pressing Tab appear to the left of the tab stop. In figure 10.9, the right tab is set at 5.5 inches.

Centered. The text or numbers you type after pressing Tab are centered at the tab stop. In figure 10.9, the centered tab is set at 3 inches.

Decimal. The numbers you type after pressing Tab are aligned by decimal points; text is aligned right. In figure 10.9, a decimal tab is set at 4 inches. (Notice that the numbers in the column are aligned by decimal points.)

In addition to these four custom tabs, you can set a *vertical* tab stop, which places a vertical line at the position at which you set the tab (see the two vertical lines in fig. 10.9). These vertical lines aren't characters you can wipe out or misalign by typing over them; the lines remain in place unless you remove the vertical tab stop. You can use vertical tabs to create vertical lines in tables.

Setting Custom Tabs

You can set custom tabs in two ways: by using the tab icons in the ruler or by using the Tabs dialog box, which you open by clicking the Tabs command button in the Paragraph dialog box. The following sections explain both procedures.

Setting Tabs with the Ruler

By far the easiest way to set, move, and cancel custom tabs is to use the ruler. To set a custom tab with the ruler, follow these steps:

1. Select the paragraph in which you want to set tabs. Alternatively, press Return to start a new paragraph.

2. Click the ruler icon that represents the kind of tab you want to set. From left to right, these icons are Left, Centered, Right, Decimal, and Vertical Bar.

3. In the ruler, click where you want to set the tab.

To move an existing tab with the ruler, follow these steps:

1. Select the paragraph that contains the tab you want to move.

2. On the ruler, drag the tab marker to its new position.

As you drag a tab marker, keep your eye on the page-number area, which shows the tab stop's location as you move the marker.

To remove a tab with the ruler, follow these steps:

1. Select the paragraph that contains the tab you want to remove.

2. Drag down the tab marker and release the mouse button away from the ruler scale.

To use the ruler to change a tab stop from one kind to another, follow these steps:

1. Clear the existing tab by dragging it down and off the ruler.

2. Click the icon that represents the kind of tab you want to set.

3. In the ruler, click where you want to set the tab.

The following section explains how to use the Tabs dialog box to clear all the tabs you set in a document and how to add leaders.

Using the Tabs Dialog Box

Although the ruler provides the easiest way to set tabs, in three specific circumstances you may need to use the Tabs dialog box:

■ *When precision is crucial.* You can type precise measurements in the Tabs dialog box.

■ *When you want to set leaders.* You can choose dot, dash, and underscore leaders (see fig. 10.10).

Fig. 10.10
Leaders.

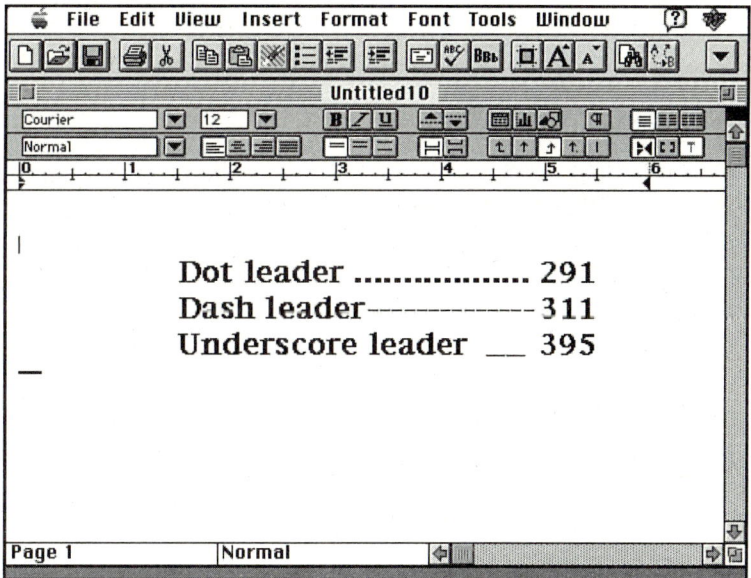

Word enters the leaders when you press Tab to move to the stop that includes the leaders. Word automatically adjusts the leader to provide room for text you type.

■ *When you want to clear all tabs from your document at once.* To clear tabs from the ruler, you must drag them off the ruler one at a time. Using the Tabs dialog box is much faster.

To display the Tabs dialog box, follow these steps:

1. Choose Paragraph from the Format menu or press ⌘-M. The Paragraph dialog box appears.

2. Click the Tabs command button. The Tabs dialog box appears over the Paragraph dialog box (see fig 10.11).

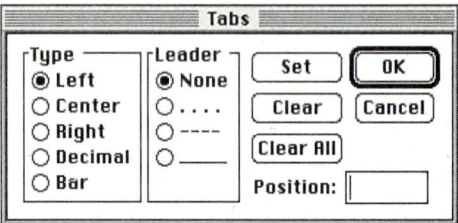

Fig. 10.11

Tabs dialog box.

To return to your document without choosing any options, click the Cancel button; when the Paragraph dialog box reappears, click Cancel in that dialog box.

To display the Tabs dialog box quickly, use the ruler to set a tab and then double-click the tab marker. The Tabs dialog box pops up, its settings reflecting the characteristics of the tab you double-clicked; if you make changes in the Tabs dialog box, those changes affect that tab.

To set a tab to a precise measurement, follow these steps:

1. Choose Paragraph from the Format menu or press ⌘-M. The Paragraph dialog box appears.

2. Click the Tabs button. The Tabs dialog box appears.

3. To set a tab other than a left-justified tab, choose an option in the Type area.

4. Type a measurement in the Position text box.

5. Choose OK to confirm your choices and close the Tabs dialog box. The Paragraph dialog box reappears.

6. Choose OK to close the Paragraph dialog box.

To create a leader, follow these steps:

1. Use the ruler to set a tab; this tab receives the leader formatting. (For a table of contents, for example, set a right-justified tab at the right margin.)

2. Double-click the tab marker that you just placed in the ruler. The Tabs dialog box appears.

3. Click the tab stop on the ruler you set in step 1.

4. In the Leader area of the Tabs dialog box, choose a leader format (dot, dash, or underscore).

5. Click the Set button.

6. Choose OK.

To enter the leader in your document, type some text and press Tab. The insertion point jumps to the tab stop you set, leaving the specified leader characters in its wake.

To clear all the custom tabs in a selected paragraph and restore the default tabs, follow these steps:

1. Choose Paragraph from the Format menu or press ⌘-M. The Paragraph dialog box appears.

2. Click the Tabs button. The Tabs dialog box appears.

3. Click Clear All.

4. Choose OK to confirm your choices and close the Tabs dialog box. The Paragraph dialog box reappears.

5. Choose OK to close the Paragraph dialog box.

Searching for Paragraph Formats

In the preceding chapter, you learned about Word's enhanced Find command, which helps you locate text to which you have applied one or more character formats. You also can search for any text that has paragraph formats of any kind.

Chapter 10

Formatting Paragraphs

The following sample of searches you can conduct with the Find dialog box illustrates how you can use this much-improved capability.

- Find in a document every location at which you typed an extended quotation with a 1-inch indentation on both sides.

- Find in a document the heading after which you added three blank lines instead of two.

- Find the paragraph that has a decimal tab at 4 1/2 inches and a right-justified tab at 6 inches.

- Find the next paragraph that has an automatic 1/2-inch first-line indentation.

The Find dialog box can come in handy when you have made formatting mistakes in a long document and want to correct the error quickly and completely.

The best way to avoid formatting inconsistencies is to create and define styles for a document. When you define a style, all the paragraphs to which you apply the style have the same format. Changing the style, when necessary, is much easier than making format corrections manually. (For more information on styles, see Chapter 14, "Formatting with Styles.")

To search for a paragraph format, follow these steps:

1. Choose Find from the Edit menu or press ⌘-F. The Find dialog box appears (see fig. 10.12).

Fig. 10.12
Find dialog box.

Find
Find What: [   ]   Find Next
Format ▾   Cancel
Special ▾
☐ Match Whole Word Only ☐ Match Case   Search: Down ▾

2. Use one of the following techniques to choose a paragraph format for which you want Word to search (you can choose more than one format):

- Use the ruler, the Paragraph dialog box, or the keyboard shortcuts to choose formats. (To display the Paragraph dialog box, choose Paragraph from the Format menu or press ⌘-M. Alternatively, select Paragraph in the Format drop-down list box of the Find dialog box.)

■ To search for text to which you have applied one blank line before the paragraph and also double line spacing, for example, click the Blank Spacing and Double Line Spacing icons in the ruler.

■ You can search for character formats, such as double-spaced text typed in Palatino 12. To add character formats to your search, use any character-formatting technique (see Chapter 9) to identify the formats, or select Character in the Format drop-down list box of the Find dialog box to display the Character dialog box.

After you choose the search formats, those formats are listed below the Find What text box (see fig. 10.13).

Fig. 10.13
Find dialog box displaying several paragraph formats.

```
┌─────────────────────────────────────────────────────────────┐
│ ▢▤                          Find                              │
│ Find What: [                              ]      ┌──────────┐ │
│            ┌─────────┐                           │ Find Next│ │
│            │ Format ▼│ Tab stops: 3 in Number Aligned ...; 4.5 in │
│            └─────────┘                           ┌──────────┐ │
│            ┌─────────┐                           │  Cancel  │ │
│            │Special ▼│                           └──────────┘ │
│            └─────────┘                           Search:      │
│            ☐ Match Whole Word Only  ☐ Match Case ┌────────┬─┐ │
│                                                  │ Down   │▼│ │
│                                                  └────────┴─┘ │
└─────────────────────────────────────────────────────────────┘
```

Notice that the search specified in figure 10.13 is for a paragraph with a number-aligned tab stop at 3 inches and a flush-left tab stop at 4.5 inches.

3. To search for specific text that has the specified formats, type that text in the Find What text box. To search for any text with the specified formats, leave the text box blank.

4. If you want to change the direction of the search, make a selection in the Search drop-down list box.

5. Choose Find Next. When Word finds text with the specified format, Word highlights the text. Choose Find Next again to find the next occurrence of the format or click Cancel to return to your document.

If Word cannot find any text with the format you have specified, an alert box appears, asking whether you want to extend the search from the beginning of the document (or from the end, if you are searching up). Choose Yes to extend the search or click No to cancel.

Chapter 10
Formatting Paragraphs

CAUTION

After you use Find to search for a format, Word retains, for the duration of the current operating session, the search-format setting and any text you typed in the Find What text box. If you choose Find again, you must clear these settings to perform a different search. To clear the text from the Find What text box, select the text and press Delete. To clear the format, pull down the Format list box and select Clear.

Replacing Paragraph Formats

As you learned in the preceding chapter, Word can replace one format with another throughout a document. You even can replace a group of formats (such as double-spaced, justified paragraphs) with another group (such as single-spaced, left-justified paragraphs with one blank line between them) throughout a document. The addition of the Format drop-down list box to the Replace dialog box makes possible this significant new capability.

Following are some examples of situations in which replacing formats can save you up to several hours of manual formatting:

- You added two blank lines under some of the headings in your document and then discover that you were supposed to insert only one line of blank space.

- The bulleted lists you added to your document with a 0.19-inch indentation don't look right; you want to increase the indentation to 0.25 inch.

- You used double line spacing throughout your document with a blank line before each paragraph, but the spacing is unattractive. You want to close the blank spaces.

Word's Replace command (Edit menu) can perform all these tasks and more, thanks to the Format drop-down list box. In the preceding chapter, you learned how to use the Replace dialog box to replace character formats. (In Word 5.1, you can access this dialog box by clicking the Replace tool.) The following sections show you how to replace paragraph formats.

To replace one paragraph format with another throughout a document, follow these steps:

1. Choose Replace from the Edit menu, press ⌘-H, or click the Replace tool. The Replace dialog box appears (see fig. 10.14).

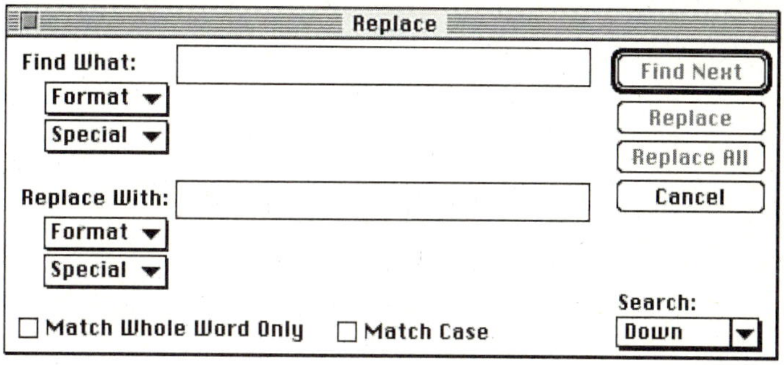

Fig. 10.14

Replace dialog box.

2. Use one of the following techniques to choose a paragraph format for which you want Word to search (you can choose more than one format):

   ■ Use the ruler, the Paragraph dialog box, or the keyboard shortcuts to choose formats. (To display the Paragraph dialog box, choose Paragraph from the Format menu or press ⌘-M. Alternatively, select Paragraph in the Format drop-down list box in the Find What section of the Replace dialog box.)

   ■ To search for paragraphs that you formatted with one blank line before the paragraph and double line spacing, for example, click the Blank Spacing and Double Line Spacing icons in the ruler.

   ■ You also can search for character formats. For example, you can search for double-spaced text formatted in Palatino 12. To add character formats to your search, use any character-formatting technique to identify the formats. Alternatively, select Character in the Find What Format drop-down list box to display the Character dialog box, where you can choose the formats.

   After you choose the search formats, those formats are listed below the Find What text box.

3. Use any of the preceding techniques to choose the format you want Word to insert in place of the original format.

   In figure 10.15, the replacement format appears below the Replace With text box. The settings in this example tell Word to find all paragraphs preceded by 12 points of blank space and then to remove the blank space.

Chapter 10

Formatting Paragraphs

Fig. 10.15

Replace dialog box after
choosing replacement
formats.

Replace
Find What: [   ]
Format ▼ SpaceBefore 12 pt
Special ▼
Replace With: [   ]
Format ▼ SpaceBefore 0 pt
Special ▼
☐ **Match Whole Word Only**   ☐ **Match Case**

Buttons: **Find Next**, **Replace**, **Replace All**, **Cancel**

Search: **Down** ▼

4. To search for specific text that has the formats you specified in the Find What area, type the text in the Find What text box. To search for all text with the specified formats, leave this text box blank.

5. To insert specific text that has the formats you specified in the Replace With area, type the text in the Replace With text box. To replace only the formatting, leave this text box blank.

6. To change the direction of the search, make a selection in the Search drop-down list box.

7. Choose Find Next to find the first occurrence of the specified format. When Word finds the first occurrence, an alert box appears, asking whether you to want to replace the highlighted text. Choose Find Next to find and confirm the next occurrence of the format, or click Cancel to return to your document.

   Alternatively, if you are sure that you want to perform the replacement throughout your document without confirmation, click Replace All instead of Find Next.

If Word cannot find any text with the specified format, an alert box appears, asking whether you want to extend the search from the beginning of the document (or from the end, if you are searching up). Choose Yes to extend the search or click No to cancel.

CAUTION

After you use the Replace dialog box to search for a format, Word retains, for the duration of the current operating session, the search-format settings and any text in the Find What and Replace What text boxes. The format and text also appear in the Find dialog box. To use Replace or Find to perform a different search, you must clear these settings. To clear the text from the Find What or Replace What text box, select the text and press Delete. To clear the format, pull down the Format list box and select Clear.

Repeating and Copying Paragraph Formats

If you have created a complex paragraph format and want to use it elsewhere in your document, you don't have to choose the commands again. Immediately after using a format, you can repeat it. If you have typed or issued commands since you applied the format, you can reuse the format by copying it. The following sections detail the procedures for performing these tasks.

Repeating Paragraph Formats

To repeat a paragraph format you have just applied, follow these steps:

1. Apply paragraph formats, using any technique discussed in this chapter.

2. Select the next paragraph that you want to format in the same way.

3. Choose Repeat from the Edit menu or press ⌘-Y.

Copying Paragraph Formats

If you have typed some text or chosen another command since you applied the paragraph format, you cannot use the technique described in the preceding section to repeat the format. You can, however, copy the format by pressing ⌘-Option-V. (As you learned in Chapter 9, you can copy character formats with this command. The procedure for copying paragraph formats, however, differs slightly.)

To copy paragraph formats, follow these steps:

1. Select the paragraph that contains the formats you want to copy. (You must highlight the entire paragraph. To select the entire paragraph, move the mouse pointer to the selection bar left of the paragraph and then double-click.)

2. Press ⌘-Option-V.

3. Click in the paragraph to which you want to apply the formats. A dotted insertion point appears.

4. Press Return to copy the formats or ⌘-period (.) to cancel the operation.

Quick Review

This section summarizes the most useful information in this chapter. Check "Productivity Tips" for a review of high-productivity tips and tricks—the ones that Macintosh and Word pros use every day. Review "Techniques" whenever you need a quick reminder about a specific procedure.

Productivity Tips

■ Remember that Word defines paragraphs in a mechanical way. Every time you press Return, you start a new paragraph. By Word's definition, a paragraph can be a blank line (because a blank line ends in a paragraph mark), a one-word heading, or a paragraph of body text.

■ The ruler is the fastest way to choose paragraph formats. Keep in mind, however, that the ruler limits your line-spacing and blank-spacing options. Use the Paragraph dialog box for formats that you cannot choose in the ruler.

■ To access the Paragraph dialog box quickly, double-click the right-indent marker in the ruler.

■ Don't create blank lines by pressing Return. If you do, you cannot use the Keep With Next option to control page breaks because the next paragraph is an empty paragraph. To add blank lines, click the Blank Spacing icon in the ruler or type measurements in the Before and After text boxes in the Paragraph dialog box. (For more information on the Keep With Next option, see Chapter 11.)

■ Use the ruler to set, move, and cancel custom tabs. You should use the Tabs dialog box only when you choose leaders, need precisely measured tabs, or want to clear all tabs quickly. To add leaders quickly, set a tab and then double-click the tab marker in the ruler; the Tabs dialog box appears. The Tabs dialog box (otherwise accessible through the Paragraph dialog box) also enables you to clear all tabs with a single command.

■ If you plan to create a table, use Word's Table command (Insert menu) rather than set tabs. (For more information on the Table command, see Chapter 15.)

- To create a bulleted list quickly in Word 5.1, select a series of paragraphs and then click the Bulleted List tool.

- Always use tabs to indent text. Don't press the space bar to add indents to your document, because Word may not align the text properly when you print your document.

- You can use Word's Find and Replace commands to search for and replace paragraph formats, but formatting with styles enables you to avoid formatting inconsistencies. (For more information on styles, see Chapter 14.)

Techniques

This section provides concise summaries of all the procedures introduced in this chapter.

Aligning Text

To center paragraphs:

1. Place the insertion point in the paragraph you want to format or select multiple paragraphs.

2. Click the Centered alignment icon in the ruler or press ⌘-Shift-C.

To align paragraphs left:

1. Place the insertion point in the paragraph you want to format or select multiple paragraphs.

2. Click the Left alignment icon in the ruler or press ⌘-Shift-L.

To align paragraphs right:

1. Place the insertion point in the paragraph you want to format or select multiple paragraphs.

2. Click the Right alignment icon in the ruler or press ⌘-Shift-R.

To justify paragraphs:

1. Place the insertion point in the paragraph you want to format or select multiple paragraphs.

2. Click the Justified alignment icon in the ruler or press ⌘-Shift-J.

Indenting Text

To use keyboard shortcuts or the Toolbar to indent text from the left margin:

1. Select the paragraph you want to format.

2. Press ⌘-Shift-N or click the Nest tool. Word positions the left-indent and first-line indent markers at 1/2 inch on the ruler.

3. To increase the indentation by 1/2 inch, use the command again. To decrease the indentation by one tab stop, press ⌘-Shift-M or click the Unnest tool.

To use the ruler to create a left or right indentation:

1. Select the paragraph you want to format.

2. Drag the left-indent marker to the position at which you want to indent the paragraph. (The first-line indent marker moves also.)

   To create an indentation from the right margin, drag the right-indent marker.

To use the Paragraph dialog box to create an indentation:

1. Select the paragraph you want to format.

2. Choose Paragraph from the Format menu or press ⌘-M. The Paragraph dialog box appears.

3. In the Indentation area, type measurements in the Left and Right text boxes.

4. Choose OK.

Using Automatic First-Line Indentation

To create automatic first-line indentation:

1. Select the paragraph you want to format.

2. Drag the first-line indent marker to create the indentation. Alternatively, type a measurement in the First text box in the Indentation area of the Paragraph dialog box or press ⌘-Shift-F.

Using Hanging Indentation

To use keyboard shortcuts to create a hanging indentation:

1. Select the paragraph you want to format.

2. Press ⌘-Shift-T. Word positions the first-line indent marker at 0 inches and the right-indent marker at 1/2 inch.

3. To increase the indentation 1/2 inch, use the command again.

To use the ruler to create a hanging indentation:

1. Select the paragraph you want to format.

2. Drag the left-indent marker to the position at which you want to indent the paragraph's second and subsequent lines (the turnover lines). The first-line indent marker moves also.

3. Drag the first-line indent marker back to the position at which you want the first line to begin.

To use the Paragraph dialog box to create a hanging indentation:

1. Select the paragraph you want to format.

2. Choose Paragraph from the Format menu or press ⌘-M. The Paragraph dialog box appears.

3. In the Indentation area, type a negative measurement (such as **-0.5**) in the First text box and a positive measurement (such as **1.0**) in the Left text box.

4. Choose OK.

Using Bulleted Lists

To create a bulleted list:

1. Select a series of paragraphs.

2. Click the Bulleted List tool.

Specifying Line Spacing

To double-space your document:

1. Select the paragraphs you want to format.

2. To double-space your document if you are using 12-point type, click the Double Line Spacing icon in the ruler.

   If you are using another font size, choose Paragraph from the Format menu or press ⌘-M to open the Paragraph dialog box.

Select At Least in the Line drop-down list box. Then multiply by 2 the font size you are using, type the result in the Line text box, and choose OK to confirm your choice.

To use a fixed-size line spacing that Word doesn't adjust automatically:

1. Select the paragraphs you want to format.

2. Choose Paragraph from the Format menu or press ⌘-M. The Paragraph dialog box appears.

3. Select Exactly in the Line drop-down list box.

4. In the Line text box, type the line spacing you want.

5. Choose OK.

Adding Blank Space

To add 12 points of blank space before paragraphs:

1. Place the insertion point where you want the line-spacing option to begin. Alternatively, select the paragraphs you want to format.

2. Click the Blank Spacing icon in the ruler.

To choose other blank-spacing options:

1. Place the insertion point where you want the line-spacing option to begin. Alternatively, select the paragraphs you want to format.

2. Choose Paragraph from the Format menu or press ⌘-M. The Paragraph dialog box appears.

3. To add blank space before paragraphs, type a measurement (in printer's points) in the Before text box.

4. To add blank space after paragraphs, type a measurement (in printer's points) in the After text box.

5. Choose OK.

Setting Tabs

To change the default tab width for the current document:

1. Choose Document from the Format menu. The Document dialog box appears.

2. Type the new tab width in the Default Tab Stops text box.

3. Choose OK.

To change the default tab width for all documents:

1. Choose Document from the Format menu. The Document dialog box appears.

2. Type the new tab width in the Default Tab Stops text box.

3. Click the Use As Default button.

4. Choose OK.

To use the ruler to set custom tabs:

1. Select the paragraph that will contain the tabs. Alternatively, press Return to start a new paragraph.

2. Click the ruler icon that represents the kind of tab you want to set.

3. In the ruler, click where you want to set the tab.

To use the ruler to move tabs:

1. Select the paragraph that contains the tabs you want to move. The tab markers appear in the ruler.

2. Drag the tab markers to their new position.

To use the ruler to remove tabs:

1. Select the paragraph that contains the tabs you want to remove.

2. Drag the tab marker off the ruler.

To use the ruler to change a tab from one kind to another:

1. Clear the tab by dragging the tab marker down and off the ruler.

2. Click the ruler icon that represents the kind of tab you want to set.

3. In the ruler, click where you want to set the tab.

To clear all the custom tabs in a selected paragraph and restore Word's default tabs:

1. Choose Paragraph from the Format menu or press ⌘-M. The Paragraph dialog box appears.

2. Click the Tabs command button. The Tabs dialog box appears.

3. Click Clear All.

4. Choose OK to close the Tabs dialog box. The Paragraph dialog box reappears.

5. Choose OK to close the Paragraph dialog box.

To set a tab with a precise measurement:

1. Choose Paragraph from the Format menu or press ⌘-M. The Paragraph dialog box appears.

2. Click the Tabs command button. The Tabs dialog box appears.

3. To set a tab other than a left-justified tab, choose an option in the Type area.

4. Type a measurement in the Position text box.

5. Choose OK to close the Tabs dialog box. The Paragraph dialog box reappears.

6. Choose OK to close the Paragraph dialog box.

To create leaders:

1. Set a tab in the ruler.

2. Double-click the tab marker. The Tabs dialog box appears.

3. Click the tab stop on the ruler that you set in step 1.

4. In the Leader area of the Tabs dialog box, choose the leader format you want (dot, dash, or underscore).

5. Click the Set button.

6. Choose OK to close the Tabs dialog box. The Paragraph dialog box reappears.

7. Choose OK to close the Paragraph dialog box.

Searching for and Replacing Paragraph Formats

To search for paragraph formats:

1. Choose Find from the Edit menu or press ⌘-F. The Find dialog box appears.

2. Use any paragraph-formatting technique to choose paragraph formats for which you want Word to search. Alternatively, select Paragraph in the Format drop-down list box to display the Paragraph dialog box, where you can choose the formats.

3. If you want to search for specific text that has the formats you indicated, type the text in the Find What text box. To search for any text with those formats, leave this text box blank.

4. If you want to change the direction of the search, make a selection in the Search drop-down box.

5. Choose Find Next to begin the search or click Cancel to return to your document.

To replace one paragraph format with another throughout your document:

1. Choose Replace from the Edit menu or press ⌘-H. The Replace dialog box appears.

2. Use any paragraph-formatting technique to choose the formats for which you want Word to search. Alternatively, choose Paragraph from the Find What Format drop-down list box to display the Paragraph dialog box, where you can choose the formats.

3. Use any paragraph-formatting technique to choose the formats you want Word to insert in place of the search formats. Alternatively, choose Paragraph from the Find What Format drop-down list box to display the Paragraph dialog box, where you can choose the formats.

4. If you want to search for specific text that has the formats you indicated, type the text in the Find What text box. To search for any text with those formats, leave this text box blank.

5. If you want to insert specific text that has the formats you indicated, type the text in the Replace With text box. To replace only the formatting, leave this text box blank.

6. If you want to change the direction of the search, make a selection in the Search drop-down list box.

7. Choose Find Next to begin the search or click Replace All to make replacements throughout your document without confirmation.

Duplicating Paragraph Formats

To repeat a paragraph format:

1. Apply paragraph formats, using any of the techniques discussed in this chapter.

2. Select the paragraph to which you want to apply the same format.

3. Choose Repeat from the Edit menu or press ⌘-Y.

To copy paragraph formats:

1. Select the paragraph that contains the format you want to copy. (You must highlight the entire paragraph. To select the entire paragraph, move the pointer to the selection bar left of the paragraph and then double-click.)

2. Press ⌘-Option-V.

3. Place the insertion point in the paragraph to which you want to apply the formats.

4. Press Return.

CHAPTER 11

Formatting Pages

The third of Word's four formatting domains, page formatting, controls the apportionment of your text to the printed page. By default, Word determines page breaks automatically and prints your document with standard margins (1 inch top and bottom, and 1 1/4 inch left and right) on standard U.S. letter paper (8 1/2 by 11 inches). For all but the simplest documents, however, many users change the page design.

Following is an overview of the page-design topics covered in this chapter:

- *Adding page numbers.* By default, Word doesn't print page numbers. In this chapter, you learn a simple technique for placing page numbers in your document. In Chapter 19, you learn how to add page numbers to headers and footers (text repeated in the top or bottom margins of all pages).

- *Changing the margins.* You easily can change Word's default margins by using the ruler or the Document dialog box. You even can adjust margins dynamically and visually in Print Preview.

- *Controlling page breaks.* Word automatically begins a new page when you fill the current page with text. At any place in a document, however, you can begin a new page manually. You also can format paragraphs so that Word inserts a page break before a paragraph, keeps a paragraph with the next one, or keeps all the lines of a paragraph together on one page.

USING
WORD 5.1
FOR THE MAC
SPECIAL EDITION

■ *Choosing paper sizes and page orientation.* Depending on your printer's capabilities, you may be able to choose paper sizes other than 8 1/2 by 11 inches or to change the page orientation so that lines of text run across the longer dimension of the page (*landscape orientation*). Word enables you to change its default paper-size and page-orientation settings.

This chapter covers the fundamentals of page formatting. The chapters noted in the following list contain additional information to guide you in designing your document's pages.

■ Chapter 19 discusses headers, footers, and footnotes.

■ Chapter 20 covers Word's Frame command and how it anchors paragraphs in absolute positions on the page.

■ Chapter 21 covers techniques for creating more than one page design in your document.

■ Chapter 31 covers envelope formatting.

■ Chapter 34 covers paper-size and page-formatting procedures for printing mailing labels.

Adding Page Numbers

Word doesn't print page numbers on documents unless you instruct the program to do so. You can turn on page numbering in three ways:

■ *Using Print Preview.* The Page Number icon in Print Preview is the easiest way to activate page numbering. Use this technique to position page numbers anywhere on a page quickly.

■ *Using the Section dialog box.* You can add page numbers by activating the Margin Page Numbers option in the Page Number area of the Section dialog box. You can suppress page numbers on the first page and specify that the second page be numbered 2 (or 1, if the first page is a title page). You can change the number format (options include the default Arabic numerals, Roman numerals, and uppercase or lowercase letters) and specify an exact location on the page for your page numbers. Use this option when you want to specify how Word handles the first page.

■ *Using headers and footers.* A third way to add page numbers is to include them in headers or footers. Use this technique when you want page numbers to appear in the same area as a header or footer.

The following sections explain the first two of these techniques; see Chapter 19 for information on adding page numbers to headers or footers.

NOTE Word applies the default font and font size to page numbers. If you want to format page numbers differently, you can put your page numbers in headers or footers, a technique that enables you to format the numbers directly. Alternatively (as explained in Chapter 14, "Formatting with Styles"), you can change Word's default page-number style for the current document or for all new documents.

Managing Page Numbers with Print Preview

Word's Print Preview feature enables you to add, reposition, and remove page numbers. Double-click the Page Number icon to add page numbers at the default location (the upper right corner), or drag the page number to another location.

To add page numbers in Print Preview, follow these steps:

1. Choose Print Preview from the File menu or press ⌘-Option-I. Word displays your document in a Print Preview window (see fig. 11.1).

Fig. 11.1
Previewing a page design in Print Preview.

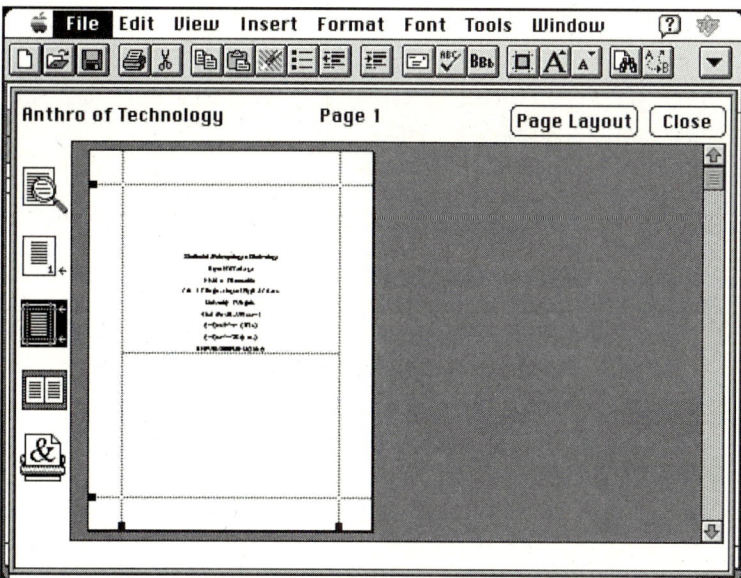

2. Add page numbers by using the Page Number icon.

   To add page numbers in the upper right corner of the page (1/2 inch from the top margin and 1/2 inch from the right margin), double-click the Page Number icon.

   To position page numbers elsewhere, click the Page Number icon and hold down the mouse button. The pointer changes to a page number. Position the pointer where you want to locate the page number and then release the mouse button.

3. Click Close to return to your document or click the Printer icon to print your document.

After you add page numbers to your document, you can reposition or remove them in Print Preview.

To reposition or remove page numbers in Print Preview, follow these steps:

1. Choose Print Preview from the File menu or press ⌘-Option-I. Word displays your document in a Print Preview window.

2. Place the mouse pointer on a page number in the document. When positioned over a page number, the pointer changes to a crosshair pointer.

3. Drag the page number to its new location (watch the page-number area to track the position of the pointer), or drag it off the page to remove it.

4. Click Close to return to your document.

Adding Page Numbers with the Section Dialog Box

The Section dialog box provides a second way to add page numbers to your document. The options in this dialog box enable you to suppress page numbers on the first page, specify the starting page number, and choose numeral formats other than Arabic.

By dividing your documents into sections, you can change page formats within your document. These formats include newspaper columns, headers and footers, and page numbers. If you are creating a complex document, such as a newsletter or a doctoral dissertation, you may want to change formats several times within a document. To create sections, choose Section Break from the Insert menu or press ⌘-Enter. To format sections, use the Section dialog box.

Changing a page number's position or removing a page number affects all the pages in the document, not just the one on which you made the change. If you divide your document into sections (see Chapter 21), the change affects only the current section.

If you haven't divided your document into sections, Word considers the entire document to be a section. You can use the Section dialog box to choose newspaper-column, header/footer, and page-number formats for your entire document.

To add page numbers with the Section dialog box, follow these steps:

1. Choose Section from the Format menu or press Option-F14. The Section dialog box appears (see fig. 11.2).

Fig. 11.2
Section dialog box.

Section	
Start: No Break ▼	□ Include Endnotes [OK]
┌Columns─	┌Page Numbers─
Number: 1	**Format:** 1 2 3 ▼ [Cancel]
Spacing: 0.5 in	□ Restart at 1 [Apply]
	☒ Margin Page Numbers
┌Header/Footer─	
From Top: 0.5 in	**From Top:** 0.5 in [Use As Default]
From Bottom: 0.5 in	**From Right:** 0.5 in [Line Numbers...]
□ Different First Page	

2. Click the Margin Page Numbers check box to turn on page numbering. By default, Word places page numbers in the upper right corner of the page, 1/2 inch from the margins, as you can see in the From Top and From Right text boxes. These text boxes become active when you click the Margin Page Numbers check box.

3. If you want to change the page-number position, type new measurements in the From Top and From Right text boxes.

4. Choose OK to confirm your page-number choices and close the dialog box.

Suppressing Page Numbering

In many documents, you suppress page numbers on the first page. When you print a long letter, for example, you don't number the first (letterhead) page; you begin numbering on Page 2. Standard practice is not to number the title page of a report or article, either; the first text page is Page 1. The Section dialog box enables you to specify both of these common page-numbering configurations.

Later in this chapter, you learn how to begin numbering on pages after Page 1. To suppress page numbering on the first page, follow these steps:

1. Position the insertion point at the beginning of the second page of your document.

2. Choose Section Break from the Format menu or press ⌘-Enter. Word places a section break (a double row of dots) in your document.

3. Choose Section from the Format menu or press Option-F14. The Section dialog box appears.

4. Click the Margin Page Numbers check box to turn on page numbering.

5. Click the Different First Page check box. This option suppresses the printing of page numbers on the first page of your document.

6. If you want to change the page-number position, type new measurements in the From Top and From Right text boxes.

7. Choose OK to confirm your page-number choices and close the dialog box.

Changing the Number Format

You also can use the Section dialog box to change the number format. The Format list box offers five options: Arabic (1, 2, 3), uppercase Roman (I, II, III), lowercase Roman (i, ii, iii), uppercase letters (A, B, C), and lowercase letters (a, b, c). Many writers use non-Arabic page numbers for appendixes, introductions, and prefaces.

To change the number format, follow these steps:

1. Choose Section from the Format menu or press Option-F14. The Section dialog box appears.

2. Activate the Margin Page Numbers option to turn on page numbering.

3. If you want to change the page-number position, type new measurements in the From Top and From Right text boxes.

4. Drop down the Format list box and select a number format (see fig. 11.3).

Fig. 11.3
Format list.

Page-number format list

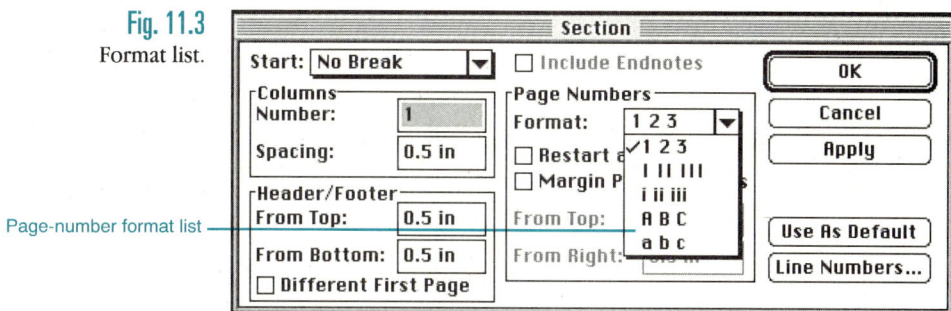

5. Choose OK to confirm your page-number choices.

Repositioning Page Numbers with the Section Dialog Box

After you add page numbers with the Section dialog box, you can reposition or remove them in Print Preview—and vice versa. Print Preview's Page Number icon is directly linked to the Section dialog box. When you make a page-number change in Print Preview, Word updates the Section dialog box. Likewise, changes you make in the Section dialog box are reflected in Print Preview's display of page numbers.

To reposition page numbers with the Section dialog box, follow these steps:

1. Choose Section from the Format menu or press Option-F14. The Section dialog box appears.

2. Type new measurements in the From Top and From Right text boxes. To center page numbers at the bottom of the page, for example, type **10.5**" in the From Top box and **4.5**" in the From Right box.

3. Choose OK to confirm your page-number choices.

Removing Page Numbers

To remove page numbers with the Section dialog box, follow these steps:

1. Choose Section from the Format menu or press Option-F14. The Section dialog box appears.

Chapter 11

Formatting Pages

2. Deactivate the Margin Page Numbers option.

3. Choose OK to confirm your page-number choice.

CAUTION

If you add page numbers in Print Preview or in the Section dialog box but later decide to add page numbers to headers or footers, be sure to remove the original page numbers. Otherwise, Word will print page numbers in two places.

Starting Page Numbering with a Number Other than 1

When you are writing a long document, you may want to place each chapter or section in a separate file. This practice improves Word's performance (the program scrolls small files faster) and lessens your chance of losing the entire document through an accident or mistake. In Chapter 27, "Working with Long Documents," you learn how to link separate files so that they print with continuous pagination. If you prefer, you can set the starting page number of each document manually, as described in the following steps:

1. With the insertion point anywhere in your document, choose Document from the Format menu or press ⌘-F14. The Document dialog box appears.

2. Click the File Series button. The File Series dialog box appears (see fig. 11.4).

Fig. 11.4

File Series dialog box.

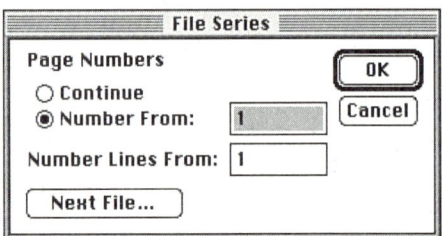

3. Type the starting page number in the Number From text box.

4. Choose OK to close the File Series dialog box. The Document dialog box reappears.

5. Choose OK to close the Document dialog box. Word numbers the pages of your document, using the number you typed in the File Series dialog box as the starting page number.

Changing Margins

In Word, indents are paragraph formats and margins are document formats; Word treats the two formats differently. You can choose a different indent for each paragraph, including single-line paragraphs such as headings. You also can vary indents as you please, creating complex patterns to highlight important text in your document.

By contrast, you can choose only one margin setting for the entire document. You cannot vary the margin setting, even if you break your document into sections (see Chapter 21 for more information on sections).

Figure 11.5 illustrates one of the design possibilities that stem from the difference between indents and margins.

Fig. 11.5
Document with outdented headings.

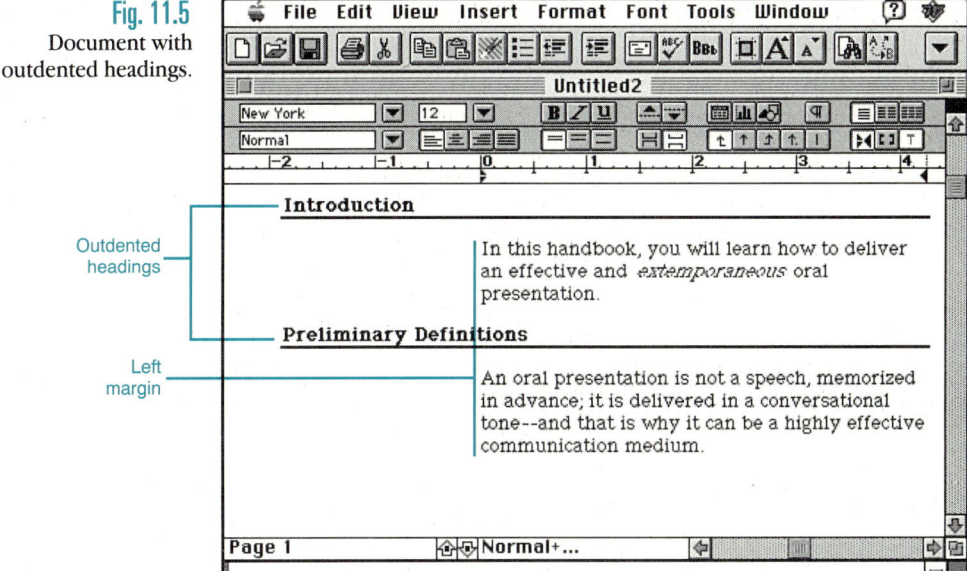

In this document, the left margin is set at 0 inches from the left edge of the page. (The Page Layout view of the document displays the left-margin indicator as a pair of triangles extending below the 0 mark on the ruler. The 0 mark always shows the position of the document's left margin.) The paragraphs containing the headings, however, are formatted with a negative indent of 2 inches. A thick line under each heading, added with the Border command, creates a visually pleasing effect. (For more information on the Border command, see Chapter 17, "Using Borders and Shading.") To sum up this example, you set *margins* for the entire document, but you can set *indents* separately for individual paragraphs, including *outdents* (negative indents).

By default, Word uses 1-inch top and bottom margins and 1 1/4-inch left and right margins. These margins work well for business letters, but the left and right settings may not be appropriate for reports or articles. You may need to add extra space on the page (called a *gutter*) to make room for binding your document. The following sections explain the procedures you use to change the margins and add a gutter.

Understanding Margin-Changing Options

Word provides several techniques for changing margins. In Print Preview, for example, you can change any margin—top, bottom, left, or right—simply by dragging its boundary marker.

You also can use the ruler to change margins. When you click the Margin Marker icon in the ruler, Word displays brackets showing the current locations of the left and right margins. You can change the left and right margins by dragging these brackets. The change affects the entire document.

The Document dialog box provides the greatest degree of flexibility for changing the margins in your document. The options in this dialog box enable you not only to change all the margins, but also to create gutters; define mirror margins for two-sided printing; and control the way Word adjusts the top and bottom margins to make room for headers, footers, and footnotes.

Changing Margins in Print Preview

In Print Preview, boundary markers indicate the margin settings. Dotted lines, each with a black square at one end, show all four margins (see fig. 11.6).

These black squares are called *handles* because you can use them to manipulate the margins. To change the margins, drag the handles.

To change margins in Print Preview, follow these steps:

1. Choose Print Preview from the Print menu or press ⌘-Option-I. Word displays your document in Print Preview.

2. If you do not see the boundary markers, activate the Boundary Marker icon.

3. Move the mouse pointer to one of the handles. The pointer changes to a crosshair pointer.

4. Drag the handle. While you drag it, keep your eye on the area that normally displays the page number. Word informs you of the pointer's current position.

5. When the margin is where you want it, release the mouse button.

6. Click Close to exit Print Preview or click the Printer icon to print your document.

After you set margins in Print Preview, you can use the same technique to adjust them at any time.

Fig. 11.6
Boundary markers and handles (Print Preview).

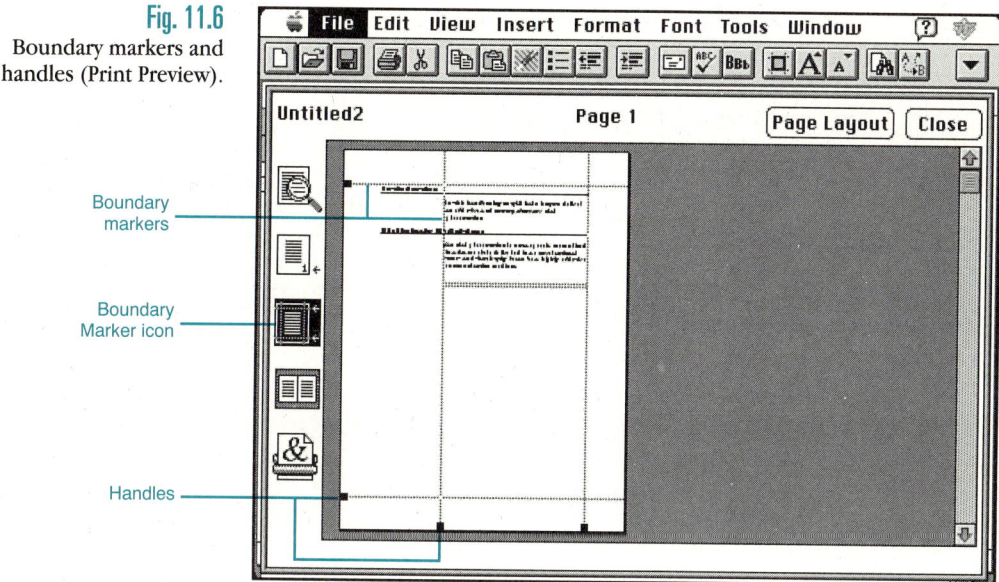

Boundary markers

Boundary Marker icon

Handles

Changing Margins with the Ruler

The ruler provides a fast and convenient way to change the right or left margin. You cannot change the top and bottom margins with the ruler; use Print Preview or the Document dialog box to change top and bottom margins.

To change the left or right margin with the ruler, follow these steps:

1. Click the Margin Marker icon in the ruler. After you click this icon, brackets replace the indent markers in the ruler (see fig. 11.7).

Fig. 11.7

Brackets showing current margin settings.

Left margin

Right margin

Margin Marker icon

Indent Marker icon

2. To change the left margin, drag the left bracket. To change the right margin, drag the right bracket. When you drag a bracket, watch the page-number area to see the pointer's current location.

3. When the bracket is in the desired location, release the mouse button.

4. Click the Indent Marker icon to restore the indent markers in the ruler.

NOTE

Your changes affect the entire document, regardless of section breaks.

Changing Margins with the Document Dialog Box

The Print Preview and ruler techniques for changing margins have some limitations. When you drag a boundary marker or a margin bracket, you can make changes only in 1/16-inch increments. Further, you cannot use these techniques to create gutters or mirror margins. To specify more precise margin measurements and to create gutters or mirror margins, you must use the Document dialog box.

To set margins in the Document dialog box, follow these steps:

1. Choose Document from the Format menu or press ⌘-F14. The Document dialog box appears (see fig. 11.8).

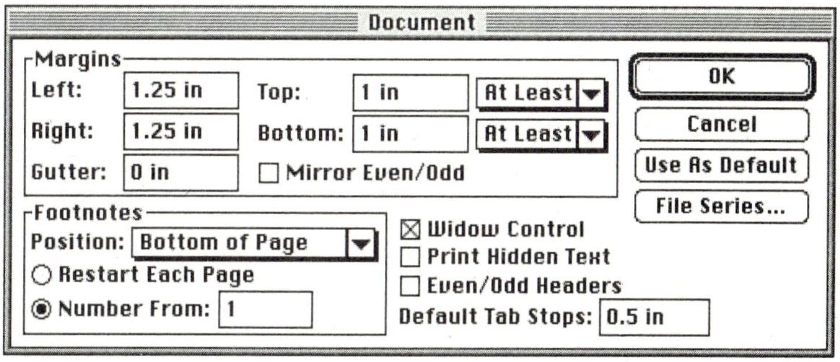

Fig. 11.8
Document dialog box.

```
▒▒▒▒▒▒▒▒▒▒▒▒▒▒▒▒▒▒▒ Document ▒▒▒▒▒▒▒▒▒▒▒▒▒▒▒▒▒
┌─Margins────────────────────────────────┐   ┌─────────────────┐
│ Left:   [1.25 in]  Top:    [1 in]  [At Least ▼]  │   OK        │
│ Right:  [1.25 in]  Bottom: [1 in]  [At Least ▼]  └─────────────────┘
│ Gutter: [0 in]     ☐ Mirror Even/Odd        │   ┌─ Cancel ──────┐
│                                             │   └─────────────────┘
┌─Footnotes───────────────────────────────┐  ┌ Use As Default ┐
│ Position: [Bottom of Page    ▼]           │  └─────────────────┘
│ ○ Restart Each Page    ☒ Widow Control    │  ┌ File Series... ┐
│ ◉ Number From: [1]     ☐ Print Hidden Text│  └─────────────────┘
│                        ☐ Even/Odd Headers │
│                        Default Tab Stops: [0.5 in]
└──────────────────────────────────────────┘
```

2. Type measurements in the Left, Right, Top, and Bottom text boxes. If you do not type a measurement abbreviation, Word uses its default measurement (inches).

3. Choose OK to confirm your choices and to close the dialog box. Your choices affect the entire document.

When you choose top and bottom margins in the Document dialog box, you can specify that Word adjust these margins to make room for long headers or footers. In the drop-down list boxes to the right of the Top and Bottom text boxes, you can select either of two options: At Least (the default) and Exactly. The At Least option tells Word to make room, if necessary, for multiple-line headers or footers.

When you choose the Exactly option, Word always prints the designated margins. Many newsletters and other desktop-published documents look better with consistent margins. For such documents, you do not want Word to adjust the margins.

Accommodating Binding

If you are planning to bind your printed document, you can add extra space to make room for the binding. Word can accommodate binding for one-sided or two-sided pages. You can add the necessary extra space in any of three ways:

■ *Increase the left margin.* Use this option if your document's pages are one-sided. Try adding 1/2 inch to the left margin and leaving the right margin as it is.

■ *Add a gutter.* Use this option if you plan to bind your document with facing pages. Word adds the binding gutter on the left side of odd-numbered pages and on the right side of even-numbered pages. To add a gutter, type a measurement in the Gutter text box in the Document dialog box. Figure 11.9 shows a binding gutter.

Fig. 11.9
Gutters for facing pages.

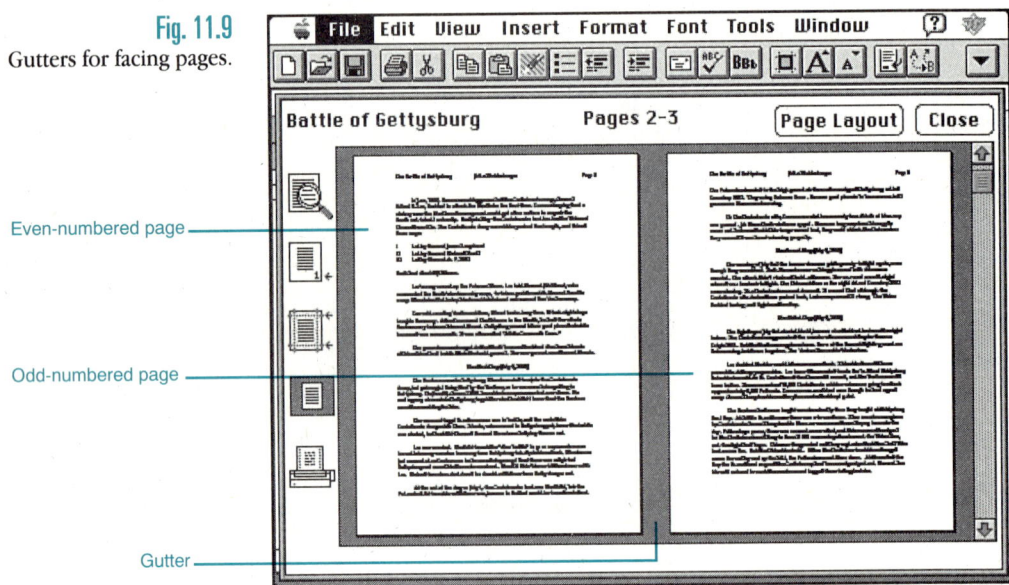

■ *Use mirror margins.* Use this option if you plan to use two-sided pages in your document and want to create different running heads for the odd and even pages. When you use this option, you add extra space to the left margin. When Word prints your document, the program reverses the left and right margin settings on even-numbered pages, producing the effect shown in figure 11.10.

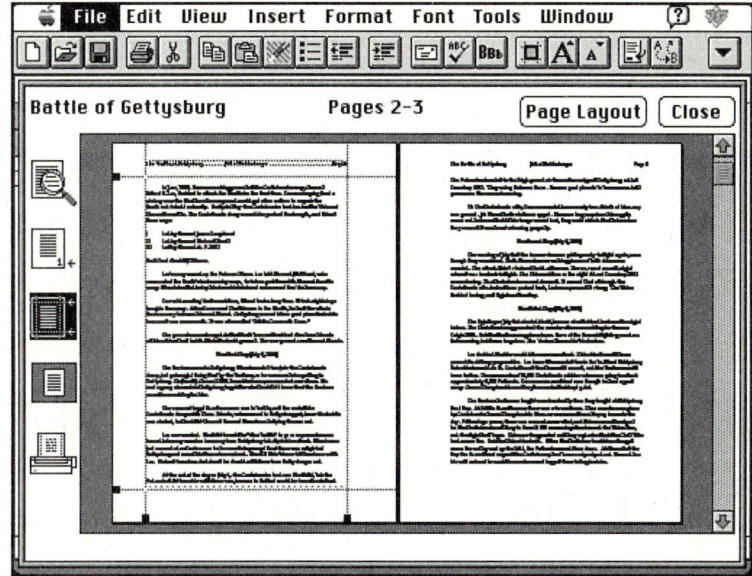

Fig. 11.10
Mirror margins.

To print your document with mirror margins, type a larger left-margin measurement in the Left text box in the Document dialog box and activate the Mirror Even/Odd option.

NOTE

Gutters prevent anything from printing in the space set aside for binding.

Controlling Page Breaks

After you fill a page with text, Word automatically starts a new page by inserting a *soft page break*. In Normal view, a soft page break looks like a row of dots, interspersed with spaces, across the screen. If you later add or delete text above the page break, Word adjusts the soft page break's location.

You can force Word to start a new page even before you fill a page with text. You might want to start a new page, for example, to begin a new chapter of a book or dissertation. To force Word to start a new page, choose Page Break from the Insert menu; Word inserts a *hard page break* at the insertion-point location. In Normal view, a hard page break

Chapter 11

Formatting Pages

looks like a solid row of dots across the screen. Even if you add or delete text above the hard page break, Word still breaks the page at the hard page break's location.

Hard page breaks are not the only way to determine how and where Word breaks pages. *Section breaks* also are useful, especially if you plan to duplicate your document on both sides of the paper. A section break looks like a double row of dots across the screen.

In addition to hard page breaks and section breaks, Word provides other ways to control page breaks, including the Keep Lines Together and Keep with Next options in the Paragraph dialog box. You also can choose an option that suppresses *widows* (the last line of a paragraph left alone at the top of a page) and *orphans* (the first line of a paragraph left alone at the bottom of a page).

If you add hidden text to your document, be sure to turn off the display of hidden text before deciding whether your page breaks are accurate. When displayed, hidden text alters the positions of page breaks in documents. To turn off the display of hidden text, choose Preferences from the Tools menu to open the Preferences dialog box; click the View icon to display the View options; deselect the Hidden Text option; and then click the close box to confirm your choice and close the dialog box.

Repaginating Your Document

By default, Word updates soft page breaks while you create and edit your text. This active updating is called *background repagination*. If your Mac is slow (an SE or Plus, for example), you may want to turn background repagination off by deactivating the Background Repagination option in the Preferences dialog box (General options). When this option is deactivated, Word doesn't paginate your document until you print it.

If you turn background repagination off, the page breaks in your document may not be accurate while you are editing. You can force pagination at any time, however, by choosing Repaginate Now from the Tools menu or clicking the Repaginate tool (see inside front cover).

Inserting Hard Page Breaks

Word gives you more than one way to insert a hard page break. You can use the Page Break command in the Insert menu, press the Page Break keyboard shortcut, or use Print Preview.

To insert a hard page break with the Page Break command or its keyboard shortcut, follow these steps:

1. Position the insertion point in your document where you want the hard page break to occur.

2. Choose Page Break from the Insert menu or press Shift-Enter. Word enters a row of dots across the screen.

Word does not print your document if you inadvertently format the page break as hidden text. If you are using hidden text extensively in your document, select the page break and then choose Character from the Format menu or press ⌘-D to open the Character dialog box. If the hidden-text option is activated, turn it off.

To insert a hard page break in Print Preview, follow these steps:

1. Position the insertion point in your document where you want the page break to occur.

2. Choose Print Preview from the File menu or press ⌘-Option-I. Word displays your document in a Print Preview window.

3. Move the mouse pointer to the soft page break (the dotted horizontal line just above the bottom margin shown in fig. 11.11). The pointer changes to a crosshair pointer.

Fig. 11.11
Soft page break in Print Preview.

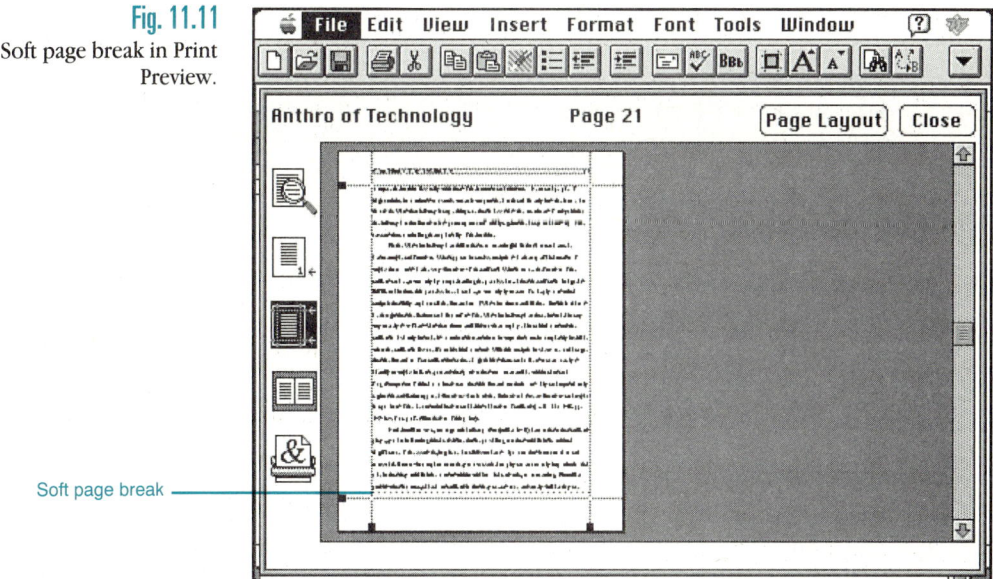

Soft page break

4. Drag the page break up the screen. As you drag, keep your eye on the page-number area to track the pointer's location.

5. When the page break is where you want it, release the mouse button. Word repaginates your document.

6. Click the Close button to return to your document or click the Printer icon to print your document.

Use hard page breaks to control page breaks as a last resort, however. Suppose that you added headings to your document and discover in Print Preview that one of the headings is widowed at the bottom of the page; the text that follows the heading has been moved to the following page. You can insert a hard page break just above the heading to correct the break. If you later add or delete text before the heading, however, the hard page break remains in your document and forces a page break in an inappropriate location.

To avert problems that can arise when you edit text after inserting hard page breaks, use hard page breaks only to begin new parts (such as new chapters) of a document. To control page breaks in other situations, use the Paragraph dialog box's Keep With Next and Keep Lines Together options (described later in this chapter).

Removing Hard Page Breaks

If a hard page break has outlived its usefulness, you can delete it. To delete a hard page break in Print Preview, drag the page break off the page. To delete a hard page break in Normal or Page Layout view, follow these steps:

1. Select the hard page break by moving the mouse pointer to the selection bar next to the hard page break and clicking the mouse.

2. Press Backspace or Delete.

Searching for Hard Page Breaks

If you want to remove hard page breaks from your document, first use Word to find them. To search for hard page breaks, follow these steps:

1. Choose Find from the Edit menu or press ⌘-F. The Find dialog box appears.

2. Select Page Break in the Special drop-down list box. Word enters the page-break code (^d) in the Find What box, as shown in figure 11.12. (You can type this code in the text box instead of selecting Page Break, if you prefer.)

Fig. 11.12

Searching for hard page breaks.

```
┌──────────────────────────────────────────────────────────────┐
│ ▪▪▪                         Find                               │
├──────────────────────────────────────────────────────────────┤
│  Find What:     │^d                             │  ┌──────────┐│
│                 └───────────────────────────────┘  │Find Next ││
│      ┌─────────────┐                                └──────────┘│
│      │ Format  ▼   │                                ┌──────────┐│
│      └─────────────┘                                │ Cancel   ││
│      ┌─────────────┐                                └──────────┘│
│      │ Special ▼   │                                            │
│      └─────────────┘                               Search:     │
│   ☐ Match Whole Word Only   ☐ Match Case        ┌────────────┐ │
│                                                 │Down      ▼ │ │
│                                                 └────────────┘ │
└──────────────────────────────────────────────────────────────┘
```

3. Choose Find Next to find the first hard page break.

Using Section Breaks

The Section dialog box provides page-break options that are not available elsewhere in Word. (Sections and section breaks are discussed thoroughly in Chapter 21, "Dividing a Document into Sections.") You can insert a section break anywhere in your document by choosing Section Break from the Insert menu or by pressing ⌘-Enter.

Normally, you insert a section break to restart headers, footers, footnote numbers, or page numbers, as you might when you start a new chapter or an appendix in a long document.

When you use section breaks, you also can choose page-break options. For example, you can choose to break the page so that the next text appears on an odd-numbered page. (If necessary, Word can leave an entire page blank.)

In documents duplicated with facing pages, new sections and chapters always begin on odd-numbered pages, because odd-numbered pages appear to the right of the binding. For such documents, always use the Section Break command to start a new chapter or section of your document.

To insert a section break that moves the next text to an odd-numbered page, follow these steps:

1. Place the insertion point in the document where you want the break to occur.

2. Choose Section Break from the Insert menu or press ⌘-Enter. Word inserts a double row of dots (called a *section mark*) across the screen and positions the insertion point just below the section mark.

3. Choose Section from the Format menu or press Option-F14. The Section dialog box appears.

4. Select Odd Page in the Start drop-down list box.

5. Choose OK.

You can create a style for chapter titles and add the Page Break Before format to the styles. (For information on styles, see Chapter 14.) When you choose the style, Word automatically enters the chapter title's character and paragraph formats and also the page break.

Forcing a Page Break Before a Paragraph

Another way to control page breaks is to choose a paragraph-formatting option that automatically inserts a page break before the paragraph. If you add this format to chapter titles, for example, Word breaks the page before each new chapter.

To force Word to break a page before a paragraph, follow these steps:

1. Position the insertion point in the paragraph you want to format.

2. Choose Paragraph from the Format menu or press ⌘-M. The Paragraph dialog box appears.

3. Activate the Page Break Before option.

4. Choose OK.

You can create heading styles for the headings in your document (see Chapter 14). If you want Word to break a page before a major heading (such as a chapter title), you can add this format to the heading style.

Keeping Lines Together

If you want to prevent page breaks from occurring within paragraphs, you can use the Keep Lines Together option in the Paragraph dialog box. When you choose this option, you prevent Word from inserting page breaks that separate the lines of a paragraph. When a paragraph is too long to fit in a page's remaining space, Word moves the entire paragraph to the top of the next page, keeping all the lines of the paragraph together.

To keep all the lines of a paragraph together on one page, follow these steps:

1. Position the insertion point in the paragraph you want to format.

2. Choose Paragraph from the Format menu or press ⌘-M. The Paragraph dialog box appears.

3. Activate the Keep Lines Together option.

4. Choose OK.

Preventing Unwanted Page Breaks between Paragraphs

Some of your document's headings may be orphaned at the bottom of the page, with a page break dividing them from the body text that follows. When you are in a rush to get your document out the door, you may forget to check for this common formatting problem before printing. A good practice, therefore, is to prevent orphaned headings from occurring. You can format a heading so that Word automatically keeps the heading paragraph with the following paragraph.

To prevent Word from inserting a page break after a paragraph, follow these steps:

1. Position the insertion point in the paragraph you want to format.

2. Choose Paragraph from the Format menu or press ⌘-M. The Paragraph dialog box appears.

3. Activate the Keep With Next option.

4. Choose OK.

Chapter 11

Formatting Pages

Displaying and Using Invisible-Format Marks

After you format a paragraph with the Page Break Before, Keep Lines Together, or Keep with Next option, Word inserts a black square in the selection bar next to the paragraph, indicating that you have chosen an *invisible format* (see Chapter 10, "Formatting Paragraphs")—one that you cannot see on-screen. To display the square, choose Show ¶ from the View menu or click the paragraph-mark icon in the ribbon.

When you see a black square next to a paragraph, you can double-click the square to display the dialog box containing the format you entered. The dialog box reminds you what format you used and also enables you to change or delete the format.

Turning off Widow-and-Orphan Control

By default, Word suppresses widows and orphans by preventing the first or last lines of paragraphs from printing by themselves at the bottoms or tops of pages. If you want to print the same number of lines on each page, however, turn off widow-and-orphan control by following these steps:

1. Choose Document from the Format menu or press ⌘-F14. The Document dialog box appears.

2. Turn off the Widow Control option.

3. Choose OK.

Choosing Paper Size and Page Orientation

Your Macintosh is designed for an international market, and Word easily can accommodate paper sizes other than the default, which is the standard U.S. letter size (8 1/2 by 11 inches). Table 11.1 lists the paper-size settings you can use in Word. Your options may vary , depending on your printer's capabilities.

Name	Size (width by height)
US Letter	8.5 by 11 inches
US Legal	8.5 by 14 inches
A4 Letter	8.5 by 11.67 inches
B5 Letter (LaserWriter II)	7.2 by 10.1 inches
Tabloid	11 by 17 inches
International Fanfold	8.25 by 12 inches
Computer Paper	14 by 11 inches

Table 11.1
Word Paper Sizes

You can choose any of these paper sizes as your default paper size for formatting and printing, or you can define a custom paper size. You also can choose portrait or landscape printing orientation. The following sections detail the procedures for choosing paper sizes and page orientation.

Choosing a Predefined Paper Size

Your printer must be equipped to handle paper-size options other than US Letter. Many printers are adjustable, however, and can accommodate a variety of paper sizes. If you are not sure about your printer's specifications, check its manual.

To choose one of Word's predefined paper sizes, follow these steps:

1. Choose Page Setup from the File menu. The Page Setup dialog box appears (see fig. 11.13).

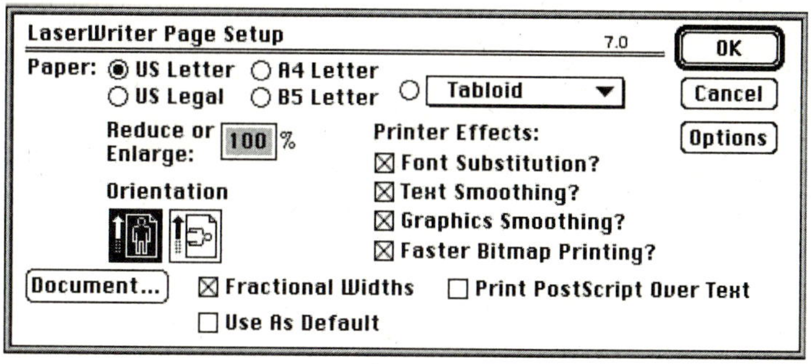

Fig. 11.13
Page Setup dialog box.

Chapter 11
Formatting Pages

2. Choose one of the paper-size options by clicking the appropriate radio button or by selecting an option in the drop-down list box.

3. To make your choice the default for all documents, activate the Use as Default option.

4. Choose OK.

Defining a Custom Paper Size

Some printers can print custom paper sizes, and Word is flexible enough to accommodate virtually any size of paper that a printer can hold. The following procedure enables you to define and use a custom paper size.

To define a custom paper size, follow these steps:

1. Choose Preferences from the Tools menu. The Preferences dialog box appears, with the General icon highlighted and the General options listed.

2. In the Custom Paper Size area, type the appropriate measurements in the Width and Height text boxes.

3. If necessary, select a measurement unit other than inches (the default) in the Measurement Unit drop-down list box.

4. Click the close box to confirm your choice and close the dialog box.

5. Choose Page Setup from the File menu. The Page Setup dialog box appears.

6. Select Custom in the drop-down list box.

7. To make your choice the new default for all documents, activate the Use as Default option.

8. Choose OK.

Some printers, such as the LaserWriter NT, do not accept custom paper sizes. If Word has dimmed the Custom Paper Size boxes in the Preferences dialog box (General options), you cannot choose a custom paper size for your printer.

Specifying the Page Orientation

Normally, you print your document in the default orientation, called *portrait orientation*, in which lines of text run across the shorter dimension of the page. You also can choose *landscape orientation* to position the lines of text across the longer dimension of the page (see fig. 11.14).

Fig. 11.14

Print Preview of document with landscape orientation.

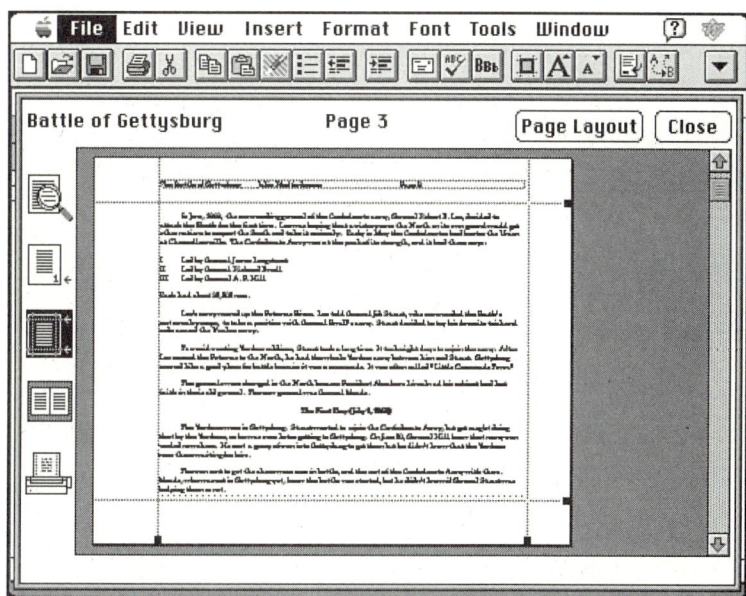

You may want to use landscape orientation to print a wide table or figure that doesn't fit on the page with portrait orientation.

To choose a page orientation, follow these steps:

1. Choose Page Setup from the File menu. The Page Setup dialog box appears.

2. Click the Portrait or Landscape orientation icon.

3. Choose OK.

Your Page Setup orientation choice applies to the active document only.

Quick Review

This section summarizes the most useful information in this chapter. Check "Productivity Tips" for a review of high-productivity tips and tricks—the ones that Macintosh and Word pros use every day. Review "Techniques" whenever you need a quick reminder about a specific procedure.

Productivity Tips

■ Use Print Preview to turn on page numbering unless you want to suppress page numbers on the first page. In Print Preview, double-click the Page Number icon to place page numbers in the default location (upper right corner).

■ To change margins quickly, adjust them in Print Preview. Alternatively, click the Margin Marker icon in the ruler and drag the margin brackets.

■ Don't use a hard page break unless absolutely necessary (such as when you are starting a new chapter in a long document). If you plan to duplicate your document on facing pages, use a section break and format the new section so that it begins on an odd-numbered page.

■ Use the Keep Lines Together and Keep With Next options (Paragraph dialog box) extensively to prevent undesirable page breaks. Always format headings with the Keep With Next option, and be sure to add blank space beneath the headings by using the blank-spacing options rather than pressing Return.

Techniques

This section provides concise summaries of all the procedures introduced in this chapter.

Using Page Numbers

To add page numbers with Print Preview:

1. Choose Print Preview from the File menu or press ⌘-Option-I. Word displays the document in a Print Preview window.

2. To add page numbers in the upper right corner of the page, double-click the Page Number icon.

   To position page numbers elsewhere, click the Page Number icon and hold down the mouse button. The pointer changes to a page number. Drag the page number to the position where you want Word to print page numbers and then release the mouse button.

3. Click the Close button to return to your document or click the Printer icon to print your document.

To add page numbers with the Section dialog box:

1. Choose Section from the Format menu or press Option-F14. The Section dialog box appears.

2. Activate the Margin Page Numbers option to turn on page numbering.

3. If you want to change the default page-number position, type new measurements in the From Top and From Right text boxes.

4. Choose OK.

To suppress page numbering on the first page and number the second page Page 2:

1. Choose Section from the Format menu or press Option-F14. The Section dialog box appears.

2. Activate the Margin Page Numbers option to turn on page numbering.

3. If you want to change the default page-number position, type new measurements in the From Top and From Right text boxes.

4. Activate the Different First Page option, which suppresses the printing of page numbers on the first page of your document.

5. Choose OK.

To suppress page numbering on the first page and number the second page Page 1:

1. Position the insertion point at the beginning of the second page.

2. Choose Section Break from the Format menu or press ⌘-Enter. Word inserts a section break at the insertion-point location.

3. Choose Section from the Format menu or press Option-F14. The Section dialog box appears.

4. Activate the Margin Page Numbers option to turn on page numbering.

5. If you want to change the default page-number position, type new measurements in the From Top and From Right text boxes.

6. Activate the Restart at 1 option.

7. Choose OK.

To reposition or remove page numbers in Print Preview:

1. Choose Print Preview from the File menu or press ⌘-Option-I. Word displays the document in a Print Preview window.

2. Position the mouse pointer on the page number in your document. The pointer changes to a crosshair pointer.

3. To reposition the page number, drag it to its new location. To remove the page number, drag it off the page.

4. Click Close to return to your document.

To reposition page numbers with the Section dialog box:

1. Choose Section from the Format menu or press Option-F14. The Section dialog box appears.

2. Type new measurements in the From Top and From Right text boxes.

3. Choose OK.

To remove page numbers with the Section dialog box:

1. Choose Section from the Format menu or press Option-F14. The Section dialog box appears.

2. Deactivate the Margin Page Numbers option.

3. Choose OK.

To change the page-number format:

1. Choose Section from the Format menu or press Option-F14. The Section dialog box appears.

2. Activate the Margin Page Numbers option to turn on page numbering.

3. If you want to change the default page-number position, type new measurements in the From Top and From Right text boxes.

4. Select the number format you want in the Format drop-down list box.

5. Choose OK.

Moving Margins

To change margins in Print Preview:

1. Choose Print Preview from the Print menu or press ⌘-Option-I. Word displays the document in a Print Preview window.

2. To display the boundary markers, click the Boundary Marker icon.

3. Move the pointer to one of the handles (the black squares). The pointer changes to a crosshair pointer.

4. Drag the handle.

5. When the margin is where you want it, release the mouse button.

6. Click the Close button to return to your document or click the Printer icon to print your document.

To change the left or right margin with the ruler:

1. Click the Margin Marker icon. Brackets appear at the margin locations in the ruler.

2. To change the left margin, drag the left bracket. To change the right margin, drag the right bracket.

3. When a bracket is where you want the margin to be, release the mouse button.

4. Click the Indent Marker icon to restore the indent markers in the ruler.

To set margins with the Document dialog box:

1. Choose Document from the Format menu or press ⌘-F14. The Document dialog box appears.

2. Type new measurements in the Top, Bottom, Left, and Right text boxes.

3. To prevent Word from adjusting the top or bottom margins to make room for long headers or footers, select Exactly in the drop-down list box next to the Top or Bottom text box.

4. Choose OK.

Adding Gutters for Binding

To add a gutter to a document duplicated with one-sided pages:

1. Choose Document from the Format menu or press ⌘-F14. The Document dialog box appears.

2. Type a new measurement (try adding half an inch) in the Left text box.

3. Choose OK.

To add a gutter to a document duplicated on both sides of the page:

1. Choose Document from the Format menu or press ⌘-F14. The Document dialog box appears.

2. Perform one of the following actions:

   ■ Type a new measurement in the Gutter text box (try **0.5"**).

   or

   ■ Type a new measurement in the Left text box (try **0.5"**) and then activate the Mirror Margins option.

3. Choose OK.

Repaginating a Document

To turn off background repagination:

1. Choose Preferences from the Tools menu. The Preferences dialog box appears, with the General icon highlighted and the General options listed.

2. Turn off the Background Repagination option.

3. Choose OK.

To repaginate your document after turning off background repagination:

Choose Repaginate Now from the Tools menu or click the Repaginate tool.

Breaking Pages

To insert a hard page break with the Page Break option:

1. Position the insertion point in the document where you want the hard page break to occur.

2. Choose Page Break from the Insert menu or press Shift-Enter.

To insert a hard page break in Print Preview:

1. Position the insertion point in the document where you want the page break to occur.

2. Choose Print Preview from the File menu or press ⌘-Option-I. Word displays the document in a Print Preview window.

3. Move the mouse pointer to the soft page break. The pointer becomes a crosshair pointer.

4. Press and hold the mouse button while you drag the page break up the page.

5. When the page break is where you want it, release the mouse button.

6. Click the Close button to return to your document or click the Printer icon to print your document.

To delete a hard page break in Normal or Page Layout view:

1. Select the hard page break.

2. Press Backspace or Delete.

To delete a hard page break in Print Preview:

Drag the page break off the page.

To force Word to break a page before a paragraph:

1. Position the insertion point in the paragraph you want to format.

2. Choose Paragraph from the Format menu or press ⌘-M. The Paragraph dialog box appears.

3. Activate the Page Break Before option.

4. Choose OK.

To insert a section break that starts the next text on an odd-numbered page:

1. Place the insertion point in the document where you want the break to occur.

2. Choose Section Break from the Insert menu or press ⌘-Enter. Word inserts a section break at the insertion-point location.

3. Choose Section from the Format menu or press Option-F14. The Section dialog box appears.

4. Select Odd Page in the Start drop-down list box.

5. Choose OK.

Keeping Text Together

To create text that Word will keep together:

1. Position the insertion point in the paragraph.

2. Choose Paragraph from the Format menu or press ⌘-M. The Paragraph dialog box appears.

3. Activate the Keep Lines Together option.

4. Choose OK.

To prevent Word from inserting a page break after a paragraph:

1. Position the insertion point in the paragraph you want to format.

2. Choose Paragraph from the Format menu or press ⌘-M. The Paragraph dialog box appears.

3. Activate the Keep With Next option.

4. Choose OK.

Keeping the Same Number of Lines on Each Page

To turn off widow-and-orphan control so that the same number of lines print on each page:

1. Choose Document from the Format menu or press ⌘-F14. The Document dialog box appears.

2. Turn off the Widow Control option.

3. Choose OK.

Choosing a Paper Size

To choose one of Word's predefined paper sizes:

1. Choose Page Setup from the File menu. The Page Setup dialog box appears.

2. Choose one of the paper-size options by clicking a radio button or making a selection in the drop-down list box.

3. To make the paper size you chose the default for all documents, activate the Use as Default option.

4. Choose OK.

To define a custom paper size (if your printer can print a custom size):

1. Choose Preferences from the Tools menu. The Preferences dialog box appears, with the General icon highlighted and the General options listed.

2. In the Custom Paper Size area, type the appropriate measurements in the Width and Height text boxes.

3. Click the close box to confirm your choices and close the dialog box.

4. Choose Page Setup from the File menu. The Page Setup dialog box appears.

5. Select Custom in the drop-down list box.

6. To make your paper-size choice the new default for all documents, activate the Use as Default option.

7. Choose OK.

Choosing Page Orientation

To choose a page orientation:

1. Choose Page Setup from the File menu. The Page Setup dialog box appears.

2. Click the Portrait or Landscape orientation icon.

3. Choose OK.

Checking Spelling and Grammar

Y our writing should be free of errors in spelling, usage, style, and grammar. Even the most attractively printed document loses its authority when the reader encounters errors.

Word cannot detect every writing error you make, but the program can detect many common errors—the errors that an unfriendly reader might use to justify an adverse opinion of you and your organization.

Word is equipped with a spelling checker (called Spelling) and with a usage, style, and grammar checker (called Grammar). These features support the program's status as the premier writing program for business and the professions.

Word 5.1 offers an improved Spelling utility that gives you more feedback on the progress of a spelling check, so you're not left waiting and wondering whether your Mac has crashed. In addition, you can cancel a spelling check by pressing ⌘-period (.) or Esc at any time. Word 5.1 offers improved handling of large custom dictionaries, which used to consume a great deal of spell-checking time. The program also has improved its handling of words you choose to ignore during a spelling check: the Ignore All button now tells Word to ignore the word for the rest of the current Word session, not just in the current document. These Word 5.1 changes affect only the performance of the spell checker, so if you're using 5.0, the material in this chapter still applies.

USING
WORD 5.1
FOR THE MAC
SPECIAL EDITION

This chapter details the use of Spelling and Grammar. Following is an overview of this chapter's contents:

- *Checking spelling.* In this section, you learn how to make Spelling work for you by customizing the way Word runs this utility. You learn how to choose among Spelling's many options and how to create custom dictionaries.

- *Checking grammar.* In this section, you learn how to use Word's new Grammar utility, which can help you write more strongly and clearly.

CAUTION

Keep in mind that running Spelling and Grammar will not save you from criticism if your document is poorly organized. Writing experts agree that the main determinants of writing quality are organization and coherence. A poorly organized brochure or proposal, or one that doesn't make sense, will not impress your clients and customers, even if the spelling is letter-perfect. If you need help organizing your ideas, try using Word's Outline utility, discussed in Chapter 22, "Organizing Documents with Outlining."

Checking Spelling in a Document

Business and professional writing requires perfect spelling. Many people consider spelling or typographical errors to be signs of limited intelligence, lack of professionalism, or carelessness. You cannot afford to make a negative impression, and with Word's spell-checking feature, you can make sure that you don't. Run Word's spell-checking utility in every document that will leave your computer.

Spell Checking a Document

Like all computer spell-checking utilities, Word's Spelling utility doesn't really check spelling; it actually compares the words in your document, one by one, with correctly spelled words stored in the program's dictionaries. When Spelling cannot find a match, it indicates that the word is unknown.

A word categorized as unknown, however, may be spelled correctly. Many proper nouns—the names of people and places, for example— aren't in the program's dictionaries. To prevent Spelling from flagging a frequently used proper noun, you can add the word to the dictionary. Be aware, too, that the spell-checking utility skips over a correctly spelled word used in the wrong context. Spell check your document, but remember that nothing can substitute for final proofreading.

Spelling doesn't check the spelling of hidden text unless the text is displayed. To display hidden text, choose Show Hidden Text in the Preferences dialog box (View options), which you access from the Tools menu.

To speed spell checking, switch to Normal view. In Page Layout view, Spelling runs slower because more time is required to scroll to each error's location.

You can check spelling in your entire document or only a selected portion (a word, sentence, paragraph, or block of text). If you don't select any text, Spelling begins checking your document from the insertion point's location. When Spelling reaches the end of the document, an alert box appears, asking whether you want to continue checking from the beginning of the document. If you choose OK, Spelling continues from the beginning until it reaches the insertion point again.

To check spelling, follow these steps:

1. To check the entire document, click the location at which you want the spell check to start. To check a selection, select the text.

2. Choose Spelling from the Tools menu or press ⌘-L.

   If you're using Word 5.1, you also can click the Spelling tool.

   The Spelling dialog box appears when the spell checker finds the first word that cannot be matched in the built-in spelling dictionaries (see fig. 12.1). The unknown word is displayed after `Not in Dictionary`.

Fig. 12.1
Spelling dialog box, displaying an unknown word and suggestions.

Spelling	
Not in Dictionary: thier	
Change To: their	Ignore / Ignore All
Suggestions: their, there, Thai, thinner	Change / Change All / Add / Close / Suggest / Options...
Add Words To: <NONE>	

Chapter 12
Checking Spelling and Grammar

By default, Spelling displays a list of potentially correct spellings in the Suggestions list box and places the first suggestion in the Change To box. If the spell checker cannot suggest any words, (No Suggestions) appears in the Suggestions list box, as shown in figure 12.2, and the unknown word also appears in the Change To box.

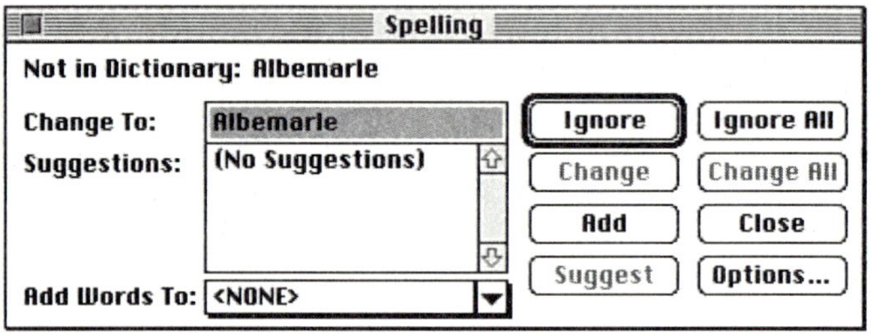

Fig. 12.2
Spelling dialog box,
displaying no suggestions.

```
┌────────────────────────────────────────────────────────────┐
│ ▣ ▤▤▤▤▤▤▤▤▤▤▤▤▤▤▤▤▤  Spelling  ▤▤▤▤▤▤▤▤▤▤▤▤▤▤▤▤▤       │
│  Not in Dictionary: Albemarle                                │
│                                                              │
│  Change To:    [Albemarle        ]   ┌─Ignore──┐  ┌Ignore All┐│
│  Suggestions:  [(No Suggestions) ⇧]    Change     Change All  │
│                [                 ]     Add        Close       │
│                [                ⇩]     Suggest    Options...  │
│  Add Words To: [<NONE>          ▾]                            │
└────────────────────────────────────────────────────────────┘
```

3. Perform one of the following actions:

   ■ *Accept Spelling's suggestion.* Click Change to accept the suggestion that Spelling placed in the Change To text box. Then click Change All if you want to make this change throughout the document without asking for confirmation of each change.

   ■ *Choose another suggested word.* If Spelling suggested the correct spelling but didn't place it in the Change To box, choose the correct spelling by highlighting it and then clicking Change (or by double-clicking the word). Then click Change All if you want the spell checker to make this change throughout the document without asking for confirmation of each change.

   ■ *Change the word in the Change To box.* If Spelling cannot make a suggestion for an incorrectly spelled word, edit the word in the Change To box. After you correct the spelling, click Change. Then click Change All if you want the spell checker to make this change throughout your document without asking for confirmation of each change.

   ■ *Close the Spelling dialog box (or simply click in the document window) and make the change in your document.* You may prefer this procedure if you see additional errors, such as a garbled sentence, that mandate rewriting as well as correcting the spelling error. To return to Spelling, choose Spelling from the Tools menu, press ⌘-L, or click the Spelling tool. Spell checking resumes from the insertion point's location.

VERSION 5.1

■ *Leave the word unchanged and continue.* If the word is correctly spelled but you will not use it in any other document, choose Ignore to skip the word once, or click Ignore All to skip all occurrences of this word in your document.

If you're using Word 5.1, Ignore All tells Spelling to skip this word during this session and all future Word sessions.

■ *Add the word to a custom dictionary.* If the word is correctly spelled and you plan to use it frequently, click Add to add the word to the current dictionary. (By default, no custom dictionary is selected, as indicated by <NONE> in the Add Words To drop-down list box.)

■ *Delete a repeated word.* If the spell checker finds a repeated word (such as *the the*), the message Repeated Word appears instead of Not in Dictionary, and the Change button becomes the Delete button (see fig. 12.3).

Fig. 12.3
Correcting a repeated word.

```
┌─────────────────────────────────────────────────────┐
│ ▣                      Spelling                       │
│ Repeated Word:   the                                  │
│                                                       │
│ Change To:    [              ]    ┌─────────┐ ┌──────────┐
│                                   │ Ignore  │ │Ignore All│
│ Suggestions:  [              ]↑   └─────────┘ └──────────┘
│               [              ]    ┌─────────┐ ┌──────────┐
│               [              ]    │ Delete  │ │Change All│
│               [              ]    └─────────┘ └──────────┘
│               [              ]↓   ┌─────────┐ ┌──────────┐
│                                   │  Add    │ │  Close   │
│ Add Words To: [<NONE>       ▼]    └─────────┘ └──────────┘
│                                   ┌─────────┐ ┌──────────┐
│                                   │ Suggest │ │Options...│
│                                   └─────────┘ └──────────┘
└─────────────────────────────────────────────────────┘
```

To delete the repeated word from your document, click Delete.

4. Repeat step 3 until Spelling informs you that it has reached the end of the document or the selection.

If Spelling reaches the end of the document or selection without checking all your text, an alert box appears, asking whether you want to continue checking spelling from the beginning. Choose OK to continue checking, or click Cancel to stop checking.

Choosing Spelling Options

By default, Spelling checks the spelling of all the text in your document, including words typed in uppercase letters and words containing numbers. The utility also suggests correct spellings by default. If you're

Chapter 12
Checking Spelling and Grammar

typing a document that contains many acronyms or technical expressions, you might want to choose options that tell Spelling to skip such words. If you're using one of the slower Macs, such as a Plus or Classic, you also may want to disable suggestions so that Spelling checks documents faster. You can change these defaults by using the Spelling options in the Preferences dialog box.

To choose spelling options, follow these steps:

1. Choose Preferences from the Tools menu to open the Preferences dialog box, and then click the Spelling icon. The Spelling options appear in the dialog box.

   Alternatively, click Options in the Spelling dialog box. The Preferences dialog box appears with the Spelling options already listed (see fig. 12.4).

Fig. 12.4

Preferences dialog box (Spelling options; Word 5.1).

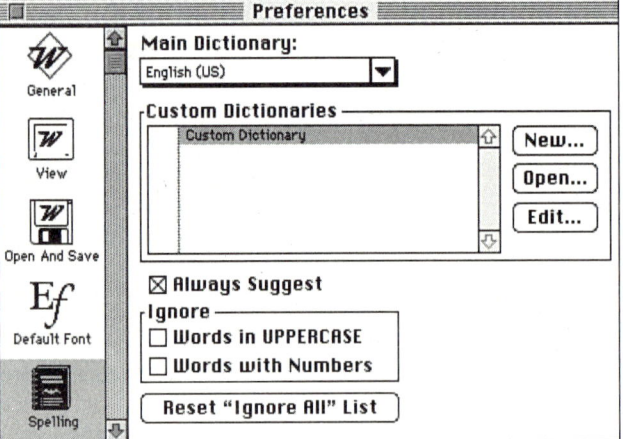

2. To turn off automatic suggestions of changes for correctly spelled words, deactivate the Always Suggest option.

3. To skip words in uppercase letters, activate the Words in UPPER-CASE option in the Ignore section.

4. To skip words that contain numbers, activate the Words with Numbers option in the Ignore section.

5. Click the close box to confirm your choices and close the Preferences dialog box.

Word 5.1 users also see a button called Reset "Ignore All" List in the Preferences dialog box. In this version of Word, clicking Ignore All while Spelling is running tells the program to ignore the word in all documents for the rest of the current operating session. If you previously chose Ignore All but now want Spelling to flag all unknown words, click this button to cancel Ignore All.

Using Custom Dictionaries

As you learned in the preceding section, you can add correctly spelled words to Spelling's dictionary. You should add frequently used proper nouns, such as your name, street name, town name, company name, and the names of colleagues and co-workers. After you add these words, Spelling does not flag them as unknown, and spell checking proceeds more quickly.

You cannot access the words in the main dictionary, which are stored in a special compressed file format. When you add words to Spelling's dictionary, Word doesn't add them to the main dictionary, for good reason: if you add an incorrectly spelled word to this dictionary, you cannot repair the error.

Rather than add words to the main dictionary, Spelling adds them to the default custom dictionary. A *custom dictionary* is a user-accessible dictionary that contains the words you add. You can remove a word you added to a custom dictionary by following the procedure detailed later in this chapter.

If no custom dictionary is activated, you see <NONE> in the Add Words To drop-down list box (Spelling dialog box). To activate a custom dictionary, click the Options command button. The Options dialog box appears. In the Custom Dictionaries list box, click next to the name of the custom dictionary you want so that a check mark appears. Then click the close box to resume spell checking.

Using More Than One Custom Dictionary

You can create more than one custom dictionary, if you want, and then choose the one to which you want to add words during a spell-checking session.

Although Word 5.1 enables you to create additional custom dictionaries, this capability is of interest mainly to Word 5.0 users. In Word 5.0, custom dictionaries are limited to 1,000 words. Good practice with Word 5.0 requires creating several custom dictionaries, differentiated by subject, and adding words to the appropriate dictionary. In Word 5.1, you can add an unlimited number of words to a custom dictionary.

Following are some examples of custom dictionaries divided by subject:

- *General Correspondence.* This dictionary could contain the names of friends and family members with whom you correspond frequently, and also important proper nouns in your personal life (street names, city names, and so on).

- *Business Correspondence.* This dictionary could contain the names of business associates, contacts, organizations, and companies. The dictionary also could list important proper nouns in your business life (the name of your boss, the name of your boss' spouse, and so on).

- *Technical/Legal.* This dictionary could contain terms, jargon, and proper nouns needed for spell checking technical or legal reports, proposals, and similar documents.

After you decide on a way to divide your user dictionaries, you can create new custom dictionaries as follows:

1. Choose Preferences from the Tools menu. The Preferences dialog box appears.

2. Click the Spelling icon to list the Spelling options.

3. In the Custom Dictionaries area, click New. The Save As dialog box appears, displaying the message `Save new custom dictionary as`.

4. Type a name (no longer than 31 characters) for the new custom dictionary.

5. If necessary, use the current-folder list box to open the Word Commands folder so that your new custom dictionary is placed in the same folder as Word's main dictionary.

6. Choose Save. Word creates the new custom dictionary and opens it.

You can tell which dictionary is open by looking at the Custom Dictionaries list in the Preferences dialog box. A check mark indicates that a custom dictionary is open (see fig. 12.5).

Fig. 12.5
Selecting a custom dictionary.

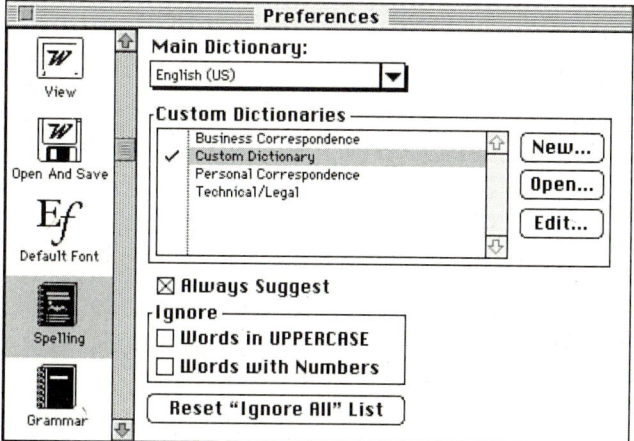

You can open more than one custom dictionary at a time. To open a dictionary, click next to its name so that a check mark appears. When more than one custom dictionary is open, Word uses all the open dictionaries to spell check your document. In addition, the names of the open dictionaries appear in the Add Words To drop-down list box (Spelling dialog box).

To add words to your new custom dictionary, you first must activate the dictionary by selecting it in the Add Words To list box. Thereafter, when you click the Add button in the Spelling dialog box, Word adds the word to that dictionary.

To close a custom dictionary, follow these steps:

1. Choose Preferences from the Tools menu. The Preferences dialog box appears.

2. Click the Spelling icon to list the Spelling options.

3. In the Custom Dictionaries list box, click the check mark next to the name of the current custom dictionary. The check mark disappears.

4. Click the close box to confirm your choice and close the dialog box.

Chapter 12
Checking Spelling and Grammar

After you close a custom dictionary, you can reopen it quickly. To open a custom dictionary, follow these steps:

1. Choose Preferences from the Tools menu. The Preferences dialog box appears.

2. Click the Spelling icon to list the Spelling options.

3. In the Custom Dictionaries list box, click to the left of the name of the custom dictionary you want to open. A check mark appears next to the name.

4. Click the close box to confirm your choice and close the Preferences dialog box.

Deleting Words from a Custom Dictionary

If you add an incorrectly spelled word to a custom dictionary, don't be concerned; you can remove the word easily with the following procedure.

To remove a word from a custom dictionary, follow these steps:

1. Choose Preferences from the Tools menu. The Preferences dialog box appears.

2. Click the Spelling icon to list the Spelling options.

3. In the Custom Dictionaries list box, select the custom dictionary you want to edit.

4. Click Edit. The Edit Custom Dictionary dialog box appears (see fig. 12.6).

Fig. 12.6
Edit Custom Dictionary dialog box.

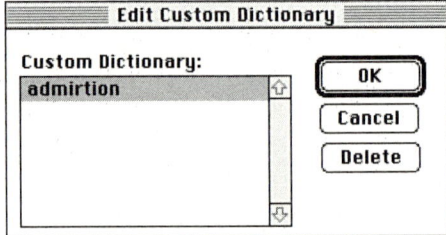

5. Highlight the word you want to delete.

6. Click Delete.

7. Repeat steps 5 and 6 until you have removed all the words that you want to delete.

8. Choose OK to close the Edit Custom Dictionary dialog box and return to the Preferences dialog box. (If you click Cancel, Spelling disregards your deletion and closes the Edit Custom Dictionary dialog box without making changes in the dictionary.)

9. Click the close box to confirm your choices and close the Preferences dialog box.

Checking Grammar in a Document

Computers cannot actually check grammar. To proofread a document for all possible grammatical errors, a program would have to understand the meaning of the words you typed. The technology needed to perform such a task lies decades in the future.

Relying on the same pattern-matching technique that Spelling uses, however, Word's Grammar utility checks your document against a built-in dictionary of text patterns, each of which may indicate certain errors in style, usage, and grammar. When Grammar finishes proofing your document, it displays statistics that can help you assess the readability of your document.

In the following sections, you learn how to use Grammar, how to get the most out of the utility despite its limitations, and how to choose grammar-checking options.

Understanding Grammar's Limitations

Like the Spelling utility, which cannot find spelling errors that occur when a correctly spelled word is used in the wrong context ("Their you go again!"), Grammar cannot ensure that your document is without error. Following is a list of Grammar's shortcomings, which you should understand clearly before using this utility:

- *Grammar flags only those errors in usage, style, and grammar that can be detected by pattern matching.* Many errors, such as subject-verb agreement and the use of incorrect articles, cannot be detected easily by pattern matching.

- *Grammar questions many passages in which a word or phrase is used correctly.* Called false positives, these questionable passages may not need revision. For example, Grammar flags all occurrences of passive voice. You may use passive voice legitimately, however, when no need exists to state the sentence's subject.

Whereas using Spelling requires relatively little judgment, you must consider virtually every word, phrase, or passage that Grammar questions. In the end, only you can decide whether the utility truly has flagged an error.

- *Grammar stresses the themes of good business writing: positiveness, clarity, conciseness, freshness, and directness.* Grammar's suggestions may not apply to academic, legal, or professional documents. Passive voice, for example, is common in formal reports and scientific papers. If you use Grammar to check such a document, you may want to disable the passive-voice rule and other rules. (For information on disabling specific rules, see "Choosing Grammar Options" later in this chapter.)

- *Grammar cannot detect organizational or logic problems.* Grammar looks on the surface for patterns in sentences and phrases, but serious writing problems often lie deeper, at the level of the document's overall structure and logic. The utility might place its stamp of approval on an incomprehensible document.

Grammar's shortcomings are shared by all style, usage, and grammar checkers. Given these shortcomings, is running Grammar worthwhile? Unequivocally, the answer is yes—if you understand that Grammar cannot detect all possible errors in your document. Despite its shortcomings, Grammar might find an error that could cause you considerable embarrassment if the uncorrected document were released to the public. But don't let the use of Grammar lull you into thinking that *all* possible errors have been detected.

To use Word's grammar checker wisely, follow these steps before running Grammar:

1. Without paying attention to spelling or other surface errors, read your document and try to judge how well it is organized. Does each paragraph express and develop one idea? Is the organization of the document right for the subject? Can you reorganize the material so that the document would be clearer?

2. Look for coherence flaws. Think about your audience. Did you omit (or fail to define) key facts or perspectives? Does your audience have enough knowledge to understand what you're trying to say? Did you use examples and analogies to explain unfamiliar material?

You should run Grammar only *after* you scrutinize your document. Think of this utility as a final step in proofing your document—one last way to catch an error that might have escaped your attention. Grammar cannot, however, take the place of manual revision.

Using Grammar

Like Spelling, Grammar searches a document sentence by sentence, comparing words and phrases with those in its built-in dictionary. By default, Grammar checks spelling, too. If the grammar checker finds a spelling error, the Spelling dialog box appears.

If you don't want Grammar to check spelling, click the Options command button in the Grammar dialog box to display the Preferences dialog box and then deactivate the Spelling Errors option. To find the Spelling Errors option, click the Grammar radio button in the Rule Groups area and then scroll down the list box. Click the check mark to deactivate the Spelling Errors option and then click the close box to continue.

To proof your document with Grammar, follow these steps:

1. Position the insertion point in your document where you want Grammar to begin checking. (Grammar checks your entire document but begins at the insertion point's location.)

   Alternatively, select part of your document so that Grammar will check only the selection.

2. Choose Grammar from the Tools menu. The Grammar dialog box appears when the program finds the first error (see fig. 12.7).

Fig. 12.7
Grammar dialog box.

Grammar

Sentence:

The **reason why** is that your shipment arrived SIX MONTHS after we placed our order!

Suggestions:

Redundant. Rephrase or simplify by using either **the reason** or **why** alone.

Ignore
Change
Next Sentence
Ignore Rule
Close
Explain...
Options...

If the Spelling dialog box appears instead, deal with the unknown word as you would when running Spelling. (For more information, refer to "Checking Spelling in a Document" earlier in this chapter.)

3. Perform one of the following actions:

   ■ *Click Explain to view an explanation of the error and suggestions for its revision.* When you click Explain, the Grammar Explanation window appears (see fig. 12.8).

Fig. 12.8

Grammar Explanation window.

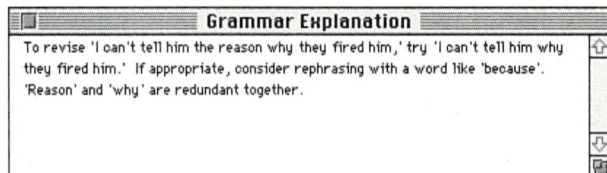

Click the close box to return to the Grammar dialog box.

   ■ *Correct the error.* Click the document window to activate the document and then edit the sentence. To continue checking grammar, choose Grammar from the Tools menu again.

   ■ *Choose Ignore to skip this occurrence of the error and continue.* Grammar shows you any additional occurrences of this error in your document as it checks the rest of the document.

   ■ *Click Next Sentence to skip the rest of the errors in this sentence.* Grammar skips to the next sentence and continues checking the document.

   ■ *Choose Ignore Rule to tell Grammar to stop flagging this kind of error during this session and subsequent sessions.* Choosing this option is the same as deactivating one of Grammar's rules in the Preferences dialog box, as explained later in this section.

4. Repeat step 3 until the grammar checker informs you that it has reached the end of the document or the selection.

If Grammar reaches the end of the document or the selection without proofing all your text, an alert box appears, asking whether you want to continue checking from the beginning. Choose OK to continue, or click Cancel to stop checking.

When Grammar finishes checking your document, the Document Statistics window appears. The following section explains this window.

Understanding Document Statistics

Figure 12.9 shows the Document Statistics window, which reports the results of several assessments of your document's readability.

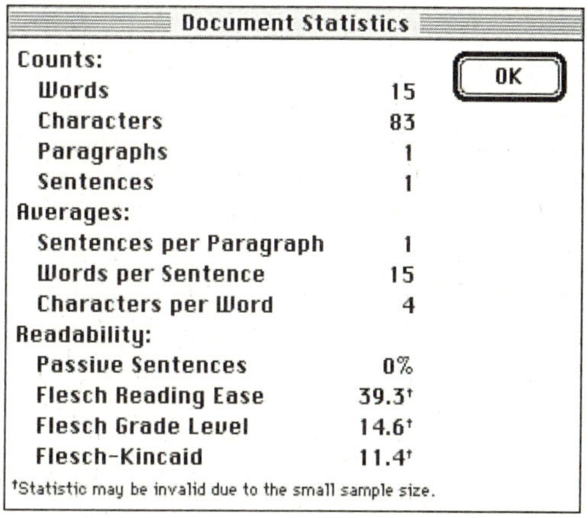

Fig. 12.9
Document Statistics window.

Document Statistics		
Counts:		OK
Words	15	
Characters	83	
Paragraphs	1	
Sentences	1	
Averages:		
Sentences per Paragraph	1	
Words per Sentence	15	
Characters per Word	4	
Readability:		
Passive Sentences	0%	
Flesch Reading Ease	39.3†	
Flesch Grade Level	14.6†	
Flesch-Kincaid	11.4†	

†Statistic may be invalid due to the small sample size.

The Flesch Grade Level and Flesch-Kincaid scales assess readability by academic grade level. The document measured in figure 12.9, for example, is written at a level suitable for readers with two to four years of college education. These scales, however, are only spuriously accurate (as suggested by the disagreement among them), so you should think of them in more general terms, as shown in Table 12.1 (This table also interprets the Flesch Reading Ease scales, which do not reflect grade levels.)

Table 12.1
Readability Levels

Reading level	Grade equivalent	Flesch Reading Ease Index
Very difficult	Postgraduate	0 to 30
Difficult	College	30 to 50
Somewhat difficult	High school	50 to 60
Standard	Junior high school	60 to 70

continues

Table 12.1
Continued

Reading level	Grade equivalent	Flesch Reading Ease Index
Fairly easy	Sixth grade	70 to 80
Easy	Fifth grade	80 to 90
Very easy	Fourth grade	90 to 100

These readability scales actually are a crude numerical measurement of your text. The Flesch-Kincaid test, for example, divides the number of words by the number of sentences and multiplies the result by an arbitrary constant. As a result, you could create an unreadable nonsense document that includes sentences like "Colorless green ideas sleep furiously" (Noam Chomsky) and get an excellent readability score.

In short, don't take these scales too seriously; use them only as one measure of your document's readability.

If you get a readability score higher than your readers' abilities, you can lower it by following these suggestions:

- Shorten sentences.

- Eliminate wordy expressions ("It will be seen that…").

- Eliminate grammatical expletives ("It is" and "There are").

- Rewrite passive-voice sentences ("The ball was kicked by John") unless you disguised or omitted the sentence's subject for a good reason.

- Use simple, familiar words.

Choosing Grammar Options

When you click the Options command button in the Grammar dialog box, the Preferences dialog box appears, with the Grammar options automatically displayed, as shown in figure 12.10. (You also can access Grammar options by choosing Preferences from the Tools menu and clicking the Grammar icon on the left side of the Preferences dialog box.)

The following list describes the Grammar options.

Rule Groups. Grammar enables you to activate or deactivate individual style and grammar rules. By default, all the rules are turned on. To disable a rule, click the check mark next to the rule's name; the check mark disappears. To turn a rule back on, click the check column next to the rule name; the check mark reappears.

Fig. 12.10

Grammar options in the Preferences dialog box.

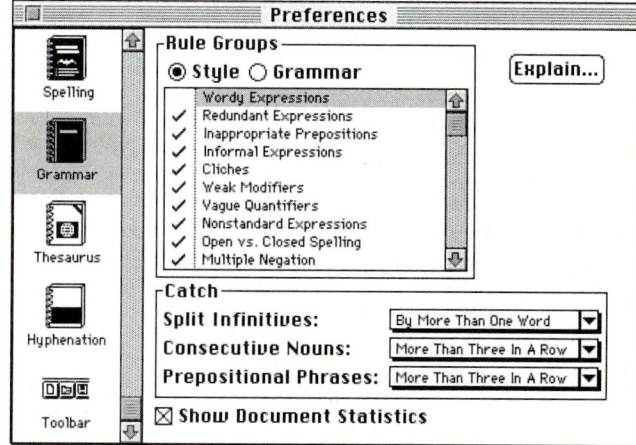

Style and Grammar radio buttons. Word displays only one rule group at a time in the Rule Groups list box. To see the style rules, click the Style button; to see the grammar rules, click the Grammar button.

Explain command button. If you don't understand a style or grammar rule, highlight the rule's name in the Rule Groups list box and then click Explain. A dialog box appears, briefly explaining the rule.

Catch area. In this area, you control how Grammar detects split infinitives ("To boldly go"), consecutive nouns ("failure detection feedback analysis procedure"), and repeated prepositional phrases ("in a box on a track on the way to town").

Split Infinitives list box. By default, Grammar doesn't flag split infinitives unless they're split by more than one word. You can restrict Grammar's search for split infinitives by selecting By More Than Two Words or By More Than Three Words ("To boldly, bravely, and perhaps foolishly go"). You also can select Always, to catch all split infinitives (this choice would catch "To boldly go"), or Never, to skip all split infinitives.

Chapter 12

Checking Spelling and Grammar

Consecutive Nouns list box. By default, Grammar flags consecutive nouns when more than three in a row occur; you can select More Than Two In A Row or More Than Four In A Row instead. To prevent Grammar from flagging consecutive nouns, select Never.

Prepositional Phrases list box. By default, Grammar flags more than three prepositional phrases in a row. You can select More Than Two In A Row, More Than Four In a Row, or Never instead.

Show Document Statistics check box. By default, Grammar displays the Document Statistics window at the end of a grammar check. To skip Document Statistics, deactivate this check box.

Quick Review

This section summarizes the most useful information in this chapter. Check "Productivity Tips" for a review of high-productivity tips and tricks—the ones that Macintosh and Word pros use every day. Review "Techniques" whenever you need a quick reminder about a specific procedure.

Productivity Tips

■ Switch to Normal view before you run Spelling.

■ Add all the proper nouns you use—including your name, your address, your boss' name, and your company's name—to a custom dictionary so that Spelling doesn't flag these words in future spelling checks.

■ If Spelling runs slowly, use the Preferences dialog box to turn off Spelling's suggestions.

■ If you are using Word 5.0 and need to add more than 1,000 words to a custom dictionary, create more than one custom dictionary— one for each type of document that you routinely create.

■ Don't let Grammar take the place of careful proofreading of your document. Grammar cannot catch many serious usage, style, and grammar errors.

■ Disable irrelevant rules to speed Grammar's operation.

- To lower your document's readability score, avoid the passive voice, shorten sentences, and use simple words. Don't place too much emphasis on readability scores, however; coherence and clarity matter more than readability scores do.

Techniques

This section provides concise summaries of all the procedures introduced in this chapter.

Checking Spelling

To check spelling, follow these steps:

1. To check your entire document, click the location at which you want the spell check to start. To check only part of the document, select that text.

2. Choose Spelling from the Tools menu, press ⌘-L, or click the Spelling tool. Spelling begins to check your document.

3. When Spelling flags an error, perform one of the following actions:

   - Click Change to accept the suggestion that appears in the Change To text box. If you want to make this change throughout the document without confirmation, click Change All.

   - Choose the correct spelling in the Suggestions list box by highlighting the word and clicking Change (or by double-clicking the word in the list box). If you want to make this correction throughout the document without confirmation, click Change All.

   - Correct the spelling in the Change To box and then click Change. If you want to make this correction throughout the document without confirmation, click Change All.

   - Close the Spelling dialog box by clicking the document window and then make the change in your document.

   - Choose Ignore to skip the word once, or click Ignore All to skip all occurrences of this word in the document.

   - Click Add to add the word to the current dictionary. (By default, the current dictionary is Custom Dictionary.)

- If Spelling finds a repeated word, click the Delete button to delete the word. (This button is available only when Spelling finds a repetition.)

4. Repeat step 3 until Spelling informs you that it has reached the end of the document or the selection.

Using Spelling Options

To choose spelling options:

1. Choose Preferences from the Tools menu to open the Preferences dialog box and then click the Spelling icon to list the Spelling options. (You also can click Options in the Spelling dialog box.)

2. To turn off automatic suggestions of changes for correctly spelled words, deactivate the Always Suggest option in the Ignore area.

3. To skip words in uppercase letters, activate the Words in UPPER-CASE option in the Ignore area.

4. To skip words that contain numbers, activate the Words with Numbers option in the Ignore area.

5. Click the close box to confirm your choices and close the Preferences dialog box.

Working with Custom Dictionaries

To create a custom dictionary:

1. Choose Preferences from the Tools menu. The Preferences dialog box appears.

2. Click the Spelling icon to list the Spelling options.

3. In the Custom Dictionaries area, click New. The Save As dialog box appears, displaying the message `Save new custom dictionary as`.

4. Type a name for the new custom dictionary (no longer than 31 characters).

5. If necessary, use the current-folder list box to open the Word Commands folder so that your new custom dictionary is placed in the same folder as Word's main dictionary.

6. Choose Save.

To open a custom dictionary:

1. Choose Preferences from the Tools menu. The Preferences dialog box appears.

2. Click the Spelling icon to list the Spelling options.

3. In the Custom Dictionaries list box, click to the left of the custom dictionary's name. A check mark appears.

4. Click the close box to confirm your choice and close the Preferences dialog box.

To close a custom dictionary:

1. Choose Preferences from the Tools menu. The Preferences dialog box appears.

2. Click the Spelling icon to list the Spelling options.

3. Click the check mark next to the name of the custom dictionary you want to close. The check mark disappears.

4. Click the close box to confirm your choice and close the Preferences dialog box.

To remove a word from a custom dictionary:

1. Choose Preferences from the Tools menu. The Preferences dialog box appears.

2. Click the Spelling icon to list the Spelling options.

3. In the Custom Dictionaries list box, select the custom dictionary you want to edit.

4. Click Edit. The Edit Custom Dictionary dialog box appears.

5. Highlight the word you want to delete.

6. Click Delete.

7. Repeat steps 5 and 6 until you have removed all the words that you want to delete.

8. Choose OK to close the Edit Custom Dictionary dialog box, or click Cancel to close the dialog box without making changes to the dictionary. The Preferences dialog box reappears.

9. Click the close box to confirm your choices and close the Preferences dialog box.

Checking Grammar

To proof your document with Grammar:

1. Position the insertion point where you want Grammar to begin checking. You also can select part of your document, and Grammar will check only the selection.

2. Choose Grammar from the Tools menu. Grammar begins checking your document.

3. When Grammar flags an error, perform one or more of the following actions:

   - Click Explain to view an explanation of the error and suggestions for its revision.

   - Click the document window to activate the document and edit the sentence.

   - Choose Ignore to skip this occurrence of the error and continue checking.

   - Click Next Sentence to skip the rest of the errors in this sentence and go on to the next sentence.

   - Click Ignore Rule to tell Grammar to quit flagging this kind of error during this session and all future Grammar sessions.

4. Repeat step 3 until Grammar informs you that it has reached the end of the document or the selection.

Using Grammar Options

To choose grammar options:

1. Choose Preferences from the Tools menu to open the Preferences dialog box, and then click the Grammar icon to list the Grammar options. Alternatively, you can click Options in the Grammar dialog box.

2. Perform any of the following actions:

   - To list Style rules in the Rule Groups list box, click the Style radio button. To list Grammar rules in this list box, click the Grammar radio button.

   - To disable a Style or Grammar rule, deactivate the check mark next to the rule's name in the Rule Groups list box.

- To view an explanation of a style or grammar rule, highlight the rule in the Rule Groups list box and then click Explain.

- If you don't want Grammar to check your document's spelling, deactivate the Spelling Errors option in the Preferences dialog box (Grammar options).

- Change the default settings for split infinitives, consecutive nouns, or prepositional phrases.

- Deactivate the Show Document Statistics check box.

3. Click the close box to save your choices and close the dialog box.

Printing Documents

ompared with other computers, the Macintosh makes printing a breeze. After you hook up your printer and use the Chooser to tell your Mac which printer you're using, printing is a simple, straightforward process. You probably have printed successfully already.

See Chapter 1, "Reviewing Mac Basics and Installing Word 5.1," for information on installing your printer.

This chapter, which reviews the basics of printing and shows you how to use Word's many print options, covers the following topics:

- *Printing your document.* You learn how to use the Print command to print your document (and also learn what to do if something goes wrong).

- *Choosing print options.* This section surveys Word's many printing options. You learn, for example, how to print a selected range of pages and multiple copies of a document. You also learn how to use the printing options in the Page Setup dialog box.

- *Preparing a document for printing on another system.* You learn how to use the Chooser to change your printer to print your file on another Macintosh system that has a different printer. You also can use the Chooser to switch printers if you have two printers or obtain a new one.

USING
WORD 5.1
FOR THE MAC
SPECIAL EDITION

Other chapters also cover subjects related to printing, as follows:

- Chapter 27, "Working with Long Documents," explains how to link documents so that they print as if they were one document, with continuous pagination.

- Chapter 31, "Storing Addresses and Printing Envelopes," explains how to print envelopes.

- Chapter 32, "Creating Form Letters," explains how to merge names and addresses from a mailing list and then print one letter for each name.

- Chapter 34, "Printing Mailing Labels," explains how to print mailing labels with Word.

Printing a Document

After you check spelling and preview document formats, you are ready to print your document. Make sure that your printer is turned on, loaded with paper, and selected (*on-line*). Normally, printing is a simple process.

Before you start printing, make sure that you added page numbers. Otherwise, you may waste a great deal of paper before you notice the omission.

To print a document, follow these steps:

1. Choose Print from the File menu or press ⌘-P. Alternatively, click the Print tool. The Print dialog box for your printer appears.

2. Choose Print to accept the current printing settings and to begin printing.

You can cancel printing at any time by pressing ⌘-period (.) or Esc.

You can choose many print options in the Print dialog box and in the Page Setup dialog box. The following sections examine these options.

Choosing Options in the Print Dialog Box

The appearance of the Print dialog box depends on which printer you have installed. If you're using a StyleWriter, for example, you see the Print dialog box shown in figure 13.1.

Part II
Word 5.1 Fundamentals

Fig. 13.1
Print dialog box
(StyleWriter).

StyleWriter   7.2.2   [Print]

Copies: [1]   Quality: ⦿ Best   ○ Faster   [Cancel]

Pages: ⦿ All   ○ From: [   ]   To: [   ]

Paper: ⦿ Sheet Feeder   ○ Manual

Print Pages: ⦿ All   ○ Odd Pages Only   ○ Even Pages Only
Section Range: From: 1   To: 1   ☐ Print Selection Only
☐ Print Hidden Text   ☐ Print Next File

Fig. 13.1
Print dialog box
(StyleWriter).

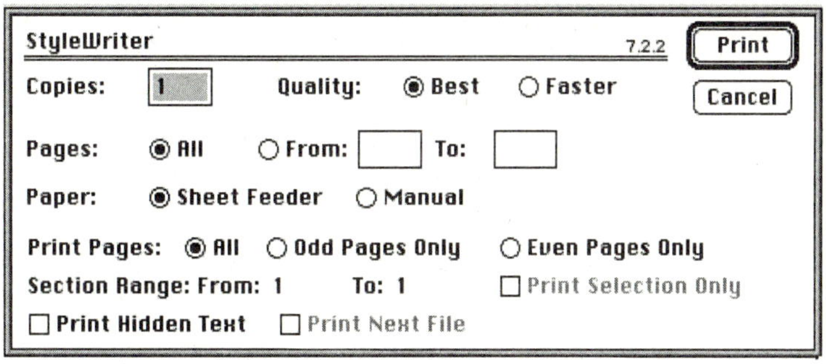

If you're using a LaserWriter, however, the Print dialog box looks like the one shown in figure 13.2.

LaserWriter "LaserWriter"   7.0   [Print]

Copies: [1]   Pages: ⦿ All ○ From: [   ] To: [   ]   [Cancel]
Cover Page: ⦿ No ○ First Page ○ Last Page
Paper Source: ⦿ Paper Cassette ○ Manual Feed
Print: ⦿ Black & White   ○ Color/Grayscale
Destination: ⦿ Printer   ○ PostScript® File
Print Pages: ⦿ All   ○ Odd Pages Only   ○ Even Pages Only
Section Range: From: 1   To: 1   ☐ Print Selection Only
☐ Print Hidden Text   ☐ Print Next File   ☐ Print Back To Front

Fig. 13.2
Print dialog box
(LaserWriter).

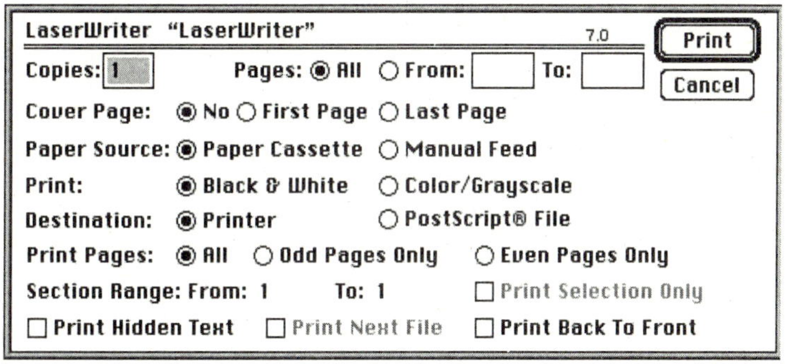

Despite the changes, all versions of this dialog box contain certain options—for example, the options that enable you to control the number of copies to be printed, the range of pages to be printed, and the type of paper to be used. Table 13.1 lists the options available in all Print dialog boxes.

Table 13.1
Print Dialog Box Printing
Options

Option	Function
Copies	By default, Word prints one copy of a document. To print more than one copy, type the number in the Copies text box. This box is highlighted when you open the Print dialog box.

continues

Chapter 13
Printing Documents

Table 13.1
Continued

Option	Function
Pages	To print a range of pages, click the From radio button and type the beginning page number of the range in the adjacent text box. Then type the last page number in the To text box (or leave this box empty to print to the end of your document). To print one page, type the same number in the From and To boxes.
Print Pages	By default, Word prints all pages of a document. If you are using Word 5.1, you can use the Odd Pages Only and Even Pages Only options to print on both sides of the page. (For more information, see "Printing on Both Sides of the Page" later in this chapter.)
Section Range	To print a range of sections in a multisection document, type the section range in the Section Range text boxes.
Print Hidden Text	Click this check box to print hidden text, even if this text is not displayed on-screen.
Print Next File	This check box is grayed unless you link files for printing by clicking the File Series button in the Document dialog box. (For more information on this dialog box, see Chapter 21, "Dividing a Document into Sections.")
Print Selection Only	This check box is grayed unless you selected some text before choosing Print. Click this option to print only the text you selected.

Some options vary, depending on your printer's capabilities. Some printers offer the additional options listed in Table 13.2.

Table 13.2
Additional Printing Options

Option	Description
Cover Page	Prints a cover page that states the document title, the time of printing, and the user identification code (for networked Macs). You can print the cover page before the document (First Page) or after the document (Last Page). When several Mac users are sharing one printer, the person operating the printer will find it easier to untangle the printed output when you choose this option.

Part II
Word 5.1 Fundamentals

Option	Description
Paper Source	Normally, your printer takes paper from its paper cassette. Some printers, however, enable you to feed paper or envelopes manually through a special manual-feed slot or by means of a second paper tray. To print an envelope on a LaserWriter II NT, for example, choose Manual Feed; Word prompts you to insert the paper manually before the printer tries to load the paper.
Color/Grayscale	If you have a color or gray-scale printer, you can choose the Color/Grayscale option to print the colors you selected in the Character dialog box. If you have a black-and-white printer that is capable of printing gray scales, the colors appear in corresponding shades of gray. To print gray text on a black-and-white LaserWriter printer, for example, use the Character dialog box to format the text with a color other than black and then choose Color/Grayscale in the Print dialog box.
Destination	Normally, Word sends print information directly to the printer, but you can choose PostScript File to print your document to a PostScript file instead. You then can take the file to a printing service bureau and have your document printed on a high-resolution printing device for a professional appearance. (For more information on PostScript, see Appendix B.)
Print Back to Front	If you find that you must manually recollate your printouts after printing so that the pages will be in the correct order, choose this option to print the last page first, and so on.
Quality	Choose Best for the highest-quality output; choose Faster for a lower-resolution copy that shows how your fonts and graphics will appear. Choose Draft for a quick printout without your font choices or graphics.

Some printers lack one or more of these options.

Printing on Both Sides of the Page

A new feature of Version 5.1 enables you to print on both sides of the page—a useful feature in these ecology-minded days. To use this feature, you first print the odd-numbered pages only and then print the even-numbered pages on the backs of the odd ones.

How you perform this operation depends on the order in which your printer produces output, as follows:

■ *Front-to-back order.* The printer places page 1 on the top of the stack of printed output, followed by page 2, and so on. If your printer works this way, you must select the Print Back to Front option in the Print dialog box before printing the even pages.

■ *Back-to-front order.* The printer places page 1 on the bottom of the stack of printed output. If your printer works this way, you can print your odd and even pages the same way.

To print double-sided pages, follow these steps:

1. Choose Print from the File menu. Alternatively, press ⌘-P or click the Print tool. The Print dialog box appears.

2. In the Print Pages area, click the Odd Pages Only radio button.

3. Choose Print. Word prints only the odd pages of your document.

4. Place the printed pages back in your printer's paper tray, with the unprinted sides facing up.

5. Choose Print from the File menu. Alternatively, press ⌘-P or click the Print tool. The Print dialog box reappears.

6. In the Print Pages area, click the Even Pages Only radio button.

7. If your printer normally places page 1 of your document on the top of the stack of output, click the Print Back to Front check box. Otherwise, proceed to step 8.

8. Choose Print. Word prints the even pages on the backs of the odd ones.

   If your document has an odd number of pages, the last page will be left in the paper tray. Retrieve the last page and place it at the end of the output stack.

Choosing Print Options in the Page Setup Dialog Box

The Page Setup dialog box enables you to choose additional print options, including paper type, paper orientation, and printing effects. To open this dialog box, choose Page Setup from the File menu or press Shift-F8.

Like the Print dialog box, the Page Setup dialog box is based on the printer you use. Figure 13.3 shows the StyleWriter Page Setup dialog box, and Figure 13.4 shows the LaserWriter version.

Fig. 13.3
Page Setup dialog box (StyleWriter).

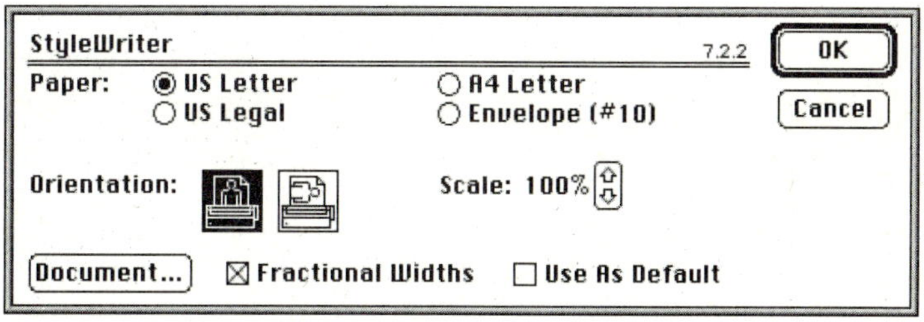

Fig. 13.4
Page Setup dialog box (LaserWriter).

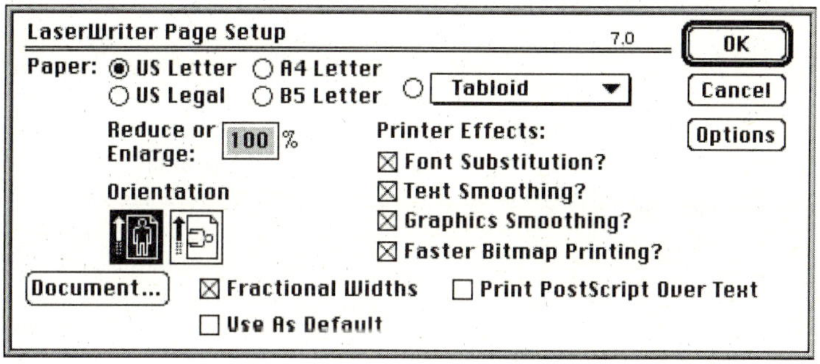

The choices you make in the Page Setup dialog box remain in effect until you change them.

The following section explains the Page Setup options available for all or most printers. Later sections discuss the special printing capabilities of ImageWriter and LaserWriter printers.

Chapter 13
Printing Documents

Understanding Page Setup Options

Table 13.3 lists the Page Setup options that you find in most Page Setup dialog boxes.

Table 13.3
Page Setup Dialog Box
Printing Options

Option	Description
Paper	You can choose among several standard paper sizes. (For more information on choosing paper size, see Chapter 11, "Formatting Pages.")
Orientation	Click the appropriate icon to print in *portrait mode* (across the width of the page) or *landscape mode* (across the length of the page).
Size	You can choose among a variety of reductions, ranging from 25% to 400%. Word changes the right margin setting on-screen to show you how much text will fit on a printed line. The ruler measurements and font sizes, however, do not change in Normal or Page Layout view. To see how your document will look when printed, choose Print Preview.
Fractional Widths	This option tells Word to simulate on-screen the character spacing of proportionally spaced fonts (such as New Century Schoolbook, Times Roman, and Helvetica). Some fonts may be difficult to read when this option is active (especially if you're using a small font size) because your Macintosh screen does not have sufficient resolution to perform this task accurately. If the text is difficult to read, try turning this option off. Be sure, however, to turn Fractional Widths back on before printing, or the line and page breaks that appear on-screen will not match the line and page breaks in your printed document. This option is on by default.
Use As Default	Click this check box to make your Page Setup choices the default for all documents.
Document	To set margins or make other page-formatting choices, click this command button, which displays the Document dialog box.

Understanding ImageWriter Page Setup Options

If you're using an ImageWriter printer, which now is something of an antique in the Macintosh world (but useful nonetheless), you can choose additional Page Setup options. Table 13.4 lists the special printing options available with this printer.

Table 13.4
ImageWriter Page Setup Options

Option	Description
Tall Adjusted	Choose this option if the bit-mapped graphics you print look stretched horizontally (so that a circle prints like an oval, for example).
50% Reduction	Prints the page half-size. You can choose this option to produce high-resolution printouts. Before printing, choose a 24-point font size (which Word prints at 12 points). Word automatically doubles the margins.
No Gaps Between Pages	If you're using continuous mailing labels, you can choose this option to omit page breaks and vertical margins.

Understanding LaserWriter Page Setup Options

If you're using a laser printer, you have additional printing options. Table 13.5 lists the printing options available in the Page Setup dialog boxes of current Apple laser printers.

Table 13.5
Laser Printer Page Setup Options

Option	Description
Precision Bitmap Alignment	This option reduces bit-mapped (paint format) graphics so that they print more attractively and sets aside large amounts of your printer's memory for graphics. Turn this option off to print if you're using download-able fonts, or your document may fail to print.
Exact Bit Images	This option reduces bit-mapped (paint format) graphics to the precise proportions of their on-screen appearance so that the graphics print more attractively. (This option is the same as Precision Bitmap Alignment.)

continues

Chapter 13
Printing Documents

	Option	Description
Table 13.5 Continued	Text Smoothing	This option (selected by default) smooths the edges of bit-mapped fonts. If you're not using bit-mapped fonts, deactivate this option, which slows your printer and can blur some fonts and graphics.
	Font Substitution	This option (selected by default) prints Geneva in Helvetica, New York in Times Roman, and Monaco in Courier. The word spacing, however, will look irregular when the document is printed, so you should choose Helvetica, Times Roman, and Courier in your document.
	Graphics Smoothing	This option (selected by default) smooths the edges and contours of graphics that appear jagged when printed. If you're not using bit-mapped graphics, deactivate this option, which slows your printer and can blur some fonts and graphics.
	Faster Bitmap Printing	This option (selected by default) speeds the printing of bit-mapped fonts and graphics. Disable this option if the document doesn't print correctly.
	Fractional Widths	This option (selected by default) tells Word to simulate on-screen the character spacing of proportionally spaced fonts such as New Century Schoolbook, Times Roman, and Helvetica. Deactivate this option to improve Word's speed.

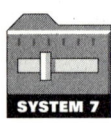 

If you like the laser-printer output generated by the TrueType versions of Geneva, New York, and Monaco in System 7, be sure to disable the Font Substitution option so that Word does not translate these fonts to Helvetica, Times Roman, or Courier. If you're not using bit-mapped fonts or bit-mapped graphics, turn off the Smoothing options.

If you're using a PostScript laser printer, you can click the Options command button to see additional printing options (see fig. 13.5).

Part II

Word 5.1 Fundamentals

Fig. 13.5
LaserWriter page-setup options.

```
LaserWriter Options                    7.0    ┌──────────┐
                                              │    OK    │
                                              └──────────┘
    ┌──────┐  ☐ Flip Horizontal            ┌──────────┐
    │      │  ☐ Flip Vertical              │  Cancel  │
    │  🐕  │  ☐ Invert Image               └──────────┘
    │      │  ☐ Precision Bitmap Alignment (4% reduction)
    └──────┘  ☐ Larger Print Area (Fewer Downloadable Fonts)
              ☐ Unlimited Downloadable Fonts in a Document
```

Table 13.6 lists these options.

Table 13.6
LaserWriter Page Setup Options

Option	Description
Flip Horizontal	This option prints text and graphics backward, so that you need a mirror to read the document.
Flip Vertical	This option reverses the page top to bottom, so that the bottom of the page comes out of the printer first.
Invert Image	This option prints white text or graphics on a black background (like a photographic negative) for special effects.
Precision Bitmap Alignment	This option improves printing of bit-mapped graphics.
Larger Print Area	This option expands the print area by reducing the minimum margins (and also reduces the number of downloadable fonts you can use).
Unlimited Downloadable Fonts in a Document	This option removes the limitation on the number of downloadable fonts you can use in a given document. If you print a document with many fonts, printing may be slow.

Using Background Printing

If you're using a LaserWriter or StyleWriter printer, you can use the PrintMonitor—a utility provided with Apple's System software—to print in the background while you work in Word (or other applications).

Chapter 13

Printing Documents

If you use System 6, you must choose MultiFinder before you can use PrintMonitor. System 7, however, enables you to use PrintMonitor at any time.

Background printing with PrintMonitor is simple and convenient, enabling you to print several documents at once. By bringing up the PrintMonitor dialog box during printing, you can monitor the status of each print job, cancel printing, change the order in which documents print, and even set the time and date at which you want each document printed. You can continue to work on your Macintosh while your documents are printing.

If your printer runs out of paper or if PrintMonitor encounters a problem while printing, an alert box appears.

To turn on background printing, choose On in the Background Printing area of the Chooser dialog box. (To display this dialog box, select Chooser from the Apple menu.) Background printing remains active until you turn it off by choosing the Off button in this dialog box.

When you print with PrintMonitor, Word quickly saves printing information to a temporary file and returns control of the keyboard to you. You can continue to work, but your Macintosh will pause frequently as it sends information to the printer.

While a document is printing, you can check the status of printing by displaying the PrintMonitor dialog box, shown in figure 13.6.

Fig. 13.6

PrintMonitor dialog box.

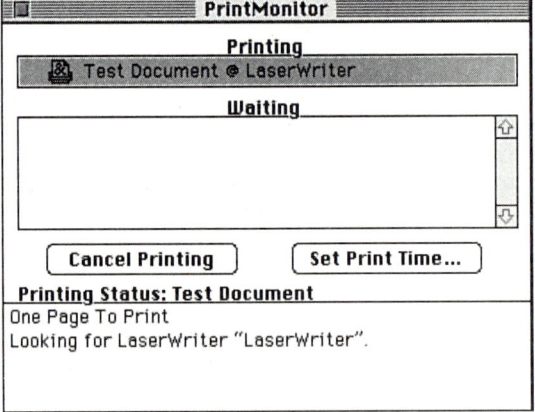

To display the PrintMonitor dialog box in System 6, click the MultiFinder icon (on the right end of the menu bar) until the dialog box appears. To display the PrintMonitor dialog box in System 7, choose PrintMonitor from the Applications menu. (To pull down the Applications menu within Word, click the Word icon—the italic *W*—at the right end of the menu bar.)

In the PrintMonitor dialog box, the name of the document that currently is printing appears in the Printing window, and a list of documents that are in line to be printed appears in the Waiting window. (These documents are printed in the order in which they're listed.)

The following sections explain how to use the PrintMonitor dialog box to cancel printing and to control the time and date of printing.

Canceling a Print Job

To cancel printing a document, follow these steps:

1. Click the MultiFinder icon until the PrintMonitor dialog box appears (System 6), or choose PrintMonitor from the Applications menu (System 7).

2. Highlight the name of the document you don't want to print. (If you're printing more than one document, this name could be listed in the Waiting window.)

3. Click the Cancel Printing command button.

4. Click the close box to exit the PrintMonitor dialog box.

Postponing a Print Job

When you postpone printing a document, you tell PrintMonitor not to print the document until you are ready. To postpone printing a document, follow these steps:

1. Click the MultiFinder icon until you see the PrintMonitor dialog box (System 6), or choose PrintMonitor from the Applications menu (System 7).

2. In the Waiting window, highlight the name of the document you want to print later.

3. Click the Set Print Time command button. The Set Print Time dialog box appears (see fig. 13.7).

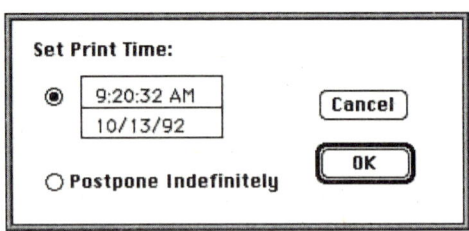

Fig. 13.7
Set Print Time dialog box.

4. Perform one of the following actions:

■ Click the Set Print Time radio button. When the dialog box appears, change the time. (You also can change the date this way.)

■ Click the Postpone Indefinitely radio button. If you choose this option, you must choose Set Print Time again and set a printing time for the document.

5. Choose OK.

6. Click the close box to exit the PrintMonitor dialog box.

Switching Printers

If you want to save your document to a floppy disk for printing on a different Macintosh system (one that has a printer other than the one you're using), you can use the Chooser to change printers temporarily. When Word formats your document, it uses settings specific to a particular printer; therefore, you should use the Chooser to select the printer you intend to use to print your document, even if that printer isn't the one connected to your system. After you save this document, remember to switch back to the printer that's connected to your system.

To change printers temporarily, follow these steps:

1. Select Chooser from the Apple menu. The Chooser dialog box appears, with the available printers displayed in the list box (see fig. 13.8).

2. Click the appropriate printer icon to select that printer.

3. Choose port, AppleTalk, and background-printing options.

4. Click the close box to close the dialog box.

Fig. 13.8
Chooser dialog box.

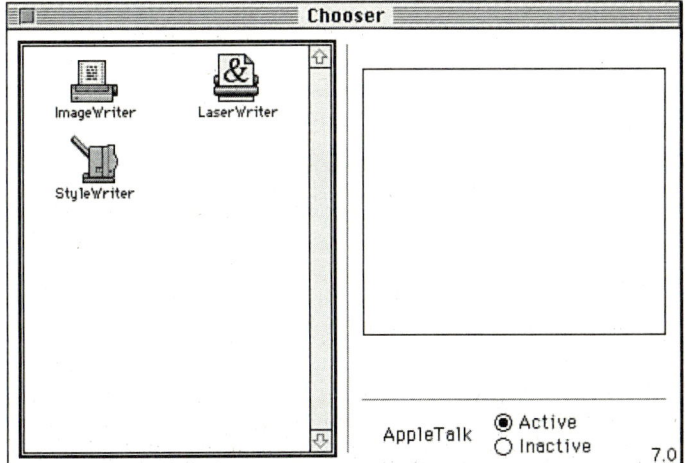

5. If Word was running when you selected Chooser, choose Page Setup from the File menu or press Shift-F8, and choose OK when the Page Setup dialog box appears.

6. Format, save, and close your document.

7. Repeat steps 1 through 5 to restore your system's printer.

If two different printers are connected to your system, you can use this procedure to choose one of them for a printing job.

Quick Review

This section summarizes the most useful information in this chapter. Check "Productivity Tips" for a review of high-productivity tips and tricks—the ones that Macintosh and Word pros use every day. Review "Techniques" whenever you need a quick reminder about a specific procedure.

Productivity Tips

■ If you want your document to have page numbers, be sure to add them to your document before printing.

Chapter 13
Printing Documents

- If more than one person uses your printer, choose the Cover Page option in the Print dialog box.

- If you're using an ImageWriter or StyleWriter, choose the Faster option to print a quick draft of your document; use the Best option for the final copy only.

- Activate background printing so that you can continue to work with Word while documents print.

Techniques

This section provides concise summaries of all the procedures introduced in this chapter.

Printing Your Work

To print your document:

1. Choose Print from the File menu. Alternatively, press ⌘-P or click the Print tool. The Print dialog box appears.

2. Choose Print to accept the current printer settings and to begin printing.

To cancel printing at any time, press ⌘-period (.) or Esc.

Choosing Print Options

To print only selected text:

1. Select the text you want to print.

2. Choose Print from the File menu. Alternatively, press ⌘-P or click the Print tool. The Print dialog box appears.

3. Click the Print Selection Only check box.

4. Choose Print.

To print hidden text:

1. Select the text you want to print.

2. Choose Print from the File menu. Alternatively, press ⌘-P or click the Print tool. The Print dialog box appears.

3. Click the Print Hidden Text check box.

4. Choose Print.

To print more than one copy:

1. Choose Print from the File menu. Alternatively, press ⌘-P or click the Print tool. The Print dialog box appears.

2. In the Copies text box, type the number of copies you want to print.

3. Choose Print.

To print a range of pages:

1. Choose Print from the File menu. Alternatively, press ⌘-P or click the Print tool. The Print dialog box appears.

2. Click the From radio button and type the beginning page number of the range in the adjacent text box.

3. In the To text box, type the last page number in the range. (To print to the end of your document, leave this box empty.) To print one page, type the same page number that you typed in the From text box.

4. Choose Print.

To print a section range:

1. Choose Print from the File menu. Alternatively, press ⌘-P or click the Print tool. The Print dialog box appears.

2. In the Section Range area, type the number of the first section you want to print in the From text box.

3. Type the last section number in the To text box. (To print to the end of your document, leave this box empty.) To print one section, type the same section number that you typed in the From text box.

4. Choose Print.

Printing on Both Sides

To print on both sides of the page:

1. Choose Print from the File menu. Alternatively, press ⌘-P or click the Print tool. The Print dialog box appears.

2. Click the Odd Pages Only radio button.

3. Choose Print.

4. Place the printed pages back in your printer's paper tray, with the unprinted sides facing up.

5. Choose Print from the File menu. Alternatively, press ⌘-P or click the Print tool. The Print dialog box reappears.

6. Click the Even Pages Only radio button.

7. If your printer normally places page 1 of your document on the top of the stack of output, click the Print Back to Front check box. Otherwise, proceed to step 8.

8. Choose Print.

Choosing Page Setup Print Options

To change printing orientation:

1. Choose Page Setup from the File menu or press Shift-F8. The Page Setup dialog box appears.

2. Click the Landscape or Portrait icon.

3. Choose OK.

4. Print your document.

To change printing size:

1. Choose Page Setup from the File menu or press Shift-F8. The Page Setup dialog box appears.

2. Type a size in the Reduce or Enlarge text box or click a size option, depending on the printer you are using.

3. Choose OK.

4. Print your document.

Activating Background Printing

To turn on background printing (if your printer permits it):

1. Select Chooser from the Apple menu. The Chooser dialog box appears.

2. Click your printer's icon.

3. Choose On in the Background Printing area.

4. Choose OK.

To cancel printing a document in the background:

1. Click the MultiFinder icon until the PrintMonitor dialog box appears (System 6), or choose PrintMonitor from the Applications menu (System 7).

2. Highlight the name of the document you don't want to print.

3. Click the Cancel Printing button.

4. Click the close box to exit the PrintMonitor dialog box.

To postpone printing a document:

1. Click the MultiFinder icon until the PrintMonitor dialog box appears (System 6), or choose PrintMonitor from the Applications menu (System 7).

2. In the Waiting window, highlight the name of the document you want to print later.

3. Click the Set Print Time command button. The Set Print Time dialog box appears.

4. Perform one of the following actions:

   ■ Click the Set Print Time radio button. When the dialog box appears, change the time. You also can change the date this way.

   ■ Click the Postpone Indefinitely radio button.

5. Choose OK.

6. Click the close box to exit the dialog box.

Changing Printers Temporarily

To change printers temporarily:

1. Select Chooser from the Apple menu. The Chooser dialog box appears.

2. Click one of the printer icons.

3. Choose port, AppleTalk, and background-printing options.

Chapter 13
Printing Documents

4. Click the close box to exit the dialog box.

5. If Word was running when you selected Chooser, choose **Page Setup** from the File menu or press Shift-F8, and then choose OK when the Page Setup dialog box appears.

6. Format, save, and close your document.

7. Repeat steps 1 through 5 to restore your system's printer.

PART

III

Using Advanced Formatting Techniques

USING
WORD 5.1
FOR THE MAC
SPECIAL EDITION

Formatting with Styles

Styles are simple but perhaps unfamiliar tools for Word users. In brief, a *style* is a named, stored collection of formats that you can apply to one or more paragraphs in your document. When you create a style, you can include emphases (such as bold or italic), fonts, font sizes, indents, alignment options, blank space, and tabs.

Creating styles is easy and based on the manual formatting skills that you already know. (*Manual formatting* refers to ribbon, ruler, dialog-box, and keyboard-shortcut techniques that format a paragraph directly.) When you apply a style, Word formats the selected paragraph with all the formats in the style definition. Using styles as your building blocks, you can create a beautifully formatted document quickly.

A style called Heading, for example, might include centered alignment, bold emphasis, the 14-point Helvetica font, 24 points of blank space before and 24 points of blank space after the heading, and the Keep with Next option to prevent Word from inserting a page break under the heading. You also could create a style called Body Text with a 1/2-inch first-line indentation, the 10-point Times font, and justified alignment.

Using these two styles, you could quickly create a document such as the one shown in figure 14.1.

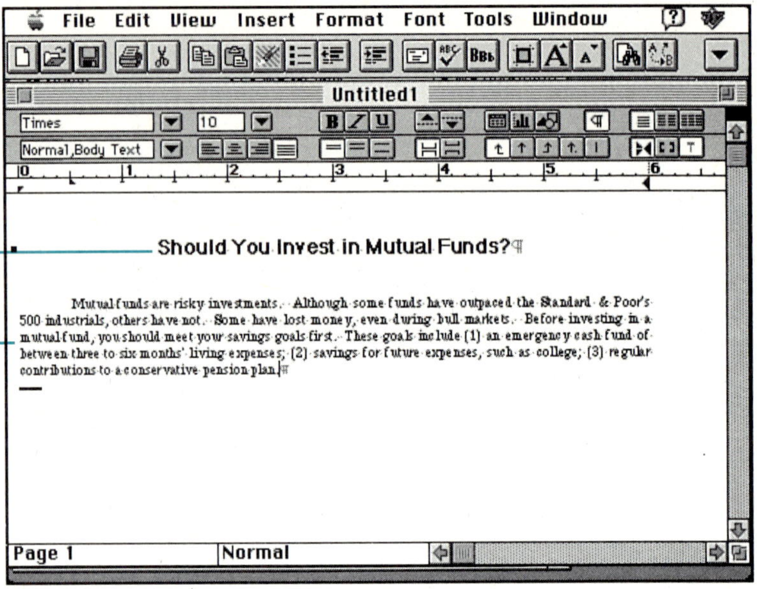

Fig. 14.1
A document formatted
with Heading and Body
Text styles.

Heading style

Body Text style

When you choose the Heading style to type a heading, Word instantly enters all the formats you have chosen: centered alignment, bold emphasis, 14-point Helvetica, 24 points of blank space before and after, and the Keep with Next option. Then you choose Body Text to type your document's body-text paragraphs, and Word instantly enters all the Body Text formats.

When you switch to the Heading style again, Word enters all the formats simultaneously (see fig. 14.2). This procedure involves no copying, no repetitive formatting commands—just fast, productive writing.

After you grow adept with styles, style formatting will become your basic formatting approach, and you will reserve manual formatting for adjusting text that you previously formatted with styles.

Following are some of the advantages of using styles:

■ *You can enter several formats quickly.* Suppose that you create a style for a hanging indentation that combines Palatino 12, justified alignment, a 3/10-inch hanging indent, and the Keep Lines Together option. You plan to use this format to create bulleted lists. If you define this style as Bulleted List, Word enters all these formats instantly whenever you apply the Bulleted List style to a paragraph.

Part III

Using Advanced Formatting Techniques

■ *You can reformat your document quickly.* Suppose that you create a Body Text style that calls for Times Roman 12, right justification, auto line spacing, and 12 points of blank space before each paragraph. At the last moment, you decide to use the Garamond typeface instead of Times Roman. Does this mean you must reformat every body-text paragraph manually? Not when you use styles. You can change the style, and Word instantly updates all the paragraphs to which you applied the style.

■ *You can redefine many of Word's default formats.* These formats include headers, footers, footnote reference marks, footnote text, page numbers, line numbers, and headings. After you redefine automatic styles, the formats you choose apply automatically to all new documents.

Fig. 14.2
Formatting another heading by choosing a style.

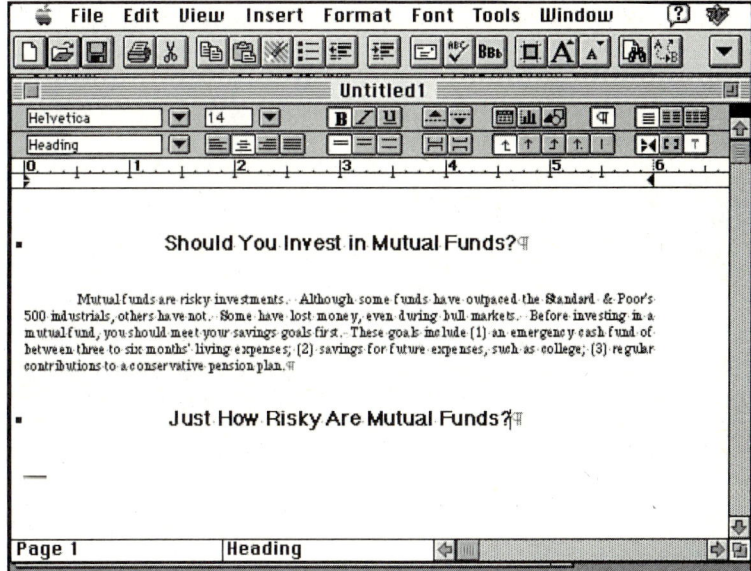

Style skills are fundamental to your knowledge of Word, so they are discussed in Part I of this book. This chapter, which is designed to get you up and running with styles, covers the following topics:

■ *Creating styles.* In this section, you learn how to record styles from already-formatted text and how to define styles with the Style command (Format menu). In addition, you learn how to create a *master style* on which all the other styles in your style sheet are based.

Chapter 14

Formatting with Styles

- *Applying styles.* Like other Word formats, styles can be applied before or after you type. In this section, you learn three different techniques for applying styles.

- *Revising and managing styles.* You can edit, rename, and delete styles after you create them, and even copy them to another document. This section explains these procedures.

- *Using styles with manual formatting.* In this section, you learn how to combine styles with manually applied formats.

- *Using standard styles.* In addition to the styles you create, Word provides many standard styles that cover formats such as page numbers, headers and footers, headings, footnote reference marks, and footnote text. This section explains how to modify these styles.

- *Searching for and replacing styles.* Word's Search and Replace commands enable you to search for styles, as you learn in this section. You also can replace one style with another throughout your document.

Understanding Style Sheets

Far too few Word users employ style sheets, perhaps because the word *style* is misleading. Most people associate the word with character emphasis. Getting past such a minor terminology block, however, is worth the potential gains in productivity. This section introduces the fundamental concepts of style-sheet formatting. You learn what styles are, and you learn where they are stored.

Users of previous versions of Word will find only minor changes in Word's style commands. The most obvious change is in the Format menu, in which one style command (Style) replaces the Define Styles and Define All Styles commands. Another change involves terminology; the new term for *automatic styles* is *standard styles*.

Word 5.0 and 5.1 can use all the styles you created with earlier versions of the program.

What Styles Do

In Word, a *style* is a named, stored collection of formats—the ones that you now apply manually. When you apply a style to text in your document, the text takes on that style. As with any other Word format, you can format with styles before or after you type.

Part III

Using Advanced Formatting Techniques

Figure 14.3 introduces styles graphically. Three styles have been applied to the document represented in this graphic: *Body Text* (justified, Palatino, 12 points of blank space after), *Heading 1* (centered, bold, Helvetica, 24 points of blank space after), and *Quotation* (left indent 0.5 inch, right indent 0.5 inch, justified, Palatino, 12 points of blank space after).

Fig. 14.3
A document with three sample styles.

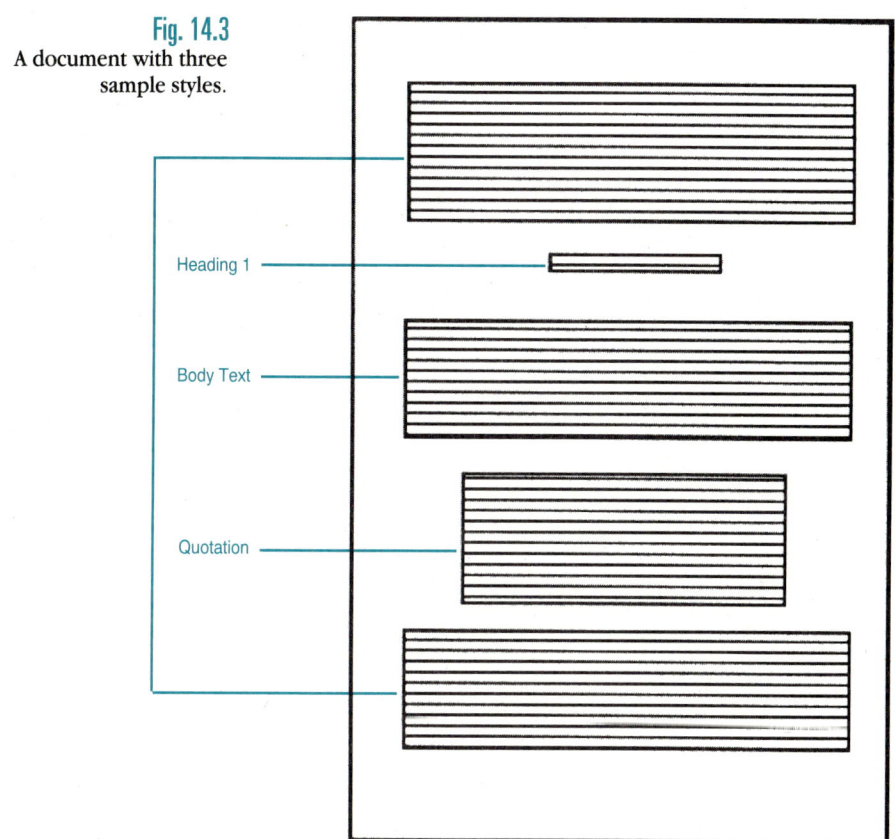

Styles enable you to reconsider your formatting decisions. Suppose that after formatting this document, you decide that you don't like the Palatino font you chose for the Body Text style and want to use Times Roman instead. Instead of reformatting all the paragraphs one by one, you simply change the Body Text style. Word automatically modifies all the paragraphs to which you applied the Body Text style; the reformatting is nearly instantaneous.

Where Styles Are Stored

When you create a style, you can store it in the default style sheet or in the document style sheet. A *document style sheet* is a storage area, attached to a specific document but invisible on-screen, in which your styles are stored. The *default style sheet* contains styles that are automatically available in all documents. You learn how to create and store your styles later in this chapter. For now, all you need to learn is the distinction between the default style sheet and the document style sheet.

If you store your style in the default style sheet, that style becomes available to all new documents you create. Suppose that you create a style called Body Text. Every time you open a new document, you see this style as an option in the ruler's Style selection drop-down list box (see fig. 14.4).

Fig. 14.4
Dropping down the Style selection list box.

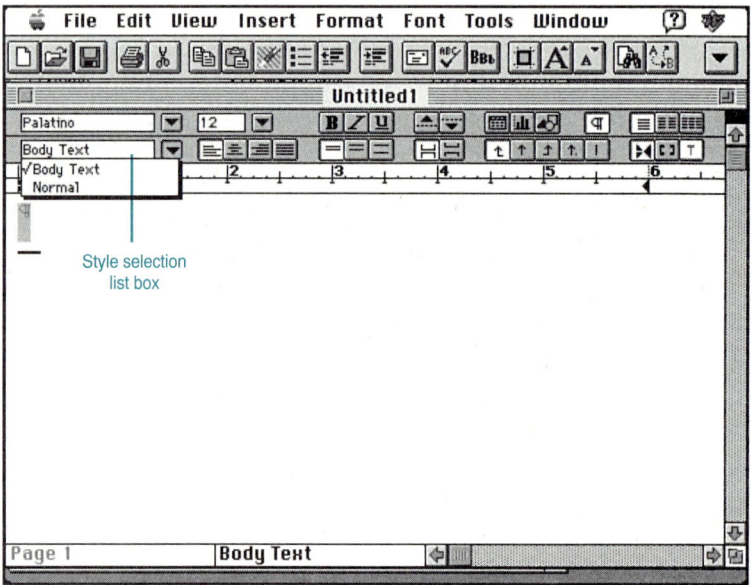

If you store your style in the document style sheet, that style is available only for the current document. You see the style in the Style selection list for the current document, but you will not see it if you open or create another document. (Later in this chapter, you learn how to copy a document style sheet from one document to another.)

What the Normal Style Is

While you have been using Word, you have been using the default style sheet. You probably noticed the word Normal in the ruler's Style selection list box. When you open a new Word document and start typing, Word applies the default style sheet's Normal style to the text you type. The Normal style formats this text with the default font and font size you chose when you installed Word. In addition, this style uses plain text (no emphasis), auto line spacing (single spacing), left paragraph alignment, no blank space before or after paragraphs, and Word's default tab settings.

CAUTION

Think twice before adding many styles to your default style sheet. If you add too many styles (more than 10 or 15), working with styles becomes cumbersome. For now, while you are learning to use styles, add styles only to your document style sheets.

Creating Styles

You can create up to 221 styles in a document, although in practice, you will find that 10 or 15 usually are sufficient. You can create styles by recording them or by using the Style command.

The easiest way to create styles is to record them from text you already have formatted. You begin by choosing formats manually, and then you record and name the style. This technique is easy but has important limitations. When you create styles this way, for example, you can save them only to the document style sheet, not the default style sheet.

You also can create styles by using the Style dialog box, which gives you more options. When you use the Style dialog box (shown later in fig. 14.7), you can save styles to the default style sheet as well as to the document style sheet. Moreover, the full range of Style options are available when you use this command.

T I P

If you want to create a style quickly and store it in the document style sheet, use the recording technique. To save a style to the default style sheet, use the Style command in the Format menu.

Rather than create your own heading styles, you may want to use (and perhaps redefine) Word's standard heading styles, such as Heading 1 and Heading 2, which are linked to outline heading levels. If you use these styles for your document headings, you get a handsome payoff when you switch to Outline view: your document headings become outline headings, and you can restructure your entire document simply by moving the headings on the screen. For more information on standard styles, see "Using Standard Styles" later in this chapter. For more information on heading styles and outlining, see Chapter 22, "Organizing Documents with Outlining."

Recording a Style

To record a style you already have created, follow these steps:

1. Format the paragraph, using manual formatting techniques.

   You can use any of the following formats: font, font size, emphasis, alignment, indentation, blank space, page-break control, tabs, borders, and frame positions (see Chapter 20). All the formats you choose become part of the style definition. When you apply the style, Word formats all the selected text with these formats.

When you create styles, be sparing in your use of character emphasis, such as bold and italic. The emphasis must apply to all the text to which you apply the style. You should include bold, for example, only when you're creating a style in which all the text should be bold (such as headings, headers, and footers).

To make sure that Word doesn't include any character emphasis in your style definition, highlight the paragraph and press ⌘-Shift-Z before defining the style.

2. If the ruler isn't displayed, choose Ruler from the Format menu or press ⌘-R.

3. Click the Style selection list box. Word highlights the box.

4. Type a name for the style.

   You can type up to 254 characters, including spaces (but excluding commas). Because the Style dialog box and the Style selection list box can display only 16 characters, however, keep your style names short.

5. Press Return. An alert box appears, asking whether you want to define the style (see fig. 14.5).

Fig. 14.5
Style-definition alert box.

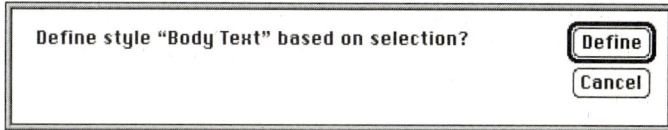

Define style "Body Text" based on selection? [Define] [Cancel]

6. Choose Define. Word records the style and stores it under the name you specified.

After you record a style, Word lists the style's name in the Style selection list box. The style becomes part of the document style sheet, and you can use it in the current document but not in other documents. To use this style in other documents, you must copy the entire style sheet (see "Copying a Document Style Sheet to a New Document" later in this chapter).

Using the Style Command

Creating a style with the Style dialog box isn't as straightforward as recording styles, but this procedure has two advantages:

- You can save the style to the default style sheet.

- You can use the Based On and Next Style options (discussed later in this chapter).

Before proceeding, notice that the style-name area at the bottom of the screen shows the current style name, as shown in figure 14.6.

To display the Style dialog box, choose Style from the Format menu, press ⌘-T, or double-click the style name in the status bar. The Style dialog box appears, displaying the current document's name in the title bar. This title indicates that you are looking at the document style sheet (see fig. 14.7).

Chapter 14
Formatting with Styles

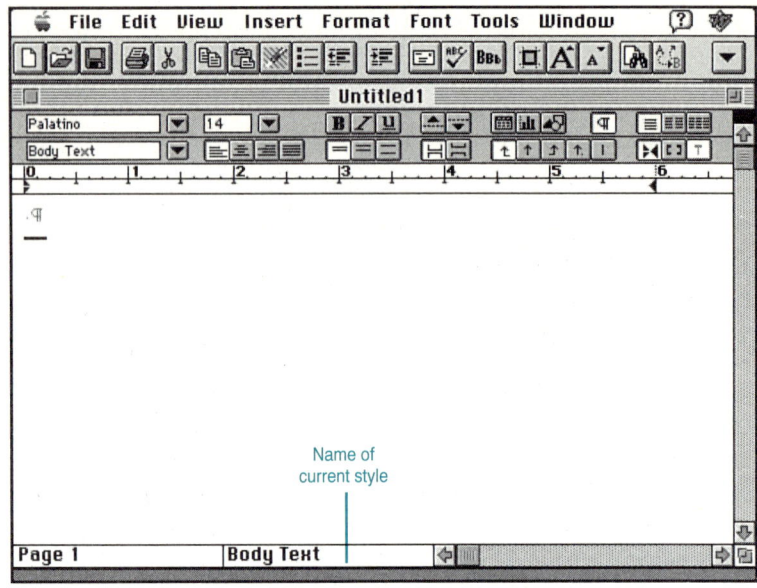

Fig. 14.6
Style-name area showing
the current style name.

Fig. 14.7
Style dialog box.

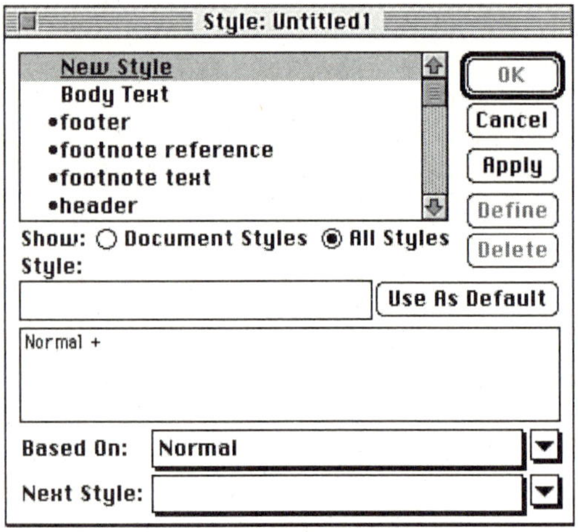

You see the following items in the Style dialog box:

Style list box. This list box displays the styles that currently are available in your document. If you select New Style, you can define a new style that will appear in this list.

Document Styles and All Styles radio buttons. By default, Word displays only the current-document styles: the default Normal style and the styles you defined for this document (if any). If you click All Styles, you see all of Word's standard styles.

Style text box. When you select a style, this box contains the name of the currently selected style; the larger box below it (the Style definition box) displays the current style's definition. In Figure 14.8, for example, the larger box shows the formats stored with the style Body Text.

Fig. 14.8

Style box displaying the current style.

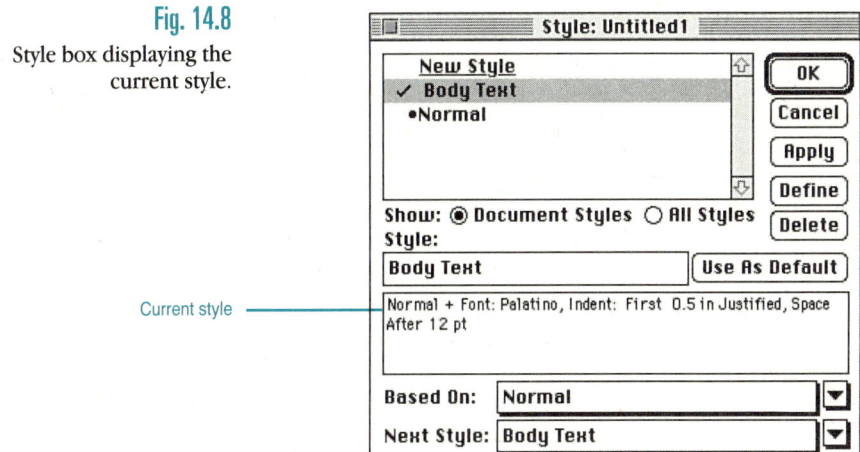

Current style

You do not type in the larger Style box directly; instead, you choose formatting commands, and Word enters the definition for you.

Based On drop-down list box. Every style can be based on another, which means that the style definition starts with the other style's formats. By default, most styles are based on the Normal style, which has an important implication: if you change Normal, all the styles based on Normal also change.

Next Style drop-down list box. This box enables you to specify which style Word will enter after you finish typing a paragraph in the current style and press Return. For example, you can define a Heading style so that Word returns to a Body Text style after you type the heading and press Return.

Command buttons. After you finish choosing formats for a new style, you click Define to save the style. Alternatively, you can click the Use as Default button to save the style to the default style sheet. Click the Apply button to see how the style looks without closing the Style dialog box. If you want to delete a style, you can highlight the style and click Delete.

To save some time when you choose formatting commands, position the insertion point in a paragraph that contains some or all of the formats you want to include in the style, and then choose the Style command. Word begins the New Style definition with the current paragraph's formats.

To create a document style in the Style dialog box, follow these steps:

1. Choose Style from the Format menu, press ⌘-T, or double-click the style name in the status bar. The Style dialog box appears, with New Style highlighted in the list box.

Notice that Word displays the formats for the paragraph in which the insertion point is positioned. If you don't want to use these formats, use any manual formatting technique to change them before you choose the Style command.

2. Type a style name in the Style text box. You can use up to 254 characters, but using fewer than 16 characters guarantees that the name will fit in the Style selection list box.

3. Use any manual formatting technique to choose formats, including using the pull-down menus and dialog boxes, making changes in the ribbon or ruler, or using keyboard commands.

4. If you want to see what the style looks like in your document without leaving the Style dialog box, click Apply.

5. Choose OK to define the style and apply the style to the selected paragraph(s). Alternatively, click Define to define the style and then click Cancel to exit the dialog box without applying the style you have created.

If you drop down the Style selection list box in the ruler, you see the style you just defined. This style is available in the current document only.

To create a default style in the Style dialog box, follow these steps:

1. Choose Style from the Format menu, press ⌘-T, or double-click the style name in the status bar. The Style dialog box appears, with New Style highlighted.

2. Type a style name in the Style text box.

3. Choose formats for the style.

4. **Important:** Click Use as Default (not Define). Clicking this command button ensures that Word will record the style in the default style sheet. An alert box appears, displaying the message OK to record style in default style sheet?

5. Choose OK to define the style and apply the style to the selected paragraph(s). The style you created now is available in all your Word documents.

   Alternatively, click Define to define the style and then click Cancel to exit the dialog box without applying the style you created.

After you define a style, you can change its definition or delete it. For more information, see "Revising and Managing Styles" later in this chapter.

Basing One Style on Another

As you see from the Style dialog box, you can base one style on another. By default, Word bases new styles on the Normal style. The Normal style, one of Word's standard styles, is defined by default to include your default font and font-size choice, as well as auto line spacing, left alignment, and tabs every 1/5-inch across the screen. If you want, you can base a new style on any other style you see in the list of styles.

When you base a new style on an existing one, the style you create includes the formats of the existing style. If you choose new formats that contradict the existing ones, however, Word uses your new choices instead of the formats of the base style. If you base a new style on the default Normal format and then choose justified alignment, for example, the new format will have justified alignment, not left alignment. The new style, however, will have any Normal formats that are not specifically contradicted by your formatting choices. If you do not choose a new font, for example, the new style will have the default font and font-size character formatting, which are part of the Normal style.

Always define the default font for a document by redefining the Normal style with the font and size you want, and then base all new styles on Normal. If you create your styles this way, you can change the font of every style simply by changing Normal.

Suppose that you define Normal to include Geneva 12. When you create several new styles based on Normal, each style is formatted with Geneva 12. Later, you decide that the document would look better in Helvetica 12. To reformat your whole document with Helvetica 12, you simply redefine Normal so that it specifies Helvetica 12 instead of Geneva 12. For instructions on modifying existing styles, see "Revising Styles" later in this chapter.

Defining the Next Style

After you create a style, apply it, and type some text in the style. You find that when you press Return, Word returns to Normal formatting instead of copying the style to the next paragraph. In other words, Word applies the Normal style automatically when you press Return. If you like, however, you can control the style Word applies when you press Return. You can change the Next Style setting in the Style dialog box (when you create the style, or later) so that Word applies the style you want when you press Return.

Controlling the next style is useful when you know that one style is always followed by another. For example, many corporate style guidelines instruct writers to type their department name below the document title. In such a case, you can create a Document Title style that is followed by a Department Name style. Every time you apply the Document Title style, type some text, and press Return, Word automatically applies the Department Name style to the following paragraph.

To define the next style while you are creating a style, simply type that style's name in the Next Style text box of the Style dialog box. You can change the Next Style setting after you create the style; choose the Style command, type the style name in the Next Style box, and choose OK.

Word applies the next style automatically only when you press Return to create a new paragraph. If you don't press Return, Word doesn't change the style of the next paragraph.

Overriding the Next Style

When you apply a style and type, Word always enters the style you specified in the Next Style box when you press Return. For example, if you type **Text Paragraph** in the Next Style box when you define the Heading 1 style, Word enters the Text Paragraph format when you press Return after typing with Heading 1. You can, however, override the Next Style setting in two ways:

- If you use the New Line command (Shift-Return) to start a new line without starting a new paragraph, Word continues using the current style without starting a new paragraph.

- If you want to start a new paragraph in the same style, press ⌘-Return.

As you define additional styles, think about which style you want Word to enter when you press Return. Most bulleted lists are followed by text paragraphs, for example, so you would type **Text Paragraph** in the Next Style box when you create a style for a bulleted list.

Applying Styles

After you create or redefine a style, you can apply it. When you apply a style, Word formats the selected paragraph (or paragraphs) with the formats stored in the style's definition. These formats apply uniformly to the entire paragraph. If the style definition includes bold or italic, for example, the entire paragraph receives this character emphasis.

To apply the styles to selected paragraphs in your document, you can use the Style selection box, the Style command, or a keyboard command.

Undo and Repeat are useful commands after you apply styles. If you apply a style to the wrong paragraph, immediately choose Undo from the Edit menu or press ⌘-Z. To apply the style again, select another paragraph and choose Repeat from the Edit menu or press ⌘-Y.

You can undo or repeat a command only if you haven't chosen another command or typed any additional text since you chose the command.

Applying Styles in the Style Selection List Box

By far the easiest way to apply a style is to use the Style selection drop-down box in the ruler. To apply a style by using the Style selection list box, follow these steps:

1. If the ruler isn't displayed, choose Ruler from the View menu or press ⌘-R.

2. Select the paragraph or paragraphs to which you want to apply the style, or press Return to start a new paragraph.

   If you are selecting only one paragraph, don't bother highlighting the entire paragraph; simply place the insertion point anywhere in the paragraph.

3. Point to the arrow next to the Style selection list box, and hold down the mouse button. Word drops down the Style selection list (shown earlier in fig. 14.4).

4. Drag the mouse down the list until you have highlighted the style that you want to apply.

5. Release the mouse button. Word applies the style to the selected text and displays the current style name in the Style box at the bottom of the document window as well as in the Style selection list box.

Applying Styles with the Style Dialog Box

The Style dialog box is useful mainly for creating, editing, and deleting styles, but you also can use it to apply styles. This technique is of interest mainly to users of small Classic screens, who may work with the ruler hidden so that they can see more text in the document window.

To apply a style with the Style dialog box, follow these steps:

1. Select the paragraph or paragraphs to which you want to apply the style, or press Return to start a new paragraph.

   If you are selecting only one paragraph, don't bother highlighting the entire paragraph; simply place the insertion point anywhere in the paragraph.

2. Choose Style from the Format menu or press ⌘-T. The Style dialog box appears.

3. Highlight the style name in the Style selection list box and then choose OK. (Alternatively, double-click the style name.) Word applies the style to the selected text and displays the current style name in the Style box at the bottom of the document window. If you are displaying the ruler, you also see the style name in the Style selection list box.

Applying Styles with the Keyboard

The third way to apply a style is to use the ⌘-Shift-S keyboard shortcut. This technique is fast but has one drawback: you don't see a list of style names, so you must memorize the names of the styles that you want to apply.

To apply a style with the keyboard, follow these steps:

1. Select the paragraph or paragraphs to which you want to apply the style, or press Return to start a new paragraph.

2. Press ⌘-Shift-S. The word Style appears in the status bar.

3. Type the style name. You need not type the entire name—only enough of it to enable Word to distinguish the style from other styles with similar names.

4. Press Return. Word applies the style to the selected text and displays the current style name in the Style box at the bottom of the document window. You also see the style name in the Style selection list box.

Chapter 35 contains important suggestions for customizing Word's menus and keyboard, including two important style tips: you can add style names to a special custom menu (called Work), and you can assign styles to keyboard commands.

Applying Styles to Manually Formatted Text

If you plan to apply styles to the paragraphs in your document after you type, you shouldn't bother choosing manual formats before you type, for the following reasons:

Chapter 14

Formatting with Styles

■ *A style's paragraph formats overwrite any manual formatting choices you made earlier.* Suppose that you manually choose tabs, blank-space options, indents, and New York 10, and then apply a style. You lose all your manual formatting choices.

■ *If a style includes character emphasis (such as bold, italic, underlining, or small caps), the style applies to all the text to which you apply it.* Suppose that you format a few words in a paragraph as boldface and then apply a style that includes bold in its definition. Word formats the entire paragraph in boldface—except for the words you manually formatted as bold! For those words, applying the style is like turning off the format. To avoid this unwanted effect, apply character emphasis *after* you apply styles, not before.

Revising and Managing Styles

You can edit, rename, or delete a style after you create it. When you edit a style, the redefined style automatically applies to all the paragraphs in the current document to which you applied the original style. If you revise a default style, the change affects all the Word documents to which you applied the original default style. After you change a default style, Word automatically updates the affected documents when you open them.

Revising Styles

If you aren't happy with a style's appearance, you can change the style definition in several ways. The easiest way is to make the changes in the document manually and then use the Style selection list box. You also can use the Style dialog box to edit the style.

To change a style definition using the Style selection list box, follow these steps:

1. Use manual formatting techniques to reformat a paragraph to which the style has been applied.

2. With the insertion point positioned in the paragraph you just formatted, click the Style selection list box to highlight the current style name.

3. Press Return. The alert box shown in figure 14.9 appears.

Fig. 14.9
Style alert box.

Style: Body Text
◉ Reapply the style to the selection?
○ Redefine the style based on selection?

OK
Cancel

4. Click the Redefine the Style Based on Selection? radio button.

5. Choose OK.

To change a style using the Style dialog box, follow these steps:

1. Position the insertion point in the text that contains the style.

2. Choose Style from the Format menu or press ⌘-T. The Style dialog box appears.

3. In the list box, select the style that you want to edit.

4. Use any manual formatting technique (the Format and Font menu, the ribbon, the ruler, or keyboard shortcuts) to change the existing formats. You also can add new formats.

5. Choose OK to define the style and apply the style to the selected text. Alternatively, click Define to define the style and then click Cancel to exit the dialog box without applying the style you created.

Renaming Styles

You can rename a style if the new name isn't already being used for a different style. To rename a style, follow these steps:

1. Choose Style from the Format menu or press ⌘-T. The Style dialog box appears.

2. In the list box, select the style that you want to rename.

3. Type the new name in the Style text box.

4. Choose OK. An alert box appears, asking whether you want to change the old style to the new style.

5. Choose OK to change the style.

Deleting Styles

You can delete any style you have added to a style sheet, whether that style is stored in the document or in the default style sheet. You cannot delete any of Word's standard styles, however. (See "Using Standard Styles" later in this chapter.) If you try to delete a standard style—identified by a dot next to its name in the Style dialog box—Word takes no action.

To delete styles, use the following procedure:

1. Choose Style from the Format menu or press ⌘-T. The Style dialog box appears.

2. In the list box, select the style name. If you want to delete a default style and you don't see the name in the list box, click the All Styles radio button to display the style name.

3. Click the Delete command button. An alert box appears, asking whether you really want to delete the style.

4. To confirm the deletion, choose OK.

If you formatted any text with the deleted style, the text takes the Normal style after you delete the style. If the style also is part of the default style sheet, you are asked to confirm the deletion from that style sheet as well.

Adding Formats to Text Formatted with Styles

After you apply a style to a paragraph, you can add additional character or paragraph formats. You should keep a few points in mind, however, when you manually apply additional formats to a paragraph formatted with a style:

■ *The formats that you add manually affect only the selected text.* The added formats do not change the style definition, and they do not apply to other paragraphs with the same style. (If you like the change, use the procedures for revising styles.)

■ *If a format that you add manually conflicts with the style definition, the manual format overrides the style format, but Word leaves the other style formats intact.* Suppose that you format a paragraph with the Body Text style, which includes Palatino 12 and justified alignment, and then you highlight the paragraph and choose Times Roman 10. Word changes the font and font size but leaves the alignment alone.

After you format manually, you can restore all the style's formats or only its character formats.

To restore the style's character formats and remove any character formats you added manually, choose Revert to Style from the Format menu or press ⌘-Shift-space bar.

To restore all the style's formats and remove the formats that you added manually, reapply the style. When the alert box appears, choose Reapply the Style to the Selection? and then choose OK.

If you want to remove the style from the paragraph completely, choose another style or press ⌘-Shift-P. This command reapplies the Normal style to the selection.

You can tell at a glance whether you added any character emphasis to a paragraph that you previously formatted with a style by looking at the Revert to Style option in the Format menu. If a check mark appears beside this option, you have not added character emphasis.

Using Standard Styles

Certain commands automatically apply Word's standard styles. Footnote reference marks and footnote text, for example, are standard styles that Word applies automatically when you use the Footnote command (Insert menu). These styles, which are part of the default style sheet, are automatically copied to every document's style sheet. To see these styles in your document style sheet, choose the All Styles option in the Style dialog box. As shown in figure 14.10, dots designate the standard styles in the Style list box.

Because these styles are applied automatically, why bother learning about them?

First, you can change any of the standard styles for the current document's style sheet. Suppose that you want to print footnotes in 12-point characters rather than in the default 9-point characters. By changing the footnote reference style, you change the size of footnote reference marks throughout your document. (The change affects only the current document.)

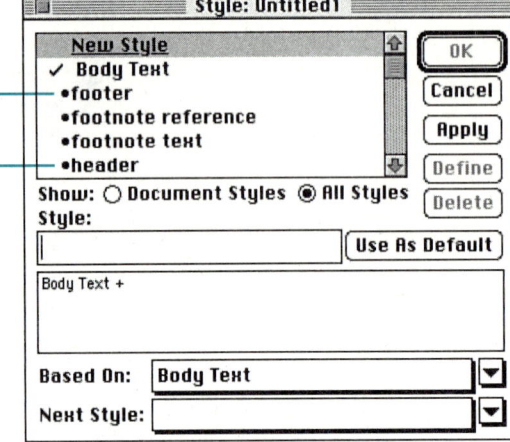

Fig. 14.10

Dots designating standard
styles in the Style
dialog box.

Standard styles

Second, you can change Word's defaults for any of the formats controlled by standard styles so that these changes automatically apply to all
your documents. Suppose that you always want 12-point footnote
reference marks. When you redefine the footnote reference style, you
can click the Use as Default button, which redefines the style in Word's
default style sheet so that all your footnotes in all your documents have
12-point footnote reference marks.

Reviewing Standard Styles

Many of Word's standard styles are based on the Normal style. When you
redefine Normal, all the styles based on Normal also change. (For more
information about basing one style on another, see "Basing One Style on
Another" earlier in this chapter.) Following is an overview of the kinds of
styles you find among the standard styles:

Header and footer styles. These styles control the character and
paragraph formats of running heads and footers, which are
positioned within the top and bottom margins of your document.
(For more information on headers and footers, see Chapter 19.)

Heading styles. These styles control the formatting of the heading
levels that Word automatically inserts when you define heading
levels in an outline (see Chapter 22).

Footnote styles. The footnote reference mark style controls the
formatting of footnote reference marks (the superscript number

placed in your document to indicate a footnote or endnote). The footnote text style applies to the footnote or endnote text (see Chapter 19).

Index styles. These styles control the formatting of the various index entries created by Word's Index command (see Chapter 26).

Line-number style. This style controls the format of the line numbers that Word can insert into the margins of your document automatically (see Chapter 16).

Normal style. By far the most important style in Word, Normal is the default style for all text-entry purposes. When you open a new document and start typing, you create text in Normal style. Changing the Normal style has dramatic effects because many other styles are based on Normal.

Page-number style. This style automatically formats page numbers inserted with the Margin Page Numbers option (Section dialog box) and page numbers inserted in Print Preview. If you insert page numbers into a header or footer, you can control the formatting manually.

Table-of-contents styles. The table-of-contents (*toc*) styles control the formatting of the table-of-contents entries that Word automatically creates when you use the Table of Contents command (see Chapter 26).

Table 14.1 lists all the standard styles and their default definitions.

Table 14.1
Default Format Definitions of Automatic Styles

Format name	Format definition
footer	Normal + Tab stops: 3 inches centered, 6 inches flush right
footnote reference	Normal + Font: 9 point, superscript 3 point
footnote text	Normal + Font: 10 point
header	Normal + Tab stops: 3 inches centered, 6 inches flush right
heading 1	Helvetica Bold Underline, 12 point, space before 12 point
heading 2	Helvetica Bold, 12 point, space before 6 point

continues

Chapter 14
Formatting with Styles

	Format name	Format definition
Table 14.1 Continued	heading 3	Normal + Bold, 12 point, indent left 0.25 inch
	heading 4	Normal + Underline, 12 point, indent left 0.25 inch
	heading 5	Normal + Bold, 10 point, indent left 0.5 inch
	heading 6	Normal, 10 point, underline, indent left 0.5 inch
	heading 7	Normal, 10 point, italic, indent left 0.5 inch
	heading 8	Normal, 10 point, italic, indent left 0.5 inch
	heading 9	Normal, 10 point, italic, indent left 0.5 inch
	index 1	Normal
	index 2	Normal + left indent 0.25 inch
	index 3	Normal + left indent 0.5 inch
	index 4	Normal + left indent 0.75 inch
	index 5	Normal + left indent 1.0 inch
	index 6	Normal + left indent 1.25 inch
	index 7	Normal + left indent 1.5 inch
	line number	Normal
	Normal	Default font and font size, flush left
	PostScript	Normal + 10 point, hidden, bold
	page number	Normal
	toc 1	Normal + 0.5 inch right indent, Tab stops: 5.75 inches flush left with leader dots and 6 inches flush right
	toc 2	Normal + left indent 0.5 inch, 0.5 inch right indent, Tab stops: 5.75 inches flush left with leader dots and 6 inches flush right
	toc 3	Normal + left indent 1.0 inch, 0.5 inch right indent, Tab stops: 5.75 inches flush left with leader dots and 6 inches flush right

Part III

Using Advanced Formatting Techniques

Format name	Format definition
toc 4	Normal + left indent 1.5 inch, 0.5 inch right indent, Tab stops: 5.75 inches flush left with leader dots and 6 inches flush right
toc 5	Normal + left indent 2.0 inch, 0.5 inch right indent, Tab stops: 5.75 inches flush left with leader dots and 6 inches flush right
toc 6	Normal + left indent 2.5 inch, 0.5 inch right indent, Tab stops: 5.75 inches flush left with leader dots and 6 inches flush right
toc 7	Normal + left indent 3.0 inch, 0.5 inch right indent, Tab stops: 5.75 inches flush left with leader dots and 6 inches flush right
toc 8	Normal + left indent 3.5 inch, 0.5 inch right indent, Tab stops: 5.75 inches flush left with leader dots and 6 inches flush right
toc 9	Normal + left indent 4.0 inch, 0.5 inch right indent, Tab stops: 5.75 inches flush left with leader dots and 6 inches flush right

Choosing Standard Styles Manually

Although Word applies most standard styles automatically (when you add a footnote, for example), you may want to choose certain styles (such as the heading styles) manually.

To apply a standard style with the Style selection list box, follow these steps:

1. Holding down the Shift key, click the arrow next to the Style selection list box, and hold down the mouse button. Word lists all the standard styles in addition to your document styles.

Chapter 14

Formatting with Styles

2. Drag the mouse down the list until the style you want is high-lighted.

3. Release the mouse button.

To choose a standard style with the Style dialog box, follow these steps:

1. Choose Style from the Format menu or press ⌘-T. The Style dialog box appears.

2. Click the All Styles radio button to display all the standard styles in the list box.

3. Highlight the name of the style you want.

4. Click Apply, if you want to see the effects of the style without exiting the Style dialog box.

5. Choose OK.

Redefining a Standard Style

To redefine a standard style, follow these steps:

1. Choose Style from the Format menu or press ⌘-T. The Style dialog box appears.

2. Click the All Styles radio button. You see all the styles in the list box, including your document styles and the standard styles.

3. Highlight the name of the style you want to change. Word shows the current formats in the Style definition box.

4. Use any manual formatting technique (the Format and Font menu, the ribbon, the ruler, or keyboard shortcuts) to change the style.

5. To redefine the style for the current document only, choose OK. To change the default style, click the Use as Default button and then choose OK when the alert box appears.

Searching for Styles

The Find command can help you quickly locate that style you applied in your document—for example, if you formatted one paragraph with a quotation format and want to preview its appearance.

You also can use styles to create a more focused search. Suppose that you want to find a paragraph that mentions Civil War battlegrounds. You know that you typed this text using the Bulleted List style. If you add the Bulleted List style to the search, Word searches only the paragraphs formatted with the Bulleted List style.

To search for a style, follow these steps:

1. Choose Find from the Edit menu or press ⌘-F. The Find dialog box appears.

2. Select a style in the Style selection list box (ruler).

   or

   Select the Style option in the Format drop-down list box (Find dialog box), and select the style in the list that appears.

3. Choose OK. After you choose the style, Word displays the style's name under the Find What text box, as shown in figure 14.11.

Fig. 14.11
Finding a style.

You can choose only one style at a time in the Find dialog box.

4. If you want to search for specific text that has the style you selected, type that text in the Find What text box. To search for any text with this style, leave the text box blank.

5. If you want to change the direction of the search, make a selection in the Search drop-down list box.

6. Choose Find Next to begin the search.

   If Word finds text with the style you specified, the program highlights that text in your document. Choose Find Next to find the next occurrence of the style or click Cancel to return to your document.

If Word cannot find any text with the style you specified, an alert box appears, asking whether you want to extend the search from the beginning of the document (or from the end, if you are searching up). Choose Yes to extend the search, or click No to cancel.

After you use the Find dialog box to search for a style, Word retains that style setting and any text in the Find What text box for the duration of the current operating session. If you choose Find again, you have to clear these settings to perform a different search. To clear text from the Find What text box, select the text and press Delete or Backspace. To clear the style, pull down the Format list box and select Clear.

Replacing Styles

The Replace command enables you to replace one style with another throughout your document. Suppose that you inadvertently formatted a few paragraphs with the Lead Paragraph style (no first-line indentation) when you should have used Text Paragraph style (0.5" first-line indentation). You can use Replace to search for all the paragraphs that have the Lead Paragraph style and then change the style to Text Paragraph by clicking Replace.

To replace one style with another throughout your document, follow these steps:

1. Choose Replace from the Edit menu or press ⌘-F. The Replace dialog box appears.

2. To choose the style you want Word to find, select the style name in the Style selection drop-down list box (ruler), or select Style in the Format drop-down list box (Replace dialog box) and then select the style in the list that appears.

3. Choose the replacement style (the one you want Word to insert in place of the style you just chose). Select the style name in the Style selection box (ruler), or select Style in the Format drop-down list box and then select the style in the list that appears. Your choice appears below the Replace With text box, as shown in figure 14.12.

4. If you want to search for specific text that has the style listed below the Find What text box, type that text in the Find What text box. To search for any text with that style, leave the text box blank.

Fig. 14.12
Replacing one style with
another.

Replace

Find What: [_____]   (**Find Next**)

[Format ▼] Style: Body Text   (Replace)

[Special ▼]   (**Replace All**)

Replace With: |[_____]   (Cancel)

[Format ▼] Style: Hanging Indent

[Special ▼]

☐ Match Whole Word Only   ☐ Match Case

Search:
[Selection ▼]

5. If you want to replace specific text that has the style listed below the Replace With text box, type the replacement text in the Replace With text box. To replace only the style, leave the text box blank.

6. If you want to change the direction of the search, make a selection in the Search drop-down list box.

7. Choose Find Next, or if you are sure that you want to perform the replacement throughout your document, click Replace All.

   Word highlights text with the style you specified. Choose Find Next to find the next occurrence of the format or click Cancel to return to your document.

   If Word cannot find any text with the style you specified, an alert box appears, asking whether you want to extend the search from the beginning of the document (or from the end, if you are searching up). Choose Yes to extend the search, or click No to cancel.

After you use the Replace dialog box to search for a style, Word retains the style settings and any text in the text boxes for the duration of the current operating session. Those styles and text also appear in the Find dialog box. If you choose Replace or Find again, you have to clear these settings to perform a different search. To clear text from the Find What text box, select the text and press Delete or Backspace. To clear the style, pull down the Format drop-down list box and select Clear.

Copying a Document Style Sheet to a New Document

After you create a useful document style sheet, you may want to copy it to a new document. When you do, all the styles in that style sheet are available in the new document.

When you copy document styles, bear in mind what happens when the *target document* (the document to which you're copying the styles) contains one or more styles with the same name: Word merges the two style sheets, and if two styles have the same name, the program over-writes the target document's styles.

Suppose that Document 2 contains a style called Body Text. Into this document, you are copying Document 1's style sheet, which also contains a style called Body Text. When Word copies Document 1's styles into Document 2, the program overwrites Document 2's Body Text style.

Be aware, too, that style names are case-sensitive. As far as Word is concerned, body text and Body Text are two different styles, so one will not overwrite the other.

To copy a document style sheet, follow these steps:

1. In the new document, choose Style from the Format menu or press ⌘-T. The Style dialog box appears.

2. Choose Open from the File menu, press ⌘-O, or click the Open tool. The Open dialog box appears.

3. In the Open dialog box, select the name of the document that contains the styles you want to copy.

4. Choose Open. Word combines the new document's style sheet with the style sheet of the document you just opened. If a style name in the new document conflicts, Word uses the incoming style's name and formats.

5. Click Close in the Style dialog box to return to your document.

Using Stationery Documents To Store Frequently Used Styles

 If you're using System 7, you can use stationery documents to store generic versions of documents, such as letters and memos. Many Word users don't realize, however, that stationery documents also can store document styles. When you open a stationery document, you get all the

formats you saved with the template, including styles—even if the document contains no text. Word's stationery-document capabilities provide an excellent resource for managing document styles.

In System 7, you can create an authoritative version of document styles easily. Suppose that you create the following series of stationery documents (with or without template text):

- *Proposal Styles.* This stationery document contains the document styles you use for proposals.

- *Article Styles.* This stationery document contains the document styles you use for the articles you contribute to scientific journals.

- *Correspondence Styles.* This stationery document contains the document styles you use for letters and memos.

When you create a new document, you can open the appropriate stationery document (such as Correspondence Styles), which contains all the styles you want to use.

Quick Review

This section summarizes the most useful information in this chapter. Check "Productivity Tips" for a review of high-productivity tips and tricks—the ones that Macintosh and Word pros use every day. Review "Techniques" whenever you need a quick reminder about a specific procedure.

Productivity Tips

- Apply styles before you type. If you use the Next Style option intelligently, Word can enter the style that is most likely to follow a paragraph every time you press Return.

- Applying styles before you type saves you the trouble of applying styles paragraph by paragraph in your document.

- Avoid adding too many styles to your default style sheet. Instead, save styles to a document style sheet and then save that document as a stationery document (see Chapter 5, "Managing Documents and Files"). When you open the document, all the document styles will be available in a new Untitled document.

- Keep your style names short enough to appear in the Style selection list box.

- If you want to use a font or font size other than the defaults, redefine the Normal style. Your change will affect most of the standard styles and all new styles you create because Word uses the Normal style as the Based On style by default.

- Create styles in the Style dialog box instead of recording them because only the Style dialog box enables you to choose the next style. Think carefully about which style is most likely to follow a paragraph to which you apply the style you are creating and then type the name of that next style in the Next Style text box.

- If you prefer to apply styles after you type, avoid adding character emphases before you apply styles.

- While you are learning the program, use Word's default heading styles for your document headings. (You probably will want to redefine them eventually.) Be sure to include the Keep With Next option, coupled with some blank space after the heading, to keep Word from breaking a page after the heading. Define the display type for headings by modifying the Heading 1 style, and then use the Based On option to base all the other heading styles on Heading 1.

Techniques

This section provides concise summaries of all the procedures introduced in this chapter.

Creating a Style

To record a style you have already created:

1. Format the paragraph, using manual formatting techniques.

2. If the ruler isn't displayed, choose Ruler from the Format menu or press ⌘-R.

3. With the insertion point in the paragraph you just formatted, click the Style selection list box in the ruler.

4. Type a name for the style.

5. Press Return.

6. When the message box appears, click Define.

To create a document style with the Style dialog box:

1. Choose Style from the Format menu or press ⌘-T. The Style dialog box appears.

2. Type a style name in the Style text box.

3. Choose formats for the style.

4. If you want to see what the style will look like in your document without leaving the Style dialog box, click Apply.

5. Choose OK to define the style and apply the style to the selected text. Alternatively, click Define to define the style and then click Cancel to exit the dialog box without applying the style you created.

To modify a default style with the Style dialog box:

1. Choose Style from the Format menu or press ⌘-T. The Style dialog box appears.

2. Type a style name in the Style text box.

3. Choose formats for the style.

4. **Important:** Click Use as Default (not Define).

5. Choose OK to define the style and apply the style to the selected text. Alternatively, click Define to define the style and then click Close to exit the dialog box without applying the style you have created.

Applying a Style

To apply a style using the Style selection list box:

1. Select the paragraph or paragraphs to which you want to apply the style, or press Return to start a new paragraph.

2. Point to the arrow next to the Style selection list box and hold down the mouse button.

3. Drag the mouse down the list until you highlight the style that you want to apply.

4. Release the mouse button.

To apply a style with the Style dialog box:

1. Select the paragraph or paragraphs to which you want to apply the style, or press Return to start a new paragraph.

2. Choose Style from the Format menu or press ⌘-T. The Style dialog box appears.

3. Highlight the style name in the Style list box and choose OK. Alternatively, double-click the style name.

To apply a style with the keyboard:

1. Select the paragraph or paragraphs to which you want to apply the style, or press Return to start a new paragraph.

2. Press ⌘-Shift-S.

3. Type the style name.

4. Press Return.

Revising a Style

To change a style definition using the Style selection list box:

1. Use manual formatting techniques to reformat a paragraph to which the style has been applied.

2. Click the Style selection list box to highlight the style name.

3. Press Return. An alert box appears.

4. Click the Redefine the Style Based on Selection? radio button.

5. Choose OK.

To change a style using the Style dialog box:

1. Choose Style from the Format menu or press ⌘-T. The Style dialog box appears.

2. If you want to revise a standard style, click the All Styles radio button.

3. In the list box, select the style that you want to edit.

4. Use any manual formatting technique (the Format and Font menu, the ribbon, the ruler, or keyboard shortcuts) to change the existing formats. You also can add new formats.

5. Choose OK to define the style and apply the style to the selected text. Alternatively, click Define to define the style and then click Cancel to exit the dialog box without applying the style you created.

Renaming a Style

To rename a style:

1. Choose Style from the Format menu or press ⌘-T. The Style dialog box appears.

2. In the list box, select the style you want to rename.

3. Type the new name in the Style text box.

4. Choose OK. An alert box appears, asking whether you want to replace the old style with the new one.

5. Choose OK.

Deleting a Style

To delete an existing style:

1. Choose Style from the Format menu or press ⌘-T. The Style dialog box appears.

2. In the list box, select the style name. If you want to delete a default style and you don't see the name in the list box, click the All Styles radio button to display the style name.

3. Click Delete. An alert box appears.

4. Confirm the deletion by choosing OK.

Canceling a Style

To remove a style from text to which the style has been applied:

Press ⌘-Shift-P to reformat the paragraph in Normal style.

or

Apply another style.

To cancel character emphases that you added to a paragraph after applying the style:

1. Highlight the paragraph or paragraphs that contain the unwanted emphasis.

2. Press ⌘-Shift-space bar or choose Revert to Style from the Format menu.

To cancel all manual formatting that you added to a paragraph after applying the style:

1. Place the insertion point in the paragraph or select more than one paragraph.

2. Click the Style selection list box.

3. Press Return. An alert box appears.

4. Click the Reapply the Style to the Selection? radio button.

5. Choose OK.

Finding a Style

To search for a style:

1. Choose Find from the Edit menu or press ⌘-F. The Find dialog box appears.

2. Select a style in the Style selection list box (ruler), or select the Style option in the Format drop-down list box (Find dialog box) and then select the style in the list that appears.

3. If you want to search for specific text that has the style listed below the Find What text box, type that text in the Find What text box. To search for any text with this style, leave the text box blank.

4. If you want to change the direction of the search, make a selection in the Search drop-down list box.

5. Choose Find Next to begin the search.

Replacing a Style

To replace one style with another throughout your document:

1. Choose Replace from the Edit menu or press ⌘-F. The Replace dialog box appears.

2. To choose the style you want Word to find, select a style in the Style selection list box (ruler), or select the Style option in the Format drop-down list box (Find dialog box) and then select the style in the list that appears.

3. To choose the replacement style, select a style in the Style selection list box, or select the Style option in the Format drop-down list box and then select the style in the list that appears.

4. If you want to search for specific text that has the style listed below the Find What text box, type that text in the Find What text box. To search for any text with that style, leave the text box blank.

5. If you want to replace specific text that has the style listed under the Replace With text box, type the replacement text in the Replace With text box. To replace only the style, leave the text box blank.

6. If you want to change the direction of the search, make a selection in the Search drop-down list box.

7. Choose Find Next, or if you are sure that you want to perform the replacement throughout your document, click Replace All.

Copying a Document Style Sheet

To copy a document style sheet:

1. In the new document, choose Style from the Format menu or press ⌘-T. The Style dialog box appears.

2. Choose Open from the File menu, press ⌘-O, or click the Open tool. The Open dialog box appears.

3. In the Open dialog box, select the document that contains the styles you want to copy.

4. Choose Open. Word copies the styles to the target document.

5. Click Close in the Style dialog box.

Creating Tables

I f you frequently type tables, you know how tedious this task can be. First, you set up tab stops. Next, you type the text. But what happens if one of the items requires more than one line? What if you left something out and need to add a column? In many cases, typing a tabbed table leads to much fussing and frustration. Adding a word you left out, for example, can throw off the whole row. To make creating tables easier, Word now offers a Table command.

What does the Table command do? In brief, this command inserts a spreadsheetlike matrix of rows and columns into your document. To create the table, you type in the cells of this table.

Using the Table command has many advantages over typing a table with tabs. Following are some of those advantages:

- If an entry requires more than one line, Word wraps the lines within that cell and adjusts the height of all the other cells in the row automatically (see fig. 15.1).

- If you need to add a column, you simply select the column where you want the new column to appear and use Word's Table Layout command.

- If you need to add a word or two to an entry, Word simply adjusts the size of the cell to accommodate the added text.

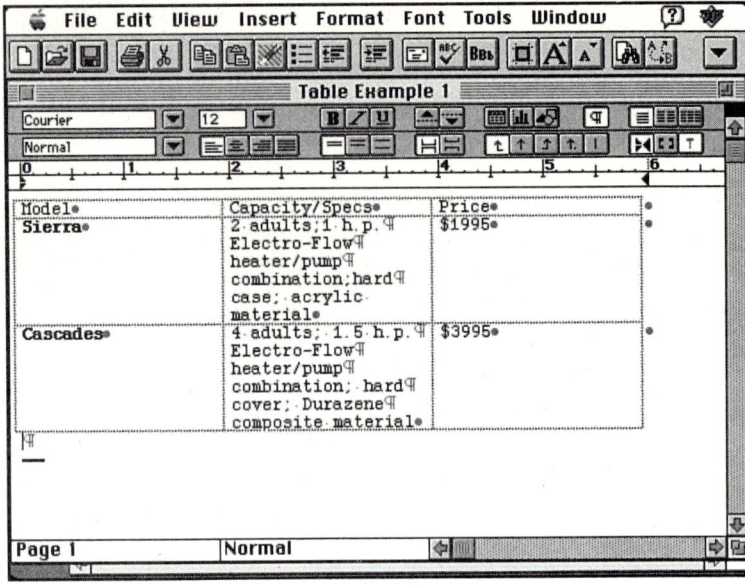

Fig. 15.1
Table cells enlarged to accommodate text.

The Table command has other advantages, most of which are covered in this chapter (Chapter 16 covers the use of Word's Sort command for sorting tables). In particular, the chapter covers the following topics:

- *Learning about Word's tables.* In this section, you explore Word's Table command, learning how you can use this command not only to create tables but also to create side-by-side paragraphs and even to place text next to graphics.

- *Creating a table.* In this section, you learn how to create a table in any Word document and how to create a table from existing tabbed text.

- *Moving the insertion point and selecting text.* When you create a table, special procedures for moving the insertion point and selecting text become available. These procedures are covered in this section.

- *Editing the table matrix.* A table's rows and columns aren't like ordinary text; you cannot delete them the way you delete characters. In the section on editing, you learn how to insert or delete rows, columns, and individual cells.

Part III

Using Advanced Formatting Techniques

- *Formatting a table.* After you insert a table, you can change the table's layout easily by adjusting column widths and changing row alignment. The procedures are covered in the section on formatting.

If you're using Word 5.1, you can take advantage of a welcome new feature: the Table icon in the ribbon. You can use this icon to create a table; to convert existing tabbed text to a table; and to insert cells, columns, or rows into a table. To find out how to use the Table icon, look for the Word 5.1 icons in this chapter.

Learning About Word's Tables

This section introduces tables. Specific information about creating, editing, and formatting tables appears later in the chapter. For now, you need to know a few terms so that you can work effectively with tables.

When you use the Table command to create a table, you first must specify how many columns and rows you want to use. Word calculates column width automatically so that each column is the same width. (You learn later in this chapter how to adjust column widths.) In figure 15.2, for example, Word created a table with 5 columns and 15 rows. Each column is 1.2 inches wide. The matrix of row and column lines does not print. You can, however, add borders for printing, as explained in Chapter 17, "Using Borders and Shading."

When you choose Show ¶ from the View menu, you see the *end-of-cell markers*—the black dots that appear in figure 15.2. Comparable to paragraph marks, these markers move right and down when you enter text.

When you choose Show Ruler from the View menu and when the Table Boundary icon in the ruler is activated, the ruler uses table-boundary markers, which are shaped like the letter *T*, to show the column boundaries (refer to fig. 15.2). As you learn later in this chapter, you can change column widths by dragging the table-boundary markers.

With this overview of tables in mind, think of tables in terms of the following procedures:

- *Creating tables.* To create a table, choose the Table command from the Insert menu. Word inserts the matrix of rows and columns into your document.

Fig. 15.2
A table of 5 columns and 15 rows.

```
 File  Edit  View  Insert  Format  Font  Tools  Window      ?
```

Table-boundary marker

End-of-cell marker

Table Boundary icon

Page 1   Normal

- *Editing tables.* As you add text to the table, you may need to add rows or columns or to move columns. To insert or delete rows, columns, and cells, use the Table command in the Edit menu. To move and copy rows, columns, and cells, use the Cut, Copy, and Paste commands in the Edit menu.

- *Formatting tables.* Changing the appearance of a table is easy. You can change column width, row height, and text alignment within columns; you also can add borders so that the cell boundaries will print.

If you worked with side-by-side paragraphs in earlier versions of Word, you will be delighted by how much more easily you can create side-by-side paragraphs (paragraphs formatted so that they always print next to each other) with the Table command.

Part III

Using Advanced Formatting Techniques

Creating a Table

To create a table in Word 5.0 or 5.1, you can choose the Table command from the Insert menu. (Word 5.1 users, however, probably will prefer to use the Table icon, discussed in "Creating a Table with the Table Icon" later in this chapter.) When you choose the Table command, the Insert Table dialog box appears, providing text boxes in which you specify how many columns and rows the table should have (see fig. 15.3).

Fig. 15.3

Insert Table dialog box.

The Table command inserts a two-column-by-two-row table by default. You may want to change these dimensions.

Before you create your table, decide whether you want to display the *grid lines*—the lines that mark cell boundaries, rows, and columns. Grid lines don't print unless you choose to print them, even though by default, they are visible on-screen.

Grid lines are a handy way to visualize your table's overall form. To control the grid lines, use the Table Gridlines check box in the Preferences dialog box. To turn off grid lines on-screen, choose Preferences from the Tools menu to display the Preferences dialog box, click the View icon to display the View options, and then deactivate the Table Gridlines check box.

You also should decide whether you want to see the *end-of-cell markers*—the bullet characters that Word places in each cell. When these markers are displayed, you easily can see the alignment options you chose. If you formatted a column with centered alignment, for example, all the end-of-cell markers are centered in the cells. To display these markers, choose Show ¶ from the View menu, press ⌘-J, or click the paragraph-mark icon in the ribbon.

Creating a New Table with the Table Command

When Word creates a table, each cell takes on the current paragraph format. If you want each cell to have centered text, choose centered alignment for the paragraph in which the insertion point is positioned before you choose the Table command.

To create a table with the Table command, follow these steps:

1. Position the insertion point in your document where you want the table to appear.

2. Choose Table from the Insert menu. The Insert Table dialog box appears.

3. Type the number of columns you want in the Number of Columns text box and the number of rows you want in the Number of Rows box. (If you're not sure how many rows or columns you need, don't worry—you can add or delete rows and columns later.)

   Word automatically calculates the column width, assuming that each column is to be the same width, and displays this measurement in the Column Width text box.

4. To specify a different column width and override Word's automatic column-width calculation, type a number in the Column Width text box.

5. Choose OK. Word inserts the table matrix into your document.

Creating a Table from Existing Text

You can convert text that you created with tabs to a table format. To convert existing text to a table, select the text and choose the Table command from the Insert menu. When you see the Insert Table dialog box, the options in the Convert From area are available. These options are as follows:

■ *Paragraphs*. Choose the Paragraphs option to transform a series of vertical paragraphs into table cells. When you choose this option, Word proposes one column by default. You can choose more than one column. Suppose that you select six paragraphs and choose a three-column format. Word places paragraphs 1, 2, and 3 in Row 1 and paragraphs 4, 5, and 6 in Row 2.

- *Tab Delimited*. Choose the Tab Delimited option to convert a table you created with tabs. Word transforms each line into a table row, even if a line ends in a soft return or a new-line character. The program counts the number of tab characters in each line and uses this figure for the number of columns.

- *Comma Delimited*. Choose the Comma Delimited option to make a table out of comma-delimited text imported from a database-management program. Word transforms each line into a table row, even if a line ends in a soft return or a new-line character. The program counts the number of commas in each line and uses this figure for the number of columns.

- *Side by Side Only*. Choose this option only to convert paragraphs formatted with Version 3.0's side-by-side paragraph format.

To convert an existing tab-formatted table to a Word table, follow these steps:

1. Select all text that you want to include in the table. (Don't forget to include the paragraph marks.)

2. Choose Text to Table from the Insert menu. The Insert Table dialog box appears, displaying Word's proposed specifications for the table. You can change the Column Width figure, if you want.

3. In the Convert From area, choose the option that best describes the selected text: Paragraphs, Tab Delimited, Comma Delimited, or Side by Side Only.

4. Choose OK. Word displays the selected text in table format.

Creating a Table with the Table Icon

In Word 5.1, you can create tables even more easily by using the Table icon in the ribbon. This icon enables you to bypass the Insert Table dialog box but still create the table with exactly the number of rows and columns you want.

To create a table with the Table icon, follow these steps:

1. Place the insertion point in your document where you want the table to appear.

2. Click the Table icon and hold down the mouse button. You see a 5-by-5 matrix of rows and columns with a Cancel bar at the bottom (see fig. 15.4).

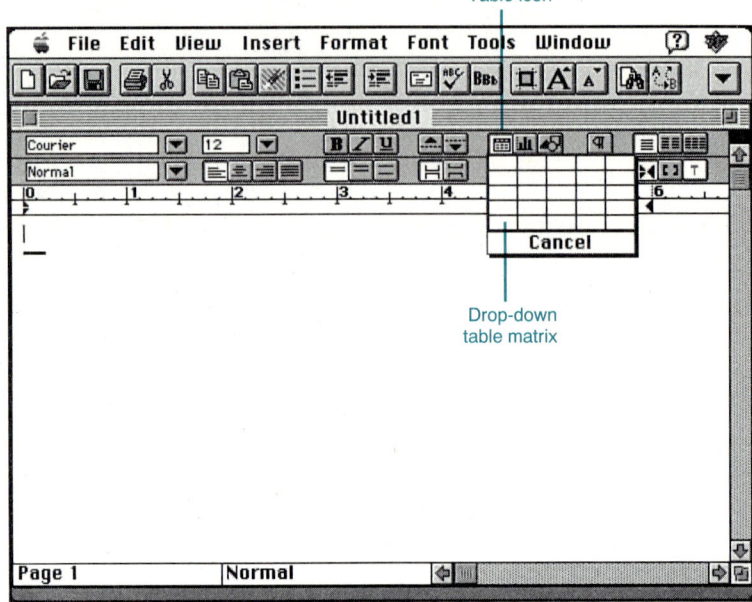

Fig. 15.4

Table icon and
table matrix.

3. Drag the mouse across and down the matrix to indicate the number of rows and columns you want. The matrix expands as you drag right and down; you are not limited to five rows or columns (see fig. 15.5).

   As you drag, notice that the Cancel bar changes to show you how many rows and columns you have selected. To cancel the table, drag the mouse up and left until the highlight disappears.

4. When the matrix displays the number of rows and columns you want, release the mouse button. Word inserts a table of the specified dimensions into your document.

Moving the Insertion Point and Selecting Text

After you create a table and place the insertion point in that table, the functions of the Return and Tab keys change, so take some time now to learn how to navigate within the table. You also need to learn a few additional text-selection techniques.

Part III

Using Advanced Formatting Techniques

Fig. 15.5
Indicating the number
rows and columns with the
Table icon.

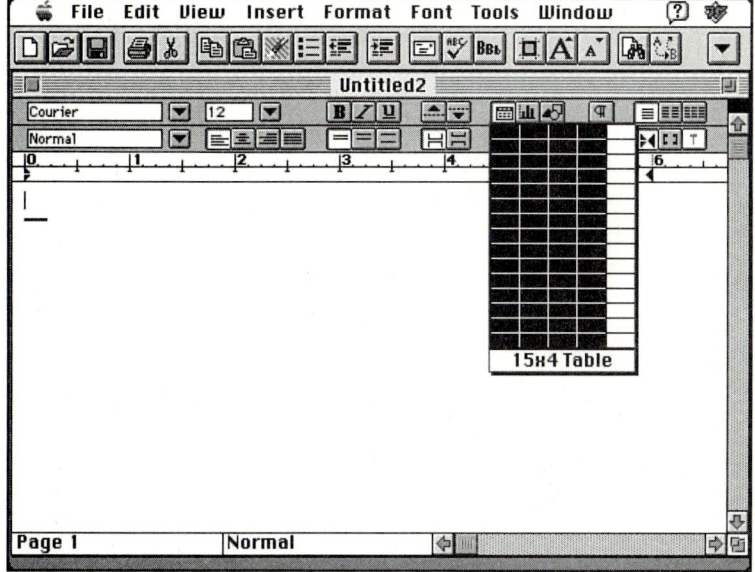

Fig. 15.5
Indicating the number
rows and columns with the
Table icon.

Using the Keyboard

The following keys and key combinations have unique functions within a
table:

- **■** *Return.* Return does not start a new row in a table. On the
  contrary, the Return key starts a new paragraph within the cell.
  Don't press Return unless you want to start a new paragraph
  inside the selected cell.

- **■** *Tab.* Tab advances the insertion point to the next cell. If the
  insertion point is at the end of a row, pressing Tab advances the
  insertion point to the first cell in the next row down.

- **■** *Shift-Tab.* This key combination moves the insertion point back to
  the preceding cell. If the insertion point is at the beginning of a
  row, pressing Shift-Tab moves the insertion point to the last cell of
  the next row up.

- **■** *Option-Tab.* This key combination advances the insertion point to
  the next tab stop in a cell. You can set tabs in a cell, although tabs
  are unnecessary in most cases. If you do set tabs, remember that
  pressing Tab advances the insertion point to the next cell, so you
  need to press Option-Tab to advance the insertion point to the
  next tab stop within a cell.

Selecting Rows and Columns

All the normal Word selection procedures operate in tables. In addition, each column has its own invisible selection bar, which runs down the left border of the column. If you move the mouse pointer to the selection bar, the pointer changes shape, enabling you to select an entire cell, row, or column.

Table 15.1 summarizes mouse methods for selecting text in a table.

Table 15.1
Using the Mouse To Select Text in a Table

Text to select	Mouse action
A cell's contents	Click the column's selection bar at the left cell boundary.
A row of a table	Double-click the selection bar next to the first cell in the row you want to select.
A column of a table	Move the mouse pointer to the top border of the top cell in the column. When the pointer changes to a down arrow, click. Alternatively, hold down the Option key and click any cell in the column.
An entire table	Hold down the Option key and double-click anywhere in the table.

To type ordinary text in the middle of a table, position the insertion point below where you want the text to appear and then press ⌘-Option-space bar. Word breaks the table into two parts and inserts a normal paragraph between the parts.

Editing Table Text

One of the major advantages of using the Table command is that after you create a table and add text, you can use any of Word's normal text-editing commands to insert, copy, move, or delete text in the table. Your actions do not affect the table matrix, as they would in a tab-created table. (You use special commands to edit the table matrix by inserting or deleting rows, columns, or cells. These commands are discussed in "Editing the Table Matrix" later in this chapter.)

Copying, moving, and deleting, however, work slightly differently in tables. When you copy or move cells, exactly what Word copies or moves depends on whether you select the end-of-cell marker (the black dot, which you can see when you have chosen Show ¶ from the View menu).

If you copy or move without selecting the end-of-cell marker, Word copies or moves the cell contents but not the cell itself. Use this technique to copy or move text into an existing cell or outside the table matrix.

If you include the end-of-cell marker, Word copies or moves the cell contents and the cell. Use this technique to add cells as you copy or move. You also can use this technique to copy or move an entire table from one location to another. Be aware, though, that when you use the Cut command to move the table, Word doesn't delete the table matrix. To remove the table matrix from your document, you have to select the table and then use the Delete command in the Table Layout dialog box (covered later in this chapter).

To store a frequently used table matrix as a glossary entry, select the entire table, including the end-of-cell markers; choose Glossary from the Edit menu or press ⌘-K; and define the glossary entry. For more information on glossaries, see Chapter 23.

When you select text in more than one cell, pressing Backspace or Delete cuts only the text in the first cell you select. To delete the text in all the selected cells (but without removing the cells themselves), select the cells and choose Cut from the Edit menu, press ⌘-X, or click the Cut tool.

If you select only one character outside the table matrix in addition to selecting some or all table cells, the Cut command deletes the table matrix of the selected cells as well as the text within it. Normally, Cut doesn't delete the table matrix, only the cell contents, so be careful how you select text when you want to leave the cells intact. You can, however, turn this peculiarity into an advantage. To cut the entire table, text and matrix included, select the whole table and one character (such as a paragraph mark) positioned outside the table, and then choose Cut.

You can rearrange the rows in your table quickly and easily by using Outline view. To move a row up or down in your table in Outline view, follow these steps:

1. Choose Outline from the View menu. Word displays your document in Outline view.

2. Select the row that you want to move.

3. To move the row, press the up- or down-arrow key, or drag the selection square that precedes the row.

Chapter 15
Creating Tables

4. Choose Normal or Page Layout from the View menu to return to your document.

To move a column, you must insert a new blank column, following the instructions in the section "Editing the Table Matrix." After moving the contents of the column to the newly inserted column, you can delete the blank column or use the column for additional data.

Formatting a Table

You can format table cells in many ways. For example, you can choose alignment options for the text in cells. By default, Word aligns cell text left, but you also can align cell text right, justified, or centered. In figure 15.6, for example, the text in the first column is aligned right, the text in the second column is centered, and the text in the third column is aligned left.

Fig. 15.6
Text alignment in cells.

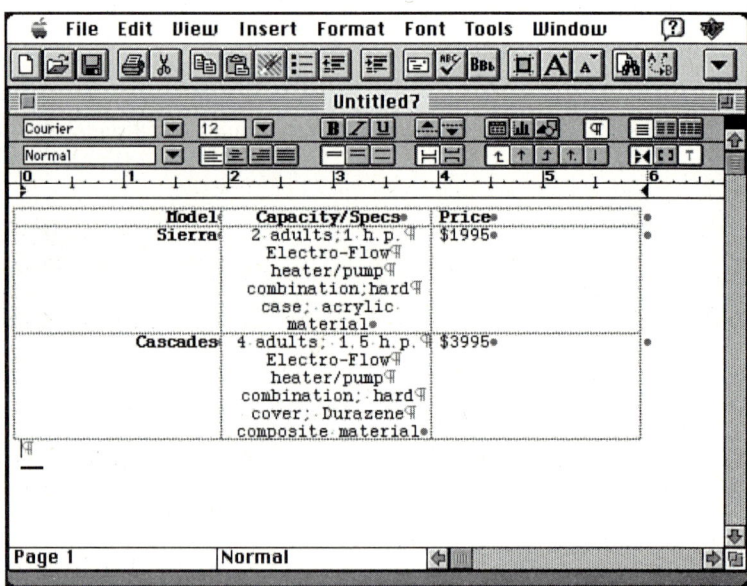

As far as Word is concerned, each cell is an independent paragraph, so you can format a cell's contents with any alignment or indentation option you choose. For example, you can center text by clicking the Centered Alignment icon in the ruler.

Part III

Using Advanced Formatting Techniques

If you want to change the indentation of table cells, follow these steps:

1. Select the cells that you want to format.

2. If necessary, click the Indent Marker icon in the ruler to display the indent markers.

3. Drag the indent markers.

To change the default indentation for all cells, follow these steps:

1. Select the cells that you want to format.

2. Choose Table Cells from the Format menu. The Table Cells dialog box appears.

3. Type a new measurement in the Indent text box.

4. Choose OK.

Understanding Table-Formatting Options

Following is an overview of the formats you can control within table cells:

- *Character formats.* Choose fonts, font sizes, and character emphasis in the usual ways.

- *Paragraph formats.* You can format text in each cell independently. You can use the normal alignment, blank-line, line-spacing, and indentation options. You even can apply styles.

- *Row alignment.* Just as you can align text within cells, you can align an entire row of cells. Your options are left (the default), centered, and right.

- *Column width.* After you create a table, you can change individual columns' widths or specify a new uniform width for all the columns.

- *Row height.* By default, Word uses auto line spacing to control row height, but you can specify a different row height (in printer's points).

- *Space between columns.* By default, Word inserts 0.11 inch of white space between columns. You can change this setting.

- *Indentation.* To indent text in every cell, you can specify an indentation. By default, Word uses no indentation.

You can use any of the normal Word formatting techniques in tables, including keyboard shortcuts, pull-down menus, and the ribbon.

When you position the insertion point in a table, the ruler changes, positioning the 0 mark above the active column (the one in which the insertion point is located).

In figure 15.7, for example, the insertion point is in the third column. Word has inserted the default 0.11-inch spacing between columns, so the 0 mark isn't aligned exactly with the left-column boundary.

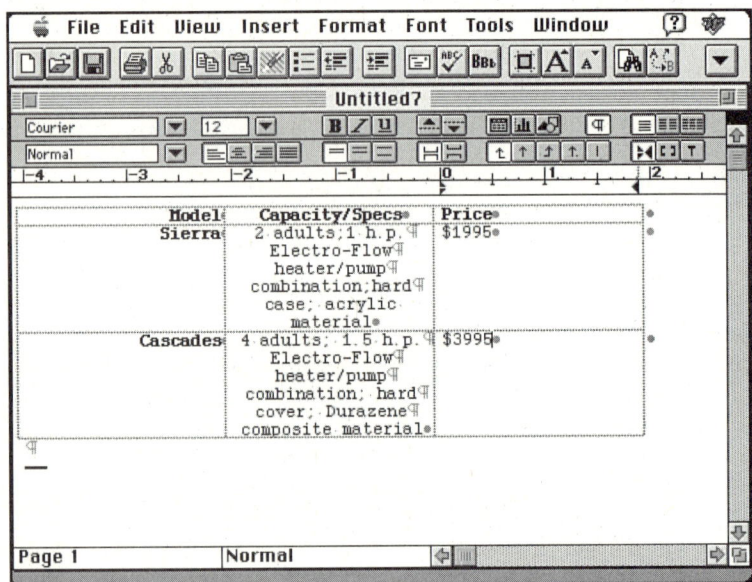

Fig. 15.7

The ruler when the insertion point is positioned in a table.

If you click the Table icon, the ruler changes again, positioning the 0 mark at the left margin of the document and displaying boundary markers (see fig. 15.8).

To adjust individual column widths quickly, click the Table icon to display boundary markers in the ruler and then drag one of the markers. If you don't see the ruler, choose Show Ruler from the View menu or press ⌘-R.

Another change that occurs when you position the insertion point within a table is that a previously grayed option, Table Cells, becomes available in the Format menu. When you choose Table Cells, the Table Cells dialog box appears (see fig. 15.9).

Part III

Using Advanced Formatting Techniques

Fig. 15.8

The ruler with boundary markers.

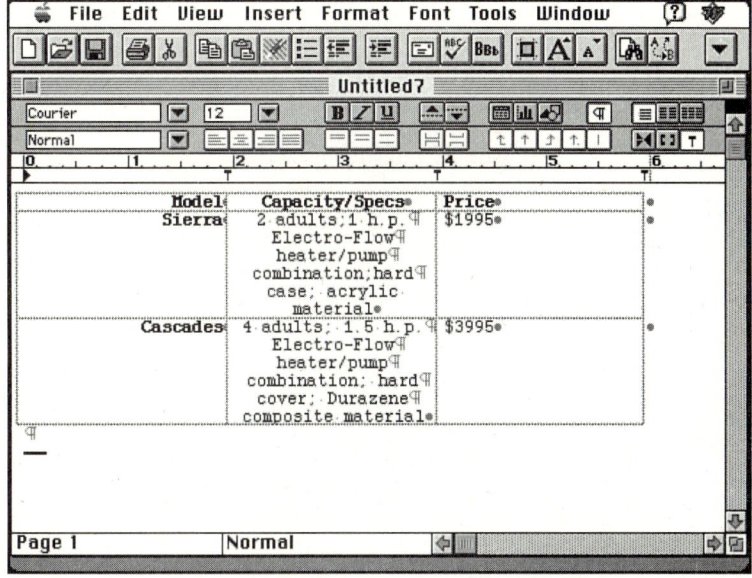

Fig. 15.9

Table Cells dialog box.

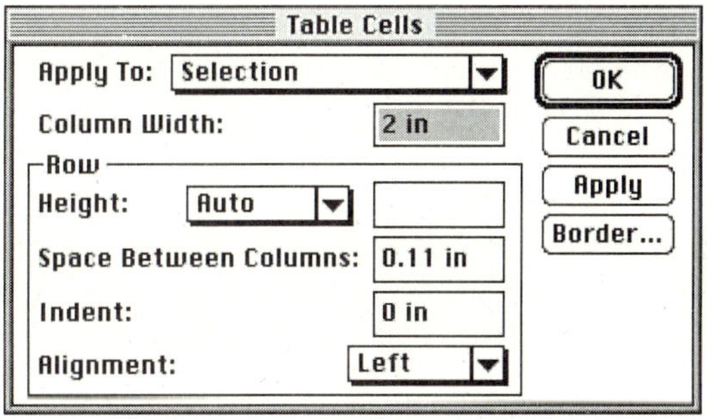

You can choose this command to change column width, row height, spacing between columns, automatic indentation within each cell, and row alignment. You also can choose this option to apply borders to your table, as explained later in this chapter.

When you use the Table Cells command, you can choose options that apply to a block of selected cells (the default option in the Apply To list box), to each cell in the table, to one or more columns, or to one or more rows.

Chapter 15

Creating Tables

478

In addition to these options, you can apply styles to the text in tables. If you frequently create tables that contain numbers, create a style (which you can call Table Numbers) that sets up a format with a decimal tab. When you apply this style to numbers in a cell, Word aligns the numbers by their decimal points.

Editing the Table Matrix

When you enter data into a table, you use ordinary Word techniques to insert, modify, or delete text and numbers in the cells. To edit the matrix of rows and columns, however, you need special techniques. These techniques include commands for inserting and deleting rows and columns and for copying or moving cells.

In Word 5.1, you can edit your table matrix easily (although you still can use the Word 5.0 techniques, if you want). Look for the Word 5.1 icons in the following sections for instructions on using the Table icon to change your table's layout.

Inserting Rows or Columns

You can add a new row or column to a table easily. When you add a new row, Word pushes existing rows down to make room. When you add a new column, Word pushes existing columns right to make room.

To insert a row or column, follow these steps:

1. Position the insertion point in the row below which you want the new row to appear. If you're inserting a column, position the insertion point in the column to the left of the new column's location. To insert two or more rows or columns, select two or more rows or columns.

2. Choose Table Layout from the Format menu. The Table Layout dialog box appears (see fig. 15.10).

Fig. 15.10
Table Layout dialog box.

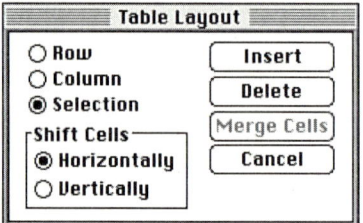

By default, Word activates the Selection option. This option tells Word to apply your choice only to the portion of the table that you selected.

3. Click the Row or Column radio button. (When you choose the Row or Column option, the options in the Shift Cells area of the dialog box are grayed.)

4. Click Insert.

To insert rows or columns with the Table icon, select the row(s) or column(s) as explained in step 1 and then click the Table icon. Word inserts the row(s) or column(s) with no further ado.

To add a row to the end of a table, follow these steps:

1. Position the insertion point before the last end-of-cell marker in the table.

2. Press Tab. Word adds a new row at the end of the table.

To add a column at the right edge of your table, follow these steps:

1. Position the insertion point before the end-of-cell marker at the end of the first row.

2. Choose Table Layout from the Format menu. The Table Layout dialog box appears.

3. Choose the Column option.

4. Click Insert.

5. To insert additional columns, choose Repeat from the Edit menu or press ⌘-Y.

Deleting Rows and Columns

As a safeguard against accidental deletion of rows or columns as you edit, you cannot delete cells by pressing Delete or by using the Cut command after you select the cells; the Delete key and the Cut command delete only the cells' contents. You must use the Table Layout command to delete rows or columns.

To delete a row or column, follow these steps:

1. Place the insertion point in the row or column that you want to delete. (To delete two or more rows or columns, select two or more rows or columns.)

2. Choose Table Layout from the Format menu. The Table Layout dialog box appears.

3. Choose Row or Column, depending on what you selected.

4. Click Delete.

Inserting and Deleting Individual Cells

In the preceding section, you learned how to insert or delete rows or columns. You also can insert or delete individual cells. In figure 15.11, for example, one cell has been added in the second row of the table, with one of the existing cells having been resized to make room for the new cell.

Fig. 15.11

A cell inserted into the second row of a table.

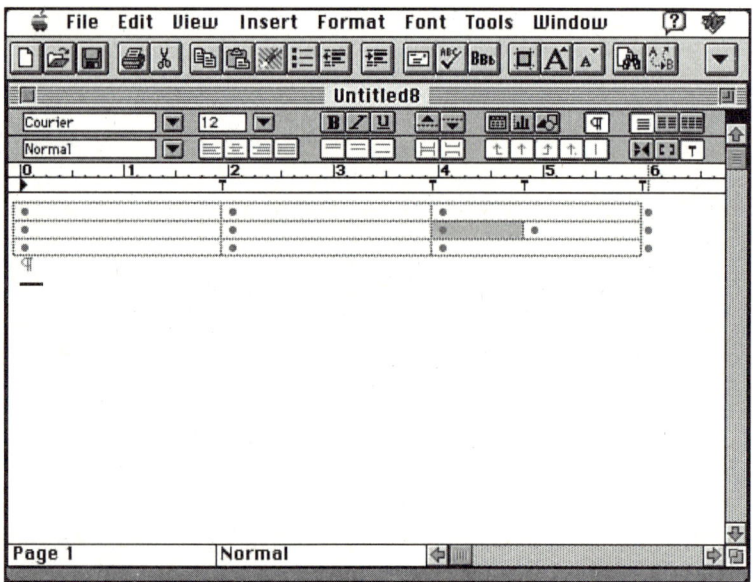

In addition to adding a cell to a row, you can push the cells of a column down (without affecting adjacent columns) by inserting cells into a column. Figure 15.12 shows the effect of inserting a cell into the second column of the third row.

Part III

Using Advanced Formatting Techniques

Fig. 15.12
A table with cells shifted vertically to accommodate an inserted cell.

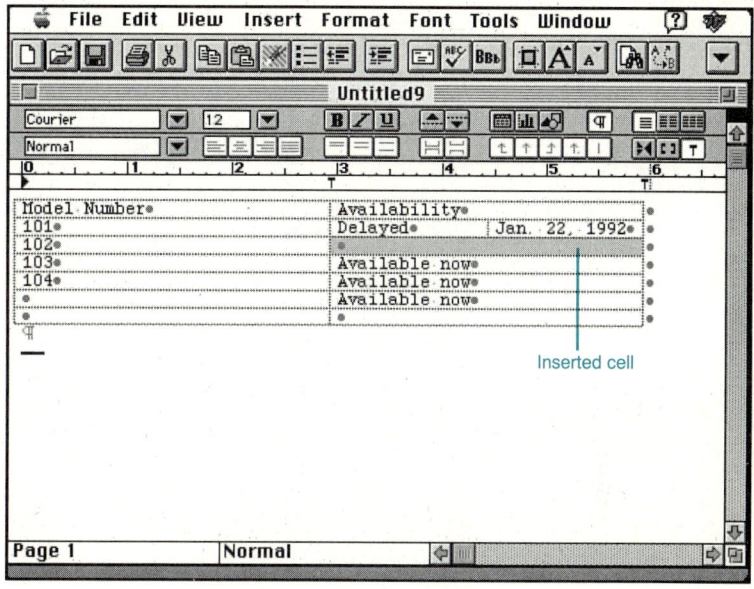

Notice that this insertion has thrown the table text out of alignment. In a situation such as this one, adding a new row would be better.

To insert a cell into a table, follow these steps:

1. Select the cell below or to the right of which you want the new cell to appear.

2. Choose Table Layout from the Format menu. The Table Layout dialog box appears.

3. Click the Selection radio button, if it isn't already selected. Word activates the Shift Cells area.

4. To shift the selected cells down, click the Vertically button. (When you click Vertically, Word adds a row to the bottom of the table.) To shift the selected cells right, click the Horizontally button.

5. Click Insert.

Merging and Splitting Cells

Sometimes you need to merge two cells into one. In a complex table, for example, a *decked head* (also called a *box head*) is useful for organizing data (see fig. 15.13).

Chapter 15
Creating Tables

Fig. 15.13
Three cells merged to
create a decked head.

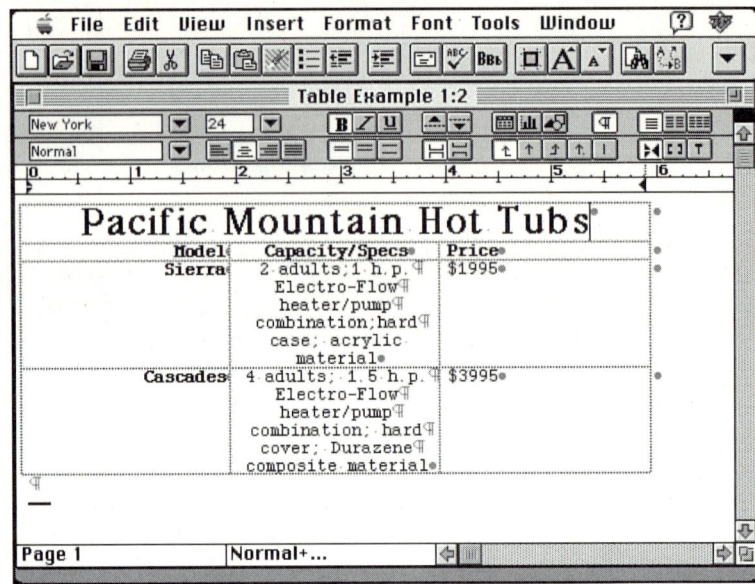

A decked head can span the column headings and contain text that clarifies the table's contents. To create a decked head, you merge two or more cells into one larger cell. (If you find the effect displeasing, you can split the merged cells.)

To merge cells, follow these steps:

1. Select the cells that you want to merge.

2. Choose Table Layout from the Format menu. The Table Layout dialog box appears.

3. Click the Merge Cells command button. Word merges the selected cells.

You cannot split a cell that you have not previously merged. To split a merged cell, follow these steps:

1. Select the merged cell that you want to split.

2. Choose Table Layout from the Format menu. The Table Layout dialog box appears, now displaying a Split Cell command button.

3. Click the Split Cell button. Word splits the selected cell.

Changing Row Height

By default, Word automatically adjusts row height to accommodate the largest font size (or a graphic) in the row. You can set row height manually, however. You can set a minimum row height with the At Least option or a fixed row height with the Exactly option.

To change row height, follow these steps:

1. Select one or more rows.

2. Choose Table Cells from the Format menu. The Table Cells dialog box appears.

3. Type a new measurement in the Height text box.

4. In the Height drop-down list box, select At Least or Exactly.

5. In the Apply To drop-down list box, choose Selection to change the row height for the selection only; Entire Rows Selected to change the row height for all the cells in the rows containing a selection, even if you didn't select all the cells in the row; or All Cells in Table to change the row height for the entire table.

6. Choose OK.

Changing the Space Between Columns

By default, Word inserts 0.11 inch of space between columns. You can change this setting by following these steps:

1. Place the insertion point in the table or select the columns that you want to format.

2. Choose Table Cells from the Format menu. The Table Cells dialog box appears.

3. Type a new measurement in the Space Between Columns text box.

4. In the Apply To drop-down list box, choose Selection to change the column spacing for the selection only; Entire Columns Selected to change the column spacing for the entire column, even if you didn't select all the cells; or All Cells in Table to change the column spacing for the entire table.

5. Choose OK.

Aligning Rows

Word aligns rows left by default. You can choose centered or right alignment instead, if you want.

To change row alignment, follow these steps:

1. Select the rows that you want to align.

2. Choose Table Cells from the Format menu. The Table Cells dialog box appears.

3. In the Apply To drop-down list box, choose Selection to format only the rows you selected or All Cells in Table to format all rows.

4. Select an alignment option in the Alignment drop-down list box.

5. Choose OK.

Converting a Table to Text

If you want to abandon the table matrix and work only with the text it contains, you can delete the matrix and convert the table to text. Word inserts tabs to delimit the columns.

To remove the table matrix, follow these steps:

1. Select the entire table.

2. Choose Table to Text from the Insert menu. Word removes the table matrix, leaving the text on-screen. (The text will require some cleanup after this procedure.)

Learning More Table Techniques

Important techniques that expand the usefulness of Word's Table command are discussed elsewhere in this book. Following is an overview of the chapters that discuss these techniques:

- Chapter 16, "Numbering and Sorting Lines, Lists, and Paragraphs," includes instructions on adding numbers automatically to items in tables and lists and on using Word's automatic sorting capabilities to place the items in numerical or alphabetical order.

- Chapter 17, "Using Borders and Shading," explains how to add lines and borders to a table. Figure 15.14 shows a Word table to which graphics and borders have been added.

Part III

Using Advanced Formatting Techniques

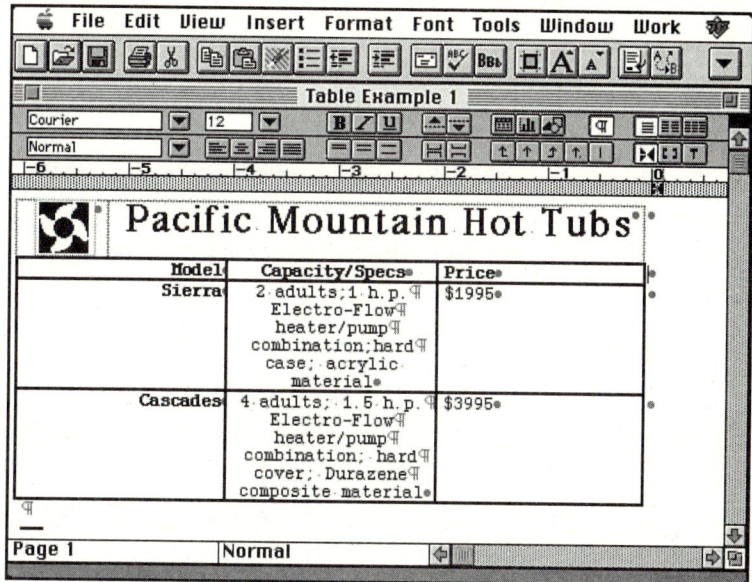

Fig. 15.14
A table with borders and graphics.

■ As figure 15.14 suggests, tables provide handy tools for placing text next to graphics. To position text next to graphics in your document, you may want to create a single-row table. For more information, see Chapter 20, "Positioning Text and Graphics."

■ Chapter 25, "Using Math and Typing Equations," explains how to use Word's on-screen math capabilities to add a column or row of numbers quickly.

■ Chapter 30, "Linking Data Dynamically," explains how to import spreadsheet data and convert that data into a Word table.

Quick Review

This section summarizes the most useful information in this chapter. Check "Productivity Tips" for a review of high-productivity tips and tricks—the ones that Macintosh and Word pros use every day. Review "Techniques" whenever you need a quick reminder about a specific procedure.

Productivity Tips

■ Use the Table command rather than tabs to create tables in your document. The table matrix enables you to move text into and out of a table without accidentally deleting your formatting.

■ To edit tables easily, learn the mouse commands for selecting cells, rows, and columns.

■ Switching to Outline view and dragging rows up or down is the quickest way to rearrange rows in a table.

■ Remember that you must use the Table Cells command to align table rows left, centered, or right. Standard paragraph-alignment commands affect only the text in the cells, not the table rows themselves.

■ Merge cells to create headings that span two or more columns.

■ Learn how the ruler works when the insertion point is in a table.

■ Read the chapters that discuss ways you can enhance your tables by adding features such as lines, borders, and graphics.

■ In tandem with Word's on-screen math (discussed in Chapter 25), use a table to create a miniature spreadsheet in your Word document.

Techniques

This section provides concise summaries of all the procedures introduced in this chapter.

Creating a New Table

To insert a new table into a document:

1. Place the insertion point in the document where you want the table to appear.

2. Choose Table from the Insert menu. The Insert Table dialog box appears.

3. In the Number of Columns text box, type the number of columns you want. In the Number of Rows text box, type the number of rows you want.

4. To choose a column width other than the one Word chooses automatically, type a measurement in the Column Width text box.

5. Choose OK. Word inserts a table of the specified dimensions into your document.

Converting Text into a Table

To convert existing text in a document into a table:

1. Select the text.

2. Choose Text to Table from the Insert menu. The Insert Table dialog box appears.

3. Choose a Convert From option: Paragraphs, Tab Delimited, Comma Delimited, or Side by Side Only.

4. Choose OK.

To convert an existing tab-formatted table to a Word table:

1. Select all text that you want to include in the table, including the paragraph marks.

2. Choose Text to Table from the Insert menu. The Insert Table dialog box appears, displaying Word's proposed specifications for the table. (You can change the Column Width setting, if you want.)

3. Choose a Convert From option: Paragraphs, Tab Delimited, Comma Delimited, or Side by Side Only.

4. Choose OK. Word displays the selected text in table format.

Using the Table Icon

To create a table with the Table icon:

1. Place the insertion point in your document where you want the table to appear.

2. Click the Table icon and hold down the mouse button to drop down the table matrix.

Chapter 15
Creating Tables

3. Drag the mouse across and down the matrix to indicate the number of rows and columns you want. As you drag, the Cancel bar at the bottom of the matrix shows how many rows and columns you have selected. (To cancel the table, drag the mouse up and left until the highlight disappears.)

4. When the matrix displays the number of rows and columns you want, release the mouse button. Word inserts a table of the specified dimensions into your document.

Displaying Grid Lines and End-of-Cell Markers

To display table grid lines and end-of-cell markers:

Choose Show ¶ from the View menu, press ⌘-J, or click the paragraph-mark icon in the ribbon.

Rearranging Rows

To move a row up or down in your table in Outline view:

1. Choose Outline from the View menu. Word displays your document in Outline view.

2. Select the row that you want to move.

3. To move the row, press the up- or down-arrow key, or drag the selection square that precedes the row.

4. Choose Normal or Page Layout from the View menu to return to your document.

Moving a Column

To move a column:

1. Insert a new blank column into the table.

2. Select the column that you want to move.

3. Choose Cut from the Edit menu, press ⌘-X, or click the Cut tool.

4. Position the insertion point where you want to move the column.

5. Choose Paste Cells from the Edit menu.

6. If you want, delete the blank column.

Changing Column Width

To change the width of a column:

1. Place the insertion point in the table.

2. Display the boundary markers by clicking the Table icon in the ruler.

3. Drag the appropriate markers.

To change the width of all the columns in a table:

1. Place the insertion point in the table.

2. Choose Table Cells from the Format menu. The Table Cells dialog box appears.

3. Type a new measurement in the Column Width text box.

4. Choose OK.

Adjusting Row Height

To change row height:

1. Select one or more rows.

2. Choose Table Cells from the Format menu. The Table Cells dialog box appears.

3. Type a new measurement in the Height text box.

4. In the Height drop-down list box, select At Least or Exactly.

5. In the Apply To drop-down list box, choose Selection to change the row height for the selection only; Entire Rows Selected to change the row height for all the cells in the rows containing a selection, even if you didn't select all the cells in the row; or All Cells in Table to change the row height for the entire table.

6. Choose OK.

Changing Column Spacing

To change the space that Word automatically inserts between columns:

1. Place the insertion point in the table or select the columns that you want to format.

Chapter 15
Creating Tables

2. Choose Table Cells from the Format menu. The Table Cells dialog box appears.

3. Type a new measurement in the Space Between Columns text box.

4. In the Apply To drop-down list box, choose Selection to change the column spacing for the selection only; Entire Columns Selected to change the column spacing for the entire column, even if you didn't select all the cells; or All Cells in Table to change the column spacing for the entire table.

5. Choose OK.

Indenting Text in Cells

To change the default cell indentation:

1. Select the cells that you want to format.

2. Choose Table Cells from the Format menu. The Table Cells dialog box appears.

3. Type a new measurement in the Indent text box.

4. Choose OK.

Aligning Tables

To align text in a cell:

1. Select the cell.

2. Use any alignment technique, such as the Paragraph dialog box, the keyboard shortcuts, or the alignment icons in the ruler.

To align rows within the document's margins:

1. Select the rows that you want to align.

2. Choose Table Cells from the Format menu. The Table Cells dialog box appears.

3. In the Apply To drop-down list box, choose Selection to format only the rows you selected or All Cells in Table to format all rows.

4. Select an alignment option in the Alignment drop-down list box.

5. Choose OK.

Copying and Moving Cell Contents and Cells

To copy or move a cell's contents without affecting the cell itself:

1. Select the text but not the end-of-cell marker.

2. Choose Copy or Cut from the Edit menu, press ⌘-C or ⌘-T, or click the Copy or Cut tool.

3. Move the insertion point to where you want the text to appear.

4. Choose Paste from the Edit menu, press ⌘-V, or click the Paste tool.

To copy or move the cell contents and the cell:

1. Select the text, including the end-of-cell marker.

2. Choose Copy or Cut from the Edit menu, press ⌘-C or ⌘-T, or click the Copy or Cut tool.

3. Move the insertion point to where you want the text to appear.

4. Choose Paste Cells from the Edit menu.

Deleting Text in a Table

To delete the contents of a single cell:

1. Select the cell.

2. Use any deletion command, such as Backspace, Delete, or Cut (Edit menu).

To delete the contents of two or more cells without removing the cell matrix:

1. Select the cells.

2. Choose Cut from the Edit menu, press ⌘-X, or click the Cut tool.

Deleting a Table

To delete an entire table, including the text and table matrix:

1. Select the entire table by placing the insertion point anywhere in the table and then holding down the Option key and double-clicking the mouse button.

Chapter 15

Creating Tables

2. Choose Table Layout from the Format menu. The Table Layout dialog box appears.

3. Click Delete to delete all the rows of the table.

Inserting Rows and Columns

To insert rows into a table:

1. Beginning below where you want the new rows to appear, select the number of rows that you want to insert.

2. Choose Table Layout from the Format menu. The Table Layout dialog box appears.

3. Click the Row radio button.

4. Click Insert.

To insert columns into a table:

1. Beginning to the right of where you want the new columns to appear, select the number of columns that you want to insert.

2. Choose Table Layout from the Format menu. The Table Layout dialog box appears.

3. Click the Column radio button.

4. Click Insert.

To add a row at the end of a table:

1. Place the insertion point at the end of the last cell.

2. Press Tab.

To add a column at the right edge of a table:

1. Position the insertion point before the end-of-cell marker at the end of the first row.

2. Choose Table Layout from the Format menu. The Table Layout dialog box appears.

3. Click the Column radio button.

4. Click Insert.

5. To insert additional rows, choose Repeat from the Edit menu or press ⌘-Y.

Deleting Rows and Columns

To delete a row, including the cell matrix and cell contents:

1. Select the row that you want to delete.

2. Choose Table Layout from the Format menu. The Table Layout dialog box appears.

3. Click the Row radio button.

4. Click Delete.

To delete a column, including the cell matrix and cell contents:

1. Select the column that you want to delete.

2. Choose Table Layout from the Format menu. The Table Layout dialog box appears.

3. Click the Column radio button.

4. Click Delete.

Inserting Cells

To insert cells into a table:

1. Beginning to the right of or below where you want the new cells to appear, select the number of cells that you want to insert.

2. Choose Table Layout from the Format menu. The Table Layout dialog box appears.

3. Click the Selection radio button.

4. In the Shift Cells area, choose Horizontally or Vertically.

5. Click Insert.

Merging Cells

To merge two or more cells into one:

1. Select the cells.

2. Choose Table Layout from the Format menu. The Table Layout dialog box appears.

3. Click Merge Cells.

Splitting Cells

To split a cell that you previously merged:

1. Select the cell.

2. Choose Table Layout from the Format menu. The Table Layout dialog box appears, displaying a Split Cell command button.

3. Click the Split Cell button.

Converting a Table into Text

To convert a table to ordinary text:

1. Select the entire table.

2. Choose Table to Text from the Insert menu.

Part III

Using Advanced Formatting Techniques

Numbering and Sorting Lines, Lists, and Paragraphs

I n professional writing, you have many occasions to number and sort items on the page. In the legal and scholarly fields, line numbers provide critical readers line-by-line reference numbers that they can use to discuss a disputed text. In technical writing, instructions are numbered (like the instructions in this book). In many other fields, you will find many uses for Word's paragraph-sorting capabilities, which place selected lines or paragraphs in alphabetical order. The next time you type a bibliography, Word can do the alphabetizing for you.

This chapter covers all aspects of numbering and sorting with Word. Following is an overview of this chapter's contents:

- *Numbering lines.* In this section, you learn how to add line numbers to the left of the text columns in your document, how to choose line-numbering options, and how to change the line-number increment (for example, you can choose to number every fifth line). You also learn how to turn off line numbering for selected paragraphs in your document.

- *Numbering paragraphs.* In this section, you learn how to choose options when you number paragraphs, how to number paragraphs of different levels, how to number headings in Outline view, and how to number only selected paragraphs.

■ *Numbering lists.* With Word 5.1's new Bulleted List tool, you can number items in a list quickly.

■ *Sorting paragraphs and tables.* This section explains how to sort paragraphs and tables in alphabetical or numerical order and how Word sorts text, paragraphs, and tables. You also learn how to undo a sort.

Numbering Lines in a Document

Line numbers often are used in legal documents and in critical editions of poems, stories, and scripts to give readers reference points for a careful study of the text. Adding line numbers to a document is a good idea when you are preparing the document for staff or committee discussion. Figure 16.1 shows a draft of an employee handbook, including line numbers.

Numbering every line in a document doesn't always make sense. In figure 16.1, for example, the headings aren't numbered. Later in this chapter, in "Numbering Lines Selectively," you learn how to suppress line numbering for headings or for other selected text.

Use the Section dialog box to add line numbers to your document. The Section dialog box contains several line-numbering options that you can use to control how Word counts lines (by page, by section, or continuously) and to specify the distance of the line numbers from the text. (By default, Word positions line numbers 0.25 inch from single-column text and 0.13 inch from multiple columns.)

Line numbers are not visible on-screen in Normal or Page Layout view. To preview line numbers, use Print Preview (File menu).

If you want to number the lines of your document, don't add blank lines by pressing Return; add them by adding blank spacing to paragraphs. If you add blank lines by pressing Return, Word numbers each blank line.

In figure 16.2, notice the paragraph mark before the paragraph that begins *At orientation, you'll learn*…. This paragraph mark indicates that blank space was added with the Return key. In figure 16.3, which shows the same page after line numbers were added, Word has numbered this line.

Fig. 16.1
Draft with line numbers.

 Pacific Mountain Hot Tubs

Handbook for New Employees

Welcome

1 Welcome to Pacific Mountain Hot Tubs. This training notebook is
2 designed to introduce you to the company. You will find that it
3 answers most of your questions. Don't hesitate to ask if you have
4 others.

Orientation

5 Your departmental representative will enroll you in an employee
6 orientation session on the first Monday after you begin work.

7 At orientation, you'll learn some of the general policies of Pacific
8 Mountain Hot Tubs. You'll complete some forms for the Benefits and
9 Insurance office. And you'll meet your guide for the day—most
10 often a member of your department.

Checklist for the First Day

11 During your first day, you will meet the people you'll be working
12 with, and become acquainted with the Pacific Mountain Hot Tub
13 facilities--including your Employee Spa, naturally!--and
14 procedures. Your guide will help you complete the checklist
15 below.

Meeting Your Group Manager

16 During your first day at work, you'll get to meet your group
17 manager. He or she is the person who keeps things moving
18 smoothly, coordinating projects and people assigned to your
19 group.

Tour

20 Pacific Mountain Hot Tubs' production site, situated in the
21 historic Nevada City region of California's Sierra Nevada
22 mountains, includes the company's production and
23 administrative buildings. During the tour, you'll see just how
24 Pacific Mountain Hot Tubs are made--and why we believe they're
25 the finest hot tubs available today.

To keep Word from numbering blank lines, always add blank space by using the Before and After text boxes in the Spacing area of the Paragraph dialog box. Alternatively, click the Blank Spacing icon in the ruler to add 12 points of blank space before a paragraph.

Chapter 16
Numbering and Sorting Lines, Lists, and Paragraphs

Fig. 16.2
A blank line added by
pressing Return.

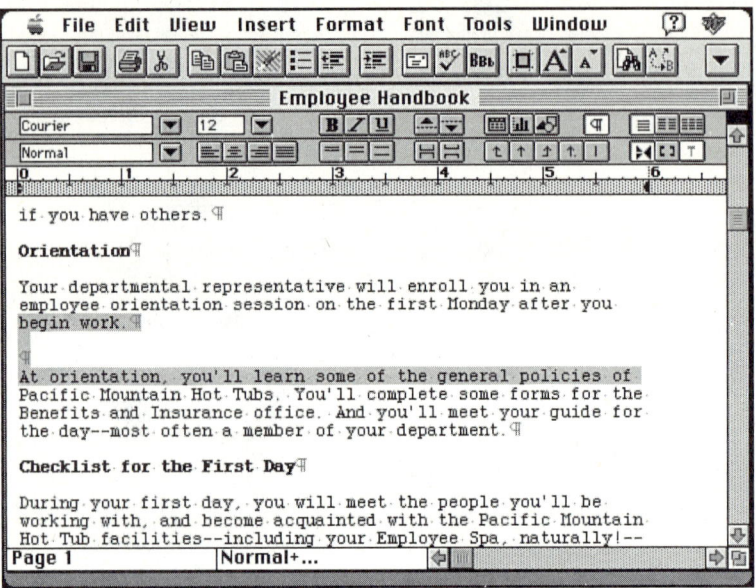

Fig. 16.3
A line-numbering problem
caused by adding a blank
line with Return.

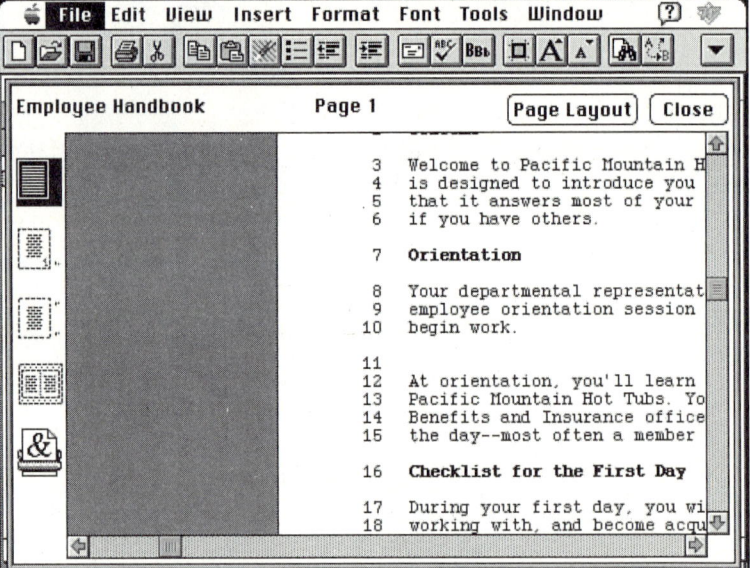

Part III

Using Advanced Formatting Techniques

Adding Line Numbers

To add line numbers to your document, follow these steps:

1. To add line numbers to only some of the paragraphs in your document, select those paragraphs. If you don't select anything, Word adds line numbers to your whole document (or to the current section, if you have divided your document into sections).

2. Choose Section from the Format menu or press Option-F14. The Section dialog box appears (see fig. 16.4).

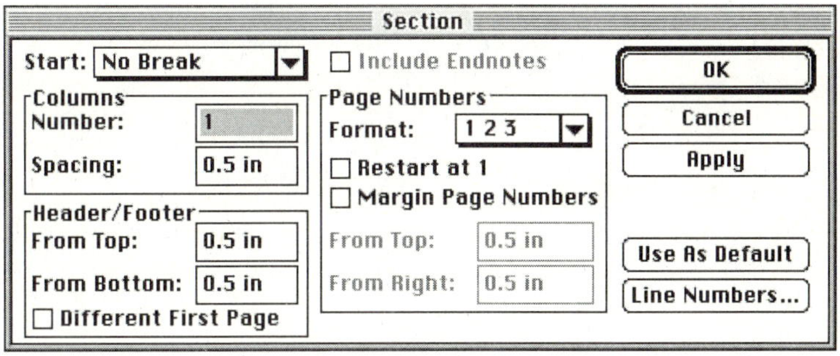

Fig. 16.4

Section dialog box.

3. Click the Line Numbers command button. The Line Numbers dialog box appears (see fig. 16.5).

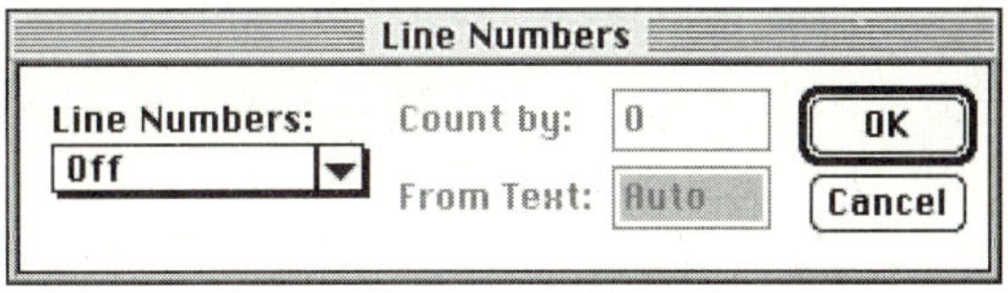

Fig. 16.5

Line Numbers dialog box.

By default, the Off option is selected, and the line-numbering options are grayed. When you choose a line-numbering option in the Line Numbers drop-down list box, the other options in this dialog box become available.

4. Select an option in the Line Numbers list box. You can choose By Page (starts numbering lines with 1 at the beginning of each page), By Section (starts numbering lines with 1 at the beginning of each section), or Continuous (numbers lines sequentially throughout the document).

Chapter 16

Numbering and Sorting Lines, Lists, and Paragraphs

5. In the Count By text box, type the line-number increment you want to use. By default, Word numbers every line. If you type **5** in the Count By box, for example, Word numbers every fifth line.

6. In the From Text text box, you can specify a distance from the end of the line number to the beginning of the text. The Auto setting places numbers 0.25 inch from the text in a single-column document and 0.13 inch from the text in a multiple-column document.

7. Choose OK. You return to the Section dialog box.

8. Choose OK to confirm your choices and close the dialog box.

To preview line numbers, choose Print Preview from the File menu.

If you have divided your document into sections, the line-numbering options you choose affect only the section in which the insertion point is positioned. To add line numbers to the whole document, choose Select All from the Edit menu or press ⌘-A before choosing Section from the Format menu and adding line numbers.

Numbering Lines Selectively

In figure 16.1, the headings are unnumbered. In this section, you learn how to suppress line numbering for any paragraph. To suppress the printing of line numbers for selected paragraphs, follow these steps:

1. If you haven't done so already, add line numbers to your document.

2. Select the paragraph or paragraphs for which you don't want line numbers to print.

3. Choose Paragraph from the Format menu or press ⌘-M. The Paragraph dialog box appears (see fig. 16.6). The Suppress Line Numbers option, which ordinarily is grayed, now is available.

4. Click the Suppress Line Numbers check box.

5. Choose OK to confirm your choices and return to your document.

6. To suppress line numbers for another paragraph, move the insertion point to that paragraph and choose Repeat from the Edit menu or press ⌘-Y.

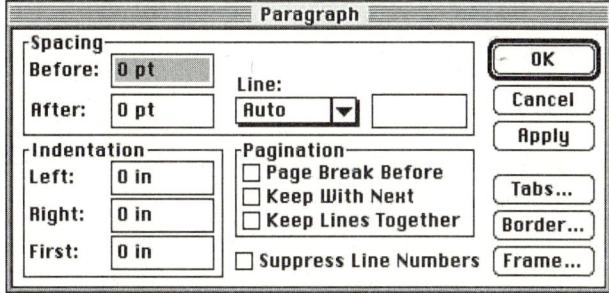

Fig. 16.6

Suppress Line Numbers
option in the Paragraph
dialog box.

If you format with styles, you can suppress line numbering for any style you have defined. You can suppress line numbers for all headings, for example, by adding the Suppress Line Numbers option to the Heading styles. (For more information on styles, see Chapter 14.)

Numbering Paragraphs in a Document

Word's Renumber command (Tools menu) enables you to add numbers to the beginning of paragraphs automatically. You can choose the format of the numbers (Arabic numerals, Roman numerals, or letters), and you can choose any character to follow the number that Word inserts (normally, a period). You also can number paragraphs differently by level and choose which paragraphs you want to number.

If you want to number paragraphs in your document, be sure to plan the paragraphing carefully. Use the New Line command (Shift-Return) to group all the lines that you want to number together.

To see why you should use the New Line command to group lines together, examine figure 16.7, which shows a set of instructions that should have only two steps, not three. The paragraphs beginning with *Before opening the door* and *Close the door securely* should be numbered 1 and 2, respectively.

What went wrong? The text beginning with *Feel the door*, which explains the first sentence, was typed in a separate paragraph—and when Word numbered the list, this paragraph got its own number.

Figure 16.8 shows how the New Line command (Shift-Return) can be used to ensure that Word numbers the paragraphs correctly. Notice the arrows entered by the New Line command.

Fig. 16.7
Poor paragraphing for
paragraph numbering.

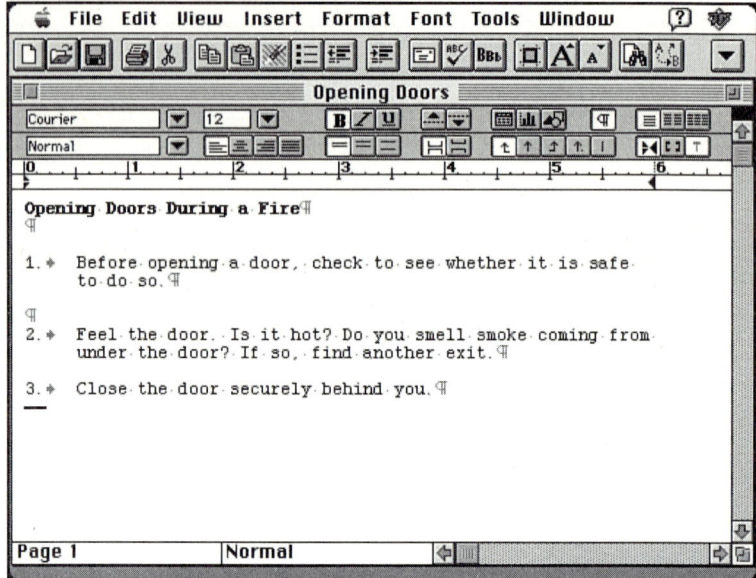

Fig. 16.8
Correct paragraphing for
paragraph numbering.

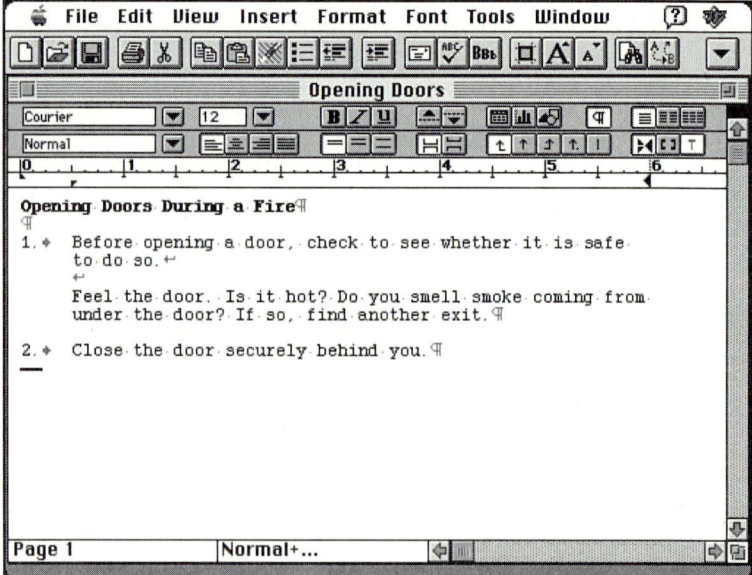

Part III

Using Advanced Formatting Techniques

Adding Paragraph Numbers

To add paragraph numbers to your document, follow these steps:

1. Select the paragraphs that you want to number. If you don't select any paragraphs, Word numbers all the paragraphs in your document.

2. Choose Renumber from the Tools menu or press ⌘-F15. The Renumber dialog box appears (see fig. 16.9).

Fig. 16.9

Renumber dialog box.

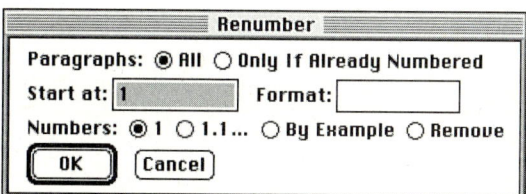

3. To start numbering with a number other than 1, type that number in the Start At text box. Type an Arabic number (1, 2, 3, and so on) to control numbering even if you plan to use a number format other than Arabic, as explained in the following step.

   For example, if you want to use capital letters to number paragraphs and want to start numbering with C, you would type **3** in the Start At box.

4. If you want to use a number format other than Arabic, use the Format text box to specify the number format and the separator character you want to use. (The tables following this numbered list provide the codes and characters you can use.) Type the codes and characters in the Format text box the way you want the numbers to appear. Some examples of valid entries follow:

   -1-

   (1)

   {1}

   A)

   I)

5. Choose OK.

Chapter 16

Numbering and Sorting Lines, Lists, and Paragraphs

If renumbering produces an unwanted result, immediately choose Undo from the Edit menu or press ⌘-Z. If you perform some other action after using the Renumber command so that you can't use Undo to remove the numbers, follow the instructions in "Updating and Removing Paragraph Numbers" later in this chapter.

Tables 16.1 and 16.2 list the number-format codes and separator characters you can use in the Renumber dialog box.

Table 16.1
Number-Format Codes

Code	Number format
1	Arabic numbers (1, 2, 3)
I	Uppercase Roman numerals (I, II, III)
i	Lowercase Roman numerals (i, ii, iii)
A	Uppercase letters (A, B, C)
a	Lowercase letters (a, b, c)

Table 16.2
Separator Characters

Character	Effect
none	1. (period added by default)
, (comma)	1,
- (hyphen)	1-
/ (slash)	1/
; (semicolon)	1;
: (colon)	1:
) (right parenthesis)	1)
( ) (double parentheses)	(1)
[ ] (double brackets)	[1]
{ } (double braces)	{1}
^t (tab code)	1. followed by tab

Creating Numbered Paragraphs with the Bulleted List Tool

If you're using Word 5.1, you can create a numbered list quickly by using the following trick:

1. Type all the paragraphs in the list.

2. Select the paragraphs.

3. Click the Bulleted List tool. Word creates a hanging-indent format, indenting all the paragraphs 1/4 inch and placing bullets at the beginning of each paragraph.

4. Hold down the Option key and use the mouse in column-selection mode to carefully select all the bullets. Be careful not to erase the tab marks that trail the bullets. If you can't see the tab marks, click the paragraph-mark icon in the ribbon or choose Show ¶ from the View menu.

5. Press Delete to erase the bullets.

6. Select the text to be numbered.

7. Use the Renumber command to add numbers to each paragraph.

8. Choose OK.

Numbering Paragraphs of Different Levels

In Word, you can use paragraph indentation to indicate logical relations among ideas in a document. In figure 16.1, for example, the indentations show that three of the topics—Checklist for the First Day, Meeting Your Group Manager, and Tour—are part of the Orientation section. If you indent paragraphs in this way, you can choose a numbering option that shows the logical subordination of indented paragraphs. When you choose this option (the 1.1 radio button in the Renumber dialog box), Word uses a numbering scheme that indicates subordination. Figure 16.10 shows how the employee handbook looks after the document was numbered this way.

Figure 16.11 shows the effect of using two levels of indents beyond normal left-justified paragraphs. Word can number up to seven levels of indents.

Pacific Mountain Hot Tubs

Handbook for New Employees

1. Welcome

Welcome to Pacific Mountain Hot Tubs. This training notebook is designed to introduce you to the company. You will find that it answers most of your questions. Don't hesitate to ask if you have others.

2. Orientation

Your departmental representative will enroll you in an employee orientation session on the first Monday after you begin work.

At orientation, you'll learn some of the general policies of Pacific Mountain Hot Tubs. You'll complete some forms for the Benefits and Insurance office. And you'll meet your guide for the day—most often a member of your department.

2.1. Checklist for the First Day

During your first day, you will meet the people you'll be working with, and become acquainted with the Pacific Mountain Hot Tub facilities--including your Employee Spa, naturally!--and procedures. Your guide will help you complete the checklist below.

2.2. Meeting Your Group Manager

During your first day at work, you'll get to meet your group manager. He or she is the person who keeps things moving smoothly, coordinating projects and people assigned to your group.

2.3. Tour

Pacific Mountain Hot Tubs' production site, situated in the historic Nevada City region of California's Sierra Nevada mountains, includes the company's production and administrative buildings. During the tour, you'll see just how

Word recognizes different levels of paragraphs no matter how you indent the paragraphs—by moving the indent markers on the ruler, by typing indents in the Paragraph dialog box, or by pressing Shift-⌘-N or Shift-⌘-M.

The Shift-⌘-N (indent one tab stop) and Shift-⌘-M (move indent back one tab stop) keyboard shortcuts are useful in a document you want to number by indent levels. Both commands are additive. If you press Shift-⌘-N three times, for example, Word indents the paragraph three default tab stops (1.5 inches), producing a Level 4 indentation. To bring the indent back one level, press Shift-⌘-M.

Fig. 16.11
Two subordinate levels
of indentation.

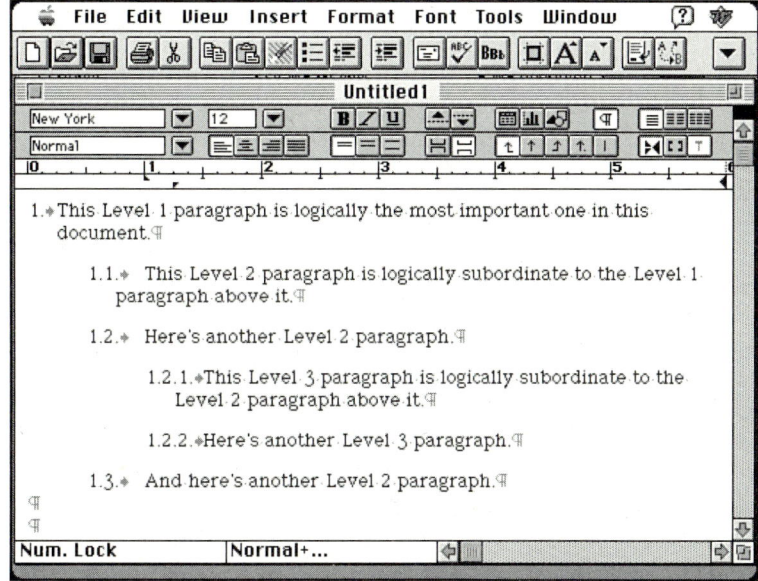

To number paragraphs of different levels, follow these steps:

1. Select the paragraphs that you want to number. If you don't select paragraphs, Word numbers all the paragraphs in your document.

2. Choose Renumber from the Tools menu or press ⌘-F15. The Renumber dialog box appears.

3. To start numbering with a number other than 1, type that number in the Start At text box.

4. To use a number format other than Arabic (1, 2, 3), type in the Format text box the number format and the separator character you want to use. (See tables 16.1 and 16.2 for the number formats and separator characters you can use.)

   Word indicates subordinate levels with Arabic numbers (II.1, II.2, II.2.1) and drops the right bracket, brace, or parenthesis for Level 2 and subsequent levels. Therefore, don't enclose numbers for subordinate levels in brackets, braces, or parentheses.

5. To turn on subordinate-level numbering, click the 1.1 radio button in the Numbers area.

6. Choose OK.

Numbering Paragraphs Selectively

If you don't want to number all the paragraphs in a document, you can use the New Line command (Shift-Return) to define two or more paragraphs as one paragraph. Word then attaches only one number to each paragraph you select. Rather than perform this procedure many times, however, you can type a number and press Tab at the beginning of each paragraph that you want Word to number. When you choose Renumber, select an option that numbers only those paragraphs that you have indicated.

To number paragraphs selectively, follow these steps:

1. At the beginning of every paragraph that you want Word to number, type a number, followed by a period (for example, **1.**), and then press Tab.

    You can type any number; Word replaces the typed numbers with the correct numbers. To repeat the number you typed, move the insertion point to the beginning of the next paragraph you want Word to number and then choose Repeat from the Edit menu or press ⌘-Y.

2. Choose Renumber from the Tools menu or press ⌘-F15. The Renumber dialog box appears.

3. To start numbering with a number other than 1, type that number in the Start At text box.

4. To use a number format other than Arabic (1, 2, 3), type in the Format text box the number format and the separator character you want to use.

5. **Important:** Click the Only If Already Numbered radio button. If you forget to choose this option, Word numbers all the paragraphs in your document.

6. Choose OK. If the numbering does not work correctly, immediately choose Undo from the Edit menu or press ⌘-Z.

Updating and Removing Paragraph Numbers

When you insert or delete paragraphs, Word doesn't automatically update the numbers in your document, as some programs do. You must select the paragraphs and use the Renumber command to number the paragraphs correctly. You also can use the Renumber command to remove numbers from a document.

To update numbers, follow these steps:

1. If you add paragraphs that need numbers, type a number followed by a period (**1.**) and then press Tab at the beginning of every newly inserted paragraph you want Word to number.

2. Choose Renumber from the Tools menu or press ⌘-F15. The Renumber dialog box appears.

3. **Important:** Click the Only If Already Numbered radio button. If you don't choose this option, Word numbers all the paragraphs in your document.

4. To change the starting number and/or the number format, you can choose subordinate numbering (the 1.1 option), even if you didn't choose this option the first time you inserted the numbers.

5. Choose OK.

To remove paragraph numbers from your document, follow these steps:

1. Choose Renumber from the Tools menu or press ⌘-F15. The Renumber dialog box appears.

2. Click the Remove radio button.

3. Choose OK.

Sorting Paragraphs and Tables

Alphabetizing can be a tedious job. Don't alphabetize paragraphs by moving paragraphs around; let Word do the job. Word's Sort command (Tools menu) can sort paragraphs or table rows in ascending order (a, b, c or 1, 2, 3) or descending order (c, b, a or 3, 2, 1).

To sort paragraphs, plan your document with sorting in mind. Use the New Line command (Shift-Return) to group lines so that they aren't separated during a sort. In figure 16.12, the New Line command keeps the program from separating the parts of each bibliographic citation.

Understanding How Word Sorts Text

To use Word's sorting capabilities effectively, you need to know that the program sorts text in ASCII order: text that begins with punctuation marks comes first, followed by text beginning with numbers. Then Word sorts text beginning with uppercase characters, followed by text beginning with lowercase characters. The program ignores diacritical marks such as accents and umlauts.

Fig. 16.12
Bibliographic citations entered with the New Line command.

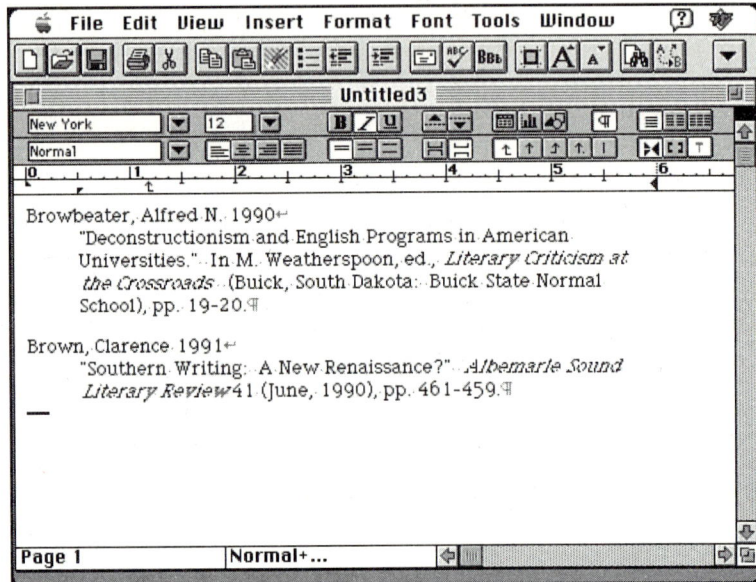

Because Word sorts in ASCII order, a sort may not conform to your expectations. For example, notice that the last two items in the price list in figure 16.13 are out of order because uppercase and lowercase are used inconsistently. To avoid this problem, use case consistently at the beginning of the paragraphs that you want to sort.

Sorting Paragraphs in a Document

Word sorts by using the first character of each paragraph you select. If the first character is a letter, Word sorts alphabetically. If the first character is a number, Word sorts numerically. If two paragraphs begin with the same character, the program uses additional characters—letters or numbers—to place the paragraphs in order. You can choose an ascending sort (the default sort order) or a descending sort (3, 2, 1).

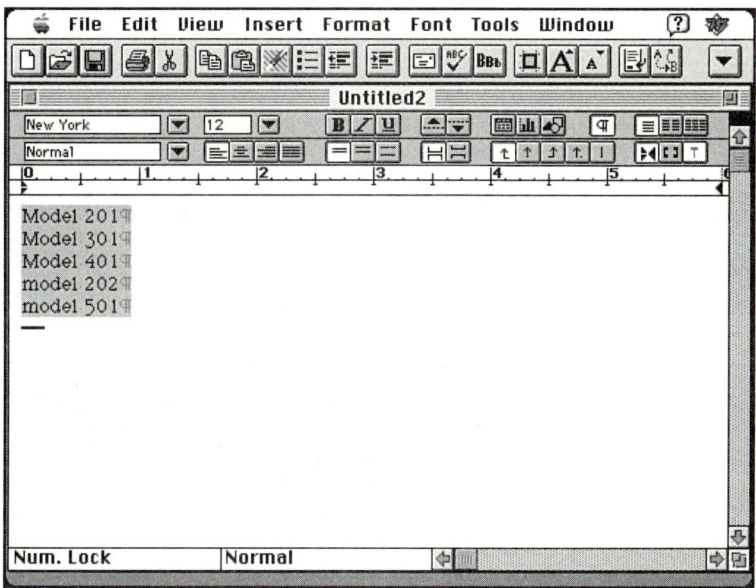

Fig. 16.13
Incorrect sort due to
inconsistent use of
uppercase and lowercase
letters.

To sort paragraphs, follow these steps:

1. Save your document before you begin to sort.

2. Select the paragraphs that you want to sort. If you don't select any paragraphs, the Sort option is grayed. To select the whole document, choose Select All from the Edit menu or press ⌘-A.

3. For an ascending sort, choose Sort from the Tools menu. For a descending sort, hold down the Shift key and choose Sort Descending from the Tools menu. Word performs the sort.

4. If you don't like the result of the sort, immediately choose Undo from the Edit menu or press ⌘-Z.

Sorting Tables

As you learned in Chapter 15, you can create tables by using tabs or by using Word's Table command. No matter which way you created a table, you can use the Sort command to sort the table.

When you sort a table, you can use column selection to show Word which column you want to use as a guide for the sort. In figure 16.14,

Chapter 16

for example, four cells in the Quantity column are selected. Selecting these cells tells Word to sort these four rows but to use this column as a guide for the sort.

Fig. 16.14

A column selected for sorting.

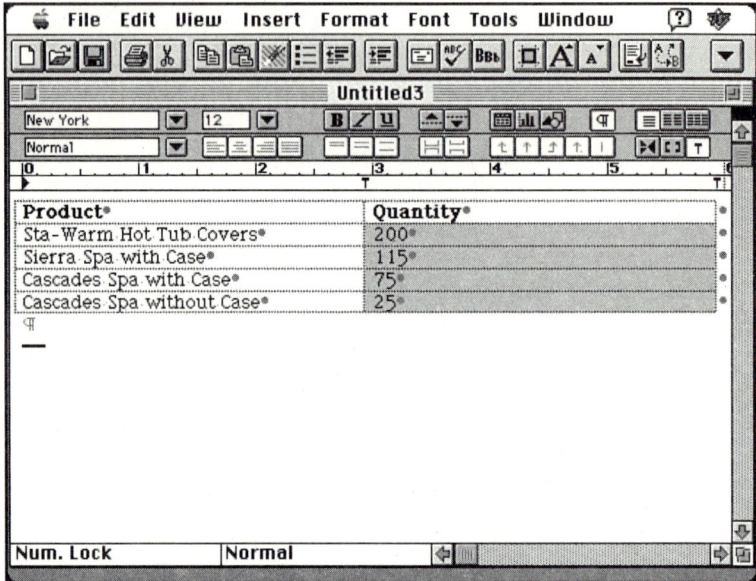

Figure 16.15 shows the result of the sort. Word has placed the rows in ascending numerical order by Quantity (Cascades Spa without Case is first, because its quantity—25—is the smallest). Notice that Word has kept the row items together without scrambling them.

To sort a table, follow these steps:

1. Select the rows that you want to sort or select one of the columns. Word uses the column you select as the guide for the sort. (Don't include the table headings in the selection; if you do, Word sorts the headings, too. If you leave the table headings out of the selection, the headings stay in place, as in figures 16.14 and 16.15.)

   To select a column in a tabbed table that uses right-aligned or decimal-aligned numbers, hold down the Option key and begin the selection at the lower right or upper right corner of the column.

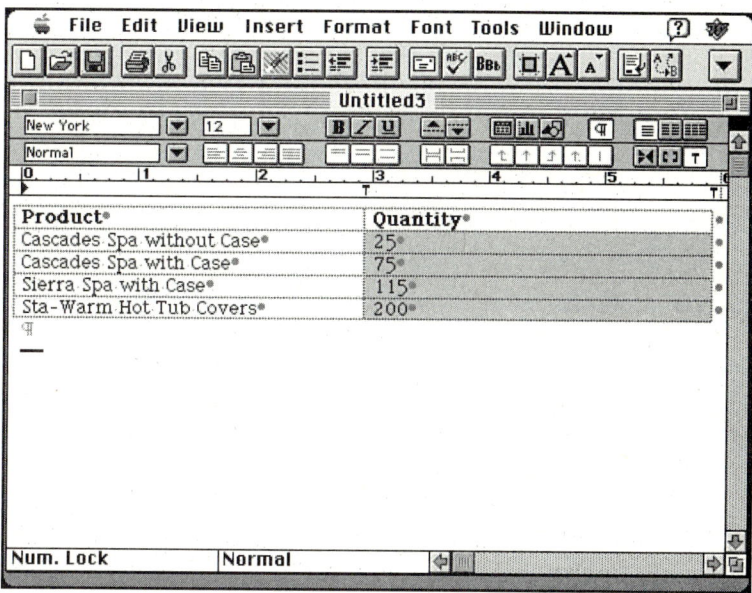

Fig. 16.15
Result of a sort with a
column selected.

Fig. 16.15
Result of a sort with a
column selected.

2. To sort in ascending order, choose Sort from the Tools menu. To sort in descending order, hold down the Shift key and choose Sort Descending from the Tools menu.

3. If the sort does not work correctly, immediately choose Undo from the Edit menu or press ⌘-Z.

Quick Review

This section summarizes the most useful information in this chapter. Check "Productivity Tips" for a review of high-productivity tips and tricks—the ones that Macintosh and Word pros use every day. Review "Techniques" whenever you need a quick reminder about a specific procedure.

Productivity Tips

■ If you want to add line numbers to a technical or legal document, plan ahead. Add blank lines by using the Spacing options in the Paragraph dialog box or the Blank Spacing icon in the ruler, not by pressing Return.

- To keep Word from numbering lines that contain headings, format your heading styles with the Suppress Line Numbers option and apply these styles to your headings.

- If you plan to number paragraphs in your document, use the New Line command (Shift-Return) to keep together, in one paragraph, all the text you want numbered with only one number.

- To add paragraph numbers only to those paragraphs that you want Word to number, type a number, a period, and a tab at the beginning of each paragraph you want to number and then use the Renumber command. Remember to choose the Only If Already Numbered option in the Renumber dialog box.

- If you want to sort text, plan ahead. Group all the lines you want to keep together in the sort by typing them with the New Line command. Use case consistently.

- Save your work before renumbering or sorting. If you perform another action and then decide that you don't like the result of the sort, you can abandon the changes by reloading the saved version of your document.

- When you sort a table, you don't have to sort the table by the text or values in the first column. If you select a column other than the first one, Word uses the selected column as a guide for the sort.

- If numbering or sorting doesn't work out as you anticipated, remember that you can choose Undo to retrieve your document in its original condition. You must choose Undo immediately, however, before you perform another action (such as typing text or choosing a command).

Techniques

This section provides concise summaries of all the procedures introduced in this chapter.

Numbering Lines

To add line numbers:

1. Select the paragraphs to which you want to add line numbers. If you don't select any text, Word adds line numbers to the whole document (or to the current section, if your document is divided into sections).

2. Choose Section from the Format menu or press Option-F14. The Section dialog box appears.

3. Click the Line Numbers command button. The Line Numbers dialog box appears.

4. In the Line Numbers drop-down list box, select By Page (numbers lines starting with 1 at the beginning of each page), By Section (numbers lines starting with 1 at the beginning of each section), or Continuous (numbers lines sequentially throughout document).

5. In the Count By text box, type the line-number increment that you want to use.

6. In the From Text text box, specify a distance from the end of the line number to the beginning of the text.

7. Choose OK. You return to the Section dialog box.

8. Choose OK to confirm your choices and close the dialog box.

Numbering Paragraphs

To add paragraph numbers to your document:

1. Select the paragraphs that you want to number. If you don't select any paragraphs, Word numbers all the paragraphs in your document.

2. Choose Renumber from the Tools menu or press ⌘-F15. The Renumber dialog box appears.

3. To start numbering with a number other than 1, type that number in the Start At text box.

4. To use a number format other than Arabic (1, 2, 3), type the number format and the separator character you want to use in the Format text box.

5. Choose OK. If the numbering is not correct, immediately choose Undo from the Edit menu or press ⌘-Z.

To number paragraphs of different levels:

1. Select the paragraphs that you want to number. If you don't select paragraphs, Word numbers all the paragraphs in your document.

2. Choose Renumber from the Tools menu or press ⌘-F15. The Renumber dialog box appears.

3. To start numbering with a number other than 1, type that number in the Start At text box.

4. To use a number format other than Arabic (1, 2, 3), type the number format and the separator character you want to use in the Format text box.

5. In the Numbers area, click the 1.1 radio button to turn on subordinate-level numbering.

6. Choose OK. If you don't like the way the numbering worked, immediately choose Undo from the Edit menu or press ⌘-Z.

To number paragraphs selectively:

1. Type a number followed by a period (**1.**) and then press Tab at the beginning of every paragraph you want to number.

2. Choose Renumber from the Tools menu or press ⌘-F15. The Renumber dialog box appears.

3. To start numbering with a number other than 1, type that number in the Start At text box.

4. To use a number format other than Arabic (1, 2, 3), type the number format and the separator character you want to use in the Format text box.

5. **Important:** Choose Only If Already Numbered.

6. Choose OK. If the numbering does not work correctly, immediately choose Undo from the Edit menu or press ⌘-Z.

To create a numbered list with the Bulleted List tool:

1. Type all the paragraphs in the list.

2. Select the paragraphs.

3. Click the Bulleted List tool. Word creates a hanging-indent format, indenting all the paragraphs 1/4 inch and placing bullets at the beginning of each paragraph.

4. Holding down the Option key, use the mouse to select all the bullets. Be careful not to erase the tab marks that trail the bullets. If you can't see the tab marks, click the paragraph-mark icon in the ribbon or choose Show ¶ from the View menu.

5. Press Delete to erase the bullets.

6. Select the text to be numbered.

7. Use the Renumber command to add numbers to each paragraph.

8. Choose OK.

Suppressing Line Numbers for Selected Paragraphs

To suppress line numbers for selected paragraphs:

1. If you haven't already done so, add line numbers to your document.

2. Select the paragraphs for which you don't want line numbers to print.

3. Choose Paragraph from the Format menu or press ⌘-M. The Paragraph dialog box appears.

4. Click the Suppress Line Numbers check box.

5. Choose OK.

6. To suppress line numbers for another paragraph, move the insertion point to that paragraph and then choose Repeat from the Edit menu or press ⌘-Y.

Updating Paragraph Numbers

To update numbers:

1. When you add paragraphs that need numbers, type a number followed by a period (**1.**) and press Tab at the beginning of every newly inserted paragraph you want to number.

2. Choose Renumber from the Tools menu or press ⌘-F15. The Renumber dialog box appears.

3. **Important:** Choose Only If Already Numbered.

4. You can change the starting number and the number format. You also can choose subordinate numbering (the 1.1 option), even if you didn't choose this option the first time you inserted the numbers.

5. Choose OK.

Removing Paragraph Numbers

To remove paragraph numbers from your document:

1. Choose Renumber from the Tools menu or press ⌘-F15. The Renumber dialog box appears.

2. Click the Remove radio button.

3. Choose OK.

Sorting Paragraphs

To sort paragraphs:

1. **Important:** Save your document.

2. Select the paragraphs that you want to sort. If you don't select any paragraphs, the Sort option is grayed.

3. To perform an ascending sort, choose Sort from the Tools menu. To perform a descending sort, hold down the Shift key and choose Sort Descending from the Tools menu.

4. If you don't like the result of the sort, immediately choose Undo from the Edit menu or press ⌘-Z.

Sorting a Table

To sort a table:

1. Select the rows that you want to sort or select a single column.

2. To sort in ascending order, choose Sort from the Tools menu. To sort in descending order, hold down the Shift key and choose Sort Descending from the Tools menu.

3. If the result of the sort is not what you want, immediately choose Undo from the Edit menu or press ⌘-Z.

Using Borders and Shading

Borders (lines and boxes) and shading effects can transform an otherwise plain document into one that looks as though it has been professionally designed. Figure 17.1 shows a newsletter that takes full advantage of Word's border and shading capabilities. Notice the single and double lines (called *rules*) below the newsletter's banner.

Fig. 17.1
Print Preview of document with borders and shading.

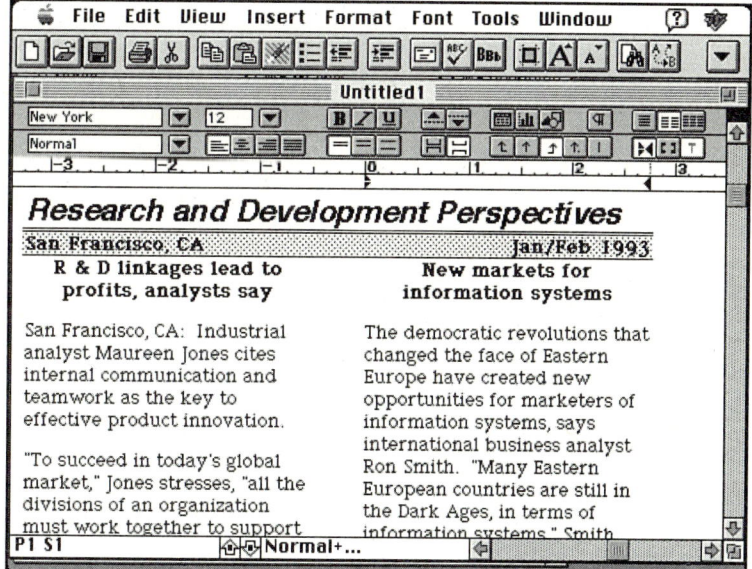

Word enables you to add borders and shading to any of the following elements of a document:

- *Text.* You can add borders and shading to any amount of selected text (one or more paragraphs). In figure 17.1, a double rule appears below the newsletter's title; the paragraph below the title has 25 percent shading with a single rule below.

- *Table.* Word automatically treats a table as a unit, as far as borders and shading are concerned. You can surround the table with a border and also print a gray screen (light gray shading) behind the table.

- *Cells.* Within a table, you can format borders and shading patterns independently for each cell. Thus, you can easily and quickly create lines that make a table look less like a spreadsheet and more like a formal table (with lines only where you want them). In addition, you can choose options that add borders and shading to rows, columns, or all the cells in a table.

- *Graphics.* Word treats each graphics element as a unit for border and shading purposes. You can add a box around a graphic.

This chapter surveys Word's border and shading capabilities. Following is an overview of the topics covered in this chapter:

- *Understanding the Border dialog box.* This section explains Word's border and shading options.

- *Adding borders and shading.* In this section, you learn how to add lines, boxes, and shading to text, graphics, and tables.

- *Aligning paragraph borders.* This section explains how to use indents and tables to control text borders.

- *Changing and removing borders and shading.* This section shows you how to alter or remove the border and shading options you have chosen.

Word considers borders and shading to be paragraph formats. If you format a paragraph of text with borders and/or shading, Word repeats the format when you press Return. Chances are that you don't want to repeat the format, however—after all, borders and shading should be used sparingly, for emphasis. For this reason, waiting to apply shading until you finish writing and editing your document is advisable.

Part III

Using Advanced Formatting Techniques

Understanding the Border Dialog Box

To add borders and shading, choose the Border command from the Format menu or click the Border tool to open the Border dialog box (see fig. 17.2).

Fig. 17.2
Border dialog box when text is selected.

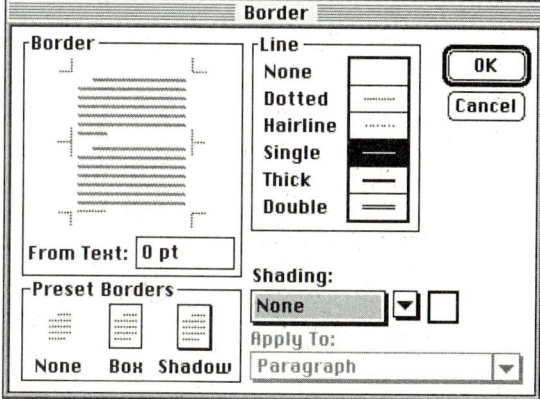

You also can bring up the Border dialog box by clicking the Border button in the Paragraph, Table Cells, or Picture dialog box.

Following is an overview of the elements in the Border dialog box:

Line area (default: Single). In this area, you choose the line width you want to use: Dotted, Hairline, Single, Thick, and Double. The hairline option prints a hairline on laser printers only; if you are using another kind of printer, this option has the same result as Single. Use the None option to blank a line in the Border area.

Preset Borders area (default: None). This area contains icons that you can click to select a box or shadow box quickly. If you click Box, you get a box using the line width currently in effect in the Line area. If you choose Shadow, you get a shadow box.

Border area. This area represents the selected text, graphic, or table on the page and enables you to add lines along the *border guides*, which are indicated by the registration marks on the simulated page. If you click the top border guide in this area, for example, Word adds a line across the top of the selected guide;

Chapter 17
Using Borders and Shading

if you click the left side of this area, Word adds a line on the left side of the selected guide. If you click the middle of this area, Word prints lines between paragraphs in selected text. After adding a line by clicking, you can click again (or choose None in the Line area) to remove the line. When you click to add a line, Word uses the line thickness or type that currently is selected in the Line area.

Figure 17.3 shows the Border area with a graphic selected; figure 17.4 shows the Border area with a table selected.

Fig. 17.3
Border dialog box when a graphic is selected.

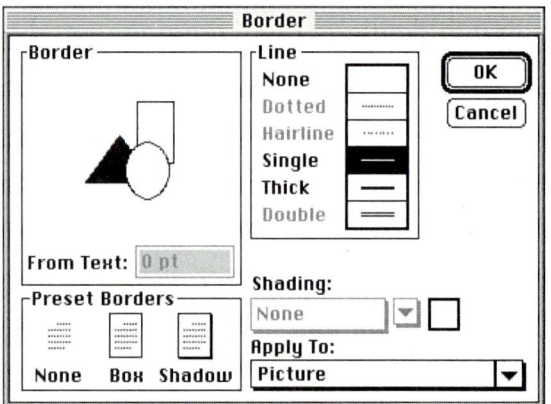

Fig. 17.4
Border dialog box when a table is selected.

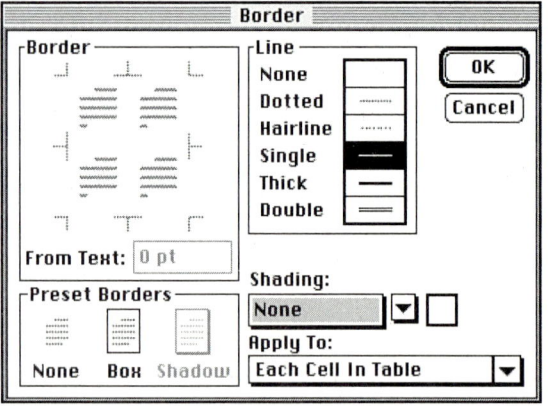

From Text text box (default: 0 pt). In this box, you type the *additional* distance you want the lines to be separated from the text. By default, Word enters 2 points of extra space, even though the From Text box shows 0 pt. If you type a number (1 to 31) in this box, Word increases the default 2-point distance by the number of points you type. (*Note:* 72 points equal 1 inch.)

Apply To drop-down list box. This box becomes active when you need to indicate where you want Word to apply borders. When you select a graphic, for example, you can apply the border to the graphic only or to the paragraph in which the graphic appears. When you select a table, you can apply the border to one cell, all the cells in the table, the entire table (with no lines within), a selected column, or a selected row. The options in this list box are explained later in this chapter, in "Adding Borders and Shading to Tables."

Shading drop-down list box. When you click the Shading list box, you see the shading options shown in figure 17.5.

Fig. 17.5
Shading options.

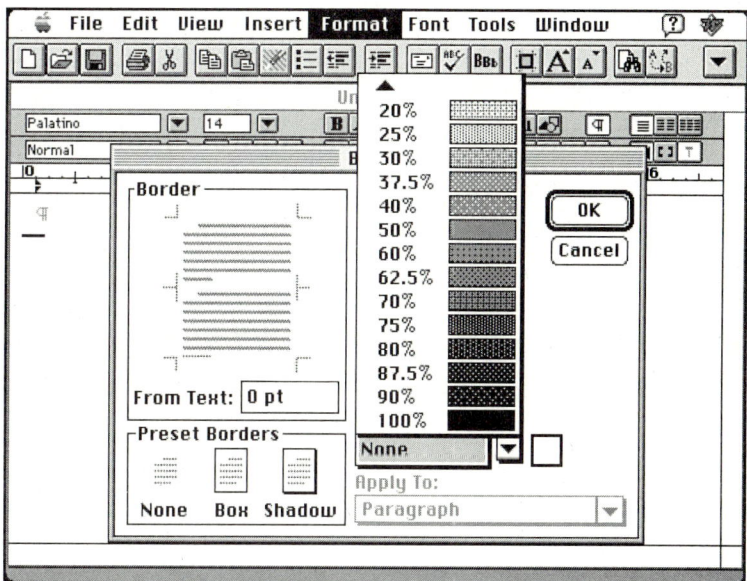

If you are using an ImageWriter, you will get the best results if you choose shading options that are multiples of 12.5 percent: 12.5, 25, 37.5, and so on. If you are using a laser printer or a 300-dots-per-inch (dpi) inkjet printer, you can choose any of the shading options in this list box.

Chapter 17

Using Borders and Shading

Adding Borders and Shading

The procedures you use to add borders and shading vary, depending on whether you have selected text, a graphic, or a table. The following sections cover all three procedures.

Adding Borders and Shading to Text

You can format one or more paragraphs of text. If you select more than one paragraph, Word treats the selection as a block and places the border around the entire selection.

When you add borders or shading to text, these elements become part of the paragraph format. As is true of all other paragraph formats, the border or shading options are "contained" in the paragraph mark. If you delete the mark, you delete the borders or shading along with all the other formats you have chosen for the paragraph.

To add borders and shading to text, follow these steps:

1. Select the text.

2. Choose Border from the Format menu or click the Border tool. The Border dialog box appears.

3. To add borders, choose a line width in the Line area.

4. Choose Box or Shadow in the Preset Borders area, or click the Border area to indicate the borders you want. If you click the middle, Word places lines between paragraphs if you have selected more than one paragraph.

5. If you want, increase the border's default distance from the text (2 points) by typing a number (1 to 31) in the From Text text box.

6. To add shading, select a shading percentage or type a percentage in the Shading drop-down list box.

7. Choose OK.

Figure 17.6 shows thick borders above and below a paragraph of text.

You can include borders and shadings in styles. If you frequently use borders or shadings for a text element, such as a title or heading, create a style that includes the border or shading formats. For more information on styles, see Chapter 14, "Formatting with Styles."

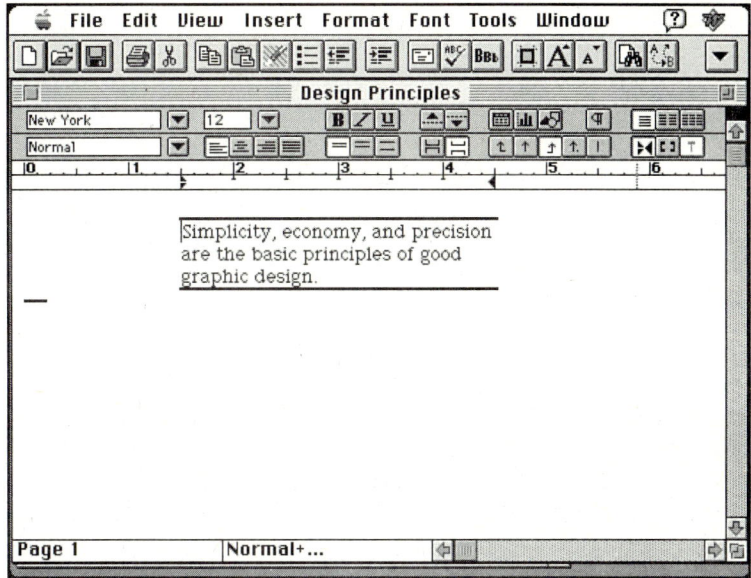

Fig. 17.6
Borders above and below a paragraph of text.

Adding Borders to a Graphic

The procedures you use to add borders to graphics are similar to those for adding borders or shading to text, with the following differences:

- You can add borders to only one graphic at a time. If you want to add borders to two or more graphics, you must format the graphics one at a time.

- You cannot use the Border command to add shading to a graphic; you must use the Edit Picture window to add shading (see Chapter 7, "Creating and Importing Graphics").

- If the borders are too close to the graphic, you can enlarge the graphic frame by selecting the frame and dragging the handles.

To add borders to a graphic, follow these steps:

1. Select the graphic.

2. Choose Border from the Format menu. The Border dialog box appears, with a graphic in the Border area.

3. To add borders, choose a line width in the Line area.

Chapter 17
Using Borders and Shading

4. Choose Box or Shadow in the Preset Borders area, or click the Border area to indicate the borders you want.

5. If you want to add shading, select a shading percentage or type a percentage in the Shading drop-down list box.

6. In the Apply To drop-down list box, select Paragraph if you want the border to surround the paragraph in which the graphic is situated. Select Picture (the default) to place the border around the picture only.

7. Choose OK.

Figure 17.7 shows a graphic surrounded by a box that was added with the Picture option (Apply To drop-down list box). Because the Picture option was used, Word did not include the paragraph mark that follows the graphic within the selection.

Fig. 17.7
Border surrounding
a graphic (but not
the paragraph).

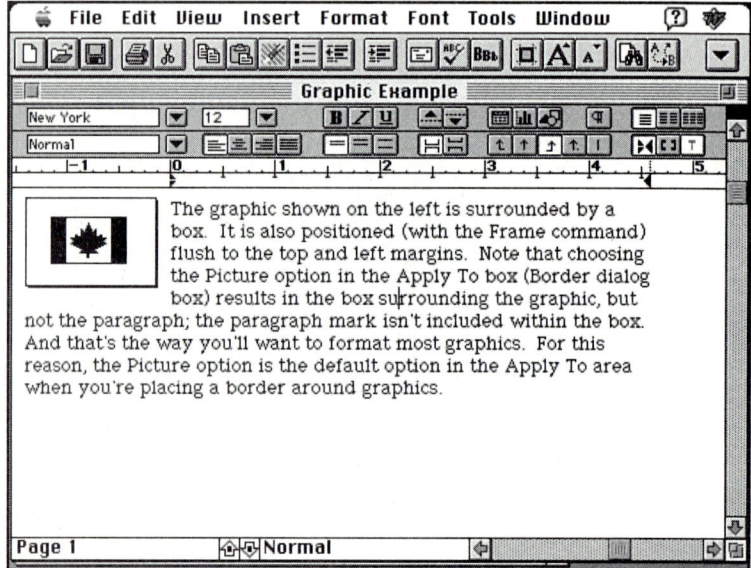

Adding Borders and Shading to Tables

When you add borders and shading to tables, you begin by selecting the cells to which you want to add these features. If you want, you can add borders to all the cells; Word places the borders where the table grid lines are located, producing a spreadsheetlike appearance. Most tables look better, however, without all the possible borders. You can add borders as you please: to one row or column, to several rows or columns, to selected cells only, or to the entire table.

To add borders and shading to a table, follow these steps:

1. Select the table by placing the insertion point anywhere in the table, holding down the Option key, and double-clicking. Alternatively, select one or more cells, one or more columns, or one or more rows.

2. Choose Border from the Format menu. The Border dialog box appears. What the Border area shows depends on what you selected. If you selected at least two rows and two columns, the Border area appears as a two-by-two table, as shown earlier in figure 17.4. If you selected one column, the Border area looks like the area shown in figure 17.8.

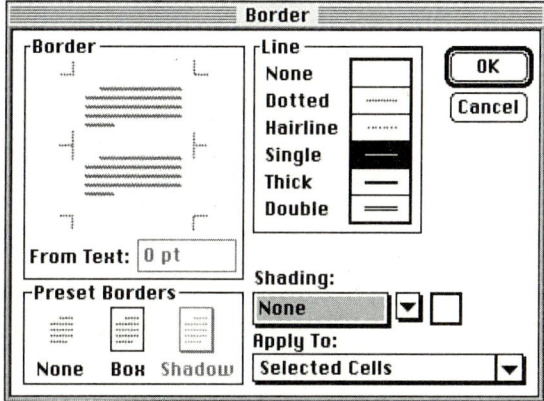

Fig. 17.8
Border dialog box when one column of a table is selected.

If you selected one row, the Border area looks like the area shown in figure 17.9.

3. To add borders, choose a line width in the Line area.

4. Choose Box or Shadow in the Preset Borders area, or click the Border area to indicate the borders you want.

To place a box around the selected cells, double-click outside the border guides (see fig. 17.10).

Chapter 17
Using Borders and Shading

Fig. 17.9
Border dialog box when
one row of a table
is selected.

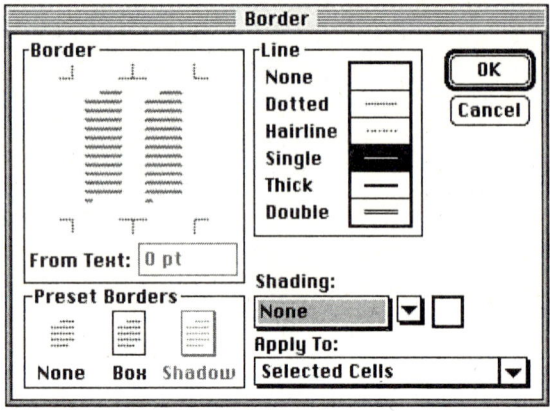

Fig. 17.10
Box added around
selected cells.

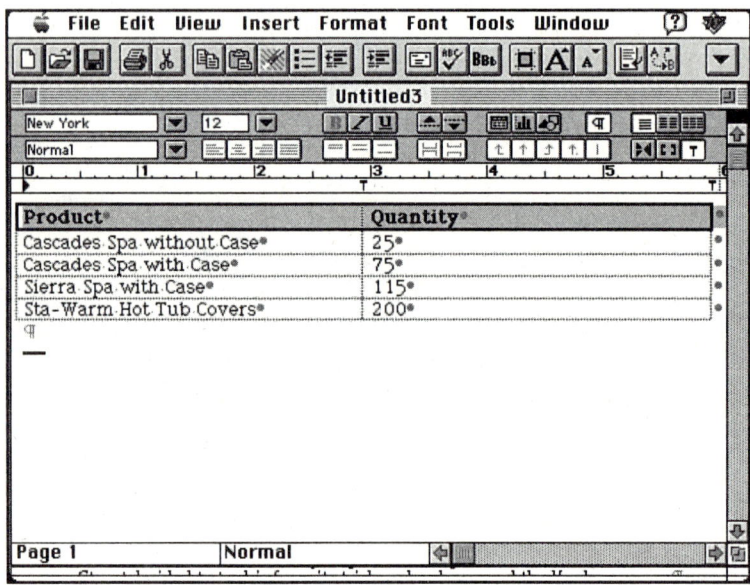

To add rules to the columns inside the table, click the vertical
border guide (see fig. 17.11).

Fig. 17.11
Column rules added.

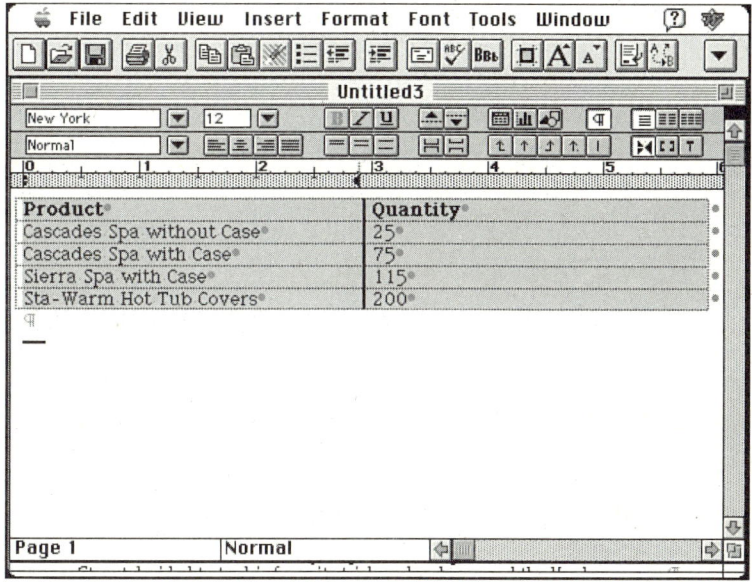

To add rules to the rows inside the table, click the horizontal border guide (see fig. 17.12).

Fig. 17.12
All borders added.

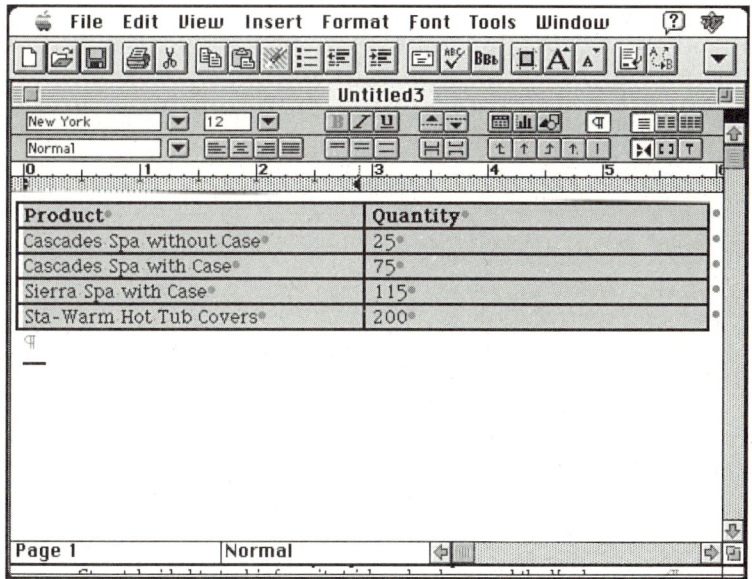

Chapter 17
Using Borders and Shading

5. If you want to add shading, select a shading percentage or type a percentage in the Shading drop-down list box.

6. In the Apply To list box, choose one of the following options:

   ■ *Selected Cells.* Applies the borders only to selected cells, as a block.

   ■ *Entire Columns Selected.* Applies the borders to all the cells in columns that contain a selected cell.

   ■ *Entire Rows Selected.* Applies the borders to all the cells in rows that contain a selected cell.

   ■ *All Cells in Table.* Applies the borders to all the cells in the table, whether or not you selected them.

7. Choose OK.

You can vary the borders and shadings you add to produce attractive results. Simply use the Border command several times, making different selections each time. In figure 17.13, for example, two line widths combine with two shading patterns to produce an attractive result.

Fig. 17.13
Combined border and shading patterns.

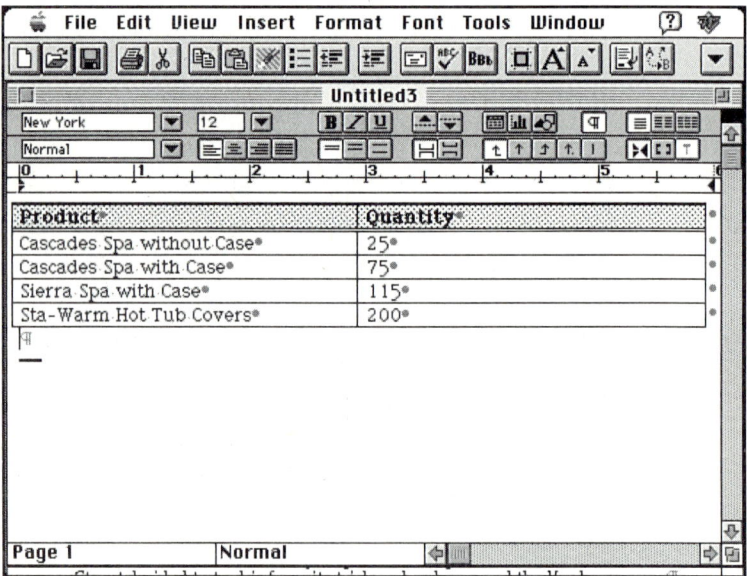

Part III
Using Advanced Formatting Techniques

Aligning Paragraph Borders

When you add vertical borders to text, Word places the borders just outside the left and right margins. In addition, the top and bottom borders extend the full width of the paragraph, from the left margin to the right. In figure 17.14, the thick rule below the heading extends from the left to the right indents. As the bulleted list shows, however, indentations affect the placement of borders.

Fig. 17.14

Default alignment of paragraph borders.

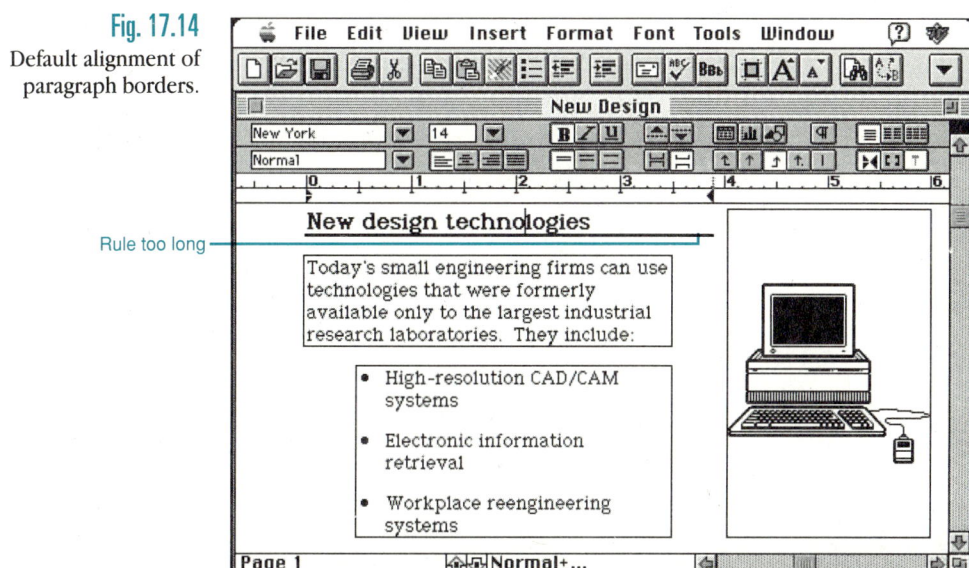

You can control the length of the top and bottom borders by indenting the text. In figure 17.15, the paragraph containing the heading has been indented from the right so that the thick rule below the heading doesn't extend to the right margin of the frame. Now the rule aligns with the boxes below it.

As you can see in figures 17.14 and 17.15, indentations can cause problems when you add borders. Suppose that you want the bulleted list to be enclosed in the same box as the text above it. You can convert all this text to a single-column table and then enclose the table in a box, as shown in figure 17.16.

Chapter 17

Using Borders and Shading

Fig. 17.15
Shortening the thick rule
under the heading.

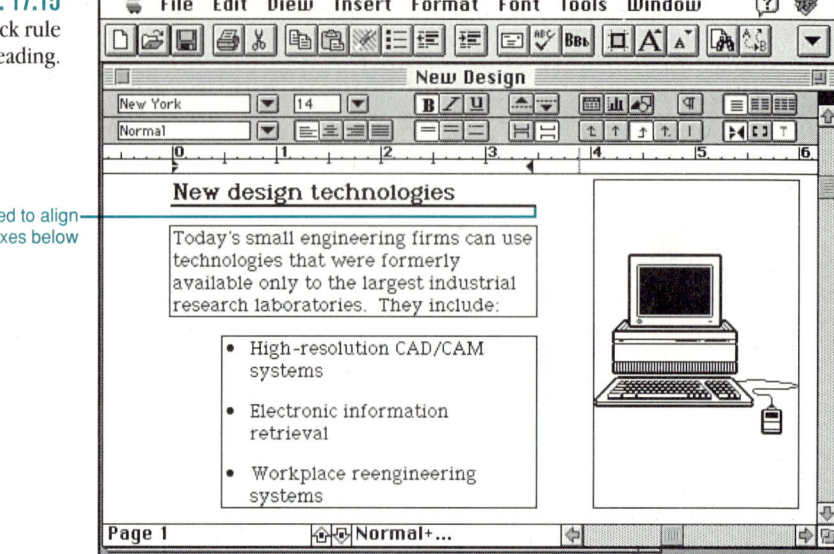

Rule indented to align
with boxes below

Fig. 17.16
Converting text
to a table to box all
selected paragraphs.

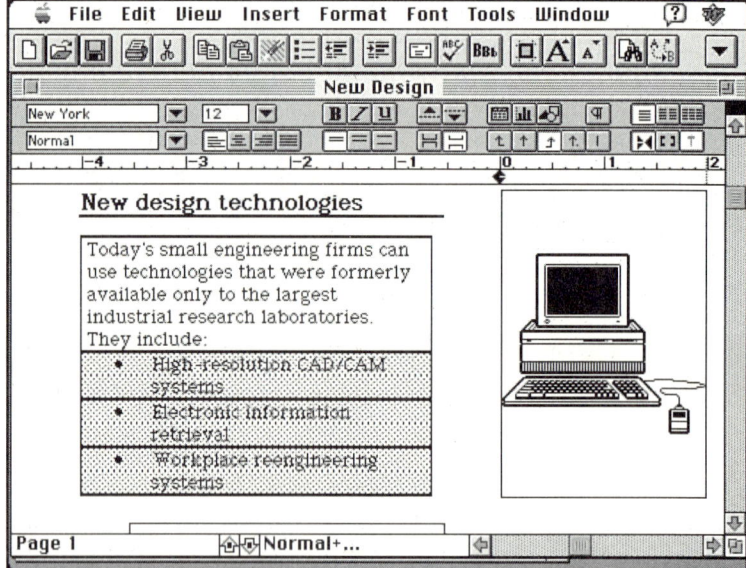

Changing and Removing Borders and Shading

After you apply borders and shading to text, graphics, or tables, you can change or remove the borders or shading.

To change a border or shading, follow these steps:

1. Select the text, graphic, or table cells that contain the border or shading.

2. Choose Border from the Format menu. The Border dialog box appears, with the Border area showing the current borders of the selected element.

3. In the Line area, choose the line width you want to use. You see black triangles at the ends of the line, indicating that the line is selected.

4. In the Border area, click the borders you want to change. (To remove an unwanted border, click that border and then choose None in the Line area.)

5. If you want to change the shading, select a different shading percentage in the Shading drop-down list box.

6. Choose OK.

To remove all borders and shading, follow these steps:

1. Select the text, graphic, or table cells that contain the border or shading.

2. Choose Border from the Format menu. The Border dialog box appears.

3. To remove all borders, choose None in the Preset Borders area.

4. To remove all shading, choose None in the Shading drop-down list box.

5. Choose OK.

Quick Review

This section summarizes the most useful information in this chapter. Check "Productivity Tips" for a review of high-productivity tips and tricks—the ones that Macintosh and Word pros use every day. Review "Techniques" whenever you need a quick reminder about a specific procedure.

Chapter 17

Using Borders and Shading

Productivity Tips

- Remember that borders and shading are paragraph formats; if you add these formats to a paragraph, Word duplicates the formats when you press Return. Because this duplication normally isn't desirable with borders and shading, which you should use sparingly, wait to apply borders and shading until you finish writing and editing your document.

- You can add borders and shading to styles. If you frequently use a text element that includes borders or shading, include the border or shading options in the style definition. When you apply the style, Word enters the border or shading automatically.

Techniques

This section provides concise summaries of all the procedures introduced in this chapter.

Adding Borders or Shading

To add borders and shading to text:

1. Select the text.

2. Choose Border from the Format menu or click the Border tool. The Border dialog box appears.

3. To add borders, choose a line width in the Line area.

4. Choose Box or Shadow in the Preset Borders area, or click the Border area to indicate the borders you want. If you click the middle border guide, Word places lines between paragraphs (if you selected more than one paragraph).

5. If you want, increase the border's default distance from the text (2 points) by typing a number (1 to 31) in the From Text text box.

6. If you want to add shading, select a shading percentage or type a percentage in the Shading drop-down list box.

7. Choose OK.

Part III

Using Advanced Formatting Techniques

To add borders to a graphic:

1. Select the graphic.

2. Choose Border from the Format menu or click the Border tool. The Border dialog box appears.

3. To add borders, choose a line width in the Line area.

4. Choose Box or Shadow in the Preset Borders area, or click the Border area to indicate the borders you want.

5. If you want to add shading, select a shading percentage or type a percentage in the Shading drop-down list box.

6. In the Apply To list box, select Paragraph if you want the border to surround the paragraph in which the graphic is situated. Select Picture (the default) to place the border around the picture only.

7. Choose OK.

To add borders and shading to a table:

1. Select the table or table cells.

2. Choose Border from the Format menu or click the Border tool. The Border dialog box appears.

3. To add borders, choose a line width in the Line area.

4. Choose Box or Shadow in the Preset Borders area, or click the Border area to indicate the borders you want.

5. If you want to add shading, select a shading percentage or type a percentage in the Shading drop-down list box.

6. In the Apply To list box, select one of the following options:

   ■ *Selected Cells.* Applies the borders only to selected cells, as a block.

   ■ *Entire Columns Selected.* Applies the borders to all the cells in columns that contain a selected cell.

   ■ *Entire Rows Selected.* Applies the borders to all the cells in rows that contain a selected cell.

   ■ *All Cells in Table.* Applies the borders to all the cells in the table, whether or not you selected them.

7. Choose OK.

Chapter 17

Using Borders and Shading

Changing Borders and Shading

To change a border or shading:

1. Select the text, graphic, or table cells that contain the border or shading.

2. Choose Border from the Format menu or click the Border tool. The Border dialog box appears.

3. In the Line area, choose the line width you want to use.

4. In the Border area, click the borders you want to change. (To remove an unwanted border, click that border and then choose None in the Line area.)

5. If you want to change the shading, choose a different shading percentage in the Shading drop-down list box.

6. Choose OK.

Removing Borders and Shading

To remove all borders and shading:

1. Select the text, graphic, or table cells that contain the border or shading.

2. Choose Border from the Format menu or click the Border tool. The Border dialog box appears.

3. To remove all borders, choose None in the Preset Borders area.

4. To remove all shading, choose None in the Shading drop-down list box.

5. Choose OK.

CHAPTER

18

Creating
Newspaper Columns

Word can format your text in multiple columns, like the columns you see in newspapers and magazines. These columns are called *snaking columns* because the text, when it reaches the bottom of a column, snakes to the top of the next one. Word can create up to 100 columns, but for most purposes you need only two or three columns.

If you add newspaper columns to your document, you probably will want to print some of your document in a one-column layout and the rest in a two-column or three-column layout, like the newsletter shown in figure 18.1. The newsletter's title is printed across the top of the page as one column, and the text is printed in a two-column format.

To switch from one column format to another, you divide your document into sections and format each section with a different column layout. (Sections are covered in more detail in Chapter 21, "Dividing a Document into Sections.") For now, be aware that you can break your document into two or more sections, each of which has its own distinctive margins, header and footer location, page-number format, and column format. If you divide your document into sections, you can change column formats as often as you want.

In this chapter, you learn how to choose multiple-column formats and how to change column formats after you create them. You also learn how to start new columns and how to use the keyboard to move the cursor from one column to the next.

USING
WORD 5.1
FOR THE MAC
SPECIAL EDITION

Fig. 18.1
Print Preview of
a newsletter.

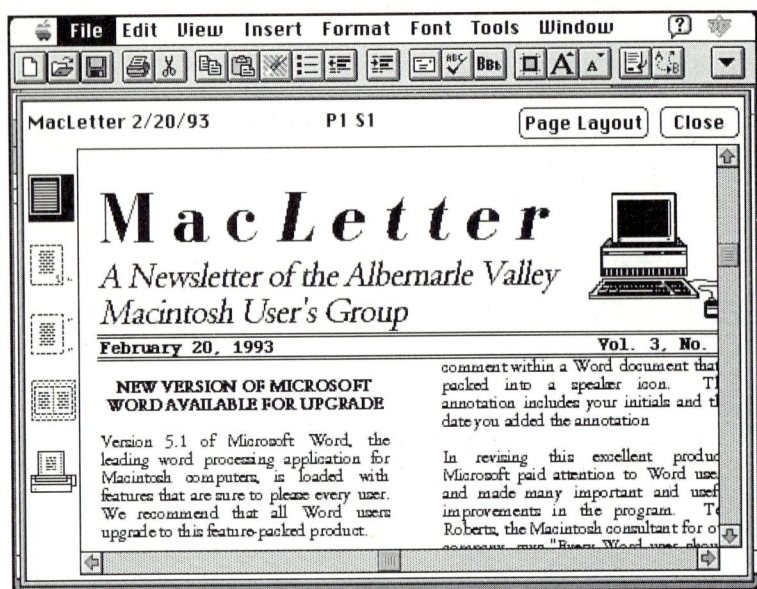

This chapter covers the following topics:

- ◼ *Viewing multiple columns.* You learn how to view multiple-column formats in Page Layout view and what the ruler shows when more than one column is visible.

- ◼ *Creating columns.* You learn how to create columns with the ribbon and with the Section dialog box.

- ◼ *Using the newsletter sample document.* You learn to use this sample document to create a newsletter quickly.

- ◼ *Controlling column breaks manually.* You learn how to control column breaks so you can adjust a column's length.

- ◼ *Changing column width.* You learn how to change column width by adjusting the white space between columns.

- ◼ *Balancing the text on the page.* You learn how to adjust your layout when columns don't completely fill the page.

NOTE

If you want to keep a specific paragraph of text adjacent to another specific paragraph, newspaper columns aren't a good layout choice. Word moves column text up or down as you insert or delete text, so a paragraph in column 1 may not appear adjacent to a specific paragraph in column 2. Use a table (see Chapter 15) if you need to keep paragraphs in two or more columns adjacent.

Viewing Multiple Columns

Before you create multiple columns, you should learn how Word displays them on-screen. In Normal view, Word displays one column, and the ruler shows the column width (measured from the left margin of the column), as shown in figure 18.2.

Fig. 18.2

Normal view of a multiple-column document.

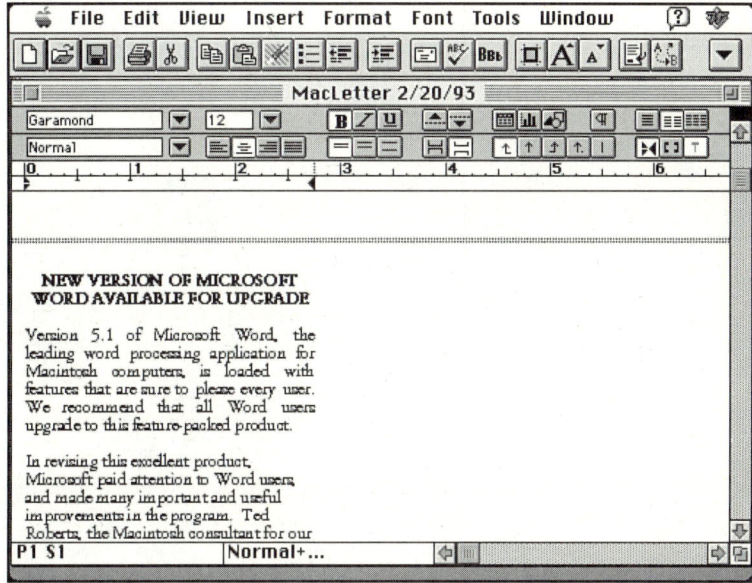

In Page Layout view, Word displays the columns as they will appear when printed (see fig. 18.3). Notice that the 0 mark in the ruler always appears at the left margin of the column in which the insertion point is positioned.

If you click the Margin Marker icon in the ruler so that Word displays margin brackets rather than indent markers, the ruler measures the page with the 0 mark positioned at the left edge of the page. The brackets measure the column boundaries. When the Margin Marker icon is activated, the ruler works this way in Normal view and Page Layout view. (See figure 18.4 for an illustration of this display in Page Layout view.)

Fig. 18.3

Page Layout view of a multiple-column document.

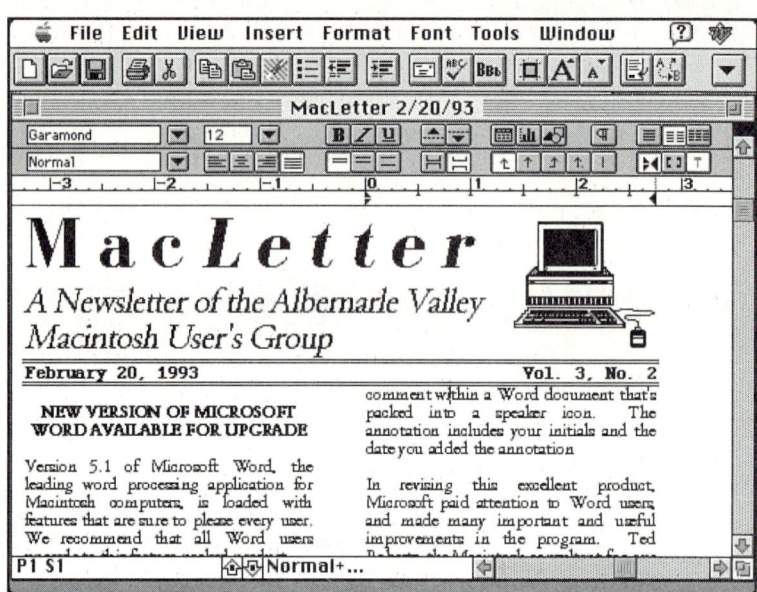

Fig. 18.4

Page Layout view of a multiple-column document (Margin Marker icon activated).

0 mark

Column boundaries

Margin Marker icon

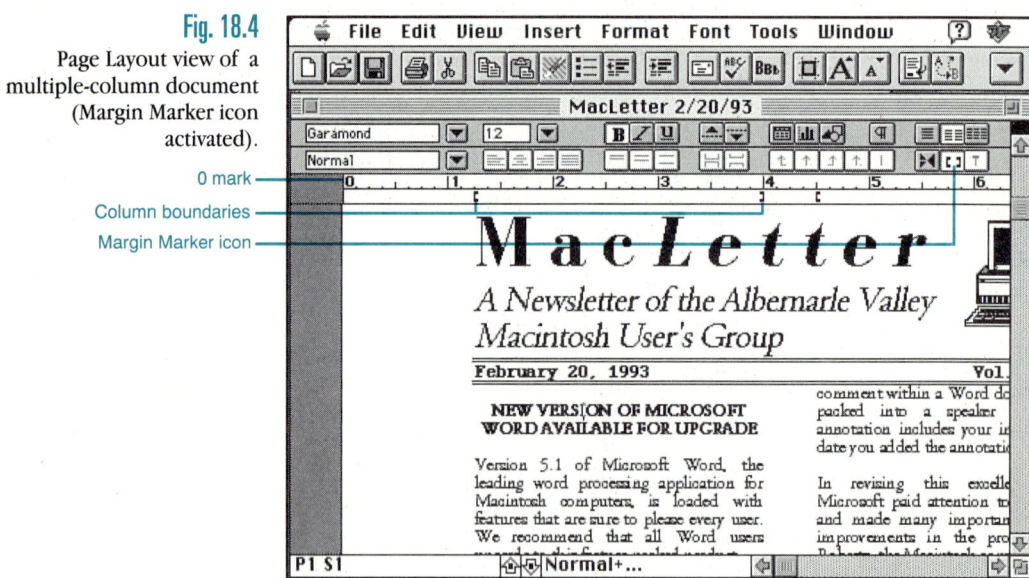

Creating Columns

You can add newspaper columns in two ways:

- *Ribbon.* Use the column-format icons in the ribbon (refer to fig. 18.7 later in this chapter) to add two- or three-column formats to your document quickly. Word uses the default column spacing (0.5 inch).

- *Section dialog box.* Use this dialog box to specify more than three columns or to use column spacing other than 0.5 inch.

  As you have learned, column formats apply to sections. Your documents contain one section by default. To break your document into two or more sections, position the insertion point where you want the break to occur and then press ⌘-Enter (the Section Break command). In Normal view, you see a double row of dots across the screen (see fig. 18.5). Word positions the insertion point below the break. Notice that the page-number area now indicates the current page number and section number.

  Section breaks are harder to see in Page Layout view. Word tries to show your document as it will appear when printed, so the section marks do not span the screen. If you display paragraph marks, you can see an abbreviated section mark in Page Layout view (see fig. 18.6).

If you want newspaper columns to appear in only part of your document, use the Section Break command (⌘-Enter) before the place where you want the columns to start. If you want to follow the newspaper-column section with single-column text or some other column format, use the Section Break command again where you want the newspaper columns to end.

By default, Word starts a new page at a section break. To prevent the program from starting a new page, place the insertion point after the section break and choose Section from the Format menu or press Option-F14. When the Section dialog box appears, select No Break in the Start drop-down list box and then choose OK.

Fig. 18.5
A section break.

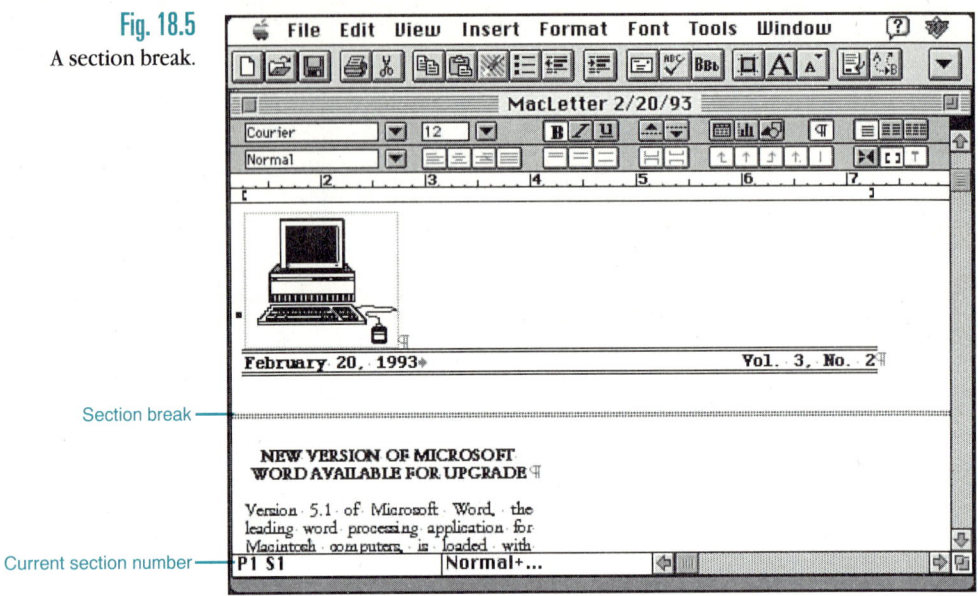

Section break —

Current section number —

Fig. 18.6
Section mark (Page
Layout view).

Section mark

Part III

Using Advanced Formatting Techniques

Why would you want to prevent a page break at the section break? Suppose that you are creating a newsletter that features a single-column title and banner across the top of the front page. You want newspaper columns to appear below this banner. To specify this format, you must format the newspaper-column section with the No Break option; otherwise, Word would start printing the newspaper columns on page 2 of your document.

Creating Columns with the Ribbon

To assign a two- or three-column format to a document with the ribbon, follow these steps:

1. Position the insertion point in the section you want to format. (If you haven't divided your document into sections, the formatting will apply to the entire document.)

2. Click the two- or three-column icon in the ribbon (see fig. 18.7).

Fig. 18.7
Column-format icons in the ribbon.

Two-column icon

Single-column icon

Three-column icon

To cancel a multiple-column format quickly, simply place the insertion point within the format and then click the single-column icon in the ribbon.

Creating Columns with the Section Dialog Box

To assign multiple-column format to your document by using the Section dialog box, follow these steps:

1. Place the insertion point in the section you want to format. (If you haven't divided your document into sections, the formatting will apply to the entire document.)

2. Choose Section from the Format menu or press Option-F14. The Section dialog box appears (see fig. 18.8).

Chapter 18
Creating Newspaper Columns

Fig. 18.8
Section dialog box.

```
┌─────────────────────────────────────────────────────────┐
│ ▦▦▦▦▦▦▦▦▦▦▦▦ Section ▦▦▦▦▦▦▦▦▦▦▦▦                          │
│ Start: │No Break          ▼│  ☐ Include Endnotes  ┌──────────┐│
│ ┌Columns────────────┐ ┌Page Numbers──────────┐  │    OK    ││
│ │Number:      │  1  ││ │Format:  │ 1 2 3  ▼│ │  └──────────┘│
│ │             └─────┘│ │                     │  ┌──────────┐│
│ │Spacing:    │0.5 in││ │☐ Restart at 1       │  │  Cancel  ││
│ └────────────└─────┘┘ │☐ Margin Page Numbers│  └──────────┘│
│ ┌Header/Footer──────┐ │                     │  ┌──────────┐│
│ │From Top:   │0.5 in││ │From Top:  │0.5 in│ │  │  Apply   ││
│ │                   │ │                     │  └──────────┘│
│ │From Bottom:│0.5 in││ │From Right: │0.5 in││  ┌──────────────┐│
│ │☐ Different First Page                     │ │Use As Default│ │
│ └───────────────────┘ └─────────────────────┘ └──────────────┘│
│                                               ┌──────────────┐│
│                                               │Line Numbers...│ │
│                                               └──────────────┘│
└─────────────────────────────────────────────────────────┘
```

3. In the Number text box (Columns area), type the number of columns you want to create.

   You can create up to 100 columns, but doing so doesn't make much sense unless you want columns that contain only one or two characters each. For most projects, such as newsletters or price lists, use two or three columns.

4. (Optional) In the Spacing text box, you can type a measurement to indicate how much white space you want Word to insert between columns. By default, Word inserts 0.5 inch of white space between the columns. If you're using a three-column layout, try using 0.25-inch spacing.

5. If you entered a section break before adding the column format, you can prevent Word from starting a new page at the section break by selecting No Break in the Start drop-down list box.

6. If you want, click Apply to see how the format changes will affect your document.

7. Choose OK. Word creates the section format.

If you want to change the format, position the insertion point in the multiple-column text and choose Section from the Format menu or press Option-F14 to display the Section dialog box. You then can change the text back to single-column layout, choose a different column number, change the page break, and choose other formatting options. (You also can change the column format by clicking a column-format icon in the ribbon.)

If you specify narrow columns, Word may have problems in justifying the right margin of each column. You can improve your document's appearance by hyphenating your document. For information on hyphenation, see Chapter 12, "Checking Spelling and Grammar."

Using the Newsletter Sample

Word 5.1 comes with a variety of sample documents (stored in the Sample Document folder) that you can use to start a document quickly. Figure 18.9 shows the newsletter sample.

The newsletter contains the following formats:

- A title (in 50 point Times) at the top of the page, with a graphic positioned in the middle.

- A banner below the title, created with a border above and below.

- A table below the banner (in which you can position graphics, a table of contents, or other information). Using this table enables you to position text and graphics side by side, as shown in figure 18.9.

- A line below the table, consisting of two headlines. (This paragraph ends with a section break.)

- A three-column newspaper-column section below the headlines, ending with another section break.

- A table at the bottom of the page.

If you have a PostScript printer, you can use an entry in the Page Layout glossary (stored in Word's Glossary folder) to add lines between columns. For more information, see Appendix B, "Using PostScript."

You can use this document to create your own newsletter simply by retyping the existing text. The document also enables you to experiment with table formats, graphics, and borders.

Chapter 18

Creating Newspaper Columns

Fig. 18.9
Newsletter sample document.

ARBOR REPORT

Arbor Footwear   Vol. II • No. 12 • Dec. 5, 1991

Foot Facts The children's shoe division walked away with this month's production award, exceeding their production goal by 7 percent!

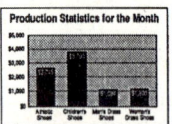

Robot added to work force

Our athletic shoe division took a step toward the twenty-first century this month when it purchased a robot to assist with manufacturing.

The robot threads shoelaces into track shoes at an astounding rate of speed. Human co-workers report that the robot is pleasant to work with and "doesn't complain much." In fact, the robot doesn't talk at all.

Nicknamed "TongueTied" by his co-workers, the 5'6" tall robot was originally programmed to whistle as he worked. Fellow workers soon voted to shut off this function. Does TongueTied make any noise at all now? Supervisor Paul Martin reports, "At the end of the day his hydraulic system decompresses and he sort of sighs."

For Martin's fortieth birthday, workers dressed the robot in a company T-shirt and a party hat. It gave TongueTied so much personality that Martin left him that way.

Autographs, anyone?

TongueTied, our company robot, seems to have a competitive side to him. As a publicity gimmick, marketing entered him in a nation-wide computer games contest last week. Along with 1,200 kids, ages 9 to 14, TongueTied competed for top scores on arcade computer games. TongueTied rolled away with not only top honors, but the world-record score for all three games.

Although all prizes went to the humans, the company sponsoring the contest created a special plaque for TongueTied to commemorate his win. And what did the kids think of their automated competitor? They had nothing but admiration for his quick reflexes.

As top scorer in the contest, TongueTied will have his name displayed in arcades around the world, along with the names of the top five human contestants. Marketing modified its sales strategy for our juvenile athletic footwear to capitalize on the robot's newfound celebrity status. Marketing director Veronique Caspary announced in a televised press conference yesterday that TongueTied will soon begin autographing each pair of high-tech track shoes that he laces.

Will celebrity status change our mild-mannered TongueTied? He already lost a day of work while he practiced signing his name. Programmers say his natural writing is "rather flamboyant." They're trying to tone it down to fit on the side of a shoe. NM

On the move

Facilities reports that our new administration wing is almost complete. The sound of hammering has finally given way to the dull thumps of the carpet layers. By the first of next month, departments should be relocated as indicated on the map.

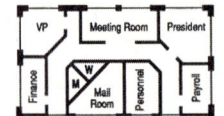

Employee News

Soccer team wins!

Congratulations to the Arbor Footwear soccer team! They took first place in the recent city competition. Special thanks to team captain **Bruno Martin** (manufacturing), who told a TV reporter, "Great shoes are part of a sound strategy."

Writing contest winner

Marla Selva took second place in the city's humorous essay contest. Co-workers encouraged her to write down the stories she tells on break time. Her winning story, "I wasn't born to ski," was their all-time favorite, told while they were signing the cast on her leg.

Wedding bells

Best wishes to **Thomas Bendel** (women's dress shoe division) and **Isabelle Mendel** (administration), who married last Friday night. For fun, co-workers prepared a hyphenated name plate for Isabelle's office door. It reads: "Dr. Isabelle Mendel-Bendel."

New baby

Arbor Footwear delivered our traditional welcome-to-the-world booties to celebrate the birth of Jeanne Loren. Parents Bernard and **Helene Loren** (men's dress shoes) report that Jeanne has her father's eyes and her mother's feet.

Small volunteers needed

We need babies less than a year old to home test our experimental Polar Baby Booties. Anne Gabor in our research and development department reports, "Our goal is to keep their tootsies toasty to 40 degrees below." Contact Anne if you know of a small, barefoot volunteer.

Controlling Column Breaks

When you're creating a multiple-column document, you may want to start a new column before the bottom of the page. You can start a new column anywhere on a page by inserting a manual column break.

Part III

Using Advanced Formatting Techniques

To prevent unwanted column breaks, format paragraphs with the Keep with Next option (see Chapter 11, "Formatting Pages"). Word does not insert a column break after a paragraph formatted with this option.

To insert a manual column break, follow these steps:

1. Place the insertion point where you want to break the column.

2. Choose Page Break from the Insert menu or press Shift-Enter. In a multiple-column section, this command breaks a column, not a page.

As you just learned, the Page Break command breaks a column, rather than a page, when the insertion point is positioned in a multiple-column section. To insert a page break into a multiple-section document, follow these steps:

1. Position the insertion point where you want to break the page.

2. Choose Section Break from the Insert menu or press ⌘-Enter to enter a section break. Word moves the insertion point below the section break.

3. Choose Section from the Format menu or press Option-F14. The Section dialog box appears.

4. Select a page-break option in the Start drop-down list box. Your options are New Page, Odd Page (starts the new page on the next odd-numbered page), and Even Page (starts the new page on the next even-numbered page).

5. Choose OK.

Changing Column Width

When you create a multiple-column format, Word calculates the width of each column based on the margins and the column spacing you have chosen (0.5 inch is the default). You can change the column spacing in two ways:

- *Changing the column-spacing setting.* By default, Word inserts 0.5 inches of white space between columns. Change this measurement in the Section dialog box to specify wider or narrower columns.

Chapter 18
Creating Newspaper Columns

■ *Dragging the margin brackets on the ruler.* Click the Margin Marker icon in the ruler to replace the indent markers with margin brackets. Dragging these brackets changes the width of the columns by increasing or decreasing the amount of blank space between them.

You cannot use the Section dialog box to create columns of unequal width. To create a format in which column widths differ, you must add a table to your document (see Chapter 15, "Creating Tables").

Balancing the Text on the Page

If you create a multiple-column section that doesn't completely fill the page, the page may look unbalanced in Print Preview, as shown in figure 18.10.

Fig. 18.10
A multiple-section document with unbalanced text.

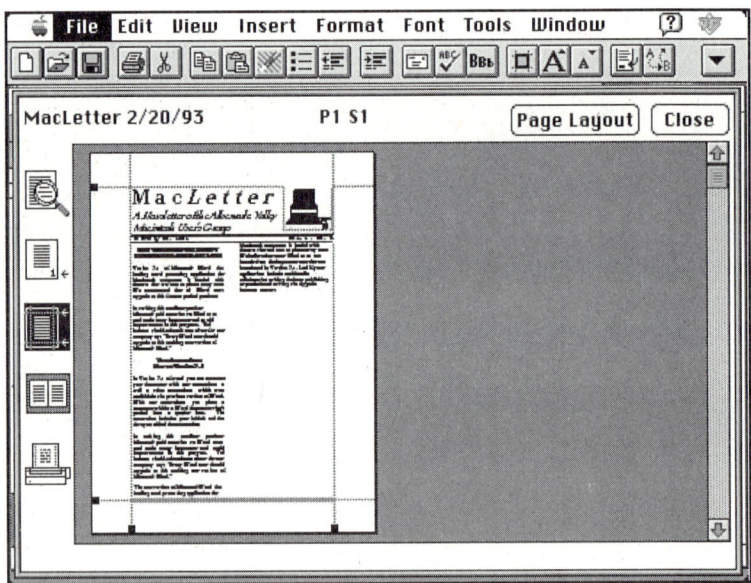

In this section, you learn how to balance the text on the page, as shown in figure 18.11.

Fig. 18.11
A multiple-section
document with
balanced text.

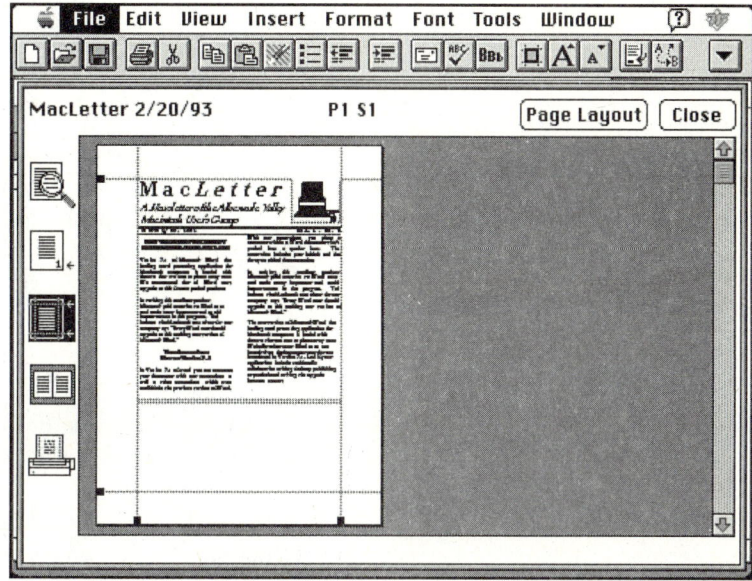

To balance text on the page, follow these steps:

1. Place the insertion point at the end of the text.

2. Choose Section Break from the Insert menu or press ⌘-Enter to create a section break.

3. With the insertion point positioned in the new section, choose Section from the Format menu or press Option-F14. The Section dialog box appears.

4. Select No Break in the Start drop-down list box. This option prevents Word from breaking the page after the section break.

Quick Review

This section summarizes the most useful information in this chapter. Check "Productivity Tips" for a review of high-productivity tips and tricks—the ones that Macintosh and Word pros use every day. Review "Techniques" whenever you need a quick reminder about a specific procedure.

Chapter 18
Creating Newspaper Columns

Productivity Tips

- You can use section breaks to divide your document into sections so that you can use more than one column format in your document. The front pages of newsletters, for example, commonly begin with a single column that contains the newsletter's title and banner, with multiple-column text beginning below the banner. If you haven't divided your document by choosing Section Break from the Insert menu or pressing ⌘-Enter, your document has only one section.

- To create a two- or three-column format quickly, click a multiple-column icon in the ribbon.

- Bear in mind that after you enter a section break, Word places the insertion point *after* the break. If you choose Section, your choices in the Section dialog box affect the section below the section break.

- To use more than one multiple-column format on a page, create a section break and then use the No Break option in the Section dialog box when you format the new section.

Techniques

This section provides concise summaries of all the procedures introduced in this chapter.

Creating Newspaper Columns

To add a two- or three-column format to your document using the ribbon's column icons:

1. Place the insertion point in the section you want to format.

2. Click the two- or three-column icon in the ribbon.

To add a multiple-column format using the Section dialog box:

1. Choose Section from the Format menu or press Option-F14. The Section dialog box appears.

2. In the Number text box, type the number of columns you want to create.

3. (Optional) Change the default column spacing (0.5 inch) by typing a measurement in the Spacing text box.

4. Choose OK.

Changing Column Formats

To change column formats without starting a new page:

1. Position the insertion point where you want the new column format to begin.

2. Choose Section Break from the Insert menu or press ⌘-Enter to create a section break.

3. With the insertion point positioned below the section break, choose Section from the Format menu or press Option-F14. The Section dialog box appears.

4. In the Number text box, type the number of columns you want.

5. (Optional) Change the default column spacing (0.5 inch) by typing a measurement in the Spacing text box.

6. Select No Break in the Start drop-down list box.

7. Choose OK.

Controlling Breaks

To control column breaks after entering a section break:

1. Place the insertion point in the section you want to format.

2. Choose Section from the Format menu or press Option-F14. The Section dialog box appears.

3. Select a page-break option in the Start drop-down list box.

4. Choose OK. Alternatively, click Apply to see how the format change will affect your document and then choose OK or click Cancel.

Starting a New Column

To start a new column:

1. Place the insertion point where you want to break the column.

2. Choose Page Break from the Insert menu.

Starting a New Page in a Multicolumn Section

To break a page in a multiple-section document:

1. Position the insertion point where you want to break the page.

2. Choose Section Break from the Insert menu or press ⌘-Enter to enter a section break.

3. Choose Section from the Format menu or press Option-F14. The Section dialog box appears.

4. Select a page-break option in the Start drop-down list box.

5. Choose OK.

Changing Column Width

To widen or narrow the columns with the ruler:

1. Click the Margin Marker icon in the ruler. Margin brackets appear in place of the indent markers.

2. Drag one of the margin brackets left or right.

To widen or narrow the columns with the Section dialog box:

1. Choose Section from the Format menu or press Option-F14. The Section dialog box appears.

2. Type a new measurement in the Spacing text box.

3. Choose OK.

Adding Headers, Footers, and Footnotes

19

I f you're creating reports, proposals, or even longer documents, you probably will want to add headers, footers, or both. A *header* is text—often a short version of the document's or chapter's title—positioned in the top margin. A *footer* is text positioned in the bottom margin. Word makes creating headers and footers easy; you type the header or footer text once, and Word inserts the text on each page. Word can automatically insert page numbers, the date, and the author's name.

You also may want to add footnotes or endnotes. A *footnote* is a reference note that prints at the bottom of the page; an *endnote* prints at the end of a document or a section.

Adding footnotes is easy with Word. The program automatically numbers the notes and renumbers them if you insert or delete footnotes while editing. Word also automatically positions the footnotes, reserving as much space as necessary at the bottom of the page. Endnotes are automatically grouped at the end of a document or section. Footnotes and endnotes can be more than one paragraph long, and you can format the notes—and their reference marks—as you please.

In Word's treatment of headers, footers, footnotes, and endnotes, the program's keynote is flexibility. Although Word's default settings for the placement of headers, footers, and footnotes are appropriate for many documents, you can position these elements virtually anywhere you want. You also control how headers, footers, and footnotes are formatted, and you even can add borders and graphics.

USING
WORD 5.1
FOR THE MAC
SPECIAL EDITION

The following topics are covered in this chapter:

- *Using headers and footers.* You learn how to add headers and footers to your document and how to take advantage of the elements Word can automatically include in a header or footer, including page numbers, the date, and the author's name. You learn how to view, edit, format, position, and delete headers and footers. You also learn how to set up different headers and footers for odd and even pages when you prepare documents that will be duplicated on both sides of the page.

- *Creating and editing footnotes and endnotes.* You learn how to add reference notes that Word automatically numbers. You also learn how to view, edit, move, format, and delete notes and how to customize the *footnote separator*—the line that separates the notes from the document's text. In addition, you learn how to control the position and numbering of footnotes.

If you're creating a long document with more than one section, be sure to read Chapter 21, "Dividing a Document into Sections." That chapter contains additional information about headers, footers, footnotes, and endnotes in multiple-section documents.

Using Headers and Footers

Headers and footers—text repeated at the top or bottom of each page—provide valuable information and remind the reader of the document's title or topic. These elements also help the reader identify and reassemble a document that wasn't securely bound and thus comes apart on a cluttered desktop.

Word gives you the following header and footer options:

- You can add page numbers, the current date, or the current time to your header or footer quickly by clicking an icon in the Header or Footer window.

- While you're creating a header or footer, you can add any item from Word's glossaries, including such Summary Info items as Author, Title, and Subject. (For more information on glossaries, see Chapter 23, "Using Glossaries.")

- Headers and footers are preset with a special tab format—a centered tab stop in the middle of the page and a flush-right tab stop at the right margin. This feature simplifies and speeds formatting. You can set new tabs, if you want.

■ You can create multiple-paragraph headers and footers. Word automatically adjusts the top or bottom margin to accommodate the header or footer.

■ By default, Word aligns headers or footers with the document's right and left margins. (The default setting is 1.25 inches left and right.) You can extend the header or footer into the left and right margins, however, by outdenting the header or footer paragraph.

■ You can format header and footer text any way you want. By default, Word uses the default font and font size for header and footer text. You can change the formatting, using manual formatting techniques or style formatting. If you change the default font, for example, the header and footer text appears in the font and font size you chose. You also can use manual formatting techniques to modify headers and footers. (For more information on styles, see Chapter 14, "Formatting with Styles.")

■ You can create different headers and footers for odd and even pages. If your document will be duplicated on both sides of the page, you can create a visually pleasing pattern with page numbers printing on the outside margin.

■ You can suppress the printing of headers or footers on the first page of a document. You also can create a special header or footer that prints only on the first page.

■ If you haven't divided your document into sections, the header or footer you create applies to the entire document and prints on every page (unless you suppress headers or footers on the first page). If you want to print one header or footer in one part of your document and then change the header or footer in another part, you can divide your document into sections. (For more information, see Chapter 21.)

Headers and footers improve the appearance of any document more than two or three pages long. In the following sections, you learn how to add page numbers and headers or footers at the same time.

The procedure for adding headers or footers varies depending on which view you're using: Normal view or Page Layout view.

■ *Normal view.* You type the header or footer in a Header or Footer window and click icons to add the time, date, and page number. You don't see the header or footer on-screen, however.

■ *Page Layout view.* Word moves the insertion point to the header or footer location. You can add the time, date, and page number by choosing options from menus. In this view, you can see the header or footer on-screen.

In the following sections, you learn how to use both techniques to create and edit headers and footers. You also learn how to suppress the printing of headers or footers on the first page of your document and how to create special first-page headers or footers. These techniques are useful for any document that contains a title or letterhead that might conflict with a header.

In addition, you learn how to change the vertical position at which headers and footers print. This technique is useful if you change the document's top or bottom margin. You also learn how to set up different headers and footers for odd and even pages. This technique is useful when you're duplicating a document on both sides of the page.

Adding a Header or Footer in Normal View

In Normal view, you add a header or footer by typing and formatting text in the Header or Footer window. To display the window, choose Header or Footer from the View menu. Figure 19.1 shows the Header window. (The Footer window is the same as the Header window except for its name.)

The Header and Footer windows have the following features:

Page Number icon. Click this icon to insert a page number at the insertion point's location.

Date icon. Click this icon to insert the current date at the insertion point's location.

Time icon. Click this icon to insert the current time at the insertion point's location.

Same as Previous. This command button becomes available only when you divide your document into sections (see Chapter 21).

When you open the Header or Footer window, Word automatically applies the Header or Footer style to the text you type in that window. This style is based on the Normal style you assigned to your document. In addition, Header or Footer style includes tab stops at 3 inches (centered) and 6 inches (flush right). Using these preset tabs, you easily can add text, a date, and the page number to your header or footer, as shown in figure 19.2.

Fig. 19.1
Header window.

Page Number icon

Date icon

Time icon

Same as
Previous
button

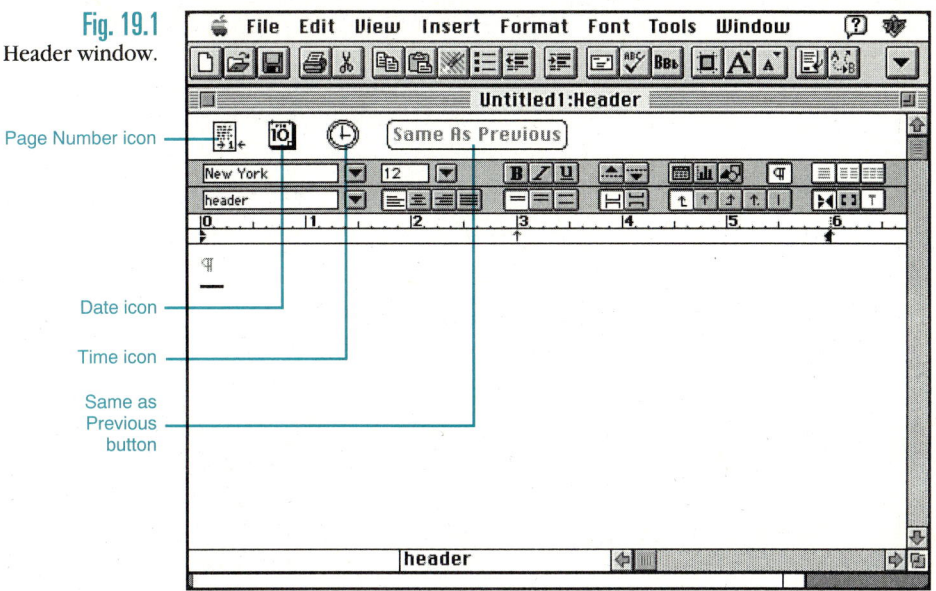

Fig. 19.2
Using the preset Header
style tabs.

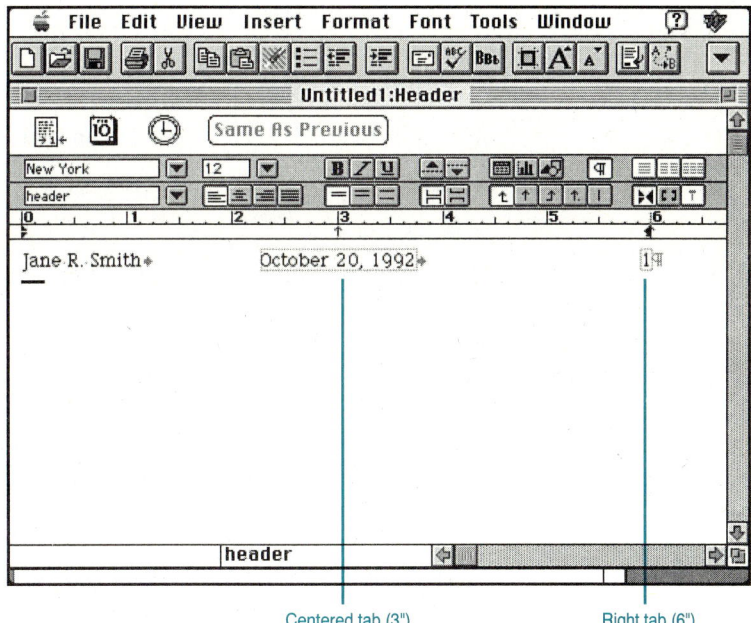

Centered tab (3")

Right tab (6")

Chapter 19

Adding Headers, Footers, and Footnotes

To add a header or footer to your document in Normal view, follow these steps:

1. Choose Header or Footer from the View menu. The Header or Footer window appears (refer to fig. 19.1).

2. Type the header or footer text in the window. This text will appear on all the pages of your document.

3. Format the header or footer as you choose. You can choose character emphases, fonts, alignments, or indentations by using any of the usual character- or paragraph-formatting techniques (see chapters 9 and 10).

   The Header and Footer windows have preset tabs at 3 inches (centered) and 6 inches (right). You can change these tabs or add tabs by using the ruler. (If you don't see the ruler, choose Show Ruler from the Format menu or press ⌘-R.)

   To position header or footer text beyond the document's margins, drag the indent markers on the ruler or type negative numbers in the Left and Right text boxes of the Paragraph dialog box. (To display the Paragraph dialog box, choose Paragraph from the Format menu or press ⌘-M.)

4. To add page numbers, the current time, or the current date, click the insertion point where you want the number, the time, or the date to appear. Use the preset tabs to align the page number, date, or time. Then click the appropriate icon. To delete the page number, time, or date, select it and press Delete or Backspace.

5. Click the close box to close the Header or Footer window.

To edit or delete a header or a footer, follow these steps:

1. Choose Header or Footer from the View menu. The Header or Footer window appears.

2. Edit the text or delete it to cancel the header or footer.

3. Click the close box to close the Header or Footer window.

If you have filled out Summary Info for the current document, you can enter the document's title, author, subject, or other information into your header or footer quickly. Open the Header or Footer window and then choose Glossary from the Edit menu or press ⌘-K. The Glossary dialog box appears. Choose one or more of the Summary Info glossaries (such as Author, Title, or Subject). Word inserts the glossary directly into the header or footer. (For more information on glossaries, see Chapter 23.)

Part III

Using Advanced Formatting Techniques

You usually don't want a header to print on the first page of a document, where it might conflict with the document's title. A Section dialog-box option, Different First Page, suppresses the printing of headers and footers on the first page of your document or section. When you choose this option, the View menu displays two new commands, First Header and First Footer, which enable you to create headers or footers that print on only the first page. For more information on this option, see "Managing First-Page Headers and Footers" later in this chapter.

Adding a Header or Footer in Page Layout View

When you add a header or a footer in Page Layout view, you do not see the Header or Footer window when you choose the Header or Footer command. Instead, the insertion point moves to the first header or footer area in your document (see fig. 19.3).

Fig. 19.3
Header displayed in Page Layout view.

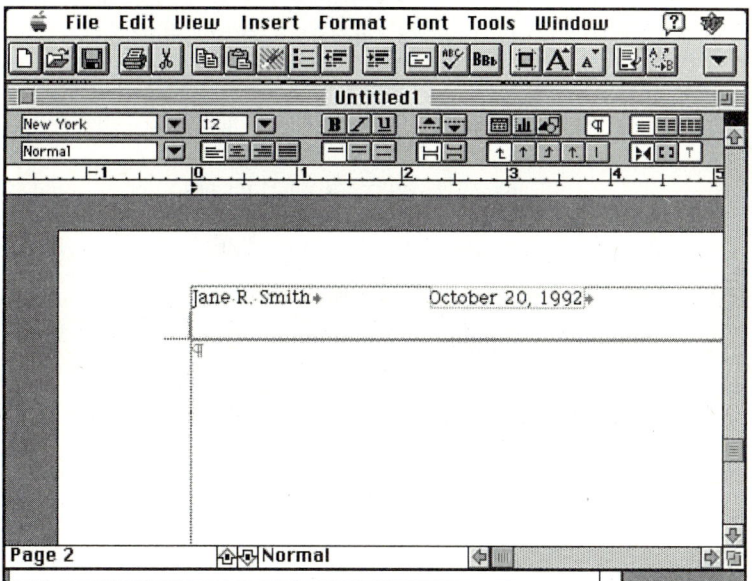

The ruler measures the header or footer with the 0 set at the left margin. You type the header or footer directly in the header or footer area.

To create a header or a footer in Page Layout view, follow these steps:

1. In Page Layout view, choose Header or Footer from the View menu. Word opens the header or footer area and scrolls the screen, if necessary, to display the header or footer.

2. Type the header or footer text and, if you want, format the text. You can use any manual formatting technique to format the header or footer text.

   Word automatically applies the Header or Footer style to this text. By default, this style calls for the Normal font and font size, a centered tab at 3 inches, and a right tab at 6 inches. If you redefine the Header or Footer style, the changes you make automatically apply to the text you're entering.

3. To enter the date, choose Date from the Insert menu. Alternatively, choose Glossary from the Edit menu or press ⌘-K and then choose one of the Date glossaries. (For more information on glossaries, see Chapter 23.)

4. To enter the time, choose Glossary from the Edit menu or press ⌘-K and then choose one of the Time glossaries.

5. When you finish creating the header or footer, click outside the header or footer area and continue working on your document.

After you create a header or footer in Page Layout view, you can edit it by scrolling up or down to bring the header or footer into view and then using the usual text-editing techniques. To display the header or footer text quickly, choose Header or Footer from the View menu.

The text you place in a header or footer appears on all the pages of your document, so if you want to change this text, you can make the change on any page of the document. Suppose that you're viewing your document in Page Layout view and want to change the header. You make the change on page 14. The change applies to your entire document, even to the pages before page 14. This feature may seem slightly weird, but remember: the header or footer you create applies to an entire document (or to an entire section, if you divided your document into sections).

If you change Word's default margins, text aligned with the preset header and footer tab stops may not look correct on-screen. Suppose that you redefine the default margins so that they're set at 1 inch left and right, producing a 6.5-inch text line. You then decide to redefine the default header and footer tab stops, from 3 inches centered and 6 inches right to 3.25 inches centered and 6.5 inches right. The best way to change these tab stops is to redefine the Header or Footer style with the tab stops you want and then save the redefined style to the default style sheet. To learn how to redefine the Header and Footer styles, see Chapter 14, "Formatting with Styles."

Managing First-Page Headers and Footers

By default, Word prints on every page of your document the header or footer you create. If you use the header shown in figure 19.4 on the first page of a two-page letter, for example, the header would conflict with your organization's letterhead and logo.

Fig. 19.4
Header for a two-page letter.

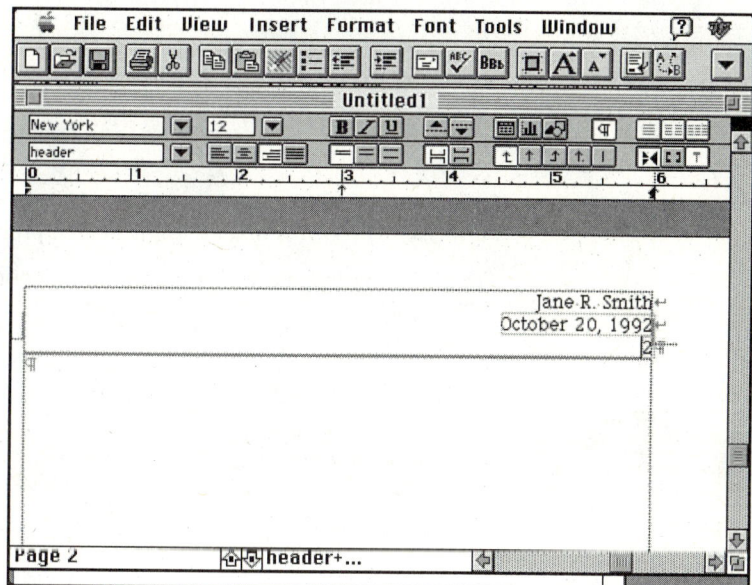

For this document and other documents in which this header would be unsatisfactory, you can suppress the printing of the header on the first page by choosing the Different First Page option in the Section dialog box. If you want, you can make this option the default for all documents.

When you choose the Different First Page option, the View menu gains two new commands: First Header and First Footer (see fig. 19.5).

Fig. 19.5
First Header and First
Footer commands
(View menu).

```
┌─────────────────────────────┐
│ View                        │
├─────────────────────────────┤
│ ✓Normal            ⌘⌥N      │
│  Outline           ⌘⌥O      │
│  Page Layout       ⌘⌥P      │
├─────────────────────────────┤
│ ✓Ribbon            ⌘⌥R      │
│ ✓Ruler             ⌘R       │
│  Print Merge Helper...      │
│  Toolbar                    │
├─────────────────────────────┤
│  Hide ¶            ⌘J       │
├─────────────────────────────┤
│  Header                     │
│  Footer                     │
│  First Header               │
│  First Footer               │
│  Footnotes         ⌘⇧⌥S     │
│  Annotations...             │
│  Voice Annotations          │
├─────────────────────────────┤
│  Play Movie...              │
└─────────────────────────────┘
```

Choose these commands to add special headers that print only on the first page of your document, following the procedures in this section.

The Different First Page option, which you choose in the Section dialog box, applies to the current section. (If you haven't divided your document into sections, the document has only one section.) If you create section breaks, as explained in the next chapter, the first-page choices you make in this dialog box apply only to the current section. If you want to suppress the printing of headers or footers throughout your document, choose Select All from the Edit menu or press ⌘-A before choosing the Section command from the Format menu.

To suppress the printing of headers or footers on the first page of your document or section, follow these steps:

1. With the insertion point positioned in your document and not in the header or footer, choose Section from the Format menu or press Option-F14. The Section dialog box appears.

2. Activate the Different First Page option.

3. To make this choice the default for all documents, click Use as Default.

4. Choose OK.

Word activates the Different First Page option for the current section.

Part III

Using Advanced Formatting Techniques

The program does not print a header or footer on the first page; the header or footer begins on page 2.

Your choice affects the current section (or the entire document, if you haven't divided your document into sections). For information on dividing your document into sections, see Chapter 21.

After you activate the Different First Page option, you can create a header or footer that prints only on the first page. To print a special first-page header or footer in Normal view, follow these steps:

1. If necessary, activate the Different First Page option in the Section dialog box.

2. Choose First Header or First Footer from the View menu. A First Header or First Footer window appears. (This window looks the same as the Header or Footer window you used previously.)

3. Create the header or footer for the first page.

4. Click the close box to close the First Header or First Footer window.

The First Header and First Footer commands are not available in Page Layout view. To add a header or footer on the first page, display the first page, choose the Header or Footer command from the View menu, and then create the header or footer. As long as the Different First Page option is activated, Word prints this header or footer only on page 1.

Adjusting the Vertical Position of Headers and Footers

By default, Word prints headers or footers 0.5 inch from the top or bottom margin. If you choose margins wider or narrower than Word's default margins (1 inch top and bottom), you may want to change the vertical locations of headers or footers so that they print in the middle of the margin. If you choose a 1.25-inch top margin, for example, you would position the headers at 0.675 inch.

To change the vertical position of headers or footers, follow these steps:

1. Choose Section from the Format menu or press Option-F14. The Section dialog box appears (see fig. 19.6).

2. In the Header/Footer area, type a measurement in the From Top text box to change the vertical position of the header.

Fig. 19.6
Section dialog box.

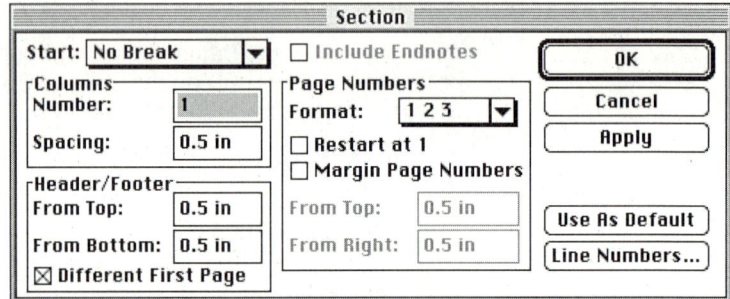

3. Type a measurement in the From Bottom text box to change the vertical position of the footer.

4. Choose OK.

Creating Different Headers and Footers for Facing Pages

If you're planning to duplicate your document on both sides of the page, take advantage of the Word feature that enables you to define different headers and footers for odd and even pages. The even-page header appears to the left of the binding, and the odd-page header or footer appears to the right of the binding.

Figure 19.7 shows a Page Layout view of the even header (Window 1) and the odd header (Window 2). Notice that the page number always appears on the outside of the page, as shown in figure 19.8.

You cannot create even/odd headers in Page Layout view. To create the headers, switch to Normal view first. After creating the headers, you can switch back to Page Layout view and edit them, if you want.

Fig. 19.7
Different headers for
facing pages.

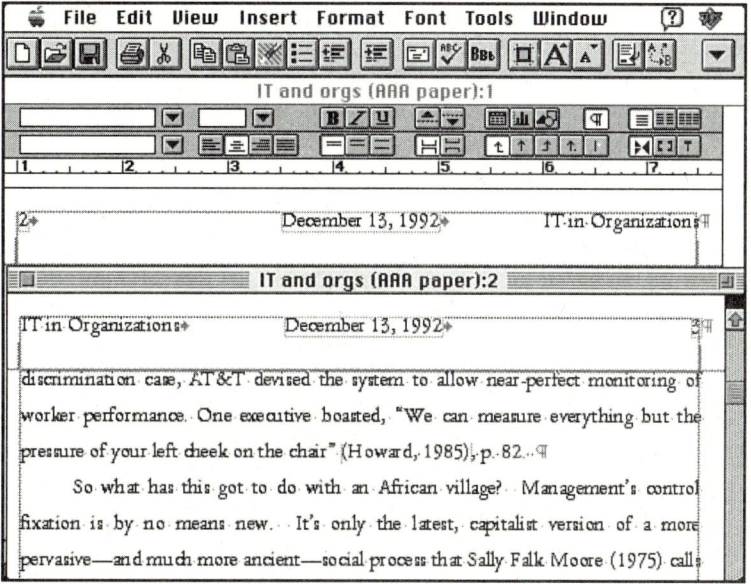

Fig. 19.8
Page numbers on
facing pages.

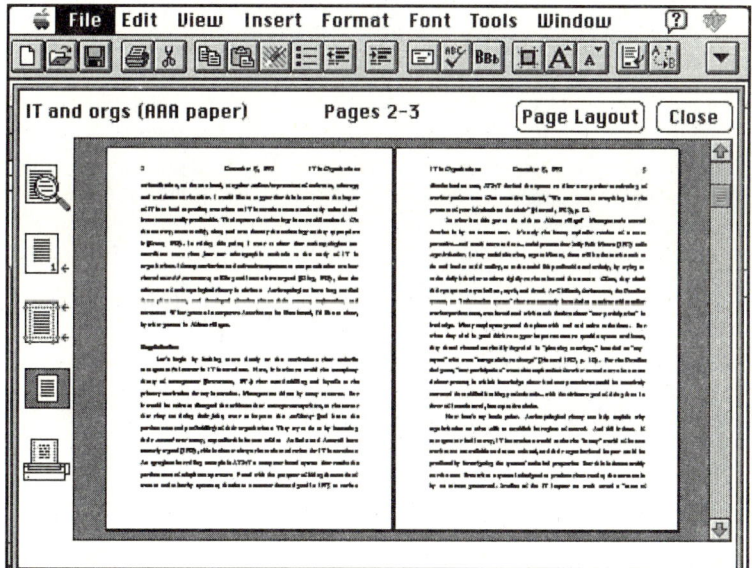

To create different headers for odd and even pages in Normal view, follow these steps:

1. Choose Document from the Format menu or press ⌘-F14. The Document dialog box appears (see fig. 19.9).

Fig. 19.9

Document dialog box.

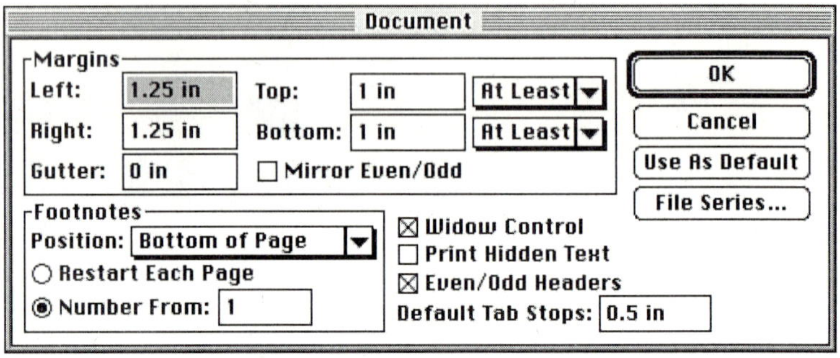

Document
Margins
Left: `1.25 in` Top: `1 in` `At Least ▼`
Right: `1.25 in` Bottom: `1 in` `At Least ▼`
Gutter: `0 in` ☐ Mirror Even/Odd
Footnotes
Position: `Bottom of Page ▼`
○ Restart Each Page
◉ Number From: `1`
⊠ Widow Control
☐ Print Hidden Text
⊠ Even/Odd Headers
Default Tab Stops: `0.5 in`
OK Cancel Use As Default File Series...

2. Activate the Even/Odd Headers option.

3. Choose OK.

4. Pull down the View menu. You see four new options in the View menu: Even Header, Even Footer, Odd Header, and Odd Footer (see fig. 19.10).

Fig. 19.10

Odd and Even Header and Footer options (View menu).

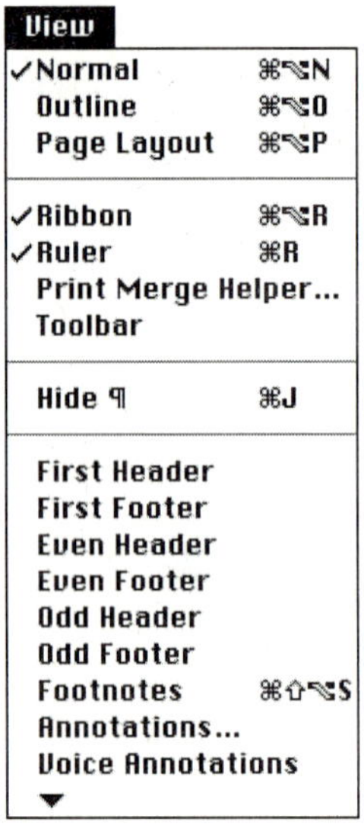

View

✓Normal	⌘⌥N
Outline	⌘⌥O
Page Layout	⌘⌥P
✓Ribbon	⌘⌥R
✓Ruler	⌘R
Print Merge Helper...	
Toolbar	
Hide ¶	⌘J
First Header	
First Footer	
Even Header	
Even Footer	
Odd Header	
Odd Footer	
Footnotes	⌘⇧⌥S
Annotations...	
Voice Annotations	
▼	

5. Choose one of these new options. The Header or Footer window appears.

6. Create the header or footer and then click the close box.

7. Repeat steps 5 and 6 until you have created all the headers or footers you want.

To create a pleasing effect, position the page numbers flush right on odd pages and flush left on even pages. Add lines below the headers and above the footers to frame the text on the page.

If you're working in Page Layout view, the Odd and Even Header and Footer options aren't available in the View menu. To create an odd or even header or footer, activate Even/Odd Headers in the Document dialog box, scroll to an odd or even page, and choose Header or Footer from the View menu. If you're displaying an odd-numbered page, Word creates the header or footer only on odd-numbered pages. If you're displaying an even-numbered page, Word creates the header or footer only on even-numbered pages.

Using Footnotes and Endnotes

Many business and professional writers, not just scholars, must back up their claims by citing other experts. A simple way to refer to other works is to include a bibliographic reference in the text and then attach a reference list at the end of the document. In many cases, however, writers use footnotes or endnotes referenced in the text by numbers (usually superscripted).

Word's footnote capabilities are superb. By default, Word numbers footnotes automatically and places them at the bottom of the page, with a two-inch line separating the notes from the body text. You also can customize Word's footnote capabilities in many ways, including the following examples:

■ The program can automatically number your footnotes and renumber them if you insert or delete any.

■ You can create footnotes with reference marks other than numbers, such as asterisks.

■ When you create a footnote, Word automatically applies its standard Footnote Reference and Footnote Text styles to the footnote reference mark and footnote text. These styles call for footnote reference marks to be superscripted, boldfaced, and formatted with the Normal font in a 9-point font size. Footnote text would be printed in a 10-point version of the Normal font. By changing the Footnote Reference and Footnote Text styles, you can change the format for footnote reference marks and footnote text throughout your document.

■ After you create a footnote in Normal view, Word opens a "smart" footnote window, which displays the text of the note referenced in the document window above. As you scroll through your document, the footnote window also scrolls so that the relevant notes always are visible.

■ Word automatically prints a two-inch separator line between the body text and the footnotes. If you want, you can delete the separator or create your own separator.

■ If the footnote text is too long to fit on one page, Word floats the rest of the footnote text to the following page and prints a *continuation separator* above the notes. A line spanning the page, the continuation separator is longer than the usual separator. This greater length alerts the reader that the first note is a continuation of a note begun on the preceding page.

■ The program also can print a *continuation notice* telling the reader that the rest of the footnote's text appears on the following page.

■ If you prefer using endnotes, you can print the notes at the ends of sections or at the end of the document.

Creating a Footnote

The procedure for adding footnotes and endnotes to a document is the same, as detailed in the following steps. You learn how to choose endnotes instead of footnotes later in this chapter, in the section "Specifying Where Footnotes Will Print."

To create a footnote, follow these steps:

1. Position the insertion point in your text at the point where you want the footnote reference mark to appear.

2. Choose Footnote from the Insert menu or press ⌘-E. The Footnote dialog box appears (see fig. 19.11).

Fig. 19.11
Footnote dialog box.

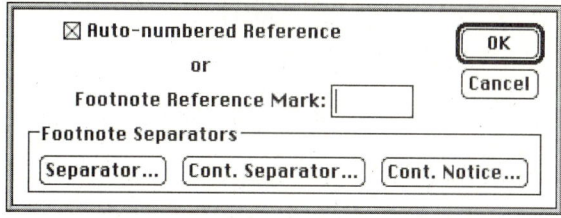

3. Choose OK to have Word number the note automatically. Word inserts a 9-point superscripted number after you choose OK.

   To insert a footnote reference mark other than a number (such as an asterisk), type the mark in the Footnote Reference Mark text box before you choose OK. Word uses that mark rather than a number to identify the note. (If you have added other notes for which Word uses automatic numbering, an unnumbered reference mark does not affect the number sequence; Word simply skips that note as it numbers and renumbers the notes.)

   If you're viewing your document in Normal view, Word splits the screen after you choose OK. The footnote window appears below the document window, separated from it by a split bar (see fig. 19.12).

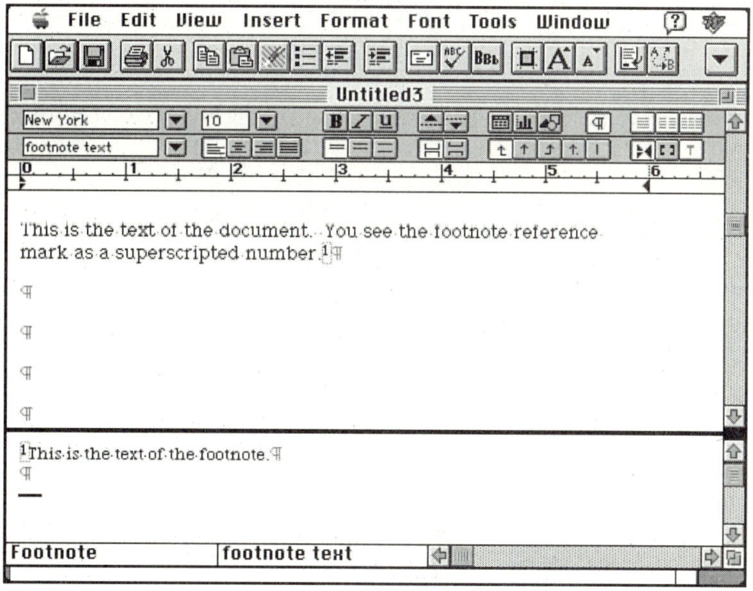

Fig. 19.12
Footnote window in
Normal view.

Chapter 19

Adding Headers, Footers, and Footnotes

Word echoes the footnote reference mark in the footnote window and positions the insertion point so that you can type the note.

If you're viewing your document in Page Layout view, Word moves the insertion point to the page's footnote area when you choose OK, as shown in figure 19.13.

Fig. 19.13
Footnote area in Page Layout view.

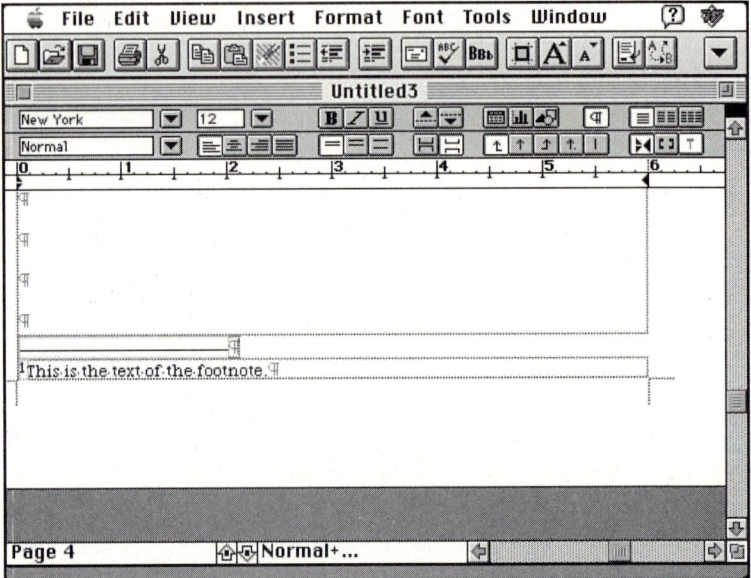

4. Type the text of the note. By default, Word formats the footnote text with 10-point characters.

5. When you finish typing the note, close the footnote window. If you're in Normal view, double-click the split bar; if you're in Page Layout view, use the Go Back command (⌘-Shift-Z).

You can change the default formats for footnote reference marks (superscript 9-point characters) and footnote text (single-spaced, left-justified 10-point characters). For details, see Chapter 9, "Formatting with Fonts and Character Styles."

CAUTION

The footnote reference mark in your document isn't an ordinary number but a special character that links the reference mark to the footnote text. If you delete the footnote reference mark, you delete all the footnote text, too. If you accidentally delete the reference mark, immediately choose Undo from the Edit menu.

Editing, Deleting, and Moving Footnotes and Endnotes

After you have created a footnote or an endnote, you can delete the note, move it to another location in your document, edit existing text, or add other notes.

To add footnotes, place the insertion point in your document where you want the footnote reference mark to appear, choose Footnotes from the Insert menu, and create the note in the usual way. Word adds the note, renumbering the existing ones automatically.

To edit footnote text, follow these steps:

1. If you're working in Page Layout view, scroll down to view the footnotes. If you're working in Normal view, you can open the footnote window in three ways:

   ■ Double-click the footnote reference mark.

   ■ Choose Footnotes from the View menu.

   ■ Hold down the Shift key and drag the split bar down from the top of the screen.

2. Edit the note.

To delete a footnote, follow these steps:

1. Select the footnote reference mark—*not* the footnote text.

2. Press Backspace or Delete. Alternatively, you can choose Cut from the Edit menu, press ⌘-X, or click the Cut tool.

To move a footnote, follow these steps:

1. Select the footnote reference mark. (You don't have to select the footnote text—only the mark.)

2. Choose Cut from the Edit menu, press ⌘-X, or click the Cut tool.

3. Position the insertion point where you want to move the footnote reference mark.

4. Choose Paste from the Edit menu, press ⌘-V, or click the Paste tool. Word moves the footnote reference mark *and* the footnote text, even though you selected only the mark.

Unless your monitor can show the entire page (including footnotes), switch to Normal view when you're editing your document and then choose Footnotes from the View menu to open the footnote window. As you scroll through your document, Word automatically displays the notes whose reference marks are visible in the document window.

Chapter 19

If you're writing for a typographically conservative journal that requires you to use a short version of a citation (for example, "Jones, *Challenge of Technological Innovation*") after the initial reference, create a new glossary, add to it the short version of the citation, and then use the glossary to enter later citations. Be sure to type the citation the same way every time. (For more information on glossaries, see Chapter 23.)

Modifying the Separator Line

By default, Word enters a two-inch separator line between footnotes and the body text. The program automatically enters a longer line when a long footnote is continued to the next page, but Word does not print a continuation notice automatically. You can change any of these separator options.

The separator lines are graphics objects, not characters, so you cannot shorten or lengthen separator lines by deleting or adding characters; you must delete the entire line and enter a new one. To add a new line, use Word's Draw capabilities (discussed in Chapter 7, "Creating and Importing Graphics") to create the line, select the line, and copy it to the Clipboard before proceeding.

To change the separator line, follow these steps:

1. From anywhere in your document, choose Footnotes from the Insert menu or press ⌘-E. The Footnote dialog box appears.

    Although you usually use this procedure to add a footnote, Word does not enter a footnote reference mark after this operation.

2. Click Separator, Cont. Separator, or Cont. Notice. Depending on which command button you choose, you see the Footnote Separator window (see fig. 19.14), the Footnote Cont. Separator window (see fig. 19.15), or the Footnote Cont. Notice window (see fig. 19.16).

Fig. 19.14

Footnote Separator window.

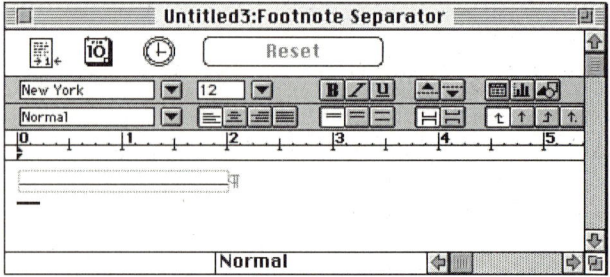

Fig. 19.15

Footnote Cont.
Separator window.

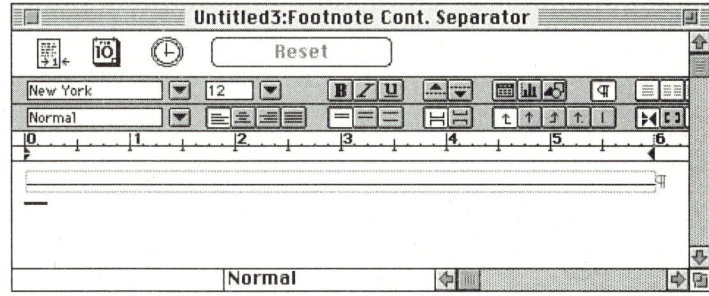

Fig. 19.16

Footnote Cont.
Notice window.

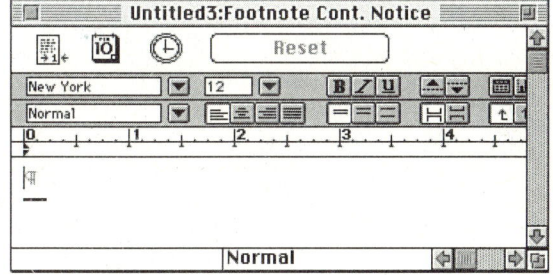

3. To delete the separator line, select it in the window and then press Backspace or Delete. If you copied a shorter or longer line to the Clipboard before choosing the Footnotes command, select the existing line and then replace it with the line in the Clipboard by choosing Paste from the Edit menu, pressing ⌘-V, or clicking the Paste tool.

To add a continuation notice, type the text in the window.

4. Click the close box to return to your document without adding a footnote.

Specifying Where Footnotes Will Print

To see your options for footnote locations, choose Document from the Format menu or press ⌘-F14 to display the Document dialog box. Then drop down the Position list box, which contains the following options:

Bottom of Page. Choose this option to place footnotes at the bottom of the page, even if the last page isn't completely filled with text.

Chapter 19

Adding Headers, Footers, and Footnotes

Beneath Text. Choose this option to place footnotes at the bottom of the page, except on the last page or any other page that the text does not fill (Word positions the notes on these pages after the last line of text).

End of Section. Choose this option if you have created a multisection document and want the notes for each section to be collected and printed as endnotes at the end of each section.

End of Document. Choose this option to print all endnotes at the end of your document, even if you have divided the document into sections.

After you choose the option you want, choose OK. The choice you make affects the entire document.

As mentioned, you can use the End of Section option to collect and print all the endnotes for each section at the end of that section (for example, at the end of a chapter). As you will learn in Chapter 21, sometimes you must create a section break for reasons other than starting a new chapter. For example, you must create a section break to change from single- to multiple-column formatting. To stop Word from collecting and printing the endnotes for such a section, place the insertion point in the section, choose Section from the Format menu or press Option-F14, and then deactivate the Include Endnotes option in the Section dialog box. Word does not print the endnotes until the end of the following section.

Controlling Footnote Numbering

You can control footnote numbering in two ways:

- *Resetting the starting number.* Many writers like to break large documents, such as books and dissertations, into separate files. To print these files with the footnotes numbered consecutively, you must manually reset the starting number for each file so that the numbering begins where the preceding file ended; otherwise, each file starts with 1. Suppose that Chapter 2 is contained in the file THESIS-CHAPTER 2. Because the last footnote in Chapter 1 was 119, you want to start Chapter 2's footnotes with 120.

- *Restarting the sequence at page or section breaks.* If you chose to run footnotes at the bottom of the page, the Document dialog box contains an option called Restart Each Page. If you choose this option, Word restarts the numbering sequence at 1 at the beginning of each page. If you chose to group endnotes at the end of sections, you see an option called Restart Each Section. This option tells Word to restart the numbering sequence at the beginning of each section.

The following procedures detail both methods of controlling footnote numbering.

To reset the starting number, follow these steps:

1. Choose Document from the Format menu or press ⌘-F14. The Document dialog box appears.

2. Type the starting number in the Number From text box.

3. Choose OK.

To restart the sequence at page or section breaks, follow these steps:

1. Choose Document from the Format menu or press ⌘-F14. The Document dialog box appears.

2. In the Position drop-down list box (Footnotes area), select one of the Page options (Bottom of Page or Beneath Text) or the End of Section option.

3. Choose Restart Each Page or Restart Each Section.

4. Choose OK.

Quick Review

This section summarizes the most useful information in this chapter. Check "Productivity Tips" for a review of high-productivity tips and tricks—the ones that Macintosh and Word pros use every day. Review "Techniques" whenever you need a quick reminder about a specific procedure.

Productivity Tips

- Quickly add page numbers to your document by switching to Normal view, choosing Header or Footer, and clicking the Page Number icon in the Header or Footer window. You also can add the time and date by clicking the Time and Date icons.

- Use the Summary Info glossaries to add your name, your document's title, and other information to a header or footer.

Chapter 19

Adding Headers, Footers, and Footnotes

- By default, Word uses the Normal style's font and font size for headers and footers. If you want to change the font, the font size, or both for body text in your document, change the Normal style, not the text. When you change the style instead of the text, your change also affects the Header and Footer styles, which are based on the Normal style. (For an explanation of styles and basing one style on another, see Chapter 14, "Formatting with Styles.")

- You seldom want headers to print on the first page of your document. To suppress first-page headers, choose Different First Page in the Section dialog box. To make this choice the default for all your documents, also click the Use as Default command button.

- If you chose header or footer margins other than 1.25-inch margins left and right, redefine the Header and Footer styles to position header and footer tab stops at the center of the page and at the right margin. If you're using 1-inch margins left and right, for example, set the centered tab at 3.25 inches and the right tab at 6.5 inches.

Techniques

This section provides concise summaries of all the procedures introduced in this chapter.

Adding a Header or Footer

To add a header or footer to your document in Normal view:

1. Choose Header or Footer from the View menu. The Header or Footer window appears.

2. Type the header or footer text in the window.

3. Format the header or footer as you choose.

4. To add page numbers, the current time, or the current date, click the insertion point where you want the number, the time, or the date to appear. Use the preset tabs to align the page number, date, or time. Then click the appropriate icon in the window.

5. Click the close box to close the Header or Footer window.

To add a header or footer to your document in Page Layout view:

1. Choose Header or Footer from the View menu. Word moves the insertion point to the header or footer area of the page.

2. Type the header or footer text and, if you want, format the text.

3. To enter the date, choose Date from the Insert menu. Alternatively, choose Glossary from the Edit menu or press ⌘-K and then choose one of the Date glossaries.

4. To enter the time, choose Glossary from the Edit menu or press ⌘-K and then choose one of the Time glossaries.

5. When you finish creating the header or footer, click outside the header or footer area, or click the close box, and continue working on your document.

To add a special first-page header or footer in Normal view:

1. If necessary, activate the Different First Page option in the Section dialog box.

2. Choose First Header or First Footer from the View menu. The First Header or First Footer window appears.

3. Create the header or footer for the first page.

4. Click the close box or the body of the document to close the window.

To add a special first-page header or footer in Page Layout view:

1. If necessary, activate the Different First Page option in the Section dialog box.

2. Scroll to the first page of your document.

3. Choose Header or Footer from the View menu. Word moves the insertion point to the header or footer area of the page.

4. Create the header or footer for the first page.

5. Click outside the header or footer area and continue working on your document.

Editing a Header or Footer

To edit a header or footer in Normal view:

1. Choose Header or Footer from the View menu. The Header or Footer window appears.

2. Edit the text.

3. Click the close box or the body of the document to close the window.

To edit a header or footer in Page Layout view:

1. Scroll the screen to display the header or footer.

2. Edit the header or footer text.

Deleting a Header or Footer

To delete a header or footer in Normal view:

1. Choose Header or Footer from the View menu. The Header or Footer window appears.

2. Delete all the text.

3. Click the close box or the body of the document to close the window.

To delete a header or footer in Page Layout view:

1. Scroll the screen to display the header or footer.

2. Delete all the header or footer text.

Suppressing a First-Page Header or Footer

To suppress the printing of a header or footer on the first page of your document or section:

1. Choose Section from the Format menu or press Option-F14. The Section dialog box appears.

2. Activate the Different First Page option.

3. Click Use as Default to make this choice the default for all your future documents.

4. Choose OK.

Changing the Vertical Position of a Header or Footer

To change the vertical position of a header or footer:

1. Choose Section from the Format menu or press Option-F14. The Section dialog box appears.

2. Type a new measurement in the From Top text box (Header/Footer area) to change the vertical position of the header.

3. In the From Bottom text box, type a new measurement to change the vertical position of the footer.

4. Choose OK.

Creating Different Headers or Footers for Facing Pages

To create different headers for odd and even pages in Normal view:

1. Choose Document from the Format menu or press ⌘-F14. The Document dialog box appears.

2. Activate the Even/Odd Headers check box.

3. Choose OK.

4. Pull down the View menu.

5. Choose one of the header or footer options. The Header or Footer window appears.

6. Create the header or footer.

7. Repeat steps 5 and 6 until you have created all the headers or footers you want.

To create different headers for odd and even pages in Page Layout view:

1. Choose Document from the Format menu or press ⌘-F14. The Document dialog box appears.

2. Activate the Even/Odd Headers check box.

3. Choose OK.

4. Scroll to an odd-numbered page.

5. Choose Header or Footer from the View menu. Word moves the insertion point to the header or footer area of the page.

6. Create the header or footer.

7. Scroll to an even-numbered page and then choose Header or Footer again.

8. Create the header or footer.

Adding a Footnote

To create a footnote:

1. Position the insertion point in your text at the point where you want the footnote reference mark to appear.

2. Choose Footnote from the Insert window or press ⌘-E. The Footnote dialog box appears.

3. Choose OK to have Word automatically number the note. Word splits the page to create a footnote area.

4. Type the text of the note.

5. If you are working in Normal view, close the footnote area by double-clicking the split bar. If you are in Page Layout view, use the Go Back command (⌘-Shift-Z).

Editing a Footnote

To edit a footnote:

1. If you're working in Page Layout view, scroll down to view the footnotes. If you're working in Normal view, you can open the footnote window in three ways:

   - Double-click a footnote reference mark.

   - Choose Footnotes from the View menu.

   - Hold down the Shift key and drag the split bar down from the top of the screen.

2. Edit the note.

Deleting a Footnote

To delete a footnote:

1. Select the footnote reference mark—*not* the footnote text.

2. Press Backspace or Delete. Alternatively, choose Cut from the Edit menu, press ⌘-X, or click the Cut tool.

Moving a Footnote

To move a footnote:

1. Select the footnote reference mark. (You don't have to select the footnote text—only the mark.)

2. Choose Cut from the Edit menu, press ⌘-X, or click the Cut tool.

3. Position the insertion point where you want to move the footnote reference mark.

4. Choose Paste from the Edit menu, press ⌘-V, or click the Paste tool.

Modifying Footnote Separators

To modify footnote separators:

1. From anywhere in your document, choose Footnotes from the Insert menu or press ⌘-E. The Footnote dialog box appears.

2. Click Separator, Cont. Separator, or Cont. Notice.

3. To delete the separator line, select it and press Backspace or Delete. (If you copied a shorter or longer line to the Clipboard before choosing this command, select the existing line and paste it from the Clipboard by choosing Paste from the Edit menu, pressing ⌘-V, or clicking the Paste tool.)

   To add a continuation notice, type the text.

4. Click the close box to return to your document without adding a footnote.

Resetting the Starting Footnote Number

To reset the number Word uses to start numbering the footnotes in a document:

1. Choose Document from the Format menu or press ⌘-F14. The Document dialog box appears.

2. Type the starting number in the Number From text box.

3. Choose OK.

To restart the sequence at page or section breaks:

1. Choose Document from the Format menu or press ⌘-F14. The Document dialog box appears.

2. In the Position drop-down list box (Footnotes area), select one of the Page options (Bottom of Page or Beneath Text) or the End of Section option.

3. Choose Restart Each Page or Restart Each Section.

4. Choose OK.

Positioning Text and Graphics

Word isn't a desktop-publishing program, but you can use Word to create an attractive page design quickly and easily. A page layout program (such as PageMaker) includes tools for creating a page design complete with areas into which you can "pour" text, just as you fill a graphics element with a color or pattern. Word does not have these capabilities, but you can place paragraphs of text or graphics on the page in a fixed location—for example, in the center of the page (see fig. 20.1). A paragraph, graphic, or table positioned on a page in a fixed location is called a *frame*.

Word's Frame command enables you to fix the location of a paragraph of text or graphics on the page *absolutely*; no matter how much text you add or delete, the text or graphic you formatted stays put. The Frame command is easy to use because you can position the frame visually without leaving the Frame dialog box.

This chapter shows you how to use the Frame command to position paragraphs, graphics, and tables in a document. Following is an overview of the chapter:

■ *Positioning a frame on the page.* In this section, you learn the three ways you can position text, graphics, or tables in an absolute position on the page.

Fig. 20.1

A graphic positioned in the center of the page.

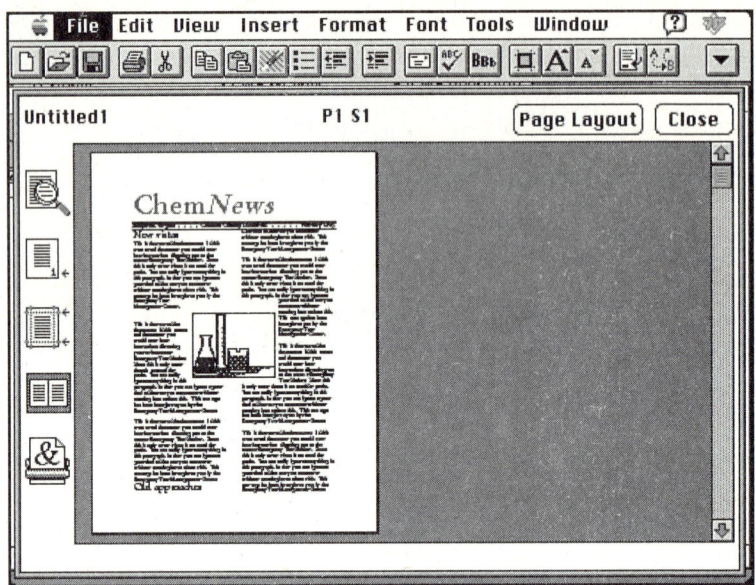

As you consider how to position graphics elements on the page, be aware that a single-row table often provides the ideal solution to the problem of positioning a graphic next to explanatory text. (For information on tables, see Chapter 15, "Creating Tables.")

■ *Formatting text in a frame.* In this section, you learn about text formatting in a frame and how the ruler measures frames in Page Layout view.

■ *Using positions in styles.* This section explains how to add Frame position information to styles so that Word enters the frame information automatically when you apply the style.

■ *Understanding position-formatting examples.* In this section, you learn how to create drop caps and other page-design elements with the Frame command.

■ *Creating drop caps.* Word 5.1 enables you to create a *drop cap*—a large initial letter—at the beginning of a paragraph.

Several other chapters contain information relevant to frames. Chapter 14, "Formatting with Styles," provides information on defining and applying styles. As you learn in this chapter, you can create styles that contain Frame position information so that when you apply the style, Word positions the text, graphic, or table according to the Frame positions included in the style. Chapter 7, "Creating and Importing Graphics," provides information on including graphics in your documents; you can position the graphic so that text flows around it on the page. Chapter 17, "Using Borders and Shading," provides information on adding borders to frames.

Positioning a Frame on the Page

Frames provide the basis for many page-design possibilities. Using Word's capability to rotate text that has been converted to a graphic (see Chapter 7) and the program's capability to position text and graphics absolutely on the page, you can create an attractive page design (see fig. 20.2). Text that normally would print where the frame is located flows around the frame instead.

Fig. 20.2
Rotated text title positioned flush with the left and top margins.

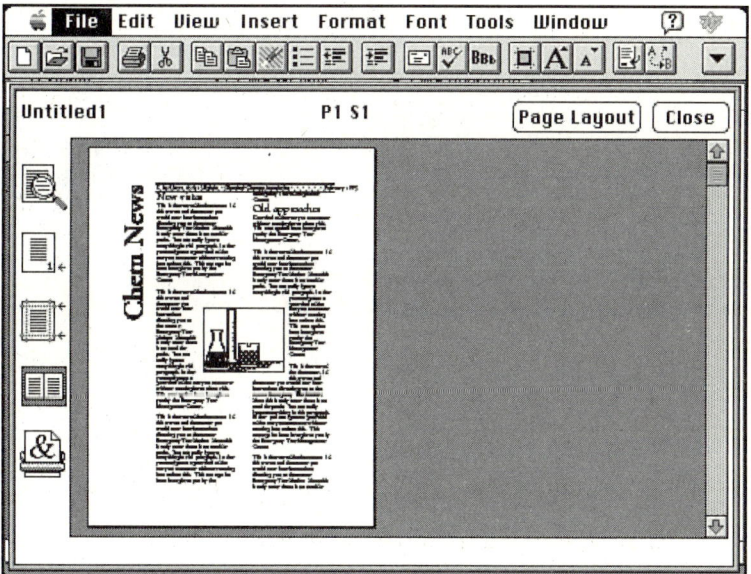

You specify the frame's location on the page—for example, beyond the margins or spanning two or more columns in a multiple-column layout. You can control the width of the frame, and you can add borders and shading for more attractive effects (see fig. 20.3).

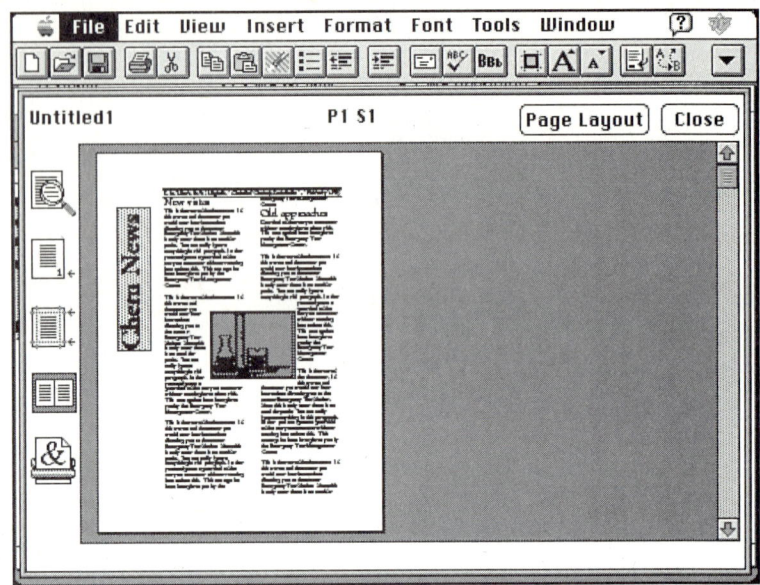

Fig. 20.3

Shading added to the positioned title and graphic.

You can position one or more paragraphs, graphics, or tables in a frame. To position the frame, you select the element or elements you want to frame (such as one or more paragraphs or graphics) and then use the Frame command, which you access through the Format menu. You then can click the Position button in the Frame dialog box to display the page in a Print Preview window, where you can position the frame by dragging it.

When you position a frame, you tell Word to disregard the position in which the selected elements originally appeared in your text. Word removes the selected elements and places them in the positions that you specify.

The Frame command enables you to fix a frame's position on the page. If you want the frame to appear on a specific page, however, the text, graphic, or table that you want to position must be placed within the text that prints on that page. If you want the frame to appear in a specific column in a multiple-column layout, the element must be positioned within the text that prints in that column.

What you see after positioning a frame depends on the view you are using. Normal view does not show the page layout; instead, you see the elements in line with surrounding text as if you had not used the Frame

Part III

Using Advanced Formatting Techniques

command. Page Layout view shows the frame's position on-screen, but unless you are working with a fast Macintosh, you may find Page Layout view too sluggish for writing and editing.

You can position a frame in three ways:

- *Position the frame visually.* When you click the Position button in the Frame dialog box, Word shows you a Print Preview of the page on which you are working. You then can drag the frame to its position. This technique is easy and fast but may not be the best choice if you want to center the frame or align it to the page edge, margins, or column boundaries.

- *Position the frame by choosing position options.* This technique is best if you want to center a frame or align it to the page edge, margins, or column boundaries. You choose these options from drop-down list boxes in the Frame dialog box.

- *Position the frame by typing measurements.* This technique is best if you want to place the frame in an exact location on the page. You type the measurements in the Frame dialog box.

The following sections explain all three methods.

Positioning a Frame Visually

You can position a frame visually by viewing the page on which you are working in Print Preview. To position a frame on the page in Print Preview, follow these steps:

1. Select the text, table, or graphic that you want to position, as shown in figure 20.4.

   Each element that you select must constitute a paragraph. You can select more than one element as long as the elements are contiguous (next to one another).

   To select a graphic, click the graphic to display the handles. To select a table, hold down the Option key and double-click anywhere in the table.

2. Choose Frame from the Format menu. The Frame dialog box appears (see fig. 20.5).

3. If you are framing text, type a width for the text in the Frame Width list box. The default setting, Auto, chooses a text-frame width equal to the width of the column in which the frame is situated. If you want text to flow around the frame, type a

measurement narrower than the column width. If you have a single-column layout (6-inch line length), for example, you can type **3.5** in the Frame Width list box to ensure that text flows around the frame.

Fig. 20.4
Selecting text to position.

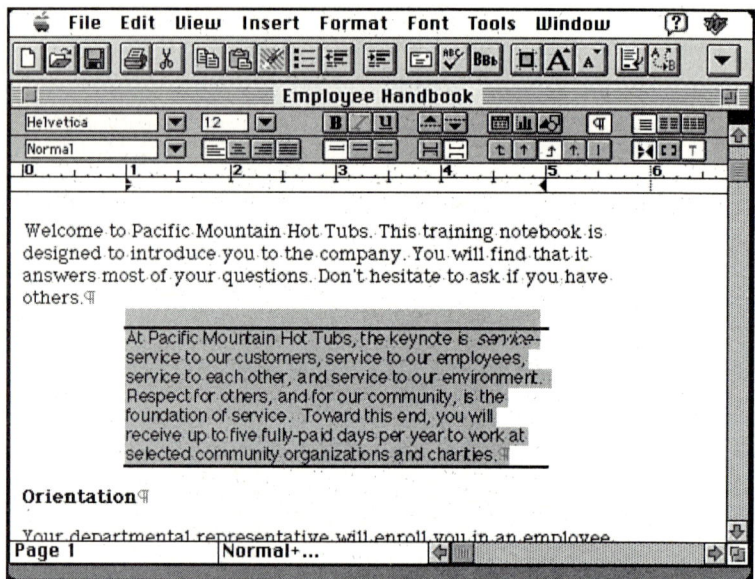

Fig. 20.5
Frame dialog box.

If you are framing a graphic or a table, Word automatically determines the width of the graphic or table and displays this figure in the Frame Width list box. If you want, you can change the default spacing from text by typing a new measurement in the From Text text box.

Part III

Using Advanced Formatting Techniques

4. Click Position. Word displays the page on which you are working in Print Preview (see fig. 20.6). When you move the mouse over the frame that you are creating, the mouse pointer changes to a crosshair pointer.

Fig. 20.6
Print Preview of the frame position.

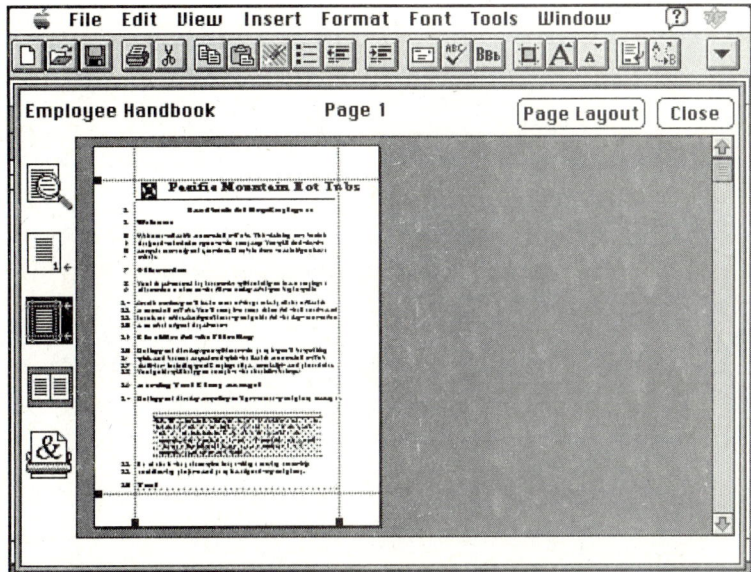

5. Click and drag to position the frame anywhere on the page. As you drag, keep your eye on the page-number area at the top of the Print Preview window; as you move the frame, this area shows the horizontal position of the left frame border (measured from the left of the page) and the vertical position of the top frame border (measured from the top of the page).

If you position the frame over existing elements, Word reformats the page so that text flows around the frame if enough room exists on the page (see fig. 20.7).

If a frame is too wide, text cannot flow around it. To reduce the frame's width (and get text to flow around the frame), select the framed element and choose the Frame command again. When the Frame dialog box appears, type a smaller number in the Frame Width list box.

Chapter 20
Positioning Text and Graphics

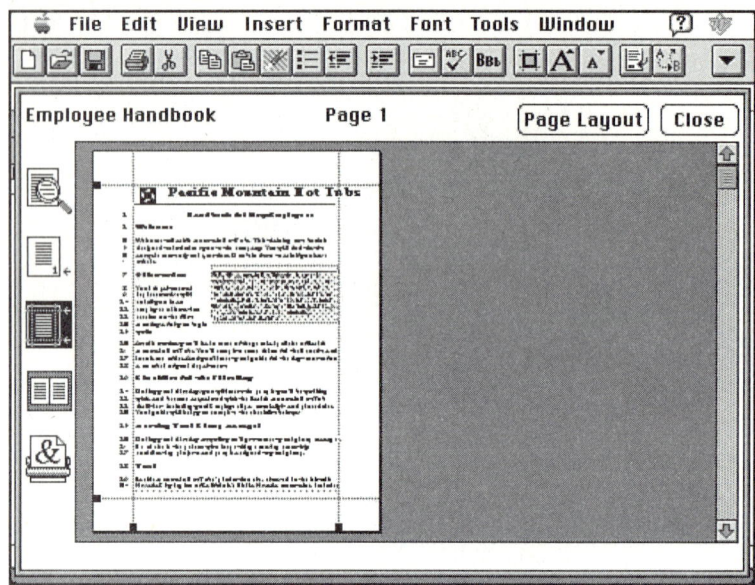

Fig. 20.7
Text flowing around a
framed element.

6. When you are satisfied with the frame's position, click Page Layout
to return to Page Layout view of your document or click Close to
return to Normal view.

If you are using a laser printer, remember that most laser printers cannot
print within a half-inch of the edge of the page. If part of the frame is cut
off when the document prints, reposition the frame farther from the
page edge. (For information on repositioning a frame, see "Repositioning a Frame and Unframing" later in this chapter.)

Choosing Position Options

When you want to center the frame horizontally or vertically or to
position the frame flush to the page edge, margins, or column boundaries, the best technique is to choose position options. When you
position a frame, you specify the horizontal and vertical positions by
choosing options from the Horizontal and Vertical drop-down list boxes
in the Frame dialog box.

For each option (such as Left or Center) that you choose, you also can
choose an option from the Relative To list box. These options are
Relative To Page and Relative To Margin for vertical positions; for
horizontal positions, the list includes Relative To Column (used for

multiple-column layouts). You can use these options to position a frame centered horizontally relative to the left and right margins and positioned flush with the top margin, for example.

The following options are available in the Horizontal list box in the Frame dialog box:

> **Left.** This option aligns the left edge of the frame to the page edge, margin, or column.

> **Center.** This option centers the frame horizontally relative to the page edges, margins, or columns.

> **Right.** This option aligns the right edge of the frame to the page edge, margin, or column.

> **Inside.** If you have chosen the Mirror Even/Odd option in the Document dialog box so that you can produce your document on both sides of the page, this option appears in the Horizontal list box. The Inside option aligns the element flush right (relative to the page edge, margin, or column) on even-numbered pages and flush left (relative to the page edge, margin, or column) on odd-numbered pages.

> **Outside.** If you have chosen the Mirror Even/Odd option, this option appears in the Horizontal list box. The Outside option aligns the element flush left (relative to the page edge, margin, or column) on even-numbered pages and flush right (relative to the page edge, margin, or column) on odd-numbered pages.

The following options are available in the Vertical list box:

> **In Line.** This option maintains the vertical position of the frame in the sequence of paragraphs in your document. If you add or delete text, the frame moves down or up in the document. Text does not flow around the frame.

> **Top.** This option positions the top edge of the frame flush with the top of the page or the top margin.

> **Center.** This option centers the frame vertically on the page relative to the page edges or the margins.

> **Bottom.** This option positions the bottom edge of the frame flush with the bottom of the page or the bottom margin.

Figure 20.8 graphically shows some position options. Notice the two-column layout and the large bottom margin. An element centered vertically relative to the page is lower than an element centered vertically relative to the margins. Notice, too, the element centered horizontally relative to the column.

Chapter 20
Positioning Text and Graphics

Fig. 20.8

Some position options.

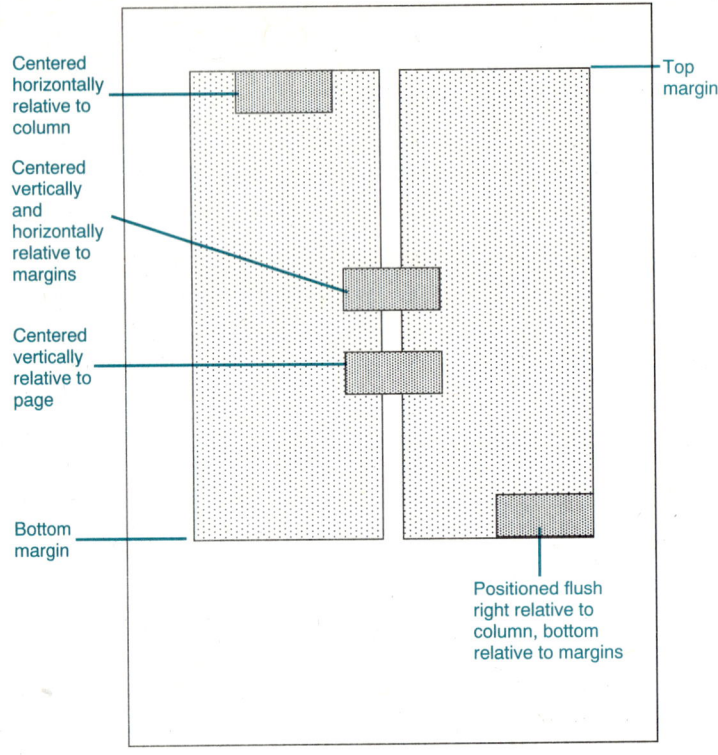

Centered horizontally relative to column

Centered vertically and horizontally relative to margins

Centered vertically relative to page

Bottom margin

Top margin

Positioned flush right relative to column, bottom relative to margins

You may have been surprised to see the In Line option in the Vertical list box. After all, the purpose of the Frame command is to change the position of a text element so that the element doesn't print in the same sequence with other paragraphs. Sometimes, however, you may want the positioned element to stay with the text above and below it. Figure 20.9, for example, shows a graphic positioned in line with the surrounding text, but framed horizontally so that it prints within the document's wide left margin.

When you position an element using the Frame command, you see a black square in the selection bar next to the element. This square indicates that the paragraph has hidden formats. To display the Frame dialog box quickly, double-click the square. (If you don't see the square, choose Show ¶ from the View menu or click the paragraph-mark icon in the ribbon.)

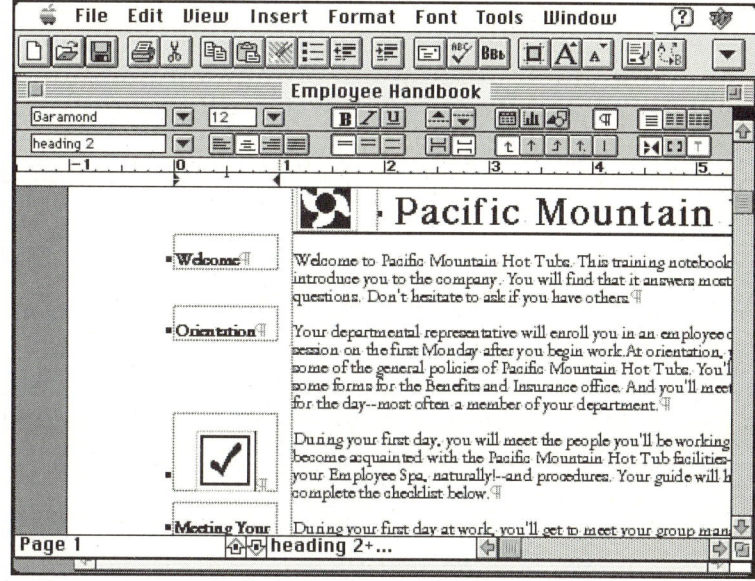

Fig. 20.9
Frame placed left relative
to the page and in
line vertically.

To position the frame by choosing position options, follow these steps:

1. Select the text, table, or graphic that you want to position.

2. Choose Frame from the Format menu. The Frame dialog box appears.

3. If you are framing text, type a width for the text in the Frame Width list box.

4. Choose an option in the Horizontal list box; in the Relative To list box, choose Column, Page, or Margin.

5. Choose an option in the Vertical list box; in the Relative To list box, choose In Line, Top, Center, or Bottom.

6. If you want, you can change the default spacing from Text by typing a new measurement in the From Text text box.

7. Choose OK to confirm the frame position.

Chapter 20
Positioning Text and Graphics

Typing Measurements

In addition to the two position techniques explained in the preceding sections, you also can type measurements in the Vertical and Horizontal list boxes in the Frame dialog box. No matter which default measurement you have chosen, you can type the distance in inches (" or in), points (pt), centimeters (cm), or picas (pi).

Repositioning a Frame and Unframing

If you have positioned an object but are not happy with the results, you can change the frame's location, or you can unframe the elements to return them to their original, sequential locations in your document.

To reposition a frame, follow these steps:

1. Choose Print Preview from the Print menu. Word displays the page in a Print Preview window.

2. Position the mouse over the frame until the pointer changes to a crosshair pointer.

3. Drag the frame to its new location.

4. Click Page Layout to return to Page Layout view or click Close to return to Normal view.

To cancel frame positioning, follow these steps:

1. Select all the elements in the frame.

2. Choose Frame from the Format menu. The Frame dialog box appears.

3. Click Unframe.

Formatting Text in a Frame

You can format text in a frame the same way you format any text in a Word document. After you create a frame and place the insertion point in that frame in Page Layout view, the ruler changes to show the boundaries of the frame, as shown in figure 20.10.

Fig. 20.10

The ruler measuring frame boundaries (Page Layout view).

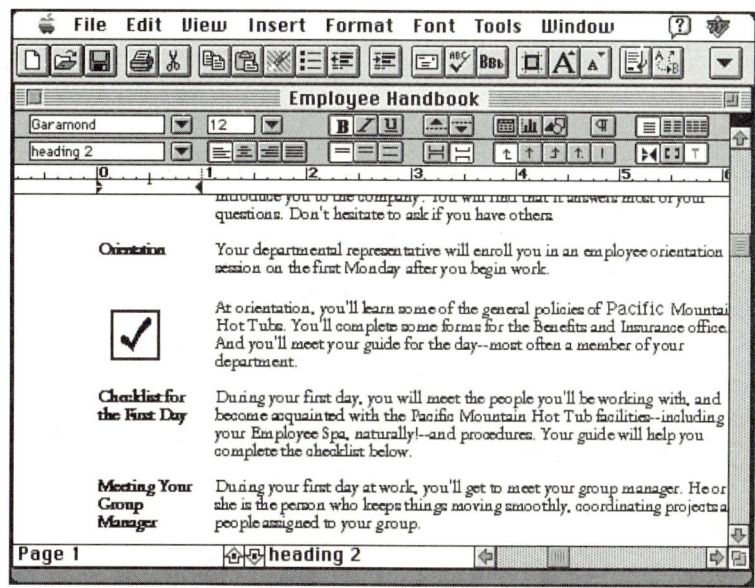

The right boundary of the frame acts like a right margin; when you are typing in the frame, text that reaches the right boundary wraps down to the next line.

You can use paragraph indents in a frame just as you do in a normal text column. If you indent the text past the left or right frame boundary, the text prints outside the frame (but Word cuts that text off if it interferes with other text).

Using Frame Positions in Styles

Because the choices you make in the Frame dialog box are paragraph formats as far as Word is concerned, you can include frame-position information in styles (see Chapter 14, "Formatting with Styles"). In figure 20.10, for example, the heading Orientation is a positioned version of the Heading 2 style. If you modify a style in this way, Word automatically enters the frame-position information when you apply the style.

To add position information to a style, create the style as usual, apply the Frame command to the text, and define the style by recording it. Alternatively, use the Style command to create the style and then use Frame to choose the position.

Understanding Position-Formatting Examples

So far in this chapter, you have learned how to position text elements, and you have seen many examples of the use of the Frame command in page design. This section presents additional examples that you may find useful.

Figure 20.11 shows a *sidebar*—text set apart for emphasis. This frame is positioned in line vertically and centered horizontally within the text column; the width is set manually at 2.75 inches. Thick borders have been added above and below the frame. (For information on borders, see Chapter 17, "Using Borders and Shading.") This effect is pleasing in a two-column document.

Fig. 20.11

Text positioned as a sidebar.

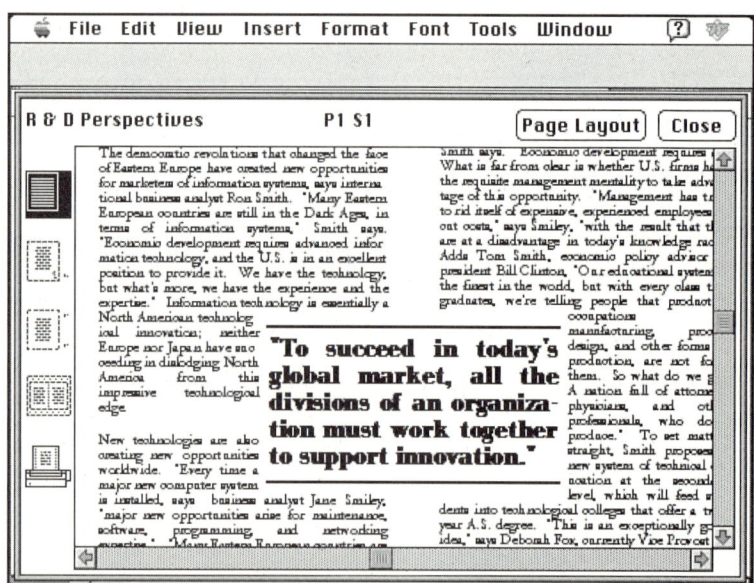

In figure 20.12, you see a graphic positioned within a newsletter header. The frame is positioned flush with the top and right margins, balancing the newsletter title on the left.

Fig. 20.12
A graphic positioned in a
newsletter header.

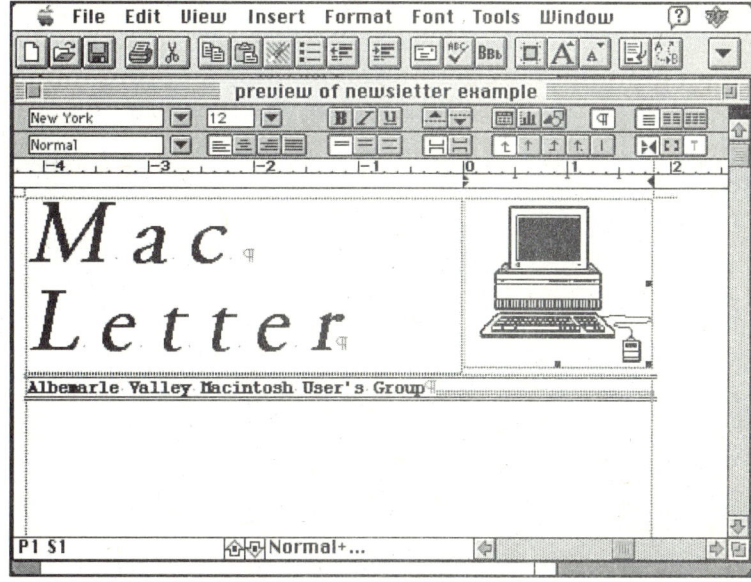

Creating Drop Caps

A welcome new feature of Word 5.1 is the Drop Caps command (Insert menu). You can use this command to create a large initial letter at the beginning of a paragraph, such as the three-line drop cap shown in figure 20.13.

Other effects you can add with this command include those shown in figure 20.14: the first word formatted as a two-line drop cap, a drop cap positioned in the margin, and special formatting (outline character) applied to the drop cap.

You cannot add drop caps to tables, headers, footers, multiple-column text, or text with spacing other than single line spacing.

To create a drop cap, follow these steps:

1. Place the insertion point at the beginning of the paragraph that you want to format. You also can select the character or characters that you want to format as a drop cap.

Chapter 20
Positioning Text and Graphics

Fig. 20.13
A drop cap.

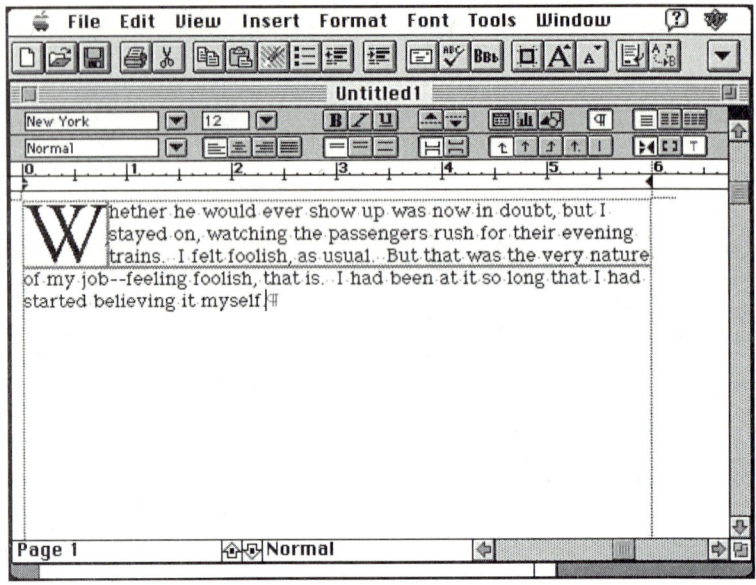

Fig. 20.14
Drop-cap variations.

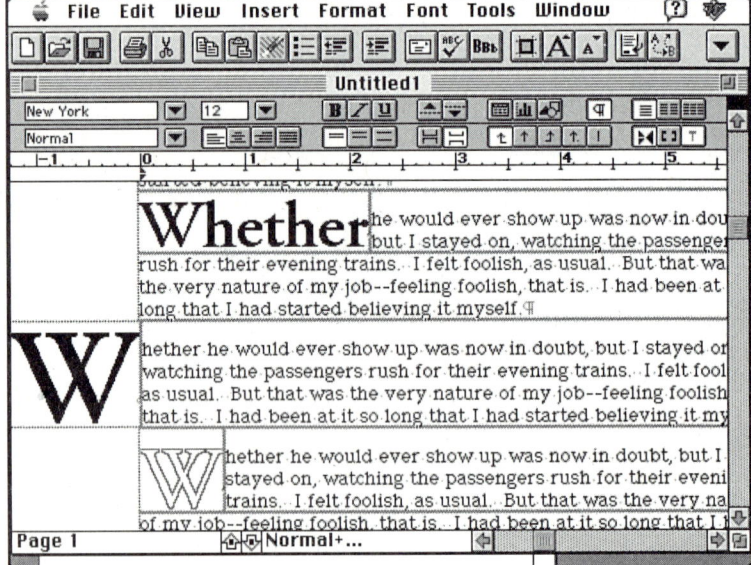

Part III

Using Advanced Formatting Techniques

2. Choose Drop Cap from the Insert menu or click the Drop Cap tool (see inside front cover). The Drop Cap dialog box appears (see fig. 20.15).

Fig. 20.15
Drop Cap dialog box.

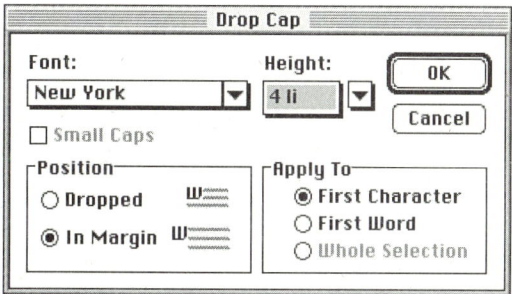

3. Select the font you want in the Font drop-down list box.

4. Select the height of the drop cap (in lines) in the Height drop-down list box. You can choose 2 to 5 lines. (If you prefer, you can type a height in points.)

5. Perform one of the following actions:

   ■ To format the first character of the current paragraph as a drop cap, click the First Character radio button.

   ■ To format the first word of the current paragraph as a drop cap, click the First Word radio button. If you want to use small caps in this word, also click the Small Caps check box, which becomes available after you activate the First Word option.

   ■ To format selected text as a drop cap, click the Whole Selection radio button. (This option is dimmed unless you selected some text before choosing the Drop Cap command.) If you want to use small caps in this text, also click the Small Caps check box, which becomes available after you activate the Whole Selection option.

6. Choose OK to confirm the drop cap.

Drop caps are position formats, so you won't see them in Normal view. To see how drop caps look, choose Page Layout from the View menu. When you create a drop cap, Word automatically switches to Page Layout view.

Chapter 20
Positioning Text and Graphics

You can create margin notes, like the ones shown in figure 20.16, by selecting text and using the Drop Cap command to place the selected text in the margin. For the height, type a point size suitable for body text (such as 12 points) in the Height text box.

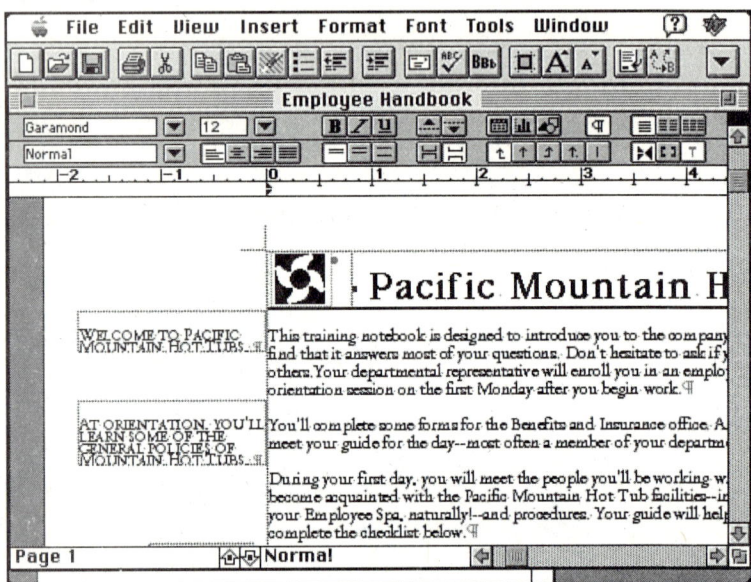

Quick Review

This section summarizes the most useful information in this chapter. Check "Productivity Tips" for a review of high-productivity tips and tricks—the ones that Macintosh and Word pros use every day. Review "Techniques" whenever you need a quick reminder about a specific procedure.

Productivity Tips

■ Use the Frame command to position text, graphics, and tables in an absolute position on the page. Be aware that a single-row table may be the best solution if you are trying to position text next to a graphic.

Part III

Using Advanced Formatting Techniques

- Before you position an element, make sure that the element is positioned somewhere on the page or in the column where you want it to appear.

- To position a graphics element quickly, use the Position button in the Frame dialog box so that you can visually place the frame on the page in Print Preview. Use the Vertical and Horizontal drop-down list boxes if you want to align the frame to the page edges, margins, or column boundaries, or if you want to center the element horizontally or vertically.

- You can reposition an element quickly by selecting it and then choosing the Frame command (Format menu). Double-clicking the black square in the selection bar next to the frame to open the Frame dialog box is even faster.

- Use Word 5.1's new drop-cap capabilities to add drop caps to your document. You also can use the Drop Cap command to place notes in the margin.

Techniques

This section provides concise summaries of all the procedures introduced in this chapter.

Positioning a Frame

To position a frame on the page using Print Preview:

1. Select the text, table, or graphic that you want to position.

2. Choose Frame from the Format menu. The Frame dialog box appears.

3. If you are framing text, type a width for the text in the Frame Width list box.

4. Click Position. Word displays the page in a Print Preview window.

5. Click and drag to position the frame anywhere on the page.

6. When you are satisfied with the frame's position, click Page Layout to return to Page Layout view or click Close to return to Normal view.

To position the frame by choosing position options or by typing measurements:

1. Select the text, table, or graphic that you want to position.

2. Choose Frame from the Format menu. The Frame dialog box appears.

3. If you are framing text, type a width for the text in the Frame Width list box.

4. Choose an option or type a measurement in the Horizontal list box.

5. Choose an option in the Relative To list box next to Horizontal.

6. Choose an option or type a measurement in the Vertical list box.

7. Choose an option in the Relative To list box next to Vertical.

8. If you want, you can change the default spacing from text by typing a new measurement in the From Text text box.

9. Choose OK to confirm the frame position.

Repositioning a Frame

To reposition a frame:

1. Choose Print Preview from the Print menu. Word displays the page in a Print Preview window.

2. Position the mouse over the frame until the pointer changes to a crosshair pointer.

3. Drag the frame to its new location.

4. Click Page Layout to return to Page Layout view or click Close to return to Normal view.

Canceling Frame Positioning

To cancel frame positioning:

1. Select all the elements in the frame.

2. Choose Frame from the Format menu. The Frame dialog box appears.

3. Click Unframe.

Creating a Drop Cap

To create a drop cap:

1. Place the insertion point at the beginning of the paragraph that you want to format. You also can select the character or characters that you want to format as a drop cap.

2. Choose Drop Cap from the Insert menu. The Drop Cap dialog box appears.

3. Select the font you want in the Font drop-down list box.

4. Select the height of the drop cap (in lines) in the Height drop-down list box. (You also can type a height in points.)

5. Perform one of the following actions:

   ■ To format the first character of the current paragraph as a drop cap, click the First Character radio button.

   ■ To format the first word of the current paragraph as a drop cap, click the First Word radio button. If you want to use small caps in this word, also click the Small Caps check box.

   ■ To format selected text as a drop cap, click the Whole Selection radio button. If you want to use small caps in this text, also click the Small Caps check box.

6. Choose OK.

Creating Professional Documents

Includes

Dividing a Document into Sections

ord defines a section as a portion of a document that has been demarcated by a section break. In this chapter, you learn how to enter section breaks into your document. Most Word users employ section breaks for two purposes:

- *Dividing a document into chapters.* Many of the documents commonly used in business and professional writing (such as proposals, technical reports, and business reports) are organized into chapters. By using section breaks to divide a report, proposal, or other long document into chapters, you can give each chapter a distinctive header and footer, footnote-number sequence, page-number sequence, and starting-page format. For example, you can format chapters with continuous Arabic numbers located in the upper right corner of the page but use lowercase letters centered at the bottom of the page for appendixes.

- *Changing column formats.* In Word, you can switch column formats as many times as you want, even in one page. For example, you can create a newsletter with a banner across the top of the page and three columns of text below the banner. To change column formats, you must enter a section break.

This chapter covers the following topics:

- *Creating and removing section breaks.* You learn how to divide documents into sections so that you can create separate chapters. (For information on column formats, see Chapter 18, "Creating Newspaper Columns.")

- *Understanding the options in the Section dialog box.* In this chapter, you also explore various features of the Section dialog box that enable you to create multiple columns (newspaper columns) and to control page breaks, headers and footers, and footnotes.

Because Word's performance becomes sluggish in a long document, you may want to make your document's chapters separate Word documents instead of sections if your document exceeds 100 pages. You still can compile a table of contents and an index for the entire document and print the document with continuous pagination. If you want continuous footnote numbering, however, you have to type the beginning footnote number at the beginning of each document. For more information, see Chapter 27, "Working with Long Documents."

Formatting Sections

You should begin your document by choosing the section formats that you want to apply to the whole document. Suppose that you want to begin each chapter on an odd page, with page numbers printed at the center of the top margin. You also want to suppress the printing of page numbers on the first page of each chapter. When you begin your document, choose Section from the Format menu and choose these options in the Section dialog box. When you insert section breaks to divide your document into chapters, Word copies the current section formats to the new section.

Understanding the Default Section Formats

If you don't use the Section command at all in a document, Word uses the default section formats, which are listed in Table 21.1.

	Format	Default setting
Table 21.1 Default Section Formats	Start	No Break
	Columns	1
	Spacing	0.5 in
	Header/Footer from Top	0.5 in
	Header/Footer from Bottom	0.5 in
	Different First Page	deactivated (page numbers, if any, print on first page)
	Include Endnotes	activated (endnotes, if any, are grouped and printed at end of section)
	Format	Arabic (1 2 3)
	Restart at 1	deactivated (page numbers print continuously across section break)
	Margin Page Numbers	deactivated (no page numbers, unless numbers are entered in headers or footers or in Print Preview)
	Page Numbers from Top	0.5 in
	Page Numbers from Bottom	0.5 in

Changing Section Formats

You can change section formats in two ways:

■ *Format one section.* To change one section's format, place the insertion point anywhere in that section and then choose Section from the Format menu or press Option-F14. The Section dialog box appears, showing the formats that currently are in effect. Make the necessary changes in the dialog box.

■ *Format two or more sections.* If you select two or more sections, you still can choose section formats that affect all the selected sections. When you select more than one section and then use the Section command, the Section dialog box appears with all the options blank (see fig. 21.1).

Chapter 21

Dividing a Document into Sections

Fig. 21.1

Section dialog box when
two or more sections
are selected.

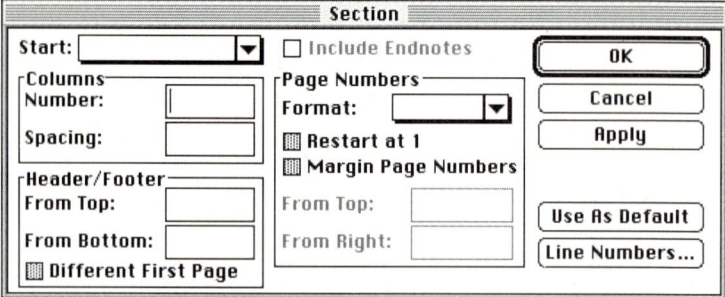

Word applies only the formats you choose; the program does not interfere with any other section formats in the selected sections.

Creating and Removing Section Breaks

When you start a new document, the whole document is one section, and any formats you choose apply to the whole document. In order to use different section formats in different parts of a Word document, you must divide the document into sections by adding section breaks.

To enter a section break, follow these steps:

1. Place the insertion point where you want the section break to occur.

2. Choose Section Break from the Insert menu or press ⌘-Enter. Word enters a *section mark*—a double row of dots—across the screen and places the insertion point below the section mark so that the insertion point is in the new section (see fig. 21.2).

Word distinguishes between the Return key and the Enter key (in the numeric keypad). To enter a section break, press ⌘-Enter.

After you enter a section break, the document has two sections. The page-number area of the document window changes to show the page number and the section number (using the abbreviations P and S, as in P2 S2).

Fig. 21.2
Document with a
section break.

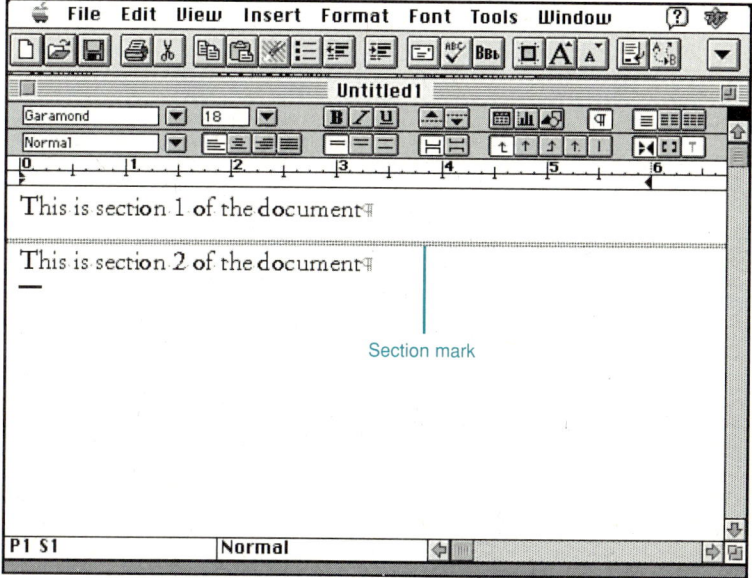

To remove a section break, follow these steps:

1. Select the section mark by clicking the selection bar to the left of the section mark.

2. Press Backspace or Delete.

CAUTION

Like paragraph marks, section marks store section formats. If you delete a section mark, you lose the formats you stored in the section above the mark. If you accidentally delete a section mark, immediately choose Undo from the Edit menu or press ⌘-Z.

Understanding and Using the Section Dialog Box

When you choose Section from the Format menu or press Option-F14, the Section dialog box appears. You can control section formatting in this dialog box, which is shown in figure 21.3.

Chapter 21

Dividing a Document into Sections

Fig. 21.3
Section dialog box.

Section

Start: [No Break ▼]   ☐ Include Endnotes   [OK]

┌ Columns ─────────┐   ┌ Page Numbers ──────┐   [Cancel]
Number: [1]   Format: [1 2 3 ▼]   [Apply]

Spacing: [0.5 in]   ☐ Restart at 1
                        ☐ Margin Page Numbers
┌ Header/Footer ───┐
From Top: [0.5 in]   From Top: [0.5 in]   [Use As Default]

From Bottom: [0.5 in]   From Right: [0.5 in]   [Line Numbers...]
☐ Different First Page

For example, you can choose to have footnotes printed at the end of each section as endnotes by clicking the Include Endnotes check box. The following sections discuss the major areas of section formatting that you control in this dialog box.

Controlling Page Breaks

By default, Word starts a new page after a section mark. If you place the insertion point in the new section and then use the Section command, you can take advantage of several options in the Section dialog box for breaking pages at the start of a new section.

You can choose the following options in the Start drop-down list box:

No Break. This option tells Word not to break a page at the section mark. If you create a document with multiple columns, Word balances the columns above the section mark.

New Page. This option (the default) tells Word to start a new page at the section mark.

New Column. This option, which you use in documents with newspaper columns, tells Word to leave the rest of the column blank and to start the next section at the top of the next column.

Odd Page. This option tells Word to start the next section on the next odd-numbered page. Odd Page is the usual choice for documents divided into chapters, because chapters always begin on odd-numbered pages. If necessary, Word leaves a page blank so that the program can start the next section on an odd page. Headers, footers, and page numbers are printed on this blank page, however, even though the page contains no text.

Even Page. This option tells Word to start the next section on the next even-numbered page. As with Odd Page, Word leaves a page blank (except for headers/footers and page numbers), if necessary.

To control page breaks after entering a section break, follow these steps:

1. Place the insertion point in the section you want to format. Alternatively, select two or more sections, or select the entire document by choosing Select All from the Edit menu or pressing ⌘-A.

2. Choose Section from the Format menu or press Option-F14. The Section dialog box appears.

3. Select a page-start option in the Start drop-down list box.

4. Choose OK.

    Alternatively, click Apply to see how the format will affect your document; the Section dialog box remains on-screen, and you can see the format behind the dialog box in the document window. Choose OK to confirm your choices or click Cancel to close the dialog box without affecting your document.

Controlling Page Numbers

Chapter 11, "Formatting Pages," explained how to turn on page numbers with the Section dialog box's Margin Page Numbers option and how to add page numbers in Print Preview. In this section, you learn how section breaks affect page numbers.

Page numbers added in Print Preview work the same way as numbers added with the Margin Page Numbers option.

When you break a section, Word continues the current page-number options unless you deliberately change these options after the section break. Suppose that you place the insertion point in Section 1 of your document and choose Margin Page Numbers in the Section dialog box. Although you chose this option only in Section 1, Word prints page numbers throughout all sections.

Now suppose that you place the insertion point in Section 3 of the same document and deactivate the Margin Page Numbers option. Word stops printing page numbers after the Section 3 break, and subsequent sections don't have page numbers.

This same rule applies to page numbers added in headers and footers (see Chapter 19). If you add page numbers in a header or footer in Section 1, Word continues printing the header or footer and page numbers throughout your document unless you change the header or footer in a subsequent section and delete the page numbers.

To add page numbers throughout a multisection document, follow these steps:

1. Position the insertion point in Section 1.

2. Choose Section from the Format menu or press Option-F14. The Section dialog box appears.

3. Perform one or more of the following actions:

   ■ To suppress the printing of page numbers on the first page of a section throughout your document, activate the Different First Page option.

   ■ To turn on page numbering, activate the Margin Page Numbers option.

   ■ To change the page-number position, type new measurements in the From Top and From Right text boxes.

   ■ To begin each section's page numbers with the number 1, activate the Restart at 1 option.

   ■ To use a page-number format other than Arabic numbers (1, 2, 3), select the format in the Format drop-down list box.

4. Choose OK.

Controlling Headers and Footers

Headers and footers (introduced in Chapter 19) work the same way as page numbers do; when you break a section, Word continues the current header and footer until you change them. If you want your document to have different headers or footers for each section, you must change the header or footer after each section break. You also can change the header and footer positions.

To start a new header or footer after a section break, follow these steps:

1. Place the insertion point in the section you want to format.

2. Choose Header or Footer from the View menu. The Header or Footer window appears.

3. Enter the header or footer, following the procedures you learned in Chapter 19.

If you change a header or footer and then decide that the change was a bad idea, click the Same As Previous command button in the header or footer window to tell Word to use the preceding header or footer (see fig. 21.4).

This button becomes available in the header or footer window only when you have created a document with multiple sections and the preceding section's header or footer differs from the one you just entered.

Fig. 21.4
Same As Previous button (header or footer window).

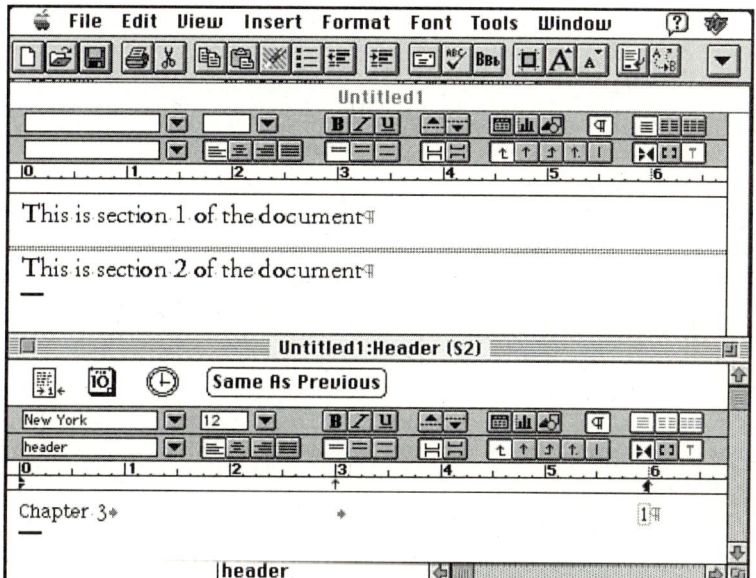

Quick Review

This section summarizes the most useful information in this chapter. Check "Productivity Tips" for a review of high-productivity tips and tricks—the ones that Macintosh and Word pros use every day. Review "Techniques" whenever you need a quick reminder about a specific procedure.

Chapter 21
Dividing a Document into Sections

Productivity Tips

■ You can use section breaks to divide your document into chapters or to change column formats in your document. If you haven't divided your document by pressing ⌘-Enter or choosing Section Break from the Insert menu, your document has one section.

■ If you're creating a brief multichapter document, such as a business report or a master's thesis, you can break the document into sections and keep the whole document in one file. For a long novel or book, however, you probably should consider keeping each chapter in its own separate file. See Chapter 27, "Working with Long Documents," for tips on printing these files with continuous pagination, a unified table of contents, and a unified index.

■ When you enter a section break, Word places the insertion point below the section mark. If you then use the Section command, your choices in the Section dialog box affect the section below the section mark.

■ You can delete a section mark just as you delete a paragraph mark. If you delete a section mark, the section above the deleted mark takes on the following section's formats.

Techniques

This section provides concise summaries of all the procedures introduced in this chapter.

Entering a Section Break

To enter a section break:

1. Place the insertion point where you want the section break to occur.

2. Choose Section Break from the Insert menu or press ⌘-Enter. Word enters a section mark into the document.

Removing a Section Break

To remove a section break:

1. Select the section mark by clicking the selection bar to the left of the section mark.

2. Press Backspace or Delete.

Controlling Page Breaks

To control page breaks after you enter a section break:

1. Place the insertion point in the section you want to format. Alternatively, select two or more sections, or select the entire document by choosing Select All from the Edit menu or pressing ⌘-A.

2. Choose Section from the Format menu or press Option-F14. The Section dialog box appears.

3. Select a page-start option in the Start drop-down list box.

4. Choose OK.

   Alternatively, click Apply to see how the format change will affect your document and then choose OK or click Cancel.

Chapter 21

Dividing a Document into Sections

Organizing Documents with Outlining

A Word outline simply is another way of looking at your document. Changes you make in your outline change your document's structure. For this reason, Word's unique outlining feature provides wonderful tools for planning, creating, and revising documents.

This chapter discusses a few of the many ways you can use Word outlines. If you create an outline for your document, you can use the outline to see instantly what your document's overall structure looks like. For long documents, you can use outlining as an alternative to scrolling. For example, by switching to Outline view, you can locate the beginning of a chapter quickly, and by returning to Normal view, you can see the page on which the chapter begins.

In short, you use Word's outlining capabilities not only for help with document planning, but also when you create long articles, business reports, books, or dissertations. If you create such documents, you can reap significant productivity gains by mastering Word's outlining features.

This chapter covers the following topics:

■ *Learning outlining concepts.* The chapter begins with an introduction to the concepts of computer outlining the Word way. You learn the meaning of key terms and functions: outline levels, promoting and demoting headings, and collapsing and expanding headings.

USING
WORD 5.1
FOR THE MAC
SPECIAL EDITION

- *Creating an outline.* In this section, you learn all the major commands you need to create an outline. You learn how to use the icons in the Outline icon bar, and then you follow a keystroke-by-keystroke tutorial to create and edit your first Word outline.

- *Restructuring the outline.* This section introduces the commands you use to restructure an outline. You learn that when you move outline headings, Word also moves the body text below these headings. This capability means that you can restructure a long document quickly and easily simply by rearranging headings in the outline.

- *Using additional outlining techniques.* In this section, you learn more about managing long documents with outlining, outlining an existing document, automatically numbering the headings in an outline, and printing the outline without the body text.

Does using outlining in every document you create make sense? No. Using outlining for short documents is overkill. In general, you need outlining only when you plan to use internal subheadings in a document. As you learn in this chapter, you can use these subheadings to get a sense of your document's overall structure, and you also can reorganize your document by rearranging subheadings.

Learning Outlining Concepts

Understanding a few key concepts and terms helps you grasp Word's outlining capabilities.

Indenting headings and subheadings is the standard arrangement for outlines. Word arranges its outlines in the same way. The first-level headings, called *Level 1*, are not indented; second-level headings, called *Level 2*, are indented once; and so on, as shown here:

Level 1 heading

Level 1 heading

    Level 2 heading

    Level 2 heading

        Level 3 heading

        Level 3 heading

Level 2 heading

Level 1 heading

In a Word outline, you can change the position of an outline heading in the hierarchy of levels. You can *promote* an outline heading (move the heading up one logical level, such as from Level 2 to Level 1), or you can *demote* an outline heading (move the heading down one logical level, such as from Level 2 to Level 3).

You also can *collapse* (hide) the subheadings under a heading so that you can see the structure of your outline more clearly. For example, you see the subheadings in the following outline:

I. Varietal wines of California

A. Chardonnay

B. Sauvignon Blanc

C. Cabernet Sauvignon

D. Merlot

II. Varietal wines of Australia

A. Chardonnay

B. Sauvignon Blanc

C. Cabernet Sauvignon

D. Merlot

If you collapse the subheadings, you have the following outline:

I. Varietal wines of California

II. Varietal wines of Australia

When you collapse the subheadings, you must *expand* them in order to see them again.

After you add text to your document, the document has *body text* (text paragraphs rather than headings) as well as outline headings. As you add text, you need to collapse the body text so that only the headings are visible in the outline. With only the headings visible, you can see your document's overall structure.

If you have used a computer outlining program before, these features are not new to you. What makes Word's outlining capability stand out, however, is its seamless integration with your document. As you make changes in your outline, the changes are reflected in your document, and as you make changes in your document's headings and subheadings, the changes are reflected automatically in your outline. You can switch to Outline view at any time for a quick view of your document's overall structure. As writing experts know, having a solid overall structure is one of the best ways to ensure high quality in reports, articles, and other long documents you create.

Creating an Outline

The first step in creating an outline is switching to Outline view by choosing Outline from the View menu or pressing ⌘-Option-O. (If you have an extended keyboard, you also can press Shift-F13.) In Outline view, you can type headings and subheadings, demoting and promoting them to the levels you prefer.

When you choose the Outline command, the Outline icon bar appears under the ribbon at the top of your document window. If the ruler was displayed, the Outline icon bar replaces it. The icons in this bar perform special functions in Outline view (see fig. 22.1).

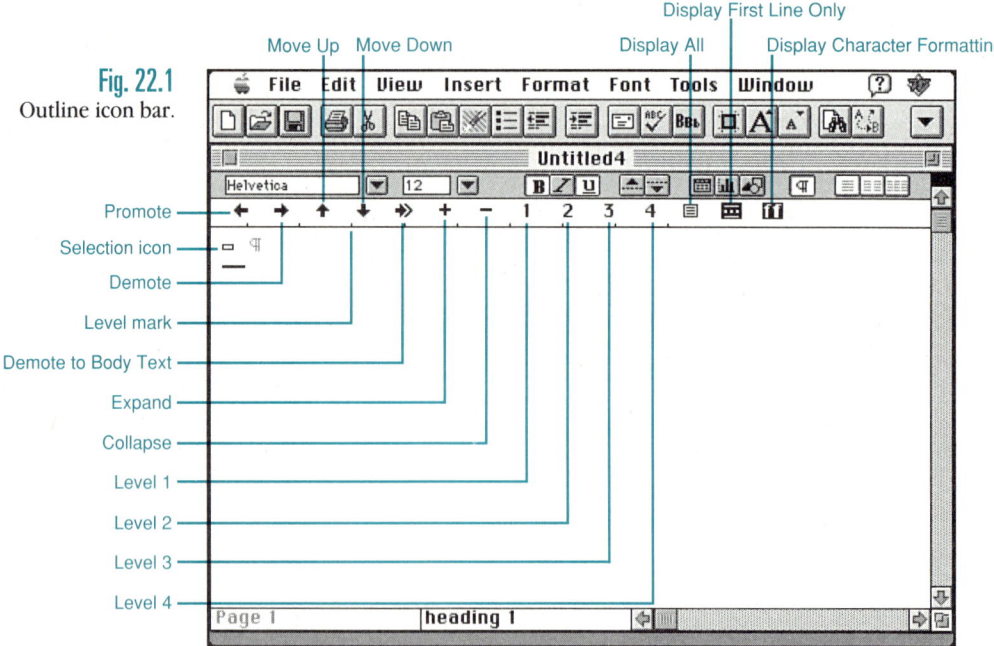

Fig. 22.1
Outline icon bar.

You learn more about what these icons do in subsequent sections. Following is a brief overview of the icons' functions and their keyboard shortcuts (where applicable):

Promote (Option-left arrow). Click the Promote icon to move a heading up one logical level.

Demote (Option-right arrow). Click the Demote icon to move a heading down one logical level.

Move Up (Option-up arrow). Click the Move Up icon to restructure the outline by moving a heading up.

Move Down (Option-down arrow). Click the Move Down icon to restructure the outline by moving a heading down.

Demote to Body Text (⌘-right arrow). Click the Body Text icon to transform a heading into ordinary body text.

Expand (keypad plus sign [+]). Click the Expand icon to show subheadings that were collapsed under the current heading.

Collapse (keypad minus sign [–]) Click the Collapse icon to hide the subheadings under the current heading.

Level 1. Click this icon to show only the Level 1 headings and collapse all others.

Level 2. Click this icon to show the Level 1 and 2 headings and collapse all others.

Level 3. Click this icon to show the Level 1, 2, and 3 headings and collapse all others.

Level 4. Click this icon to show the Level 1, 2, 3, and 4 headings and collapse all others.

Display All (keypad asterisk [*]). The Display All icon works like a toggle command. On the first click, Display All collapses all the body text under all the headings. (A dotted line below the headings indicates that body text has been hidden under the headings.) On the second click, Display All expands the body text.

Display First Line Only (keypad equals sign [=]). The Display First Line Only icon, which is highlighted by default, also works like a toggle. By default, Word displays all the body text under a heading. When you click the Display First Line Only icon to remove the highlighting, Word shows only the first line of body text under a heading.

Chapter 22

Organizing Documents with Outlining

Display Character Formatting (keypad slash [/]). The Display Character Formatting icon, which is highlighted by default, displays the outline headings with the formatting Word automatically applies or with whatever formatting you choose. If you deactivate this option, Word uses the default font and font size to display your outline.

Level marks. The small vertical lines along the bottom of the Outline icon bar are level marks, showing where Word aligns the headings by level.

The Outline icon bar is useful, but keep in mind that you can duplicate most of its functions by using mouse procedures that are unique to Outline view. For example, you can demote or promote a heading simply by dragging the *selection icon* (the outlined dash or plus sign next to each heading or subheading) to the right or left. In the tutorial that begins in the next section, you learn how to use this technique and other mouse techniques in Outline view.

Creating a Sample Outline

To explore outlining, try the tutorial in this section and the subsequent sections. This tutorial introduces outlining concepts and skills in step-by-step fashion. Follow these steps:

1. Start Word and display a new document by choosing New from the File menu. Alternatively, press F5 or click the New tool.

2. Choose Outline from the View menu, or press ⌘-Option-O or Shift-F13.

3. To display your outline in the default font and font size, deactivate the Display Character Formatting icon (the one with two *f*s).

This tutorial continues in the following sections.

Creating Headings and Subheadings

When you type in Outline view, Word enters the lines that you type as outline headings, not as body text. To create an outline for document-planning purposes, follow these steps:

1. Type your Level 1 heading, **Fall Quarter Report**, on the first line, which is preceded by an outlined dash. This selection icon indicates that the line contains a heading but no subheadings.

2. After you type the Level 1 heading, press Return. Word moves the insertion point to the next line, and another selection icon appears at the beginning of that line. The new line is the same level as the preceding line.

3. Demote the current heading (the second line in the outline), using one of the following procedures:

   ■ Drag the selection icon to the right. As you drag the icon, the mouse pointer changes to an arrow pointing both ways, indicating that you can demote or promote the heading. A dotted vertical line also appears to help you align the heading with the level marks in the Outline icon bar (see fig. 22.2). Drag the selection icon right until you have aligned it with the Level 2 mark in the Outline icon bar, and then release the mouse button.

Fig. 22.2
Aligning a heading with a level mark.

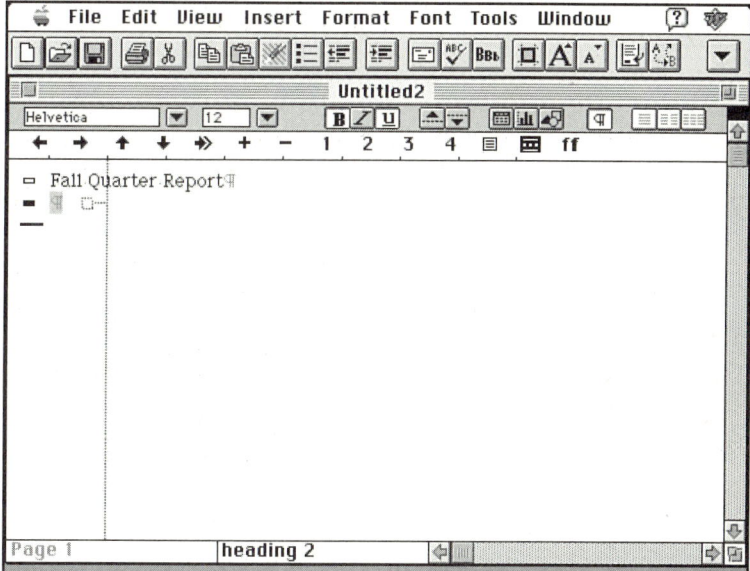

   ■ Click the Demote icon in the icon bar.

   ■ Press Option-right arrow.

   After you demote the heading, the outline heading icon in the first line changes to an outlined plus sign, indicating that the Level 1 heading now has subheadings (see fig. 22.3).

Remember that after you collapse subheadings, you have no other way to see that subheadings are hidden under a heading.

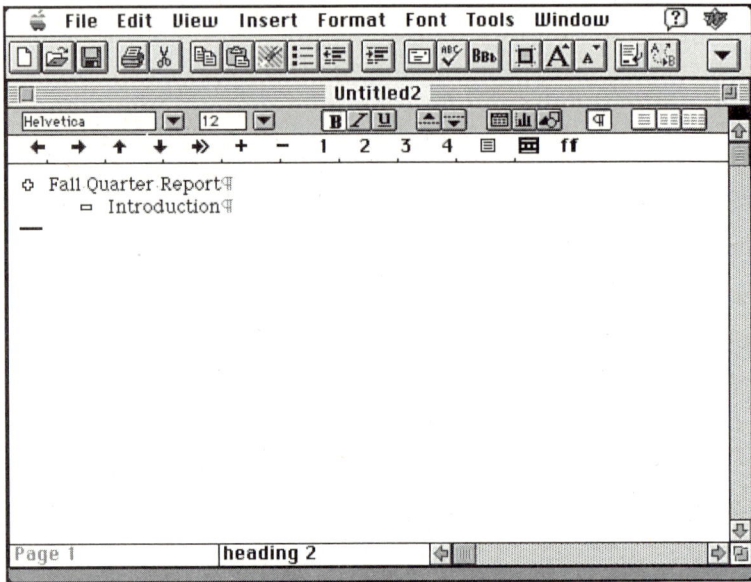

4. Type the Level 2 heading: **Introduction**.

5. Continue by typing additional headings, as follows. Demote headings as necessary by dragging the selection icon, clicking the Demote icon, or pressing Option-right arrow.

Review of Summer Quarter Performance

Fall Quarter Performance Data

Sales

Corporate

Direct

To tell which level you are working in, look at the status bar. The current heading level is displayed in the style-name area (Heading 2, Heading 3, and so on).

Your outline should look like the one shown in figure 22.4.

Fig. 22.4

An outline with
second-, third-, and
fourth-level headings.

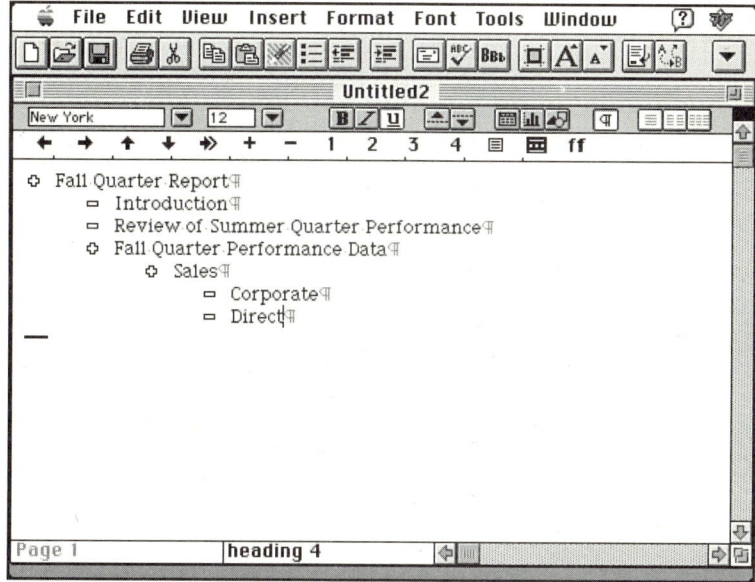

6. Press Return to start a new heading. Promote the heading one
   level, using one of the following methods:

   ■ Drag the selection icon left until the icon aligns with the
     Level 3 mark.

   ■ Click the Promote icon in the icon bar.

   ■ Press Option left arrow.

7. With the insertion point positioned in a blank Level 3 heading,
   continue typing the outline as follows, demoting and promoting
   headings as necessary:

   Inventory

   Shipping

   Quality Control

   Customer Service

      Technical Assistance

      Returns and Refunds

Accounting

Analysis of Performance Data

Recommendations

Figure 22.5 shows the outline you have created.

Fig. 22.5
Finished draft of
the outline.

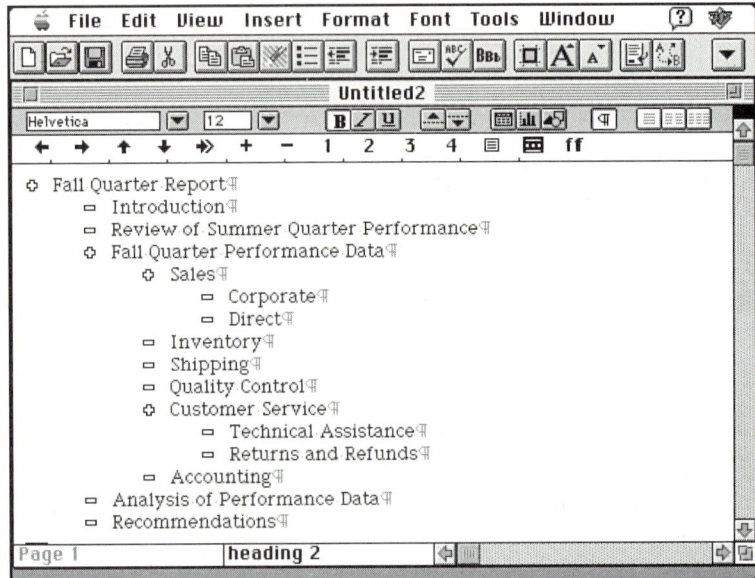

Viewing the Default Heading Styles

When you type headings in Outline view, Word automatically applies the standard heading styles (Heading 1, Heading 2, Heading 3, and so on). Each style has its own predefined format, which you can see by clicking the Display Character Formatting icon in the Outline icon bar. Figure 22.6 shows how your outline looks after you click this icon.

Returning to Normal View

After you have roughed out the overall plan for your document, you can return to Normal view to see how your headings look with the default heading styles that Word assigns when you choose outline levels (see fig. 22.7).

Part IV

Creating Professional Documents

Fig. 22.6
Outline with
default character
formatting displayed.

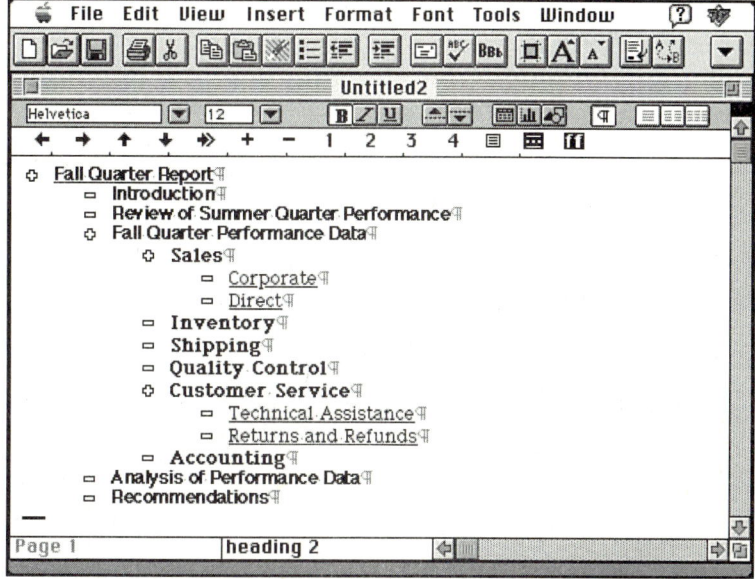

Fig. 22.7
Normal view of outline.

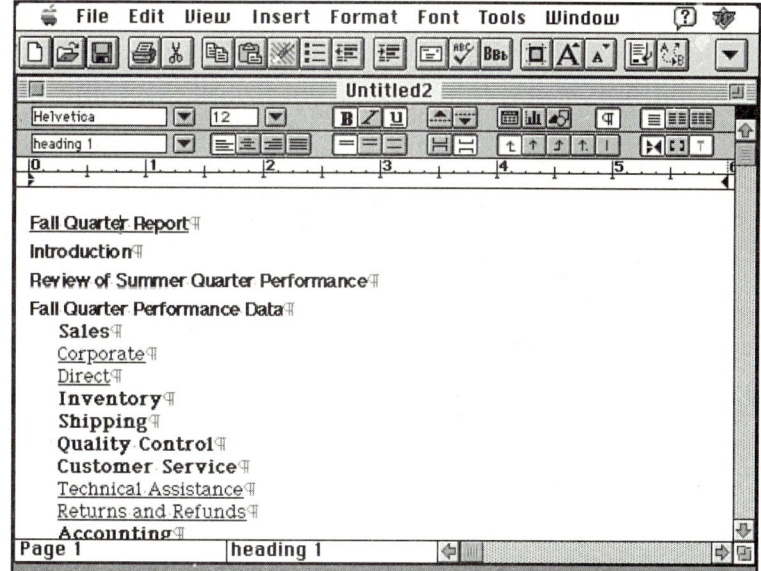

Chapter 22

Organizing Documents with Outlining

To return to Normal view, choose Normal from the View menu or press ⌘-Option-N.

If you aren't satisfied with the predefined styles for heading levels, you may want to redefine them, as explained in Chapter 14. Figure 22.8 shows how the headings look in Normal view after reformatting.

Fig. 22.8
Reformatted headings in Normal view.

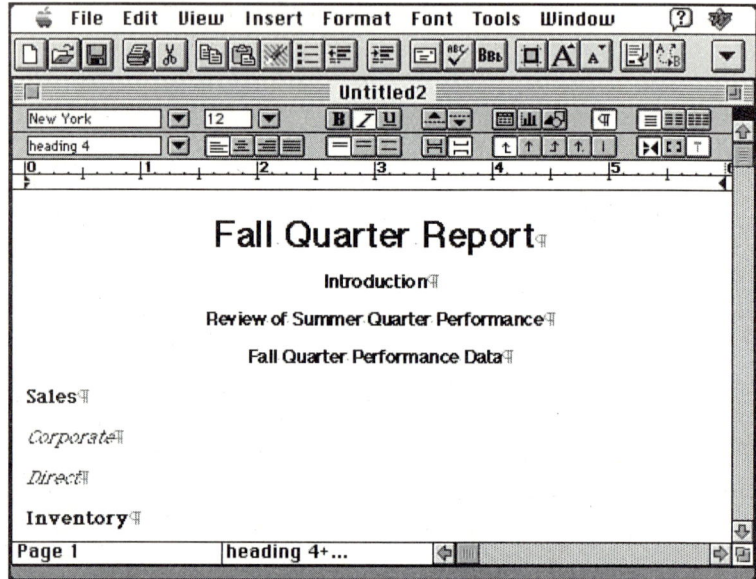

Figure 22.9 shows the reformatted headings in Outline view. Notice that Word drops the paragraph formatting (such as centering) so that you can see the outline levels.

Adding Body Text

After you create and format the pattern of headings and subheadings for your document, you're ready to add body text. To add body text to your outline, follow these steps:

1. Choose Show ¶ from the Edit menu or click the paragraph-mark icon in the ribbon, if necessary, so that you can see the paragraph marks in the outline.

Fig. 22.9
Reformatted headings in
Outline view.

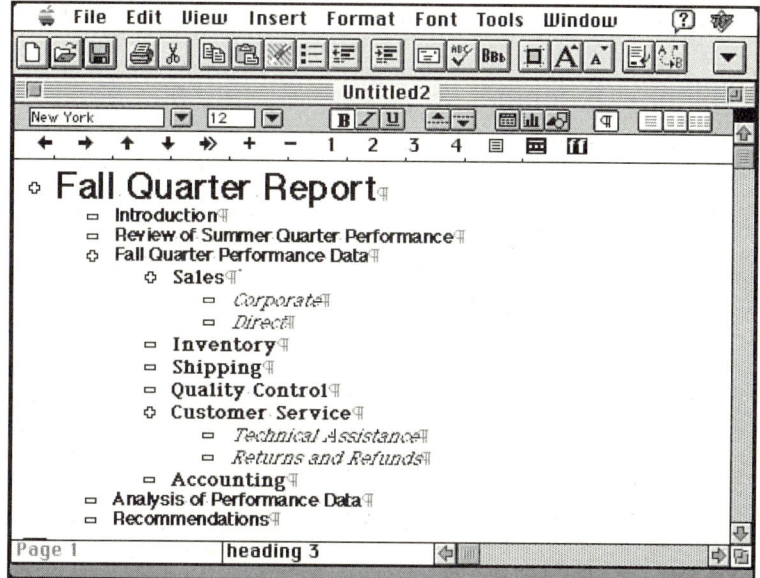

Fig. 22.9
Reformatted headings in
Outline view.

2. If your document still is in Outline view, choose Normal from the View menu or press ⌘-Option-N.

3. Place the insertion point at the end of the first Level 2 heading (*Introduction*) but before the paragraph mark, and then press Return to start a new line.

4. Type the following text (or make up your own):

   Pacific Mountain Hot Tubs recorded strong improvements in all categories this quarter. This improved performance occurred despite an overall flat economy.

5. Select the paragraph of text you just entered but not the paragraph mark at the end of it.

6. Choose Copy from the Edit menu, press ⌘-C, or click the Copy tool. You have copied the paragraph to the Clipboard.

7. Place the insertion point at the end of the next heading (*Review of Summer Quarter Performance*) but before the paragraph mark, and then press Return to start a new line of body text.

8. Type the following text:

During the past quarter, we improved sales and lowered costs. The pattern of success touched all aspects of our operation, as indicated in the following sections.

Your document should look like the one shown in figure 22.10.

Fig. 22.10
The document with body
text added below
each heading.

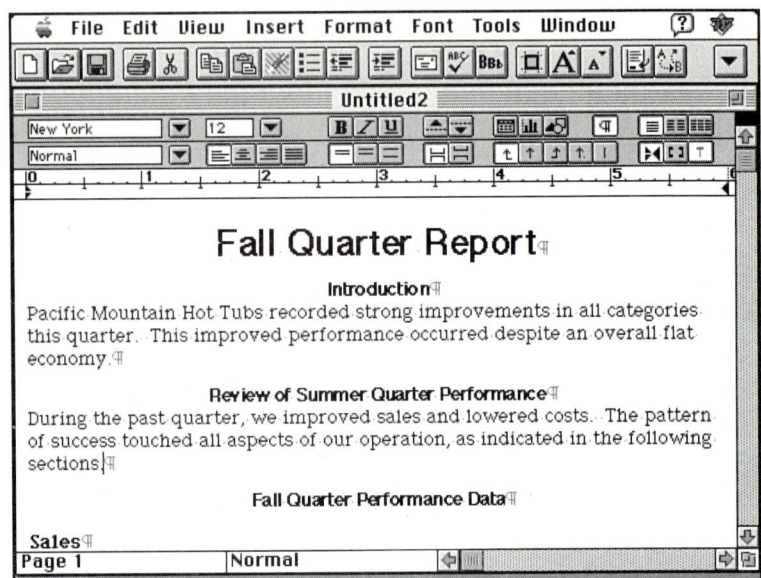

Collapsing Body Text

After you add body text, you see the body text when you return to Outline view. In this section, you learn how to collapse (hide) the body text. After you collapse the body text, you can see your document's structure.

To collapse the body text you added to the outline, follow these steps:

1. Return to the Outline view by choosing Outline from the View menu or pressing ⌘-Option-O. You see the outline with the body text visible (see fig. 22.11).

2. To view your outline with only the first line of body text showing, click the Display First Line icon in the Outline icon bar or press the keypad equals sign (=). The outline will look like figure 22.12.

Fig. 22.11
Outline with body
text visible.

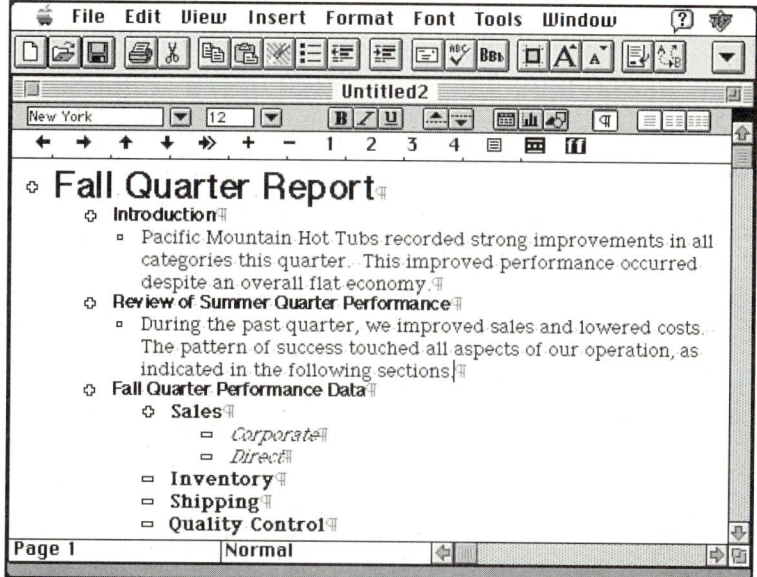

Fig. 22.12
Outline with the first line
of body text visible.

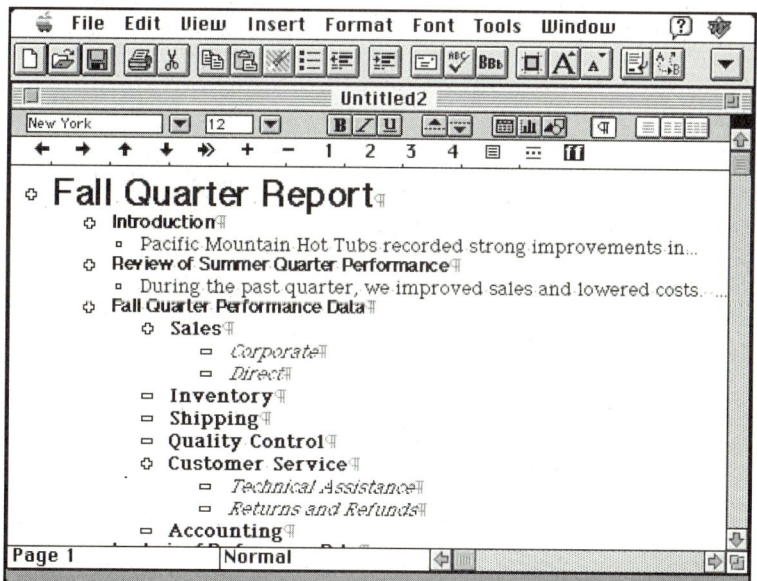

3. To collapse all the body text, click the Display All icon or press the keypad asterisk (*). After you collapse the body text, the headings with hidden body text are displayed with fuzzy gray underlining (see fig. 22.13).

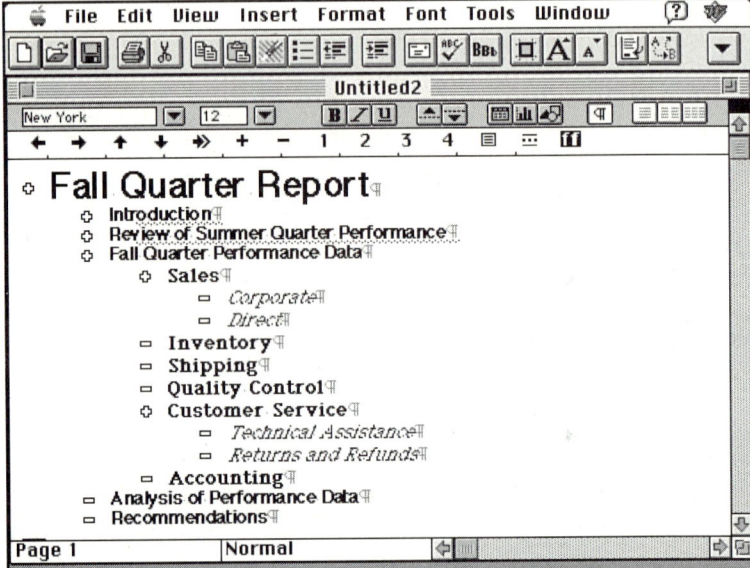

Adding and Deleting Headings

Adding and deleting headings is easy in Word. To add space for a heading, follow these steps:

1. Collapse the body text, if necessary.

2. Position the insertion point after the Level 4 subheading *Direct* (but before the paragraph mark) and then press Return. Word creates a new Level 3 line for a heading. (New lines that you create by pressing Return always take on the level of the preceding heading.)

3. Press Return again to add a line for another Level 3 heading.

To delete a heading, follow these steps:

1. Move the mouse pointer over the selection icon until the pointer changes to a four-arrow symbol.

2. Click the mouse to select the heading.

3. Press Delete or Backspace to delete the space.

Collapsing and Expanding Headings

An outline with many levels of subheadings can become so long that it no longer helps you view the overall structure of the document quickly. You can avert this problem by collapsing (hiding) subheadings. You can collapse all the subheadings under a specific heading, or you can collapse all the subheadings in your outline down to a specified level. After you collapse subheadings, you can expand them again when you need to view them.

To collapse subheadings in the document, follow these steps:

1. Place the insertion point in the Level 2 heading *Fall Quarter Performance Data*.

2. Click the Collapse icon (the minus sign in the Outline icon bar) or press the keypad minus sign (–). Word collapses the lowest-level subheading under this heading (Level 4 subheadings), leaving the list of Level 3 subheadings under the *Fall Quarter Performance Data* heading, as shown in figure 22.14.

3. Click the Collapse icon again or press the keypad minus sign (–) again. Word collapses the Level 3 subheadings this time (see fig. 22.15).

To expand the subheadings, follow these steps:

1. Click the Expand icon (the plus sign in the Outline icon bar) or press the keypad plus sign (+). Word expands the headings to show the Level 3 subheadings.

2. Click the Expand icon again or press the keypad plus sign (+) again. Now you see the Level 4 subheadings too.

3. Click the Expand icon or press the keypad plus sign (+) a third time. You see the body text, if any exists.

Chapter 22

Organizing Documents with Outlining

Fig. 22.14
Outline with Level 4
subheadings collapsed.

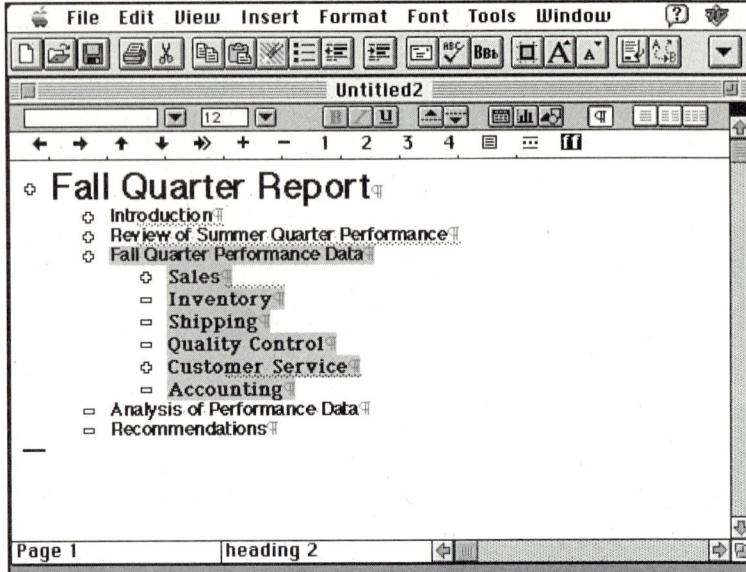

Fig. 22.15
Outline collapsed to
show only Level 1 and
Level 2 headings.

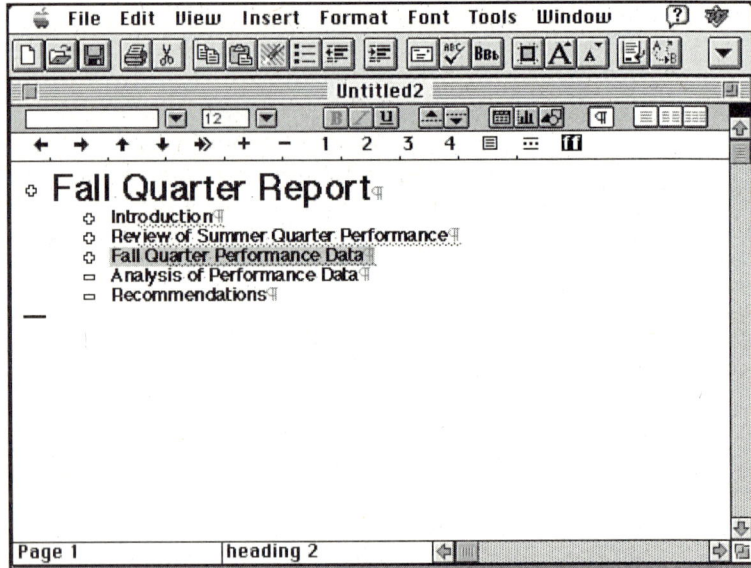

Collapsing and Expanding Headings Throughout an Outline

The procedure you just learned enables you to collapse or expand the subheadings under the selected heading. In this section, you learn how to collapse or expand headings throughout an outline.

To display the outline at a level you specify, follow these steps:

1. Click the Level 1 icon in the Outline icon bar. Only one heading—the Level 1 heading—appears on-screen.

2. Click the Level 2 icon. Only the Level 1 and Level 2 headings appear on-screen.

3. Click the Level 3 icon. Now, in addition to Level 1 and Level 2, the Level 3 headings appear on-screen.

Restructuring the Outline

When you restructure an outline by moving headings, Word moves the body text, too. You also can sort headings. Word's outlining capabilities enable you to restructure a huge document in seconds, as you learn in the following sections.

Another way to restructure your outline is to promote or demote headings. By demoting *Review of Summer Quarter Performance*, for example, you could make the heading part of the introduction section. You also can promote or demote headings after you move them. For example, you could position *Review of Summer Quarter Performance* below *Recommendations* and then demote the *Review* heading so that it becomes part of *Recommendations*.

Moving the Headings

In this section, you learn how to move a heading up and down in the outline.

To restructure your outline, follow these steps:

1. Place the insertion point in the *Accounting* subheading.

2. Click the Move Up icon in the Outline icon bar (the up arrow) or press Option-up arrow. Word moves the *Accounting* heading up one line in the outline.

3. Keep clicking Move Up or pressing Option-up arrow to see what happens. Word keeps the heading at Level 3, no matter where in the outline you place it.

4. To move the *Accounting* heading down one line again, click the Move Down icon in the Outline icon bar (the down arrow) or press Option-down arrow. Position the heading at the beginning of the Level 3 headings below *Fall Quarter Performance Data*.

You also can move a heading up or down with the mouse, as follows:

1. Move the pointer to the heading's selection icon until you see an arrow pointing four ways.

2. Drag the pointer up. You see a dotted line with an arrow indicating where the heading will be positioned (see fig. 22.16).

Fig. 22.16
Dragging a heading vertically.

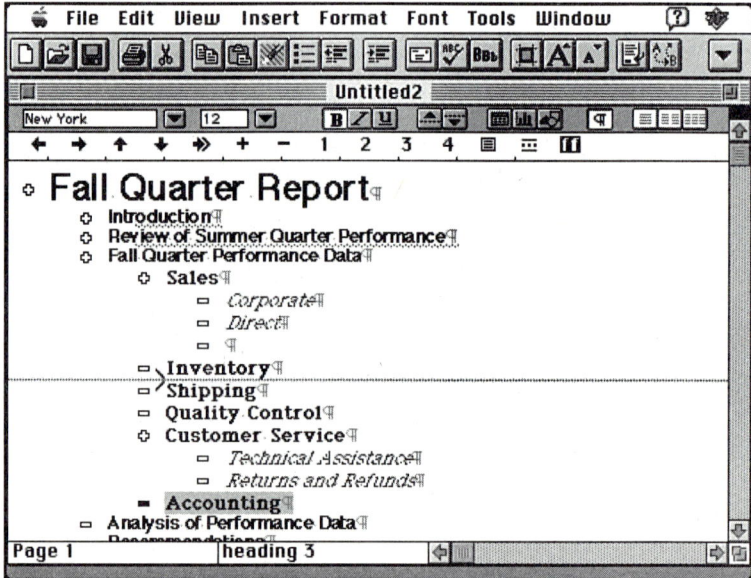

3. When the heading is where you want it, release the mouse button.

Sorting the Headings

The Level 3 headings in this outline should be in alphabetical order. You can arrange them yourself, as you did when you moved the *Accounting* heading to the top of the Level 3 headings, or you can have Word do this tedious job for you.

To sort the Level 3 headings, follow these steps:

1. Click the Level 3 icon in the Outline icon bar so that the Level 4 headings are hidden.

2. Select the Level 3 headings below *Fall Quarter Performance Data*, as shown in figure 22.17.

Fig. 22.17
Selected Level 3 headings.

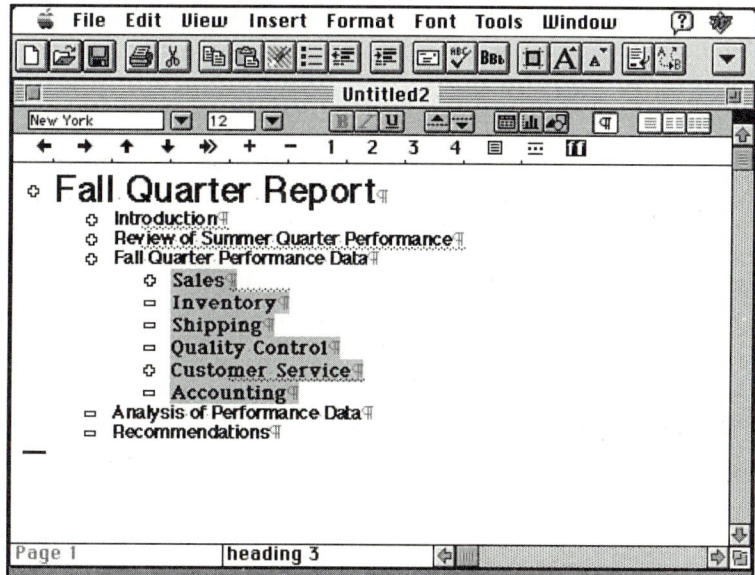

3. Choose Sort from the Tools menu. Word sorts the headings in ascending alphabetical order by default (see fig. 22.18). To sort in descending alphabetical order, hold down the Shift key before choosing Sort.

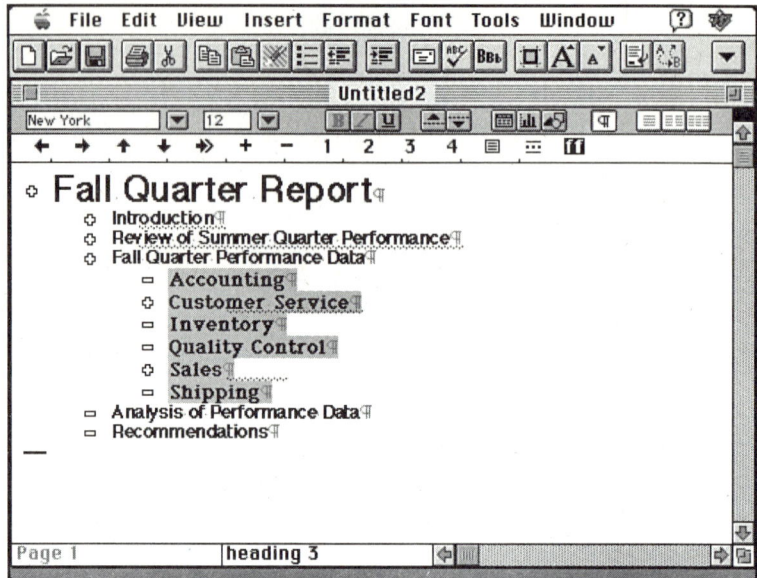

Fig. 22.18
Sorted Level 3 headings.

Fig. 22.18
Sorted Level 3 headings.

When you sort outline headings, you sort not only the headings, but also the whole document—including the body text below the headings. If you sort outline headings, you can restructure your document much more quickly than if you use ordinary cut-and-paste techniques.

Using Additional Outlining Techniques

In this section, you learn more about managing long documents with outlining. You also learn how to outline an existing document, number the headings in an outline, and print your document's outline without the body text.

Managing a Long Document with Outlining

When you create a long document, keep in mind the advantages of switching to Outline view to get a quick view of your document's structure. You can hide body text and collapse subheadings quickly by clicking one of the Level icons.

To use Outline view to move quickly through a document rather than scroll page by page, follow these steps:

1. Choose Outline from the View menu, or press ⌘-Option-O or Shift-F13. Word displays your document in Outline view.

2. Scroll the screen so that the heading you want to find in your document is positioned at the top of the window.

3. Choose Normal or Page Layout from the View menu. You see your document with the heading you want at the top of the window.

Outlining an Existing Document

To take full advantage of outlining, you can add headings to an existing document in Normal view. The key to adding headings is formatting the headings with Word's built-in heading styles, such as Heading 1 and Heading 2. (See Chapter 14, "Formatting with Styles," for information on applying Word's built-in styles to headings.)

After you format your headings this way, the headings appear as outline headings when you switch to Outline view.

Numbering Outline Headings

If you prefer a numbered outline, you can use the Renumber command in the Tools menu to add numbers quickly. In this section, you learn how to number the Level 3 headings below *Fall Quarter Performance Data* in your outline.

To add numbers to headings, follow these steps:

1. Because Word numbers only the outline headings that are visible on-screen, collapse the Level 4 headings, if necessary, by clicking the Level 3 icon.

2. Select the Level 3 headings as you did when you sorted them.

3. Choose Renumber from the Tools menu or press ⌘-F15. The Renumber dialog box appears (see fig. 22.19).

   The default settings in this dialog box are fine: Page numbering starts at 1; all selected headings are formatted; and Word uses the number series 1, 2, 3, and so on.

Fig. 22.19
Renumber dialog box.

```
┌─────────────────────── Renumber ───────────────────────┐
│  Paragraphs: ◉ All  ○ Only If Already Numbered          │
│  Start at: [1      ]      Format: [         ]           │
│  Numbers: ◉ 1  ○ 1.1...  ○ By Example  ○ Remove         │
│  ┌─ OK ─┐   [ Cancel ]                                  │
│  └──────┘                                               │
└─────────────────────────────────────────────────────────┘
```

4. Choose OK. Word numbers the Level 3 headings.

For information about the other options in the Renumber dialog box, see Chapter 16, "Numbering and Sorting Lines, Lists, and Paragraphs."

Word does not change the heading numbers if you insert or delete a heading within the numbered list. When you insert or delete a heading, you must select the headings again and then use the Renumber command again.

Printing Your Outline

Keeping a printout of your outline on hand is another way to keep the document's structure in mind. To print an outline, follow these steps:

1. Collapse headings and body text to a specific level by clicking one of the Level icons. Word prints only what appears on-screen, no matter how much body text or other material you collapsed.

2. Choose Print from the File menu, press ⌘-P, or click the Print tool. The Print dialog box appears.

3. Choose OK to print your document.

Quick Review

This section summarizes the most useful information in this chapter. Check "Productivity Tips" for a review of high-productivity tips and tricks—the ones that Macintosh and Word pros use every day. Review "Techniques" whenever you need a quick reminder about a specific procedure.

Productivity Tips

■ Learn outlining techniques if you plan to write documents (such as articles or proposals) that have internal subheadings. Word's outlining feature helps you get organized and provides powerful document-restructuring tools.

■ The icons in the Outline icon bar are useful, but you can use mouse techniques in outlining, too. For example, you can promote or demote a heading just by dragging the selection icon left or right.

■ If you don't like Word's default heading styles, redefine them before creating your document.

■ If you're working with a long document that has headings and subheadings, find your way around the document by switching to Outline view. Use the Outline view to find a section rather than scroll page after page on-screen.

■ Let Word alphabetize or number the headings in your document. Switch to Outline view, display and select the headings, and then choose Sort or Renumber from the Tools menu.

Techniques

This section provides concise summaries of all the procedures introduced in this chapter.

Displaying Character Formatting

To toggle the display of character formatting on and off:

Click the Display Character Formatting icon.

or

Use the Option-Shift-up arrow or the keypad slash (/) shortcut.

Demoting Headings

To demote a heading:

Drag the selection icon to the right.

Chapter 22

Organizing Documents with Outlining

or

Click the Demote icon in the Outline icon bar.

or

Press Option-right arrow.

Promoting Headings

To promote a heading:

Drag the selection icon to the left.

or

Click the Promote icon in the Outline icon bar.

or

Press Option-left arrow.

Displaying and Collapsing Body Text

To toggle between full display and first-line display of body text (when body text is visible):

Click the Display First Line icon in the Outline icon bar.

To hide or display body text:

Click the Display All icon or press the keypad asterisk (*).

To demote a heading to body text:

Click the Demote to Body Text icon in the Outline icon bar.

Editing the Outline

To delete a heading:

1. Move the pointer over the heading's selection icon until the pointer changes shape, and then click the mouse to select the heading.

2. Press Delete or Backspace.

To move a heading up one line in the outline:

> Click the Move Up icon or press Option-up arrow.

To move a heading down one line in the outline:

> Click the Move Down icon or press Option-down-arrow.

Collapsing Headings

To collapse the subheadings below a heading:

1. Place the insertion point in the heading.

2. Click the Collapse icon or press the keypad minus sign (–).

To collapse headings to a level you specify:

> Click one of the Level icons in the Outline icon bar.

Expanding Headings

To expand the headings below a heading:

1. Place the insertion point in the heading.

2. Click the Expand icon or press the keypad plus sign (+).

Sorting Headings

To alphabetize headings:

1. Collapse the subheadings below the headings that you want to alphabetize.

2. Select the headings.

3. Choose Sort from the Tools menu. Word sorts in ascending alphabetical order by default. To sort in descending order, hold down the Shift key before choosing Sort.

Numbering Headings

To number headings in an outline:

1. Collapse the subheadings below the headings that you want to number.

2. Select the headings.

3. Choose Renumber from the Tools menu or press ⌘-F15. The Renumber dialog box appears.

4. Choose OK.

Printing an Outline

To print your outline:

1. Display the headings that you want to print. Collapse body text if you want to.

2. Choose Print from the File menu, press ⌘-P, or click the Print tool. The Print dialog box appears.

3. Choose OK.

Using Glossaries

I f you have to say the same thing over and over, and if saying the right thing is important, Word's glossaries are for you. Using Word's glossaries, you can store carefully worded passages of text, ranging from a few words to dozens of pages, and access these glossaries quickly and easily. You also can store frequently used graphics in glossaries, using exactly the same techniques you use to store and retrieve text.

Using glossaries can increase your productivity, as shown by the following examples:

- An attorney can store and retrieve standardized passages for documents, such as wills or contracts.

- A small-business owner can create and retrieve paragraphs that respond to typical questions people ask in letters of inquiry, so that answering a letter takes only a matter of seconds.

- Because glossaries can handle graphics as well as text, a graphics designer can store frequently used graphics, such as logos or product illustrations, and retrieve them from the glossary at a keystroke.

In short, glossaries are another of Word's many features for high-productivity writing. If you're not using glossaries, you're missing ways to save time and money.

This chapter covers the following subjects:

- *Understanding glossaries.* In this section, you learn what glossaries are and how to create, store, and use them.

- *Creating and managing glossary entries.* This section details the procedures for creating glossary entries, inserting glossaries into a document, and managing glossary entries (editing, renaming, and deleting).

- *Managing glossary files.* Most Word users find the Standard Glossary file fully adequate for their needs. Some users, however, may want to create specialized glossary files for certain tasks, such as keeping a storehouse of graphics for a newsletter. In this section, you learn how to create and use specialized glossary files.

Understanding Glossaries

The term *glossary* isn't very descriptive. The term goes back to the days when this feature really was used to store a glossary of words, terms, and phrases. In the days of limited computer memory (when 64K was considered wildly luxurious), you could store only limited amounts of text in a glossary entry, so writers used glossaries to store only single words or short phrases. If you had to type *autochthonous processes of spontaneous generation* over and over, for example, you could store the phrase as a glossary item and retrieve it by typing **apsg** and entering a keyboard command.

The glossary feature is far more useful now than in the early days of personal computing. You still can use Word's glossaries to store terms and phrases, but now that storage space is limited only by the size of your disk. You can store long passages of text or graphics in glossaries. Furthermore, Word's glossaries retain the formats you applied to the text that you store in them. With such increased versatility, glossaries could be called cubbyholes for frequently accessed units of fully formatted text, such as a return address complete with a corporate logo.

Each glossary item that you create and store becomes a glossary entry in a glossary file. A *glossary entry* is a named unit of text or graphics. You can place hundreds of glossary entries in each glossary file; the only limit is the size of your disk. After creating the entry, you can insert the entry into your document quickly and easily, using a menu command or a keyboard shortcut.

You can create more than one glossary file. By default, Word uses a glossary file called the Standard Glossary. If you plan to create only a few (one or two dozen) glossary entries, you can use the Standard Glossary to store all your entries. You can add hundreds of glossary entries to the Standard Glossary, but the list of entries would become too long to scroll through conveniently. For this reason, you can create custom glossary files, in which you can place infrequently used or specialized glossary entries.

Understanding the Standard Entries

The Standard Glossary contains standard entries, all of which have special uses. These entries are available in any glossary, even the ones you create. Most of these glossary entries fall into one of the following three categories:

- *Date and time entries.* Glossary entries such as Date, Print Date, and Print Time can enter the current date or time directly into your document or add the date or time at the time of printing.

- *Summary Info entries.* Summary Info glossary entries enter text that you type in the corresponding boxes of the current document's Summary Info dialog box. These boxes include Title, Subject, Author, Version, and Keywords. If you don't fill out the Summary Info dialog box, Word doesn't enter anything when you choose the corresponding glossary entry (except Author, which uses the name that you typed when you installed Word).

  This fact suggests yet another reason for filling out Summary Info dialog boxes, which are advantageous for file-management purposes. If you fill out the Title box, for example, you can enter the document's title quickly by choosing the Title glossary.

- *File-name entries.* These glossary entries place the name of the current file in your document.

Table 23.1 lists the Standard Glossary file's standard entries.

	Entry	Description
Table 23.1 Standard Glossary Entries	Author	Enters the name of the author, as defined in the Summary Info dialog box
	Date	Enters the current date (April 1, 1992)

continues

Chapter 23

Using Glossaries

Table 23.1	*Entry*	*Description*
Continued		

Entry	Description
Date Abbreviated	Enters the current date in abbreviated form (Sat, Apr 1, 1992)
Date Long	Enters the current date in long form (Saturday, April 1, 1992)
Date Short	Enters the current date in short form (4/1/92)
Day Abbreviated	Enters the current day of the week in short form (Sat)
Day Long	Enters the current day of the week (Saturday)
Day of the Month	Enters the current day of the month (15)
File Name Only	Enters the name of the current file (Fall Quarter Report 1992)
File Name with Path	Enters the name of the current document, including volume, folder, and file name (HD80:Periodic Reports:Spring Quarter Report 1992)
Keywords	Enters the current document's keywords, as currently defined in the Summary Info dialog box
Month Abbreviated	Enters the current month in abbreviated form (Oct)
Month Long	Enters the current month in long form (December)
Month Short	Enters the number of the current month (12)
Page Number	Enters a page number at the insertion point's location; the number prints in this location on all pages of the current section
Print Date	Enters the current date (April 1, 1992)
Print Date Abbreviated	Prints the date at the time of printing, in abbreviated form (Sat, Apr 1, 1992)
Print Date Long	Prints the date at the time of printing, in long form (Saturday, April 1, 1992)
Print Date Short	Prints the date at the time of printing, in short form (4/1/92)

Entry	Description
Print Day Abbreviated	Prints the day at the time of printing, in abbreviated form (Fri)
Print Day Long	Prints the day at the time of printing, in long form (Friday)
Print Day of the Month	Prints the day of the month at time of printing (15)
Print Merge	Inserts the special symbols used to create Print Merge instructions
Print Month Abbreviated	Prints the month at the time of printing, in abbreviated form (Apr)
Print Month Long	Prints the month at the time of printing, in long form (April)
Print Month Short	Prints the month at the time of printing, in short form (12)
Print Time	Prints the time at the time of printing (10:51 AM)
Print Time with Seconds	Prints the time at the time of printing, with seconds (10:51:46 AM)
Print Year Long	Prints the year at the time of printing, in long form (1992)
Print Year Short	Prints the year at the time of printing, in short form (92)
Section	Enters the current section number
Subject	Enters the text you placed in the Subject box of the current document's Summary Info dialog box
Time	Inserts the current time (10:51 AM)
Time with Seconds	Inserts the current time, with seconds (10:51:46 AM)
Title	Inserts the current document's name (if the document has been saved)
Version	Enters the version number you placed in the Version box of the current document's Summary Info dialog box
Year Long	Enters the current year, in long form (1992)
Year Short	Enters the current year, in short form (92)

If you create stationery documents for letters, as described in Chapter 5, use the print entries to insert the date at the time of printing. Your letters always will show the correct date (the date at the time of printing).

These Standard Glossary entries always are available, even if you create your own glossary files. When you create a new glossary file, Word copies all default glossary entries to the new file. Glossary files always contain the Standard Glossary entries, which you cannot delete.

To view the Standard Glossary entries, follow these steps:

1. Choose Glossary from the Edit menu or press ⌘-K. The Glossary dialog box appears. By default, the list box shows only the user entries.

2. To display the standard entries, activate the Standard Entries check box (see fig. 23.1).

Fig. 23.1
Glossary dialog box.

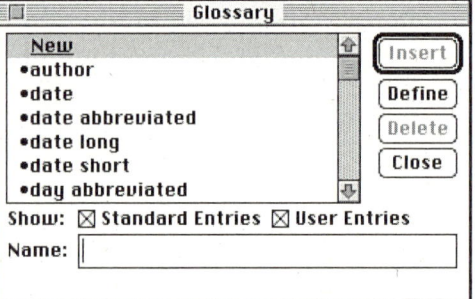

■ To help you distinguish the default glossary entries from the ones you create, bullets precede the names of the default entries in the Glossary dialog box.

Creating and Managing Glossary Entries

To create a glossary entry, select the text or graphic and then choose Glossary from the Edit menu. After creating a glossary entry, you can insert, edit, rename, or delete the entry. This section discusses these tasks.

Part IV

Creating Professional Documents

To include formatting in your glossary entries, choose Show ¶ from the View menu. Include the paragraph mark in the selection before you select the Glossary command. Because the paragraph mark contains paragraph formatting, your glossary entry retains the formats that are in effect in your document.

Creating a Glossary Entry

You can copy any amount of text to a glossary. You also can copy a graphic or text mixed with graphics. When you create the glossary entry, Word does not copy the formatting unless you include paragraph marks in the selection.

To create a glossary entry, follow these steps:

1. Select the text or graphic that you want to store in a glossary. To include paragraph formats in the glossary, be sure to include the trailing paragraph marks in the selection.

2. Choose Glossary from the Edit menu or press ⌘-K. The Glossary dialog box appears. Word highlights the New entry, which you can define (refer to fig. 23.1).

3. Type a glossary-entry name in the Name text box. You can use up to 32 characters (including spaces) to name glossary entries. Keep the name as short and as easy to remember as possible.

4. Click the Define button. Word defines the glossary entry and adds the name of the new entry to the glossary list.

5. Click Close.

Defining a glossary entry isn't the same as saving the entry. To save your glossary entries, you must use a separate procedure, described in "Managing Glossary Files" later in this chapter.

Inserting a Glossary Entry

After you create a glossary entry, you can use the menus or the keyboard to insert the entry into your text. If you use the menus to insert the entry, you don't need to know the exact name of the entry (you select the entry you want in the Glossary dialog box). To insert the entry with the keyboard, however, you must know the exact name.

To use the Glossary dialog box to insert a glossary entry, follow these steps:

1. Place the insertion point in your document where you want the glossary entry to appear.

2. Choose Glossary from the Edit menu or press ⌘-K. The Glossary dialog box appears.

3. In the list box, select the entry you want. Word displays the entry's name in the Name box and the entry's first line at the bottom of the dialog box. If the first line contains a graphic, you see a box (see fig. 23.2).

Fig. 23.2

Glossary contents shown at the bottom of the Glossary dialog box.

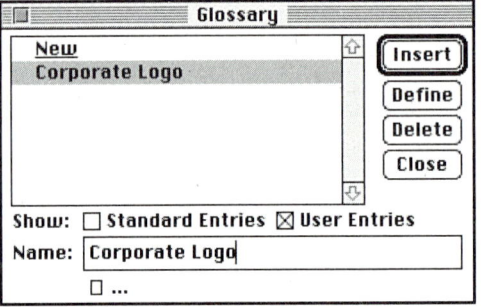

To reduce the number of entries displayed, you can deactivate the Standard Entries or User Entries check box.

4. Choose Insert. Word inserts the glossary entry into your document at the insertion point.

To insert a glossary entry with the keyboard, follow these steps:

1. Position the insertion point in your document where you want the glossary entry to appear.

2. Press ⌘-Delete or ⌘-Backspace. The message Name appears in the status bar.

3. Type the name of the glossary entry.

    You don't have to type the full name—only enough of it to help Word differentiate the entry from others. To insert the Author glossary, for example, you can type **au**, provided that no other entry begins with those letters.

4. Press Return. Word inserts the glossary entry at the insertion point.

   To cancel the operation without inserting a glossary, press Esc or ⌘-period (.).

You can add frequently chosen glossary entries to the Work menu. For more information, see Chapter 35, "Customizing Menus and Keyboard Shortcuts."

Undoing or Repeating a Glossary Entry

After you insert a glossary entry, you can cancel the insertion by immediately choosing Undo from the Edit menu or by pressing ⌘-Z. If you perform other actions after inserting the glossary entry, you need to use normal deletion techniques to remove the glossary entry from your document. You also can choose the Repeat command from the Edit menu or press ⌘-Y to insert the same entry elsewhere before you perform another action.

Editing a Glossary Entry

Editing the text that you stored in a glossary entry is easy. You simply insert the entry into a document, edit the text, and then repeat the procedure you used to define the glossary entry.

To edit a glossary entry, follow these steps:

1. Choose Glossary from the Edit menu or press ⌘-K. The Glossary dialog box appears.

2. In the list box, select the glossary entry that you want to edit.

3. Choose Insert. Word inserts the glossary entry into your document.

4. Edit and format the entry as you would edit and format any document text.

5. Select the entry.

6. Choose Glossary from the Edit menu or press ⌘-K. The Glossary dialog box reappears.

7. In the list box, select the glossary entry's name and then click Define.

8. Click Close to close the Glossary dialog box.

Chapter 23

Using Glossaries

Renaming a Glossary Entry

To rename a glossary entry, follow these steps:

1. Choose Glossary from the Edit menu or press ⌘-K. The Glossary dialog box appears.

2. Select the glossary name in the list box.

3. Select and then edit the name in the Name text box.

4. Click Define.

5. Choose Insert to enter the glossary contents into your document, or click Close to return to the document without entering the glossary.

Deleting a Glossary Entry

Eventually, some glossary entries that you create lose their usefulness. You may have created the glossary entry for a special one-time purpose, or perhaps you found an easier way to perform the same task. Whatever the reason, deleting unneeded entries makes glossaries easier to use.

To delete glossary entries, follow these steps:

1. Choose Glossary from the Edit menu or press ⌘-K. The Glossary dialog box appears.

2. In the list box, select the glossary entry that you want to delete.

3. Click Delete. An alert box appears, asking you to confirm the deletion.

4. Choose Yes to delete the glossary entry. You return to the Glossary dialog box.

5. Click Close to return to your document.

CAUTION

Word doesn't automatically save the changes you make in a glossary file: the changes are made in memory only. To make the changes permanent, you must save the glossary file, as described in the following section.

Managing Glossary Files

When you start Word, the program opens the Standard Glossary file stored in the Word folder. Don't delete or move this file. If you do, Word cannot open the Standard Glossary when you start the program.

You can save your changes to the Standard Glossary or to a custom glossary. Because Word opens the Standard Glossary when you start the program, the entries you place in that glossary are available by default, so the Standard Glossary is the best place to save glossary entries that you frequently use.

You may want to save to a custom glossary entries that you use only for certain types of documents, such as technical, medical, or legal documents. These entries are not available in the Standard Glossary. To use custom entries, you must open the appropriate custom glossary.

Saving a Glossary File

Unlike styles, which Word automatically saves when you save a document, glossary entries must be saved by choice. If you quit Word without saving your glossary changes, you lose them.

To save your glossary changes when you quit Word, follow these steps:

1. Choose Quit from the File menu or press ⌘-Q. Word closes your document, and the alert box shown in figure 23.3 appears.

Fig. 23.3
Save Changes alert box.

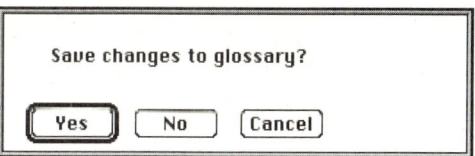

Save changes to glossary?

Yes   No   Cancel

2. Choose Yes to save your glossary entries. A Save As dialog box appears, such as the one shown in figure 23.4.

   In the Save Glossary As text box, Word suggests saving your glossary changes to the Standard Glossary—normally the best place to store your changes.

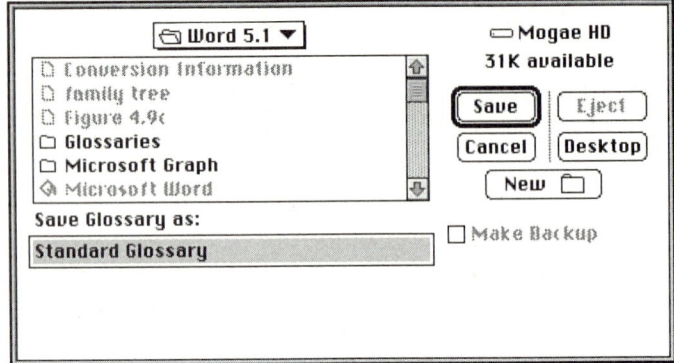

3. Perform one of the following actions:

- To save changes to the Standard Glossary, choose Save.

- To save changes to a custom glossary, select the name of the custom glossary in the list box and then choose Save.

- To create a new custom glossary, type the new glossary name in the Save Glossary As text box and then choose Save. If a glossary file with that name already exists, an alert box appears, such as the one shown in figure 23.5.

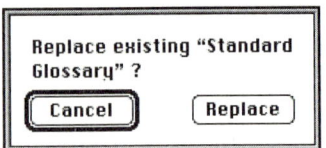

If you're sure that you want to overwrite the preceding version of the glossary, click Replace.

To save your glossary changes without quitting Word, follow these steps:

1. Choose Glossary from the Edit menu or press ⌘-K. The Glossary dialog box appears.

2. Choose Save from the File menu, press ⌘-S, or click the Save tool. A Save As dialog box appears (refer to fig. 23.4), suggesting that you save your changes to the Standard Glossary.

3. Perform one of the following actions:

- To save changes to the Standard Glossary, choose Save.

- To save changes to a custom glossary, select the name of the custom glossary in the list box and then choose Save.

- To create a new custom glossary, type the new glossary name in the Save Glossary As text box and then choose Save. If a glossary file with that name already exists, an alert box appears (refer to fig. 23.5).

If you're resaving an existing glossary, choose Replace when the alert box appears.

Creating a Custom Glossary

To create a custom glossary file, follow these steps:

1. Choose Glossary from the Edit menu or press ⌘-K. The Glossary dialog box appears.

2. Choose New from the File menu, press ⌘-N, or click the New tool. An alert box appears, asking whether you want to clear all the old entries from the new glossary file.

3. Choose Yes to clear all the old entries from the new glossary file.

4. Choose Save As from the File menu or click the Save tool. The Save As dialog box appears.

5. In the Save As dialog box, open the Glossaries folder within the Word folder.

6. Type a name for the glossary in the Save Glossary As box.

7. Choose Save.

Opening a Custom Glossary

As you already know, Word automatically opens the Standard Glossary when you start the program. To open a custom glossary, follow the procedure described in this section.

When you open a glossary, Word merges that glossary's entries with the ones currently in memory. To prevent Word from mixing the incoming entries with the ones stored in the current glossary, you must clear Word's glossary before opening the custom one. (When you clear the glossary, you clear only the entries in memory. Nothing happens to the entries stored on disk.)

To open a custom glossary, follow these steps:

1. Choose Glossary from the Edit menu or press ⌘-K. The Glossary dialog box appears.

2. Choose New from the File menu, press ⌘-N, or click the New tool. An alert box appears, asking whether you want to clear all non-standard glossary entries.

3. Choose Yes, unless you really want to merge all the current glossary entries into the custom glossary that you are opening.

   When you choose Yes, you do not erase the glossary entries or the glossary file on disk; you simply remove them from Word's memory so that the program does not merge the current entries with those in the glossary that you are opening.

4. Choose Open from the File menu, press ⌘-O, or click the Open tool. An Open dialog box appears, displaying a list of glossary files in the list box (see fig. 23.6).

Fig. 23.6
Selecting a glossary.

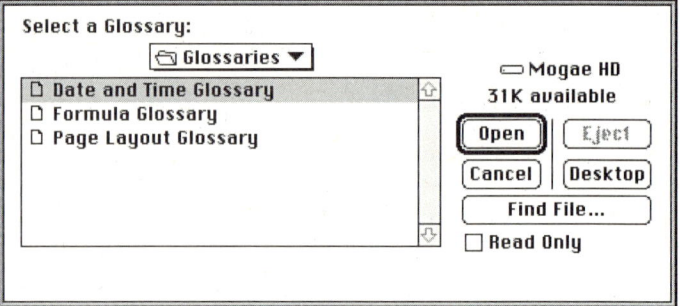

Notice that Word automatically switches to the folder in which Word's glossaries are stored. If you don't see the glossary you want to open, you can switch to another folder, or you can click Find File to search for all the glossaries in the current drive.

5. Select the glossary you want to use and then choose Open.

   If you don't see the glossary you want to use, click the Find File command button. Word opens the Find File dialog box, selects the Glossaries option in the File Type drop-down list box, and lists all the glossaries in the current drive (see fig. 23.7).

Fig. 23.7
Find File dialog box, with
Glossaries automatically
selected.

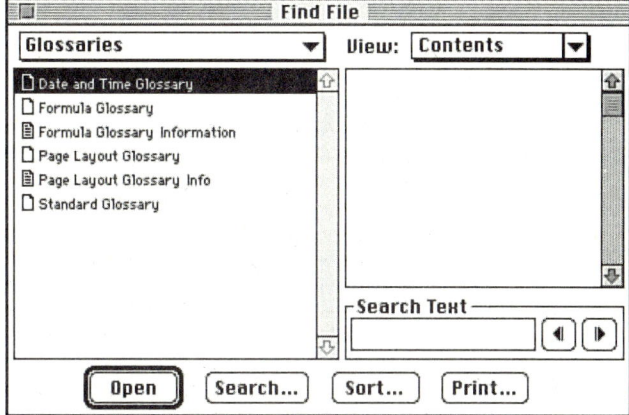

6. Select an entry to insert and then choose Insert, or click Close to return to your document.

Printing a Glossary

If you use glossaries frequently, you may want to keep a printout of the contents of your glossary files for easy reference.

In the Glossary dialog box, you see the contents (but not the graphics) of a selected entry. Word uses a system font to display the entry. Only the first few characters of text appear on-screen, but the printout shows the complete entry, alphabetized by entry names.

To print a glossary file, follow these steps:

1. Choose Glossary from the Edit menu or press ⌘-K. The Glossary dialog box appears.

2. Choose Print from the File menu, press ⌘-P, or click the Print tool. The Print dialog box appears.

3. Choose Print.

4. Click Close to close the Glossary dialog box.

Copying a Glossary Entry

After you have created two or more glossary files, you may want to copy an entry from one glossary file to another. Suppose that you create a letterhead glossary and store the information in a glossary file called Correspondence Glossary. You like the format so much that you want to copy the letterhead glossary into your Standard Glossary.

To copy a glossary entry from one glossary file to another, follow these steps:

1. Choose Glossary from the Edit menu or press ⌘-K. When the Glossary dialog box appears, select the entry you want to copy.

2. Choose Copy from the Edit menu, press ⌘-C, or click the Copy tool. Word copies the entry to the Clipboard.

3. To clear all the nonstandard glossary entries from Word's memory, choose New from the File menu, press ⌘-N, or click the New tool.

4. Choose Open from the File menu, press ⌘-O, or click the Open tool. An Open dialog box appears.

5. Select the name of the glossary file to which you want to copy the entry and then choose Open.

6. Choose Paste from the Edit menu, press ⌘-V, or click the Paste tool. Word copies the glossary entry from the Clipboard to the glossary file.

7. Click Close to close the Glossary dialog box.

Explore the custom glossaries provided with Word. In the Glossaries folder are three custom glossaries: Date and Time Glossary (which contains many entries for entering dates and times in varying formats), Formula Glossary (which is used with Word's formula-typesetting capabilities, now replaced by Equation Editor), and Page Layout Glossary. Page Layout Glossary contains sample PostScript programs that you can use to generate special text effects on a PostScript printer. For more information, see Appendix B, "Using PostScript."

Quick Review

This section summarizes the most useful information in this chapter. Check "Productivity Tips" for a review of high-productivity tips and tricks—the ones that Macintosh and Word pros use every day. Review "Techniques" whenever you need a quick reminder about a specific procedure.

Productivity Tips

■ Use a glossary entry to store and insert frequently used graphics, such as logos.

■ Explore the Standard Glossary entries. Many entries can save you time by automatically entering the date, the time, and details about the current document (such as Author, Subject, Title, and Keywords).

■ Create stationery documents that include the Print Date glossary. Word then prints the current date when you print a new document that you created from a stationery document.

■ If you want your glossary entries to include formatting, make sure that you include the trailing paragraph mark in the selection when you define an entry.

■ Save frequently used glossary entries to the Standard Glossary, which Word opens every time you start the program.

■ If you develop many glossary entries for a type of document that you create infrequently, save these entries to a custom glossary.

■ To avoid merging glossaries, always clear Word's glossary memory (by using the New command with the Glossary dialog box displayed) before you open a custom glossary or switch back to the Standard Glossary.

Techniques

This section provides concise summaries of all the procedures introduced in this chapter.

Defining Glossary Entries

To create a glossary entry:

1. Select the text or graphic you want to store in a glossary.

2. Choose Glossary from the Edit menu or press ⌘-K. The Glossary dialog box appears.

3. Type a glossary-entry name in the Name text box.

4. Click the Define button.

5. Click Close.

Chapter 23

Using Glossaries

Inserting Glossary Entries

To insert a glossary entry with the Glossary dialog box:

1. Place the insertion point in your document where you want the glossary entry to appear.

2. Choose Glossary from the Edit menu or press ⌘-K. The Glossary dialog box appears.

3. If you want, deactivate the Standard Entries or User Entries option to reduce the number of entries displayed.

4. In the list box, select the entry you want.

5. Choose Insert.

To insert a glossary entry with the keyboard:

1. Position the insertion point in your document where you want the glossary entry to appear.

2. Press ⌘-Delete. The message Name appears in the status bar.

3. Type the name of the glossary entry and then press Return.

    To cancel without inserting a glossary, press Esc or ⌘-period (.).

    To undo a glossary entry after inserting the entry (but before you perform another action), choose Undo from the Edit menu or press ⌘-Z.

    To repeat a glossary-entry insertion before you perform another action, move the insertion point to the place where you want the entry to appear and then choose Repeat from the Edit menu or press ⌘-Y.

Editing Glossary Entries

To edit a glossary entry:

1. Choose Glossary from the Edit menu or press ⌘-K. The Glossary dialog box appears.

2. In the list box, select the glossary entry you want to edit and then choose Insert. Word inserts the entry into your document.

3. Edit and format the entry as you would edit and format any document text.

4. Select the entry.

5. Choose Glossary from the Edit menu or press ⌘-K. The Glossary dialog box reappears.

6. Select the glossary entry in the list box and then click Define.

7. Click Close.

Renaming Glossary Entries

To rename a glossary entry:

1. Choose Glossary from the Edit menu or press ⌘-K. The Glossary dialog box appears.

2. Select the glossary name in the list box.

3. Select and edit the name in the Name text box.

4. Click Define.

5. Click Close.

Deleting Glossary Entries

To delete a glossary entry:

1. Choose Glossary from the Edit menu or press ⌘-K. The Glossary dialog box appears.

2. In the list box, select the glossary entry you want to delete.

3. Click the Delete button. An alert box appears, asking you to confirm the deletion.

4. Choose Yes to confirm the deletion.

Saving Glossary Files

To save your glossary changes when you quit Word:

1. Choose Quit from the File menu or press ⌘-Q. Word closes your document, and a Save Changes alert box appears.

2. Choose Yes to save your glossary entries.

3. Perform one of the following actions:

   ■ To save your changes to the Standard Glossary, choose Save.

   ■ To save your changes to a custom glossary, select the name of the custom glossary in the list box and then choose Save.

   ■ To create a new custom glossary, type the new glossary name in the text box and then choose Save. If a glossary file with that name already exists, an alert box appears.

If you're resaving an existing glossary, choose Replace.

To save your glossary changes without quitting Word:

1. Choose Glossary from the Edit menu or press ⌘-K. The Glossary dialog box appears.

2. Choose Save from the File menu, press ⌘-S, or click the Save tool. A Save As dialog box appears.

3. Perform one of the following actions:

   ■ To save changes to the Standard Glossary, choose Save.

   ■ To save changes to a custom glossary, select the name of the custom glossary in the list box and then choose Save.

   ■ To create a new custom glossary, type the new glossary name in the Save Glossary As text box and then choose Save. If a glossary file with that name already exists, an alert box appears.

If you're resaving an existing glossary, choose Replace.

Opening Custom Glossaries

To open a custom glossary:

1. Choose Glossary from the Edit menu or press ⌘-K. The Glossary dialog box appears.

2. Choose New from the File menu, press ⌘-N, or click the New tool. An alert box appears, asking whether you want to clear all non-standard glossary entries.

3. Choose Yes to delete all the nonstandard entries (so that Word doesn't merge these entries with the glossary you're opening).

4. Choose Open from the File menu, press ⌘-O, or click the Open tool. An Open dialog box appears.

5. Select the glossary you want to use and then choose Open.

6. Click Close.

Printing Glossary Files

To print a glossary file:

1. Choose Glossary from the Edit menu or press ⌘-K. The Glossary dialog box appears.

2. Choose Print from the File menu, press ⌘-P, or click the Print tool. The Print dialog box appears.

3. Choose Print.

4. Click Close to close the Glossary dialog box.

Copying Glossary Entries

To copy a glossary entry from one glossary file to another:

1. Choose Glossary from the Edit menu or press ⌘-K. When the Glossary dialog box appears, select the entry you want to copy.

2. Choose Copy from the Edit menu, press ⌘-C, or click the Copy tool. Word copies the selected entry to the Clipboard.

3. Choose New from the File menu, press ⌘-N, or click the New tool to clear all nonstandard glossary entries from Word's memory.

4. Choose Open from the File menu, press ⌘-O, or click the Open tool. An Open dialog box appears.

5. Select the name of the glossary file to which you want to copy the entry and then choose Open.

6. Choose Paste from the Edit menu, press ⌘-V, or click the Paste tool. Word pastes the glossary entry into the glossary file.

7. Click Close.

Creating Charts with Microsoft Graph

 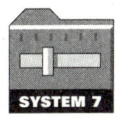

A chart can quickly and succinctly convey information that would require a great deal of text to convey. To include a chart in your Word document, you can import charts from Microsoft Excel or other programs that are capable of creating charts. Word 5.1 users who have equipped their systems with System 7, however, have another option: Microsoft Graph.

Microsoft Graph is a program that you use within compatible programs, such as Microsoft Word 5.1, to display data in graphic form. Microsoft Graph uses System 7's *object linking and embedding* (OLE) capabilities. In technical terms, Graph is an *OLE applet*, a mini program that isn't designed to run by itself but to be accessed from within other programs.

For now, all you need to know about OLE is that the charts you create with Microsoft Graph are not stored in their own files. On the contrary, the charts are *embedded* within your Word document—actually part of your Word document's file. When you use Microsoft Graph, Equation Editor, or any other OLE applet, you create a *compound document*—a file that contains portions created by more than one program. In practical terms, the benefit of a compound document becomes clear when you need to edit the data. You simply double-click the embedded

object (here, a chart), and System 7 starts the program that created the data. You can make the needed changes, and when you exit the program, your Macintosh updates the object in your Word document. You learn more about OLE in Chapter 30, "Linking Data Dynamically."

If you use Microsoft Excel for the Macintosh, Graph will seem very familiar; this program's charting capabilities are similar to those of Excel. If you already know how to use these capabilities, you will master Microsoft Graph in short order.

In this chapter, you learn how to transform data into striking visuals with Microsoft Graph. This subject is barely covered in Word's documentation, so you might think that Microsoft Graph is a simple subject. Not so! Even this long chapter cannot cover every aspect of creating charts with Microsoft Graph. For example, the chapter doesn't attempt to cover specialized applications such as typing data for x-y charts, creating charts to track stock prices, creating overlay charts with two different y-axis scales, or importing data from Excel or other spreadsheet programs. The chapter does, however, cover all the fundamentals. (For detailed information on advanced chart-making skills, consult Que's *Using Excel 4, Special Edition*.)

This chapter covers the following topics:

- *Starting and exiting Microsoft Graph.* You learn how to access Graph by using System 7's super-nifty object linking and embedding (OLE) techniques.

- *Understanding the graph windows.* You learn how to display the data underlying your graph and the graph produced from that data.

- *Creating charts.* In this section, a step-by-step tutorial walks you through the process of creating a chart with Graph.

- *Choosing a chart type.* You learn how to choose among Graph's chart-type options, including bar charts, line charts, and area charts.

- *Formatting chart data.* You can choose numeric formats for your data.

- *Enhancing a chart's appearance.* You can add text styles, change the legend position, and add grid lines and axis patterns.

- *Scaling a chart.* You can manually adjust the scale of a chart to emphasize your data.

Starting and Exiting Microsoft Graph

Because Microsoft Graph is an OLE applet, you cannot run the program by itself. You must access Graph from within another OLE-capable program, such as Microsoft Word. In this section, you learn how to start Microsoft Graph and how to return to Word.

To start Microsoft Graph, follow these steps:

1. In a Word document, position the insertion point where you want the chart to appear.

2. Choose Object from the Insert menu. The Object Type dialog box appears. Select Microsoft Graph in the Object Type list.

   Alternatively, click the Graph icon in the ribbon. Microsoft Graph starts, and you see the default chart shown in figure 24.1.

Fig. 24.1
Microsoft Graph's
initial screen.

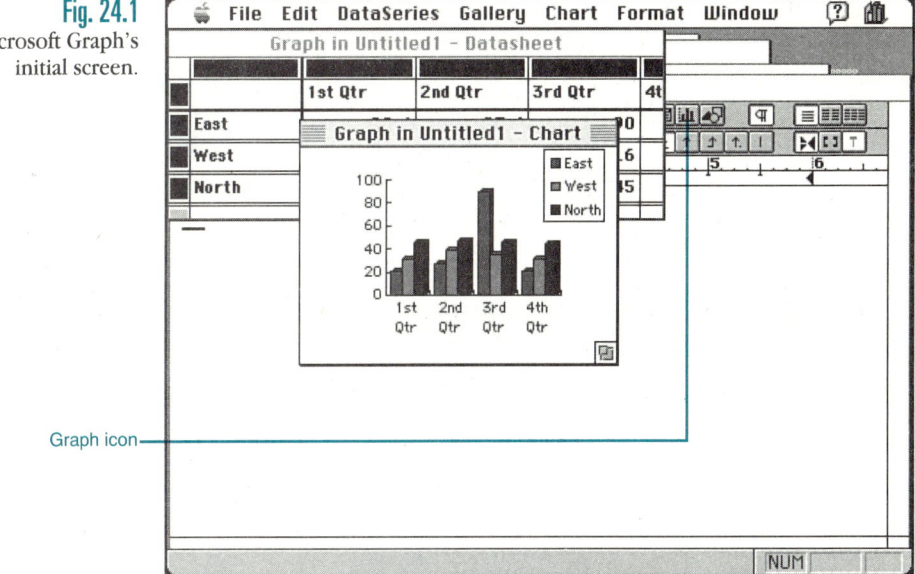

Graph icon

This chart and its underlying data always appear when you start Microsoft Graph. You can build a chart quickly by modifying the default chart.

Chapter 24
Creating Charts with Microsoft Graph

NOTE You can save one of your own charts as the default chart. Why would you want to create your own default chart? Suppose that you frequently use pie charts. If you create a pie chart and make it the default chart, you see this pie chart every time you start Microsoft Graph. You then can modify this chart. For more information, see "Setting the Default Chart" later in this chapter.

To exit Microsoft Graph, follow these steps:

1. Choose Quit and Return from the File menu (this command is followed by the name of the current Word document), or press ⌘-Q. An alert box appears, asking whether you want to update the chart in your Word document.

2. Choose Yes to include the chart. (If you click No, Word does not include the chart in your document.) The chart appears in your Word document (see fig. 24.2).

Fig. 24.2
Chart added to Word document.

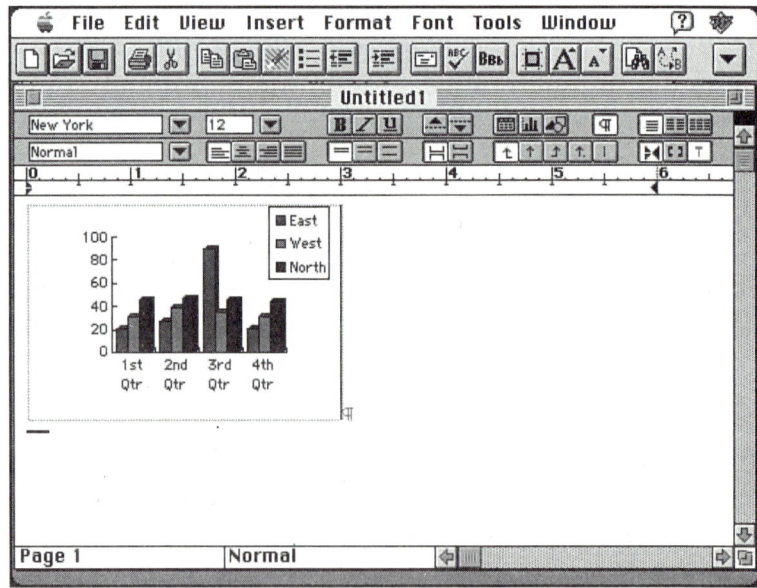

After you insert a chart into your document, you can edit it easily and quickly. Double-click the chart, and Microsoft Graph starts, displaying your chart; you can edit the chart as you please. To exit Microsoft Graph, choose Quit and Return from the File menu. When the alert box appears, choose Yes to update the chart in your Word document.

Understanding the Graph Windows

Microsoft Graph displays two windows:

■ *Datasheet window.* In this window, you type the information that underlies the chart. (You can import the data from a spreadsheet program, if you prefer.) You also type headings and titles in the datasheet window.

■ *Chart window.* This window shows the chart that is based on the data in the datasheet window. You can change the chart type (for example, bar, line, area, and pie).

If you have never created charts before, you should learn a few key terms before you use Microsoft Graph. Learning these terms helps you understand the relationship between the datasheet and the chart.

■ *x-axis (categories axis).* Most charts have two axes: a horizontal axis (x-axis) and a vertical axis (y-axis). In the simple column chart shown in figure 24.3, the x-axis shows the *categories* of the item being measured—here, sales by quarter for the East region. The categories are 1st Qtr, 2nd Qtr, and so on.

Fig. 24.3

Simple column chart.

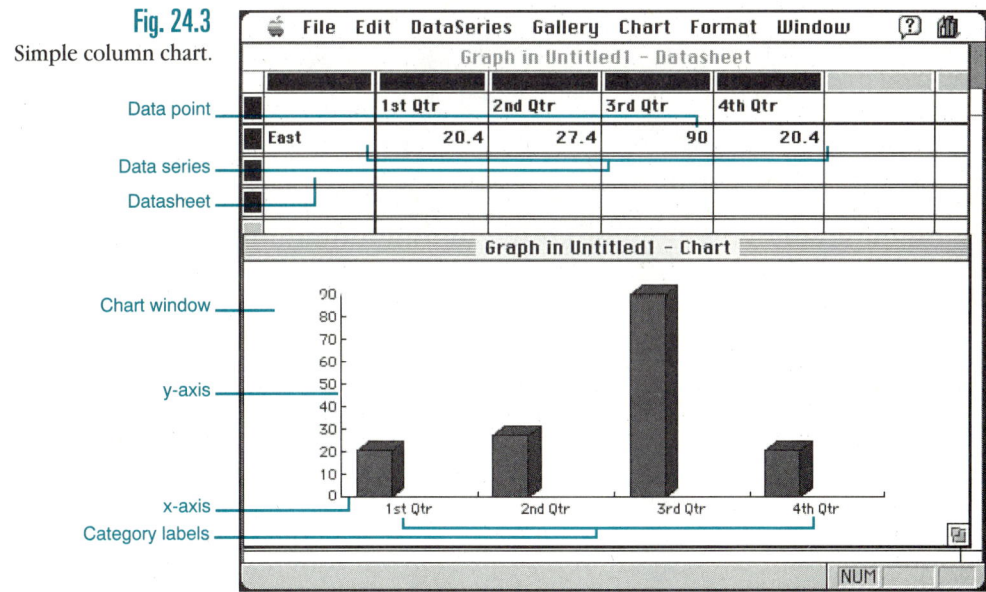

Chapter 24

Creating Charts with Microsoft Graph

■ *Category labels.* You type category labels (1st Qtr, 2nd Qtr, and so on) in the datasheet. Microsoft Graph automatically places these labels below the x-axis, as shown in figure 24.3.

■ *y-axis (values axis).* In a column chart, the vertical axis (the y-axis) measures the items being displayed. You don't have to worry about setting these values, although you can adjust or *scale* this axis. Microsoft Graph sets the scale automatically, based on the data you typed in the datasheet.

Notice the tick marks on the y-axis. You can add grid lines to the chart, if you want, to help viewers determine the magnitude of an item more easily.

■ *Data series.* A data series is a complete collection of data about one subject. In figure 24.3, for example, you see a data series consisting of quarterly sales for the East region. In many charts, however, you see more than one data series. Figure 24.4, for example, shows an enlarged version of the default datasheet and chart, which contain three data series: one each for East, West, and North.

Fig. 24.4
Column chart with three data series.

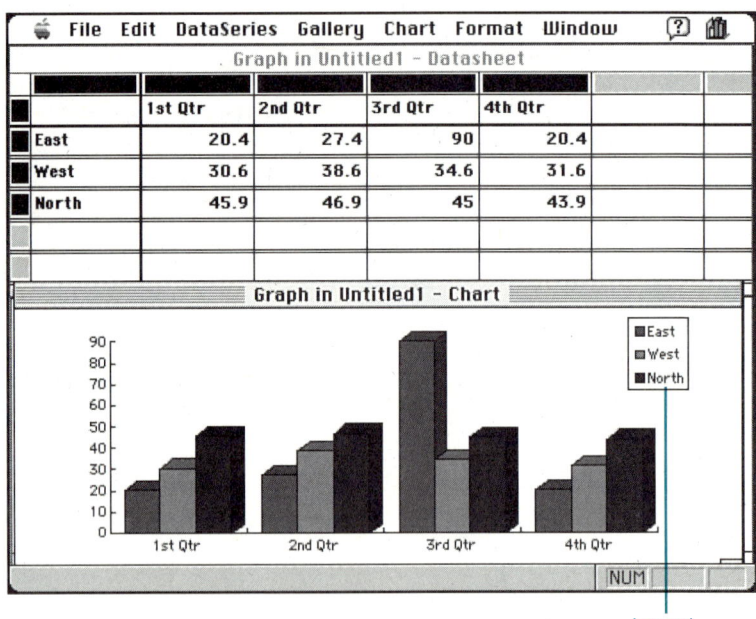

Legend

Part IV
Creating Professional Documents

■ *Data point.* A data series is made up of individual numbers called data points.

■ *Legend.* A legend, positioned in a box in the upper right corner of the chart in figure 24.4, provides a key to the data series shown in the chart. The legend is optional but helpful in a chart that shows more than one data series.

Creating Your Own Chart

Now that you know the basic terms, you can try your hand at making your own chart. This section includes a tutorial that walks you through the chart-making process. The section also introduces many additional aspects of chart-making.

Entering Data in the Datasheet

The first step in creating a chart is entering data in the datasheet. To enter the datasheet data for your chart, follow these steps:

1. Start Microsoft Graph and display the default chart. Click the datasheet window and enlarge it to fill the screen. To enlarge the datasheet window, click the zoom box in the upper right corner of the window.

2. In the cell that now says 1st Qtr, type **Napa**. As you type, Microsoft Graph replaces the existing text in that cell. Press Return to confirm the new entry.

3. Press Tab or the right-arrow key to move to the next cell (alternatively, you can click the mouse in the next cell) and then type **Sonoma**.

4. Move to the next cell and then type **Mendocino**.

5. Move to the next cell and then type **Central Coast**.

   Notice that this label is slightly too long for the cell. You can widen the cell by moving the mouse pointer to the right border of the top cell in this column (the one with the black background). When the mouse pointer changes to a line with arrows pointing left and right, drag the column boundary to the right.

   Your datasheet should look like the one shown in figure 24.5.

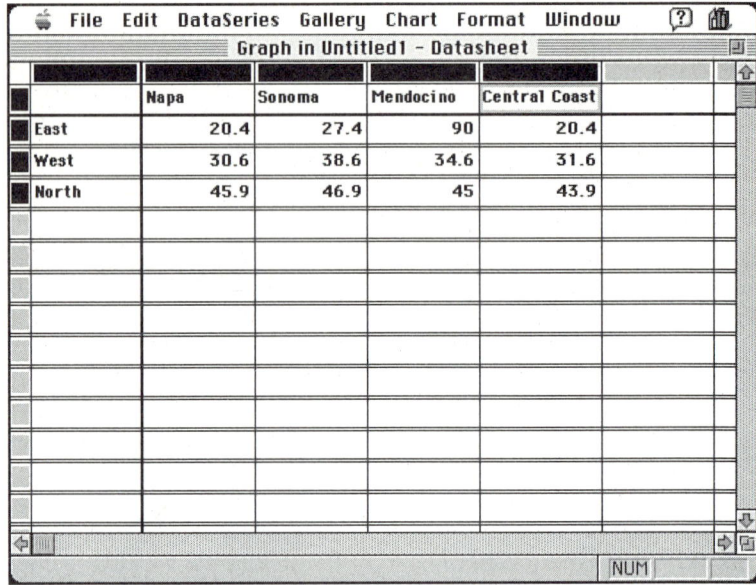

Fig. 24.5
Building your datasheet.

6. Complete the datasheet by adding the remaining data and labels, as follows (use the mouse to expand the first column so the labels will fit):

	Napa	Sonoma	Mendocino	Central Coast
Chardonnay	994	1129	2298	1675
Sauvignon Blanc	728	898	997	1358
Gewurztraminer	554	212	338	946

Your chart should look like the one shown in figure 24.6.

7. Did you make a typographical error? If so, you can edit any cell by double-clicking it. The Cell Data dialog box appears, displaying the content of the cell in a text box (see fig. 24.7). Edit the text in the text box and then choose OK.

Part IV

Creating Professional Documents

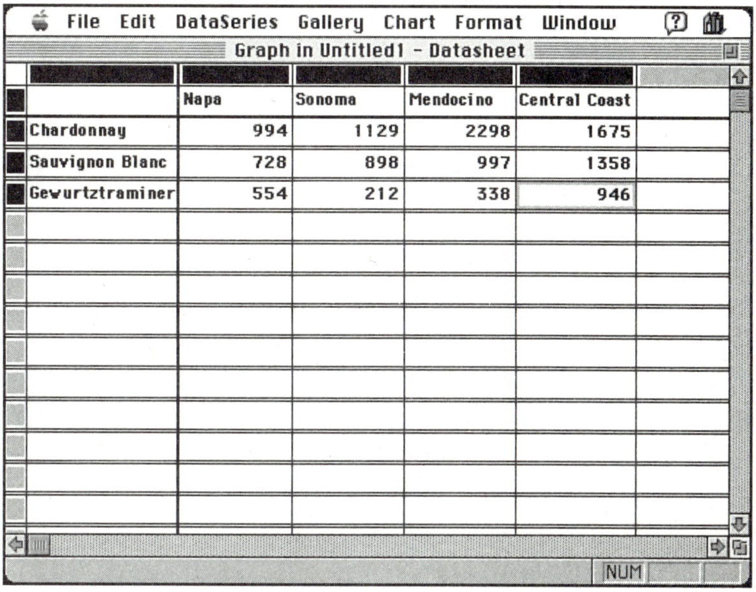

Fig. 24.6
Completed datasheet.

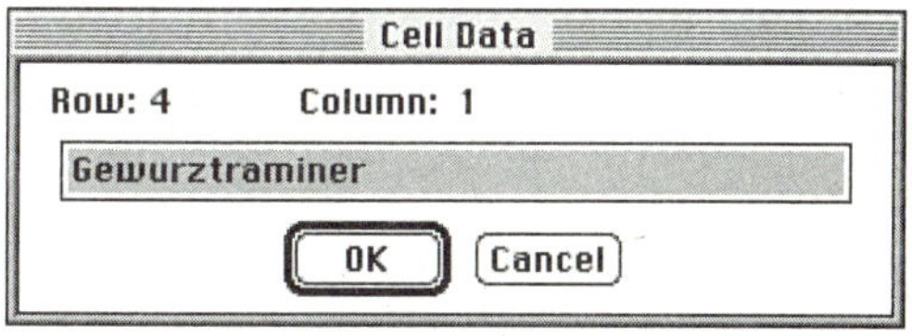

	Napa	Sonoma	Mendocino	Central Coast	
Chardonnay	994	1129	2298	1675	
Sauvignon Blanc	728	898	997	1358	
Gewurztraminer	554	212	338	946	

🍎 File Edit DataSeries Gallery Chart Format Window ⑦ 🏛

Graph in Untitled1 - Datasheet

NUM

Fig. 24.7
Cell Data dialog box.

Cell Data

Row: 4   Column: 1

Gewurztraminer

OK   Cancel

Creating the Chart

To display and embellish your chart, follow these steps:

1. Choose Chart from the Window menu. From the same menu, choose 100% View. You see your chart in a window, as shown in figure 24.8.

   As you can see from the figure, this chart looks OK, but a title would give the chart meaning.

2. Choose Titles from the Chart menu. The Attach Title dialog box appears (see fig. 24.9).

Chapter 24
Creating Charts with Microsoft Graph

Fig. 24.8
Chart produced from
data in datasheet.

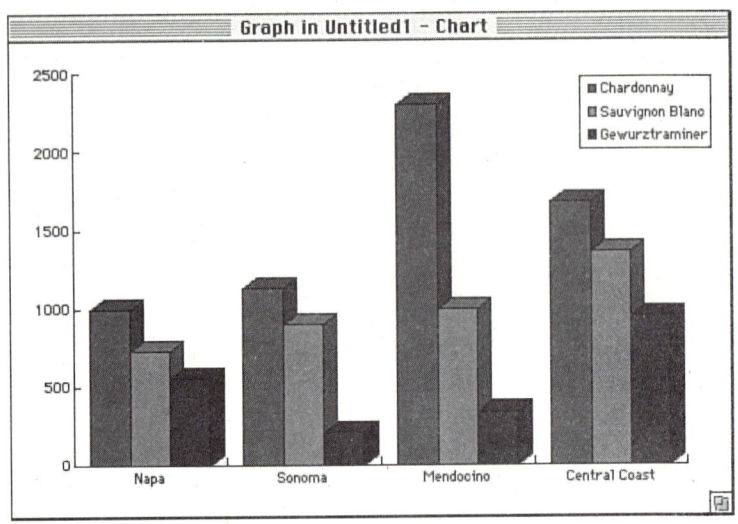

Fig. 24.9
Attach Title dialog box.

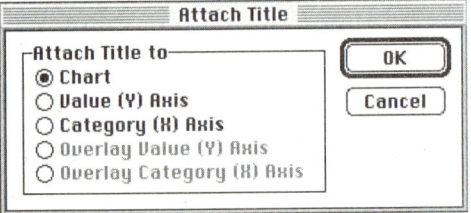

3. Choose the Chart option and then choose OK. You see a text box in your chart containing the word `Title`; the text box has eight white handles around it. The white handles indicate that the title is *attached text* and cannot be sized. (Attached text is linked to a specific area of the chart; Microsoft Graph adjusts the text's size automatically.)

4. In the text box, type **Estate-Bottled Wine Production (Cases)**. As you type, you see that you don't have enough room in the text box, but don't worry—Microsoft Graph adjusts the size of the text box to accommodate the text that you type.

5. Click outside the text box to confirm the title.

   If you see that you have made a typographical error, activate the text box by clicking it, correct the error, and then click outside the text box again to confirm the change.

6. Choose Titles from the Chart menu again and then choose the Category (X) Axis option. A text box appears at the bottom of the chart.

7. In the text box, type **Wine-Producing Regions**. Your chart should now look like the one shown in figure 24.10.

Fig. 24.10
Title added to chart.

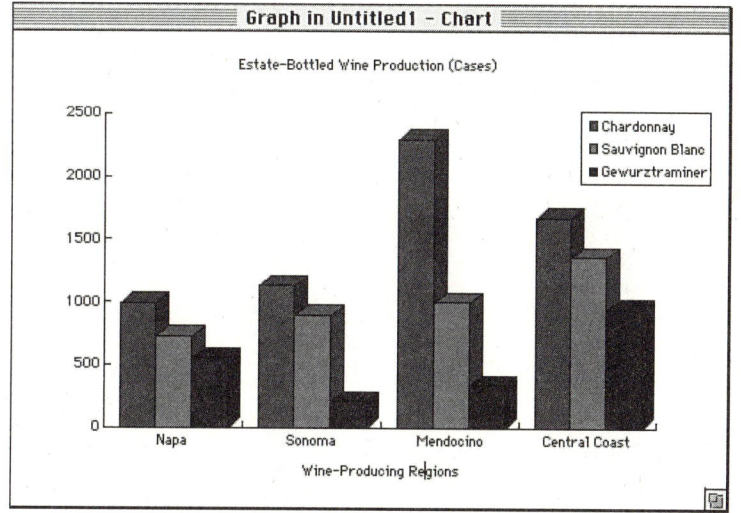

Obviously, the chart title needs formatting to make it more prominent. In the following steps, you learn how to format attached text.

8. Click the chart title, *Estate-Bottled Wine Production (Cases)*, so that the white handles appear around it.

9. Choose Font from the Format menu. The Chart Fonts dialog box appears (see fig. 24.11).

10. In the Font list box, select Helvetica. In the Size list box, select 18. In the Style area, choose Bold. Then choose OK to confirm your choices.

11. Your readers may appreciate your adding explanatory text that points out the chart's significance. You can add text anywhere in the chart simply by typing in the chart when no attached text is selected. Word places the text in a text box that (unlike attached-text boxes) you can size and move. This text is called *unattached text*.

Chapter 24

Creating Charts with Microsoft Graph

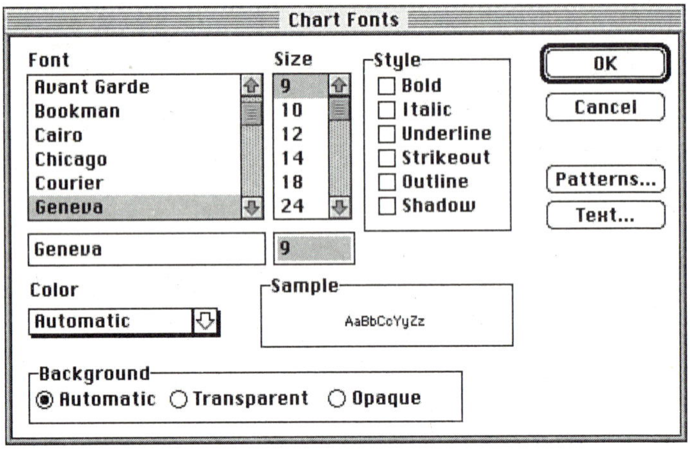

Fig. 24.11

Chart Fonts dialog box.

Fig. 24.11 Chart Fonts dialog box.

Try typing some unattached text. Place the insertion point any-where in the chart and then type the following text: **Mendocino wins the Chardonnay sweepstakes . . . [press Return] But the Central Coast has more balanced production**.

Now size and move the text to the blank area in the upper left corner of the chart area. To size the text box, drag one of the handles. To move the text box, move the mouse pointer to the edge of the box until the pointer changes shape to an arrow and then drag the box. To format the text, select the text box and choose Font from the Format menu to open the Chart Fonts dialog box, where you can make your formatting choices.

12. Add arrows to the chart by choosing Add Arrow from the Chart menu. Microsoft Graph adds the arrow with two handles, one on each end. Drag the handles to position the arrow. Your chart should resemble figure 24.12.

Inserting the Chart into a Word Document

To insert the chart you have just created into your Word document, follow these steps:

1. Choose Update from the File menu. Word adds the chart to your document.

2. Choose Quit and Return from the same menu or press ⌘-Q. The chart appears in your Word document (see fig. 24.13).

Fig. 24.12
Arrows added to chart.

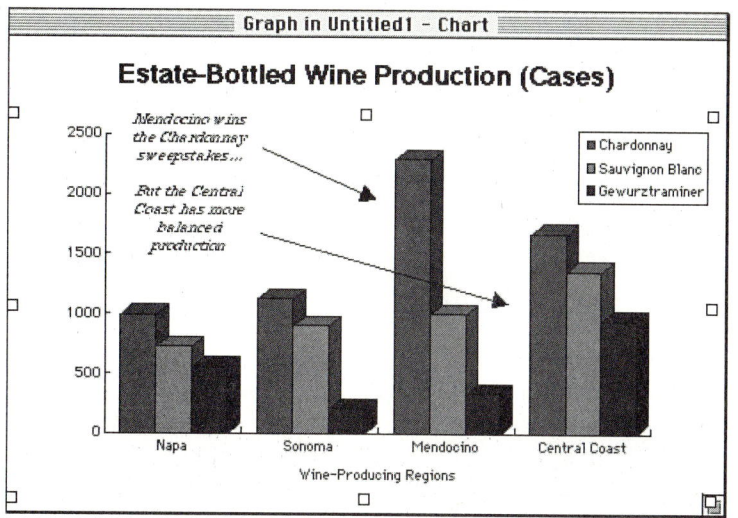

Fig. 24.13
Chart in a Word document.

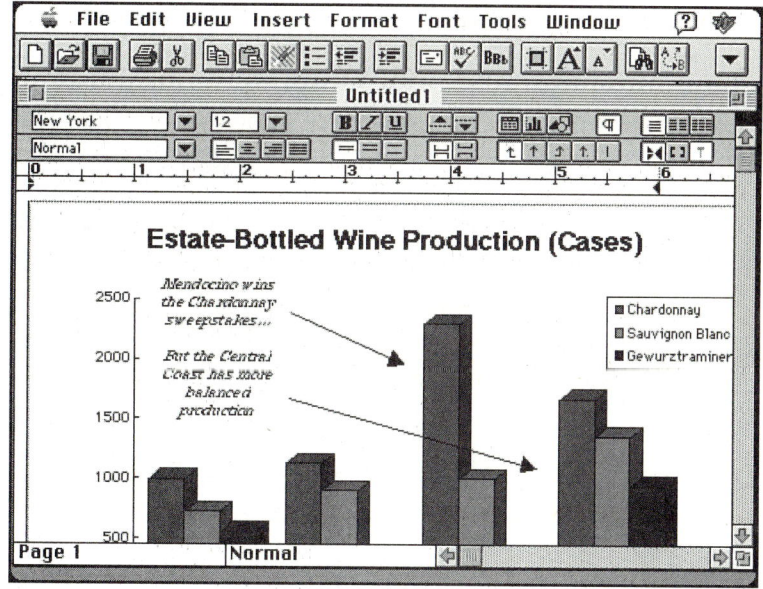

You can size, scale, move, copy, or delete this chart the way you would any other graphic element. For information on these procedures, see Chapter 7, "Creating and Importing Graphics."

Chapter 24

Creating Charts with Microsoft Graph

After you insert the chart into your Word document, save the Word document.

NOTE

You can edit the chart at any time by double-clicking anywhere in the chart area. Microsoft Graph starts, and you see your chart displayed in the Chart window.

Choosing the Chart Type

In the tutorial you just completed, you used Microsoft Graph's default chart type, the column chart. A column chart is a good choice when you want to group items by category and compare them, as the wine-production chart does. You can choose among many additional chart types, however, as the following list shows:

■ *Area charts* (see fig. 24.14) show the totals of all the data points in the chart categories as colored masses stacked on top of one another. You can use an area chart to show how individual values change over time in proportion to the total stacked values.

Fig. 24.14
Area chart.

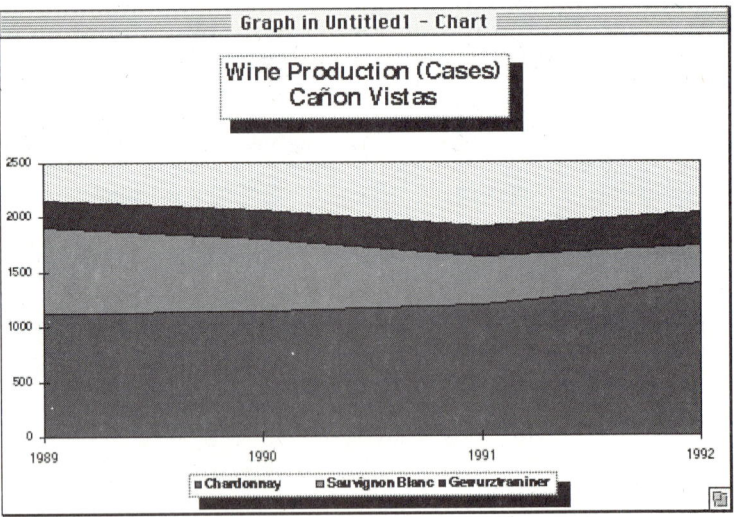

■ *Line charts* (see fig. 24.15) use continuous lines to connect the data points in a data series. Line charts highlight trends over time. A special type of line chart called·the *high-low-close-open* chart is used to track stock prices.

Fig. 24.15
Line chart.

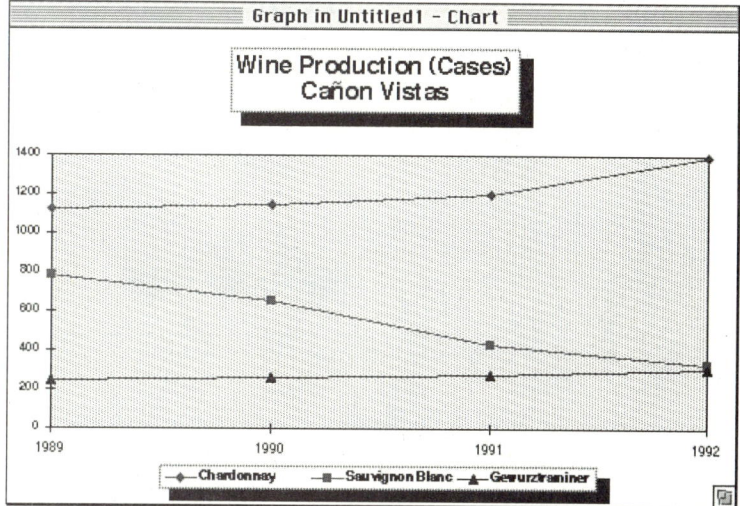

■ *Bar charts* (see fig. 24.16) invert the x- and y-axes. These charts are useful for comparing items, especially when the x-axis titles (now on the vertical axis) are long and wouldn't fit well on the horizontal axis.

■ *Pie charts* (see fig. 24.17) show the parts of a whole. A pie chart can show only one data series.

■ *100% column charts* (see fig. 24.18), like pie charts, show the parts of a whole but can show more than one data series.

■ *Combination charts* show data series in two or more chart types. Figure 24.19, for example, shows a combination column and area chart.

Chapter 24
Creating Charts with Microsoft Graph

Fig. 24.16
Bar chart.

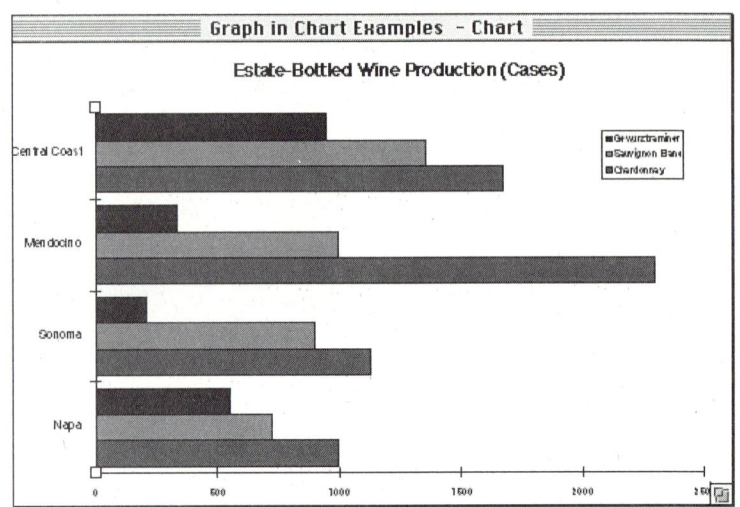

Fig. 24.17
Pie chart.

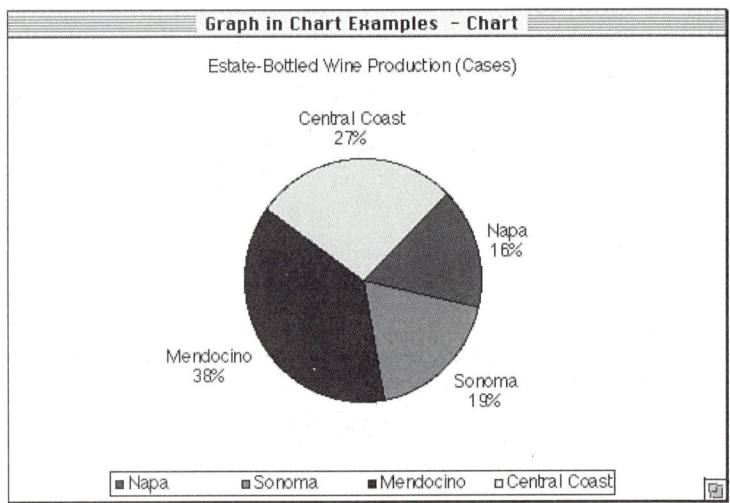

Fig. 24.18
100% column chart.

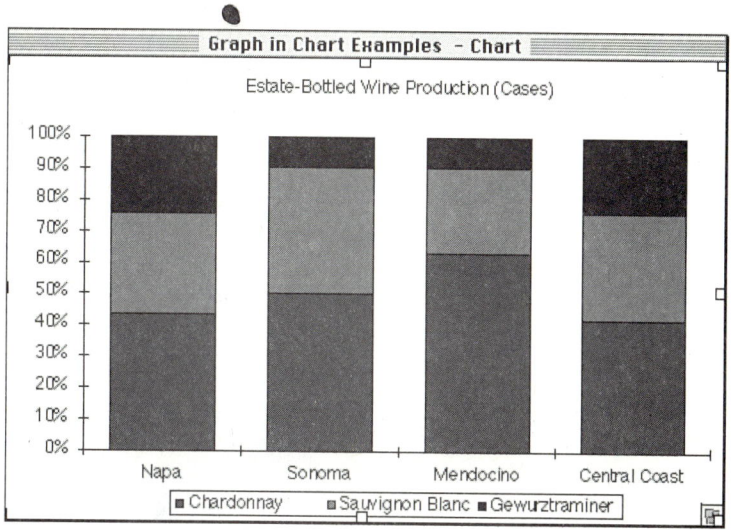

Fig. 24.19
Combination chart.

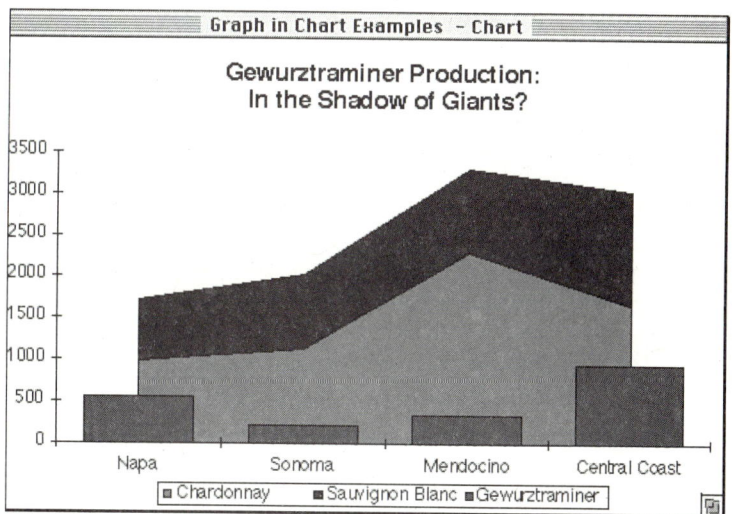

Chapter 24
Creating Charts with Microsoft Graph

■ *3-D charts* (see fig. 24.20) represent patterns and trends in dramatic three-dimensional shapes.

Fig. 24.20
3-D chart.

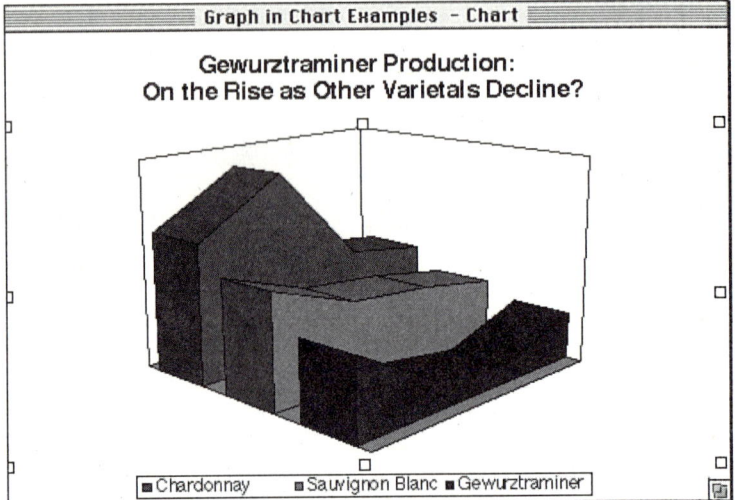

■ *x-y graphs* use two numeric scales to plot data points. You can use x-y graphs to show how increases in one area lead to corresponding effects in another area. In figure 24.21, for example, you see how advertisements appearing in all media during a given period affected wine sales.

Changing the Chart Type

You can change the chart type at any time, even after you type the underlying data. (If you type more than one data series and choose a pie chart, you see only the first data series displayed, but Microsoft Graph preserves the data you typed.) A better procedure, however, is to decide which chart type you want to use before you add custom formatting, such as grid lines. With some chart choices, you lose custom formats.

To change the chart type, follow these steps:

1. Choose a chart type from the Gallery menu. The Chart Gallery dialog box for the chart type you chose appears. Figure 24.22 shows the Chart Gallery dialog box for column charts.

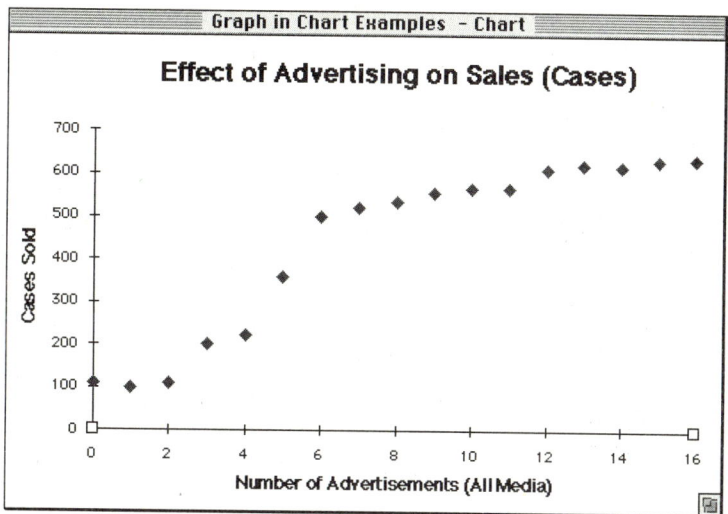

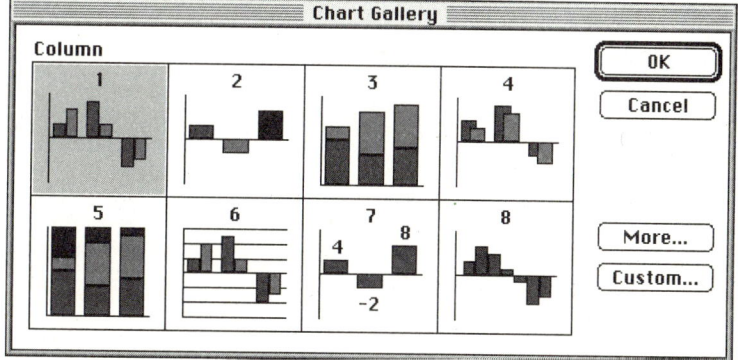

The options you see in the Chart Gallery dialog box depend on which chart type you chose, but you may be able to choose *grid lines* (lines that help you determine the values of bars, columns, lines, and areas); *data labels* (numbers placed next to the shape that measures an item); *stacking* (placing grouped values on top of one another); and *100% options*, which show all the values as proportions of a whole.

2. Click the box that contains the chart type you want. Alternatively, click More to see additional chart types.

Chapter 24
Creating Charts with Microsoft Graph

If you click Custom, you can create your own chart types by varying such aspects as bar overlap, line format, 3-D depth, and pie-slice angle.

3. Choose OK to confirm your choices.

Formatting the Data

In spreadsheet programs, you can choose a *numeric format*, such as Percent or Currency, that automatically affects the way numbers appear in your worksheet. If you choose Percent, for example, the value you type as **.06** appears on-screen as 6%. Similarly, you can choose numeric formats for the numbers displayed in your Microsoft Graph charts.

To choose a numeric format, follow these steps:

1. In the Datasheet window, select the cells you want to format.

2. Choose Number from the Format menu. The Number dialog box appears (see fig. 24.23).

Fig. 24.23
Number dialog box.

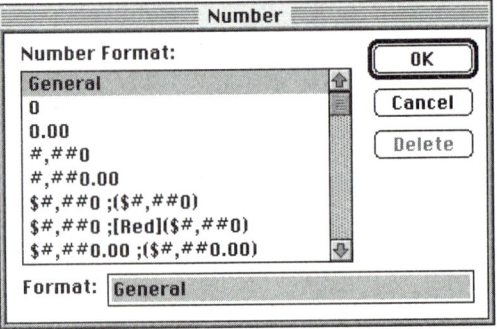

3. Select a format in the Number Format list box. (See the table following these steps for explanations of these formats.) Notice that a semicolon is used to separate positive-number formats from negative-number formats. For example, the following format displays negative numbers in red: `$#,##0.00;[Red]($#,##0.00)`. This format also displays a dollar sign, uses a comma to separate thousands, and displays two decimal places.

You also can create a custom numeric format by typing symbols in the Format text box.

4. Choose OK to confirm your choices.

Table 24.1 explains the number-format symbols in the Number dialog box.

Table 24.1
Number-Format Symbols

Symbol	Displays numbers as
0	A digit, even if the digit is 0
#	A digit, only if the digit is not 0
.	Decimal point
,	Thousands separator
%	Percentage (multiplies number entered by 100)
$	Displays this character
-	Displays this character
_	Displays this character
(	Displays this character
)	Displays this character
(space)	Enters a space
[Yellow]	Displays the number in the indicated color
d	Displays the day as a number
dd	Displays the day as a two-digit number
ddd	Displays a three-character abbreviation for the day of the week
m	Displays the month as a number
mm	Displays the month as a two-digit number
mmm	Displays a three-character abbreviation for the month
mmmm	Displays the month as a complete word
yy	Displays the last two digits of the year
yyyy	Displays all four digits of the year
h	Displays the hour
mm	Displays the minutes
ss	Displays the seconds
E-, E+, e-, e+	Displays the number in scientific notation
"text"	Displays the text within the quotation marks
*	Repeats a character to fill the column

Chapter 24
Creating Charts with Microsoft Graph

Enhancing the Chart's Appearance

You can change virtually all aspects of your chart's appearance, including text attributes, legend position, grid lines, axis patterns, and scaling.

Changing Text Attributes

In the tutorial that opened this chapter, you learned that you can change the font, font size, and emphasis style of chart text. This section fully explores your text-formatting options. You can assign patterns, font characteristics, and alignment options to the text in any text box in your chart. (For instructions on changing the appearance of text on the axes, see "Choosing Axis Attributes" later in this chapter.)

To choose patterns, follow these steps:

1. Select the text box.

2. Choose Patterns from the Format menu. The Area Patterns dialog box appears (see fig. 24.24).

Fig. 24.24
Area Patterns dialog box.

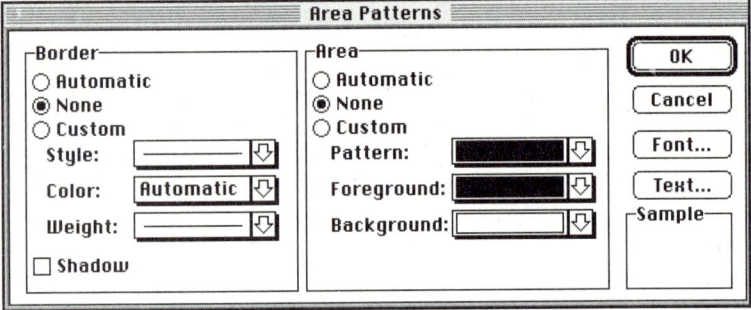

3. In the Border area, choose Automatic to apply the default border, None to hide the border, or Custom to create a custom border. If you choose Custom, also make selections in the drop-down list boxes to specify the appearance of the border (Style), the color of the line (Color), and the thickness of the line (Weight).

4. To add a shadow to your text box, click the Shadow check box.

5. In the Area area, choose Automatic to apply the default fill pattern, None to leave the background blank, or Custom to create a custom fill pattern. If you choose Custom, also select a fill pattern or color

in the Pattern drop-down list box. If you choose a pattern rather than a solid color, you also can select foreground and background colors in the Foreground and Background drop-down list boxes.

6. Choose OK to confirm you choices.

To choose fonts, follow these steps:

1. Select the text box.

2. Choose Fonts from the Format menu. The Chart Fonts dialog box appears (refer to fig. 24.11).

3. Choose the font options you want. In the Background area, you can choose Automatic, Transparent, or Opaque. The Automatic setting varies depending on the text box you select; some text boxes are opaque, whereas others are transparent.

4. Choose OK to confirm your choices.

To choose text alignment and orientation, follow these steps:

1. Select the text box.

2. Choose Text from the Format menu. The Chart Text dialog box appears (see fig. 24.25).

Fig. 24.25

Chart Text dialog box.

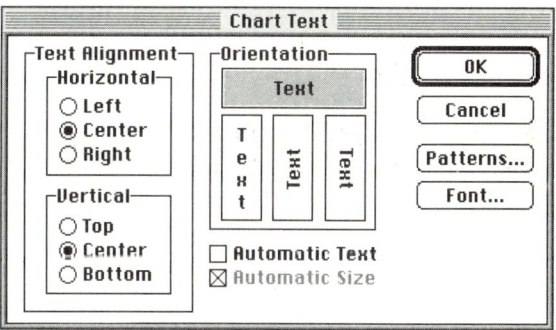

3. Choose an option in the Text Alignment area, if you want. You can choose among three vertical-orientation options and three horizontal-orientation options. (By default, text is centered horizontally and vertically in text boxes.)

4. Choose an option in the Orientation area, if you want. (The default orientation is horizontal.)

Chapter 24

Creating Charts with Microsoft Graph

5. Click the Automatic Text check box to restore the original text format.

6. Click the Automatic Size check box to size the border to fit around the text exactly.

7. Choose OK to confirm your choices.

You can access the Area Patterns dialog box quickly by double-clicking a text box. From the Area Patterns dialog box, you can access the Chart Fonts or Chart Text dialog box by clicking the Font or Text command button.

If you want to apply the same font to all the text in your chart, including the text on the axes, don't waste time formatting each text box or axis independently. Click the chart background until you select the entire chart. (When you have selected the whole chart, you see white selection handles at the corners and edges of the chart window.) Choose Font from the Format menu to open the Chart Fonts dialog box, and then choose the font options you want.

Changing the Legend Position

Some chart types add legends automatically. If your chart has no legend, you can add one by choosing Add Legend from the Chart menu. (This command is named Delete Legend if a legend already appears in your chart.)

You can change the legend's location, as explained in the following steps:

1. Select the legend.

2. Choose Legend from the Format menu. The Legend dialog box appears (see fig. 24.26).

Fig. 24.26

Legend dialog box.

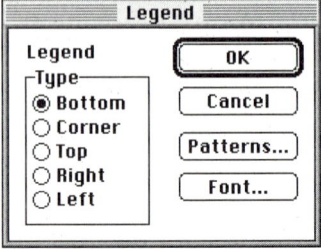

3. In the Type area, choose a location.

4. Choose OK. Optionally, you can click the Patterns or Fonts command button to access the Area Patterns or Charts Fonts dialog box.

Adding Grid Lines to the Chart

In every chart, Microsoft Graph inserts *major tick marks* and *minor tick marks*. A major tick mark shows the location of the axis data points; minor tick marks show intervals between the major tick marks. The program selects the intervals automatically, although you can change them if you want (see "Scaling Your Chart" later in this chapter). You can add grid lines that align with these tick marks and help viewers measure the magnitude of an item.

Among the chart styles you can choose in the Chart Gallery dialog box are designs that include grid lines. If you know that you want grid lines, you can save yourself some formatting by choosing one of these designs as the underlying chart type.

To add grid lines to your chart, follow these steps:

1. In the Chart window, select the chart area by clicking one of the chart axes.

2. Choose Gridlines from the Chart menu. The Gridlines dialog box appears (see fig. 24.27).

Fig. 24.27
Gridlines dialog box.

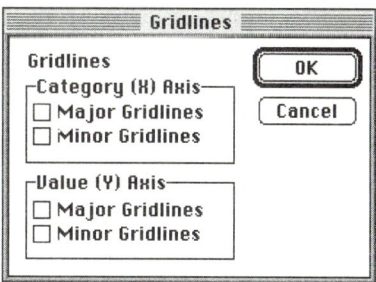

As you can see, you can add grid lines for the major tick marks, the minor tick marks, or both. You also can add grid lines for the categories axis, the values axis, or both.

CAUTION

Your chart will look very busy if you add minor and major grid lines to both axes. With the exception of x-y charts, you don't really need grid lines on the x-axis.

3. Choose the grid-line options you want.

4. Choose OK.

Choosing Axis Attributes

For both axes, you can choose axis attributes, which include line patterns (style, color, and weight), tick-mark type (inside, outside, cross, or none), and tick-label position (low, high, or next to axis). By default, Microsoft Graph creates the axis using a thin black line, cross tick marks at the major intervals, and tick labels next to the axis. When you choose axis attributes, you also have an opportunity to change the axis font and the text alignment and orientation.

To choose axis patterns, follow these steps:

1. In the Chart window, select one of the axes.

2. Double-click the axis or choose Patterns from the Format menu. The Axis Patterns dialog box appears (see fig. 24.28).

Fig. 24.28
Axis Patterns dialog box.

```
======================= Axis Patterns =======================
┌─Axis──────────────┐  ┌─Tick Mark Type──────────────┐     ┌───────────┐
│ ○ Automatic       │  │ ┌─Major──┐   ┌─Minor──┐      │     │    OK     │
│ ○ None            │  │ │ ○ None │   │ ● None │      │     └───────────┘
│ ● Custom          │  │ │ ○ Inside│  │ ○ Inside│     │     ┌───────────┐
│                   │  │ │ ○ Outside│ │ ○ Outside│    │     │  Cancel   │
│  Style:   [____⬇] │  │ │ ● Cross │  │ ○ Cross │     │     └───────────┘
│                   │  │ └────────┘   └────────┘      │     ┌───────────┐
│  Color: [Automatic⬇]│ ┌─Tick Labels──────────────┐  │     │  Font...  │
│                   │  │ ○ None      ○ High         │  │     └───────────┘
│  Weight:  [____⬇] │  │ ○ Low       ● Next to Axis │  │     ┌───────────┐
│                   │  └────────────────────────────┘  │     │  Text...  │
└───────────────────┘                                        └───────────┘
                                                             ┌───────────┐
                                                             │  Scale... │
                                                             └───────────┘
                                                             ┌─Sample────┐
                                                             │           │
                                                             └───────────┘
```

3. In the Axis area, choose Automatic to assign the default attributes to the axis, None to hide the axis, or Custom to change the attributes. If you choose Custom, also make selections in the drop-down list boxes to specify the appearance of the line (Style), the color of the line (Color), and the thickness of the line (Weight).

4. In the Tick Mark Type area, choose major and/or minor tick-mark options. Choose Inside to show the tick marks on the chart side of the axis; choose Outside to show them on the other side. Choose Cross to show the tick marks crossing the axis. If you choose None, no tick mark appears.

To see the tick marks better, turn off the grid lines.

5. In the Tick Labels area, choose the tick-label position. Choose Low to show the labels at the bottom or left of the chart; choose High to show them at the top or right of the chart. Choose Next to Axis to keep the tick labels next to the axis. If you choose None, Microsoft Graph hides the tick labels.

6. To change the font of the tick labels, click the Font command button to open the Chart Fonts dialog box, where you can choose a new font.

7. To change the text attributes of the text labels, click the Text command button to open the Chart Text dialog box, where you can choose new attributes.

8. Choose OK to confirm your choices.

Choosing Additional Attributes

In any chart, you can change the attributes of any element that you can select independently. In addition to the elements already covered in this chapter, you can format the following chart elements:

- *Data series.* Double-click one of the data series' markers, bars, or areas to change its attributes, such as color, line width, fill color, and marker style.

- *Arrows.* Double-click an arrow to change the line style, color, and weight, as well as the arrowhead style, width, and length.

- *Plot area.* This area is the rectangular area bounded by the axes. To select the plot area, click any blank space in the chart. You can change the border color, width, and style, as well as the area fill pattern and colors.

Scaling Your Chart

When you create a new chart, Microsoft Graph chooses scale values automatically. The program does so in accordance with established graphics guidelines, which call for setting the minimum value of the value axis at 0. (Setting this value higher could distort the data by exaggerating the differences among the data points.) You may want to adjust the scale, however, as long as doing so does not distort the data. If you draw a line between adjacent bars in a bar chart or use a line chart, you can judge what your chart is saying about the difference between the data points. In general, people perceive a slope of about 30 degrees as indicating significant change; a slope of 45 degrees indicates drastic change.

To scale your chart manually, follow these steps:

1. Select the axis you want to scale.

2. Choose Scale from the Format menu. The Format Axis Scale dialog box appears (see fig. 24.29).

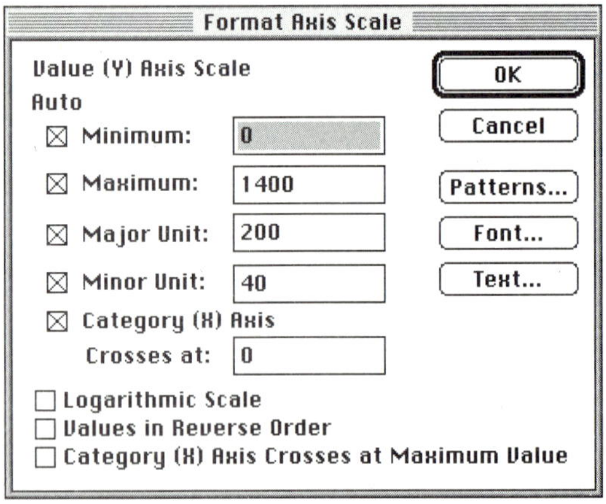

Fig. 24.29
Format Axis Scale
dialog box.

As you can see, you can change many aspects of the slope, including the minimum value, the maximum value, the major unit (major tick marks), minor unit (minor tick marks), and the point at which the other axis crosses the selected axis. In the text boxes, you see the values that Microsoft Graph has automatically chosen.

3. To change one of Microsoft Graph's preset values, click the corresponding check box and type the new setting in the text box.

4. Choose OK to confirm your choice.

Part IV
Creating Professional Documents

A good reason for scaling your graph arises when you are comparing very small values with very large ones, as shown in figure 24.30, in which the data series for the Sirah and Merlot varietals are hard to see.

Fig. 24.30
Chart comparing very large and very small values.

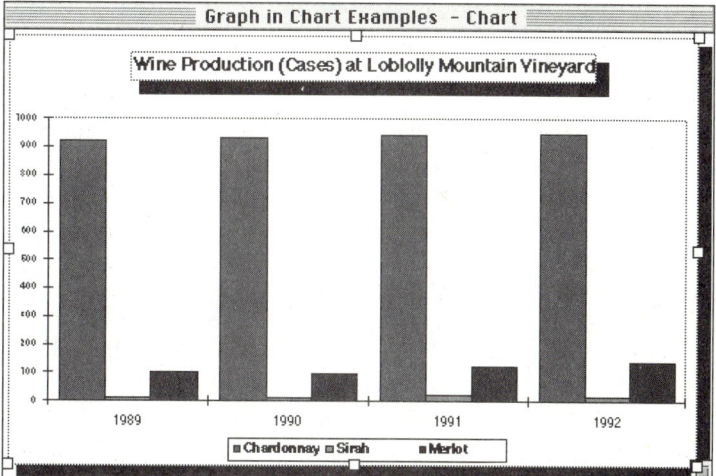

To cure this problem, use a logarithmic scale. In a logarithmic scale, the y-axis values increase *exponentially* (by 10, 100, 1,000, and so on). The effect of this scale is to magnify variations among the smallest values so that the values' data series are easier to see (see fig. 24.31).

Fig. 24.31
Logarithmically scaled chart.

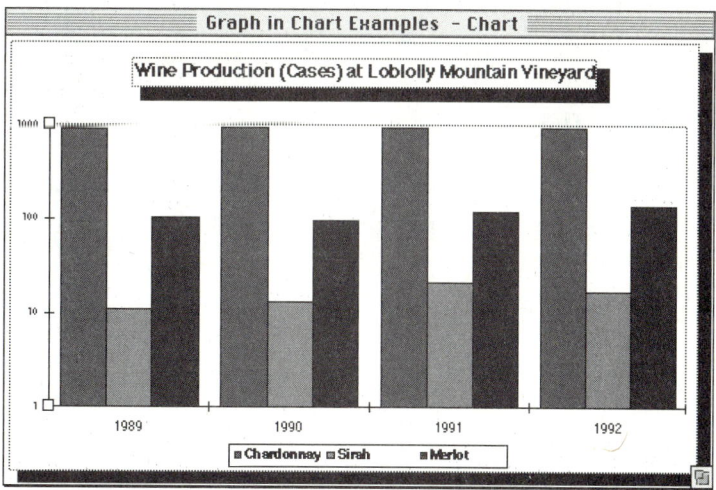

Chapter 24
Creating Charts with Microsoft Graph

To use a logarithmic scale, follow these steps:

1. Select the values axis (y-axis).

2. Choose Scale from the Format menu. The Format Axis Scale dialog box appears.

3. Click the Logarithmic Scale check box.

4. Choose OK.

When you're using a logarithmic scale, include both minor and major grid lines to accentuate the fact that you are using a logarithmic scale for your chart (see fig. 24.32).

Fig. 24.32
Logarithmic chart with major and minor grid lines.

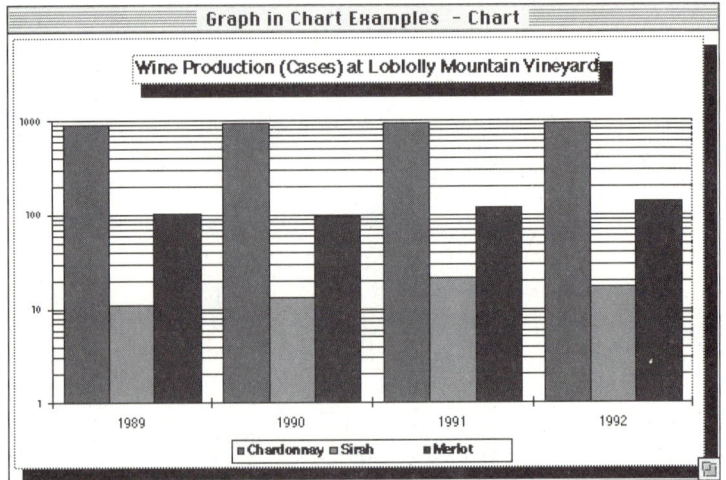

Setting the Default Chart

If you find yourself spending a great deal of time formatting charts, you should redefine the default chart—the one that appears automatically when Microsoft Graph starts. If you like the formatting in a chart you created, you can make that chart the default so that its formats become the defaults for future charts you create. Figure 24.33, for example, shows a chart with attractive formats that you might want to reuse.

To change the default chart setting, display the chart that you want to use as the default chart and then choose Save as Default Chart from the File menu.

Fig. 24.33
Potential default chart.

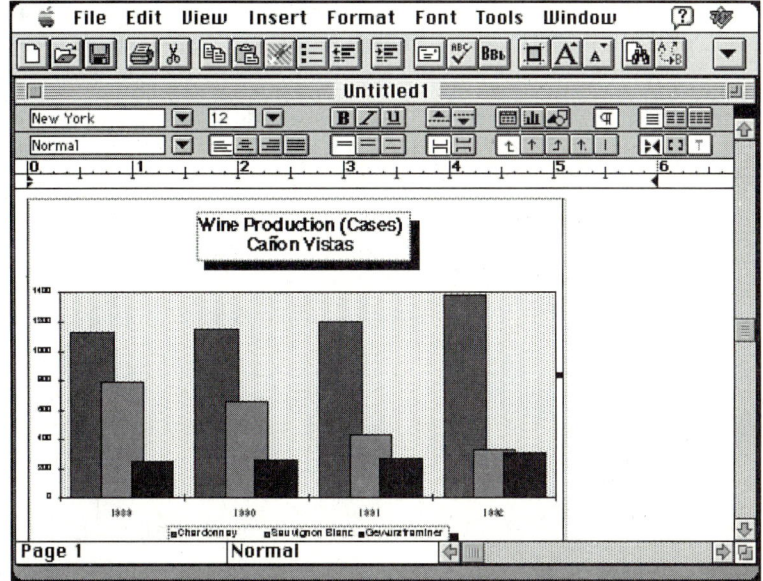

Quick Review

This section summarizes the most useful information in this chapter. Check "Productivity Tips" for a review of high-productivity tips and tricks—the ones that Macintosh and Word pros use every day. Review "Techniques" whenever you need a quick reminder about a specific procedure.

Productivity Tips

■ Microsoft Graph's chart-making capabilities closely resemble those of Microsoft Excel. If you have learned Excel, you already know how to use Microsoft Graph.

■ Choose the chart type before you do much formatting. Some chart-type choices erase the custom formats you choose.

■ To specify font attributes for the entire chart, select the chart and then choose Font from the Format menu to open the Chart Fonts dialog box, where you can make your choices.

Chapter 24

Creating Charts with Microsoft Graph

- If you're comparing tiny values with large ones, the smaller values will show up better if you choose a logarithmic scale.

- Rather than fussing with formats every time you create a chart, pick your favorite creative effort and define it as the default chart so that all of its formats will be available for your use every time you open Microsoft Graph.

Techniques

This section provides concise summaries of all the procedures introduced in this chapter.

Starting Microsoft Graph

To start Microsoft Graph:

1. In a Word document, position the insertion point where you want the graph to appear.

2. Choose Object from the Insert menu. The Insert Object dialog box appears.

3. Select Microsoft Graph in the Object Type list.

   As an alternative to steps 2 and 3, click the Graph icon in the ribbon.

Quitting Graph and Returning to Word

To exit Microsoft Graph:

1. Choose Quit and Return from the File menu or press ⌘-Q. An alert box appears, asking whether you want to update the chart in your Word document.

2. Perform one of the following actions:

   - Choose Yes to insert the graph into your Word document.

   - Click No to abandon your work and return to Word.

   - Click Cancel to return to Microsoft Graph.

Creating the Datasheet

To enter data in the datasheet:

1. Start Microsoft Graph and activate the datasheet window.

2. In the datasheet, type the x-axis categories in the top row, leaving the first cell blank. These labels appear next to the x-axis (categories axis).

3. Type the first data series in the second row. In the first cell, type the title of the data series and then type the data in the adjoining cells.

4. If you want to add a second data series, type its title in the first cell of the third row and then type the data in the adjoining cells. (You can add other data series.)

Creating a Chart

To display and embellish your chart:

1. Choose Chart from the Window menu to display the chart. Adjust the size of the window, if you want.

2. Choose Titles from the Chart menu to open the Attach Title dialog box. Use this dialog box to add chart and axis titles, if you want.

3. Select the entire chart and then choose Font from the Format menu to open the Chart Font dialog box, where you can choose font attributes for the entire chart.

4. If you want, individually choose additional chart elements, such as text boxes and arrows, and then change patterns, font, or text attributes.

   To add an arrow, choose Add Arrow from the Chart menu. An arrow appears in your chart. Drag the arrow's handles to position the arrow where you want it.

Inserting a Chart into a Document

To insert a chart into a Word document:

Choose Update from the File menu and then choose Quit and Return from the same menu, or press ⌘-Q.

Chapter 24
Creating Charts with Microsoft Graph

Editing a Chart

To edit a chart that you have inserted into a Word document:

1. Double-click the chart. Microsoft Graph starts, displaying the chart.

2. In Microsoft Graph, edit the chart.

3. Choose Update from the File menu.

4. Choose Quit and Return from the File menu.

Changing a Chart Type

To change the chart type:

1. Choose a chart type from the Gallery menu. The Chart Gallery dialog box appears.

2. Click the box that represents the chart type you want.

3. Choose OK.

Choosing Attributes

To choose border style, color, and weight, as well as fill colors and patterns:

1. Select the chart element you want to format.

2. Double-click the element or choose Patterns from the Format menu. The Area Patterns dialog box appears.

3. In the Border area, choose Automatic to assign the default attributes, None to hide the axis, or Custom to change the attributes. If you choose Custom, also make selections in the Style, Color, and Weight drop-down list boxes.

4. To add a shadow to your text box, choose the Shadow option.

5. In the Area area, choose Automatic to apply the default fill attributes, None to leave the background blank, or Custom to create a custom fill. If you choose Custom, also select a fill pattern or color in the Pattern drop-down list box. If you choose a pattern rather than a solid color, you also can choose foreground and background colors in the Foreground and Background drop-down list boxes.

6. Choose OK to confirm your choices.

Aligning and Orienting Text

To align or orient text:

1. Select the text box.

2. Choose Text from the Format menu. The Chart Text dialog box appears.

3. Choose text-alignment options, if you want.

4. Choose orientation options, if you want.

5. Click the Automatic Text check box to restore the original text format.

6. Click the Automatic Size check box to size the borders to fit around the text exactly.

7. Choose OK.

Moving the Legend

To move the legend:

1. Select the legend.

2. Choose Legend from the Format menu. The Legend dialog box appears.

3. In the Type area, select a location.

4. Choose OK. Optionally, you can click the Patterns or Fonts command button to open the Area Patterns or Chart Fonts dialog box, in which you can change the attributes of the legend.

Adding Grid Lines

To add grid lines to a chart:

1. In the Chart window, choose the chart area by clicking one of the chart axes.

2. Choose Gridlines from the Chart menu. The Gridlines dialog box appears.

3. Choose the grid-line options you want.

4. Choose OK.

Chapter 24
Creating Charts with Microsoft Graph

Scaling a Chart

To scale your chart manually:

1. Select the axis you want to scale.

2. Choose Scale from the Format menu. The Format Axis Scale dialog box appears.

3. To change one of Microsoft Graph's preset values, click the corresponding check box and type the new setting in the text box.

4. Choose OK to confirm your choice.

To use a logarithmic scale, follow these steps:

1. Select the values axis (y-axis).

2. Choose Scale from the Format menu. The Format Axis Scale dialog box appears.

3. Click the Logarithmic Scale check box.

4. Choose OK.

Specifying a Default Chart

To specify a default chart:

1. In Microsoft Graph, display the chart you want to use as the default.

2. Choose Set as Default Chart from the File menu.

Using Math and Typing Equations

n today's increasingly technical society, numbers find their way into many documents, such as technical reports and proposals, market analyses, and economic forecasts. In keeping with the increasing use of numbers in business and professional writing, Microsoft Word offers two useful features, both of which are explored in this chapter:

■ *On-screen math.* Using Word's Calculate command (Tools menu), you can add rows or columns of figures, multiply or divide numbers, and determine percentages. Word shows the result of a calculation in the page-number area in the lower left corner of the document window. The program also copies the result to the Clipboard, from which you can insert the result into your document. In tandem with Word's Table command (see Chapter 15, "Creating Tables"), you can create a mini spreadsheet within a Word document.

■ *Equation Editor.* An object linking and embedding (OLE) applet in Microsoft Graph, Equation Editor, greatly simplifies typing mathematical equations. If you have ever tried to type an equation by fussing with the Mac's Symbol font and mathematical-typesetting techniques, you are sure to find that Equation Editor represents a major improvement.

To build an equation with Equation Editor, you first select symbols and templates from on-screen palettes. After you insert a template (such as an integral), you see *slots*, or areas in which you can type numbers or insert additional symbols or templates. As you build your equation, Equation Editor automatically sizes and formats the equation so that the printed symbols look good and conform to standard mathematical practice.

This chapter covers the following topics:

- *Using math.* You learn how to perform simple calculations on-screen, such as adding a column of numbers.

- *Typing equations with Equation Editor.* You learn how to use this OLE applet to create mathematical equations of all kinds.

 **NOTE**

If you used the mathematical-typesetting capabilities of a previous version of Word to create equations, you still can use those capabilities in Word 5.0 and 5.1. Using Equation Editor, however, is by far the best way to create equations.

Using Math

Word is no spreadsheet program, but you still can use it to perform useful calculations, such as adding a column or row of numbers in a table. For more extensive computations, create and analyze the data in a spreadsheet program, such as Excel, and then transfer the data to Word by using the techniques discussed in Chapter 30, "Linking Data Dynamically."

Calculating On-Screen

You can perform calculations at any time by typing an arithmetic expression anywhere in your document, selecting the expression, and choosing the Calculate command from the Utilities menu or pressing ⌘-equals sign (=). The result appears in the page-number area of the document window. Word also places the result in the Clipboard, from which you can paste the result into your document.

Table 25.1 lists the arithmetic operators you can use with the Calculate command.

Table 25.1
Arithmetic Operators

Operator	Operation	Example	Result
+	Addition	10+5	15
(space)	Addition	10 5	15
-	Subtraction	10-5	5
(x)	Subtraction	10 (5)	5
*	Multiplication	10*5	50
/	Division	10/5	2
%	Percentage	10*5%	.5

Keep the following points in mind as you create expressions:

- Unless you use one of the operators listed in Table 25.1, Word adds the numbers that you select.

- Word calculates from left to right. If you select more than one line, the program evaluates each line left to right, moving down to the next line at the end of each line. In older spreadsheet programs, this calculation technique is called *row-wise calculation*.

- If you group numbers and operator signs within parentheses, Word evaluates the group before proceeding with the rest of the calculations. If you type **8+(2*50)**, for example, Word displays 108 in the page-number area. If you type **8+2*50**, Word displays 500. A single number enclosed in parentheses, however, indicates a negative number. The expression **10*(10)**, for example, produces a result of -100.

- If you include commas (as in 12,319) in any of the numbers in the expression, Word includes the commas in the result.

- Word calculates the result to the largest number of decimal places you used in the numbers you typed. When you type **10.1/4**, for example, you get 2.5; if you type **10.100/4**, you get 2.525.

To calculate on-screen, follow these steps:

1. Type the expression.

   You can use numbers, commas, decimal points, parentheses, and operators in the expression. If you include any letters or other punctuation marks, Word ignores them.

2. Select the expression.

Chapter 25
Using Math and Typing Equations

3. Choose Calculate from the Tools menu or press ⌘-equals sign (=). Word displays the result in the page-number area (see fig. 25.1).

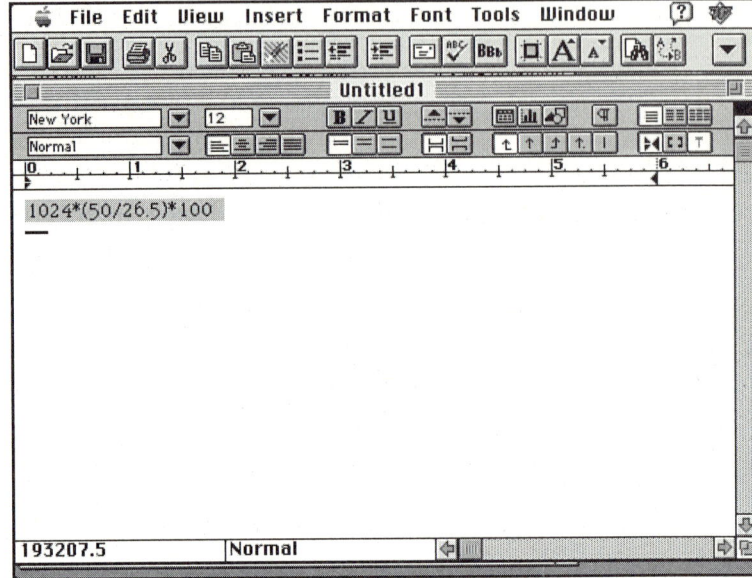

4. To insert the result into your document, position the insertion point where you want the result to appear and then choose Paste from the Edit menu, press ⌘-V, or click the Paste tool.

Calculating the Sum of Columns and Rows in a Tabbed Table

If you used tabs to create a table of numbers, you can add these numbers quickly by using column selection. Follow these steps:

1. Use decimal tabs to type columns of numbers. You also can use flush-right tabs, if all the numbers are whole numbers.

2. Select a column of numbers by holding down the Option key and positioning the insertion point on the lower right or upper right corner of the column (see fig. 25.2).

Fig. 25.2
Tabbed column correctly selected, beginning with right corner.

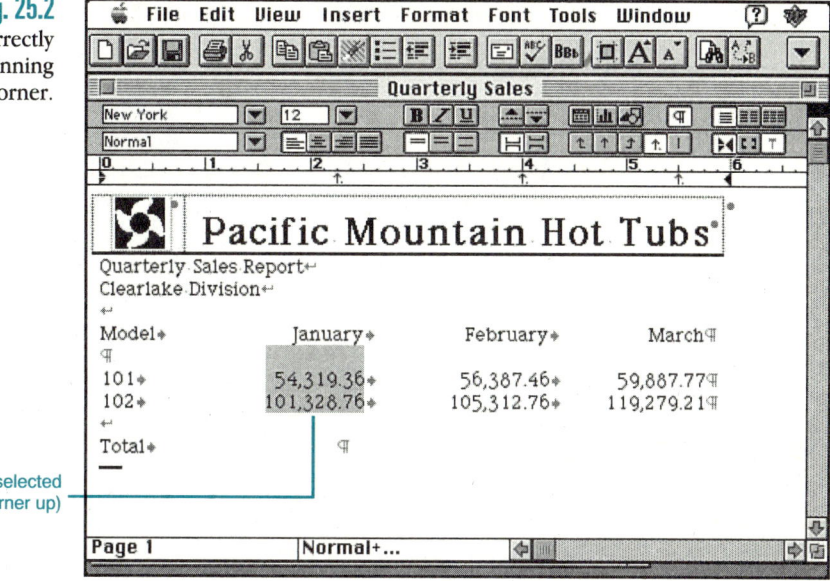

Column correctly selected
(from bottom right corner up)

If the column contains numbers that occupy varying numbers of places, you might not be able to select the longest numbers if you start selecting in the left corner. If you start selecting in the upper left corner, you leave out one of the numbers, as shown in figure 25.3, and your result will be incorrect.

3. Choose Calculate from the Tools menu or press ⌘-equals sign (=).

4. Position the insertion point where you want the result to appear and then choose Paste from the Edit menu, press ⌘-V, or click the Paste tool. Word displays the total (see fig. 25.4).

Adding rows is easy. You simply use ordinary selection techniques to select the row, as shown in figure 25.5, and then use the Calculate command.

Fig. 25.3
Tabbed column incorrectly
selected, beginning with
upper left corner.

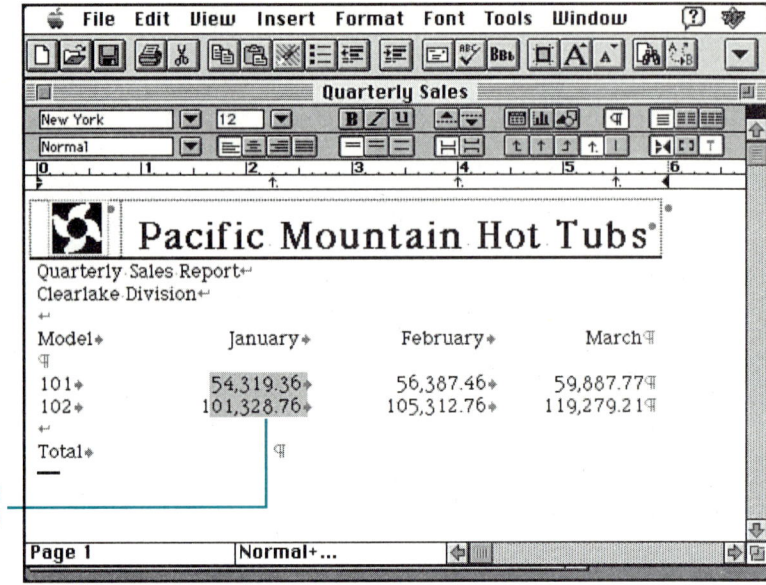

Column incorrectly selected
(from top down)

Fig. 25.4
Inserting the total.

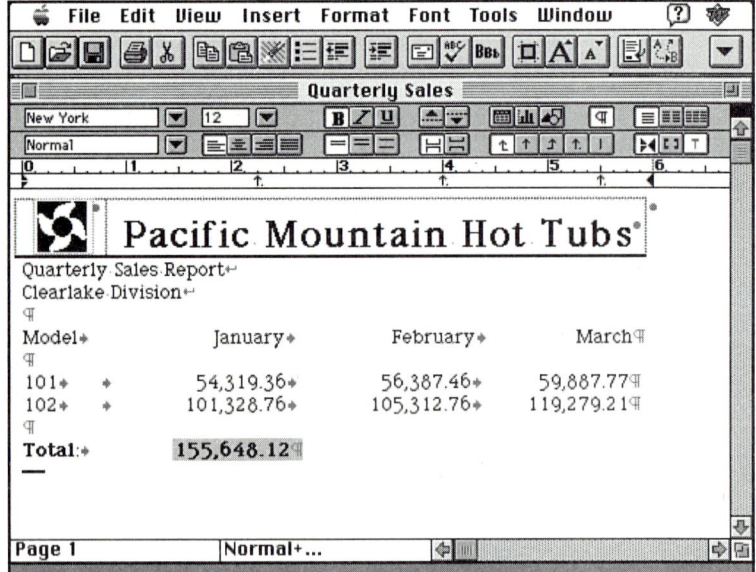

Part IV

Creating Professional Documents

Fig. 25.5

Selecting a row for calculation.

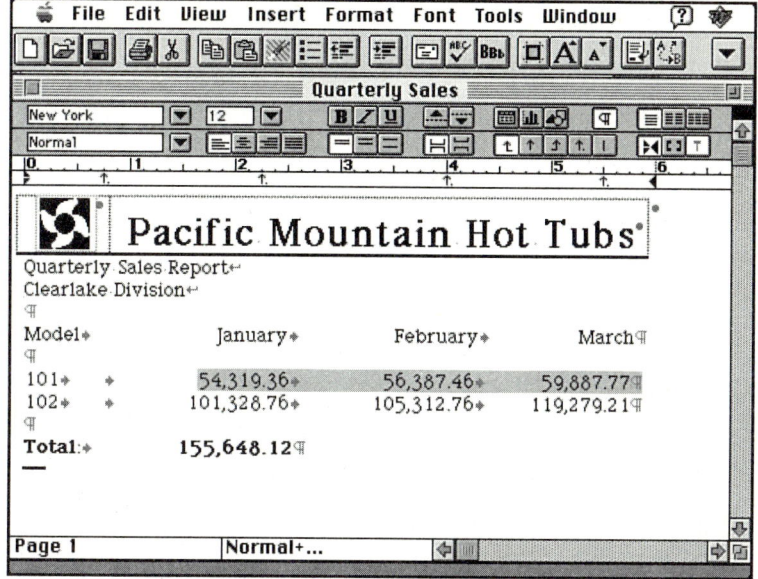

Fig. 25.5

Selecting a row for calculation.

In calculating a row or column, you're restricted to addition, but you can include negative numbers by entering them in parentheses (a standard accounting practice). In figure 25.6, for example, the new Model 102XL shows a loss in January, so Word subtracts 1,254.48 from the January total.

Calculating the Sum of Columns and Rows in a Table

In Chapter 15, you learned how to use Word's Table command to create, edit, and format tables. Using the Table command, which creates a spreadsheetlike matrix of rows and columns, has many advantages over typing a table with tabs. One advantage is that using the Calculate command is easier in a table that you created with the Table command. In a tabbed table, you can inadvertently leave out a digit if you don't start the column selection in the right place (as explained in the preceding section). When you select a column of numbers in a Table-command table, however, you don't have to worry about including every digit; you simply select the cells and then choose the Calculate command.

Chapter 25

Using Math and Typing Equations

Fig. 25.6
Including a
negative number.

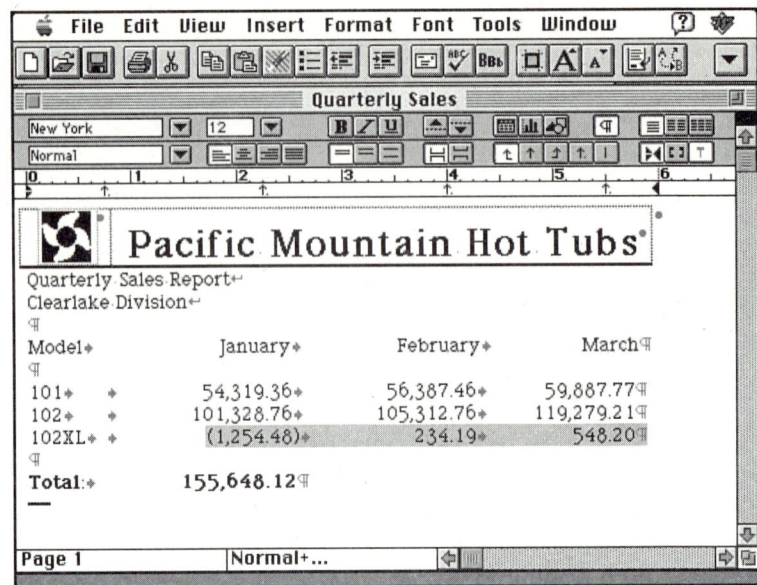

To select a column in a table for use in a calculation, hold down the Option key and click anywhere in the column (see fig. 25.7). Word ignores any cells that contain text, even if you include those cells in your selection. To perform the calculation, choose Calculate from the Tools menu or press ⌘-equals sign (=).

Tables that you create with Word's Table command aren't really spreadsheets, because you cannot embed formulas in those tables' cells. Word's capability to sum columns and rows accurately and quickly, however, is adequate for many of the tables that find their way into business reports and proposals.

Typing Equations with Equation Editor

Equation Editor, an OLE applet supplied with Word, helps you build complex equations and insert them into your Word documents. Simply by pointing at symbols and templates on an on-screen palette and clicking, you can create equations that would be extremely tedious to construct with the mathematical-typesetting techniques of earlier versions of Word.

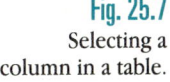

Fig. 25.7
Selecting a
column in a table.

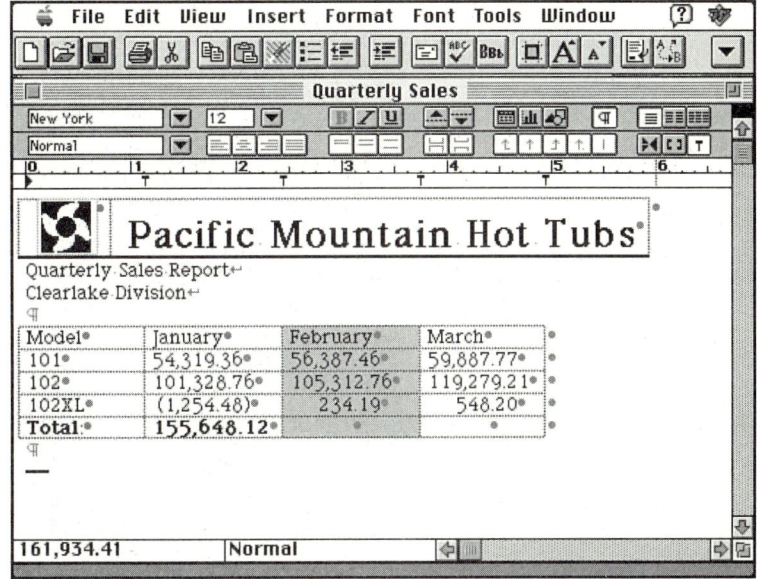

Equation Editor is so easy to use that reading about this exceptional utility takes more effort than using it does. All you need is to know a few basic concepts and techniques.

Capable of precision typesetting for professional publications, Equation Editor includes advanced features that cannot be fully discussed in this chapter. Enough information is given here, however, that you can get started with Equation Editor and create handsome-looking equations. From this starting point, you have a firm foundation from which to explore the program more fully.

If you're planning to use Equation Editor, don't delete the MT Extra font that Word installed in your System Folder. Equation Editor needs this font to display and print your equations.

WARNING

Accessing Equation Editor

You can access Equation Editor in two ways: as a stand-alone program and through object embedding.

Chapter 25

Using Math and Typing Equations

Equation Editor is a stand-alone program in your Word Commands folder. To start the program from the Finder and open the Equation Editor window, double-click the Equation Editor icon in the Word Commands folder. After you create your equation, you can copy the equation to your Word document, using Clipboard techniques.

Access Equation Editor as a stand-alone program if you're running System 6 or if your system has limited memory.

Equation Editor also fully supports object linking and embedding (OLE), which is discussed in Chapter 30, "Linking Data Dynamically." If you're running Word in System 7 and have sufficient memory to run the Word and Equation Editor applications simultaneously, you can access Equation by choosing the Object command from the Insert menu. After you create your equation and quit Equation Editor, the formula you created is embedded in your Word document as an embedded object.

With object embedding, you can produce high-quality equations no matter which way you access Equation Editor. You also can edit equations easily. Simply select an equation and choose Edit Object from the Edit menu. Word starts Equation Editor and displays the equation in Equation Editor's work space.

To start Equation Editor using the Object command (System 7 only), follow these steps:

1. Place the insertion point in your document where you want your equation to appear.

2. Choose Object from the Insert menu. The Insert Object dialog box appears (see fig. 25.8).

Fig. 25.8
Insert Object dialog box.

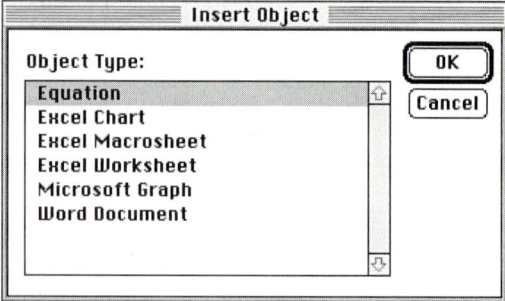

If the Equation option does not appear in the Object Type list box, you have never run Equation Editor. In such a case, click the Cancel button, switch to the Finder, locate Equation Editor in the

Word Commands folder, and start Equation Editor. Then quit Equation Editor, switch back to Word, and try again.

3. Select Equation in the Object Type list box. The Equation Editor window appears.

The following section describes the Equation Editor window.

Understanding the Equation Editor Window

As a separate program, Equation Editor has its own menu-bar options and window features. You already know how to use many of these features, including the scroll bars and arrows, the pull-down menus, and the close, zoom, and size boxes. You also are familiar with most of Word's commands. Many of the menu commands in this window are necessary only if you want to override Equation Editor's default formats, styles, and sizes. In this section, you learn how to use the Equation Editor features you haven't seen before.

Figure 25.9 shows the Equation Editor window.

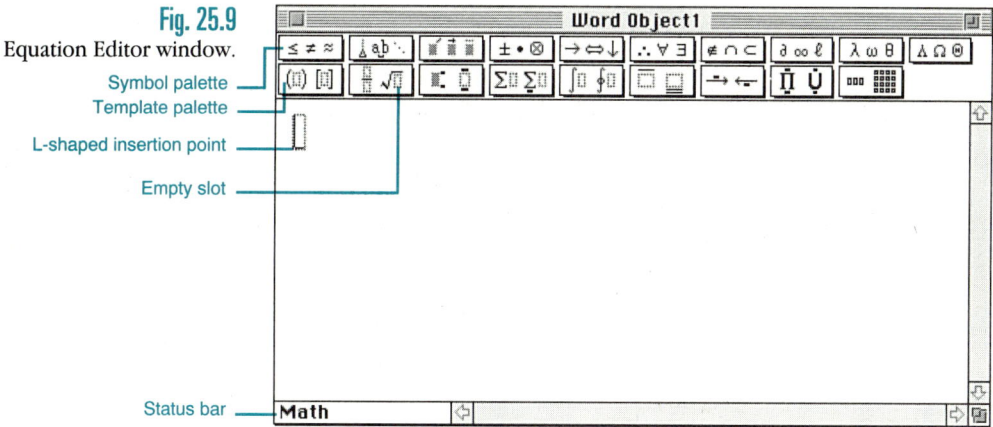

Fig. 25.9
Equation Editor window.

Symbol palette
Template palette
L-shaped insertion point
Empty slot
Status bar

Following is an overview of the components of the Equation Editor window:

> **Symbol palette.** Positioned just below the title bar, the symbol palette is the first row of options at the top of the document work area. This palette enables you to choose a wide variety of mathematical symbols. Click any of the palette icons to drop down the full palette, from which you can choose a symbol (see fig. 25.10).

Chapter 25
Using Math and Typing Equations

Fig. 25.10
Dropped-down
symbol palette.

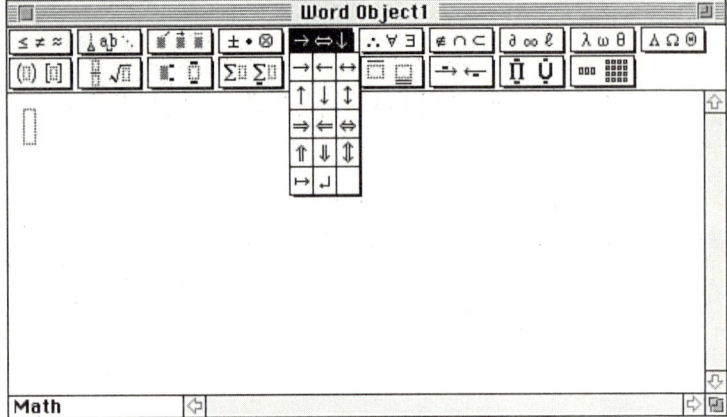

Template palette. Below the symbol palette is the template palette, which contains dozens of templates for standard mathematical relationships. A template includes areas called *empty slots*, where you can plug in numbers, symbols, or additional templates. To access the templates, drop down the palette, as shown in figure 25.11, and choose one of the options.

Fig. 25.11
Dropped-down
template palette.

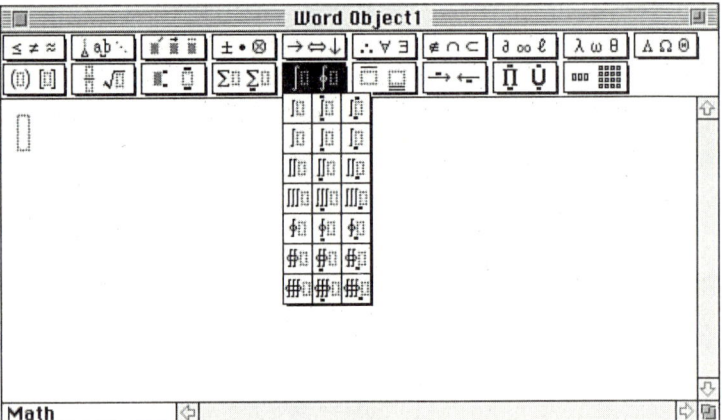

Empty slot. Equation Editor uses an empty slot (a dotted rectangle) to show where you can insert symbols, numbers, text, or templates. Many templates contain additional empty slots, into which you can plug additional templates, text, symbols, or numbers.

L-shaped insertion point. A special insertion point shows you where text, symbols, or templates will be inserted. The horizontal bar along the bottom edge of the insertion point indicates which slot is selected.

Status bar. The bottom left corner of the screen indicates which mode Equation Editor currently is using. By default, Equation Editor uses Math mode. The other modes are used to override Equation Editor's default formatting treatments of the text you enter and for advanced manual typesetting.

You choose these modes from the Style menu. The modes are Text (for entering text manually) and Function, Variable, Greek, and Vector (for decoding manual typesetting). Most users can ignore these modes and use Equation Editor in Math mode.

Building Equations

The best way to understand Equation Editor is to use it to create an equation. In the following tutorial, you produce the equation shown in figure 25.12.

Fig. 25.12
Equation created in
Equation Editor
(400% view).

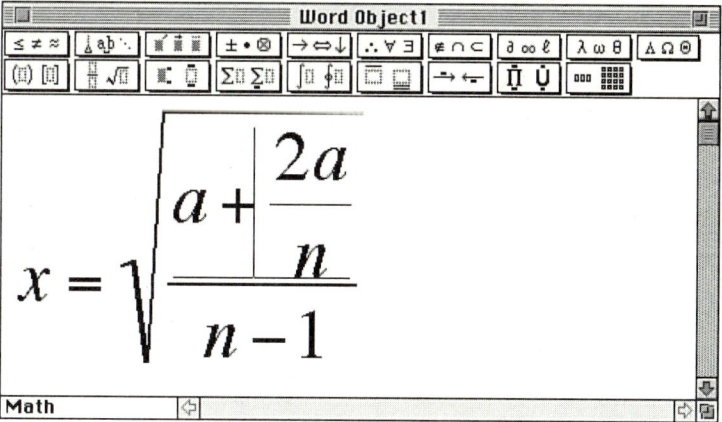

For clarity, the equation shown in figure 25.12 is shown in 400% view (four times normal size). The equation will not look this big in your document unless you choose 400% view.

To create an equation with Equation Editor, follow these steps:

1. Start Equation Editor.

2. Without pressing the space bar, type **x=** in the Equation Editor window. (Pressing the space bar has no effect in Math mode, because Equation Editor handles spacing automatically.) Equation Editor enters and formats the characters you typed, using general mathematical practices (see fig. 25.13).

Fig. 25.13

Text automatically formatted by Equation Editor.

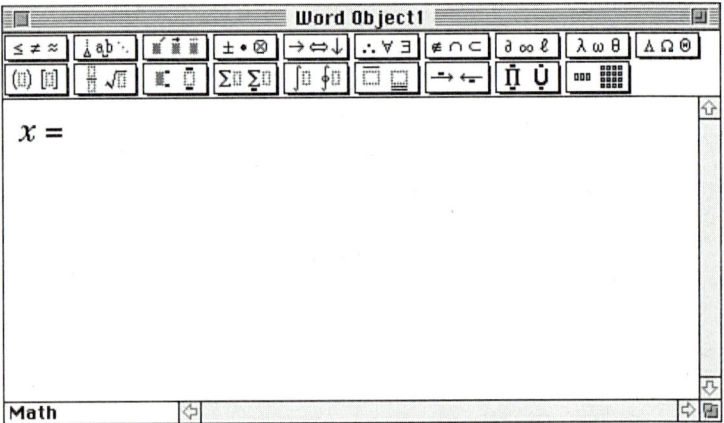

By default, Equation Editor displays the equation using a 200% view, twice normal size. The equation looks smaller in your Word document. If you want, you can choose the 100% (normal size) or 400% (quadruple size) option from the View menu.

3. Drop down the fraction/radicals template (the second template from the left) and then choose the square-root template, shown in figure 25.14.

Equation Editor places the square-root template in your document, as shown in figure 25.15. Notice that the square-root template enters the empty slot in which the L-shaped insertion point is positioned.

Fig. 25.14

Choosing the square-root template from the fraction/radicals template.

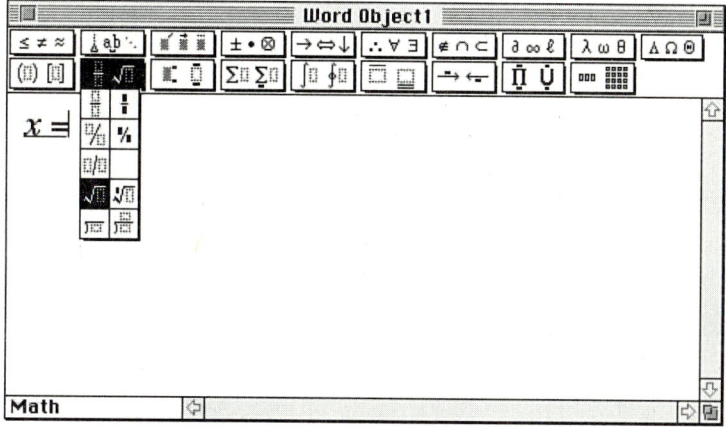

Fig. 25.15

Square-root template placed in document.

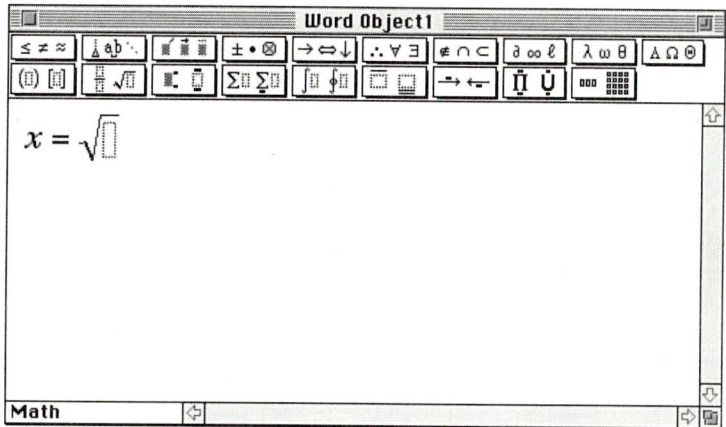

4. From the fraction/radicals template, choose the fraction template, shown in figure 25.16.

Chapter 25

Using Math and Typing Equations

Fig. 25.16
Choosing the fraction
template from the fraction/
radicals template.

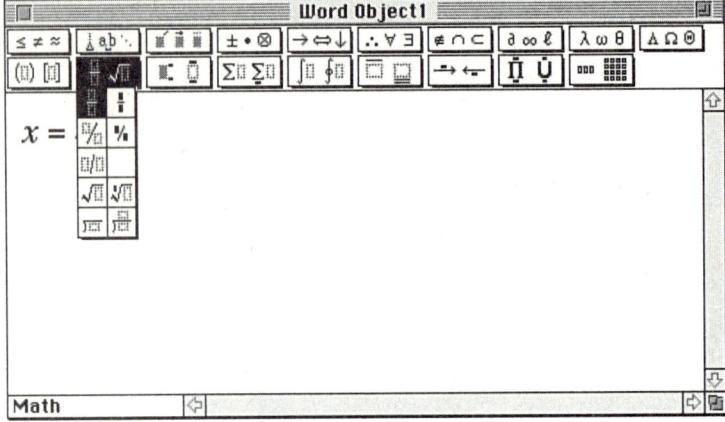

Fig. 25.16
Choosing the fraction
template from the fraction/
radicals template.

Word inserts the fraction template into your equation, as shown in figure 25.17. Notice that the fraction template includes two empty slots. Also notice that Equation Editor automatically adjusts the square-root template to make room for the fraction template.

Fig. 25.17
Fraction template
inserted within
square-root template.

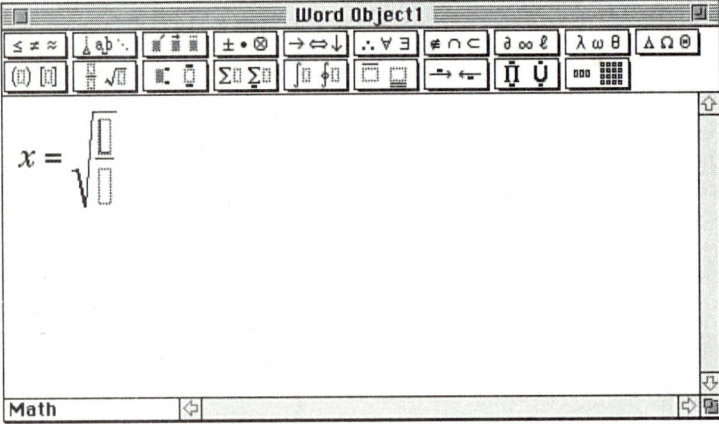

5. In the top slot of the fraction template, type the numerator **a**; type the denominator **b** in the bottom slot. (To move from the numerator slot to the denominator slot, you can click the slot, press Tab, or press the down-arrow key.) Equation Editor enters these variables and formats them according to standard mathematical practice.

6. To move the insertion point out of the denominator slot, press Tab.

7. Type **-c** (using a hyphen for a minus sign). Your equation now should look like the one shown in figure 25.18.

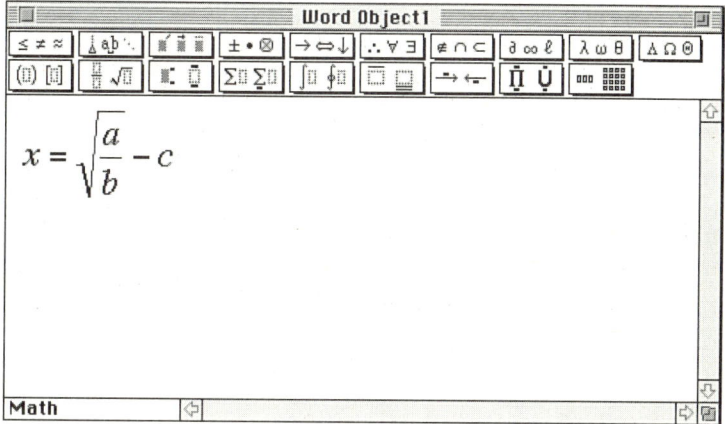

8. To add superscript formatting, choose the superscript template from the superscript/subscript template, as shown in figure 25.19.

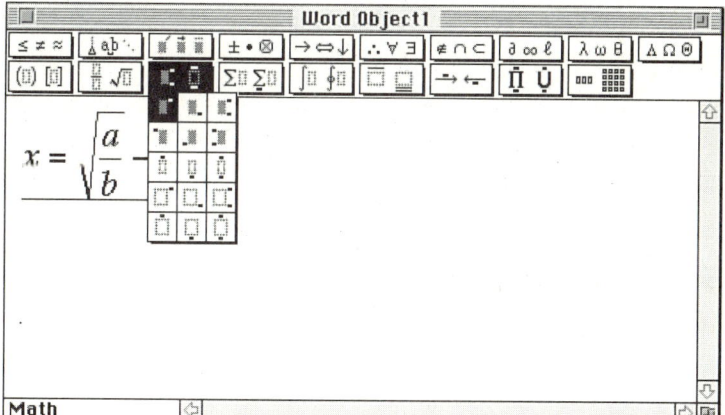

This palette has two kinds of templates. Choose the first kind, indicated by a grayed rectangle, after you enter the symbol or variable. If you choose the second kind of template, indicated by the empty slots, Equation Editor enters two empty slots: one for the variable or symbol and another for the superscript or sub-script. Because you have already typed the variable, choose the grayed kind. (Notice the many available options. The small black dots show where superscript and subscript slots will appear.)

9. Type **2** to complete the equation.

10. To add the equation to your document, perform one of the following actions:

   ■ If you used the Object command to start Equation Editor, click the window's close box to embed the equation in your Word document.

   ■ If you started Equation Editor as a stand-alone application, choose Select All from the Edit menu or press ⌘-A; and then choose Cut from the Edit menu, press ⌘-X, or click the Cut tool. Start Word, display your document, and then use the Paste command (choose Page from the Edit menu, press ⌘-V, or click the Paste tool) to insert the equation into your document.

Figure 25.20 shows how the equation appears in a Word document.

Fig. 25.20
Equation in a Word document.

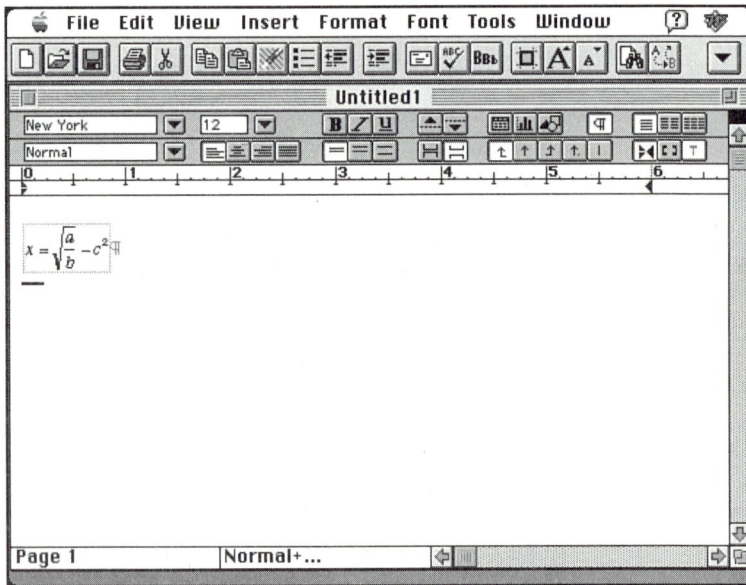

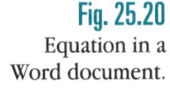

Editing Equations

Whether you use object embedding or the Clipboard method to insert your equation into a Word document, Word treats the equation like a picture. Although the equation is a single character that you can move, copy, or delete, you cannot directly edit the equation. You can edit the equation in two ways:

- If you used object embedding to insert the equation, you can edit the equation quickly by selecting the equation and then choosing Edit Object from the Edit menu. (Alternatively, you simply can double-click the equation.) Word starts Equation Editor and displays your equation in the Equation Editor window. Make the changes you want and then click the window's close box to place the edited equation in your Word document.

- If you used the Clipboard method to insert the equation, you must use the Clipboard to cut the equation back to Equation Editor for editing. Select the equation and then choose Cut from the Edit menu, press ⌘-X, or click the Cut tool. Next, quit Word; start Equation Editor; and choose Paste from the Edit menu, press ⌘-V, or click the Paste tool.

  If you use System 7 and have enough memory to run both Word and Equation Editor simultaneously, you can switch between the two programs. (System 6 users must run MultiFinder in order to take advantage of this technique.)

  When you redisplay your equation in the Equation Editor window, you can use any of the standard Macintosh techniques to edit the equation (such as pressing Backspace or Delete to erase a selection). You also can add additional symbols, templates, or text.

When you finish editing your equation, choose Update from the File menu or press ⌘-U. Then choose Quit from the File menu or press ⌘-Q to return to your document.

An even faster way to exit is to click the close box in the Equation Editor window. Word updates the equation in your document and closes Equation Editor.

Chapter 25
Using Math and Typing Equations

Understanding Additional Equation Editor Features

Because Equation Editor is a program in its own right, the program has far more features than this chapter can cover. Following are some additional features that you may want to explore on your own:

- *Getting help.* Choose Equation Editor Help from the Help menu or press ⌘-? to see extensive on-screen help for a variety of Equation Editor subjects. (In System 7, Equation Editor also supports Balloon Help.)

- *Creating and aligning a pile of equations.* You can create more than one equation at a time in the Equation Editor window. When you finish an equation, press Return to insert a blank slot below the equation. A series of lines created in this way is called a *pile*. Alignment commands in the Format menu enable you to choose how you want the lines placed: Align Left, Align Center, Align Right, Align at = (equals sign), or Align at . (decimal point). To rejoin lines, place the insertion point at the beginning of the line and then press Backspace or Delete.

- *Adding embellishments.* In mathematics, variables and symbols often have diacriticals, primes, overbars, and other embellishments. The embellishment palette offers a variety of embellishments you can add to a symbol or variable (see fig. 25.21).

Fig. 25.21
Embellishment palette.

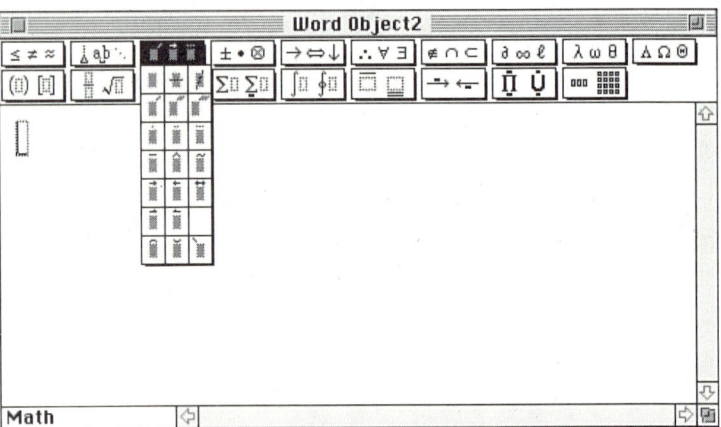

- *Selecting items in an equation with the Option key.* You can use normal selection techniques when you edit an equation, but Equation Editor offers a special technique you should learn.

Part IV

Creating Professional Documents

To select within a template an object that you cannot select through ordinary techniques, hold down the Option key and click the object.

■ *Using keyboard shortcuts.* Equation Editor includes many useful keyboard shortcuts for symbols and templates. For example, you can press ⌘-S-R to insert a square-root symbol. To view a complete list of Equation Editor keyboard shortcuts on-screen, choose Equation Editor Help from the Help menu and then select Keyboard Shortcuts in the help window.

■ *Choosing fonts.* By default, Equation Editor uses the standard Times and Symbol fonts to format your equations. You can, however, change the font assignments, using the Define option in the Style menu.

Quick Review

This section summarizes the most useful information in this chapter. Check "Productivity Tips" for a review of high-productivity tips and tricks—the ones that Macintosh and Word pros use every day. Review "Techniques" whenever you need a quick reminder about a specific procedure.

Productivity Tips

■ You don't need to keep a pocket calculator next to your computer; you can calculate on-screen in Word by typing an expression, selecting the expression, and then choosing Calculate from the Tools menu or pressing ⌘-equals sign (=). To replace the expression with the result, again select the expression you typed and then choose Paste from the Edit menu, press ⌘-V, or click the Paste tool.

■ If you plan to use Word to sum up values in a table, create the table by using the Table command rather than tabs. You can all too easily make a mistake in a tabbed table by leaving a digit out of the column selection.

■ Equation Editor enables you to create equations without any mathematical typesetting. To build an equation, choose options from on-screen palettes and then type constants and variables.

Chapter 25
Using Math and Typing Equations

■ To speed equation editing in System 7, use Word's object-embedding capabilities. Simply start Equation Editor by choosing Object from the Insert menu rather than starting the program from the Finder as a stand-alone program.

Techniques

This section provides concise summaries of all the procedures introduced in this chapter.

Using On-Screen Math

To calculate on-screen:

1. Type the expression, using operators (+, -, *, /, or %), if you want. UsEe parentheses to override the default order of evaluation (left to right, line by line).

2. Select the expression.

3. Choose Calculate from the Tools menu or press ⌘-equals sign (=).

4. To insert the result into your document, position the insertion point where you want the result to appear and then choose Paste from the Edit menu, press ⌘-V, or click the Paste tool.

Summing a Column in a Tabbed Table

To sum a column of numbers in a tabbed table:

1. Use decimal or flush-right tabs to type the column of numbers.

2. Hold down the Option key and position the insertion point on the lower right or upper right corner of the column of numbers.

3. Choose Calculate from the Tools menu or press ⌘-equals sign (=).

4. Position the insertion point where you want the result to appear and then choose Paste from the Edit menu, press ⌘-V, or click the Paste tool.

Starting Equation Editor

To start Equation Editor:

1. Open the Word Commands folder.

2. Double-click the Equation Editor icon.

To start Equation Editor from Word and create the formula as an embedded object (System 7 only):

1. Place the insertion point in your document where you want your equation to appear.

2. Choose Object from the Insert menu. The Insert Object dialog box appears.

3. Select Equation in the Object Type list box. The Equation Editor window appears.

Creating a Formula with Equation Editor

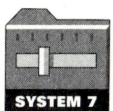

To create a formula as an embedded object:

1. Position the insertion point where you want the equation to appear.

2. Start Equation Editor by choosing Object from the Insert menu. The Insert Object dialog box appears.

3. Select Equation in the Object Type list box. The Equation Editor window appears.

4. Choose symbols and templates from the palettes, and type constants and variables.

5. When you finish creating your equation, click the window's close box to insert the equation into your Word document.

To create a formula using Equation Editor as a stand-alone program:

1. Position the insertion point where you want the equation to appear.

2. Double-click the Equation Editor icon in the Word Commands folder. The Equation Editor window appears.

3. Choose symbols and templates from the palettes, and type constants and variables.

Chapter 25
Using Math and Typing Equations

4. When you finish creating your equation, choose Select All from the Edit menu or press ⌘-A.

5. Choose Cut from the Edit menu, press ⌘-X, or click the Cut tool.

6. Choose Quit from the File menu to quit Equation Editor.

7. Start Word, display your document, and position the insertion point where you want your equation to appear.

8. Choose Paste from the Edit menu, press ⌘-V, or click the Paste tool.

Editing an Equation

To edit an equation that you inserted as an embedded object:

1. Double-click the equation. The Equation Editor window appears.

2. Edit the equation.

3. Click the window's close box to embed the corrected equation in your Word document.

To edit an equation you inserted via the Clipboard:

1. Select the equation.

2. Choose Cut from the Edit menu, press ⌘-X, or click the Cut tool.

3. Quit Word.

4. Start Equation Editor.

5. Choose Paste from the Edit menu, press ⌘-V, or click the Paste tool.

6. Edit the equation.

7. Choose Select All from the Edit menu or press ⌘-A.

8. Choose Cut from the Edit menu, press ⌘-X, or click the Cut tool.

9. Quit Equation Editor.

10. Start Word, display your document, and then position the insertion point where you want the corrected equation to appear.

11. Choose Paste from the Edit menu, press ⌘-V, or click the Paste tool.

Adding an Index and Table of Contents

f you prepare reports, dissertations, or proposals that require an index, a table of contents, and other tables (such as tables of illustrations), Word has the tools you need to make short work of these tasks. Word can compile an index and table of contents, insert correct page numbers, and print both tables for you automatically. If you make changes in your document, you can reprint these tables, and Word makes all the corrections with no intervention on your part. This feature alone is sure to save you much time as you struggle to meet deadlines.

This chapter is useful if your reports and proposals will be reproduced directly from Word printouts, because the index and table of contents refer to the pages Word creates. (If you're preparing a document to be typeset, however, you must prepare the table of contents and index from the page proofs that the printer gives you; Word isn't much help in such circumstances.)

This chapter covers the following topics:

- *Creating an index.* In this section, you learn how to mark index entries so that Word can compile them into an index.

- *Creating a table of contents.* This section shows you how you can create an accurate table of contents for your document easily, especially if you have used Word's standard heading styles for chapter and section titles.

USING
WORD 5.1
FOR THE MAC
SPECIAL EDITION

Creating an Index

When you create an index, a certain amount of tedious manual work is involved. Word saves you huge amounts of time by automating the compilation of the index, but you must read through your document and mark the words to be included.

You learn more about how to mark your document in this section, but for now, you should consider which words to mark. You should mark the main ideas in your document, the main subjects in each section, variations on chapter and section titles, special terms or nomenclature, abbreviations and acronyms, and proper nouns (such as names and places). In addition, you should include synonyms of main terms (for example, *modernization* as well as *industrialization*) and inverted versions of main terms (for example, *development, economic* as well as *economic development*).

You can identify the words or phrases to be included in your index in two ways:

- *You can mark words or phrases in your document.* This technique creates a *concordance entry*—a word in your document that you mark for indexing. As you learn in this section, you mark a word by selecting it and then choosing Index Entry from the Insert menu. Word marks the word and prints the concordance entry in the index.

- *You can type the word or phrase.* You use this technique to create conceptual entries and subentries.

  A *conceptual entry* is a word that you embed in the text (formatting the word as hidden text so that it won't print) and mark for indexing. Word doesn't print the conceptual entry, but the entry appears in the index. You use conceptual entries when the words in your document aren't quite right for indexing.

  A *subentry* is a subordinate term positioned below a main entry in a multilevel index, as follows:

  industrialization

      defined 7

      origins 9

      work roles 12

  industry

      Third World, 14-19

The following sections show you how to mark all three types of entries: concordance entries, conceptual entries, and subentries.

Before you begin experimenting with indexing, make sure that hidden text will appear on-screen. You will find it helpful to see hidden text while you work with indexed terms in your document. The display of hidden text is controlled by the View options in the Preferences dialog box (Tools menu). To see what is in figure 26.1, for example, you must activate the hidden-text option.

Marking Concordance Entries

The Index Entry command (Insert menu) automatically formats a word or phrase as a concordance entry (an entry that is printed in the document and that appears in the index). The command inserts codes that Word needs in order to recognize the word as a word to be printed in the index. These codes are formatted as hidden text.

Figure 26.1 shows a correctly coded concordance entry. Notice that the codes—the index code (.i.) before the word and the end-of-entry code (a semicolon) after the word—are formatted as hidden text, as indicated by the dotted underline.

Word adds the concordance entry to your index, using the case style you used when you typed the word in your document. If your style guidelines require all words to be capitalized when they appear in the index, you still can use the concordance technique. Simply select the entire index after Word compiles it, choose Change Case from the Format menu, and then choose the Sentence Case option in the Change Case dialog box.

To mark a word as a concordance entry, follow these steps:

1. Select the word. (To select the entire word quickly, double-click anywhere inside the word.)

2. Choose Index Entry from the Insert menu. Word marks the word automatically.

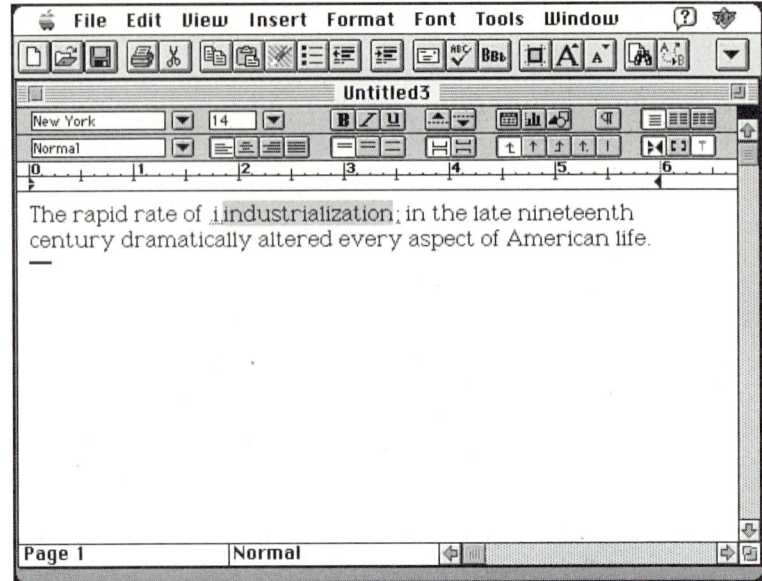

Fig. 26.1
A correctly coded
concordance entry.

Marking Conceptual Entries

When you create a conceptual entry, the word or phrase you are indexing does not appear in the text; you are indexing a concept that is not actually mentioned in the text. To create a conceptual entry, you must type the entire entry, all of which is formatted as hidden text. Because the conceptual entry is formatted as hidden text, the entry isn't printed in the text; it appears only in the index.

To create a conceptual entry, follow these steps:

1. Position the insertion point in the document where you want to type the entry. (Place the entry on the page you want to reference in the index.)

2. Choose Index Entry from the Insert menu. Word enters the index code (.i.) and the end-of-entry mark (the semicolon), and places the insertion point between the code and the mark.

3. Type the conceptual entry.

   Word formats the entire entry as hidden text. This text will not be printed within your document, but the indexed term will appear in your index (after you use Word to compile the index).

Figure 26.2 shows a correctly formatted conceptual entry (industry) at the end of a sentence.

Fig. 26.2
A conceptual entry.

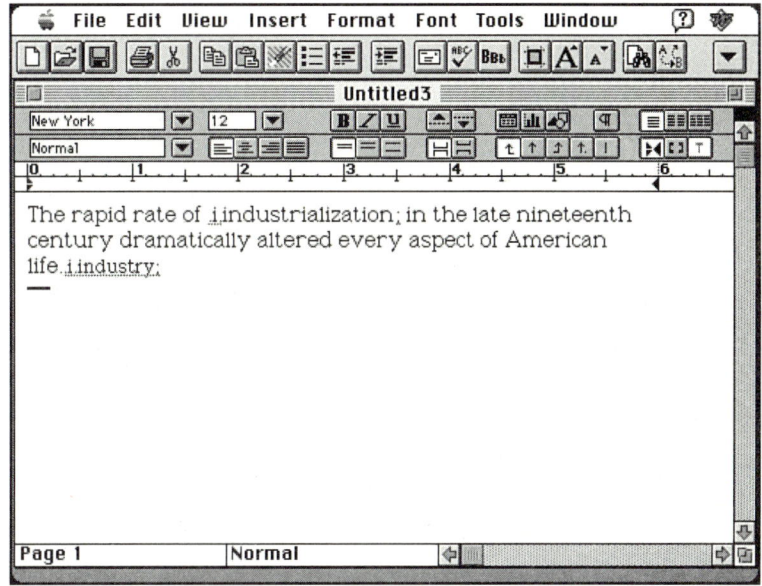

Marking Subentries

You should use subentries when an entry is to be followed by a long list of page numbers. In this case, subentries, such as the following, help the reader locate the desired information:

Industrial ventures

aluminum cookware 60

graphite processing 32

luxury goods 59

matches 38

textiles 23

Subentries resemble conceptual entries in that the whole entry is formatted as hidden text; you don't want the subentry code to appear in your document.

To create subentries, follow these steps:

1. Place the insertion point within the discussion of the topic you want to index.

2. Choose Index Entry from the Insert menu. Word positions the insertion point between the index code and the end-of-entry mark.

If you want, you can add as many as seven subordinate levels, although most style handbooks caution against using more than one or two levels. To add sublevels, simply add subentries separated by colons, as in these examples:

Industrial ventures:cookware:aluminum

Industrial ventures:cookware:pottery

Coding entries in this way produces an index that looks like the following example:

Industrial ventures

cookware

aluminum 18

pottery 29

Marking a Range of Pages

Often, you may want to index a topic that is discussed on more than one page, such as the following topic:

Industry 19-43

To create an entry that marks a range of pages, follow these steps:

1. At the beginning of the discussion of the topic, choose Index Entry from the Insert menu and then type an entry, using the following coding scheme:

.i(.subject;

The only difference between this entry and an ordinary conceptual entry is the beginning parenthesis. Notice that the parenthesis comes after the i but before the second period.

The word *subject* here refers to the topic you're indexing. If you're indexing the topic *industry*, the entry would look like the following:

.i(.industry;

2. At the end of the discussion of the topic, choose Index Entry from the Insert menu again and then type an entry, using a closing parenthesis as in the following example:

.i).subject;

Notice again that the parenthesis comes after the i but before the second period.

After Word compiles your index, the page range is indicated as follows:

Industry 19-43

Marking Cross-References

You can direct Word to print text rather than page numbers after index entries. You can use this feature to create cross-references, as in this example:

Industrial development. *See* industrialization.

To create a cross-reference, follow these steps:

1. Select the term you want to cross-reference.

2. Choose Index Entry from the Insert menu.

3. Type a number sign (**#**) followed by the text you want to print, as in the following example:

.i.Industrial development# *See* **industrialization;**

Formatting Index Entries

When you code index entries, you can add special formatting codes that affect the appearance of the entries in the index. These formatting codes do not affect the appearance of the word within the text of your document.

To boldface the page number, type **b** between the i of the index code and the code's second period, as in this example:

.ib.industrialization;

To italicize the page number, type **i** between the i of the index code and the code's second period, as in the following example:

.ii.industrialization;

To boldface and italicize the page number, type **bi** between the i of the index code and the code's second period, as in this example:

.ibi.industrialization;

To add space between the index term and the page number, press the space bar at the end of the index entry, as in the following example:

.i.industrialization ;

To add a tab between the index term and the page number, press Tab at the end of the index entry.

To add a character (such as a comma) at the end of the index entry and before the page number, type the character after the index entry, as in this example:

.i.industrialization,;

Compiling an Index

When you are certain that your document is in its final form and you have marked all the index entries, decide how you want your index to appear. You can choose either of the following formatting options:

- *Nested subentries.* Nested subentries appear below the main entry and 1/4 inch to the right. These subentries can have distinct character styles. Following is an example of a nested subentry:

  Industrial ventures

  > Batteries, 29

  > Fishing boats, 32

  > Tires, 48

- *Run-in subentries* continue on the same line and cannot have distinct character styles. The following example shows a run-in subentry:

  Industrial ventures: Batteries, 29; Fishing boats, 32, Tires, 48

To compile your index, follow these steps:

1. Choose Index from the Insert menu. The Index dialog box appears (see fig. 26.3).

2. In the Format area, click the Nested or Run-In Box radio button.

Fig. 26.3
Index dialog box.

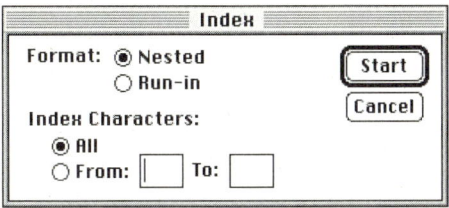

3. In the Index Characters area, click the All radio button if you want to index all letters. If you want to create an index only for selected letters of the alphabet, click the From radio button and then type the range (such as A and C) in the From and To text boxes.

4. Choose Start. Word compiles the index and places the completed index in its own section at the end of the document (see fig. 26.4).

Fig. 26.4
Index compiled from terms coded in the document.

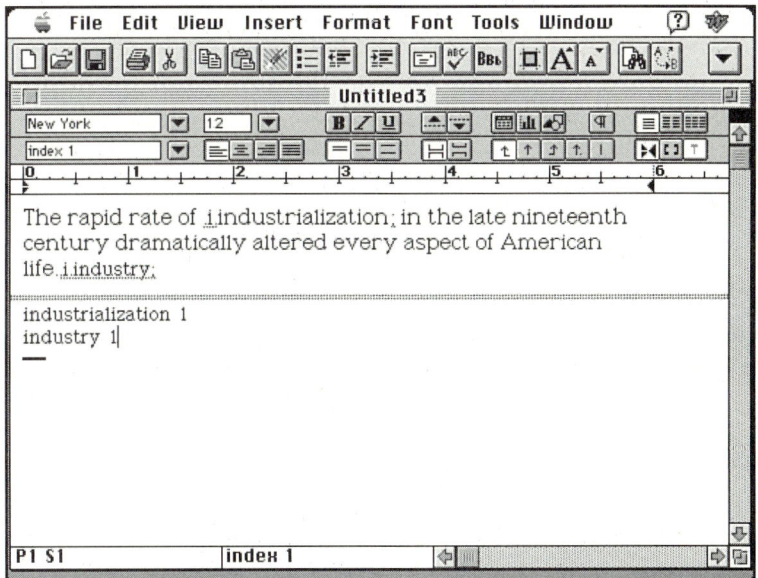

If you find that terms are missing from your index or that the index contains errors, insert or correct the codes in your document, and then use the Index command again to recompile the index. Upon your confirmation, Word deletes the existing index when it compiles the new one.

Chapter 26
Adding an Index and Table of Contents

Indexing requires a great deal of memory. If your Macintosh runs out of memory and cannot finish the index, compile the index again, but index only A through C on the first pass, D through F on the second, and so on.

Updating the Index

If you make changes in your document that affect the page breaks, you should update your index. This section describes the procedure you can use to update your index quickly.

To update your index, follow these steps:

1. Choose Index from the Insert menu. Word detects the existing index. An alert box appears, asking whether you want to replace the index.

2. Choose Yes to replace the existing index, or click No so that Word places the new index after the existing one.

Removing Index Codes

If you decide against including an index in your document, you can discard the index after your document prints. If you prefer to remove the index codes, you can do so by using the Replace command. When the Replace dialog box appears, leave the Find What text box blank but choose the hidden-text format in this box. Leave the Replace With box blank, too, and then choose OK. Word deletes all the hidden text in your document.

For more information on removing formats with the Replace command, see Chapter 9, "Formatting with Fonts and Character Styles."

Understanding Index Styles

When you have compiled the index, you will notice that Word has formatted each entry by using the standard Index styles (Index 1, Index 2, and so on). These styles format the main entry with the normal character and paragraph styles. Subentries are indented 1/4 inch.

You can change these styles, if you want. You can define the Index 1 style to print in boldface Helvetica 12, for example, and print subentries in Helvetica 10 italic.

To change index styles, redefine them as you would redefine any other automatic style. For information on redefining automatic styles, see Chapter 14, "Formatting with Styles."

Creating a Table of Contents

To help the reader and to create a professional appearance, business and professional reports and proposals require a table of contents. Normally, compiling such a table is a chore. Word, however, can do the job almost automatically, especially if you have organized your document with outlining, as recommended in Chapter 22.

If you haven't outlined your document, you can code the headings in your document so that Word can use the headings to compile a table of contents. A much easier procedure, however, is to outline your document by applying Word's standard heading styles (Heading 1, Heading 2, Heading 3, and so on) to the titles and subtitles in your document. (For more information on applying standard styles, see Chapter 14.)

Creating a Table of Contents with the Outline Method

One advantage of outlining your documents is that you can almost automatically compile a table of contents from an outline that echoes the headings in your document (see chapters 14 and 22 for more information on linking document headings and outline entries). To compile such a table, you must have used Word's heading styles for the chapter titles, headings, and subheadings in your document, as explained in Chapter 22.

To create a table of contents from a document in which you used Word's standard heading styles, follow these steps:

1. Switch to Outline view by choosing Outline from the View menu or pressing ⌘-Option-O.

2. Choose Table of Contents from the Insert menu. The Table of Contents dialog box appears (see fig. 26.5).

3. In the Collect area, click the Outline radio button.

4. In the Level area, click the All radio button to use all heading levels in your outline, or click the From radio button to use only some levels and then type those levels in the From and To text boxes. (To print chapter titles and major headings, for example, type **1** in the From box and **2** in the To box.)

Chapter 26

Adding an Index and Table of Contents

Fig. 26.5
Table of Contents
dialog box.

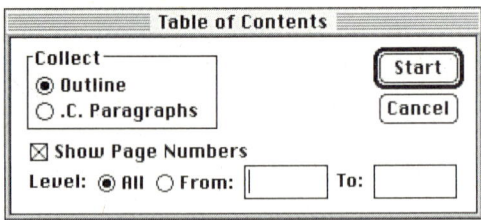

5. Choose Start. Word compiles the table of contents and places it at the beginning of your document, in its own unpaginated section (see fig. 26.6).

Fig. 26.6
Table of contents.

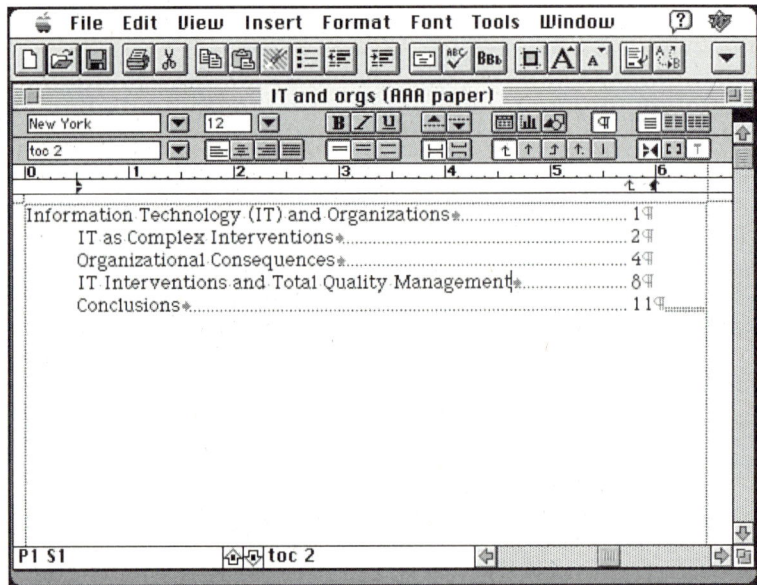

You can format the table of contents, adding character emphases, indentations, blank lines, and other formats to suit your taste and your style guidelines.

Creating a Table of Contents by Coding Entries

Marking headings for inclusion in a table of contents is much like creating concordance entries for an index. You must distinguish among three parts of each marked heading, as follows:

- *Table-of-contents code (.c.).* This code (a lowercase c surrounded by periods) must be formatted as hidden text. The code tells Word that the text to follow should be treated as a table-of-contents entry. The number after the c code (see Table 26.1) tells Word the level of the heading. (You can distinguish as many as nine levels.) If no number appears after the code, Word assumes that the heading is a first-level heading.

- *Heading.* So that the heading will print in your document, the heading should not be formatted as hidden text. If the heading contains a colon, semicolon, or quotation marks, enclose the heading in quotation marks formatted as hidden text.

- *End mark (;).* This code (a semicolon formatted as hidden text) tells Word where the table-of-contents entry stops.

Table 26.1 lists Word's table-of-contents codes.

Table 26.1
Table-of-Contents Codes

Level	Code
First level	.c. or .c1.
Second level	.c2.
Third level	.c3.
Fourth level	.c4.
Fifth level	.c5.
Sixth level	.c6.
Seventh level	.c7.
Eighth level	.c8.
Ninth level	.c9.

To create a table of contents by using the manual marking technique, follow these steps:

1. Select the heading that you want to appear in the table of contents.

Chapter 26

Adding an Index and Table of Contents

2. Choose TOC Entry from the Insert menu. Word adds the `.c.` code and semicolon, and formats these codes as hidden text.

3. After the `c` in the table-of-contents code, type the number of the heading's level. For a second-level heading, for example, type **.c2.**

4. If you want to suppress page numbers after the entry, type a colon before the semicolon, as in this example:

    .i.Chapter3:;

    Make sure that the semicolon is formatted as hidden text.

5. Continue to code the headings, as explained in step 3.

6. When you finish coding all the headings, choose Table of Contents from the Insert menu. The Table of Contents dialog box appears.

7. In the Collect area, click the .C. Paragraphs radio button.

8. Choose Start. Word compiles the table of contents and places it at the beginning of your document, in its own unpaginated section.

You can format the table of contents, adding character emphases, indentations, blank lines, and other formats to suit your taste and your style guidelines.

Word doesn't automatically update your table of contents. If you make changes in your document that affect pagination, you should recompile the table by using the Table of Contents command again. An alert box appears, asking whether you want to replace the existing table of contents. Choose Yes.

Understanding Table-of-Contents Styles

Like entries in the indexes that Word automatically creates, table-of-contents entries are formatted with the automatic styles in Word's default style sheet, but you can modify these styles.

By default, Word formats a table of contents so that the headings are formatted with the normal character format and a flush-right tab stop (with dot leaders) at six inches. Subordinate headings are formatted with additional half-inch indentations. You can reposition tab stops, redefine a character style, or change the pattern of indentations. For information on redefining automatic styles, see Chapter 14, "Formatting with Styles."

Quick Review

This section summarizes the most useful information in this chapter. Check "Productivity Tips" for a review of high-productivity tips and tricks—the ones that Macintosh and Word pros use every day. Review "Techniques" whenever you need a quick reminder about a specific procedure.

Productivity Tips

- To create a good index for your document, try to anticipate what your readers will want to look up. Distinguish between concordance entries (words that appear in the text as well as in the index) and conceptual entries (words that don't appear in the text but do appear in the index). A good index has both concordance and conceptual entries.

- Resist the temptation to use too many levels of subentries; use two levels at the most.

- To create concordance entries, type the word you want to index, select it, and choose the Insert Index Entry command from the Document menu. To create conceptual entries, first choose the Insert Index Entry command and then type the term.

- You can add page-range, major-entry, and text entries to your index. Use text entries to cross-reference other topics in your index.

- If your document needs a table of contents, format your document's headings and subheadings with Word's standard heading styles so that the headings are linked to outline levels. After formatting your document's headings and subheadings with these styles, you can compile a table of contents quickly and almost automatically.

Techniques

This section provides concise summaries of all the procedures introduced in this chapter.

Chapter 26

Adding an Index and Table of Contents

Creating Concordance Index Entries

To mark a word as a concordance entry:

1. Select the word.

2. Choose Index Entry from the Insert menu.

Creating Conceptual Index Entries

To create a conceptual entry:

1. Position the insertion point where you want to type the entry.

2. Choose Index Entry from the Insert menu.

3. Type the conceptual entry.

Creating Index Subentries

To create subentries:

1. Place the insertion point within the discussion of the topic you want to index.

2. Choose Index Entry from the Insert menu.

3. Type the main entry, a colon, and a subentry.

Creating a Page-Range Index Entry

To create a page-range index entry:

1. At the beginning of the discussion of the topic, choose Index Entry from the Insert menu and type an entry, using this coding scheme:

   .i(.subject;

2. At the end of the discussion of the topic, choose Insert Index Entry again and then type an entry using a closing parenthesis, as follows:

   .i).subject;

Creating Cross-References

To create a cross-reference (concordance entry):

1. Select the term you want to cross-reference.

2. Choose Index Entry from the Insert menu.

3. Type a number sign (#) followed by the text you want to print.

Compiling the Index

To compile your index:

1. Choose Index from the Insert menu. The Index dialog box appears.

2. In the Format area, click the Nested or Run-In Box radio button.

3. In the Index Characters area, click the All radio button if you want to index all letters. If you want to create an index only for selected letters of the alphabet, click the From radio button and then type the range (such as A and C) in the From and To text boxes.

4. Choose Start.

Updating an Index

To update an index:

1. Choose Index from the Insert menu. Word detects the existing index. An alert box appears, asking whether you want to replace the index.

2. Choose Yes to replace the existing index, or click No so that Word places the new index after the existing one.

Creating a Table of Contents from an Outlined Document

To create a table of contents from an outlined document:

1. Switch to Outline view by choosing Outline from the View menu or pressing ⌘-Option-O.

2. Choose Table of Contents from the Insert menu. The Table of Contents dialog box appears.

Chapter 26

Adding an Index and Table of Contents

3. In the Collect area, click the Outline radio button.

4. In the Level area, type the levels that you want to appear in the outline.

5. Choose Start.

Creating a Table of Contents by Marking TOC Entries

To create a table of contents by using the manual marking technique:

1. Select the heading that you want to appear in the table of contents.

2. Choose TOC Entry from the Insert menu.

3. After the letter c in the table-of-contents code, type the number of the heading's level.

4. If you want to suppress page numbers after the entry, type a colon before the semicolon.

5. Continue to code the headings, as explained in step 3.

6. When you finish coding all the headings, choose Table of Contents from the Insert menu. The Table of Contents dialog box appears.

7. In the Collect area, click the .C. Paragraphs radio button.

8. Choose Start.

Working with Long Documents

More than a few doctoral dissertations, 1,000-page novels, textbooks, and trade books are composed on Macintoshes running Word, and the book you're reading is an example. Taking up several megabytes of disk space, the text of a long book such as this one could make one heck of a big file—and easily could cause problems proportionate to its size, such as sluggish performance, low-memory messages, and all-your-eggs-in-one-basket disasters if the file became corrupt for some reason. Prudent Word users keep sections of a long document in a series of separate files.

What happens, however, when you want to print a document with continuous pagination, as well as an accurate table of contents and index? New features in Word, including the File Series option in the Document dialog box, enable you to chain documents for printing in a series without having to type complicated Print Merge commands, as users of previous versions of Word were obliged to do.

This chapter presents a complete strategy for tackling a huge writing project with Word. Following is an overview of this chapter's contents:

- *Creating a template document.* You begin by creating a stationery document that contains the styles and formatting choices you want to apply to every section of the document.

- *Linking the files in a file series.* After you complete the files and are ready to print, you link the files in a file series by following the instructions in this section.

USING
WORD 5.1
FOR THE MAC
SPECIAL EDITION

■ *Numbering pages and footnotes consecutively.* In this section, you learn how to make sure that pages and footnotes are numbered consecutively and correctly throughout your long document.

■ *Creating an index and table of contents.* This section discusses creating a unified index and table of contents after you link files in a file series.

■ *Using the INCLUDE command to assemble a document.* You can use this Print Merge command to include one long file within another, as this section explains.

Creating a Template Document

If you are creating a document that you plan to assemble from a series of linked files, all the files *must* have exactly the same formats and styles; otherwise, you could see formatting inconsistencies when you print your document. By far the best way to prevent such inconsistencies is to begin the project by creating a stationery document that serves as a template for all the sections of the document. You add to this template the styles you want to use throughout your document, and you also choose formats and add text, such as chapter titles and headers. After creating the template, you start each file by opening the template document.

To create the master template document, follow these steps:

1. In a new Word document, choose the section and document formats that you want to apply to all the files: margins, header and footer locations, footnote preferences (such as footnotes or endnotes printed at the end of sections), and page numbers (unless you want to add page numbers with headers).

   To suppress the printing of page numbers on the first page of a chapter, choose Different First Page in the Section dialog box.

   To make sure that Word starts each chapter or section on an odd-numbered page, choose Odd Page in the Start list box of the Section dialog box.

2. Create styles for your document, and redefine standard styles to suit your taste or your style guidelines.

   To create the styles, you may want to experiment by creating dummy text, as shown in figures 27.1 and 27.2. (See Table 27.1 for a list of the styles used to create this document.)

3. Add headers and footers. If you didn't choose Margin Page Numbers in the Section dialog box, add page numbers to the header or footer.

4. Choose Select All from the Edit menu or press ⌘-A to select all the dummy text.

5. To delete the text (but not the styles you created), choose Cut from the Edit menu, press ⌘-X, or click the Cut tool.

6. Choose Save from the Edit menu, press ⌘-S, or click the Save tool. The Save As dialog box appears.

7. In the Save File As Type drop-down list box, select Stationery.

8. In the File Name text box, type a name that indicates that the file is a template (for example, Report Chapter Template or Thesis Chapter Template).

Fig. 27.1

Design for a template document (page 1 of 2).

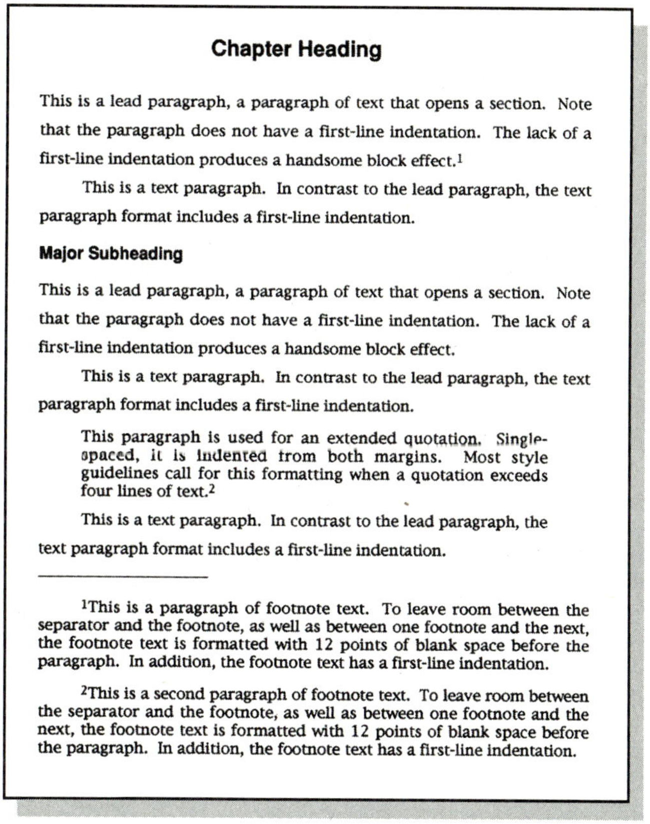

Chapter Heading

This is a lead paragraph, a paragraph of text that opens a section. Note that the paragraph does not have a first-line indentation. The lack of a first-line indentation produces a handsome block effect.[1]

This is a text paragraph. In contrast to the lead paragraph, the text paragraph format includes a first-line indentation.

Major Subheading

This is a lead paragraph, a paragraph of text that opens a section. Note that the paragraph does not have a first-line indentation. The lack of a first-line indentation produces a handsome block effect.

This is a text paragraph. In contrast to the lead paragraph, the text paragraph format includes a first-line indentation.

This paragraph is used for an extended quotation. Single-spaced, it is indented from both margins. Most style guidelines call for this formatting when a quotation exceeds four lines of text.[2]

This is a text paragraph. In contrast to the lead paragraph, the text paragraph format includes a first-line indentation.

---

[1]This is a paragraph of footnote text. To leave room between the separator and the footnote, as well as between one footnote and the next, the footnote text is formatted with 12 points of blank space before the paragraph. In addition, the footnote text has a first-line indentation.

[2]This is a second paragraph of footnote text. To leave room between the separator and the footnote, as well as between one footnote and the next, the footnote text is formatted with 12 points of blank space before the paragraph. In addition, the footnote text has a first-line indentation.

Chapter 27

Working with Long Documents

Fig. 27.2

Design for a template
document (page 2 of 2).

Chapter XX   2

Major Subheading

This is a lead paragraph, a paragraph of text that opens a section. Note
that the paragraph does not have a first-line indentation. The lack of a
first-line indentation produces a handsome block effect.

    This is a text paragraph. In contrast to the lead paragraph, the text
paragraph format includes a first-line indentation.

> This paragraph is used for an extended quotation. Single-
> spaced, it is indented from both margins. Most style
> guidelines call for this formatting when a quotation exceeds
> four lines of text.[3]

This is a text paragraph. In contrast to the lead paragraph, the
text paragraph format includes a first-line indentation. This is a text
paragraph. In contrast to the lead paragraph, the text paragraph
format includes a first-line indentation. This is a text paragraph. In
contrast to the lead paragraph, the text paragraph format includes a
first-line indentation.

> This paragraph is used for an extended quotation. Single-
> spaced, it is indented from both margins. Most style
> guidelines call for this formatting when a quotation exceeds
> four lines of text.[4]

This is a text paragraph. In contrast to the lead paragraph, the
text paragraph format includes a first-line indentation. This is a text

---

[3]This is a third paragraph of footnote text. To leave room between
the separator and the footnote, as well as between one footnote and the
next, the footnote text is formatted with 12 points of blank space before
the paragraph. In addition, the footnote text has a first-line indentation.

[4]This is a fourth paragraph of footnote text. To leave room between
the separator and the footnote, as well as between one footnote and the
next, the footnote text is formatted with 12 points of blank space before
the paragraph. In addition, the footnote text has a first-line indentation.

---

9. Choose Save. Word creates the template document and changes
   the name of the current document to Untitled. Now you can use
   this document to create the first chapter of your report or thesis.

To create additional documents based on this template, open it as you
would open any Word document. Word always opens a template as an
Untitled document, so you never overwrite the original. (For more
information on template documents, see Chapter 5, "Managing Documents and Files.")

Table 27.1 lists the styles used to create this template.

Part IV

Creating Professional Documents

Style name	Use and formats
Heading 2*	Used for chapter titles (Helvetica 24 Bold, 48 points before, 18 points after; centered; Keep With Next Paragraph)
Heading 3*	Used for major subheadings (Helvetica 14 Bold, 18 points before, 6 points after; left alignment; Keep With Next Paragraph)
Lead ¶	Used for lead paragraphs (New York 12, at least 24 points line spacing [double space]; justified alignment)
Text ¶	Used for text paragraphs (New York 12, at least 24 points line spacing [double space]; 1/2-inch first-line indentation; justified)
Quotation	Used for extended quotations (New York 12, automatic line spacing [single space]; 1/2-inch indentation left, 1/2-inch indentation right; justified alignment)
Footnote Text*	Used for footnote text (New York 12, automatic line spacing [single space]; 1/2-inch first-line indentation; 12 points before; justified alignment)

Table 27.1
Styles in the
Template Document

*Redefined standard style.

If you need to add a style later, be sure to add the style to the template document. Then copy the style from the template document to all the other files. For more information on using a template document to store styles, see Chapter 14, "Formatting with Styles."

Linking the Files in a File Series

After you create all the files that make up your long project, use the Document command (Format menu) to link the files in a series. Word numbers the pages consecutively and accurately, and you can compile an index and table of contents as though the files were part of one long document.

To link files in a series, follow these steps:

1. Open the first document.

2. Choose Document from the Format menu or press ⌘-F14. The Document dialog box appears.

3. Click the File Series command button. The File Series dialog box appears (see fig. 27.3).

Fig. 27.3

File Series dialog box.

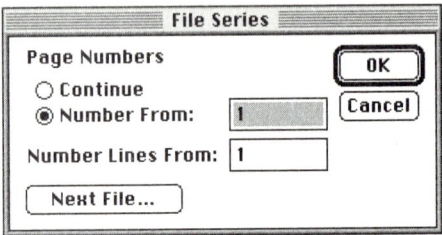

4. Click the Next File command button. An Open dialog box appears.

5. In the list box, select the next file in the series and then choose OK. The File Series dialog box reappears, with the name of the next file displayed at the bottom and the Next File command button changed to Reset Next File.

6. Choose OK.

7. Save and close the first document.

8. Open the next document and then repeat steps 2 through 7. In step 6, however, click the Continue radio button before closing the File Series dialog box so that Word will number the pages consecutively.

9. Repeat step 8 until you link all the files except the last one.

When you link files by using the File Series dialog box, Word automatically prints the next file—and the file linked to the next file, and so on—until all the documents are printed.

To print the linked files with continuous pagination, follow these steps:

1. Open the first document.

2. Choose Print from the File menu, press ⌘-P, or click the Print tool. The Print dialog box appears.

3. If you want to print a draft of only the current file, without printing all the rest of the files, deactivate the Print Next File check box.

4. Choose Print.

Numbering Footnotes Consecutively

In many style guidelines, footnote numbering starts at 1 at the beginning of every major section or chapter. Word numbers exactly this way when you place chapters in separate files and link them for printing. You may prefer, however, to number footnotes consecutively. To do so, you must specify the starting footnote number for each file in the series.

To number footnotes consecutively, follow these steps:

1. Open the first document.

2. Choose Footnotes from the View menu. The Footnote window appears on-screen.

3. Scroll to the end of the document and note the number of the last footnote.

4. Close the document.

5. Open the next document.

6. Choose Document from the Format menu or press ⌘-F14. The Document dialog box appears (see fig. 27.4).

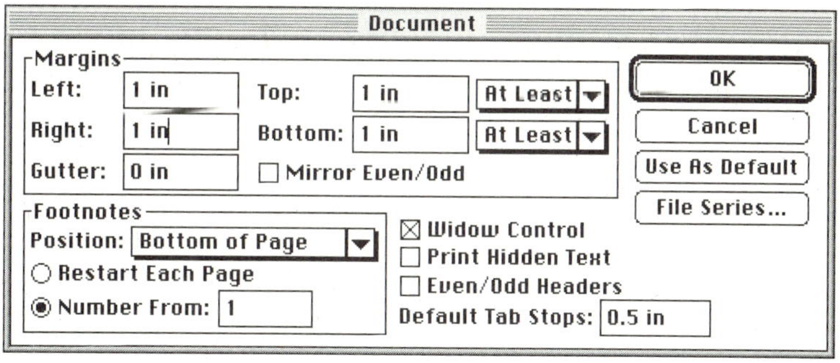

Fig. 27.4
Document dialog box.

Document

Margins
Left: 1 in   Top: 1 in   At Least ▼
Right: 1 in   Bottom: 1 in At Least ▼
Gutter: 0 in   ☐ Mirror Even/Odd

OK
Cancel
Use As Default
File Series...

Footnotes
Position: Bottom of Page ▼
☐ Restart Each Page
⦿ Number From: 1

☒ Widow Control
☐ Print Hidden Text
☐ Even/Odd Headers
Default Tab Stops: 0.5 in

7. In the Number From text box, type the number Word should use to start consecutively numbering the footnotes. (To get this number, add 1 to the number of the last footnote in the preceding document.)

8. Choose OK.

9. Choose Footnotes from the View menu to open the Footnote window again.

10. Scroll to the end of the document and note the last footnote number used.

11. Save the document.

12. Close the document.

13. Repeat steps 5 through 12 for all the rest of the documents in the series.

Creating an Index and Table of Contents

To add an index and table of contents to a series of linked files, mark the index entries in all the documents, as explained in Chapter 26. Then open the first document, and compile the index and table of contents just as you would in any other document. Word automatically opens the rest of the documents in the series and extracts the table-of-contents and index entries. The index and table of contents that Word creates include correct page numbers.

Using the INCLUDE Command To Assemble a Document

In previous versions of Word, you used the INCLUDE command—one of Word's Print Merge keywords—to link documents for printing with continuous pagination. In Word 5.0 and 5.1, the File Series dialog box provides a much easier way to chain files for printing. You still can use the INCLUDE command, however, and using this command even has one advantage: by using INCLUDE, you can *insert* a file *within* another one when you print. (You cannot insert one file into another one when you use the File Series dialog box, which always starts the next file at the end of the current one.)

Because the INCLUDE command is only a placeholder, your document doesn't grow in size beyond a few additional characters. Word inserts the text only during printing.

A good argument, though, is that you shouldn't use INCLUDE in this way unless the file you are inserting truly is enormous. If you are inserting a short or medium-size file (perhaps 20 or 30 pages), a better method may be to insert the text by using the File or Object command. (For more information on using these commands to insert one file into another, see Chapter 30, "Linking Data Dynamically.")

To include one file within another when you print, with continuous pagination, follow these steps:

1. Place the insertion point where you want the file to appear when the document is printed.

2. Choose Print Merge Helper from the View menu. An Open dialog box appears.

3. Click None to open Print Merge Helper without assigning a data document.

4. Choose INCLUDE from the Insert Keyword list box. An Open dialog box appears, with a message that asks you to select the file you want to include.

5. Select the file you want to include and then choose Open. Word inserts the INCLUDE command into your document, as shown in figure 27.5.

Fig. 27.5
INCLUDE command inserted into a document.

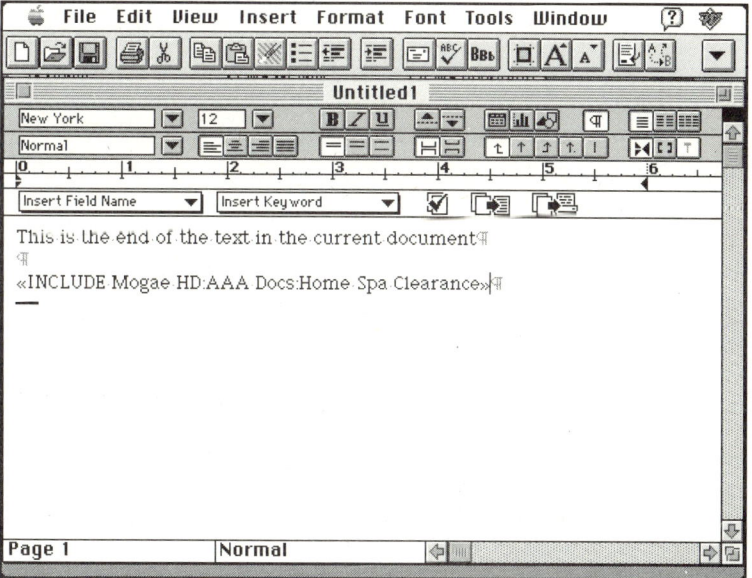

6. To insert additional documents when you print, repeat steps 3 through 5.

7. Save your document.

To print the document that contains the INCLUDE instructions, follow these steps:

1. Choose Print Merge from the File menu. The Print Merge dialog box appears (see fig. 27.6).

Fig. 27.6
Print Merge dialog box.

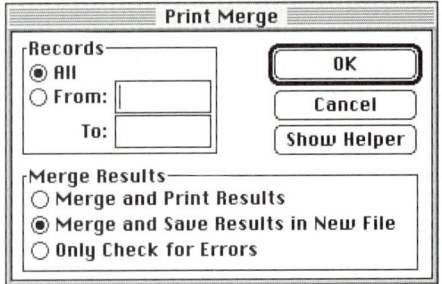

2. Choose an option in the Merge Results area. You can choose Merge and Print Results to New File or Merge and Print Results.

3. Choose OK. Word prints the linked documents with continuous pagination. The included documents take on the formatting from the document in which you placed the INCLUDE commands.

Quick Review

This section summarizes the most useful information in this chapter. Check "Productivity Tips" for a review of high-productivity tips and tricks—the ones that Macintosh and Word pros use every day. Review "Techniques" whenever you need a quick reminder about a specific procedure.

Productivity Tips

■ Before you start to write a long document, create a template to store the formats and styles you want to use in each section. Save the file as a stationery document, and retrieve this file to start each chapter or section.

Part IV

Creating Professional Documents

■ If you are creating a long document, break its chapters or sections into separate files and use the File Series dialog box to link those files. Word will run faster, and you eliminate the possibility of losing all your work if even one file becomes corrupted.

Techniques

This section provides concise summaries of all the procedures introduced in this chapter.

Creating the Master Template Document for a File Series

To create the master template document:

1. In a new Word document, choose the section and document formats you want to apply to all the files.

2. Create styles for your document, and redefine standard styles to suit your taste or your style guidelines.

3. Add headers and footers. If you didn't choose Margin Page Numbers in the Section dialog box, add page numbers to the header or footer.

4. Choose Select All from the Edit menu or press ⌘-A to select all the dummy text.

5. To delete the text (but not the styles you created), choose Cut from the Edit menu, press ⌘-X, or click the Cut tool.

6. Choose Save from the Edit menu, press ⌘-S, or click the Save tool. The Save As dialog box appears.

7. In the Save File As Type drop-down list box, select Stationery.

8. In the File Name text box, type a name that indicates that the file is a template.

9. Choose Save.

Linking the Files in a Series

To link files in a series:

1. Open the first document.

2. Choose Document from the Format menu or press ⌘-F14. The Document dialog box appears.

3. Click the File Series command button. The File Series dialog box appears.

4. Click the Next File command button. An Open dialog box appears.

5. In the list box, select the next file in the series.

6. Choose OK. The File Series dialog box reappears, with the name of the next file displayed at the bottom and the Next File command button changed to Reset Next File.

7. Save and close the first document.

8. Open the next document, and repeat steps 2 through 7. In step 6, click the Continue radio button before closing the File Series dialog box so that Word will number the pages consecutively.

9. Repeat step 8 until you link all the files except the last one.

Numbering Footnotes Consecutively in the File Series

To number footnotes consecutively:

1. Open the first document.

2. Choose Footnotes from the View menu to open the Footnote window.

3. Scroll to the end of the document, and note the number of the last footnote.

4. Close the document.

5. Open the next document.

6. Choose Document from the Format menu or press ⌘-F14. The Document dialog box appears.

7. In the Number From text box, type the number Word should use to start the footnote numbering consecutively. (To get this number, add 1 to the number of the last footnote in the preceding document.)

8. Choose OK.

9. Choose Footnotes again from the View menu to reopen the footnote window.

10. Scroll to the end of the document, and note the last footnote number used.

11. Save the document.

12. Close the document.

13. Repeat steps 5 through 12 for all the remaining documents in the series.

Adding an Index to a File-Series Document

To add an index to a file-series document:

1. In each document, mark the terms you want to index.

2. Open the first document.

3. Choose Index from the Insert menu.

4. Choose Start to begin compiling the index for all the documents in the series.

Adding a Table of Contents to a File-Series Document

To add a table of contents to a file-series document:

1. Format chapter titles, headings, and subheadings, using Word's standard heading styles.

2. Open the first document.

3. Choose Table of Contents from the Insert menu. The Table of Contents dialog box appears.

4. Click Outline.

5. In the From and To text boxes, indicate the outline levels you want to appear in the table of contents.

6. Choose Start to begin compiling the table of contents.

Printing Files Linked in a Series

To print the linked files with continuous pagination:

1. Open the first document.

2. Choose Print from the File menu, press ⌘-P, or click the Print tool. The Print dialog box appears.

3. Choose Print.

Printing Only the Current Document

To print the current document without printing the rest of the files in the file series:

1. Open the document.

2. Choose Print from the File menu, press ⌘-P, or click the Print tool. The Print dialog box appears.

3. Deactivate the Print Next File check box.

4. Choose Print.

Creating Collaborative and Dynamic Documents

Includes

Writing Collaboratively
with Annotations

Playing Movies

Linking Data Dynamically

USING
WORD 5.1
FOR THE MAC
SPECIAL EDITION

Writing Collaboratively with Annotations

When you learn how to write in school, you work individually. But on the job, much writing is done collaboratively. An author creates a draft and gives it to one or more colleagues, who make suggestions for revision or provide additional material for incorporation into the document. Thanks to Word 5.1's new Text Annotation capabilities, reviewers can add *annotations*—comments formatted in hidden text—that facilitate on-line (computer-based) revision. The author can read the reviewers' annotations and then remove those annotations or incorporate them into the text.

If you have a Macintosh equipped with a microphone, such as a II LC or IIsi, you can annotate your document with voice annotations. A *voice annotation* is a stored voice recording that appears as an icon in your document. When you click the icon, the Voice Annotation dialog box appears, enabling you to play the recording. You can play the recorded sounds on any Macintosh.

In this chapter, you learn how to use both kinds of annotations to facilitate your collaborative writing efforts.

This chapter covers the following topics:

- ■ *Creating and using text annotations.* You learn how to insert, edit, display, hide, print, review, and copy text annotations.

- ■ *Creating and using voice annotations.* You learn how to record, play, edit, and manage voice annotations.

USING
WORD 5.1
FOR THE MAC
SPECIAL EDITION

Creating and Using Text Annotations

An annotation is a comment, formatted in hidden text, that you add to a document. Word shows the annotation's location with an *annotation mark*. By default, the annotation mark is a cartoon balloon that contains the reviewer's initials, as shown in figure 28.1.

Fig. 28.1

Annotation mark embedded in text of document.

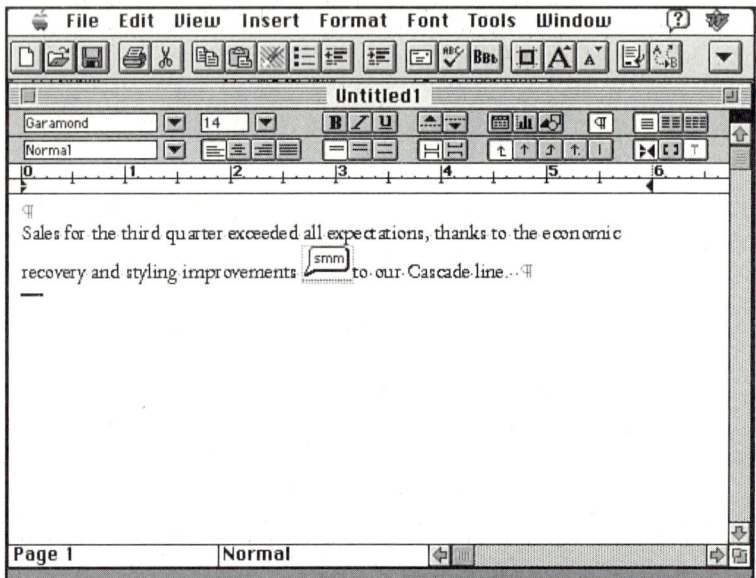

When you double-click the annotation mark, you see the text of the annotation, as shown in figure 28.2.

In the following sections, you learn how to insert annotations into your document, review and edit them, and incorporate or remove annotations made by other readers.

Inserting a Text Annotation into a Document

You can insert as many annotations as you want into a document. Word marks each annotation with an annotation mark.

To insert a text annotation, follow these steps:

1. Position the insertion point in your document where you want to place the annotation.

2. Choose Annotation from the Insert menu. The Annotation dialog box appears (see fig. 28.3).

Fig. 28.2
Text of annotation.

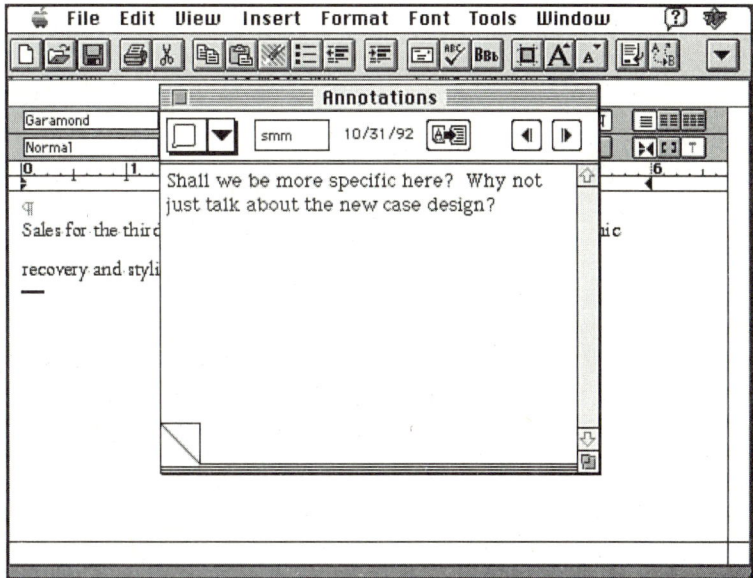

Fig. 28.3
Annotation dialog box.

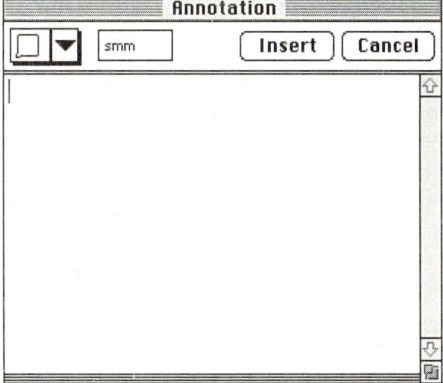

3. The first drop-down list box contains alternative annotation marks. By default, Word inserts a balloon annotation mark. You can choose among four other marks, as shown in figure 28.4, but only the balloon and the square show the reviewer's initials.

Fig. 28.4

Annotation-mark
drop-down list box.

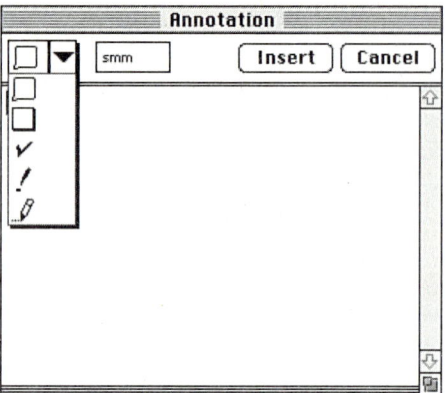

4. In the text box next to the annotation-mark list box, type your
   initials. If you type nothing, Word uses the initials typed in the
   Your Initials area of the Preferences dialog box (see fig. 28.5).

Fig. 28.5

Name and initials in the
Preferences dialog box.

When you installed Word, you typed your initials along with your name.
Word automatically inserted these initials into the Your Initials area of
the Preferences dialog box. Your initials, therefore, appear automatically
in the annotation mark—as long as you're using your own machine.
When you review a document on someone else's Macintosh, use the
initials area of the Annotation dialog box to insert your own initials into
the annotations.

Part V

Creating Collaborative and Dynamic Documents

5. Type the text of the annotation.

6. Click the Insert command button. Word places the annotation in your document and marks its location with an annotation mark.

If you don't see the annotation mark in your document, choose Preferences from the Tools menu to open the Preferences dialog box, and click the View icon to display the View options. Then activate the Show Hidden Text option and click the close box to exit Preferences.

Editing Text Annotations

After you have inserted annotations, you can edit them easily.

To edit a text annotation, follow these steps:

1. Double-click the annotation mark. The Annotations dialog box appears (see fig. 28.6 in "Reviewing Text Annotations" later in this chapter).

   This box differs slightly from the dialog box you use to insert an annotation. You learn about the additional features of the dialog box later in this chapter, in "Reviewing Text Annotations."

2. Edit the text of the annotation. You also can change the initials and the annotation mark.

3. Click the close box. An alert box appears, asking whether you want to save your annotation.

4. Choose Yes.

Displaying, Hiding, and Printing Annotation Marks

If you activated the Show Hidden Text option in the Preferences dialog box (View options), you see the annotation marks in your document. You can hide the marks, if you prefer, and you can choose to print your document with the marks displayed or hidden. For information on displaying or printing your document with the text of the annotations visible, see "Copying Text Annotations to a New Document" later in this chapter.

Displaying the annotation marks in your document does not program Word to print the marks. You must activate another option to tell Word to print the annotation marks.

Chapter 28

Writing Collaboratively with Annotations

To print annotation marks, follow these steps:

1. Choose Print from the File menu, press ⌘-P, or click the Print tool. The Print dialog box appears.

2. Activate the Print Hidden Text option.

3. Choose Print.

Word prints the annotation marks, not the text of the annotations themselves. To print the annotation text, you must copy the annotations to a new document, as explained later in this chapter.

Reviewing Text Annotations

Word enables you to review annotations quickly and easily. You need not scroll through the document to locate and display each annotation individually; after the Annotations dialog box appears on-screen, you can review in quick succession all the annotations in the document.

To review text annotations, follow these steps:

1. Position the insertion point at the beginning of your document.

2. Choose Annotations from the View menu. The Annotations dialog box appears, displaying the text of the first annotation (see fig. 28.6).

Fig. 28.6
Annotations dialog box.

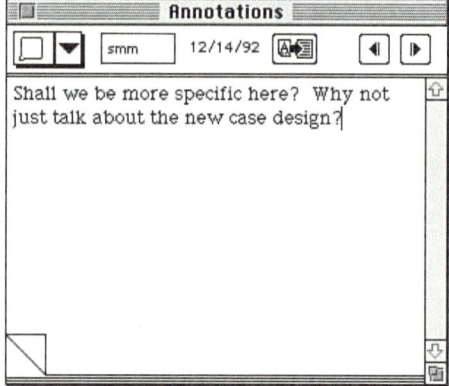

3. Size the Annotations dialog box so that you can see the document text, as shown in figure 28.7.

Fig. 28.7
Annotations dialog box sized so that document text is visible.

Next button

Previous button

Copy to New Document button

Next Page tab

Previous Page tab

> File Edit View Insert Format Font Tools Window
>
> Untitled1
>
> Garamond 14 Normal
>
> recovery and styling improvements [smm] to our Cascade line.
>
> **Annotations**
>
> smm 10/31/92
>
> Shall we be more specific here? Why not just talk about the new case design?

4. To view the following annotation, click the Next button or the Next Page tab. To view the preceding annotation, click the Previous button or the Previous Page tab.

5. When you reach the end of the annotations, an alert box appears, asking whether you want to restart viewing annotations. Choose Yes to restart or click No to stop viewing annotations.

NOTE

To incorporate the text of an annotation into your document, select the text in the Annotations dialog box and then use the Copy command. Position the insertion point in your document and then use the Paste command.

After reviewing annotations, you may want to delete them. To delete an annotation, select the annotation and then choose Delete from the Edit menu or press the Delete key. Remember, however, that Word does not print annotations unless you choose the Print Hidden Text option in the

Print dialog box. (By default, this option is inactive.) You can leave the annotations in your document and print the document as though no annotations were added.

Copying Text Annotations to a New Document

The Annotations dialog box contains a Copy to New Document button (refer to fig. 28.7). This button enables you to make a new version of your document that, when printed, is handy for editorial purposes. This document can include either of the following options:

All Annotations. Word copies the text of all the annotations to a new Untitled document. Word also copies the paragraphs that contain the annotation marks. Word places each annotation in a paragraph formatted with the Annotation style, as shown in figure 28.8.

Fig. 28.8
New document with annotations shown.

Copied annotation—

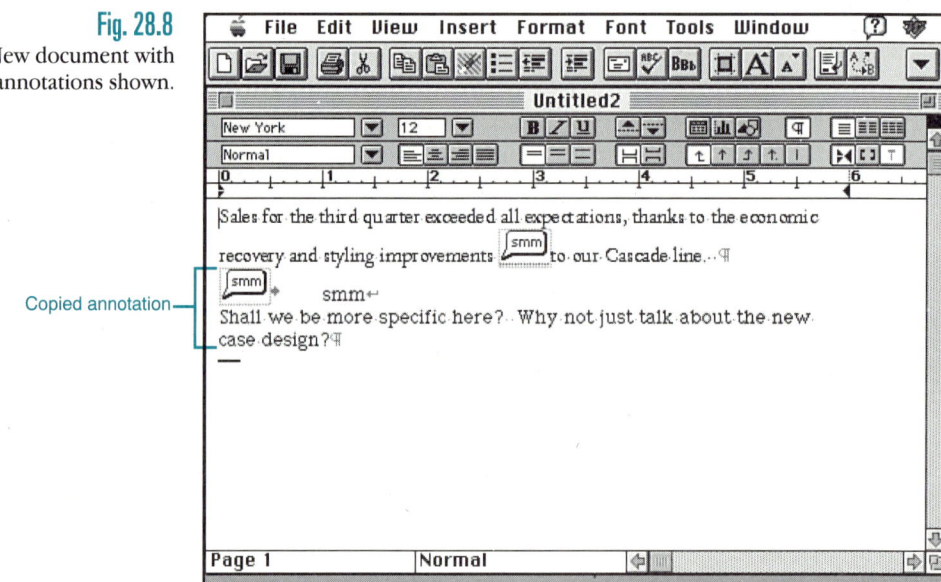

Whole Document with All Annotations. Word copies the entire document, including the text of all the annotations, to a new Untitled document. Word places each annotation in a paragraph formatted with the Annotation style.

The second option—copying the annotations and the whole document—is useful when you want to incorporate many annotations into the document's text. You reformat the annotation paragraphs with one of the text-paragraph styles from your document. To produce the finished document, you must remove the annotation marks and do some additional editing and formatting; even so, this procedure is much quicker than typing your reviewers' comments into the document.

To copy text annotations to a new document, follow these steps:

1. Choose Annotations from the View menu. The Annotations dialog box appears.

2. Click the Copy to New Document button. A dialog box appears, asking whether you want to copy all annotations or the whole document with all annotations.

3. Choose All Annotations to copy only the annotations (and surrounding text) to the new document, or choose Whole Document with All Annotations to copy the text of the document and all the annotations.

4. Choose OK. Word copies the annotations to a new document.

5. Save the new document.

Creating and Using Voice Annotations

If your Macintosh is equipped with a microphone, you can record voice annotations. Word indicates a voice annotation by displaying a speaker icon in your document.

The maximum length of your recording depends on the amount of memory available when you choose Voice Annotations and on the sound quality you choose. If you have 4M of available RAM, for example, you can record only a few seconds at best quality. You can record up to 40 seconds, however, if you choose a lower sound-quality option.

You can play back a voice annotation on any Macintosh. When you click the speaker icon, a dialog box appears, enabling you to play the recording. This dialog box shows the initials currently listed in the Your Initials area of the Preferences dialog box.

When you save your document, Word also saves the voice annotation. Alternatively, you can save your voice annotation to a separate file. You also can import sounds into an annotation. The following sections discuss the procedures you use for these operations.

Recording Voice Annotations

To record a voice annotation, you must have a Macintosh that's equipped with a microphone. When you choose Voice Annotation from the Insert menu, you see the Voice Record dialog box, shown in figure 28.9. (In Version 5.0, this dialog box is called the Voice Annotation dialog box.)

Fig. 28.9
Voice Record dialog box.

In this dialog box, you can perform the following actions:

- *Choose recording quality.* You can choose Good, Better, or Best. The lower the quality, the less disk space the recording requires. For this reason, you can record up to 40 seconds with Good and 20 seconds with Better but only 6 seconds with Best. All three options produce a file 148K in length, which is about 5 to 10 times the length of an average Word document.

- *Record a voice annotation.* You can record your annotation within a fixed time, depending on the recording-quality level you have chosen.

- *View information about the recording.* The Level indicator shows the volume of the sound, while the pie chart in the Total area shows how much of the available recording time you have used.

- *Save and open sound files.* The File menu enables you to save your sound in a separate file. The menu also enables you to open previously saved sound files.

- *Choose preferences.* You can choose the default sound quality.

CAUTION

Bear in mind that sound files eat up huge amounts of disk space. Use voice annotations sparingly.

To record a voice annotation, follow these steps:

1. Position the insertion point in your document where you want to place the annotation.

2. Choose Voice Annotation from the Insert menu. The Voice Record dialog box appears.

3. Use the microphone and the Level bar to experiment with the sound level. Try to speak at a level that fills the left half or two-thirds of the bar; don't speak so loudly that the meter goes all the way to the right edge of the bar.

NOTE

The version of Voice Record that comes with Word does not provide a re-cording-level adjustment, but you can adjust the sound level manually. To increase the level, hold the microphone closer and/or speak louder. To decrease the level, hold the microphone farther away and/or speak more softly.

4. Click the Record button or press ⌘-R to begin recording your annotation. Press Tab to pause, if necessary.

   The pie chart in the Total area indicates how much of the allotted recording time you have used. When you are out of time, Word stops recording.

5. When you finish recording, click Stop or press ⌘-period (.).

6. Click Play or press ⌘-Y to hear your annotation. If you don't like your recording and want to try again, choose Undo Recording from the Edit menu or press ⌘-Z and then repeat steps 4 and 5.

TIP

If you ran out of time while recording at Best quality, select Better or Good from the Quality menu to increase the allotted time for your annotation.

7. Choose OK. Word places the annotation in your document in the form of a speaker icon (see fig. 28.10).

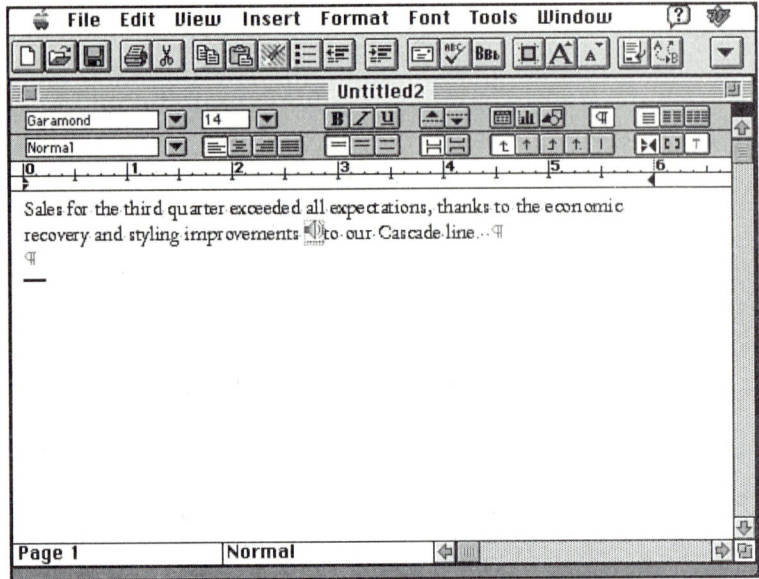

Fig. 28.10
Voice-annotation
speaker icon.

After you insert an annotation, Word assigns a number to it. The first annotation is numbered 1; subsequent annotations are numbered in sequence in your document. If you insert additional annotations, Word renumbers the existing ones, if necessary, to maintain the sequence. You don't see these numbers until you choose Annotations from the View menu, as discussed in the following section.

Because Word formats this icon as hidden text, the speaker does not appear in your printed document. To control the on-screen display of hidden text, choose Preferences from the Tools menu to display the Preferences dialog box, and then click the View icon to display the View options. To show hidden text, activate the Hidden Text option. To hide hidden text (including the annotation symbols), clear this option. Click the close box to exit the Preferences dialog box.

Need to make a longer recording? If you're willing to forgo the handy buttons and indicators in the Voice Record dialog box, you can bypass this dialog box and thereby make more memory available for recording your annotation. To record without the Voice Record dialog box, pick up the microphone and get ready to speak. Then hold down the Option key and choose Voice Annotation from the Insert menu to begin recording. You see the elapsed time in the page-number area at the bottom of the screen. To stop recording, press ⌘-Esc.

Part V

Creating Collaborative and Dynamic Documents

Playing Voice Annotations

You can play voice annotations on any Macintosh. The Voice Annotations dialog box, shown in figure 28.11, enables you to play your document's voice annotations.

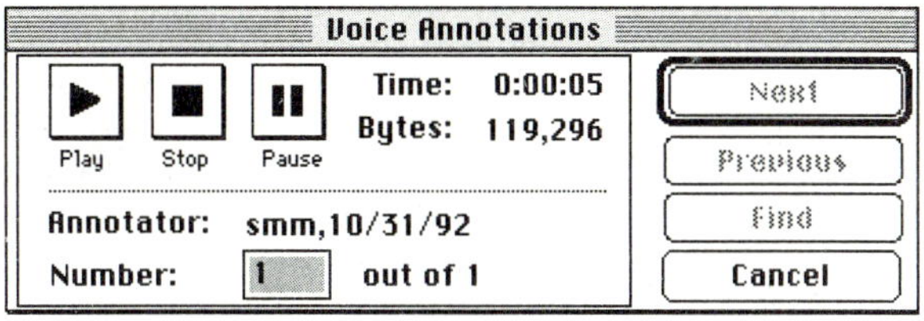

Fig. 28.11

Voice Annotations dialog box.

This dialog box shows the initials typed in the Your Initials area of the Preferences dialog box, the date the recording was made, the elapsed recording time, and the size of the disk information needed to produce the sound (in bytes).

To play voice annotations, follow these steps:

1. To play all the annotations in your document, place the insertion point at the beginning of your document and choose Voice Annotations from the View menu. The Voice Annotations dialog box appears.

   To hear just one annotation, double-click the speaker icon of the annotation you want to hear. The Voice Annotations dialog box appears.

2. To play the annotation, click Play. You can click Pause to pause the playback or Stop to stop it.

3. To play more annotations, perform one of the following actions:

   ■ To hear the next annotation, choose Next.

   ■ To hear the preceding annotation, click Previous.

   ■ To find a specific annotation, type the annotation's number in the Number text box and then click Find.

4. To exit Voice Annotations, click Cancel.

Editing Voice Annotations

After recording an annotation, you can add to it, replace the recording with a new one, or copy or move the sound from one annotation to another. You also can copy or move an annotation and its speaker icon or delete the annotation entirely.

To display the Edit Voice Annotation option in the Edit menu, you must carefully select the speaker icon without selecting any leading or trailing spaces. If you don't see this option, you inadvertently have selected neighboring characters or spaces. Select only the icon and try again.

To add to a voice annotation, follow these steps:

1. Select the annotation's speaker icon.

2. Choose Edit Voice Annotation from the Edit menu. The Voice Record dialog box appears, showing the information for the current annotation recording. If any time is left in the pie chart, you can add to the annotation.

If you want to see information about the current annotation, choose Device Info from the Help menu in the Voice Record dialog box. (This menu is represented by a question mark at the left end of the menu bar.) Device Info displays information about the sound-input device and the quality settings. To see more information, choose Current Sound from the Help menu; this option displays information about the sample rate, the compression, the file size, and the recording time.

3. Click Record to begin recording your annotation. Press Tab to pause, if necessary.

4. When you finish, click Stop to stop recording. Word appends your recording to the end of the current annotation.

5. Choose OK to return to your document.

To replace an existing annotation with a new one, follow these steps:

1. Select the annotation's speaker icon.

2. Choose Edit Voice Annotation from the Edit menu. The Voice Record dialog box appears.

3. Choose Cut or Clear from the Edit menu in the Voice Record dialog box.

4. Click Record to begin recording your annotation. Press Tab to pause, if necessary.

5. When you finish, click Stop to stop recording.

6. Choose OK to return to your document.

You can copy or move voice annotations in two ways:

■ Use the Edit Voice Annotations command to copy or move the recorded *sound* from one annotation to another. This procedure affects only the recorded sound, not the speaker icons that appear in your document.

■ Use the commands in Word's Edit menu to copy or move the entire annotation, including the speaker icon.

To copy or move a sound from one annotation to another, follow these steps:

1. Select the annotation you want to move or the one from which you want to copy a sound.

2. Choose Edit Voice Annotation from the Edit menu. The Voice Record dialog box appears.

3. To copy the sound, choose Copy from the dialog box's Edit menu.

   To move the sound, choose Cut from the dialog box's Edit menu.

4. Choose OK to exit the Voice Record dialog box.

5. Select the annotation to which you want to copy or move the recorded sound.

6. Choose Edit Voice Annotation from the Edit menu. The Voice Record dialog box appears.

7. Choose Paste from the dialog box's Edit menu.

8. Choose OK to return to your document.

To copy or move an entire annotation (both sound and icon), follow these steps:

1. Select the icon.

2. To copy the annotation, choose Copy from the Edit menu, press ⌘-C, or click the Copy tool.

   To move the annotation, choose Cut from the Edit menu, press ⌘-X, or click the Cut tool.

3. Position the insertion point in your document where you want to place the annotation.

4. Choose Paste from the Edit menu, press ⌘-V, or click the Paste tool.

To delete an annotation, follow these steps:

1. Select the annotation's speaker icon.

2. Choose Cut from the Edit menu, press ⌘-C, or click the Cut tool.

If you mistakenly delete the wrong annotation, immediately choose Undo from the Edit menu or press ⌘-Z to restore the annotation.

Managing Sound-Annotation Files

The commands in the Voice Record dialog box's File menu enable you to save your sounds to a separate file. You can choose the format in which a sound is stored so that you can use the sound in other programs.

If you are familiar with Macintosh programming, you will be pleased to learn that you can save your sounds as SND resources. An *SND resource* is a recorded sound that you can add to any program's file. For example, you can add your Word-created sounds to a HyperCard stack, where they become available for use.

After you save sound files, you can use the File menu in the Voice Record dialog box to open them. You also can use the commands in this menu to merge two annotations.

To save a sound to a separate file, follow these steps:

1. After you record a sound with the Voice Record dialog box, choose Save As from the dialog box's File menu. The Save As dialog box appears (see fig. 28.12).

Fig. 28.12
Save As dialog box.

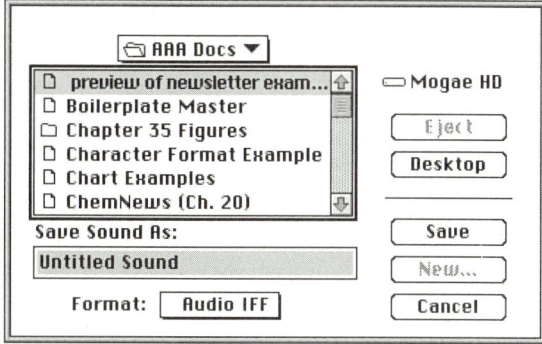

2. In the Save Sound As text box, type a file name.

3. In the Format box, choose a format for the sound. You can choose any of the following options:

   ■ *SoundWave.* Creates a sound file compatible with SoundWave and SoundEdit applications (FSSD files).

   ■ *Audio IFF.* Creates a sound file in the Audio Interchange File Format.

   ■ *Audio IFF-C.* Creates a compressed sound file in the Audio Interchange File Format.

   ■ *Resource.* Creates an SND resource that you can add to a file. If you choose this option, you must identify the file to which you want to add the sound.

4. Choose Save.

To open a sound file, follow these steps:

1. Choose Open from the File menu in the Voice Record dialog box. An Open dialog box appears.

2. Select the sound file you want to open.

   To open a sound resource in a file, select Resource in the Format list and then choose the sound file that contains the resource. Word lists the sounds that the file contains. In this list, select the sound you want to open.

3. Choose OK to open the Voice Annotations dialog box and display the sound's characteristics.

Chapter 28
Writing Collaboratively with Annotations

4. To play the sound, click Play.

5. Choose OK to confirm the sound and return to your document.

Because you can use the Open command in the Voice Record dialog box to open sound resources in files, you can gain access to many fun sounds that are stored in various software programs.

Quick Review

This section summarizes the most useful information in this chapter. Check "Productivity Tips" for a review of high-productivity tips and tricks—the ones that Macintosh and Word pros use every day. Review "Techniques" whenever you need a quick reminder about a specific procedure.

Productivity Tips

- In collaborative writing, an author gives a document to reviewers for comments. Word 5.1 enables you to make comments in text annotations and voice annotations; Word 5.0 users can use voice annotations only.

- Reviewers can type suggested revisions as annotations. Later, after reviewing and approving the annotations, you can use the Copy command to insert the text into your document.

- To incorporate several annotations into your document, copy the annotations and text to a new document and incorporate them there.

- The length of a Voice Annotation recording depends on the amount of memory available. You can increase the maximum length of a recording by choosing lower recording quality.

- You can increase the amount of available memory, and make a longer recording, by holding down the Option key when you choose Voice Annotation from the Insert menu. This procedure bypasses the Voice Record dialog box.

Techniques

This section provides concise summaries of all the procedures introduced in this chapter.

Inserting a Text Annotation

To insert a text annotation into your document:

1. Position the insertion point where you want the annotation mark to appear.

2. Choose Annotation from the Insert menu. The Annotations dialog box appears.

3. Choose an annotation mark, if you want.

4. In the text box next to the annotation-mark list box, you can type your initials. If you type nothing, Word uses the initials typed in the Your Initials area of the Preferences dialog box.

5. Type the text of the annotation.

6. Click Insert.

Editing a Text Annotation

To edit a text annotation:

1. Double-click the annotation mark in the document. The Annotations dialog box appears.

2. Edit the text of the annotation. You also can change the initials and the annotation mark.

3. Click the close box. An alert box appears, asking whether you want to save the annotation.

4. Choose Yes.

Reviewing a Text Annotation

To review a text annotation:

1. Position the insertion point at the beginning of your document.

2. Choose Annotations from the View menu. The Annotations dialog box appears.

3. Size the Annotations dialog box so that you can see the document's text.

4. To view the following annotation, click the Next button or the Next Page tab. To view the preceding annotation, click the Previous button or the Previous Page tab.

5. When you reach the end of the annotations, an alert box appears, asking whether you want to restart viewing annotations. Choose Yes to restart or click No to stop viewing annotations.

Copying Text Annotations to a Document

To copy text annotations to a document:

1. Choose Annotations from the View menu. The Annotations dialog box appears.

2. Click the Copy to New Document button.

3. Choose All Annotations to copy just the annotations (and surrounding text) to the new document, or choose Whole Document with All Annotations to copy the text of the document and all the annotations.

4. Choose OK.

5. Save the new document.

Recording a Voice Annotation

To record a voice annotation:

1. Position the insertion point in your document where you want to place the annotation.

2. Choose Voice Annotation from the Insert menu. The Voice Record dialog box appears.

3. Use the microphone and the Level box to experiment with the sound level. Record at a volume that fills the left half or two-thirds of the bar; do not record so loudly that the meter goes all the way to the right edge.

4. Click the Record button or press ⌘-R to begin recording your annotation. Press Tab to pause, if necessary.

5. When you finish recording, click Stop or press ⌘-period (.).

6. Click Play or press ⌘-Y to hear your annotation. If you don't like your recording and want to try again, choose Undo Recording from the Edit menu or press ⌘-Z and then repeat steps 4 and 5.

7. Choose OK to place the annotation in your document.

Playing a Voice Annotation

To play a voice annotation:

1. To play all the annotations in your document, place the insertion point at the beginning of your document and choose Voice Annotations from the View menu. The Voice Annotations dialog box appears.

   To hear only one annotation, double-click the speaker icon of the annotation you want to hear. The Voice Annotations dialog box appears.

2. To play the annotation, click Play. You can click Pause to pause the playback or Stop to stop it.

3. To play more annotations, perform one of the following actions:

   ■ To hear the next annotation, choose Next.

   ■ To hear the preceding annotation, click Previous.

   ■ To find a specific annotation, type the annotation's number in the Number text box and then click Find.

4. To exit Voice Annotations, click Cancel.

Copying and Moving Voice Annotations

To copy or move an entire annotation (sound and icon):

1. Select the icon.

2. To copy the annotation, choose Copy from the Edit menu, press ⌘-C, or click the Copy tool.

   To move the annotation, choose Cut from the Edit menu, press ⌘-X, or click the Cut tool.

3. Position the insertion point in your document where you want to place the annotation.

4. Choose Paste from the Edit menu, press ⌘-V, or click the Paste tool.

To copy or move a sound from one annotation to another:

1. Select the annotation you want to move or the one from which you want to copy a sound.

2. Choose Edit Voice Annotation from the Edit menu. The Voice Record dialog box appears.

3. To copy the sound, choose Copy from the dialog box's Edit menu.

    To move the sound, choose Cut from the dialog box's Edit menu.

4. Choose OK to exit the Voice Record dialog box.

5. Select the annotation to which you want to copy or move the recorded sound.

6. Choose Edit Voice Annotation from the Edit menu. The Voice Record dialog box appears.

7. Choose Paste from the Edit menu in the Voice Record dialog box.

8. Choose OK to return to your document.

Saving a Sound Annotation as a Separate File

To save a sound to a separate file:

1. After you record a sound with the Voice Record dialog box, choose Save As from the File menu in the dialog box. The Save As dialog box appears.

2. In the Save Sound As text box, type a file name.

3. In the Format box, choose a format for the sound.

Opening a Sound File

To open a sound file:

1. Choose Open from the File menu in the Voice Record dialog box.

2. Choose the sound file you want. To open a sound resource in a file, select Resource in the Format list and then select the sound file that contains the resource. Word displays a list of the sounds contained in the file. Select the sound you want.

3. Choose OK to open the sound.

4. To play the sound, click Play.

5. Choose OK to confirm the sound and return to your document.

Displaying and Hiding Annotation Marks

To hide or display text-annotation marks and/or voice-annotation speaker icons:

1. Choose Preferences from the Tools menu. The Preferences dialog box appears.

2. Click the View icon to display the View options.

3. To display the annotation marks and/or speaker icons, activate the Show Hidden Text option.

   To hide the annotation marks and/or speaker icons, clear the Show Hidden Text option.

4. Click the close box.

Deleting Annotations

To delete a text annotation:

1. Select the annotation mark.

2. Choose Cut from the Edit menu, press ⌘-C, or click the Cut tool.

To delete a voice annotation:

1. Select the annotation's speaker icon.

2. Choose Cut from the Edit menu, press ⌘-C, or click the Cut tool.

Playing Movies

ersion 5.1 of Word brings multimedia to your Word documents. In brief, *multimedia* is a combination of media—including text, sound, animation, or video—used to convey a message. In some cases, nothing less than a multimedia message will do. Suppose that you're trying to convey the precise technique for holding a wrench when accessing an awkwardly positioned drainage port on a machine. You can describe the technique in words, but wouldn't a short video do the job much better?

Thanks to Word's movie capabilities (and Apple's QuickTime multimedia support), you can include movies in your Word documents. Before you conclude that a new age of dynamic documents has arrived, however, bear the following restrictions in mind:

■ *You need special equipment to record movies.* You can buy video-capture and sound-digitizer boards for some Macintoshes that enable you to connect a VCR camera and make your own movies.

■ *Movies require enormous amounts of disk space.* Even when compressed, a very short movie (just 10 seconds in length) may require a megabyte or more of storage. If you want to get involved in multimedia applications, you need the largest hard disk you can get.

USING
WORD 5.1
FOR THE MAC
SPECIAL EDITION

- *To play commercially distributed movies, you need a CD-ROM player.* Movie files are so large that they are distributed on compact discs that can hold up to 550M of data. To play a compact-disc movie, your Macintosh must be equipped with a CD-ROM player.

- *Not all Macintoshes can play movies.* You cannot play movies on any Macintosh that lacks 32-bit color QuickDraw graphics; this category includes the Macintosh Plus, Classic, SE, Portable, and PowerBook 100. To play movies, you need a Macintosh equipped with an Apple SuperDrive and 32-bit color QuickDraw graphics: an SE/30 (with System 7), a Mac II, a Quadra, or a PowerBook 140 or 170. To show movies, you need at least 4M of RAM; you may need as much as 8M to show high-resolution movies.

- *Movies require Apple's QuickTime System extension.* If you want to use movies in Word, you must obtain Apple's QuickTime Starter Kit from your Apple dealer. This package of utility programs includes the QuickTime extensions to the Apple System software, as well as a MoviePlayer application, a Picture Compressor, a Movie Converter that converts several file formats into movies, and a CD-ROM disk that contains sample QuickTime movies.

As you can see, if the future is multimedia, your Mac may not be ready for the future—yet. Fortunately, you can try multimedia applications even if you're not willing to invest in extra equipment. Apple's QuickTime Starter Kit, for example, contains a brief low-resolution movie (called *Liftoff*) that's provided on a high-density disk. You don't need a CD-ROM player to play this movie.

This chapter covers the following topics:

- *Looking at Word's movie capabilities.* You learn what Word can do with movies.

- *Inserting movies into Word documents.* You learn how to add a movie that readers of a document can view.

- *Playing and managing movies.* You learn how to play the movie, control the volume, rewind, advance, and perform other management tasks.

- *Editing movies.* You learn how to cut, copy, and paste frames or sequences of frames within or between movies.

- *Converting movies into graphics.* You learn how to convert a movie image into a still graphic.

Part V

Creating Collaborative and Dynamic Documents

NOTE

Before trying to play movies in Word, install Apple's QuickTime extensions on your system. If you try to use the movie commands without installing QuickTime, an alert box informs you that QuickTime is not installed on your Macintosh.

Looking at Word's Movie Capabilities

Now that you know all the caveats, the following sections provide a brief introduction to Word's features for playing movies. In Word 5.1, you can perform the following tasks:

■ *Insert a movie into a Word document.* When you insert a movie, your Macintosh plays it in a movie window. After you close this window, the movie appears in your document in the form of a frozen PICT image called a *poster* (see fig. 29.1).

Fig. 29.1
Poster inserted into a Word document.

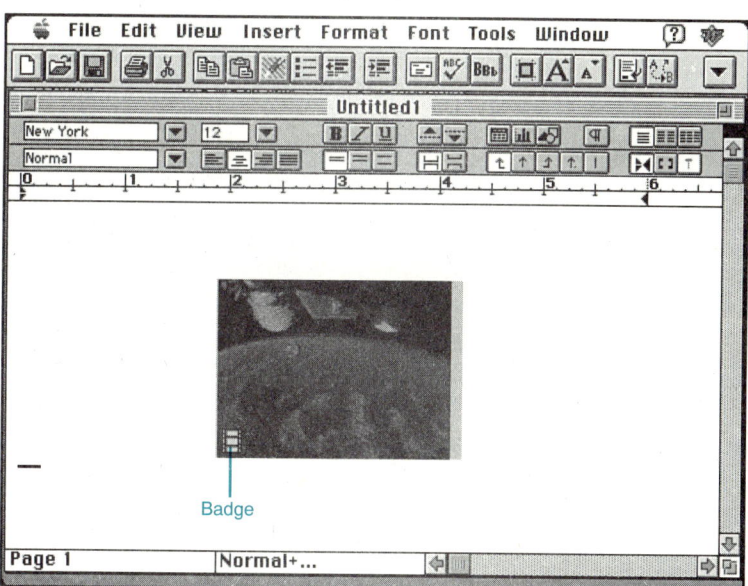

You can tell a movie from an ordinary graphic by the *badge* in the bottom left corner of the poster. The badge looks like a strip of film.

Chapter 29
Playing Movies

■ *Play a movie.* When you double-click the poster, Word plays the movie. You see VCR-like controls that enable you to rewind the movie, advance one frame, go back one frame, and adjust the volume (see fig. 29.2).

Fig. 29.2
Playing a movie.

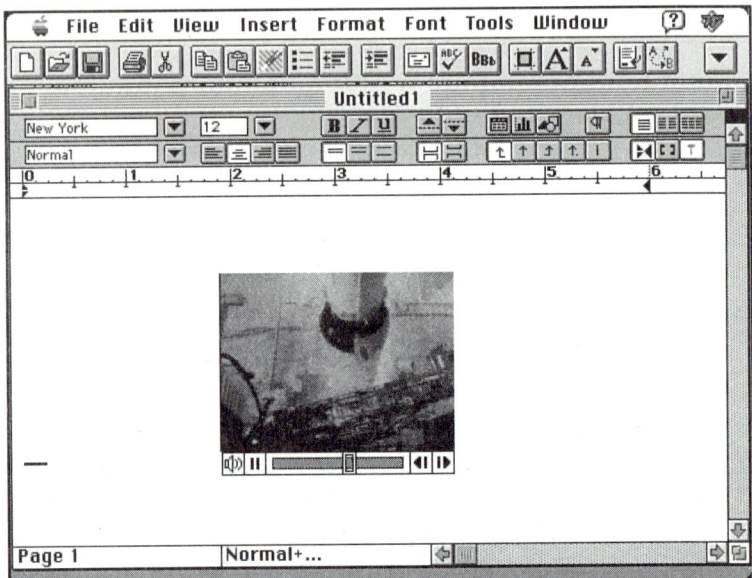

■ *Move or copy movies.* You can move or copy a movie by using techniques similar to those for moving or copying a picture.

■ *Choose movie options.* You can choose options that control how the movie appears in your document and how it plays when you double-click the poster.

■ *Edit movies.* When a movie is frozen on-screen, you can use the Edit menu commands to cut, copy, and paste movie frames. With this capability, you can copy a frame to use as an illustration elsewhere, cut unwanted frames out of a movie, or insert additional frames into the movie.

■ *Convert a movie into a graphic.* If you no longer want to play the entire movie within your document, you can convert the movie poster into a graphic.

The following sections cover each of these features in detail.

Inserting and Playing Movies

To insert QuickTime movies into your Word documents, you use the Movie command in the Insert menu. This command plays the movie and then places it in your document.

To insert a QuickTime movie into a Word document, follow these steps:

1. Place the insertion point in your document where you want to insert the movie.

2. Choose Movie from the Insert menu. The dialog box shown in figure 29.3 appears.

Fig. 29.3
Preview of movie.

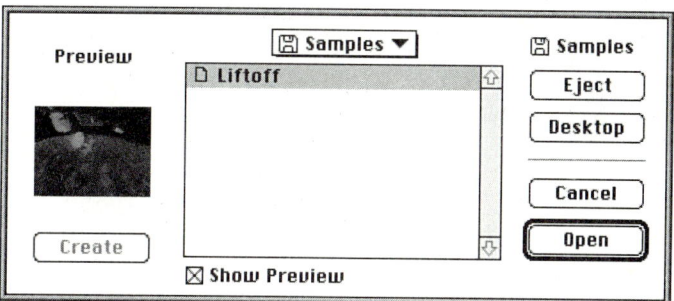

3. Select the movie that you want to insert. By default, you see a preview of the movie in the Preview area.

4. Choose Open. The movie plays in a small Movie window (see fig. 29.4).

Fig. 29.4
Movie window with
controller bar.

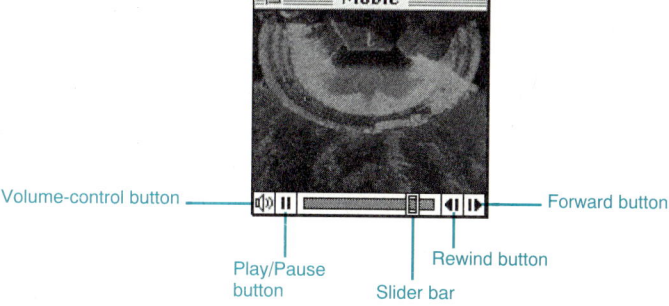

Volume-control button

Play/Pause button

Slider bar

Rewind button

Forward button

Chapter 29

Playing Movies

5. While the movie plays, you can use the buttons in the controller bar to perform the following actions, as necessary:

■ *Control the volume.* If you click the volume-control button, the volume-control slider bar appears. This bar enables you to control the speaker volume.

■ *Pause the movie.* Click the Pause button while the movie is running. The Pause button changes to the Play button when the movie finishes running.

■ *Advance one frame.* Click the Forward button while the movie is stopped.

■ *Go back one frame.* Click the Rewind button while the movie is stopped.

■ *Restart after pausing.* Double-click the movie in the window.

■ *Advance or rewind several frames.* Drag the horizontal slider bar.

■ *Play the movie again.* When the movie finishes running, click the Play button to restart the movie from the beginning.

6. To insert the movie into your document, click the Movie window's close box. Word inserts the poster, with a badge, into your document.

After you insert a poster into your document, you can format the poster as you would any graphic (except that you cannot size or scale it). You can position the poster with the Frame command, for example, and use the Border command to put borders around it.

After you insert a movie into your document, you can play it whenever you want. To play the movie, choose Play Movie from the Insert menu or double-click the poster. You then see the Movie window with the controller bar at the bottom. Using the controller bar, you can control the volume, pause the movie, advance one frame, go back one frame, restart after pausing, advance or rewind several frames, and restart the movie from the beginning. To stop the movie, click anywhere outside the movie.

CAUTION

Bear in mind that Word cannot play a movie if Word cannot find the supporting QuickTime movie file. Suppose that you insert the *Liftoff* movie into your document and then copy the document for someone who doesn't have the *Liftoff* movie on disk. When that person tries to play the movie, a dialog box appears, asking for the file's location.

Choosing Movie Options

Several Word options enable you to control various aspects of movie playback. To access these options, you first must stop the movie and then select the poster. When you do, the Edit Movie command appears in the Edit menu. You can use this command to choose the following movie-playback options:

- *Always Show Badge.* This option displays the movie badge in the bottom left corner of the poster.

- *Play Continuously.* This option replays the movie continuously whenever the movie is open.

- *Loop Back and Forth.* This option plays the movie from the beginning to the end and then runs the movie backward, from the end to the beginning. You can make the loop continuous by activating the Play Continuously option in conjunction with Loop Back and Forth.

- *Double-Click Shows Controller.* This option, which is activated by default, displays the controller bar whenever you double-click the poster. If you turn this option off, the mouse pointer changes to a pause symbol while the movie is playing. You can click the mouse to pause the movie.

- *Keep This Display Picture.* This option displays the current movie frame as the poster when the movie is stopped.

- *Always Play from First Frame.* This option plays the entire movie from the first frame after the movie has been stopped.

To choose movie-playback options, follow these steps:

1. Click the poster to select it. Be sure to select only the poster—no trailing spaces or paragraph marks.

2. Choose Edit Movie from the Edit menu. The Movie Options dialog box appears (see fig. 29.5).

Chapter 29

Playing Movies

Fig. 29.5

Movie Options dialog box.

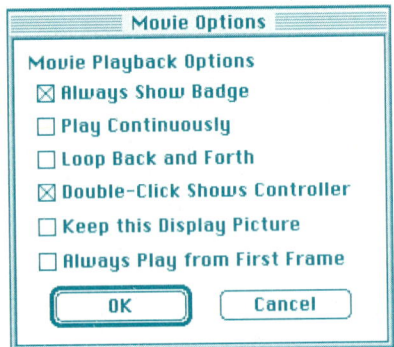

3. Choose one or more of the options.

4. Choose OK to confirm your choices and exit the dialog box.

Editing Movies

Like a real movie, every QuickTime movie is made up of a succession of still images called *frames*. In a high-resolution movie, so many frames pass per second that the eye sees the motion as continuous. When you stop the movie, you freeze the motion to display a single image or frame on-screen. After freezing a movie on-screen, you can edit the frames by performing the following actions:

■ *Cutting or copying a single frame.* Stop the movie on the frame you want to edit and then use the Cut or Copy command to copy the movie frame to the Clipboard.

■ *Cutting or copying a sequence of frames.* Stop the movie on the first frame you want to edit. Then hold down the Shift key, drag the slider to the end of the sequence you want to select, and use the Cut or Copy command to copy the frame to the Clipboard.

■ *Pasting frames into a movie.* From one movie, cut or copy single frames or sequences, using the techniques just discussed. Play another movie, stop that movie at the place where you want to paste the cut or copied frames, and then use the Paste command.

Converting Movies into Graphics

You can convert a movie into a still-frame graphic, if you want. The graphic consumes much less disk space.

If you don't want the badge to appear in the graphic, choose Edit Movie from the Edit menu and turn off the Always Show Badge option in the Movie Options dialog box.

To convert a movie into a graphic, follow these steps:

1. Stop and select the movie.

2. Choose Object Options from the Edit menu. The Object Options dialog box appears (see fig. 29.6).

Fig. 29.6
Object Options dialog box.

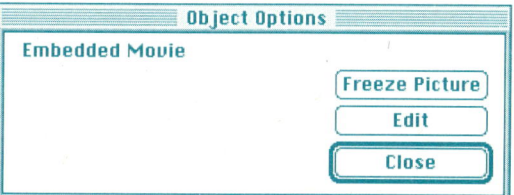

3. Click the Freeze Picture button. Word converts the movie into a graphic.

4. Choose Close to close the dialog box.

A movie converted into a graphic no longer is dependent upon the movie file; you can display the graphic in any document, even if the movie file isn't on the disk.

Quick Review

This section summarizes the most useful information in this chapter. Check "Productivity Tips" for a review of high-productivity tips and tricks—the ones that Macintosh and Word pros use every day. Review "Techniques" whenever you need a quick reminder about a specific procedure.

Productivity Tips

■ To play movies on your Macintosh, you need Apple's QuickTime extensions installed in your System Folder. To obtain the QuickTime extensions, purchase the QuickTime Starter Kit from your Apple dealer. QuickTime is not included with the Apple System software.

■ You need special equipment to create and show high-quality movies on your Macintosh. Apple's QuickTime Starter Kit, however, includes a short movie that you can play on your system without having to add expensive extra equipment, such as a CD-ROM player.

■ Even if you have inserted a movie into your document, you cannot play the movie unless the QuickTime movie file is available.

Techniques

This section provides concise summaries of all the procedures introduced in this chapter.

Inserting a Movie into a Document

To insert a QuickTime movie into a Word document:

1. Place the insertion point in the document where you want to insert the movie.

2. Choose Movie from the Insert menu.

3. In the dialog box that appears, select the movie you want to insert.

4. Choose Open. The movie plays in the Movie window.

5. To insert the movie into your document, click the Movie window's close box.

Playing a Movie

To play a movie that you have inserted into a document:

Select the poster and then choose Play Movie from the Edit menu.

or

Double-click the poster.

Part V

Creating Collaborative and Dynamic Documents

Controlling the Playback Volume

To control the playback volume:

1. Click the Volume button in the controller bar. The slider bar appears.

2. Move the slider up or down.

Pausing a Movie

To pause a movie during playback:

Click the Pause button.

Advancing and Rewinding the Movie One Frame

To advance the movie one frame:

Click the Forward button.

To rewind the movie one frame:

Click the Rewind button.

Restarting the Movie

To restart the movie after pausing:

Click the Pause button or double-click the poster.

To restart the movie from the beginning when it is finished running and at the last frame:

Click the Play button.

Stopping a Movie

To stop a movie:

Click anywhere outside the movie.

Selecting Movie Options

To choose movie options:

1. Click the poster to select it. Be sure to select only the poster—no trailing spaces or paragraph marks.

2. Choose Edit Movie from the Edit menu. The Movie Options dialog box appears.

3. Activate the options you want.

4. Choose OK to confirm your choices and exit the dialog box.

Editing a Movie

To cut or copy a single frame:

1. Stop the movie at the frame.

2. Choose Cut or Copy from the Edit menu, press ⌘-X or ⌘-C, or click the Cut or Copy tool.

To cut or copy a sequence of frames:

1. Stop the movie where the sequence begins.

2. Hold down the Shift key.

3. Drag the slider to the end of the sequence.

4. Choose Cut or Copy from the Edit menu, press ⌘-X or ⌘-C, or click the Cut or Copy tool.

To paste frames into a movie:

1. Cut or copy a single frame or a sequence to the Clipboard.

2. Start the movie into which you want to paste the frame or frames.

3. Pause the movie where you want the new frame(s) to appear.

4. Choose Paste from the Edit menu, press ⌘-V, or click the Paste tool.

Converting a Movie into a Graphic

To convert a movie into a graphic:

1. Stop and select the movie.

2. Choose Object Options from the Edit menu. The Object Options dialog box appears.

3. Click the Freeze Picture button.

4. Choose Close.

Linking Data Dynamically

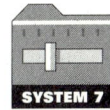

Imagine this scenario: You're writing a major report that includes several important tables of financial data that you pasted into your Word document from Excel spreadsheets. You start Excel and check the figures because the bottom line of one of the tables looks peculiar. You find and correct an error in one of the Excel formulas. An old friend shows up unexpectedly, and the two of you reminisce for a while. After this minor distraction, you print the report and hand it to your boss.

The accuracy of the bottom-line figure in the table containing the corrected formula depends on whether you're using System 6 or System 7 Apple software. Under System 6, you must update the link between the source document and the destination document manually. In the preceding example, if you are using System 6, the Word document has an incorrect figure. Under System 7, however, Word automatically reflects in the destination document the changes you make in the source document. More than any other chapter in this book, this chapter reveals the impressive technical advantages of Apple's System 7 software.

This chapter comprehensively surveys the three methods of linking data dynamically with System 7. (If you're using System 6, read on; you still can use one technique.) This chapter discusses the following topics:

USING
WORD 5.1
FOR THE MAC
SPECIAL EDITION

- ■ *Understanding dynamic linking and embedding.* In this section, you learn how to differentiate among dynamic linking, object linking and embedding, and System 7's Publish/Subscribe commands. You also learn the strengths and weaknesses of each data-linking approach.

- ■ *Creating dynamic links.* This section introduces the first of the three dynamic data-linking techniques: inserting data with the Paste Link and Paste Special commands. System 6 users can use both commands but must update the linked data manually.

- ■ *Embedding objects in a Word document.* This section covers a System 7 feature that enables you to treat other software programs like an extension of Word.

- ■ *Publishing and subscribing.* This section explains how to use Publish and Subscribe, System 7's way of making data from your Word documents available for use in other Word documents, other programs, and even other Macintoshes (if your Mac is linked to a network).

Understanding Dynamic Linking and Embedding

This section explains dynamic linking and embedding under System 7. (An explanation of document linking under System 6 appears at the end of the section.) Beginning with an explanation of the Clipboard's limitations in data exchange, this section introduces the concept of dynamic data exchange, contrasts the various data-linking methods, and indicates under which circumstances one method is preferable over the other methods.

Understanding the Limitations of the Clipboard

When Macintosh technology was new, the Clipboard provided the only means for transferring data from one program to another. Transferring data with the Clipboard is a simple process. In the source program (the one from which you're copying), you select the data and copy it to the Clipboard. In the destination program (the one to which you're copying), you use the Paste command to import the data at the insertion point's location.

The Clipboard is extremely handy, but it has two limitations:

- *You lose the original data's formatting.* In the destination document, the data appears as text and takes on the formatting of the destination document.

- *After you paste the data into the destination document, the data has no link with the source document.* The destination program cannot tell where the data came from. If you need the source program to fix an error in the data, you must remember from which document you pulled the source data, switch to the source program, open the source document, and make the changes. You also must transfer the corrected data manually.

  Suppose that you transfer data to several destination documents and then make corrections to the data in the source program. You must remember all the documents into which you pasted the erroneous data and update each document manually.

Looking at the Advantages of Dynamic Linking

The Clipboard is useful for many purposes. Better techniques exist, however, for creating *dynamic* links between documents. In a dynamic link, the changes you make to the source document are updated *automatically* to all copies of the source information.

A dynamic link has two advantages over Clipboard copying and pasting:

- The data you import retains some or all of the formatting you gave it in the source program.

- The source document retains information about the data's origin. If you make a change in the source document, the dynamic link ensures that copies of data from the source document are updated. The update occurs automatically in *all copies* of the source data. You don't have to remember all the destination documents into which you pasted the data.

Understanding the Two Dynamic-Linking Techniques

If you use System 7, you can link documents dynamically with the Paste Link and Paste Special commands, or you can use the Publish and Subscribe commands. Linking creates a dynamic link between two documents; Publish/Subscribe creates a dynamic link between one source document and an unlimited number of destination documents. The following sections provide an overview of the difference between these two techniques.

Linking with Paste Link or Paste Special

Linking two documents dynamically is similar to copying with the Clipboard. When you link documents, however, you choose Paste Link or Paste Special instead of Paste (the command used in copying). When you use these commands, Word records information about the source document, and if you make changes in the source document, Word reflects these changes in the destination document. Further, Word preserves the source document's formatting. You also can use the Update Link command to start the source program from within the destination program so that you can edit the source document easily.

You can use the Paste Link and Paste Special commands to create dynamic links between Word documents. This technique is the best choice for linking one source document and one destination document. The programs used to create the linked documents, however, must support *dynamic data exchange* (DDE). If you're not sure whether a program supports DDE, check the program's documentation.

Linking with Publish/Subscribe

Using the Publish/Subscribe dynamic linking technique enables you to bypass the Clipboard. To transfer data to other programs that support Publish/Subscribe, you create a *publisher* by selecting some or all of your document and then choosing Create Publisher from the Edit menu. You save this information in a special document called an *edition*. After you create the edition, an unlimited number of documents can *subscribe* to the edition. When you change the publisher, your Macintosh updates the edition and all the subscribers.

Publish/Subscribe is the best method of linking one source document (the publisher) with many destination documents (subscribers), especially if you're using a Macintosh connected to a network. (The Publish and Subscribe commands are designed to work well on networks.) Subscribers cannot change the source document.

Understanding Embedding

Object linking and embedding (OLE) isn't a linking technique; OLE is a way of *embedding* a document produced by one program in a document produced by another program. The result is a *compound document*—a document created by more than one program. You can embed an Excel chart, for example, in a Microsoft Word document.

What is the benefit of embedding? The answer is simple: ease of editing the embedded object. To edit an object embedded in a Word document, simply double-click the object; your Macintosh starts the program that created the object. When you finish editing the object and return to Word, you see your changes.

You embed objects by using the Object command in the Insert menu.

What is the difference between linking with Paste Link and embedding with the Insert Object command? With linking, you can create a dynamic link between one source document and as many destination documents as you like. Linking, therefore, is the right technique if you want to maintain a single authoritative version of a file. With embedding, however, only one document exists: the compound document, which contains portions created by Word and portions created by the program you used to create the embedded object. Embedding is a good technique to use when you don't plan to use the object in any other document but might need to edit or update the object.

Keep in mind that you cannot use OLE unless you have enough memory to run both programs simultaneously—a great deal of memory under System 7. To run Word and Excel simultaneously, for example, you are cutting it close with 4M of RAM.

System 7 users with plenty of disk space and 68030 or 68040 processors should activate virtual memory to extend the amount of RAM available for running programs. (To activate virtual memory, choose the Memory option in the Control Panels window.) *Virtual memory* tricks programs into thinking that much more RAM is available than actually exists. However, 1M of *total* memory still requires 1M of disk space. To configure your machine so that programs think they can use 8M of RAM, even though you only have 4M of RAM installed, you need 8M of hard disk space.

Virtual memory is slower than "real" memory. If you're short on memory, however, operating in virtual memory is much better than coping with the notorious Low on memory message, which requires you to save your work and exit the programs you're running.

Choosing the Right Method for Data Exchange

Now that you have been introduced to the three data-exchange methods you can use with Word, you can use this section to choose the correct method for various purposes.

■ *To create a dynamic link between two documents, use the Paste Link or Paste Special command.* If you use this technique to import an Excel spreadsheet into a Word document, for example, the imported spreadsheet reflects the changes you make in the source document. You even can edit the source spreadsheet without leaving Word. You cannot create such a link, however, unless both programs support Microsoft's DDE standards. (Microsoft programs support these standards, but many other programs don't.)

■ *To create a dynamic link between one source document and unlimited numbers of subscriber documents, use Publish/ Subscribe.* This linking technique is the best choice if you're using a network and want to make a document available to people who are using other Macintoshes. Many System 7-compatible programs support Publish/Subscribe.

■ *If you want to include an object in your document but don't think you will use the object elsewhere, choose embedding.* You can edit or update the object easily by double-clicking it. This action starts the program that created the object. The source program must be compatible with Microsoft's Object Linking and Embedding standards. (Microsoft programs are compatible with these standards, but many other programs aren't.)

If you have tried to run Microsoft Graph or Equation Editor within Word, you have tried embedding. Both of these programs create objects—equations or graphs—that you can incorporate into Word documents. For more information on Microsoft Graph, see Chapter 24, "Creating Charts with Microsoft Graph." For more information on Equation Editor, see Chapter 25, "Using Math and Typing Equations."

Linking Documents with System 6

If you're running System 6, you have fewer linking options. You cannot use Publish/Subscribe or OLE. You can use the Paste Link command, however, to create a link that you can update manually by choosing the Update Link command.

You cannot link two Word documents as you can with System 7. System 6 enables you, however, to link a Word document with one created by another program that supports Microsoft's DDE standards.

Creating Dynamic Links

The Paste Link command enables you to create dynamic links between a source document (created by Word or any other program that supports DDE) and a destination document (a Word document). You must store the two documents on the same Macintosh.

By default, Word automatically reflects in the destination document any changes made in the source document. After you create the link, you can specify the frequency of updates, cancel the link, change the format of the link, or open and edit the source document. The following sections introduce the procedures you use to create and edit dynamic links.

If you're using System 6, you can create links between source documents created by other programs and Word documents. (You cannot create links between Word documents in System 6.) Word does not automatically update the destination document to reflect changes made in the source document; you must update the link manually.

CAUTION

After you create links between a source document and a destination document, don't move the source document; if you do, the destination program may not be able to find the source document. If you move the source document to another folder, you must edit the link by using the Edit Link option in the Link Options dialog box (described later in this chapter).

Creating a Dynamic Link with Paste Link

In this section, you learn how to use the Paste Link command to create a link between another program's source document and a Word document. This command creates a link using the default format, based on the type of file to which you are linking.

To create a link with Paste Link, follow these steps:

1. Open the program that contains the data you want to use, and make sure that you have formatted the data correctly. After you import the data into your Word document, you cannot format individual characters in the unit of imported data.

2. Select the data you want to use.

   Figure 30.1, for example, shows all the data in an Excel spreadsheet selected.

Fig. 30.1
Selected data in an Excel spreadsheet.

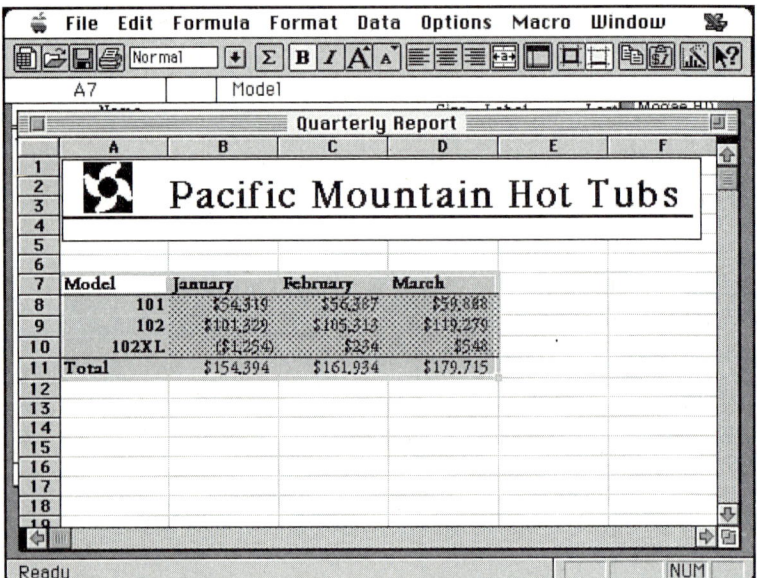

3. Choose Copy from the Edit menu, press ⌘-C, or click the Copy tool.

4. Switch to Word.

5. Open the destination document.

6. Position the insertion point where you want the data to appear.

7. Hold down the Shift key and choose Paste Link from the Edit menu or press Option-F4. Word pastes a copy of the selected portion of the source document into your Word document, as shown in figure 30.2.

Part V

Creating Collaborative and Dynamic Documents

Fig. 30.2
Data pasted into Word with
Paste Link.

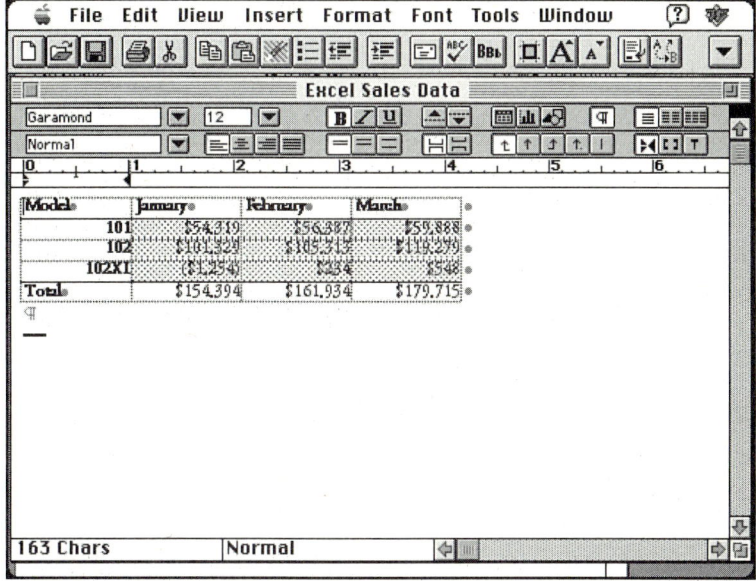

If you're copying data from an Excel spreadsheet, as in this example, Word places the data in a table. (For more information on tables, see Chapter 15.) Word surrounds the linked information with brackets that are visible only if the Show ¶ option in the Edit menu is activated.

Creating a Link with Paste Special

When you link a document with Paste Link, Word automatically uses the best possible method of importing the data so that formatting is retained. You may want to choose the format manually, however. You can import the data as unformatted text, for example, or as a picture. If you want to choose the format Word uses in creating the link, use the Paste Special command instead of Paste Link.

When you use the Paste Special command, the Paste Special dialog box appears (see fig. 30.3).

This dialog box indicates the name of the program and the file from which you are importing the data. The Paste list box displays a list of formats you can apply to the imported data. The available formats are determined by the program you used to create the imported data. With Excel, for example, three options are available: Formatted Text, Unformatted Text, and Picture.

Chapter 30
Linking Data Dynamically

Fig. 30.3

Paste Special dialog box.

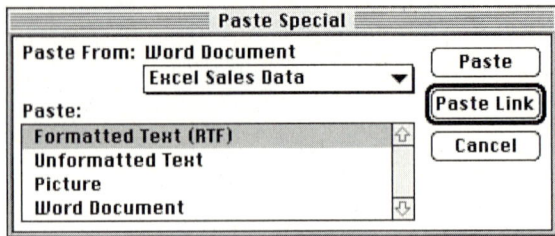

Following is a brief explanation of these formatting options in the Paste Special dialog box:

■ *Formatted Text (RTF).* This option is the default formatting option for Paste Link. Paste Special highlights this option by default.

■ *Unformatted Text.* Choose this option to create an active link without retaining formatting.

■ *Picture.* This option imports a PICT-format picture of the imported data; therefore, imported data is displayed as it appears in its native program.

Figure 30.4 shows Excel spreadsheet data that was imported in two ways. The top spreadsheet was imported as a picture; Word left the data alone. The bottom spreadsheet was imported with the RTF option; Word placed the data in a table.

Fig. 30.4

Spreadsheet data imported in PICT format (top) and RTF format (bottom).

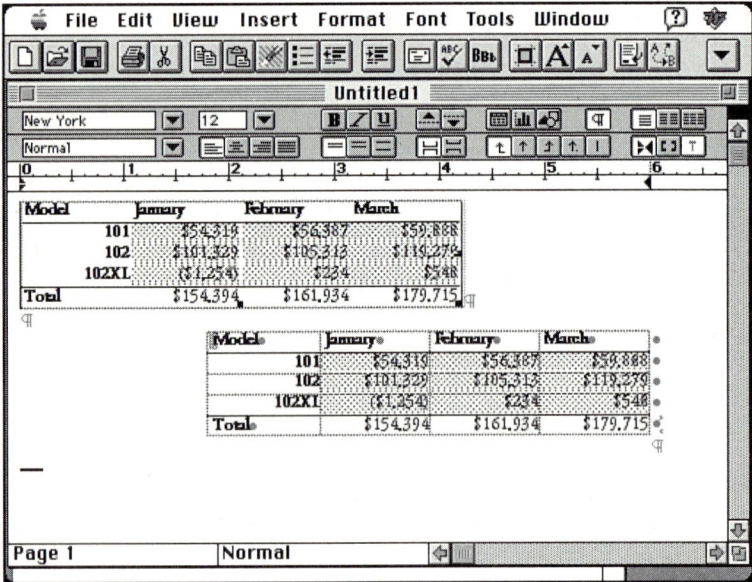

Part V

Creating Collaborative and Dynamic Documents

■ *Native Program Format.* When you choose this option, the name of which indicates the program name and file type (such as Excel Worksheet), Word imports the data as an embedded object. This option doesn't create a dynamic link between the source document and the destination, so don't choose this option if you want to use dynamic links. This option works only if the source program supports Microsoft's OLE standards.

■ *Word Document.* If you're linking to text in a Word document, you see this option, which is Word's native program format.

You need not worry about accidentally changing the data you imported; you cannot edit imported data. Word treats imported data as one huge character. You can format the data, but the formats you choose apply to all the data. You cannot format part of the imported data without breaking the link.

To create a link with Paste Special, follow these steps:

1. Open the program that contains the data you want to import.

2. Select the data.

3. Choose Copy from the Edit menu, press ⌘-C, or click the Copy tool.

4. Switch to Word.

5. Open the destination document.

6. Position the insertion point in the document where you want to place the imported data.

7. Choose Paste Special from the Edit menu. The Paste Special dialog box appears (refer to fig. 30.3).

8. Select a formatting option in the Paste list box.

9. Click Paste to import the picture without creating a link, or choose Paste Link to import the data and create a dynamic link with the source document.

Updating the Link

After you create a dynamic link, you can use the Link Options command to specify when links are updated, to change the format of the link, to edit the link, and to cancel the link.

Chapter 30
Linking Data Dynamically

Under System 7, destination-document updates occur when you make a change in the source document. You quickly discover, however, that your Macintosh runs sluggishly when you edit the source document with the destination document open. Editing the source document is easier if you switch to manual updating. If you do, however, you must use the Update Now option in the Link Options dialog box to update the link.

To update a dynamic link, follow these steps:

1. Position the insertion point in the imported data.

2. Choose Link Options from the Edit menu. The Link Options dialog box appears (see fig. 30.5).

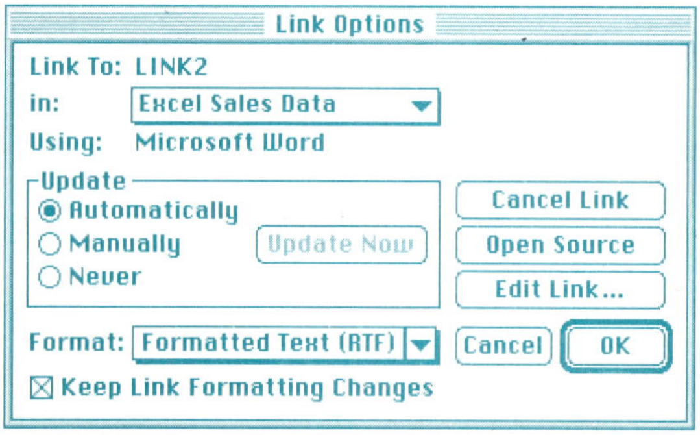

Fig. 30.5
Link Options dialog box.

In the Link To area, Word displays the portion of the document that was linked (in this example, a range of an Excel spreadsheet). Word also displays the names of the source document and the source program.

3. Perform one of the following actions:

   ■ To switch to manual updating, click the Manually radio button in the Update area. (If you have chosen Automatically in the Update area, this button is grayed.)

   ■ To update a manual link, click the Update Now command button in the Update area.

   ■ To retain the link but prevent further updates, click the Never radio button in the Update area.

   ■ Select a different format in the Format drop-down list box. (The program used to create the source document determines which formats are available.)

- ■ To break the link to the source document, click the Cancel Link command button.

- ■ To start the source program and edit the document, click the Open Source command button.

- ■ To change the path for the source document if you moved that document to a new location on your disk, click the Edit Link command button.

4. Choose OK.

If you click the Open Source command button to edit the link, keep in mind that changes you make *outside* the area you originally selected in the source document are not reflected in the destination document. If you're editing a spreadsheet, for example, only changes that fall within the originally selected range are reflected in the destination document. If you add a row or column of new data, you must re-create the link if you want Word to reflect the new data in the destination document.

Embedding Objects in a Word Document

If your computer has lots of RAM (at least 4M) and you install other programs that support Microsoft's object linking and embedding standards, you can embed objects in your Word document. Word treats embedded objects as pictures—but as pictures with special properties. If you double-click the embedded object, Word starts the program that created the object and displays the object in the native program's window. You then can edit the object.

When you choose Update from the native program's File menu, the program closes, Word appears again, and the embedded object shows your changes. When you embed an object, in some respects you also are embedding other programs in Word. If you embed in a document an Excel chart, a PowerPoint graphic, and an Equation Editor equation, all the power of these programs is available at a double-click of the mouse.

To explore embedding, try running Equation Editor and Microsoft Graph from within Word. Both programs are designed to create objects that you can embed in Word documents.

You can embed objects in Word documents in two ways:

- *Import an existing document as an object.* If the object you want to embed already exists, you can copy it into Word through the Clipboard. In your Word document, use the Paste Object command to embed the object.

- *Create the object within Word.* If you're creating a document and find that you need a chart, spreadsheet, equation, or illustration, you can start any OLE-compatible program by using the Object command (Insert menu). All the program's tools become available to you. After you create the document, use the Update command to return to Word, and Word enters the document you created as an embedded object.

The following sections discuss both techniques. You also learn how to edit an embedded object.

Importing an Existing Document as an Object

If the object you want to embed already exists in a document created in another program, follow the instructions in this section to embed the document (or part of it) in your Word document. Keep in mind that embedding does not create a dynamic link, as do the Paste Link and Paste Special commands. If you make changes in the source document, these changes are not automatically reflected in the object you embedded in your Word document.

To embed an existing document in a Word document as an object, follow these steps:

1. Start the program you used to create the document.

2. Select the portion of the document you want to embed in your Word document.

3. Choose Copy from the Edit menu, press ⌘-C, or click the Copy tool.

4. Switch to Word.

5. Hold down the Shift key and choose Paste Object from the Edit menu or press ⌘-F4. Word embeds the object as a picture in your document.

Creating an Object in Word

In this section, you learn how to extend Word's capabilities by running another OLE-compatible program from Word.

To create an object without leaving Word, follow these steps:

1. Place the insertion point in your document where you want to place the object.

2. Choose Object from the Insert menu. The Insert Object dialog box appears, listing all the programs on your Macintosh that support OLE (see fig. 30.6).

Fig. 30.6
Insert Object dialog box.

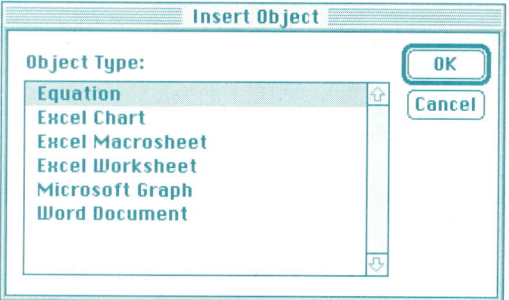

Even if a program is OLE-compatible, it doesn't appear in this list if you have never run the program on your Macintosh.

3. Choose the type of object you want to insert. Word starts the program and displays a blank program window titled Word Object.

4. Use the program's tools to create the object.

5. Choose Update from the File menu or press ⌘-Q. Word returns to the screen, and you see the object you created.

Editing an Embedded Object

Editing an embedded object is easy. Ease of editing, in fact, provides the strongest argument for using OLE instead of linking.

Chapter 30
Linking Data Dynamically

To edit an embedded object, follow these steps:

1. Position the insertion point on the object you want to edit.

2. Choose Edit Object from the Edit menu or double-click the object. Word starts the source program and displays the object in a Word Object window.

3. Use the native program's tools to edit the object.

4. To return to Word and update the object in your Word document, choose Update from the File menu or press ⌘-Q.

Publishing and Subscribing

To create a Publish/Subscribe program, you select the publisher and create the edition. You then can choose publishing intervals. To use the edition, you subscribe. You can choose options that affect the subscription. The following sections describe all the relevant procedures for using the Publish/Subscribe feature.

Create a folder called Editions to store all your editions, no matter what programs created those editions. This practice ensures that you (or anyone using your system) can find editions quickly and easily.

Defining the Publisher and Creating the Edition

To create a Publish/Subscribe program, you first must create the data you want to publish. You can create this data in Word or in any other program that supports Publish/Subscribe. The data can consist of text, graphics, or a combination of text and graphics.

To define the publisher and create the edition, follow these steps:

1. Select the information you want to publish. In figure 30.7, for example, a paragraph of boilerplate text has been selected.

2. Choose Create Publisher from the Edit menu. The dialog box shown in figure 30.8 appears. On the left side of the dialog box, you see a preview of your edition.

Fig. 30.7
Boilerplate text selected.

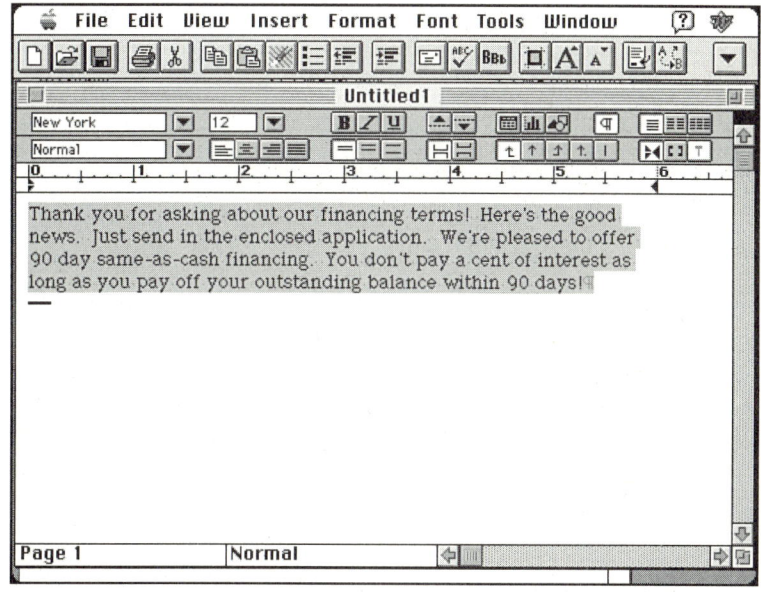

Fig. 30.8
Previewing the edition.

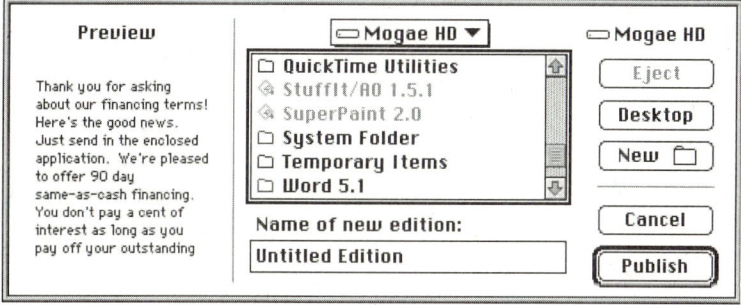

Be sure to format the publisher the way you want the edition to appear in subscriber documents. Subscribers can format the edition only in limited ways.

3. Select the Editions folder (or create one).

4. Type a name for your edition in the Name of New Edition text box.

Chapter 30

Linking Data Dynamically

5. Choose Publish. The program creates the edition. If you activated paragraph marks, you see gray brackets around the published text (see fig. 30.9).

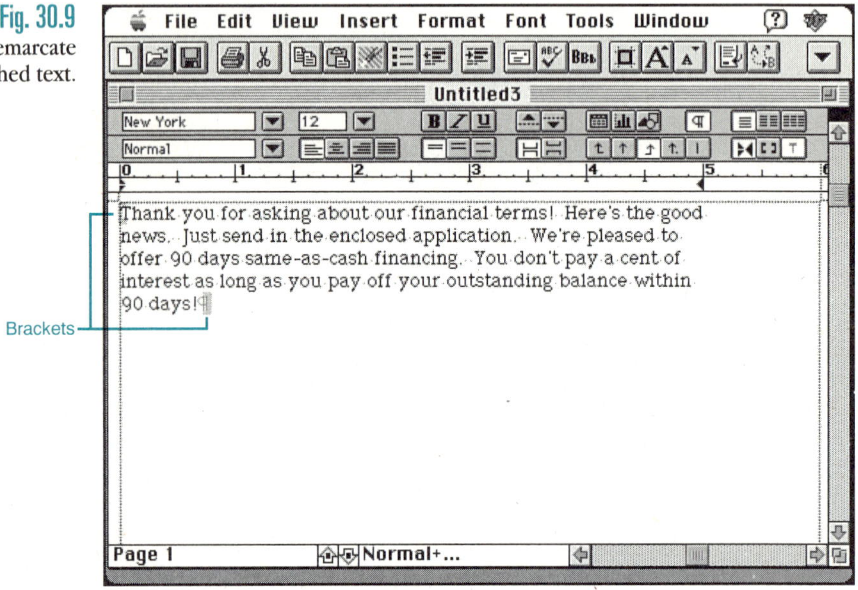

Fig. 30.9
Gray brackets demarcate published text.

Brackets

Updating the Publisher

After you create an edition, you can change the update interval. By default, Word updates the edition every time you save changes in the publisher. When you use the Update Publisher command, you can choose an option that creates a new edition every time you edit the document. You also can choose manual updating to send the edition only when you choose the Send Edition Now option, or you can cancel publication. This section explains the steps you take to accomplish these tasks.

To update the publisher, follow these steps:

1. In the document that contains the publisher, position the insertion point within the publication brackets.

2. Choose Publisher Options from the Edit menu. The dialog box shown in figure 30.10 appears.

Part V

Creating Collaborative and Dynamic Documents

Fig. 30.10
Changing the
update interval.

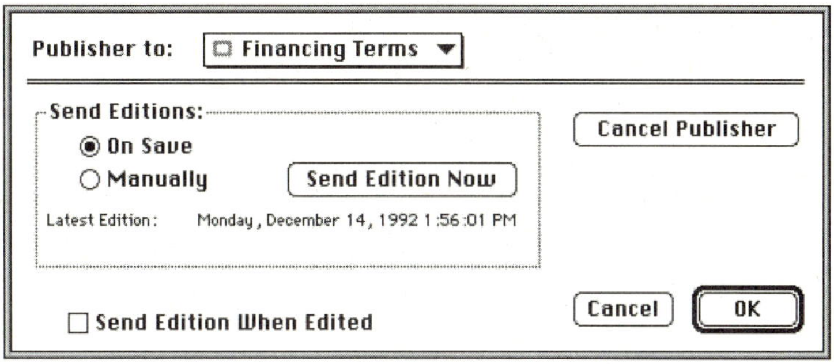

```
Publisher to:     ⬚ Financing Terms  ▼

┌─Send Editions:─────────────────────────────┐          ┌──────────────────────┐
│  ◉ On Save                                  │          │   Cancel Publisher   │
│  ○ Manually       ┌──────────────────────┐  │          └──────────────────────┘
│                   │   Send Edition Now   │  │
│                   └──────────────────────┘  │
│  Latest Edition:     Monday, December 14, 1992 1:56:01 PM │
└─────────────────────────────────────────────┘

   ☐ Send Edition When Edited              ┌──────────┐  ┌─────────┐
                                           │  Cancel  │  │   OK    │
                                           └──────────┘  └─────────┘
```

3. Perform one of the following actions:

   ■ Click the Manually radio button to update the publication
   only when you click the Send Edition now command button.

   ■ Click Send Edition Now to update an edition.

   ■ Click the Send Edition When Edited button to send all
   updates automatically.

   ■ Click the Cancel Publisher button to stop publication.

4. Choose OK.

Subscribing to an Edition

After you create an edition, subscribing is easy. To subscribe, follow
these steps:

1. Open the document in which you want to paste a copy of
   the edition.

2. Position the insertion point where you want to place the edition.

3. Choose Subscribe To from the Edit menu. The dialog box shown
   in figure 30.11 appears.

4. Select the edition you want to add. A preview of the edition's
   contents appears on the left side of the dialog box, as shown in
   figure 30.11.

5. Choose Subscribe. Word inserts the edition into your document,
   surrounded by gray brackets.

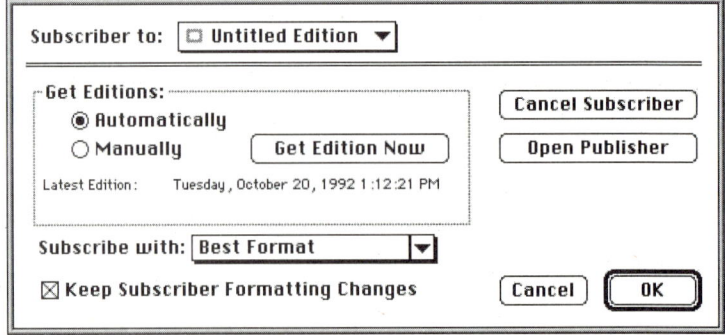

```
          Preview                  📁 System Folder ▼         ▭ Mogae HD

                              📁 Control Panels        ⬆
 Thank you for asking         📁 Extensions                      Eject
 about our financing terms!   📁 Preferences
 Here's the good news.        📁 PrintMonitor Documents          Desktop
 Just send in the enclosed    📁 Speech Synth.
 application. We're pleased    📁 Spool Folder                   Cancel
 to offer 90 day
 same-as-cash financing.      📁 Startup Items
 You don't pay a cent of      📁 Untitled Edition      ⬇      Subscribe
 interest as long as you
 pay off your outstanding

              Subscribe with: Best Format              ▼
```

The inserted edition is called a *subscriber*. Word treats all inserted text as one character. You must select all the text as a unit, and you must format all the text as a unit.

Updating a Subscription

After you subscribe to an edition, you can specify the frequency of updates. By default, your Macintosh updates the subscriber when the edition changes. You can choose manual updating or specify a specific time for updating.

To update a subscription, follow these steps:

1. Place the insertion point within the subscriber.

2. Choose Subscriber Options from the Edit menu. The dialog box shown in figure 30.12 appears.

Fig. 30.12
Subscriber options.

```
 Subscriber to:  📁 Untitled Edition  ▼

 ┌─Get Editions:──────────────────────────┐   ┌──────────────────┐
 │  ◉ Automatically                        │   │ Cancel Subscriber │
 │  ○ Manually       Get Edition Now       │   │  Open Publisher   │
 │  Latest Edition:  Tuesday, October 20, 1992 1:12:21 PM │
 └─────────────────────────────────────────┘

 Subscribe with: Best Format          ▼

 ☒ Keep Subscriber Formatting Changes        Cancel      OK
```

3. Perform one of the following actions:

- Click the Manually radio button to prevent updates until you click the Get Edition Now command button.

- Click Get Edition Now to update the edition.

- Click the Cancel Publisher button to sever the link between the edition and the subscriber.

- Click the Open Publisher button to open the program that created the publisher and display the document that contains the publisher. You then can edit the publisher.

4. Choose OK.

Quick Review

This section summarizes the most useful information in this chapter. Check "Productivity Tips" for a review of high-productivity tips and tricks—the ones that Macintosh and Word pros use every day. Review "Techniques" whenever you need a quick reminder about a specific procedure.

Productivity Tips

- To create a dynamic link, use Paste Link or Publish/Subscribe. Publish/Subscribe is the best option if the data you're importing can be used in many documents and by other programs.

- If you don't want to create a dynamic link but want ease of updating and editing from within Word, use embedding.

- If you are using a 68030-based system, such as a Mac Classic II or one of the newer Mac IIs, you can increase apparent RAM by using System 7's virtual-memory capabilities. Remember, however, that virtual memory requires a great deal of disk space.

- When you create the document that you're going to link or publish, be sure to add all the necessary formatting. You cannot format the copy of the document that is inserted into the destination document.

- If you move a linked or published source document, the dependent programs may not be able to find the source document or the publisher.

- If you edit the source document, remember that changes you make outside the originally selected area are not reflected in the linked documents. Gray brackets surround the published part of the document.

- If you're using System 6, you can use Paste Link, but you must update the link manually.

Techniques

This section provides concise summaries of all the procedures introduced in this chapter.

Creating a Dynamic Link with Paste Link

To create a link with Paste Link:

1. Open the program that contains the data you want to use.

2. Select the data.

3. Choose Copy from the Edit menu, press ⌘-C, or click the Copy tool.

4. Switch to Word.

5. Open the destination document.

6. Position the insertion point in the document where you want to place the imported data.

7. Hold down the Shift key and choose Paste Link from the Edit menu or press Option-F4.

Creating a Dynamic Link with Paste Special

To create a link with Paste Special:

1. Open the program that contains the data you want to use.

2. Select the data.

3. Choose Copy from the Edit menu, press ⌘-C, or click the Copy tool.

4. Switch to Word.

5. Open the destination document.

6. Position the insertion point in the document where you want to place the imported data.

7. Choose Paste Special from the Edit menu. The Paste Special dialog box appears.

8. Choose a formatting option.

9. Click Paste to import the picture but not create a link, or choose Paste Link to import the data and create a dynamic link with the source document.

To update the link:

1. Position the insertion point in the imported data.

2. Choose Link Options from the Edit menu. The Link Options dialog box appears.

3. Perform one of the following actions:

   ■ Click the Manually radio button to switch to manual updating of the link.

   ■ Click the Update Now command button to update a manual link.

   ■ Click the Never radio button to retain the link but prevent further updates.

   ■ Select a different format in the Format drop-down list box.

   ■ Click Cancel Link to break the link to the source document.

   ■ Click Open Source to start the source program and edit the document.

   ■ Click Edit Link to change the path for the source document if you have moved it to a new location on your disk.

4. Choose OK.

Embedding Objects in Word Documents

To embed an existing document in Word:

1. Start the program you used to create the document.

2. Select the portion of the document that you want to embed in your Word document.

3. Choose Copy from the Edit menu, press ⌘-C, or click the Copy tool.

4. Switch to Word.

5. Hold down the Shift key and choose Paste Object from the Edit menu or press ⌘-F4.

To create the object without leaving Word:

1. Place the insertion point where you want the object to appear.

2. Choose Object from the Insert menu. The Insert Object dialog box appears.

3. Choose the type of object you want to insert.

4. Use the program's tools to create the object.

5. Choose Update from the File menu or press ⌘-Q.

To edit an embedded object:

1. Position the insertion point on the object you want to edit.

2. Choose Edit Object from the Edit menu or double-click the object.

3. Use the native program's tools to edit the object.

4. To return to Word and update the object in your Word document, choose Update from the File menu or press ⌘-Q.

Publishing a Document

To define the publisher and create the edition:

1. Select the information you want to publish.

2. Choose Create Publisher from the Edit menu. A preview dialog box appears.

3. Choose a destination folder for your edition.

4. Type a name for your edition in the Name of New Edition text box.

5. Choose Publisher Options from the Edit menu.

To update the publisher:

1. In the document that contains the publisher, position the insertion point within the publication brackets.

2. Choose Publisher Options from the Edit menu.

3. Perform one of the following actions:

- Click the Manually radio button to update the publication only when you click the Send Edition Now command button.

- Click Send Edition Now to update an edition.

- Click the Send Edition When Edited button to send all updates automatically.

- Click the Cancel Publisher button to stop publication.

4. Choose OK.

Subscribing to a Published Edition

To subscribe to an edition:

1. Open the document into which you want to paste a copy of the edition.

2. Position the insertion point where you want to place the edition.

3. Choose Subscriber Options from the Edit menu. The Subscriber Options dialog box appears.

4. Select the edition you want to add.

5. Choose Subscribe.

Creating
Office Applications

Includes

Storing Addresses and
Printing Envelopes

Creating Form Letters

Creating Business Forms

Printing Mailing Labels

31

Storing Addresses and Printing Envelopes

I f you think that the Computer Revolution has arrived, you might think again after visiting a modern office. You will see people copying addresses off computer screens onto pieces of paper and then typing envelopes on office typewriters. Worse, you can tell who's using a computer: you get a beautifully printed letter, but the envelope has a hand-scrawled address.

Thanks to Word 5.1's new envelope-addressing capabilities, your days of typing or handwriting envelopes are at an end. What's more, you can store an unlimited number of addresses in Word so that the address you need always is at hand when you want it. This simple but indispensable feature will make Word 5.1 a winner in the office-automation sweepstakes.

Can your printer print envelopes? If you're using a LaserWriter, StyleWriter, or virtually any laser printer, the answer is an emphatic "Yes." These printers have envelope-feed mechanisms that enable you to insert an envelope manually. The instructions vary from printer to printer, but printing an envelope is not as hard as it sounds.

This chapter covers the following topics:

- *Storing and inserting addresses.* You learn how to store and retrieve your correspondents' addresses—and your own.

- *Printing envelopes.* You learn how to print an envelope, using the address you inserted into your document.

Storing and Inserting Addresses

You use the Addresses dialog box to store your return address and the addresses of your correspondents. In the following sections, you learn how to define your return address, add your correspondents' addresses, and insert an address into a document.

Defining Your Return Address

Your first step is to enter your return address. Word places this return address on your envelopes so you don't have to retype the address manually.

You can choose fonts and font sizes when you type addresses in the Addresses dialog box, but your choices appear only on envelopes. When Word inserts an address into a document (such as a letter you are writing), the program applies the Normal style to the address, and you lose any formatting you applied in the Addresses dialog box. Generally, however, losing the formatting is a good thing, because your letter should have a consistent appearance, with the same font and font size used throughout.

To enter your return address, follow these steps:

1. Choose Addresses from the Insert menu. The Addresses dialog box appears (see fig. 31.1).

2. In the list box, select Default Return Address.

3. In the address text box below the Address Name text box, type your return address (see fig. 31.2).

4. If you want, select the text and then choose a font and font size from the Font menu. Word will use your choices when the address prints on your envelopes.

5. Click the Use as Default button.

6. Click OK to return to your document.

Fig. 31.1

Addresses dialog box.

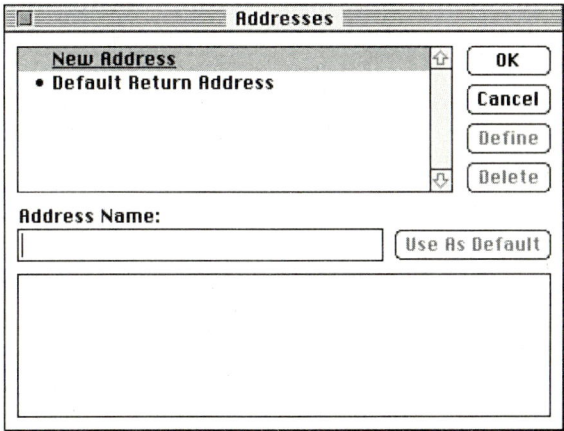

Fig. 31.2

Typing the return address.

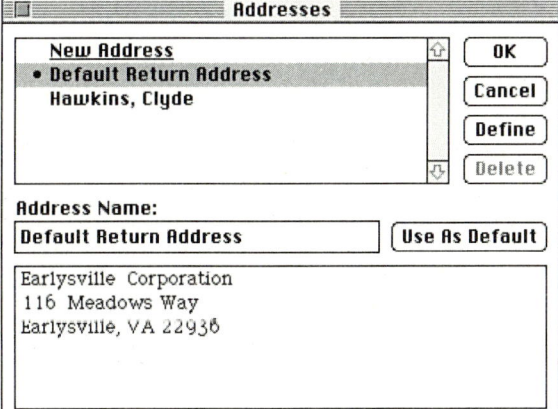

If you need to edit your return address, you can do so easily. Simply display the Addresses dialog box again and select the Default Return Address option. In the text box, make the correction, and then click Define.

Chapter 31

Storing Addresses and Printing Envelopes

Storing Correspondents' Addresses

A basic rule of high-productivity computing is "Never type the same data twice." If you find yourself typing the same address over and over, you will find Word's Addresses feature to be a genuine productivity-booster. You can store frequently accessed names and addresses in the Addresses dialog box, insert those names and addresses into your documents, and use that information to print envelopes.

Word's Addresses feature is a time-saver when it comes to typing frequently used addresses—but not the best way to store a business' mailing list. Unlike a mailing-list-management program, Word does not provide any way to store telephone numbers in the Addresses dialog box; neither does the program attach information to the names and addresses (for example, "Last contacted 12/3/92"). Moreover, you cannot search the address list automatically; you must do so manually. (You wouldn't like using this feature if you had 12,000 names in the address list!) Use the Addresses feature to store the names and addresses of people with whom you correspond frequently so that you don't have to type the same address more than once.

To store an address, follow these steps:

1. If you already have typed the address in a document, select the address and then choose Addresses from the Insert menu. When the Addresses dialog box appears, Word displays the selected address in the address text box.

   If you haven't typed the address in a document, choose Addresses from the Insert menu to open the Addresses dialog box and then type the address in the address text box.

2. In the Address Name text box, type the last name, followed by a comma, a space, and the first name. Word sorts the addresses automatically, using the name you type in the Address Name text box, so typing the name this way will help you retrieve the address later.

3. Choose the font and font size you want to use when the address prints on your envelopes.

4. Click the Define button. Word adds the name and address to the address list.

5. Click OK to exit the dialog box.

Editing and Deleting Addresses

After you define an address, you can edit or delete it easily by following the procedures in this section.

CAUTION

When you edit an address, bear in mind that Word doesn't save your changes unless you click the Define command button. If you click another name or button without clicking Define, you lose your changes.

To edit an address, follow these steps:

1. Choose Addresses from the Insert menu. The Addresses dialog box appears.

2. In the list box, select the name under which you stored the address. The address appears in the address text box (see fig. 31.3).

Fig. 31.3

Address appearing in the address text box after the address name is selected.

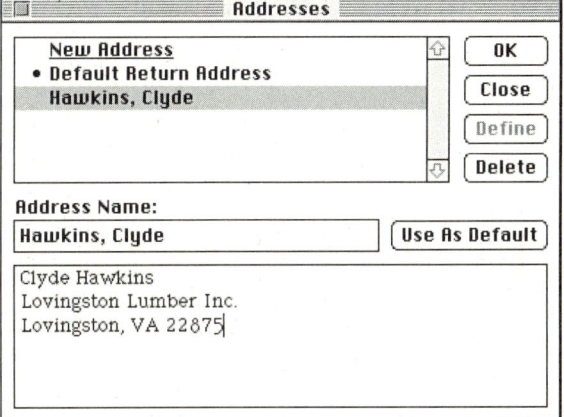

3. Edit the address.

4. Click Define. An alert box appears, asking you to confirm the changes you made.

5. Choose OK to accept the changes, or click Cancel to leave the address unchanged.

Chapter 31

Storing Addresses and Printing Envelopes

To delete an address, follow these steps:

1. Choose Addresses from the Insert menu. The Addresses dialog box appears.

2. In the list box, select the name under which you stored the address. The address appears in the address text box.

3. Click Delete. An alert box appears, asking for confirmation.

4. Choose OK to continue, or click Cancel to retain the address.

Inserting an Address into a Document

After you add an address to the Addresses list, you can insert that address into a document. Word inserts the address formatted with the Normal style. The address is one paragraph, with the lines separated by new-line marks.

To insert an address into a document, follow these steps:

1. Position the insertion point where you want the address to appear.

2. Choose Addresses from the Insert menu. The Addresses dialog box appears.

3. In the list box, select the name of the person or organization whose address you want to insert.

4. Click OK. Word inserts the address into your document at the insertion-point location.

Printing an Envelope

To print an envelope with Word, use the Create Envelope dialog box. You can copy an address from your document or insert one from the Addresses dialog box.

To print an envelope, follow these steps:

1. Perform one of the following actions:

   ■ If the address appears in your document (but not in the Addresses dialog box), select the address in your document and then choose Create Envelope from the Tools menu or click the Envelope tool (see inside front cover).

■ If the address is stored in the Addresses dialog box, choose Create Envelope from the Tools menu or click the Envelope tool. The Create Envelope dialog box appears. Click the Addresses button in the Create Envelope dialog box. When the Addresses dialog box appears, select the name you want in the list box and then click OK.

Both actions display the Create Envelope dialog box, which displays the selected address and your return address (see fig. 31.4).

Fig. 31.4
Create Envelope dialog box.

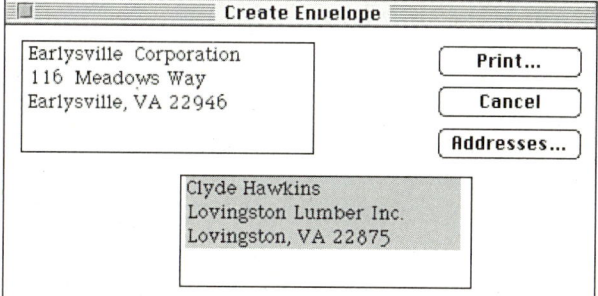

When the Create Envelope dialog box is on-screen, you can change the font and font size of both addresses by selecting the text and then making choices from the Font menu.

2. Click Print. The Page Setup dialog box for your printer appears.

In figure 31.5, you see the Page Setup dialog box for the LaserWriter printer. Notice that this dialog box differs slightly from the Page Setup dialog box that you access through the File menu. At the bottom of the dialog box, you see two additional areas that contain the envelope-alignment options and the envelope-size list box.

3. In the Envelope Alignment area, choose the alignment that your printer requires.

Some printers require you to place the envelope against the right side of the manual feed area; if you're using such a printer, click the Right radio button. For other printers, the manual-feed slot has adjustable guides that center the envelope; if you're using such a printer, click the Center radio button. Still other printers require you to place the envelope against the left side of the manual-feed area; if you're using such a printer, click the Left radio button.

LaserWriter Page Setup
dialog box for envelopes.

```
┌──────────────────────────────────────────────────────────────────────┐
│ LaserWriter Page Setup                          7.0    │    OK    │   │
│ Paper: ⦿ US Letter  ○ A4 Letter                        └──────────┘   │
│        ○ US Legal   ○ B5 Letter   ○ │ Tabloid    ▼ │  │  Cancel  │    │
│ Reduce or ┌────┐%        Printer Effects:              └──────────┘    │
│ Enlarge:  │100 │         ⊠ Font Substitution?          │ Options  │    │
│           └────┘         ⊠ Text Smoothing?                             │
│ Orientation             ⊠ Graphics Smoothing?                         │
│                         ⊠ Faster Bitmap Printing?                     │
│                                                                        │
│ Envelope Alignment:              Envelope size:                        │
│ ⦿ Left  ○ Center ○ Right         │ Size 10 (4 1/8 x 9 1/2 in) │        │
└──────────────────────────────────────────────────────────────────────┘
```

Apple printers:

Printer	Alignment choice
LaserWriter	Right
LaserWriter II NT	Center
LaserWriter II NTX	Center
LaserWriter IISC	Center
LaserWriter Plus	Right
LaserWriter SC	Right
Personal LaserWriter SC	Right
StyleWriter	Center

If your printer is not on this list, consult your printer manual to find out how to align envelopes in the manual-feed slot.

4. In the Paper area, click the US Letter radio button or (if no US Letter option appears) the Envelope radio button.

5. In the Envelope Size drop-down list box, select the size of the envelope you're using.

6. Choose OK. The Print dialog box appears.

7. If your printer has a manual envelope feed, choose Manual Feed or Hand Feed in the Paper Source area. If your printer has an envelope cassette and you have inserted this cassette into the paper-cassette slot, choose Paper Cassette.

8. Choose Print (or choose OK, if you're using System 6).

   If you chose the Manual Feed option, Word prompts you to insert the envelope into the paper's manual-feed slot. Insert the envelope and then choose OK.

   Word prints your envelope with the default return address and the address shown in the Create Envelope dialog box.

Quick Review

This section summarizes the most useful information in this chapter. Check "Productivity Tips" for a review of high-productivity tips and tricks—the ones that Macintosh and Word pros use every day. Review "Techniques" whenever you need a quick reminder about a specific procedure.

Productivity Tips

■ Don't use Word's Addresses feature to manage your business' mailing list. This feature doesn't offer the coding, sorting, analysis, and searching capabilities you need for mailing-list management. Use Addresses only to avoid retyping frequently used addresses.

■ When you enter names and addresses in the Addresses dialog box, type names last name first. Because Word automatically alphabetizes the names, typing names this way helps you retrieve addresses after you add many addresses to your list.

■ When you insert an address into a document, the address takes on the Normal format for that document. To choose a consistent font and font size for your document, reformat the Normal style.

■ Before you print envelopes, be sure that you understand how to insert envelopes into your printer's envelope-feed mechanism. Read your printer manual carefully and try a few test runs.

Techniques

This section provides concise summaries of all the procedures introduced in this chapter.

Entering Your Return Address

To enter your return address:

1. Choose Addressees from the Insert menu. The Addresses dialog box appears.

2. In the list box, select Default Return Address.

3. In the address text box below the Address Name text box, type your return address.

4. Choose the font and font size you want to use when the address prints on your envelopes.

5. Click Define.

6. Click OK to return to your document.

Managing Correspondents' Addresses

To store an address:

1. If you already have typed the address in a document, select the address and then choose Addresses from the Insert menu. When the Addresses dialog box appears, Word displays the address in the address text box.

   If you haven't typed the address in a document, choose Addresses from the Insert menu to open the Addresses dialog box and then type the address in the address text box.

2. In the Address Name text box, type the last name, followed by the first name.

3. Choose the font and font size you want to use when the address is printed on your envelopes.

4. Click Define.

5. Click OK to exit the dialog box.

Part VI
Creating Office Applications

To edit an address:

1. Choose Addresses from the Insert menu. The Addresses dialog box appears.

2. In the list box, select the name under which you stored the address. Word displays the address in the address text box.

3. Edit the address.

4. Click Define. An alert box appears, asking you to confirm the changes you made.

5. Choose OK.

To delete an address:

1. Choose Addresses from the Insert menu. The Addresses dialog box appears.

2. In the list box, select the name under which you stored the address.

3. Click Delete. An alert box appears, asking you to confirm the deletion.

4. Choose OK.

To insert an address into a document:

1. Position the insertion point where you want the address to appear.

2. Choose Addresses from the Insert menu. The Addresses dialog box appears.

3. In the list box, select the name of the person or organization whose address you want to insert.

4. Choose OK. Word inserts the address into the document at the insertion-point location.

Printing Envelopes

To print an envelope:

1. Perform one of the following actions:

   ■ If the address appears in your document (but not in the Addresses dialog box), select the address in your document and then choose Create Envelope from the Tools menu or click the Envelope tool.

Chapter 31

Storing Addresses and Printing Envelopes

■ If the address is stored in the Addresses dialog box, choose Create Envelope from the Tools menu or click the Envelope tool. The Create Envelope dialog box appears. Then click the Addresses button. When the Addresses dialog box appears, select the name you want in the list box and then click OK.

Both actions display the Create Envelope dialog box.

2. Click Print. The Page Setup dialog box for your printer appears.

3. In the Envelope Alignment area, choose the alignment option that your printer requires.

4. In the Paper area, choose the US Letter option or (if no such option appears) the Envelope option.

5. In the Envelope Size drop-down list box, select the size of the envelope you're using.

6. Choose OK. The Print dialog box appears.

7. Choose Manual Feed or Hand Feed in the Paper Source area. If your printer has an envelope cassette and you have inserted this cassette into the paper-cassette slot, choose Paper Cassette.

8. Choose Print (or choose OK, if you're using System 6).

If you chose the Manual Feed option, Word prompts you to insert the envelope into the paper's manual-feed slot. Insert the envelope and then choose OK.

Creating Form Letters

Form letters can be a help or a nuisance. At some time you probably have received a personalized form letter—a letter sent to many people but personalized by a computer to appear as though it were sent only to you, as in the following example:

> Dear Mr. or Ms. So-and-So, here's great news for you and the So-and-So family. You have definitely won at least one of the following fantastic prizes: a Lincoln Continental, a six-month trip to the South Seas, $30,000 in cash, or a cheap digital wristwatch. To claim your prize, all you have to do is visit our fine new recreational center—the Happy Acres Landfill and Hazardous Waste Repository—and endure six hours of grueling cross-examination by our sadistic sales staff!

More than likely, your name is printed slightly out of register, betraying the fact that everyone in your neighborhood is receiving the same letter.

Letters of this sort are irritating, but personalized form letters have many legitimate uses in business. Whenever you need to send the same message to many people but with a personal touch, consider sending a personalized form letter. Word offers one of the most powerful form-letter features in any word processing package: the Print Merge feature, which merges information drawn from a data document with the text in a letter or some other document. This chapter introduces you to Word's Print Merge capabilities.

USING
WORD 5.1
FOR THE MAC
SPECIAL EDITION

The Print Merge Helper (View menu) walks you through all three phases of a Print Merge application: building a data document, creating a main document (the letter that contains the text you send to everyone), and printing form letters. With Print Merge Helper, you can create a form letter quickly and easily.

This chapter covers creating form letters with Print Merge Helper. Although you can use other techniques to print form letters manually, using Print Merge Helper is so easy and convenient that it's the technique of choice for anyone who's learning how to create form letters in Word.

In this chapter, you learn about Print Merge and how a form letter works. You learn how to distinguish between the *data document* (the document that contains names and addresses) and the *main document* (the document that contains the text you send to everyone). You learn how to set up a data document to store names, addresses, and other information about your clients, customers, and contacts. You also discover how to set up the main document.

You learn how to print form letters using Print Merge and how to print only the names and addresses that meet certain criteria, such as a ZIP code. This chapter explains how to use Word's Print Merge keywords, such as IF, to print selected records. In addition, you learn how to print additional text when Word encounters a name and address that meet conditions you specify.

This chapter explains Word's advanced form-letter capabilities. You learn how to prompt the user for information to be added to letters just before they're printed, such as an up-to-the-minute interest-rate quote.

Word's Print Merge Helper creates a table to store your mailing-list data. For this reason, you should read Chapter 15, "Creating Tables," before proceeding with this chapter. In order to use Print Merge Helper effectively, you should know how to manipulate tables. In addition, read Chapter 16, "Numbering and Sorting Lines, Lists, and Paragraphs," for information on sorting tables.

This chapter covers the following topics:

- *Understanding Print Merge.* In this section, you learn the basic concepts of form letters.

- *Creating the data document.* You learn how to store names and addresses.

- *Creating the main document.* You learn how to type the text of your letter, adding codes that insert a name and address into each copy.

- *Printing selected records.* You learn how to send letters to individual addresses.

- *Using conditional instructions.* You learn powerful selection techniques that enable you to send letters only to addresses that meet certain criteria—for example, to all the addresses in a certain ZIP code.

- *Prompting the user to supply information.* You learn how to write commands that, at the time of printing, display a dialog box that prompts the user to type needed information.

Understanding Print Merge

When Print Merge is applied to form letters, it draws information from a mailing list and creates copies of a letter personalized with each person's name, address, city, state, ZIP code, and other information. This type of application requires two Word documents: the data document and the main document. The following sections explain these documents.

You can use Print Merge for purposes other than form letters, such as printing mailing labels. For information on printing mailing labels, see Chapter 34.

Understanding the Data Document

The data document contains the personalized information you want Word to insert automatically into each copy of the letter. Each line contains a *data record*—a basic unit of information, such as a person's complete name and address. Each data record contains *data fields*. Each field contains a particular kind of information, such as a street address, city, state, or last name.

To create a successful form letter, you should break the data down into as many fields as possible so that you can sort and organize your data easily. Suppose that you store names in this format: Mr. Clarence Jones, Ms. Roberta Garcia, Dr. Hiro Himekami. You cannot alphabetize this list. If you break down the names into three fields, however—Last Name, First Name, and Salutation—you can alphabetize the data easily.

The following example shows a good plan for a name-and-address data document:

Field	Entry
Last Name	Stevenson
First Name	Edwin
Salutation	Dr.
Address 1	Department of Radiology
Address 2	Albemarle University
City	Charlottesville
State	VA
ZIP	22999-4567

Notice that the example has two address fields, which are necessary if you are addressing people who work in organizations. If you are creating a mailing list for residences only, you may not need both address fields.

In the "Creating the Data Document" section later in this chapter, you learn how to create a data document with two address fields.

Formatting in the data document has no effect on the way the main document prints, so don't bother with formatting when you create the data document. To format this information, you format the field codes in the main document, as explained in the following section.

Understanding the Main Document

The main document contains the information you want to send to everyone—the text of the letter. You write this document just as you would an ordinary Word document, except that you don't fill in the particulars about the person who will receive the letter; rather, you use Print Merge Helper to insert field names. When Word prints the letter, the program substitutes the data for the field names. The data takes on the formatting that's applied to the field codes. For example, if you format your main document (including the field codes) in Palatino 12, Word uses that font to print the letter and the information merged into the letter.

After you create the data document and the main document, you use the Print Merge command (File menu) to print the main document. Word makes one copy of the main document for each record in the data document. When Word encounters a field name, the program retrieves from the data record the text you put in the specified field.

In figure 32.1, for example, the data document contains three records (for Ed, Mary, and Sue), and each record contains two fields (Name and State). The main document contains two field names: Name and State. When you use Print Merge to print the main document, you get three letters—one each to Ed, Mary, and Sue.

Fig. 32.1
An overview of mail merging.

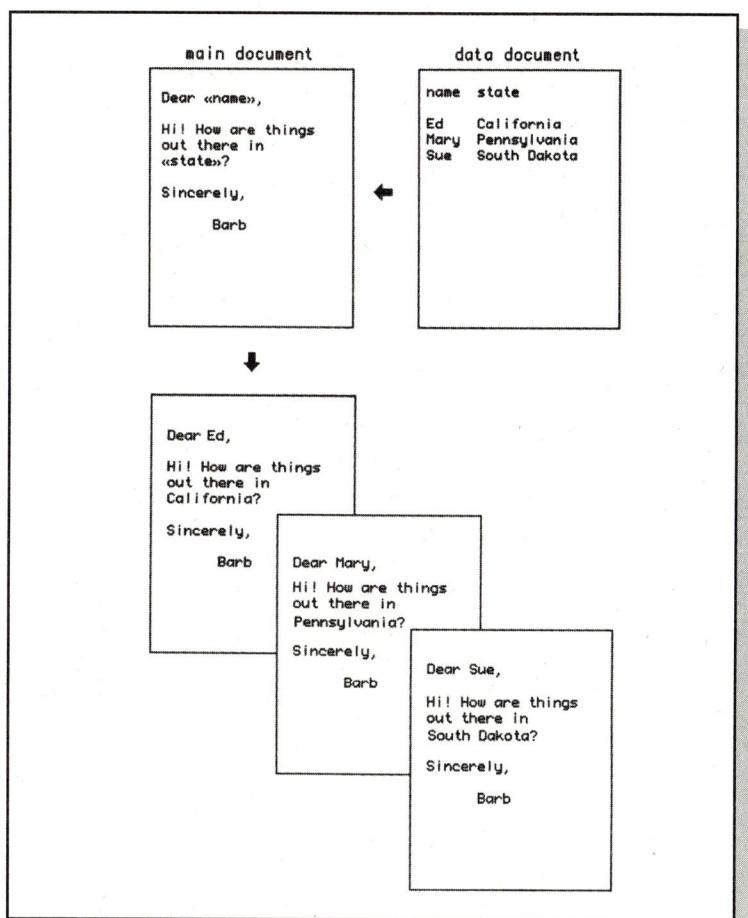

The basic concept is simple, and with Print Merge Helper, creating a successful form letter is easy. Word automatically inserts all the necessary codes.

Chapter 32
Creating Form Letters

Creating the Data Document

The first step in creating a form letter is creating the data document, which is the Word file that contains the information you want Word to insert automatically into your form letter. In this section, you learn how to create a data document with Print Merge Helper.

To create a data document, follow these steps:

1. Choose Print Merge Helper from the View menu. The Open dialog box appears.

2. Click the New button. The Data Document Builder dialog box appears (see fig. 32.2).

Fig. 32.2

Data Document Builder dialog box (Print Merge Helper).

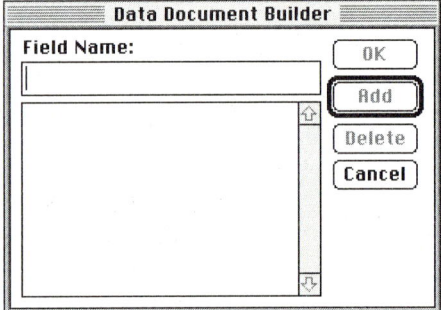

3. Type the first field name in the Field Name text box.

   Field names can have as many as 253 characters, although you should keep them shorter. If you use no more than 6 or 8 characters, you can fit more columns on-screen.

CAUTION

Don't use the words *and, not,* and *or* as separate words in field names. These words have special meaning to Print Merge. If you must use them, bracket them with underline characters (for example, Department_and_Building) so that Word doesn't recognize them as separate words.

Likewise, don't use any of the words reserved for Print Merge applications, such as *IF, NEXT, ELSE, INCLUDE,* and *DATA.*

If you are creating a name-and-address list, begin by typing **Last Name**, as shown in figure 32.3. (Whether you use uppercase or lowercase doesn't matter; Word converts the field name to lowercase letters in the following step.)

Fig. 32.3
Typing the first field name.

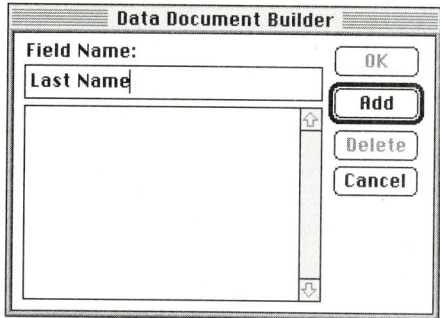

4. Choose Add. Word displays the field name in the Field Name list box, as shown in figure 32.4.

Fig. 32.4
The field name added to the field-name list.

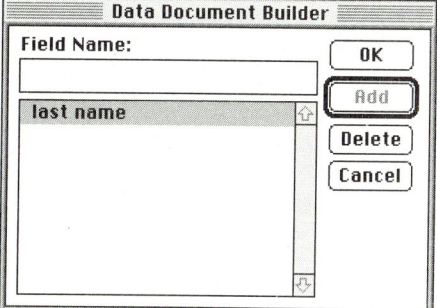

If you misspell a field name or add the same field twice, you can delete it by selecting the field and then clicking the Delete button.

---

5. Repeat steps 3 and 4 to add all the rest of the fields to your data document.

   You can define as many as 127 fields in each form letter. If you are using a table to hold your data, however, you cannot exceed the maximum number of columns (22).

   When you finish entering fields, you should see a complete field-name list, as shown in figure 32.5.

Chapter 32
Creating Form Letters

Fig. 32.5
A complete field-name list.

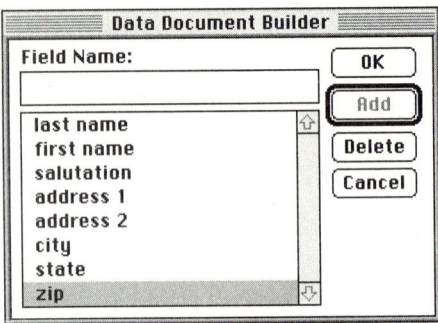

6. When you're sure that the field-name list is complete and correct, click OK. The Save As dialog box appears, prompting you to name the new data document.

7. Type a name for the document and then choose Save. Word creates the data document and places the field names in the first row of a two-row table (see fig. 32.6).

Fig. 32.6

A data document created by Print Merge Helper.

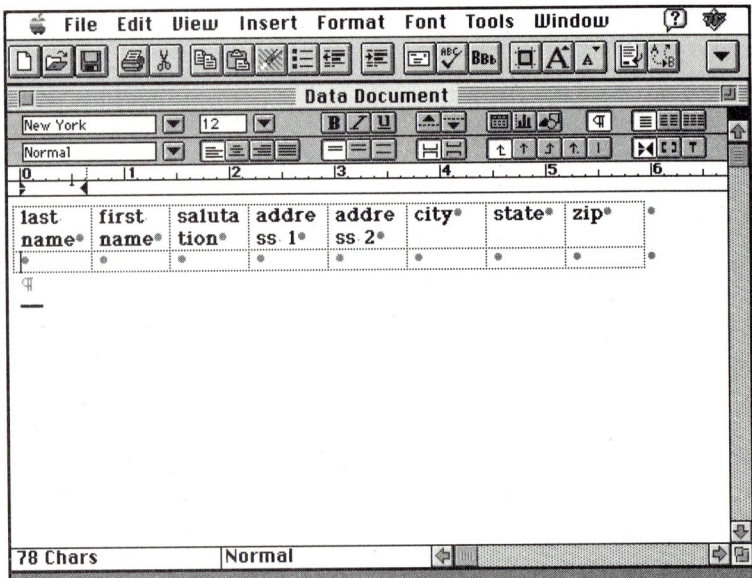

Word also opens a new Untitled document and places a DATA instruction at the beginning of the Untitled document, which serves as the nucleus of your main document.

Part VI

Creating Office Applications

As you can see in figure 32.6, the table Word created doesn't leave much room for typing names and other information. You can widen the columns, but don't make your table wider than 10 inches. You can print a 10-inch table by choosing the landscape-orientation option in the Page Setup dialog box.

8. For now, redisplay the data document, which Word displays as a table. (If you haven't read Chapter 15, do so now; you should understand Word's tables before you can use Print Merge Helper effectively.) In the first row, you see the field names you created in the Data Document Builder dialog box. The second row is blank; that row represents the first data record. In this row, you type a complete name and address. To type additional names and addresses, you extend the table.

9. Click the Table Boundary icon (the T icon in the ruler) and widen the columns, as shown in figure 32.7.

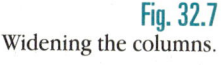
Fig. 32.7
Widening the columns.

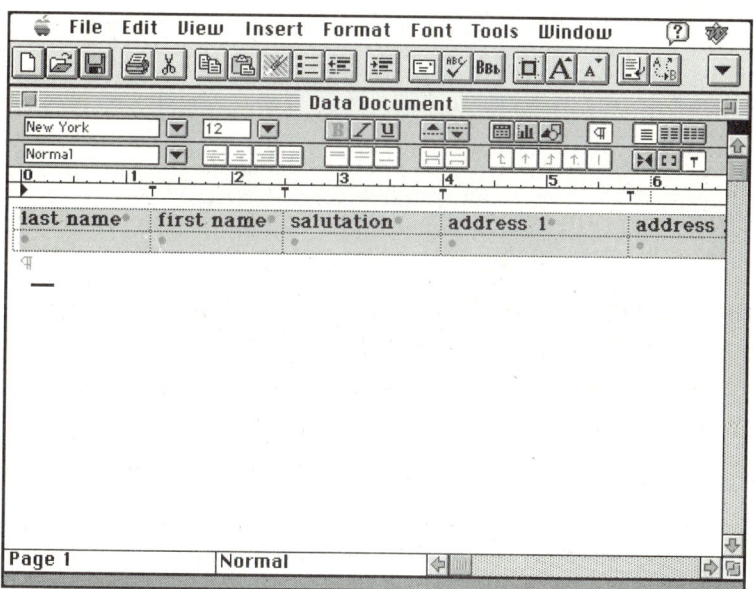

As you widen the columns, remember that you don't have to widen them to accommodate the longest possible entry in the field. If you type an entry that's longer than the field width, Word wraps the text to the next line. The entry still prints on one line in your main document, however, if enough room is available.

Chapter 32

Creating Form Letters

In figure 32.8, you can see that `Department of Radiology` doesn't fit in the space allotted for the Address 1 field; Word wrapped `Radiology` to the next line in the table cell.

Fig. 32.8
Word wrapping within a cell.

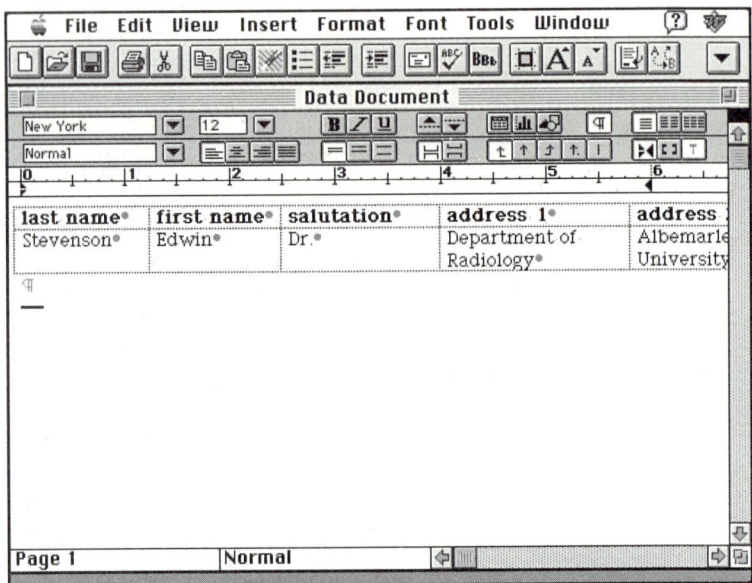

Fig. 32.8
Word wrapping within a cell.

If you were sending a letter to Dr. Stevenson, however, Word would print the address in the form letter as follows:

Dr. Edwin Stevenson
Department of Radiology
Albemarle University
Charlottesville, VA 22999-4567

NOTE

You should widen the columns to allow for convenient data entry, but not so much that the rows are longer than 10 inches. After all, you probably want to print your data document. You can print your mailing list in landscape orientation. To choose landscape orientation, choose Page Setup from the File menu and click the Landscape icon in the Page Setup dialog box before printing. (For more information on landscape printing, see Chapter 13.)

10. Type the rest of the mailing-list data. To create a new row, press Tab at the end of the last row.

Don't worry about putting the data in alphabetical order; you can sort the data easily, as the following steps explain.

Your completed data document should resemble the one shown in figure 32.9.

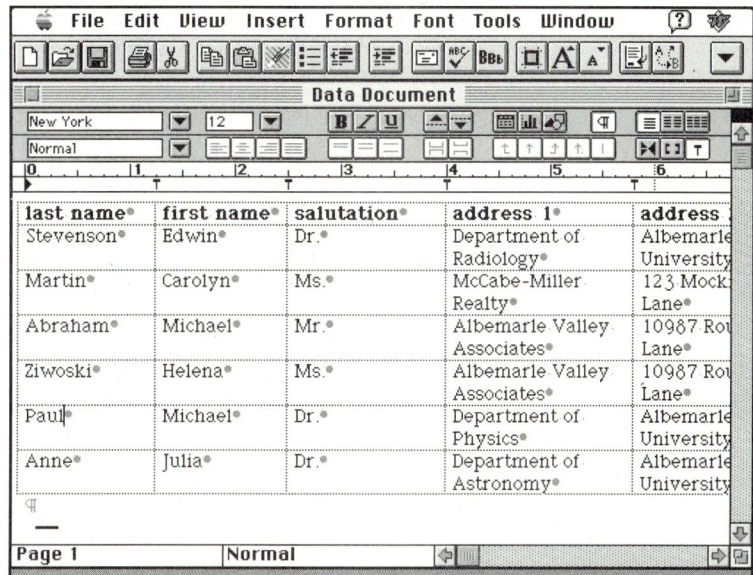

Fig. 32.9
A data document with data added.

last name●	first name●	salutation●	address 1●	address
Stevenson●	Edwin●	Dr.●	Department of Radiology●	Albemarle University
Martin●	Carolyn●	Ms.●	McCabe-Miller Realty●	123 Mock Lane●
Abraham●	Michael●	Mr.●	Albemarle Valley Associates●	10987 Rou Lane●
Ziwoski●	Helena●	Ms.●	Albemarle Valley Associates●	10987 Rou Lane●
Paul●	Michael●	Dr.●	Department of Physics●	Albemarle University
Anne●	Julia●	Dr.●	Department of Astronomy●	Albemarle University

11. Select the column that you want to use as the key for the sort (don't include the first row in the selection).

    To sort by last name, for example, select the Last Name column; to sort by ZIP code, select the ZIP Code column.

If you accidentally include the field-name cell in your sort selection, immediately choose Undo from the Edit menu or press ⌘-Z and then try again.

12. Choose Sort from the Tools menu. Word sorts the data, using the column you selected as the key (see fig. 32.10).

Fig. 32.10

The data sorted by
last name.

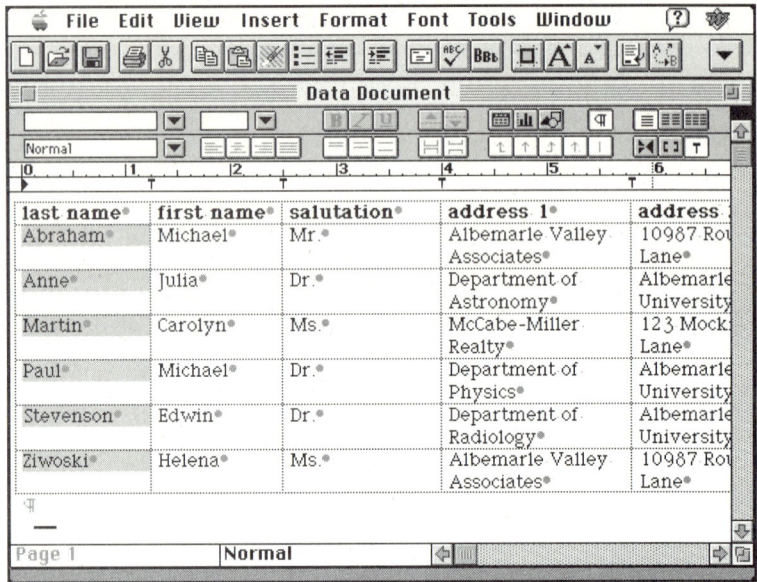

13. Save the data document. When you save, Word gives you a head start on the main document, automatically creating an Untitled document and adding the DATA instruction that references the data document. If you don't want to create the main document during the current work session, be sure to save the data document before quitting Word.

14. To print a copy of the data document, choose Page Setup from the Print menu. When the Page Setup dialog box appears, click the Landscape icon in the Orientation area, choose OK, and then choose Print from the File menu.

After you create a data document, you easily can insert a new field, such as Phone. Place the insertion point on the end-of-row mark after the last cell in the first row and choose Table Layout from the Format menu. When the Table Layout dialog box appears, click the Column option and then choose Insert. Type the new field name and add the data.

Creating the Main Document

In this section, you learn how to create the main document. This document is like any other letter you write with Word except that you leave out the specifics (name, address, city, and so on). With Print Merge Helper, adding the codes you need to fill in the specifics is easy. First, you create the main document and add the codes, and then you check your work. The following sections cover both procedures.

The following tutorial assumes that you created the data document with Print Merge Helper, so that Word automatically created an Untitled main document and added the DATA instruction to that document.

If you didn't use Print Merge Helper to create your main document, follow these steps to create the main document and insert the DATA instruction:

1. Open a new document.

2. Choose Print Merge Helper from the View menu. An Open dialog box appears.

3. Select your data document.

4. Choose OK. Word adds the DATA instruction to your document.

Starting Your Main Document

Print Merge Helper enables you to create a workable form letter on your first try. To start the main document, follow these steps:

1. Switch to your main document, which has a DATA command in its first line. This command tells Word where to find the data for the mail-merge operation.

2. **Important:** Position the insertion point after the DATA instruction. This instruction must come first.

3. Create or insert a letterhead, as shown in figure 32.11, making sure that the DATA instruction comes first.

The DATA instruction must appear at the beginning of your document, with no spaces or characters preceding it.

Chapter 32
Creating Form Letters

Fig. 32.11

Main document with letterhead and DATA instruction added automatically by Print Merge Helper.

DATA instruction

Print Merge Helper bar

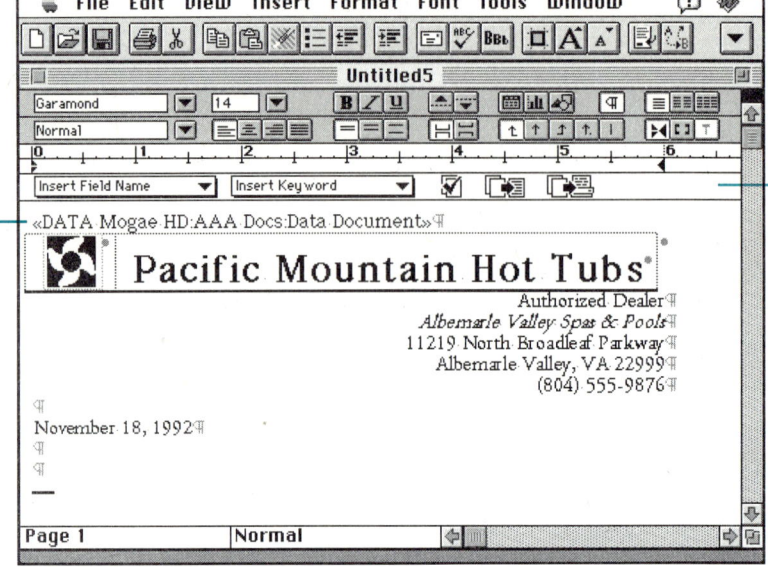

Understanding the Print Merge Helper Bar

NOTE

If the Print Merge Helper bar isn't displayed, choose Print Merge Helper from the View menu.

When you choose Print Merge Helper from the View menu, Word adjusts this command's action to suit the context. When you display your main document with Print Merge Helper active, you see the Print Merge Helper bar, shown in figure 32.11. This bar helps you add field codes to your main document.

When you drop down the bar's Insert Field Name list box (see fig. 32.12), you see the field names you created in your data document.

NOTE

If you choose Print Merge Helper while working in a document that has no DATA instruction, Print Merge Helper automatically displays an Open dialog box and asks you to select the data document. After you select the document and choose OK, Print Merge Helper adds the DATA instruction to your document.

Part VI

Creating Office Applications

Check icon   Print to File icon

Fig. 32.12
Insert Field Name drop-
down list box.

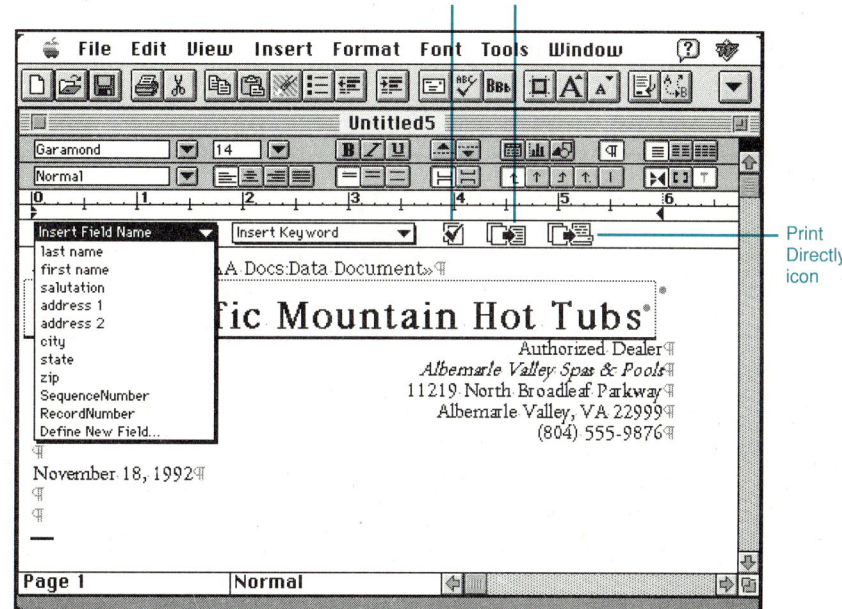

Print
Directly
icon

You will learn more about the Print Merge Helper bar in subsequent sections. For now, note that you see the following fields in the Insert Field Name list:

SequenceNumber. This field, created automatically by Word, inserts a number into your document. This number shows the sequence of the documents that Word successfully prints. For example, the first document successfully printed is 1, the second is 2, and so on. Documents that don't print (usually because of errors in the data document) aren't numbered.

RecordNumber. This field, created automatically by Word, also inserts a number into your document. This number shows the row number of the data record in your data document.

Define New Field. This option is used for special ASK and SET Print Merge applications, discussed later in this chapter.

The Print Merge Helper bar has other features, too. Following is an overview of those features:

Insert Keyword list box. You learn more about keywords later in this chapter. For simple form letters, you don't use the Insert Keyword list box.

Chapter 32

Creating Form Letters

Check icon. You click this icon to have Word check your form letters for errors. (Before using this icon, you have to add field names to your data document.)

Print to File icon. You click this icon to print form letters to new Word documents, which you then can customize and print. (Before using this icon, you have to add field names to your data document.)

Print Directly icon. You click this icon to print form letters directly, without creating intermediary files. (Before using this icon, you have to add field names to your data document.)

Inserting Field Names into Your Document

As you just learned, Print Merge Helper provides tools that enable you to perform all print-merging tasks. In this section, you learn how to insert field names from the Insert Field Name list box. The following steps describe how to add the field names to your main document, to which you already have added your return address and today's date.

To insert field names, follow these steps:

1. With the insertion point positioned just below the date in your main document, select First Name in the Insert Field Name drop-down list box. Word inserts the field into the main document at the insertion-point location and surrounds the field name with chevrons (see fig. 32.13).

WARNING

Don't delete the chevrons—without them, Word cannot tell that the text within the chevrons is a field name.

2. Repeat step 1 to add the rest of the field names. Add spaces, punctuation, and hard returns to the text as necessary.

   Examine figure 32.14 carefully to see how to enter the field names correctly. Notice that you can use the same field name more than once (<<last name>> appears twice).

3. Add text to your letter, being careful not to delete any chevrons or to disturb the field-name codes in any way.

   Figure 32.15 shows an example of text you could send to everyone in your mailing list.

Fig. 32.13
A field name added to the
main document.

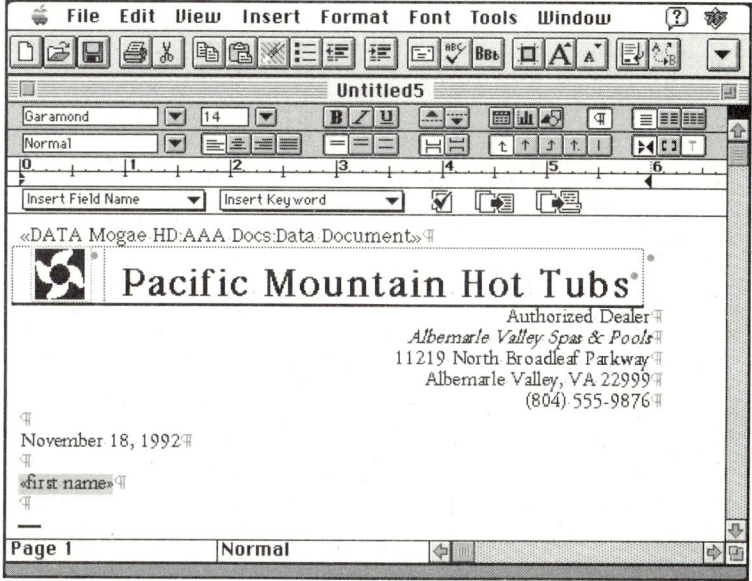

Fig. 32.14
Field names
entered correctly.

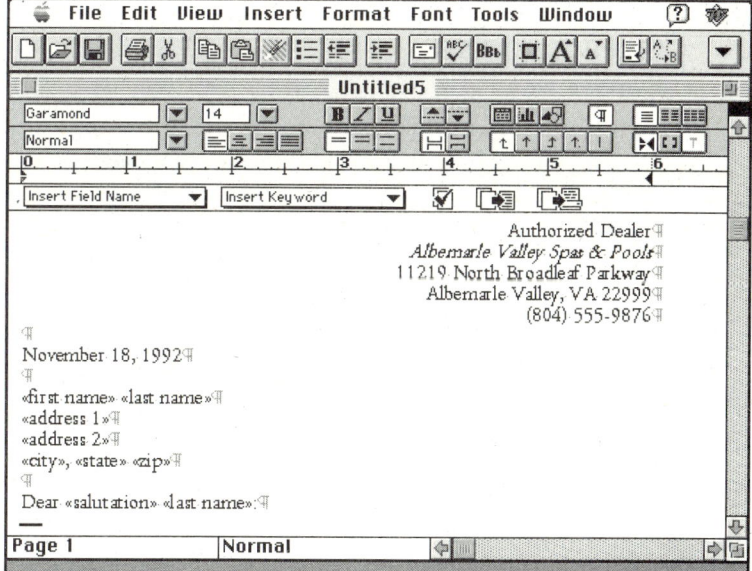

Fig. 32.15
Text added to the
main document.

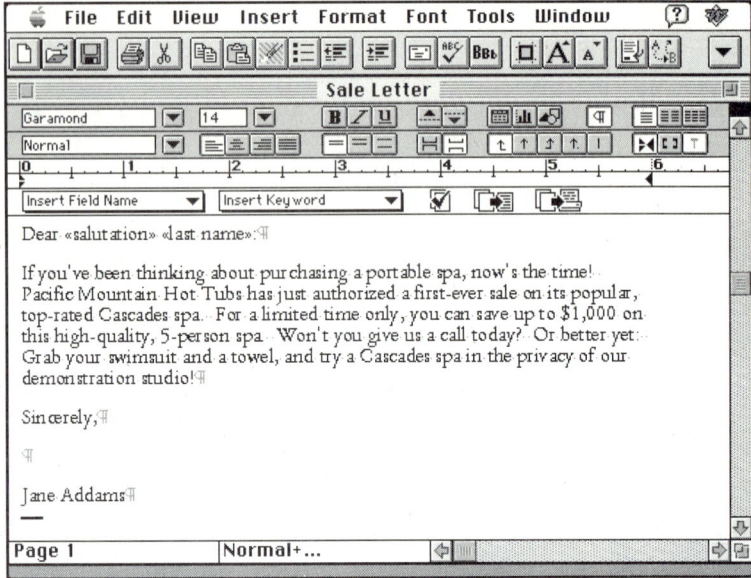

4. Save and name the data document.

After you create and save the main document, don't move your data document to a different folder. In the DATA instruction, Word saved information that shows where the data document is located. If you move this document to a different folder, Word will not be able to find the data document. (In such a case, however, all is not lost: Word asks you to help locate the document, and the merge operation proceeds.)

Checking Your Work

To check your work quickly, click the Check icon in the Print Merge Helper bar. If you carefully followed the instructions in the preceding section, Word created a temporary Merge document, and a dialog box appeared, displaying the message No errors found. If Word found an error, the program inserted an explanation at the place where the error was detected. In either case, close the temporary Merge document when you finish checking.

The most likely cause of errors in using Print Merge Helper is accidental deletion of chevrons. If you see the message Unknown Field Name in the temporary Merge document, chances are that you deleted one of the chevrons; as a result, Word cannot recognize the field name. Delete what's left of the field name and reinsert the entire field into the main document, using the Insert Field Name list box.

Printing the Form Letters

After you correctly set up Print Merge, printing form letters is easy. You can print in two ways:

■ *Printing to a new document.* If you choose this option, Word prints the letters to a new document, with each letter separated by a hard page break. You can scroll through this document and add personalized messages to letters. When you are ready to print, choose Print from the File menu.

■ *Printing directly.* When you choose this option, Word prints the form letters directly, without creating a new document. Choose this method if you don't need to add any text to the letters.

To print your form letters to a new document, follow these steps:

1. With your main document and Print Merge Helper on-screen, click the Print to File icon (refer to fig. 32.12). Word creates a Merge file containing the form letters.

2. Add text to the letters, if you want.

3. Choose Print from the File menu to print the letters.

TIP

When you print your form letters, make two copies so that you have one for your files.

To print your form letters directly, follow these steps:

1. With your main document and Print Merge Helper on-screen, click the Print Directly icon (refer to fig. 32.12). The Print dialog box appears.

2. Choose Print.

Figure 32.16 shows a completed letter generated by Print Merge.

Pacific Mountain Hot Tubs

Authorized Dealer
Albemarle Valley Spas & Pools
11219 North Broadleaf Parkway
Albemarle Valley, VA 22999
(804) 555-9876

November 18, 1992

Michael Paul
Department of Physics
Albemarle University
Charlottesville, VA 22999-9987

Dear Dr. Paul:

If you've been thinking about purchasing a portable spa, now's the
time! Pacific Mountain Hot Tubs has just authorized a first-ever sale
on its popular, top-rated Cascades spa.   For a limited time only, you
can save up to $1,000 on this high-quality, 5-person spa. Won't you
give us a call today? Or better yet: Grab your swimsuit and a towel,
and try a Cascades spa in the privacy of our demonstration studio!

Sincerely,

Jane Addams
President, Albemarle Valley Spas and Pools

Printing Selected Records

Sometimes you don't want to send letters to everyone in your mailing
list. In this section, you learn how to print only some of the records in
your mailing list.

You should use this technique only when you have a convenient and
obvious way to sort your data document so that all the records you want
to print can be grouped together. (Even if such a sort is possible, you
still may want to use an alternative technique described in "Using
Conditional Instructions" later in this chapter.)

To print selected records, follow these steps:

1. In the data document, sort the data so that the records you want to
   print are grouped together.

Suppose you want to send letters to everyone with a 22999 ZIP code but not to anyone else. Sort your data document by ZIP code so that all the 22999 addresses are grouped together. (To sort the table this way, select the column that contains ZIP codes, omitting the first cell, and then choose Sort from the Tools menu.)

2. In the main document, place the insertion point just after the return address, where you can see it without having to scroll down. The insertion-point location is where the record number will appear.

3. Select Record Number from the Insert Field Name drop-down list box in Print Merge Helper. Word adds a field name that prints the record number at the insertion-point location.

4. Choose Print Merge from the File menu. The Print Merge dialog box appears (see fig. 32.17).

Fig. 32.17

Print Merge dialog box.

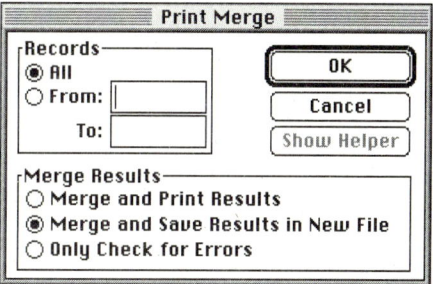

5. In the Merge Results area, click the Merge and Save Results in New File radio button, and then choose OK. Word merges the data to a new document. You see record numbers where the Record Number field name was added.

6. Scroll through the new document and note the range of record numbers you want to print (for example, 16 through 29).

7. Close the document without saving it and switch back to the main document.

8. Choose Print Merge from the File menu again to redisplay the Print Merge dialog box.

9. In the From text box, type the number of the first data record you want to print.

Chapter 32

Creating Form Letters

10. In the To text box, type the number of the last data record you want to print.

11. Choose one of the Merge Results options:

   ■ To print directly, click the Merge and Print Results radio button.

   ■ To print a new document, click the Merge and Save Results in New File radio button.

   ■ To check for errors, click the Only Check for Errors radio button.

12. Choose OK. Word merges only the documents that fall within the range you indicated.

Using Conditional Instructions

In Print Merge Helper, you probably noticed the Insert Keyword drop-down list box, into which you insert commands that perform a variety of advanced Print Merge operations. With Print Merge Helper's assistance, you can attempt one of these operations even if you're still a beginner in personal computing. One of these commands, IF, enables you to create a *conditional merge*. In a conditional merge, you instruct Word to print only certain records—ones that meet criteria you specify.

You may want to create a conditional merge for two reasons:

   ■ You can specify the records you want to print without the hassle of sorting your data document, grouping the records you want to print, and using Print Merge to print a range of documents (procedures described in the preceding sections). You can print, for example, all records in which the entries in the Last Name field begin with A or B and all records in which the ZIP Code field contains 22999 or 22998.

   ■ Using a conditional merge, you can add text only to data records that meet certain criteria. Suppose that you add to your data document a field called Bill Overdue? If an entry you typed in this field in any record contains the phrase 30 days, you can set up an IF instruction so that Word prints additional text, such as *Our records show that your bill is 30 days overdue. Won't you write us a check today?*

Adding fields to your data document increases your capability to print records selectively. In figure 32.18, for example, a Contact field has been added to show which salesperson contacted the customer. If you add this field to your data document, you easily can select only the records that have a specific entry in this field (for example, Jan).

Fig. 32.18
Contact field added to the data document.

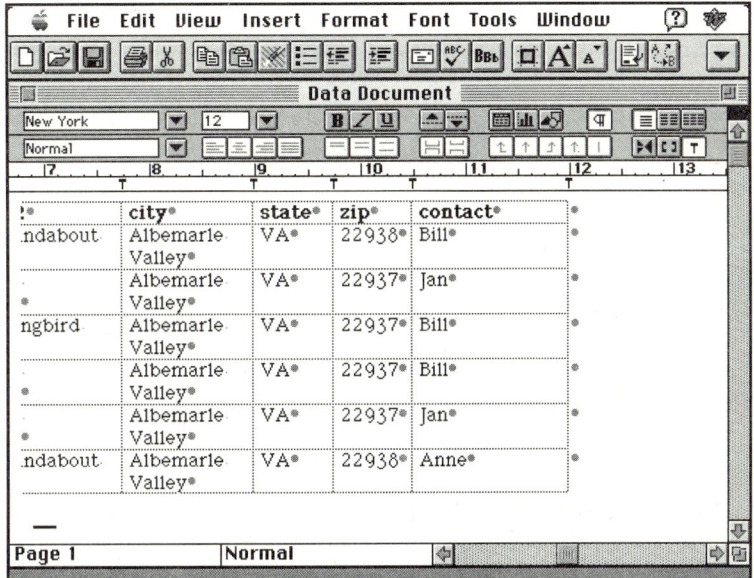

Printing Records That Meet Criteria You Specify

Printing records that meet criteria you specify is the best technique to use when you want to print only some of the records in your data document. You can, for example, print the records that contain the ZIP code 22999-9987 and skip all the others.

To print selected records, use the Insert Keyword list box to build a complex instruction—one that uses several keywords. If you have done a little computer programming, you understand what keywords mean and what they do. If you haven't done any programming, read on: the concept is easy to understand. In essence, you create an *expression*, or instruction, that tells Word, "If the current data record contains in a certain field the text I specify, print the record. If not, skip to the next one."

To print records that meet criteria you specify, follow these steps:

1. In the main document, place the insertion point above the correspondent's name and address.

Chapter 32
Creating Form Letters

2. Select IF from the Insert Keyword drop-down list box in the Print Merge Helper bar. The Insert IF dialog box appears (see fig. 32.19).

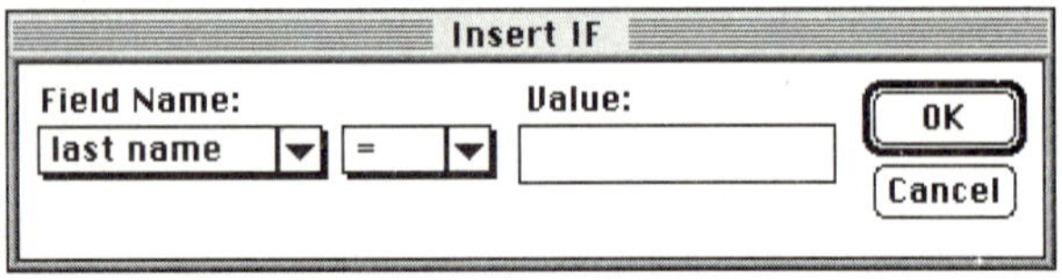

Fig. 32.19

Insert IF dialog box.

3. In the Field Name list box, select the name of the field you want to use as the selection criterion.

   The Field Name list box contains the names of all the fields you created in your data document. Only one name appears in this box at a time, but you can select others by dropping down the list. If you want to select all records that contain 22937 in the ZIP Code field, for example, select ZIP Code in the Field Name list box.

4. In the Value text box, carefully type the value you want Word to match. Figure 32.20 shows an example of a correct entry.

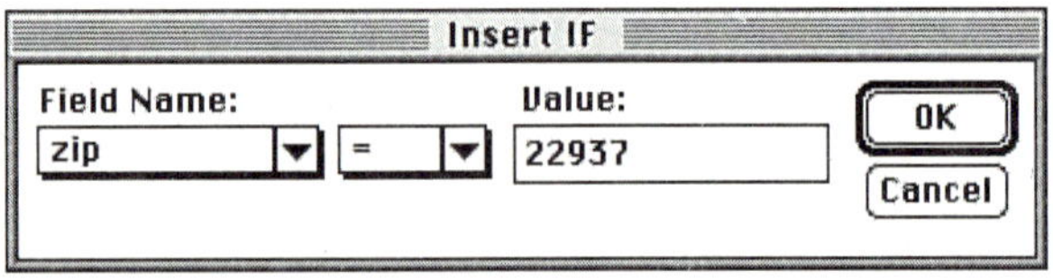

Fig. 32.20

Filling out the Insert IF dialog box.

Word inserts the IF instruction into your document, surrounded by chevrons (see fig. 32.21).

5. Without moving the insertion point, which currently is positioned at the end of the IF instruction, select Else in the Insert Keyword list box. Word inserts an ELSE instruction, surrounded by chevrons. This keyword starts an expression that tells Word what to do if the program encounters a record in which the field doesn't contain the value you specified.

6. Without moving the insertion point, select Next in the Insert Keyword drop-down list box. Word inserts a NEXT instruction, surrounded by chevrons. This instruction takes effect only when a data record's field doesn't contain the value you specified. This instruction tells Word to go on to the next record without printing anything.

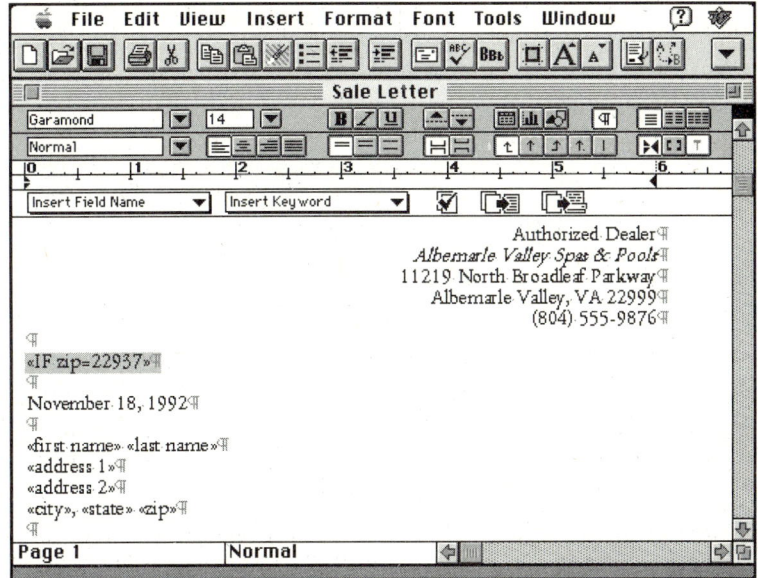

Fig. 32.21

An IF instruction added to the main document.

7. Without moving the insertion point, select ENDIF in the Insert Keyword drop-down list box. The expression must end with an ENDIF instruction, or an error message appears when you try to print. Your instruction should look like the one in figure 32.22.

8. Choose Print Merge from the File menu or click one of the printing icons in the Print Merge Helper bar to print the records that meet the criteria you specified.

Adding Text That Prints Conditionally

In this section, you learn a different conditional-merging technique. You print all the data records; however, you include an expression that tells Word to add text to some of the data records.

In figure 32.18, shown earlier, you see in the data document a new field called Contact. The field contains the first name of the salesperson who originally contacted the customer. Suppose that Bill Johnson—the Bill in the Contact column—has left your firm. You want to tell Bill's customers to contact Cindy Smith instead. In all the letters you send to customers whom Bill originally contacted, you want to add the following text:

Just give us a call and ask for Cindy Smith. A pool and spa professional with years of experience, Cindy's waiting to help you enjoy
your Pacific Mountain Spa!

Fig. 32.22

The completed
conditional-merging
expression.

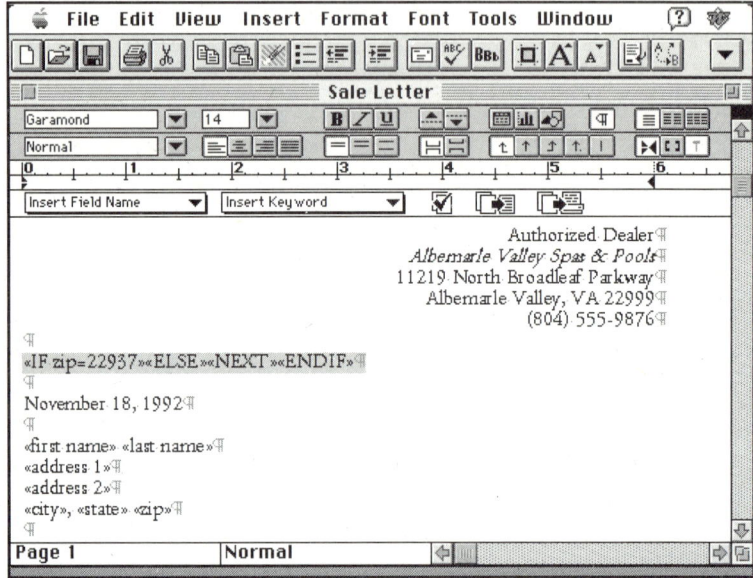

To add text that prints conditionally, follow these steps:

1. In the main document, position the insertion point where you want the text to print.

2. Select IF in the Insert Keyword drop-down list box.

3. In the Field Name list box, select the name of the field that contains the text you want to match.

4. In the Value text box, type the value you want to match.

5. Choose OK. Word inserts the IF instruction (see fig. 32.23).

6. Type the text you want to print conditionally and press Return when you reach the end of the text. (You want to add the Return keystroke to your document only if this text is to print.)

7. At the end of the text, select ENDIF in the Insert Keyword drop-down list box. Your main document should look like the one shown in figure 32.24.

Part VI

Creating Office Applications

Fig. 32.23
Adding an instruction to
print text conditionally.

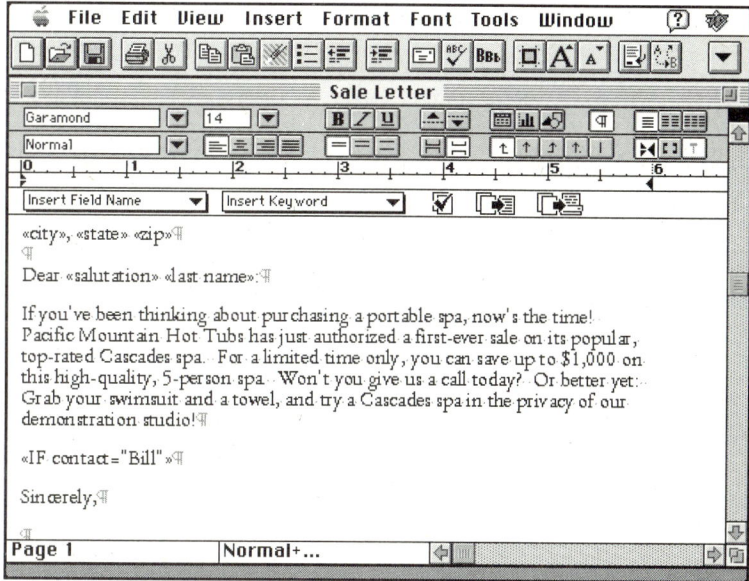

Fig. 32.24
Added text that
prints conditionally.

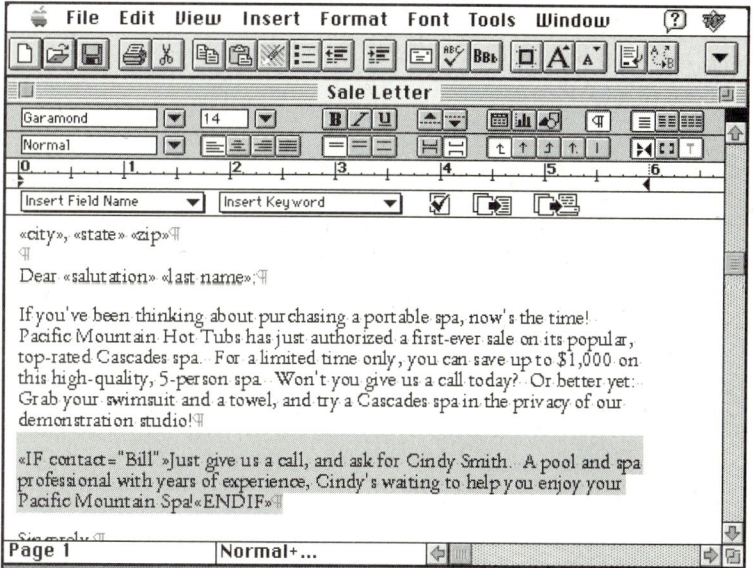

8. Print the records by choosing Print Merge from the File menu or clicking one of the printing icons in the Print Merge Helper bar.

Figure 32.25 shows a letter to which text was added conditionally.

Pacific Mountain Hot Tubs

Authorized Dealer
Albemarle Valley Spas & Pools
11219 North Broadleaf Parkway
Albemarle Valley, VA 22999
(804) 555-9876

November 18, 1992

Helena Ziwoski
Albemarle Valley Associates
10987 Roundabout Lane
Charlottesville, VA 22999-9987

Dear Ms. Ziwoski:

If you've been thinking about purchasing a portable spa, now's the time! Pacific Mountain Hot Tubs has just authorized a first-ever sale on its popular, top-rated Cascades spa. For a limited time only, you can save up to $1,000 on this high-quality, 5-person spa. Won't you give us a call today? Or better yet: Grab your swimsuit and a towel, and try a Cascades spa in the privacy of our demonstration studio!

Just give us a call, and ask for Cindy Smith. A pool and spa professional with years of experience, Cindy's waiting to help you enjoy your Pacific Mountain Spa!

Sincerely,

Jane Addams
President, Albemarle Valley Spas and Pools

As you develop your Print Merge project, think about the kinds of information you can collect and place in your data document—information that will help you take advantage of Word's conditional-instruction capabilities. Add new field names and columns to accommodate this information. If you're maintaining a membership mailing list, for example, you should record whether members have paid their dues for the current year. If the Dues Paid field in any record contains No, you can add in the next mailing an instruction that prints a request for payment.

Prompting the User To Supply Information

By now, you have learned how to use Word's Print Merge capabilities at an advanced level. This section describes one more advanced technique that you're sure to find useful. Using the SET and ASK keywords, you can include in your main document an instruction to prompt the user—you or anyone else—to supply additional information at the time you print the letters.

Using the SET Keyword

You use the SET keyword to define a variable that's not defined in the data document. You also use SET to print the same information in each version of the merged document. (A similar keyword, ASK, prints different information for each version of the merged document.)

For example, you can define a variable called RATE, which prints the current interest rate on a financing offer. The rate appears in each letter you print. When you print, a message box appears, asking you to type the rate. Word inserts this rate into each letter at the place where you inserted the Rate field name.

To include an instruction that prompts the user to supply information, follow these steps:

1. Position the insertion point below the DATA instruction, in the second line of your main document.

2. Select SET in the Insert Keyword drop-down list box in the Print Merge Helper bar. The Insert SET dialog box appears (see fig. 32.26).

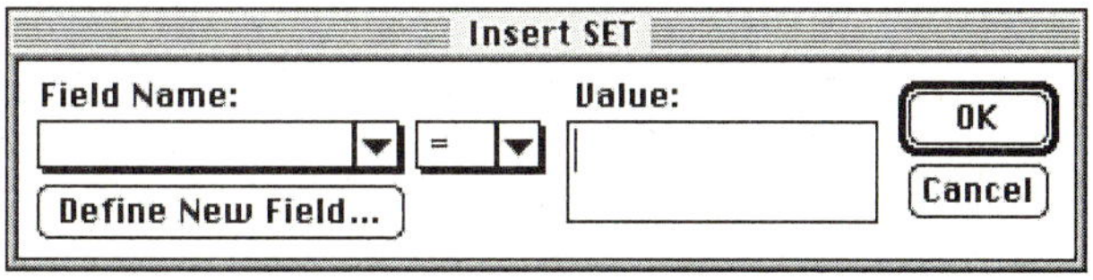

Fig. 32.26
Insert SET dialog box.

3. Click the Define New Field button. You must click this button because you are going to define a new field for the value you are asking the user to type. This new field is temporary and doesn't affect the data document.

   The Insert New Field dialog box appears (see fig. 32.27).

Chapter 32
Creating Form Letters

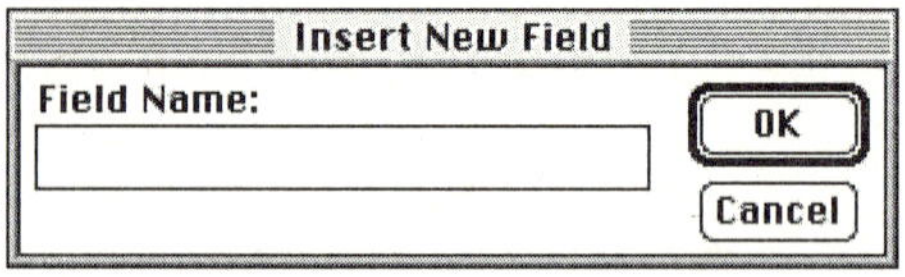

Fig. 32.27

Insert New Field
dialog box.

Fig. 32.27

Insert New Field
dialog box.

4. In the Field Name text box, type the name of the temporary field. Then choose OK. The Insert SET dialog box appears again, and you see your field name in the Field Name list box.

5. In the Prompt text box, type the message that you want Word to display to the user. (You can type as many as 253 characters; the text box scrolls to make room.)

   When you finish, the Insert SET dialog box should resemble the one shown in figure 32.28.

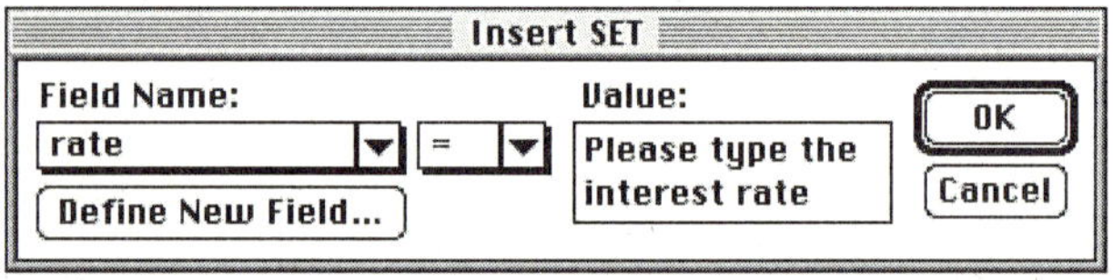

Fig. 32.28

Insert SET dialog box with
field name and prompt.

6. Choose OK. Word inserts the SET instruction into your main document (see fig. 32.29).

7. **Important:** Within the SET instruction, carefully type a question mark after the equals sign (see fig. 32.30).

   If you omit the question mark, SET does not ask the user to define the variable; instead, SET uses the text you typed in the Prompt box to define the variable.

Now that you have created the SET field, you must add it to your main document. To add the SET field, follow these steps:

1. Position the insertion point in your main document where you want the variable's value to appear.

2. In the Insert Field list box, select the name of the field you just created. Word adds the field name to your document (see fig. 32.31).

Part VI

Creating Office Applications

Fig. 32.29
The SET instruction included in main document.

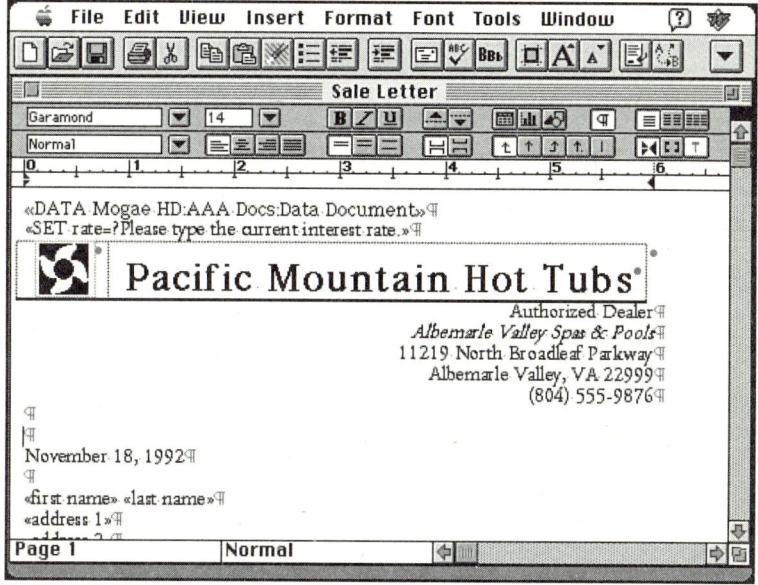

Fig. 32.30
SET instruction with question mark.

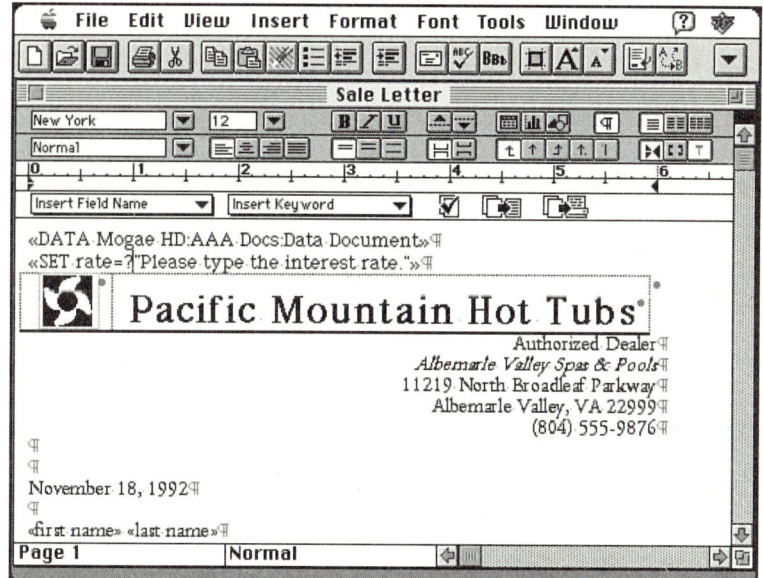

Fig. 32.31
Adding the new field to
the main document.

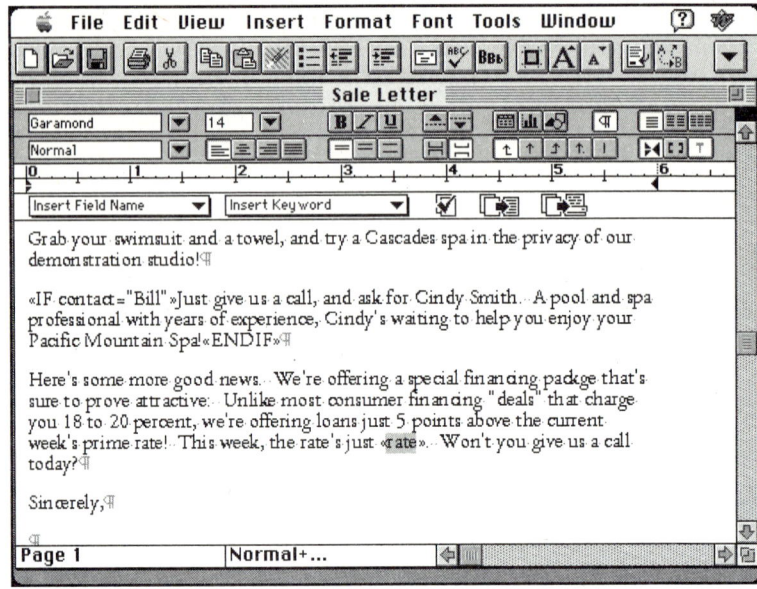

When you print the letter, you see a dialog box containing the prompt you wrote (see fig. 32.32).

Fig. 32.32
Dialog box generated by
the SET instruction.

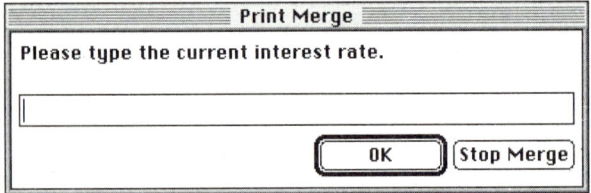

You then type the information you want Word to insert into your document and choose OK.

Figure 32.33 shows an example of a letter in which the interest rate was inserted automatically by the SET instruction.

Fig. 32.33
Merged letter with rate
automatically added by
SET instruction.

 Pacific Mountain Hot Tubs

Authorized Dealer
Albemarle Valley Spas & Pools
11219 North Broadleaf Parkway
Albemarle Valley, VA 22999
(804) 555-9876

November 18, 1992

Michael Abraham
Albemarle Valley Associates
10987 Roundabout Lane
Charlottesville, VA 22999-9878

Dear Mr. Abraham:

If you've been thinking about purchasing a portable spa, now's the
time! Pacific Mountain Hot Tubs has just authorized a first-ever sale
on its popular, top-rated Cascades spa. For a limited time only, you
can save up to $1,000 on this high-quality, 5-person spa. Won't you
give us a call today? Or better yet: Grab your swimsuit and a towel,
and try a Cascades spa in the privacy of our demonstration studio!

Here's more good news. We're offering a special financing package
that's sure to prove attractive: Unlike most consumer financing
"deals" that charge you 18 to 20 percent, we're offering loans just 5
points above the current week's prime rate! This week, the rate's
just 14.5 percent. Won't you give us a call today?

Sincerely,

Jane Addams
President, Albemarle Valley Spas and Pools

Using the ASK Keyword

The ASK keyword works the same way that the SET keyword does,
enabling you to create a new variable and prompting the user to supply
needed information. The difference is that you see a dialog box prompting you to type the requested information for each record you print.

If you use ASK instead of SET, you can insert a different value into each
letter. In the preceding example, you could type a unique interest rate
for clients who have missed a payment.

Chapter 32
Creating Form Letters

To use ASK, follow the instructions for SET except for typing the question mark (step 7).

For an example of how to use ASK, see Chapter 33, "Creating Business Forms."

Quick Review

This section summarizes the most useful information in this chapter. Check "Productivity Tips" for a review of high-productivity tips and tricks—the ones that Macintosh and Word pros use every day. Review "Techniques" whenever you need a quick reminder about a specific procedure.

Productivity Tips

- Use Word's Print Merge Helper to create a data document and main document. Print Merge Helper can help anyone create a form letter easily.

- Before you use Print Merge, learn all you can about tables and sorting (see chapters 15 and 16). Because Print Merge Helper automatically creates a table to store your data, you will have more success with Print Merge if you master tables and sorting first.

- Plan your data document. In addition to names and addresses, include information that would be helpful in future letters. The best form letters are tailored to a customer's unique situation.

- In some cases, you might find it useful to sort your data document and print a range of data records. In general, however, using the IF instruction to select records conditionally is a much better procedure.

- If you're mailing letters that could include up-to-the-minute information, use the SET command to prompt the user for information.

Techniques

This section provides concise summaries of all the procedures introduced in this chapter.

Creating a Data Document

To create a data document:

1. Choose Print Merge Helper from the View menu. The Open dialog box appears.

2. Click the New button. The Data Document Builder dialog box appears.

3. Type the first field name in the Field Name text box.

4. Choose Add.

5. Repeat steps 3 and 4 to add all the rest of the fields to your data document.

6. When you're sure that the field-name list is complete and correct, click OK. The Save As dialog box appears.

7. Type a name for the document and then choose Save. Word creates the data document and places the field names in the first row of a two-row table.

Adding Data to the Data Document and Sorting the Mailing List

To add data to the data document and sort the mailing list:

1. If necessary, create the data document (see the preceding section).

2. Click the Table Boundary icon in the ruler and widen the table columns.

3. Type the rest of the mailing-list data in the table. To create a new row, press Tab at the end of the last row.

4. Select the column you want to use as the key for the sort (don't include the first row in the selection).

5. Choose Sort from the Tools menu.

6. Save the data document.

Creating a Main Document

To create a main document:

1. Position the insertion point at the beginning of the document.

2. Choose Print Merge Helper from the View menu. The Open dialog box appears.

3. Select the data document that contains your mailing list and then choose Open.

4. Type the text that you want everyone in the list to see.

5. Position the insertion point where you want the first data field to appear and drop down the Insert Field Name list box.

6. Use the Insert Field Name list box to add the rest of the field names. Add spaces, punctuation, and hard returns to the text as necessary.

7. Save the data document.

Printing Form Letters

To print form letters to a new document:

1. With your main document and Print Merge Helper on-screen, click the Print to File icon.

2. Add text to the letters, if you want.

3. Choose Print from the File menu to print the letters.

To print form letters directly:

1. With your main document and Print Merge Helper on-screen, click the Print Directly icon.

2. Choose Print.

Printing Records

To print records that meet criteria you specify:

1. In the main document, place the insertion point above the correspondent's name and address.

2. Select IF in the Insert Keyword drop-down list box in the Print Merge Helper bar. The Insert IF dialog box appears.

3. In the Field Name list box, select the name of the field you want to use as the selection criterion.

4. In the Value text box, carefully type the value that you want Word to match.

5. Choose OK. Word inserts the IF instruction.

6. Without moving the insertion point, which currently is positioned at the end of the IF instruction, select ELSE in the Insert Keyword drop-down list box.

7. Without moving the insertion point, select NEXT in the Insert Keyword drop-down list box.

8. Without moving the insertion point, select ENDIF in the Insert Keyword drop-down list box.

9. Choose Print Merge from the File menu or click one of the printing icons to print your records.

Adding Text to Print Conditionally

To add text that prints conditionally:

1. In the main document, position the insertion point where you want the text to print.

2. Select IF in the Insert Keyword drop-down list box in the Print Merge Helper bar. The Insert IF dialog box appears.

3. In the Field Name list box, select the name of the field that contains the text you want to match.

4. In the Value text box, type the value you want to match.

5. Choose OK. Word inserts the IF instruction.

6. Type the text you want to print conditionally and press Return when you reach the end of the text.

7. At the end of the text, select ENDIF in the Insert Keyword drop-down list box.

8. Print the merge application by choosing Print Merge from the File menu or clicking one of the printing icons in the Print Merge Helper bar.

Creating Business Forms

Forms are essential tools for making sure that you get the information you need. Whether you're going through employment applications, quarterly reports, or time sheets, every form must contain all the information that your organization requires. A well-designed form—one that prompts you for all the required information—is a real asset in a business or professional setting.

You can create two kinds of forms with Word: forms that you print and reproduce in quantity, and on-screen forms that you fill in as you sit at your Macintosh.

The forms that you print and reproduce, such as employment-application forms and order forms, take the place of forms that you otherwise would have to pay a print shop to design. With Word's desktop-publishing capabilities, you no longer need to hand over substantial sums to layout artists; you easily can design a professional-looking form with Word and save your organization a tidy sum of money. If the form needs revision, you can make the necessary changes with Word in a matter of minutes and save the trouble of contacting the printer for another expensive go-around with the layout artist.

On-screen forms also have their place in your strategy to improve productivity. These forms are especially useful for invoices and reports. You learn in this chapter how you can use Print Merge instructions to set up a system that makes filling in such forms virtually automatic. You also

take advantage of Word instructions that enable you to compute subtotals and totals from information stored in data fields.

Creating your own business forms with Word can save you considerable time and money. The key to creating business forms is using Word's Table command, introduced in Chapter 15. To illustrate the use of this command for creating business forms, this chapter presents an extended tutorial. Figure 33.1 shows the form you will create.

Fig. 33.1

Business form created with Word.

Second Chance Computers
"We never sell a computer until after its time"

Specializing in Reconditioned Macintosh Computers
Used Computers Bought and Sold
Repairs of All Computer Brands
129 Stevenson Parkway
Periwinkle, VA 22998
(804) 555-1212

SALES INVOICE

First name	Middle initial	Last name		
Street address				Apt.
City			State	Zip
Phone				

Item	Quantity	Description	Price	Total
			Subtotal	
			Insurance/Shipping	
			Express Delivery	
			Total	

You also learn how to create a form that bills clients for the time you spend providing professional services.

This chapter assumes that you're familiar with the Table command (see Chapter 15, "Creating Tables") and borders (see Chapter 17, "Using Borders and Shading"). If you haven't done so, read these chapters before tackling this one.

This chapter covers the following topics:

■ *Creating business forms.* You learn how to use Word's Table and Border commands to create attractive business forms quickly.

■ *Creating on-screen forms.* You learn how to use Word's mail-merging capabilities to create forms that you can fill out on-screen.

Part VI

Creating Office Applications

Creating a Business Form

This section teaches you how to create a business form that you can print and duplicate. The form you create is designed to be filled in by hand. If you have your own business-form design in mind, you can adapt the tutorial to your needs as you go along. Even if you don't have your own design in mind, following the tutorial quickly teaches you the techniques you need to produce professional-looking business forms.

The example shown in figure 33.2 shows the banner with a graphic placed next to the firm's name and address. To create such a banner, you use a one-row, two-column table to place the graphic adjacent to the text. The tutorial that follows shows you how to create the rest of the form.

Fig. 33.2
Banner for a form.

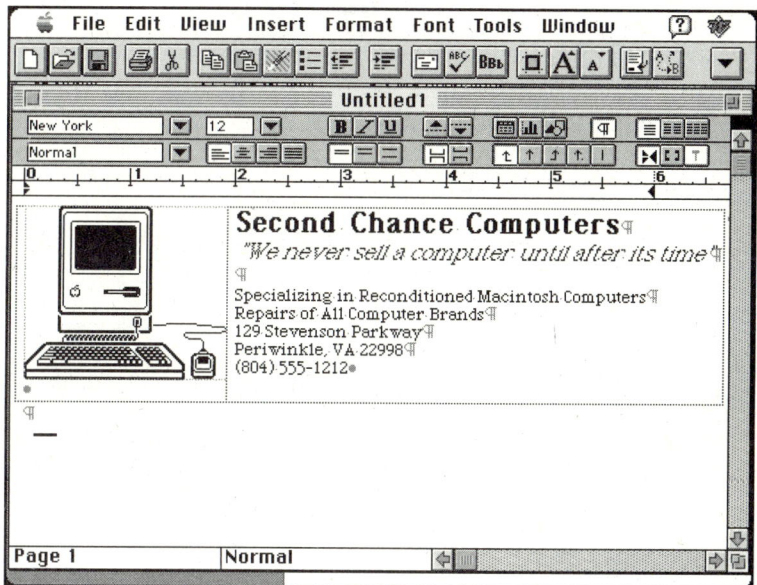

To start this tutorial, open a new Word document, and then follow these steps:

1. Type **SALES INVOICE** and press Return twice.

2. Choose Table from the Insert menu. The Insert Table dialog box appears.

Chapter 33

Creating Business Forms

3. Type **3** in the Number of Columns text box and **4** in the Number of Rows text box.

4. Choose OK. Word places the table in your document, as shown in figure 33.3.

Fig. 33.3

Table added to the form document.

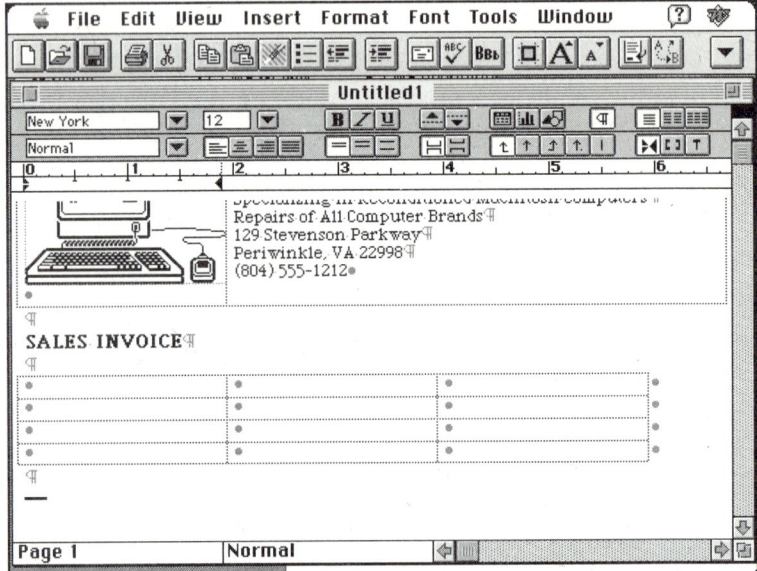

5. Click the Table Boundary icon in the ruler to show the cell boundary markers.

6. Type the headings shown in figure 33.4, pressing Return after typing each heading to double-space the cells as shown.

Removing Unwanted Cells

The Table command enters a matrix of columns and rows in which each row has the same number of cells. To create the form shown in figure 33.1, you need to remove some cells, as you learn to do in this section.

To delete unwanted cells in your form, follow these steps:

1. Select one of the empty, unwanted cells.

2. Choose Table Layout from the Format menu. The Table Layout dialog box appears.

Fig. 33.4
Headings added to
the table.

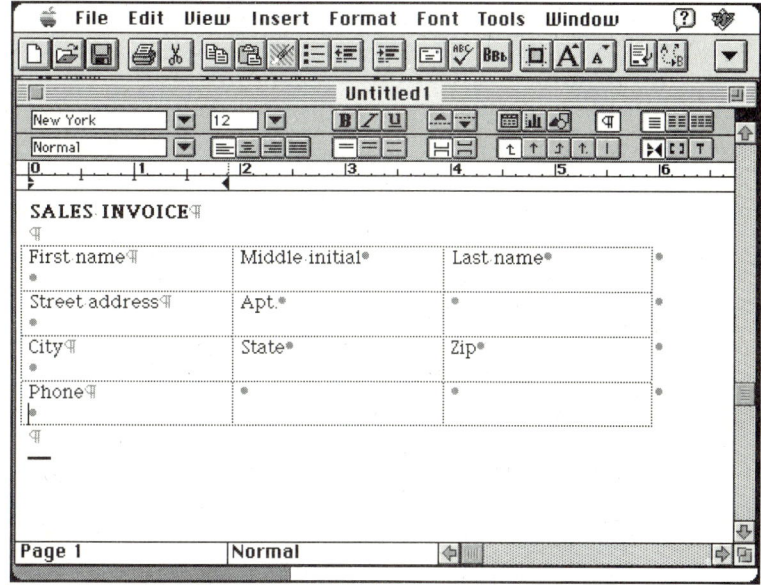

3. Click the Selection radio button.

4. Click the Delete command button. Word deletes the cell.

5. Select the next cell that you want to delete.

6. Choose Repeat from the Edit menu or press ⌘-Y to repeat the
    deletion.

After you delete the unwanted cells, your table should look like
figure 33.5.

Adding Borders

To add borders to your table, follow these steps:

1. Place the insertion point anywhere in the table, hold down the
    Option key, and double-click to select the whole table.

2. Choose Border from the Format menu. The Border dialog box
    appears (see fig. 33.6).

3. In the Line area, select the Thick option.

Fig. 33.5
Table with cells deleted.

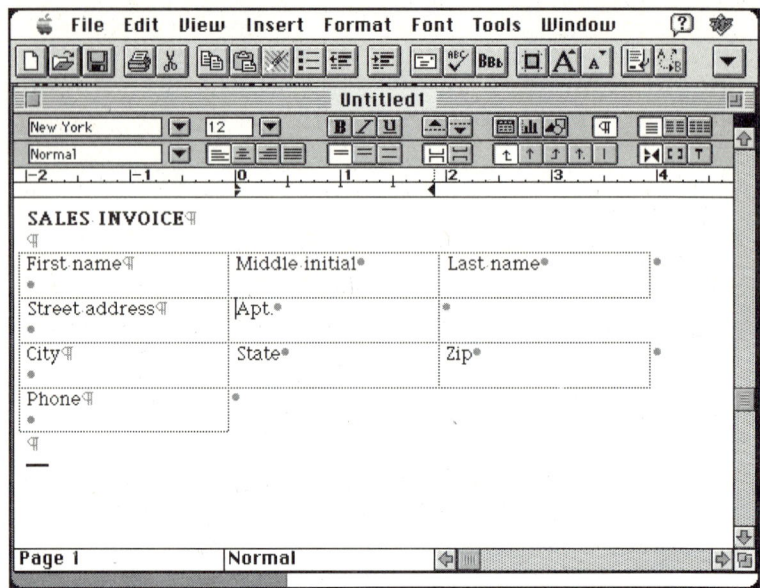

Fig. 33.6
Border dialog box.

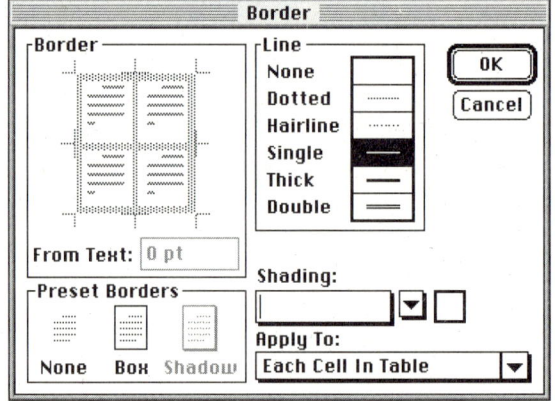

4. In the Preset Borders area, click the Box icon.

5. Click the horizontal and vertical crossbars in the Border area. This step adds borders within the table.

6. Choose OK. Word adds the borders to the table, as shown in figure 33.7.

Fig. 33.7
Borders added to
table cells.

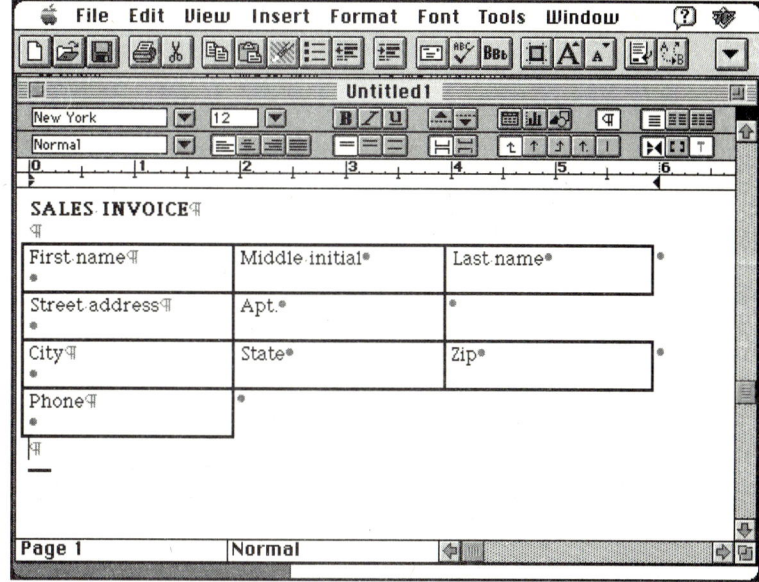

Fig. 33.7
Borders added to
table cells.

Adjusting Cell Width

As you inspect your form, you decide that you need more room for Last Name, less for Middle Initial, and even less for State and Apt. To adjust the width of those cells, follow these steps:

1. Place the insertion point in the first cell in the first row (First Name). If the boundary markers are not displayed, click the Table Boundary icon (the T icon in the ruler).

2. Drag the first boundary marker left until you have reduced the size of the first cell to about 1.3 inches. Watch the status bar as you drag the boundary marker to see the marker's current location.

3. Select the Middle Initial cell and shrink the column just enough to accommodate the cell's name.

4. Expand the Last Name cell to the right margin (the dotted line in the ruler) by dragging the boundary marker right.

5. Continue sizing cells as shown in figure 33.8.

6. Save your form under a name such as Sales Invoice.

Chapter 33

Creating Business Forms

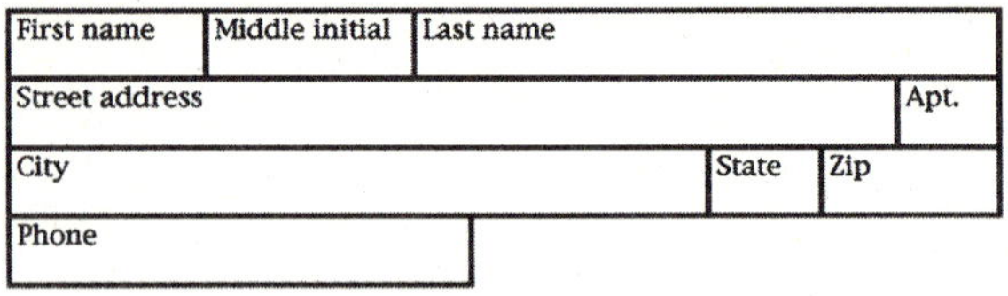

Fig. 33.8
Adjusting the cell widths.

First name	Middle initial	Last name		
Street address				Apt.
City			State	Zip
Phone				

Creating the Order-Information Section

In this section, you learn how to create the bottom half of the form shown in figure 33.1. You enter another table and then delete some cells (and merge others) to create the form.

To create the spaces for order information, follow these steps:

1. Place the insertion point below the table you just created, and then press Return twice to create a blank space.

2. Choose Table from the Insert menu. The Insert Table dialog box appears.

3. Type **5** in the Number of Columns text box and **10** in the Number of Rows text box.

4. Choose OK. Word places the table in your document.

5. Place the insertion point in the first cell of the first row and then hold down the Option key and click the mouse to select the column.

6. Click the Table Boundary icon, if necessary, to display the boundary markers, and then drag the first boundary marker to the 2-inch mark on the ruler.

7. Size the columns as shown in figure 33.9, and then type the headings.

8. Now you need to delete a block of cells in the last four rows. Select those cells, as shown in figure 33.10.

9. Choose Table Layout from the Format menu. The Table Layout dialog box appears.

10. Click the Delete button. Word deletes the selected cells.

11. Select the last four rows of the first column and then adjust their size and position as shown in figure 33.11.

Part VI
Creating Office Applications

Fig. 33.9
Adding and sizing the
order grid.

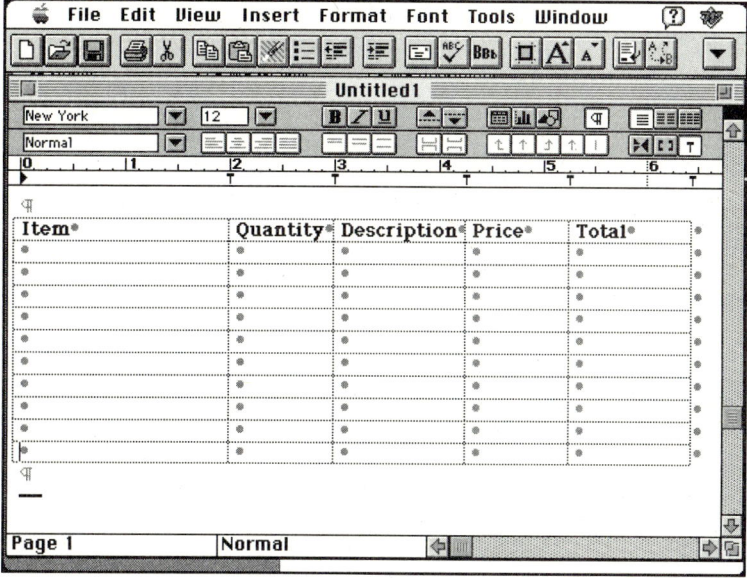

Fig. 33.10
Cells selected for deletion.

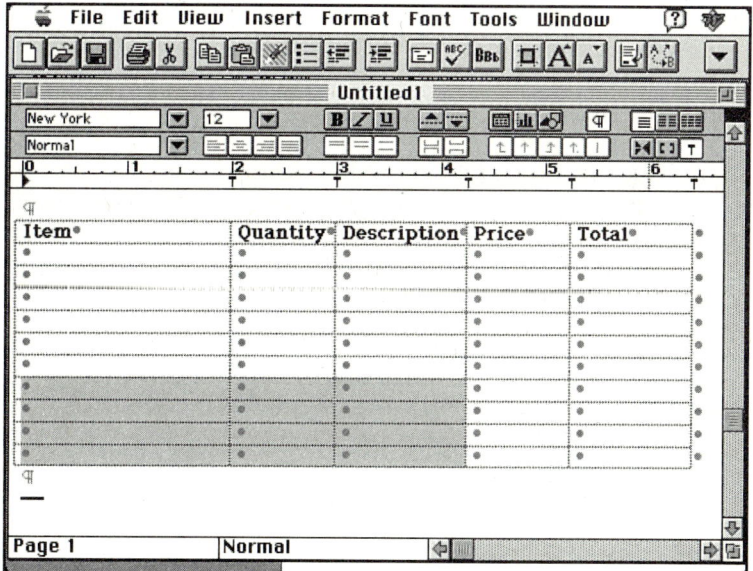

Chapter 33

Creating Business Forms

Fig. 33.11
Fig. 33.11
Sizing the last four rows.

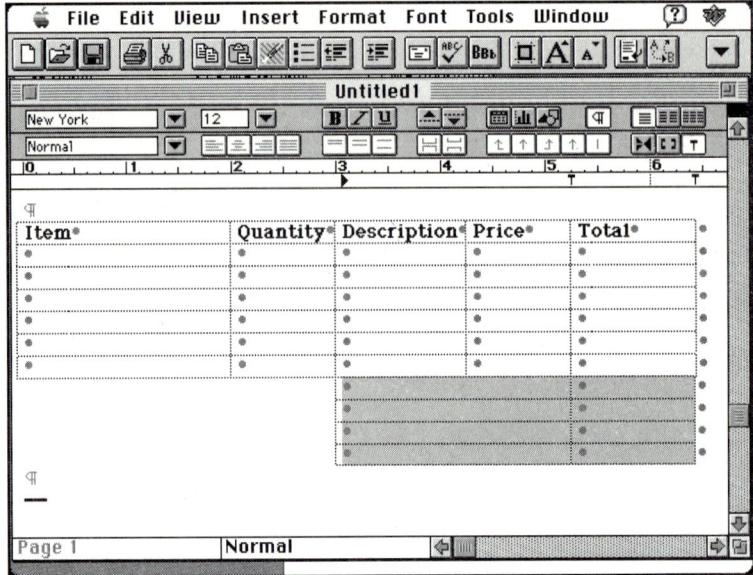

12. To add the headings to the last four rows, as shown in figure 33.12, drag the mouse down the first column in these rows, click the Table Boundary icon to remove the boundary markers from the ruler, click the Right Alignment icon in the ruler, and then type the headings.

13. Select the whole table by placing the insertion point anywhere within the table, holding down the Option key, and double-clicking. Use the Border command (Format menu) to add thick borders to all cells, as shown in figure 33.12.

You created in a matter of minutes a form that would have cost you at least $100 at a print shop. You can change this form in minutes without a time-consuming (and costly) trip to the printer.

Creating On-Screen Forms

The tutorial you just completed taught you how to create forms that you can print and then reproduce in quantity. These forms are for other people to fill in—people such as your clients, customers, and employees. To save time on the forms you fill in yourself, you can use on-screen forms—forms that you fill in as you sit at your Macintosh and then print.

Part VI

Creating Office Applications

Fig. 33.12
The completed form.

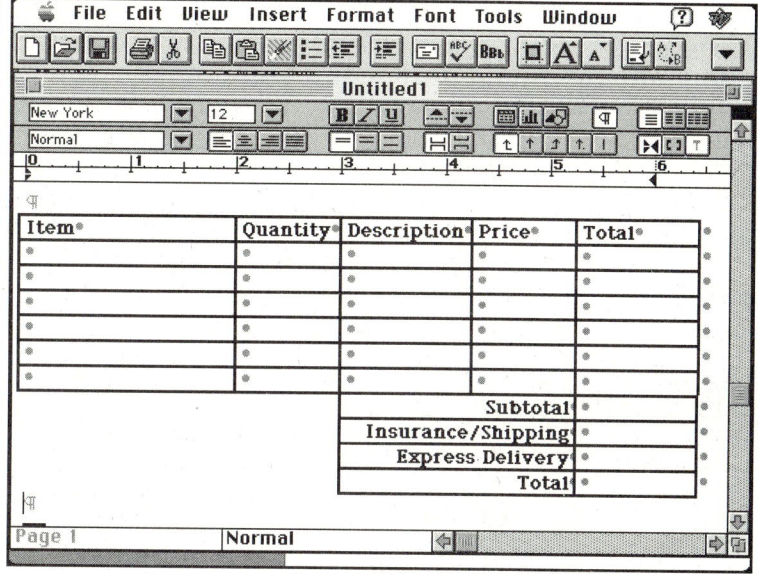

The procedure described in this section is of greatest value for creating a form that you must complete periodically—for example, a weekly time sheet, an invoice, or a quarterly report. Such forms aren't reproduced in quantity; at most, you make only two or three copies of them. To help you remember to fill in all the necessary information, this application uses the ASK instruction from Word's armada of Print Merge commands, which normally are used for form letters (see Chapter 32). You also can use this Print Merge technique to produce one copy of a completed form.

You can use ASK instructions to display a series of dialog boxes, each of which prompts you to supply an item of information that you need to fill in the form. Word completes the form from the information you supply. You can print the form right away, or Word will display the filled-in form in a new document in which you can perform calculations or add additional text.

With a little experimentation, you can see for yourself how the ASK instruction works. Try the following tutorial to learn how to use the ASK instruction.

Chapter 33
Creating Business Forms

Using the ASK Instruction

To use the ASK instruction, follow these steps:

1. In a new Word document, choose Print Merge Helper from the View menu. A dialog box appears, asking you to locate the data document. You don't need a data document, however, for a document that includes the ASK instruction.

2. Choose None. Word closes the dialog box, and you see the Print Merge Helper bar.

3. Select ASK in the Insert Keyword drop-down list box in the Print Merge Helper bar. The Insert ASK dialog box appears (see fig. 33.13).

Fig. 33.13
Insert ASK dialog box.

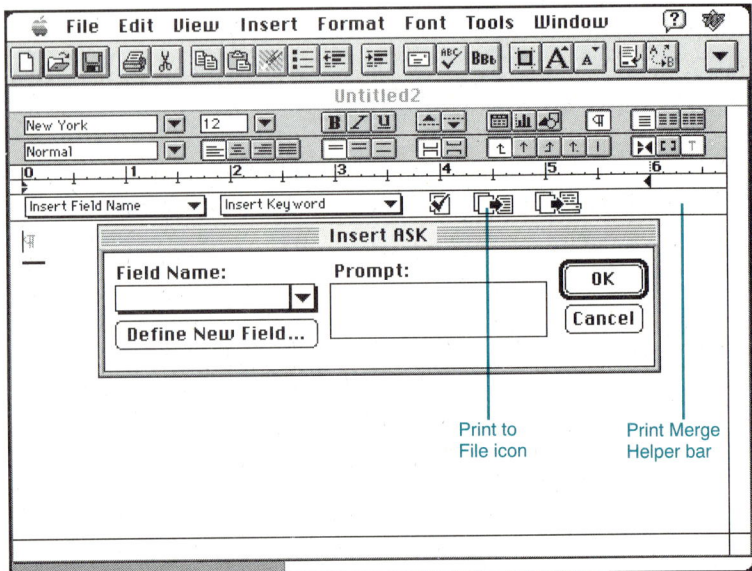

4. Click the Define New Field button. A dialog box appears, asking you to type a field name.

5. Type **your name** (the two words, not your actual name) and then choose OK. You return to the Insert ASK dialog box.

6. In the Prompt text box, type **Hi! What's your name?** Your Insert ASK dialog box should look like the one shown in figure 33.14.

Fig. 33.14
Filled-out areas of the
Insert ASK dialog box.

Insert ASK

Field Name: Prompt:
your name ▼   Hi! What's your   OK
                               name?
Define New Field...   Cancel

7. Choose OK. Print Merge Helper builds the ASK instruction and inserts it into your document.

8. Press Return and then select the new field name (your name) from the Insert Field Name drop-down list box in the Print Merge Helper bar.

9. In the Print Merge Helper bar, click the Print to File icon. A dialog box like the one shown in figure 33.15 appears.

Fig. 33.15
Dialog box asking for
user input.

Print Merge

Hi! What's your name?

[   ]

                                    OK   Stop Merge

10. Type a response in the text box and then choose OK. Word creates a new document and adds the name to the document.

11. In the Print Merge dialog box, choose Stop Merge.

You can put this feature to work for you on a regular basis; because creating an ASK application is easy. In the following section, you learn how to create an application that uses many ASK instructions.

Setting Up a Client Billing System

Suppose that you run a part-time computer-repair business. Most of your billing is a one-shot deal; you perform one service for your customer. As a result, you need to create an accurate invoice quickly.

Figure 33.16 shows a Print Merge application that prompts for all the needed information, computes the total, and prints the bill on a form. Because all the ASK instructions lack a trailing chevron, Word doesn't leave a blank line when it prints the document.

Fig. 33.16
Print Merge application for
billing clients.

«ASK first name=?What is the client's first name?
«ASK last name=?What is the client's last name?
«ASK address=?What is the client's street address?
«ASK city=?What is the client's city?
«ASK state=?What is the client's state?
«ASK zip=?What is the client's zip code?
«ASK repair=?What repair was performed?
«ASK date=?What was the date of the repair?
«ASK charge=?What was the charge for the repair?
«ASK parts=?What was the total cost for parts?

Albemarle Valley Computer Specialists
Repairing IBM and Macintosh Computers
221 University Terrace
Albemarle Valley, VA 22999

INVOICE FOR SERVICES RENDERED

«first name» «last name»
«address»
«city», «state» «zip»

Repair performed   : «repair»
Date repair performed   : «date»

Fee for «repair»		«charge»
	Parts	«parts»
	Total	«charge+parts»

The Print Merge instructions include many ASK instructions and some calculated fields (notice the expression in the Total box). When you print this main document, you see a series of ASK dialog boxes that prompt you to supply all the needed information. Word prints the document by replacing the placeholders with the data you typed (see fig. 33.17).

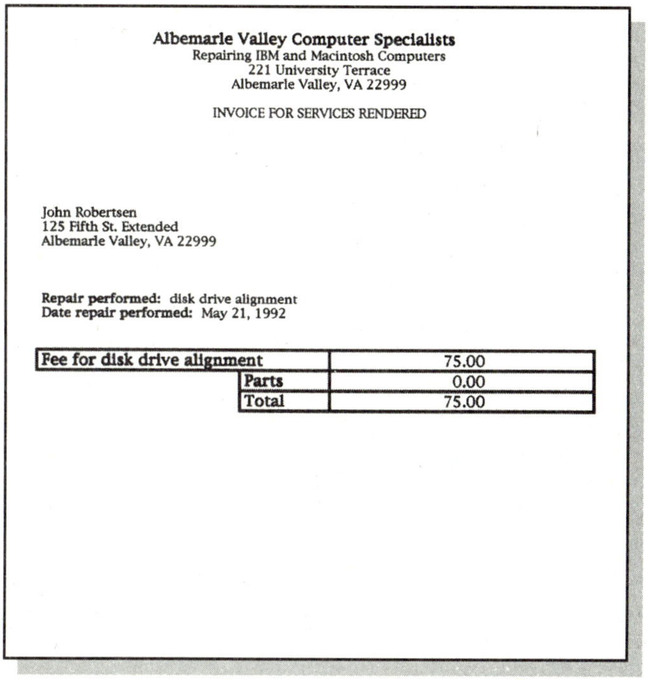

Fig. 33.17
Document generated from
ASK instructions.

Albemarle Valley Computer Specialists
Repairing IBM and Macintosh Computers
221 University Terrace
Albemarle Valley, VA 22999

INVOICE FOR SERVICES RENDERED

John Robertsen
125 Fifth St. Extended
Albemarle Valley, VA 22999

Repair performed: disk drive alignment
Date repair performed: May 21, 1992

Fee for disk drive alignment		75.00
	Parts	0.00
	Total	75.00

Quick Review

This section concisely summarizes the most useful information in this chapter. Check "Productivity Tips" for a review of high-productivity tips and tricks. The "Techniques" section is omitted here because this chapter recapitulates techniques previously presented in this book (see chapters 15 and 17).

Productivity Tips

- You can use Word's Table command to create business forms quickly. Add thick borders to all cells, and you have a form that you would have to pay a print shop $100 or more to design.

- Using the ASK instruction, you can create on-screen forms that prompt you to fill in the needed information.

Chapter 33

Creating Business Forms

Printing Mailing Labels

P roperly printed mailing labels are the key to successful mailings, ranging from newsletters to collection notices. In this chapter, you learn how to generate mailing labels from your mailing-list data document (the one you created in Chapter 32, "Creating Form Letters"). After printing the labels, you can use them for newsletters, flyers, brochures, catalogs, and anything else you can mail to your clients and customers.

Even though the procedures for creating a mailing label vary depending on the labels and printer you are using, the basic procedure is the same. You create a *main document* that includes field names. These field names draw data from your data document and print that data on the label. That's the easy part. The tough part, as this chapter describes, is getting the printed names and addresses to align correctly on the labels. You probably will have to experiment with margin settings and other formatting options to get the labels to print correctly. Plan on wasting some labels!

This chapter covers the following topics:

- *Printing one-column continuous labels on an ImageWriter.* The technique you learn in this section is by far the easiest way to print mailing labels. Hang on to that ImageWriter!

- *Printing three-column continuous labels on an ImageWriter.* In this section, you learn how to use some fancy formatting tricks to print three-column continuous labels.

■ *Printing laser labels on LaserWriter and StyleWriter printers.* In this section, you learn how to set Word to print 30 labels to a page of press-on Avery labels. You can adapt the technique to the labels you are using.

You need a mailing list in the form of a data document in order to try the applications discussed in this chapter. For information on creating a data document, see Chapter 32, "Creating Form Letters."

Buying Labels

You can buy mailing labels at any office-supplies store. For Macintosh printers, mailing labels fall into two categories: *continuous* labels and *sheet* labels.

Continuous labels—designed for use on ImageWriter printers—come in one- and three-column formats. The tops of the labels are exactly 1 inch apart. A paper backing includes the pinholes used to draw the labels through the printer, facilitating printing of one-column labels.

Some sheet labels—designed for StyleWriter and LaserWriter printers— contain 27 one-inch labels in three columns, each with nine labels. These labels often are called *laser labels*, but you can use them with inkjet printers such as the DeskWriter and StyleWriter. Other labels come 30 to a sheet.

Printing One-Column Continuous Labels on an ImageWriter

Newer, snazzier printers have supplanted the ImageWriter, but many ImageWriters are still in business. These printers have their advantages. ImageWriters are much cheaper to operate than StyleWriters or LaserWriters and are well suited for printing mailing labels. In many offices, the ImageWriter that once bore major printing responsibilities has been relegated to a background role, cranking out drafts and printing labels as needed.

With single-column labels, you have to align only one dimension: the vertical. If you choose three-column labels, you must set up a three-column format and also gauge the horizontal dimension correctly. Altogether, printing three-column labels is a longer (and trickier) process.

To print one-column labels on an ImageWriter, you first set up the main document, then set up the page, and finally print the labels.

To set up the main document, follow these steps:

1. Open a new Word document.

2. Choose Print Merge Helper from the View menu. An Open dialog box appears, prompting you to select the file that contains your data document.

3. Select your data document and then choose Open. Word inserts a DATA instruction at the beginning of your new document, identifying the file from which the data is drawn (see fig. 34.1).

Fig. 34.1
A DATA instruction inserted into a document.

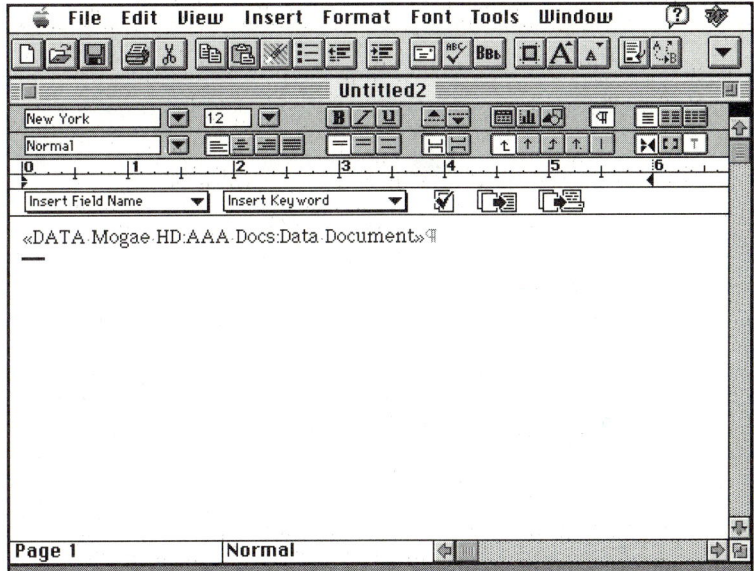

4. Without moving the insertion point, select the first field that you want to insert (the field containing your correspondent's first name) in the Insert Field Name drop-down list box (Print Merge Helper bar).

5. Press the space bar to leave a space after the first name.

6. Select the Last Name field in the Insert Field Name list box. Your main document should resemble the one shown in figure 34.2.

Chapter 34
Printing Mailing Labels

Fig. 34.2
The first line completed in
a main document.

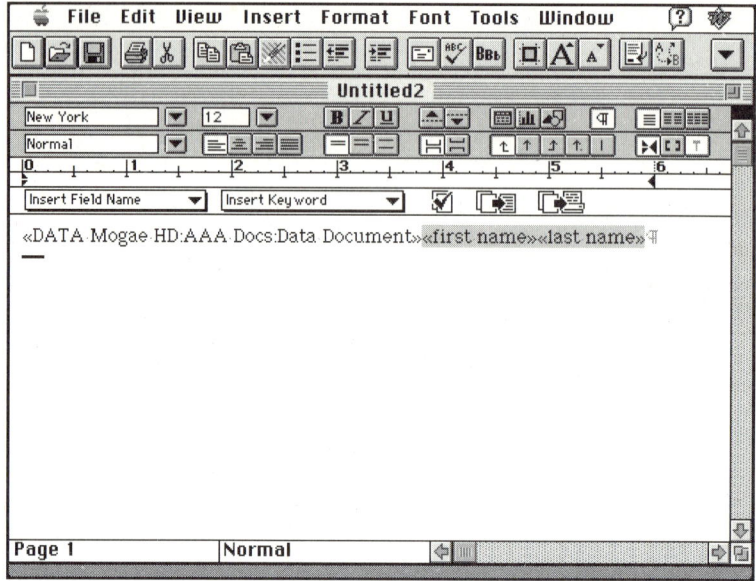

7. Press Return to start a new line.

8. Select the first address field in the Insert Field Name drop-down list box.

9. Press Return to start a new line.

10. If your data document includes a second address field, select the name of this field in the Insert Field Name list box and then press Return to start a new line.

11. Select the City field in the Insert Field Name list box, type a comma, and press the space bar.

12. Select the State field in the Insert Field Name list box and then press the space bar.

13. Select the ZIP Code field in the Insert Field Name list box. At this point, your main document should resemble the one shown in figure 34.3.

Creating Office Applications

Fig. 34.3
All the field names added
to the main document.

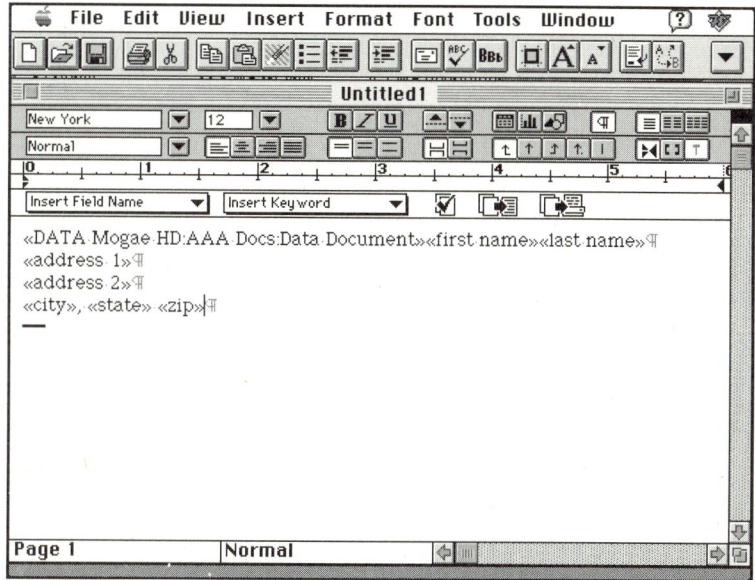

Fig. 34.3
All the field names added
to the main document.

14. Save your main document.

To set up the page, follow these steps:

1. Choose Preferences from the Tools menu. When the Preferences
   dialog box appears, displaying the General options, type the width
   of your label paper in the Custom Paper Size Width text box.

2. Type **1** (the label height in inches) in the Custom Paper Size
   Height text box. Your Preferences dialog box should look like the
   one shown in figure 34.4.

3. Click the close box to exit the dialog box.

4. Choose Page Setup from the File menu. The Page Setup dialog box
   appears (see fig. 34.5). Notice that the Custom Paper Size option
   you just defined appears in the dialog box.

Chapter 34

Printing Mailing Labels

Fig. 34.4
Custom Paper Size settings
in the Preferences
dialog box.

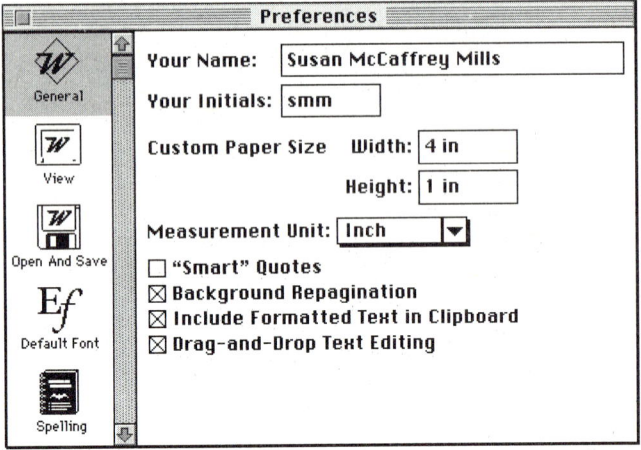

Fig. 34.5
Page Setup dialog box for
an ImageWriter.

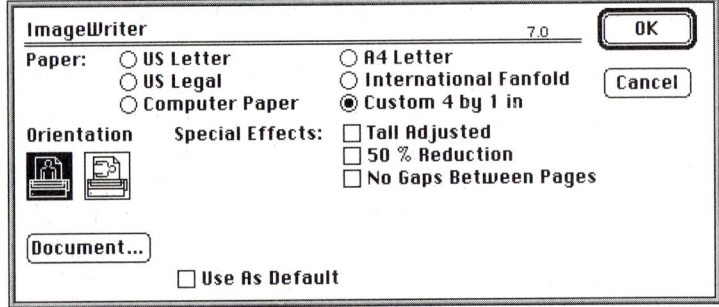

5. Choose the Custom Paper Size and No Gaps Between Pages options. (The No Gaps Between Pages option ensures that Word moves to the next label without skipping any space.)

6. Click the Document command button. The Document dialog box appears.

7. In the Margins area, type **0 in** in the Top, Bottom, and Right text boxes, and type **0.2 in** in the Left text box. Your Document dialog box should look like the one shown in figure 34.6.

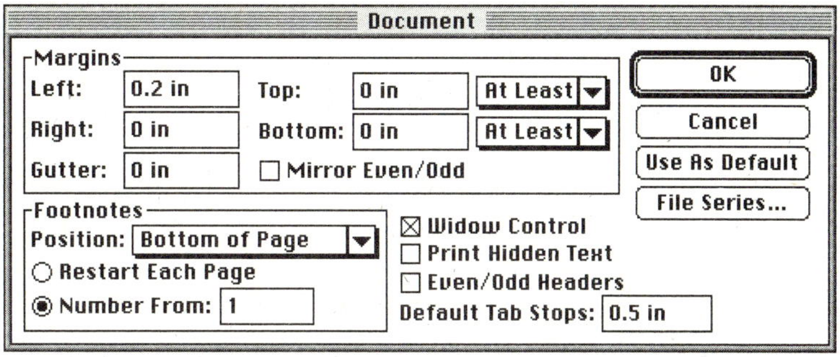

Fig. 34.6

Document dialog box.

Document

Margins
Left: 0.2 in   Top: 0 in   At Least ▼
Right: 0 in   Bottom: 0 in   At Least ▼
Gutter: 0 in   ☐ Mirror Even/Odd

OK
Cancel
Use As Default
File Series...

Footnotes
Position: Bottom of Page ▼
○ Restart Each Page
◉ Number From: 1

☒ Widow Control
☐ Print Hidden Text
☐ Even/Odd Headers
Default Tab Stops: 0.5 in

8. Choose OK.

To print the labels, follow these steps:

1. Load the continuous-label paper into the printer so that the top of the first label is even with the print head. (Remember that the paper has no top margin.)

2. Choose Print Merge from the File menu. The Print Merge dialog box appears (see fig. 34.7).

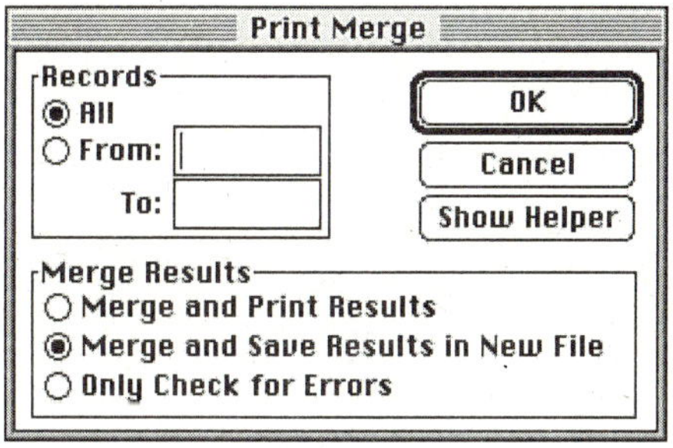

Fig. 34.7

Print Merge dialog box.

Print Merge

Records
◉ All
○ From:
To:

OK
Cancel
Show Helper

Merge Results
○ Merge and Print Results
◉ Merge and Save Results in New File
○ Only Check for Errors

3. In the Records area, click the From radio button.

4. Type **1** in the From text box and **1** in the To text box.

5. Choose OK and inspect the alignment of the first label. If you're satisfied with the printing, choose Print Merge from the File menu again and then click the All radio button in the Print Merge dialog box. If you're not satisfied with the printing, adjust the label paper, choose Print Merge from the File menu again, and repeat steps 3 through 5.

Chapter 34

Printing Mailing Labels

Printing Three-Column Continuous Labels on an ImageWriter

Printing three-column labels requires you to create a multiple-column main document. You enter three sets of address fields—one for each column. This procedure is more difficult than the single-column procedure described in the preceding section.

To set up your main document, follow these steps:

1. Open a new Word document.

2. Choose Print Merge Helper from the View menu. An Open dialog box appears.

3. Select your data document and then choose Open. Word inserts a DATA instruction at the beginning of your new document.

4. Without moving the insertion point, select the first field that you want to insert (the field containing your correspondent's first name) in the Insert Field Name drop-down list box (Print Merge Helper bar).

5. Press the space bar to leave a space after the first name.

6. Select the Last Name field in the Insert Field Name list box.

7. Press Return to start a new line.

8. Select the first address field in the Insert Field Name drop-down list box.

9. Press Return to start a new line.

10. If your data document includes a second address field, select the name of this field in the Insert Field Name list box and then press Return to start a new line.

11. Select the City field in the Insert Field Name list box, type a comma, and press the space bar.

12. Select the State field in the Insert Field Name list box and then press the space bar.

13. Select the ZIP Code field in the Insert Field Name list box.

14. Choose Section Break from the Insert menu or press ⌘-Enter to enter a section mark.

15. Select NEXT in the Insert Keyword drop-down list box.

16. Highlight the name and address field names, being careful to include the beginning and trailing chevrons as well as the section mark that comes after the ZIP Code field. Figure 34.8 shows an example of correct selection.

Fig. 34.8

Selecting field names and section marks.

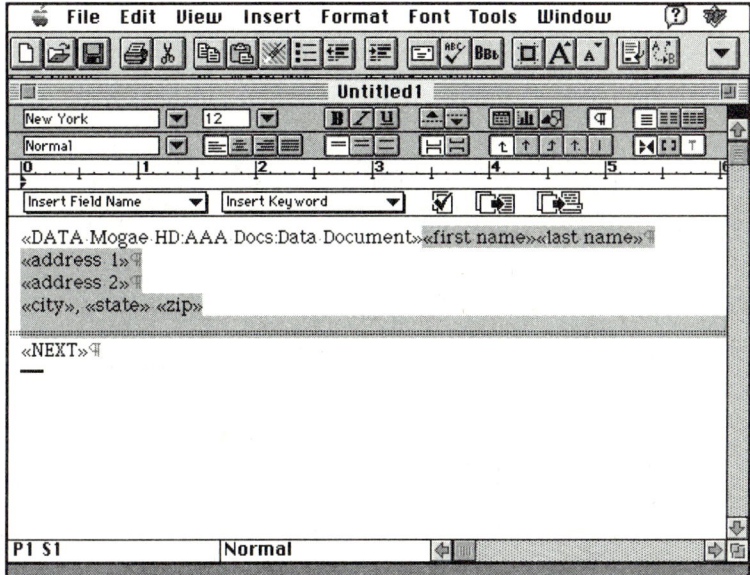

17. Choose Copy from the Edit menu, press ⌘-C, or click the Cut tool.

18. Position the insertion point after the NEXT command and then choose Paste from the Edit menu, press ⌘-V, or click the Paste tool. Word inserts the selected field names at the insertion-point location.

19. Select NEXT in the Insert Keyword drop-down list box.

20. Choose Paste from the Edit menu, press ⌘-V, or click the Paste tool. Your document should resemble the one shown in figure 34.9.

Chapter 34

Printing Mailing Labels

Fig. 34.9
Fields properly entered
for three-column
continuous labels.

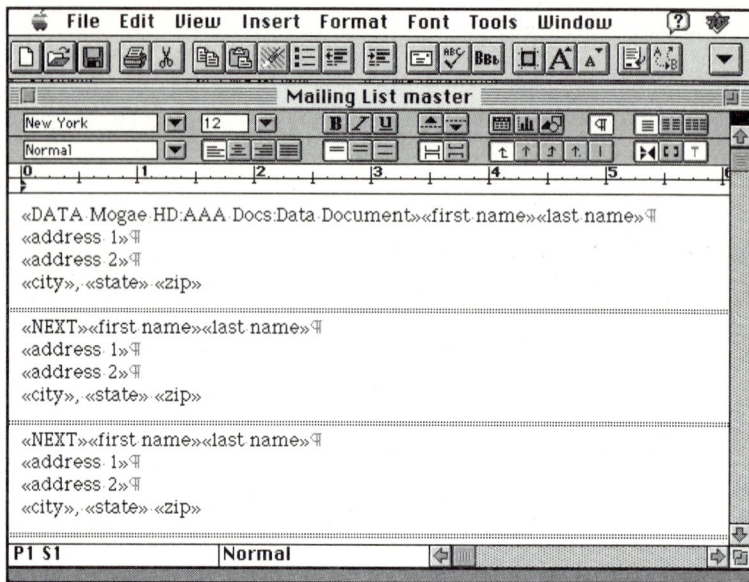

21. Select the whole document and then choose Section from the Format menu or press Option-F14. The Section dialog box appears (see fig. 34.10).

Fig. 34.10
Section dialog box.

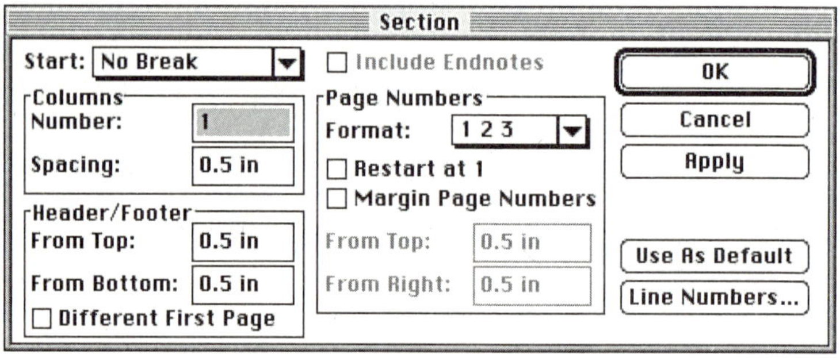

22. In the Columns area, type **3** in the Number text box and **0** in the Spacing text box.

23. Select New Column in the Start drop-down list box and then choose OK.

24. Save your data document.

Part VI
Creating Office Applications

To set up the page, follow these steps:

1. Choose Preferences from the Edit menu and, when the Preferences dialog box appears, type the width of your label paper (usually 8.5 inches) in the Custom Paper Size Width text box.

2. Type **1** (the label height) in the Custom Paper Size Height text box.

3. Click the close box to exit the dialog box.

4. Choose Page Setup from the File menu. The Page Setup dialog box appears.

5. Choose the Custom Paper Size and No Gaps Between Pages options, and then choose OK.

6. Choose Document from the Format menu or press ⌘-F14. The Document dialog box appears.

7. In the Margins area, type these margin settings: Left, **0.25 in**; Right, Top, and Bottom, **0 in**.

8. Choose OK.

To print your labels, follow these steps:

1. Load the continuous-label paper into the printer so that the top of the first label is even with the print head. (Remember that the paper has no top margin.)

2. Choose Print Merge from the File menu. The Print Merge dialog box appears.

3. In the Records area, click the From radio button.

4. Type **1** in the From text box and **3** in the To text box.

5. Choose OK and inspect the alignment of the first label. If you're satisfied with the printing, choose Print Merge from the File menu again and then click the All radio button in the Print Merge dialog box. If you're not satisfied with the printing, adjust the label paper, choose Print Merge from the File menu again, and repeat steps 3 through 5.

If all goes well, the labels should print three across (see fig. 34.11).

Fig. 34.11

A three-column continuous-label printout (printed to file).

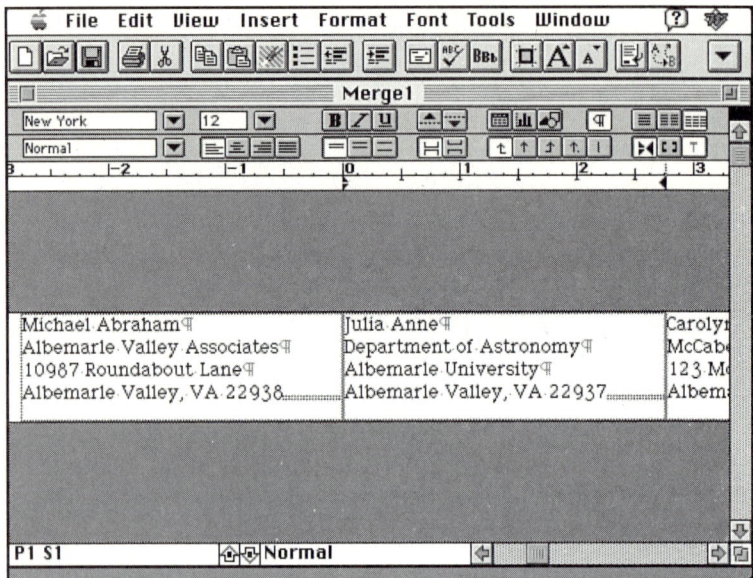

If you have trouble getting an entire name and address to fit within the allotted space, try selecting the whole document and then selecting a 10-point font size.

Printing Laser Labels on LaserWriter and StyleWriter Printers

To print laser label sheets, you must create a main document with the same number of address fields as there are labels in the sheet. One popular brand of laser labels offers 1-inch-by-3-inch labels, with 30 labels per sheet, allowing room for 1/2-inch top and bottom margins.

The following instructions work for printing four-line labels on laser printers. If you are using a LaserWriter, you may have to reduce the font size to 9 points so that the left and right columns of the labels can accommodate the 1/2-inch margin needed for printing. Almost certainly, you will have to experiment to get this technique to work correctly.

Part VI

Creating Office Applications

To set up the main document, follow these steps:

1. Open a new Word document.

2. Choose Print Merge Helper from the View menu. An Open dialog box appears.

3. Select your data document and then choose Open. Word inserts a DATA instruction at the beginning of your new document.

4. Without moving the insertion point, select the first field that you want to insert (the field containing your correspondent's first name) in the Insert Field Name drop-down list box (Print Merge Helper bar).

5. Press the space bar to leave a space after the first name.

6. Select the Last Name field in the Insert Field Name list box.

7. Press Return to start a new line.

8. Select the first address field in the Insert Field Name drop-down list box.

9. Press Return to start a new line.

10. If your data document includes a second address field, select the name of this field in the Insert Field Name list box and then press Return to start a new line.

11. Select the City field in the Insert Field Name list box, type a comma, and press the space bar.

12. Select the State field in the Insert Field Name list box and then press the space bar.

13. Select the ZIP Code field in the Insert Field Name list box.

14. Press Return.

15. Select NEXT in the Insert Keyword drop-down list box.

16. Press Return twice.

17. Carefully select all the name and address field names, including the beginning and trailing chevrons. Include the NEXT instruction (and the trailing paragraph mark) in the selection, as shown in figure 34.12. Don't forget the first chevron!

Fig. 34.12

Selecting name and address field names.

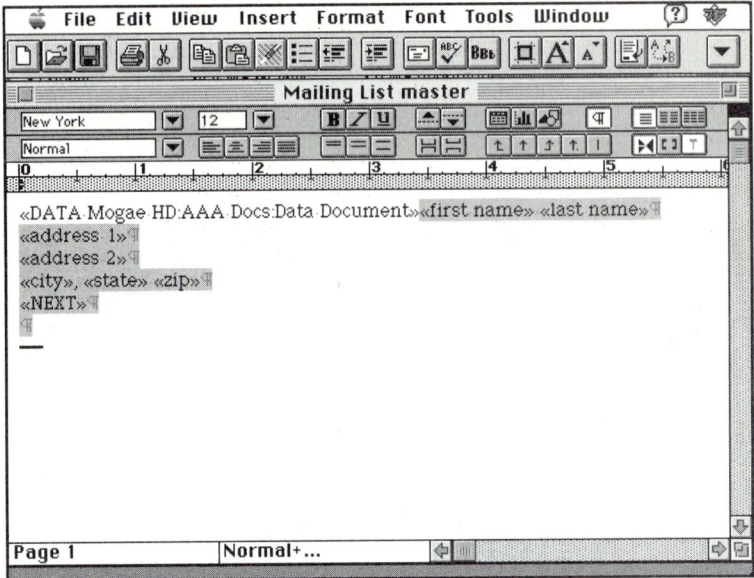

18. Choose Copy from the Edit menu, press ⌘-C, or click the Copy tool.

19. Place the insertion point at the end of the document (before the last paragraph mark).

20. Press Return.

21. Press ⌘-V, or click the Paste tool, 29 times. You have entered 29 copies of the name and address field names, making 30 in all.

22. Choose Section from the Format menu or press Option-F14. The Section dialog box appears.

23. In the Columns area, type **3** in the Number text box and **0.25** in the Spacing text box.

    Unlike three-column continuous labels, laser labels have 1/4-inch spacing between the three columns. Try this measurement initially to see whether it spaces the columns adequately.

24. Choose OK to confirm the section format.

25. Choose Select All from the Edit menu or press ⌘-A to select the entire document.

26. Choose Paragraph from the Format menu or press ⌘-M. The Paragraph dialog box appears (see fig 34.13).

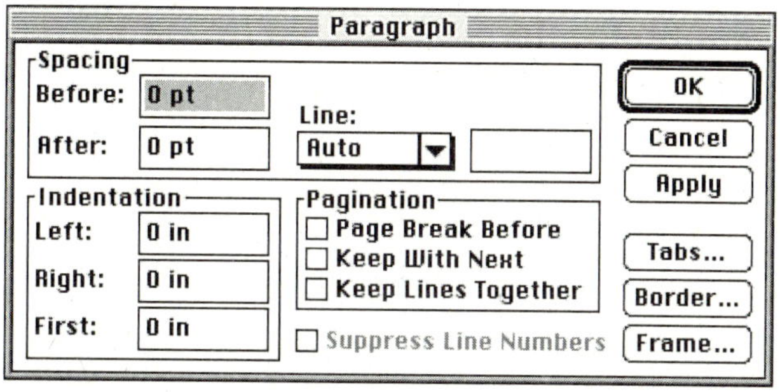

Fig. 34.13
Paragraph dialog box.

27. In the Line drop-down list box, select Exactly and then type **12** in the adjacent text box.

    You have chosen line spacing of exactly 12 points. This setting ensures that even if you select a smaller font, Word prints exactly six lines per inch.

28. Choose OK to confirm the paragraph formats.

29. With the entire document still selected, select 9 in the Font Size drop-down list box in the ribbon. (You will have a tough time packing your addresses into the allotted four lines unless you use 9- or 10-point type.)

To set up the page, follow these steps:

1. Choose Document from the Format menu or press ⌘-F14. The Document dialog box appears.

2. In the Margins area, type these margin settings: Left and Right, **0.75 in**; Top and Bottom, **0.5 in**.

3. After loading the laser label sheets into your printer, click the Print to File icon in the Print Merge Helper bar (the middle icon).

4. Try printing the first page of the new document to see how the setting works. If necessary, make changes in the margins, column width, and font size until you solve the remaining formatting problems.

5. Return to the main document, make the same changes that you made in the merge document, and click the Print Directory icon in the Print Merge Helper bar (see Chapter 32). Word prints the three-column layout in precise alignment with the labels, as shown in figure 34.14.

Fig. 34.14

A mailing list merged to three-column laser labels.

Michael Abraham Albemarle Valley Associates 10987 Roundabout Lane Charlottesville, VA 22999-9878	Edwin Stevenson Department of Radiology Albemarle University Charlottesville, VA 22999-4567	Carolyn Martin McCabe-Miller Realty 123 Mockingbird Lane Charlottesville, VA 22999-5678
Julia Anne Department of Veterinary Medicine Albemarle University Charlottesville, VA 22999-9987	Helena Ziwoski Albemarle Valley Associates 10987 Roundabout Lane Charlottesville, VA 22999-9987	Michael Paul Department of Physics Albemarle University Charlottesville, VA 22999-9987
Carolyn Martin McCabe-Miller Realty 123 Mockingbird Lane Charlottesville, VA 22999-5678	Michael Abraham Albemarle Valley Associates 10987 Roundabout Lane Charlottesville, VA 22999-9878	Edwin Stevenson Department of Radiology Albemarle University Charlottesville, VA 22999-4567
Michael Paul Department of Physics Albemarle University Charlottesville, VA 22999-9987	Julia Anne Department of Veterinary Medicine Albemarle University Charlottesville, VA 22999-9987	Helena Ziwoski Albemarle Valley Associates 10987 Roundabout Lane Charlottesville, VA 22999-9987
Edwin Stevenson Department of Radiology Albemarle University Charlottesville, VA 22999-4567	Carolyn Martin McCabe-Miller Realty 123 Mockingbird Lane Charlottesville, VA 22999-5678	Michael Abraham Albemarle Valley Associates 10987 Roundabout Lane Charlottesville, VA 22999-9878
Helena Ziwoski Albemarle Valley Associates 10987 Roundabout Lane Charlottesville, VA 22999-9987	Michael Paul Department of Physics Albemarle University Charlottesville, VA 22999-9987	Julia Anne Department of Veterinary Medicine Albemarle University Charlottesville, VA 22999-9987
Michael Abraham Albemarle Valley Associates 10987 Roundabout Lane Charlottesville, VA 22999-9878	Edwin Stevenson Department of Radiology Albemarle University Charlottesville, VA 22999-4567	Carolyn Martin McCabe-Miller Realty 123 Mockingbird Lane Charlottesville, VA 22999-5678
Julia Anne Department of Veterinary Medicine Albemarle University Charlottesville, VA 22999-9987	Helena Ziwoski Albemarle Valley Associates 10987 Roundabout Lane Charlottesville, VA 22999-9987	Michael Paul Department of Physics Albemarle University Charlottesville, VA 22999-9987
Carolyn Martin McCabe-Miller Realty 123 Mockingbird Lane Charlottesville, VA 22999-5678	Michael Abraham Albemarle Valley Associates 10987 Roundabout Lane Charlottesville, VA 22999-9878	Edwin Stevenson Department of Radiology Albemarle University Charlottesville, VA 22999-4567
Michael Paul Department of Physics Albemarle University Charlottesville, VA 22999-9987	Julia Anne Department of Veterinary Medicine Albemarle University Charlottesville, VA 22999-9987	Helena Ziwoski Albemarle Valley Associates 10987 Roundabout Lane Charlottesville, VA 22999-9987

Printing Mailing Labels with Varying Numbers of Lines

This chapter emphasizes the printing of four-line mailing labels, such as those used in sending a mailing to people at their business addresses. In all likelihood, however, your mailing list consists of a mixture of three- and four-line addresses. A four-line label should look like the following:

Dr. Ralph Johnson
Department of Epidemiology
Albemarle University
Charlottesville, VA 22999

A three-line label looks like this:

Mr. Barnaby Smith
109 Birdwhistle Drive

Periwinkle, VA 22998

The appearance of the second label, with the blank line, is far from catastrophic; it's just an aesthetic problem, which you may or may not be willing to tolerate. The mailing labels still print; every label will have the required six lines.

To keep Word from adding blank lines to your labels, you can use a special IF command that tells Word to print a line only if the field contains an entry. If the field is blank, Word will print the next line without leaving a blank one. The following instructions tell you how to type the field names and merge instructions so that Word doesn't put blank lines in addresses. You also must add a second IF instruction so that Word adds a blank line at the bottom of the label if a field is skipped; otherwise, the spacing between labels is thrown off.

To set up the fields and instructions so that Word will not leave blank lines in labels, follow these steps:

1. Position the insertion point where you want the field to print if it isn't blank.

   In figure 34.15, two fields are entered. The next field, called Company, might be blank if the address is a residential address.

2. Without pressing Return, select IF...ENDIF in the Insert Keyword drop-down list box. The Insert IF dialog box appears (see fig. 34.16).

3. In the Field Name list box, select the name of the field that might be empty.

4. In the middle drop-down list box (the Operator list), select Field Not Empty.

5. Choose OK. Word enters the IF...ENDIF instruction in your main document (see fig. 34.17).

Fig. 34.15
Positioning the insertion
point correctly.

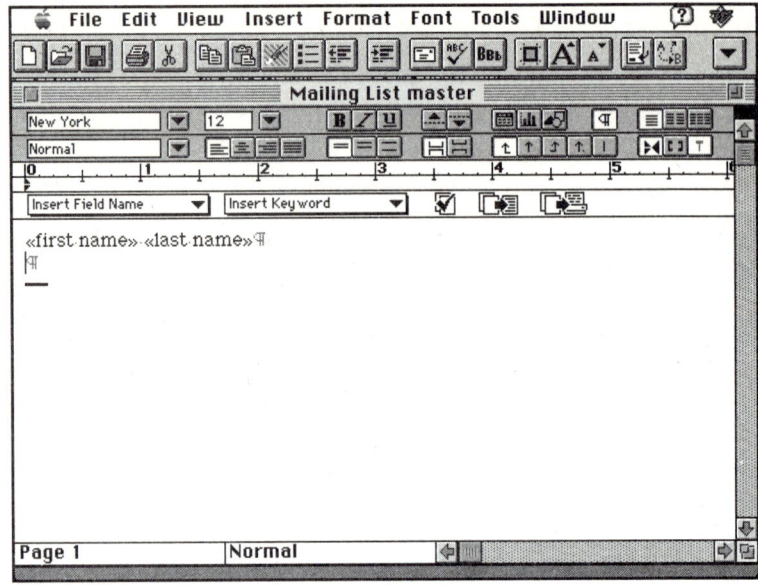

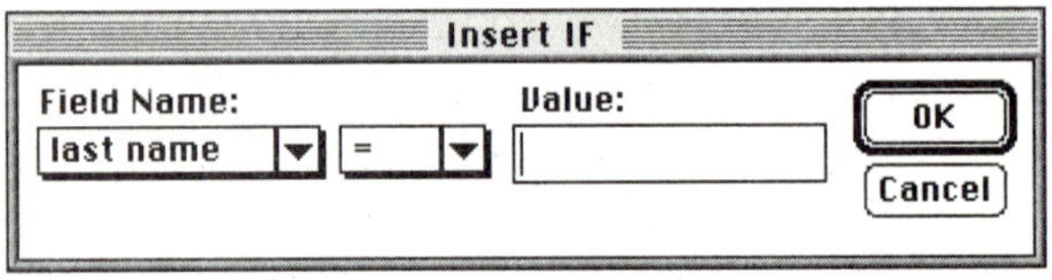

Fig. 34.16
Insert IF dialog box.

6. Without moving the insertion point, select the same field again in the Insert Field Name drop-down list box. Word adds the field name to the document.

7. Without moving the insertion point, press Return. Your instruction should resemble the one shown in figure 34.18.

Fig. 34.17
IF...ENDIF instruction
added.

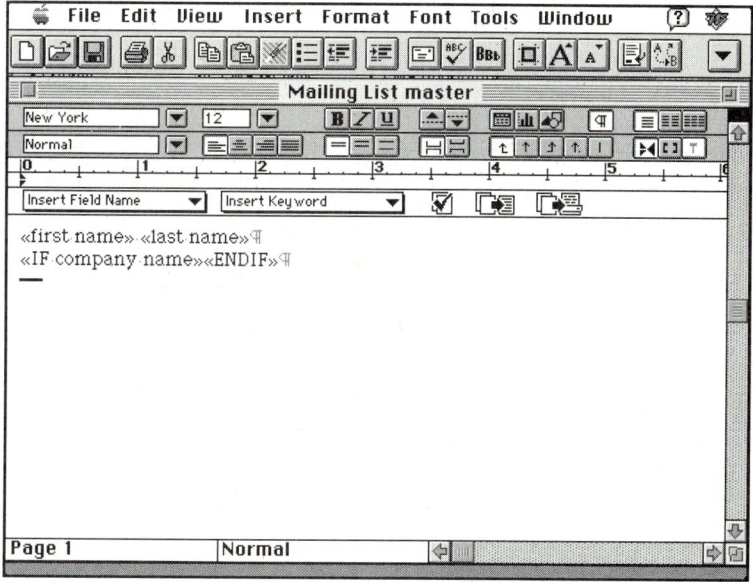

Fig. 34.18
Completed IF instruction
that tells Word to skip a
blank field.

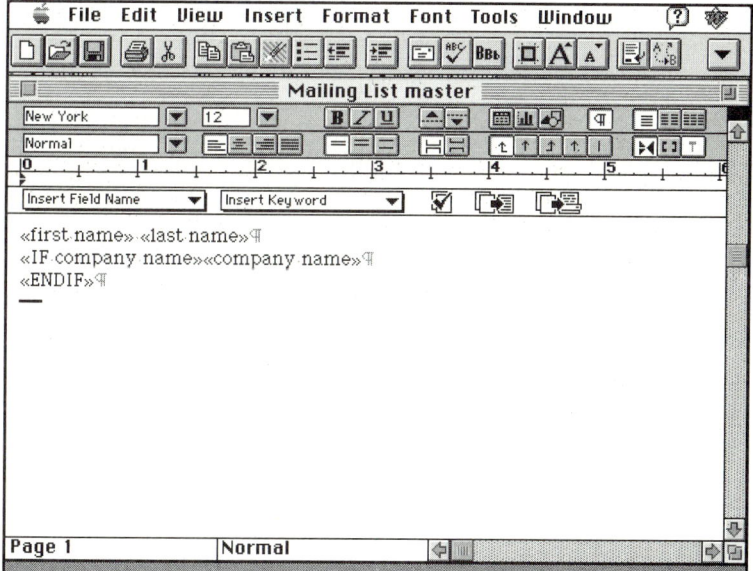

Chapter 34
Printing Mailing Labels

8. Continue adding the fields as shown in figure 34.19.

Fig. 34.19

Adding the rest of
the fields.

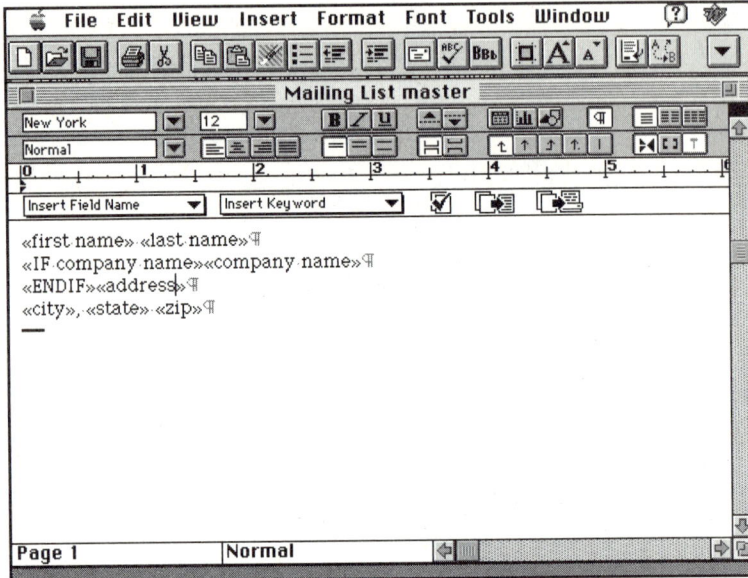

Fig. 34.19
Adding the rest of
the fields.

9. Place the insertion point at the end of the ZIP field and repeat steps 3, 4, and 5. Word enters another IF...ENDIF instruction.

10. Press Return.

11. Select NEXT in the Insert Keyword list box.

12. Place the insertion point before the ENDIF instruction and press Return twice.

13. Place the insertion point after the NEXT instruction and then select ELSE in the Insert Keyword list box. Your main document should look like the one shown in figure 34.20.

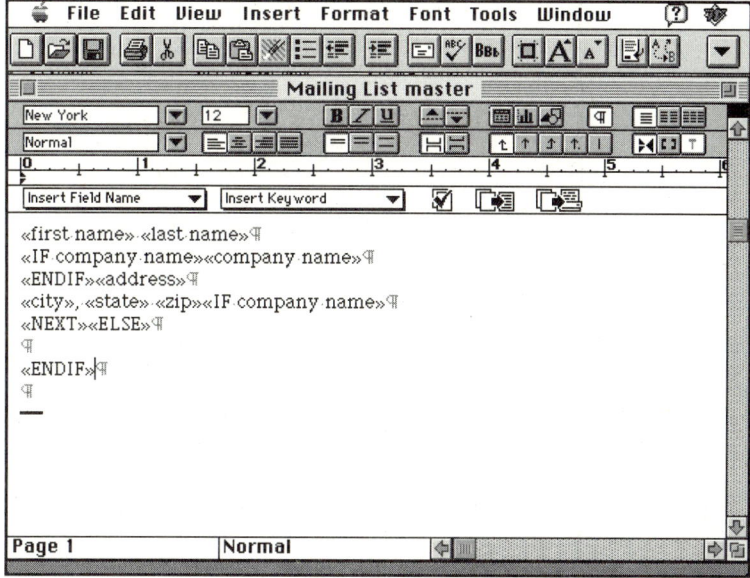

Fig. 34.20
Completed IF…ENDIF
instruction.

Quick Review

This section summarizes the most useful information in this chapter. Check "Productivity Tips" for a review of high-productivity tips and tricks—the ones that Macintosh and Word pros use every day. Review "Techniques" whenever you need a quick reminder about a specific procedure.

Productivity Tips

■ If you have invested the time and energy to set up a Word mailing-list data document, by all means learn how to print mailing labels. You will have to adjust margins and column widths to get the labels to print properly, but after the application works correctly, you can print labels whenever you want with no further hassle.

■ The easiest way to print mailing labels with Word is to crank them out on an ImageWriter, using single-column, tractor-fed continuous labels.

Chapter 34
Printing Mailing Labels

■ If you are working with a LaserWriter, look for laser labels that leave 1/2-inch margins at the top and bottom. That way, you can print all 30 labels on the sheet. The instructions in this chapter show you how to print 30 labels to a page of press-on Avery labels, commonly available in office-supplies stores.

■ Clever use of Word's merge keywords can solve problems caused by mixing three- and four-line addresses.

Techniques

This section provides concise summaries of all the procedures introduced in this chapter.

Printing One-Column Labels on an ImageWriter

To print one-column labels on an ImageWriter:

1. Open a new Word document.

2. Choose Print Merge Helper from the View menu. An Open dialog box appears.

3. Select your data document in the list box and then choose Open.

4. Without moving the insertion point, select the first field you want to insert (the field containing your correspondent's first name) in the Insert Field Name list box.

5. Press the space bar to leave a space after the first name.

6. Select the last-name field in the Insert Field Name list box.

7. Press Return to start a new line.

8. In the Insert Field Name list box, select the first address field.

9. Press Return to start a new line.

10. If your data document includes a second address field for organizational addresses, select the name of this field in the Insert Field Name list box and then press Return.

11. Select the City field in the Insert Field Name list box, type a comma, and press the space bar.

12. Select the State field in the Insert Field Name list box and then press the space bar.

13. Select the ZIP Code field in the Insert Field Name list box.

14. Save your main document.

15. Choose Preferences from the Tools menu and, when the Preferences dialog box appears, type the width of your label paper in the Custom Paper Size Width text box.

16. Type **1** (the label height in inches) in the Custom Paper Size Height text box.

17. Click the close box to exit the dialog box.

18. Choose Page Setup from the File menu. The Page Setup dialog box appears.

19. Choose the Custom Paper Size and No Gaps Between Pages options.

20. Click the Document command button. The Document dialog box appears.

21. In the Margins area, type **0 in** in the Top, Bottom, and Right text boxes, and type **0.2 in** in the Left text box.

22. Choose OK.

23. Load the continuous-label paper into the printer so that the top of the first label is even with the print head. (Remember that the paper has no top margin.)

24. Choose Print Merge from the File menu. The Print Merge dialog box appears.

25. In the Records area, click the From radio button.

26. Type **1** in the From text box and **1** in the To text box.

27. Choose OK and inspect the alignment of the first label. If you're satisfied with the printing, choose Print Merge from the File menu again and then click the All radio button in the Print Merge dialog box. If you're not satisfied with the printing, adjust the label paper, choose Print Merge from the File menu again, and repeat steps 25 through 27.

Printing Three-Column Labels on an ImageWriter

To print three-column labels on tractor-fed continuous-label paper:

1. Begin your main document by following steps 1 through 13 in the preceding section.

Chapter 34

Printing Mailing Labels

2. Choose Section Break from the Insert menu or press ⌘-Enter to enter a section mark.

3. Select NEXT in the Insert Keyword drop-down list box.

4. Highlight the name and address field names, being careful to include the beginning and trailing chevrons, as well as the section mark that comes after the ZIP Code field.

5. Choose Copy from the Edit menu, press ⌘-C, or click the Copy tool.

6. Position the insertion point just after the NEXT command and then choose Paste from the Edit menu, press ⌘-V, or click the Paste tool.

7. Select NEXT in the Insert Keyword list box.

8. Choose Paste from the Edit menu, press ⌘-V, or click the Paste tool.

9. Select the whole document and choose Section from the Format menu or press Option-F14. The Section dialog box appears.

10. In the Columns area, type **3** in the Number text box and **0** in the Spacing text box.

11. Select New Column in the Start drop-down list box and then choose OK.

12. Choose Preferences from the Edit menu and, when the Preferences dialog box appears, type the width of your label paper (usually 8.5 inches) in the Custom Paper Size Width text box.

13. Type **1** (the label height) in the Custom Paper Size Height text box.

14. Click the close box to exit the dialog box.

15. Choose Page Setup from the File menu. The Page Setup dialog box appears.

16. Choose the Custom Paper Size and No Gaps Between Pages options.

17. Choose Document from the Format menu or press ⌘-F14. The Document dialog box appears.

18. In the Margins area, type these margin settings: Left, **0.25 in**; Right, Top, and Bottom, **0 in**.

19. Choose OK.

20. Load the continuous-label paper into the printer so that the top of the first label is even with the print head. (Remember that the paper has no top margin.)

21. Choose Print Merge from the File menu. The Print Merge dialog box appears.

22. Click the From radio button.

23. Type **1** in the From text box and **3** in the To text box.

24. Save your document.

25. Choose OK and inspect the alignment of the first label. If you're satisfied with the printing, choose Print Merge from the File menu again and then click the All radio button in the Print Merge dialog box. If you're not satisfied with the printing, adjust the label paper, choose Print Merge from the File menu again, and repeat steps 3 through 5.

Printing Laser Labels

To print laser label sheets on a LaserWriter or StyleWriter printer:

1. Begin your main document by following steps 1 through 13 in the preceding section.

2. Press Return.

3. Select NEXT in the Insert Keyword drop-down list box.

4. Press Return twice.

5. Carefully select all the name and address field names, including the beginning and trailing chevrons. Include the NEXT instruction (*and* the trailing paragraph mark) in the selection.

6. Choose Copy from the Edit menu, press ⌘-C, or click the Copy tool.

7. Place the insertion point at the end of the document (before the last paragraph mark).

8. Press Return.

9. Press ⌘-V, or click the Paste tool, 29 times.

10. Choose Section from the Format menu or press Option-F14. The Section dialog box appears.

11. In the Columns area, type **3** in the Number text box and **0.25** in the Spacing text box.

12. Choose OK to confirm the section format.

13. Choose Select All from the Edit menu or press ⌘-A to select the entire document.

14. Choose Paragraph from the Format menu or press ⌘-M. The Paragraph dialog box appears.

15. In the Line drop-down list box, select Exactly and then type **12** in the adjacent text box.

16. Choose OK to confirm the paragraph formats.

17. With the entire document still selected, select 9 in the Font Size drop-down list box in the ribbon.

18. Choose Document from the Format menu or press ⌘-F14. The Document dialog box appears.

19. In the Margins area, type these settings: Left and Right, **0.75 in**; Top and Bottom, **0.5 in**.

20. Save your document.

21. After loading the laser-label sheets into your printer, click the Print to File icon in the Print Merge Helper bar.

22. Try printing the first page of the merge document to see how the settings work. If necessary, make changes in the margins, column width, and font size until you solve the remaining formatting problems.

23. Return to the main document, make the same changes you made in the new document, and click the Print to File icon in the Print Merge Helper bar.

PART

VII

Customizing Word 5.1

Includes

Customizing Menus and Keyboard Shortcuts

Customizing Word's Toolbar

USING
WORD 5.1
FOR THE MAC
SPECIAL EDITION

Customizing Menus and Keyboard Shortcuts

B y now, you have mastered the Word interface—including its menus, keyboard shortcuts, and dialog-box defaults—and you may have ideas about how you can improve the interface. In this chapter, you learn how to customize this interface so that Word works exactly the way you want.

Following is an overview of the ways you can customize this amazing program:

- You can choose Section, Document, and Page Setup defaults for all your documents. When you choose these options, Word applies them to all the new documents you create.

- You can use the Preferences dialog box to choose the operating defaults you want. For example, you can tell Word to open all documents in Page Layout view.

- You can add or remove commands from menus. Many Word commands, such as Move to Next Window, aren't listed in menus. If you want, you can add this command, and many more, to an appropriate menu.

- You can set up the keyboard the way you want by assigning a keyboard shortcut to any Word command, including many dialog-box options.

USING
WORD 5.1
FOR THE MAC
SPECIAL EDITION

■ You can create a new menu, called Work, that contains frequently accessed dialog-box items, including glossaries. If you often find yourself wading through dialog boxes to choose an option, you can save significant amounts of time by adding such an option to the Work menu.

After you change Word's interface, you save these changes to a customized settings file. Such a file lists all your Preferences dialog-box options, keyboard-shortcut assignments, menu additions or removals, and Work-menu assignments.

You even can create more than one settings file so that you can choose the one that's right for a particular task. You can create a settings file called Letters, for example, that contains keyboard shortcuts, menu items, and Work-menu assignments that are appropriate for writing letters. Another settings file called Reports could contain the proper settings for creating business reports with graphics.

The customization procedures may sound complicated, but they're not; they're as easy as the other Word operations you have learned. You cannot ruin Word by making ill-advised customization choices. With one command, you can remove all your customization choices and restore Word to its pristine default state, just as it was when you started the program after installation.

This chapter, which surveys the many techniques you can use to customize Word, covers the following topics:

■ *Redefining the default style sheet.* By redefining styles and saving them to the default style sheet, you can change Word's default formats in many ways, as you learn in this section.

■ *Choosing page-formatting defaults.* This section shows you many ways to change the default settings for page numbers, margins, and other page-formatting choices.

■ *Choosing preferences.* As you learn in this section, you can choose many different options in the Preferences dialog box (accessed from the Tools menu).

■ *Customizing Word's menus.* In this section, you learn how to add commands to menus—and how to remove menu commands that you don't use.

■ *Customizing Word's keyboard.* This section explains the different techniques you can use to assign commands to keyboard shortcuts (and to remove keyboard shortcuts that you don't use).

■ *Creating a Work menu.* This section shows you how to assign dialog-box options to a special Work menu, which Word creates and places to the right of the Window menu in the menu bar.

■ *Managing settings files.* In this section, you learn how to save your configuration choices. You also learn how to create two or more alternative-settings files to which you can switch in order to use a different set of configuration choices.

Redefining the Default Style Sheet

As you learned in Chapter 14, you can save often-used styles to the default style sheet so that these styles are available for every new document you create. You can use this technique to redefine many of Word's formatting defaults, which are encoded in the program's standard styles. Word formats footnote text using the Normal font, for example, but uses a 10-point font size. If you find yourself redefining this style every time you open a new document, you should redefine and save the style to the default style sheet.

This section summarizes the procedure you use to redefine styles in the default style sheet. For more information on choosing formats for styles, see Chapter 14, "Formatting with Styles."

To redefine a default style, follow these steps:

1. Choose Style from the Format menu or press ⌘-T. The Style dialog box appears (see fig. 35.1).

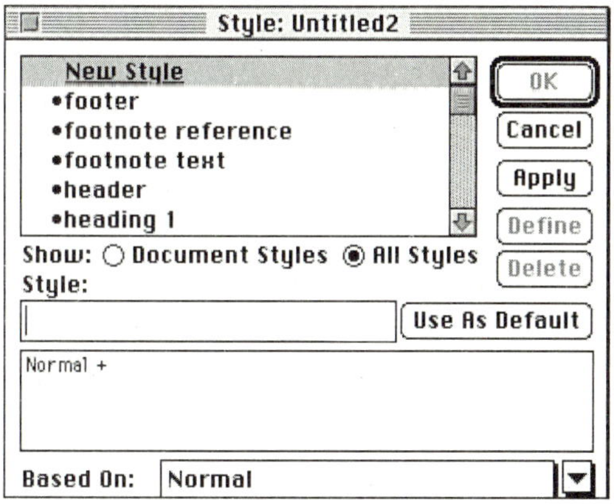

Fig. 35.1
Style dialog box.

Style: Untitled2

New Style
• footer
• footnote reference
• footnote text
• header
• heading 1

OK
Cancel
Apply
Define
Delete

Show: ○ Document Styles ◉ All Styles
Style:

Use As Default

Normal +

Based On: Normal

2. In the list box, select the name of the style you want to change. If necessary, click the All Styles radio button to display all styles in the list box.

3. Choose the formats you want.

4. Click the Use As Default command button. An alert box appears, asking `OK to record style in default style sheet?`

5. Choose OK. You return to the Style dialog box.

6. Choose Close.

Other styles you may want to redefine include Word's standard heading styles. If you redefine those styles, be sure to choose the Keep with Next option in the Paragraph dialog box so that Word doesn't insert page breaks after the headings.

Besides redefining existing styles, you can create and save new styles to the default style sheet. For example, you can create a Text ¶ style with the following formats: Garamond font, 12 points, 1/2-inch first-line indentation, one blank line before, double line spacing. If you save this style to the default style sheet, the style appears in the document style sheets of all new documents.

Choosing Page-Formatting Defaults

By redefining standard styles, you can change the default formats that Word uses when the program inserts elements such as headers, footers, page numbers, and footnotes into documents. You cannot, however, redefine page or section formats—such as margins, columns, and page size—by redefining the default style sheet. In this section, you learn how to redefine Word's default section and page formats.

Reflect on your use of Word to determine which defaults you should change. What do you do when you open a new Word document? Do you frequently change margins, turn on page numbering, or choose endnotes? If so, reset the defaults so that you don't have to perform such operations every time you create a new Word document.

Changing Section-Formatting Defaults

The Section dialog box includes many default settings that you may want to change (see fig. 35.2).

Section		
Start: No Break ▼	☐ Include Endnotes	OK
Columns	Page Numbers	Cancel
Number: 1	Format: 1 2 3 ▼	Apply
Spacing: 0.5 in	☐ Restart at 1	
Header/Footer	☐ Margin Page Numbers	Use As Default
From Top: 0.5 in	From Top: 0.5 in	Line Numbers...
From Bottom: 0.5 in	From Right: 0.5 in	
☐ Different First Page		

Suppose that you always want your documents to include page numbers printed and centered at the bottom of the page, but you never want page numbers to appear on the first page. To change these Section defaults, follow these steps:

1. Choose Section from the Format menu or press Option-F14. The Section dialog box appears.

2. Choose the Section formats you want Word to apply to the current document and to all the new documents you create.

3. Click the Use As Default command button.

4. Choose OK.

Your choices apply to the current document and to all the subsequent documents you create. Previous documents will remain intact, with their original formatting.

For more information on section formats, see Chapter 21, "Dividing a Document into Sections."

Changing Document-Formatting Defaults

To change Word's default document formats, such as margins, use the Document dialog box (see fig. 35.3).

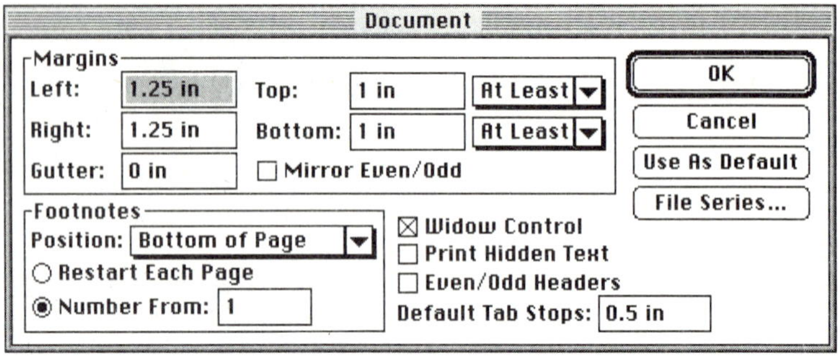

Fig. 35.3
Document dialog box.

Suppose that you always want Word to open new documents with 1-inch margins all around and that you prefer to position footnotes at the end of the document (endnotes). To change these document-formatting defaults, follow these steps:

1. Choose Document from the Format menu or press ⌘-F14. The Document dialog box appears.

2. Choose the options you want Word to apply to the current document and to all the new documents you create.

3. Click the Use As Default command button.

4. Choose OK.

For more information on document formats, see Chapter 11, "Formatting Pages."

Changing Page-Setup Defaults

The Page Setup dialog box varies, depending on which printer you use. Figure 35.4 shows the Page Setup dialog box that appears after you choose the StyleWriter option in the Chooser desk accessory.

No matter which printer you choose, however, you can choose Page Setup defaults by using the Use As Default check box, which appears in every version of the Page Setup dialog box. You may want to change the Page Setup defaults if you're using A4 paper or if you want to take advantage at all times of other Page Setup options, such as document reduction or enlargement.

To change Page Setup defaults, follow these steps:

1. If you haven't done so, choose your printer, using the Chooser desk accessory (Apple menu).

2. Choose Page Setup from the File menu or press Shift-F8. The Page Setup dialog box appears.

3. Click the Use As Default check box.

4. Choose OK.

Fig. 35.4
Page Setup dialog box (StyleWriter).

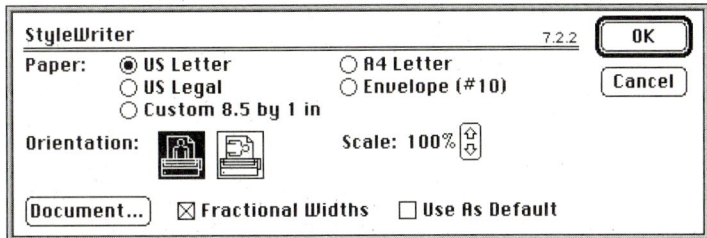

Choosing Preferences

The Preferences command (Tools menu) enables you to change many of Word's operating default settings. This section comprehensively surveys these options, many of which have been mentioned or discussed in earlier chapters.

The icons on the left side of the Preferences dialog box give you a way of choosing different categories of options. When you choose Preferences, you see the General options (discussed in the next section). Additional options are View, Open and Save, Default Font, Spelling, Grammar, Thesaurus, Hyphenation, and Toolbar. When you click one of these icons, the appropriate options appear on the right side of the dialog box.

The following sections discuss the General, View, and Open and Save options. See Chapter 9, "Formatting with Fonts and Character Styles," for information on Default Font options. See Chapter 12, "Checking Spelling and Grammar," for information on the Spelling and Grammar options. For information on the Toolbar, see Chapter 36, "Customizing Word's Toolbar."

The Thesaurus and Hyphenation options are useful only if you use thesaurus and hyphenation dictionaries other than the ones provided with Word. (You can buy such dictionaries from Microsoft.) You can use these options to choose these dictionaries so that Word uses those dictionaries instead of the ones provided with Word. If you're a North American preparing a document for publication in Great Britain, for example, you can buy and load the British versions of the thesaurus and hyphenation dictionaries.

Choosing General Options

When you choose Preferences from the Tools menu, the Preferences dialog box appears, displaying the General options (see fig. 35.5).

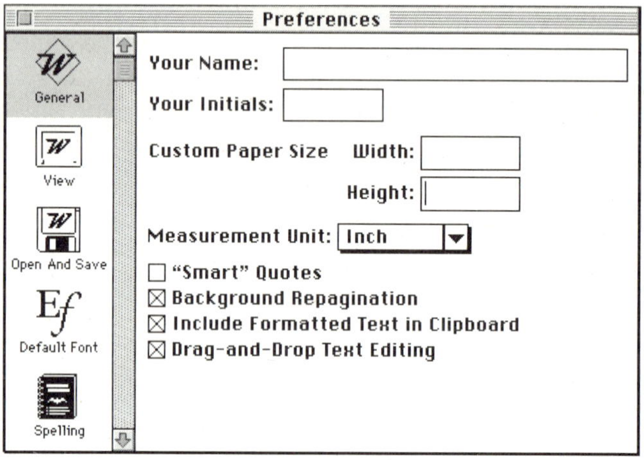

Fig. 35.5
General options (Preferences dialog box).

The General list contains fundamental options that affect the way Word works, including the name Word assigns to the files you create and the default measurement unit. You can choose the following options in the General list:

- *Your Name* (default: the name you typed when you installed Word). Make sure that the Preferences dialog box contains your name so that Word can retrieve your documents.

- *Your Initials* (default: blank). If you installed Word's Text or Voice Annotation feature, type your initials here. Word adds your initials to the annotation icons you add to your document.

- *Custom Paper Size* (default: blank or dimmed). In the Width and Height text boxes, type the dimensions of special paper you're using for printing, such as mailing labels. This option is dimmed if you're using a printer that cannot use custom paper sizes (for example, a LaserWriter).

- *Measurement Unit* (default: inch). You also can choose centimeters (cm), printer's points (pt), or picas (pi).

- *"Smart" Quotes* (default: off). If you activate "Smart" Quotes, Word enters open and close quotation marks (" ") and single quotation marks (' '), instead of using the same character.

If you're creating a document that you want to send to someone else via modem, be sure to keep the "Smart" Quotes option turned off. "Smart" Quotes enters special Macintosh characters for leading and trailing quotation marks and single quotation marks, which come across as odd control characters when you transmit your document as an ASCII text file.

- *Background Repagination* (default: on). With this option activated, Word actively repaginates your document while you're writing so that you see where page breaks occur. If you're using a sluggish Macintosh, however, you can deactivate this option to improve Word's performance.

- *Include Formatted Text in Clipboard* (default: on). By default, Word retains character formatting when you copy or cut text via the Clipboard. (Paragraph formatting is retained only if you include the paragraph mark in the selection.) Including formatting requires more memory, however. If your Macintosh's memory is severely limited, you can deactivate this option to reduce the amount of memory required for editing operations.

- *Drag-and-Drop Text Editing* (default: on). Activate this option to take advantage of Word's drag-and-drop editing feature, which enables you to move text by dragging the selection. For more information on drag-and-drop editing, see Chapter 8, "Editing Text."

Choosing View Options

When you click the View icon in the Preferences dialog box, you see the View options, as shown in figure 35.6. These options control what you see on-screen.

You can choose the following View options:

- *Show Hidden Text* (default: on). When this option is activated, you can see hidden text on-screen. Moreover, Word takes the hidden text into account in computing page breaks. To see how your document is paginated without hidden text, turn this option off.

- *Show Table Gridlines* (default: on). When activated, this option shows the table grid lines when you create a table. (The grid lines don't print.) If you prefer, turn this option off.

- *Show Text Boundaries in Page Layout View* (default: off). With this option active, Word uses gray lines to display the boundaries of columns and frames in Page Layout view. If you turn on text boundaries while working with multiple-column text and frames, you have an easier time grasping where you can enter text in your document.

Fig. 35.6
View options (Preferences dialog box).

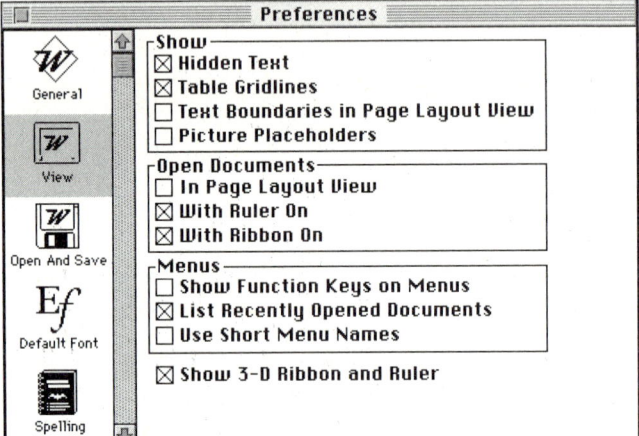

- *Show Picture Placeholders* (default: off). If you add graphics to your document, you probably know how much the graphics slow Word's scrolling speed. You can improve that speed dramatically by choosing this option, which substitutes a gray screen for your graphics. Although Word does not show them on-screen, your graphics still are in your document and still print.

- *Open Documents in Page Layout View* (default: off). If you're using a Mac based on the Motorola 68030 processor (or a Quadra), you can choose this option to open documents in Page Layout view instead of the default Normal view. If you use a slower Macintosh, leave this option off so that Word opens documents in Normal view. You always can switch to Page Layout view to preview page formats before printing.

- *Open Documents with Ruler On* (default: on). The ruler is handy for paragraph formatting, styles, and tabs, but you may want to hide the ruler by deactivating this check box if you use a Classic with a 9-inch screen. You still can toggle the ruler on and off by choosing the Ruler command from the View menu.

■ *Open Documents with Ribbon On* (default: on). Like the ruler, one of Word's best features, the ribbon, is handy for formatting (fonts, font sizes, character emphases, and multiple-column formats). You may want to hide the ribbon by deactivating this check box, however, if you use a Classic with a 9-inch screen. You still can toggle the ribbon on and off by choosing the Ribbon command from the View menu.

■ *Show Function Keys on Menus* (default: off). If you're using a Macintosh with an extended keyboard, which has function keys, choose this option to see function-key shortcuts next to menu names.

■ *List Recently Opened Documents* (default: on). This useful feature places the names of the last four documents you opened in the File menu. To open one of these documents again quickly, choose its name from the File menu.

If you're using Disk Doubler or some other file-compression program to save space on your hard disk, turn off the List Recently Opened Documents option and don't try to open documents this way. When you open a compressed document through the Open dialog box, your file-compression program detects the use of this command and decompresses the file. If you open a document through the File menu, however, the file-compression program does not decompress the file.

■ *Use Short Menu Names* (default: off). If you activate this option, Word shortens the names in the menu bar to make more room. Format becomes Fmt, Window becomes Wnd, and so on. You may want to choose this option if you're running additional programs, such as SuperClock, that require room in the menu bar to display menu names or other information.

■ *Show 3-D Ribbon and Ruler* (default: on). This new Word 5.1 option displays a "three-dimensional" ribbon and ruler, as shown in the illustrations in this book. This option consumes memory and processing time, however. You can speed Word's operation by deactivating this option.

Choosing Open and Save Options

When you click the Open and Save icon in the Preferences dialog box, you see the Open and Save options (see fig. 35.7).

Fig. 35.7
Open and Save options
(Preferences dialog box).

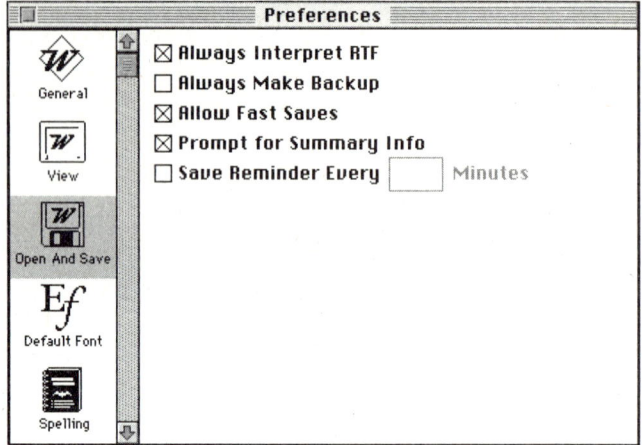

You can choose the following Open and Save options:

■ *Always Interpret RTF* (default: on). By default, Word correctly decodes formatting instructions when you import RTF documents. An RTF document has been saved with Microsoft's Rich Text Formatting codes, which enable users of different programs to exchange documents without losing formatting. Because RTF uses only standard ASCII characters, RTF enables you to exchange documents via electronic mail and other telecommunications links without losing formatting. You can save memory, though, by deactivating this option.

■ *Always Make Backup* (default: off). As explained in Chapter 5, "Managing Documents and Files," this option really doesn't make a backup of your document. If you turn on this option, Word preserves the last saved version of your file. The default setting tells Word to overwrite the most recent version of a file.

You may want to activate this option if you're the kind of writer who likes to save all preliminary drafts of your work. Turning this option on eats up disk space very quickly, however.

■ *Allow Fast Saves* (default: on). This option activates a rapid file-saving technique when you resave a file. Rather than rewrite the whole file, Word saves your changes.

The Fast Save method is as safe as the normal file-saving technique but requires more memory. If your Mac has limited memory, turn this option off. Be aware, though, that Word needs much more time to save files with the normal technique—as much as several minutes for a file that's 1M or larger.

■ *Prompt for Summary Info* (default: on). As explained in Chapter 5, many good reasons exist to fill out Word's Summary Info dialog boxes when you save a document for the first time. If you don't want to fill out these boxes, deactivate this option.

■ *Save Reminder Every x Minutes* (default: off). By all means, activate this option and type a reminder interval (such as **10** or **15** minutes) in the text box. When this option is activated, Word displays an alert box at the specified interval, reminding you to save your work. This Word feature helps avert one dangerous aspect of working with a computer: significant work loss due to disk crashes or power failures.

Customizing Word's Menus

This section discloses a remarkable Word feature: the program's pull-down menus can be completely customized, showing only the commands you want. You also can add to menus many commands that don't currently appear in the menus, such as Assign to Key (a command that enables you to assign a menu option to a key) and Copy Formats (available only via a keyboard command by default).

Word achieves its menu flexibility by separating its commands from the command names that appear in the pull-down menus.

In most programs, most or all commands are listed in the menus, and you cannot add or remove any commands. Word, however, draws a distinction between its built-in list of commands and the menu commands. You have complete control of which commands appear in menus.

By default, each command is linked to a certain menu. For example, the Set Table Ruler Scale command, which tells Word to measure the page from the left page edge rather than from the left boundary of the text area, is linked to the Window menu. If you choose this command and tell Word to add it to a menu, Word adds this command to the View menu. You can override the default menu linkage and control where the item appears in the menu, however.

Many more commands exist than you see in the menus. If you added each command to the menus, however, the menus would become ridiculously long. Figure 35.8 shows a menu with all its commands added.

Fig. 35.8
View menu with all
options added.

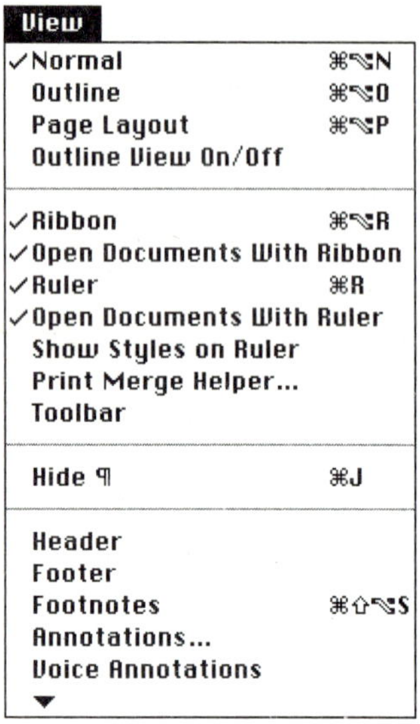

```
View
✓Normal              ⌘⌥N
 Outline             ⌘⌥O
 Page Layout         ⌘⌥P
 Outline View On/Off

✓Ribbon              ⌘⌥R
✓Open Documents With Ribbon
✓Ruler               ⌘R
✓Open Documents With Ruler
 Show Styles on Ruler
 Print Merge Helper...
 Toolbar

 Hide ¶              ⌘J

 Header
 Footer
 Footnotes           ⌘⇧⌥S
 Annotations...
 Voice Annotations
 ▼
```

Many Word commands are options available in dialog boxes and in the
ribbon and ruler. Table 35.1 lists Word's many commands and their
menu linkages. You can add any of these commands to the Word menus
with which the commands are linked. Notice that the italicized items are
plug-in modules (PIMs), whereas those with ellipses display a dialog box.

Table 35.1
Commands and
Linked Menus

Command	Linked menu
About Microsoft Word	(None)
Activate Keyboard Menus	Edit
Add to Menu	Tools
Address Entry	File
Addresses…	Insert
All Caps	Format
Allow Fast Saves	Tools
Always Interpret RTF	Tools
Always Make Backup Files	Tools
Annotations…	View
Apply Style Name:	Work
Assign to Key	Tools
Background Repagination	Tools

Command	Linked menu
Backspace	(None)
Black	Format
Blue	Format
Bold	Format
Border…	Format
Bullet	Insert
Calculate	Tools
Cancel	(None)
Centered	Format
Change Case…	Format
Change Font	Edit
Change Style	Edit
Character…	Format
Clear	Edit
Close	File
Collapse Selection	View
Collapse Subtext	View
Columns 1	Format
Columns 2	Format
Columns 3	Format
Columns 4	Format
Command from Key Assignment…	Tools
Commands…	Tools
Condensed 1.5 Pt	Format
Copy	Edit
Copy as Picture	Edit
Copy Formats	Edit
Copy Text	Edit
Create Envelope…	Tools
Create Publisher…	Edit

continues

Table 35.1
Continued

Command	Linked menu
Cut	Edit
Cyan	Format
Date	Insert
Default Font...	Font
Delete...	File
Delete Cells, Shift Left	Format
Delete Cells, Shift Up	Format
Delete Columns	Format
Delete Forward	Edit
Delete Next Word	Edit
Delete Previous Word	Edit
Delete Rows	Format
Demote Heading	Edit
Different First Page	Format
Document...	Format
Dotted Underline	Format
Double Underline	Format
Down	Font
Drag-and-Drop Text Editing	Tools
Drop Cap...	Insert
Edit Link (QuickSwitch)	Edit
Edit Object...	Edit
Even Footer	View
Even Header	View
Expand Subtext	View
Expanded:	Format
Extend to Character	Tools
File...	Insert
Files Recently Opened	(None)
Find...	Edit
Find Again	Edit

Command	Linked menu
Find File...	File
Find Formats	Edit
First Footer	View
First Header	View
First Line Indent	Format
Font Name:	Font
Font Size:	Font
Footer	View
Footnote...	Insert
Footnote Cont. Notice...	View
Footnote Cont. Notice: Default	View
Footnote Cont. Separator	View
Footnote Cont. Sep.: Default	View
Footnote Separator...	View
Footnote Separator: Default	View
Footnotes	View
Fractional Widths	File
Frame (Format)...	Format
Frame (Insert)...	Insert
Full Repaginate Now	Tools
Glossary...	Edit
Glossary Entry	Work
Go Back	Edit
Go To...	Edit
Grammar...	Tools
Green	Format
Hanging Indent	Format
Header	View
Help...	Window
Help (context-sensitive)	(None)

continues

Chapter 35
Customizing Menus and Keyboard Shortcuts

Table 35.1	
Continued	

Command	Linked menu
Hidden Text	Format
Hyphenation…	Tools
Include Endnotes in Section	Format
Include Formatted Text in Clipboard	Tools
Index…	Insert
Index Entry	Insert
Insert Cells Down	Format
Insert Cells Right	Format
Insert Columns	Format
Insert Formula	Insert
Insert Glossary Entry	Edit
Insert Nonbreaking Hyphen	Insert
Insert Nonbreaking Space	Insert
Insert Optional Hyphen	Insert
Insert ¶ Above Row	Insert
Insert Rows	Format
Insert Tab	Insert
Italic	Format
Italic Cursor	Tools
Justified	Format
Keep Lines Together	Format
Keep with Next Paragraph	Format
Larger Font Size	Font
Line Break	Insert
Line Numbers by Page	Format
Line Numbers by Section	Format
Line Numbers Continuous	Format
Line Numbers Off	Format
Line Spacing: Double	Format
Line Spacing: 1 and 1/2	Format

Part VII

Customizing Word 5.1

Command	Linked menu
Line Spacing: Single	Format
Link Options…	Edit
List All Fonts	Font
List Recently Opened Documents	Tools
Lowercase	Format
Magenta	Format
Make Backup Files	Tools
Make Body Text	Edit
Margin Page Numbers	Format
Measurement Unit: Cm	Tools
Measurement Unit: Inches	Tools
Measurement Unit: Picas	Tools
Measurement Unit: Points	Tools
Merge Cells	Format
More Keyboard Prefix	(None)
Move Down One Text Area	Tools
Move Heading Down	Edit
Move Heading Up	Edit
Move Left One Text Area	Tools
Move Right One Text Area	Tools
Move Text	Edit
Move to Bottom of Window	Tools
Move to End of Document	Tools
Move to End of Line	Tools
Move to First Text Area	Tools
Move to Last Text Area	Tools
Move to Next Cell	Tools
Move to Next Character	Tools
Move to Next Line	Tools

continues

Chapter 35
Customizing Menus and Keyboard Shortcuts

Table 35.1 Continued	Command	Linked menu
	Move to Next Page	Tools
	Move to Next Paragraph	Tools
	Move to Next Sentence	Tools
	Move to Next Text Area	Tools
	Move to Next Window	Window
	Move to Next Word	Tools
	Move to Previous Cell	Tools
	Move to Previous Character	Tools
	Move to Previous Line	Tools
	Move to Previous Page	Tools
	Move to Previous Paragraph	Tools
	Move to Previous Sentence	Tools
	Move to Previous Text Area	Tools
	Move to Previous Word	Tools
	Move to Start of Document	Tools
	Move to Start of Line	Tools
	Move to Top of Window	Tools
	Move Up One Text Area	Tools
	Movie…	Insert
	Nest Paragraph	Format
	New	File
	New Paragraph	Insert
	New ¶ After Ins. Point	Insert
	New ¶ with Same Style	Insert
	New Picture	Insert
	New Window	Window
	Normal	View
	Normal Character Position	Format
	Normal Character Spacing	Format
	Normal Paragraph	Format
	Numeric Lock	Tools

Command	Linked menu
Object…	Insert
Odd Footer	View
Odd Header	View
Open…	File
Open Any File…	File
Open Documents in Page View	View
Open Documents with Ribbon	View
Open Documents with Ruler	View
Open File Name:	Work
Open Mail…	File
Other…	Font
Outline Command Prefix	Edit
Outline (Format)	Format
Outline (View)	View
Outline View On/Off	View
Page Break	Insert
Page Break Before	Format
Page Layout	View
Page Layout View On/Off	View
Page Number	Insert
Page # Alphabetic Lowercase	Format
Page # Alphabetic Uppercase	Format
Page # Arabic	Format
Page # Roman Lowercase	Format
Page # Roman Uppercase	Format
Page Setup…	File
Palindrome Looping	File
Paragraph…	Format
Paragraph Aligned Left	Format
Paragraph Aligned Right	Format

continues

Chapter 35

Customizing Menus and Keyboard Shortcuts

Command	Linked menu
Paragraph Border:	Format
Paragraph Border...	Format
Paragraph Shading:	Format
Paste	Edit
Paste Cells	Edit
Paste Link	Edit
Paste Object	Edit
Paste Special...	Edit
Paste Special Character	Edit
Picture...	Insert
Plain Text	Format
Play Movie...	View
Preferences...	Tools
Print...	File
Print Merge...	File
Print Merge Helper...	View
Print Preview...	File
Promote Heading	Edit
Prompt for Summary Info	Tools
Quick Record Voice Annotation	View
Quit	File
Red	Format
Redefine Style From Selection	Format
Remove from Menu	Tools
Renumber...	Tools
Repaginate Now	Tools
Repeat	Edit
Replace...	Edit
Restart Page Numbering at 1	Format

Table 35.1 Continued

Part VII

Customizing Word 5.1

Command	Linked menu
Revert to Style	Format
Ribbon	View
Ruler	View
Same as Previous	View
Save	File
Save As…	File
Save Copy As…	File
Screen Test	Tools
Scroll Line Down	Tools
Scroll Line Up	Tools
Scroll Screen Down	Tools
Scroll Screen Up	Tools
Section…	Format
Section Break	Insert
Section Starts on Even Page	Format
Section Starts on New Column	Format
Section Starts on New Page	Format
Section Starts on Odd Page	Format
Section Starts with No Break	Format
Select All	Edit
Select Window:	Window
Send Mail…	File
Sentence Case	Format
—Separator—	(None)
Set Display Picture	File
Set Indent Ruler Scale	View
Set Margin Ruler Scale	View
Set Table Ruler Scale	View
Shadow	Format
Show All Headings	View

continues

Table 35.1
Continued

Command	Linked menu
Show Body Text	View
Show Clipboard	Window
Show Formatting	View
Show Function Keys on Menus	Tools
Show Heading 1	View
Show Heading 2	View
Show Heading 3	View
Show Heading 4	View
Show Heading 5	View
Show Heading 6	View
Show Heading 7	View
Show Heading 8	View
Show Heading 9	View
Show/Hide ¶	View
Show Hidden Text	View
Show Picture Placeholders	View
Show Styles on Ruler	View
Show Table Gridlines	View
Show Text Boundaries	View
Side by Side	Format
Small Caps	Format
Smaller Font Size	Font
"Smart" Quotes	Tools
Sort	Tools
Sort Descending	Tools
Space Before ¶: None	Format
Space Before ¶: 12 points	Format
Spelling…	Tools
Split Cell	Format
Split Window	View
Strikethru	Format

Command	Linked menu
Style…	Format
Subscribe To…	Edit
Subscript:	Format
Summary Info…	File
Superscript:	Format
Suppress Line # in Paragraph	Format
Symbol…	Insert
Symbol Font	(None)
Table…	Insert
Table Cells…	Format
Table Cells Border:	Format
Table Cells Border…	Format
Table Cells Shading:	Format
Table Layout…	Format
Table of Contents…	Insert
Table to Text…	Insert
Tabs…	Format
Text to Table…	Insert
Thesaurus…	Tools
Time	Insert
Title Case	Format
TOC Entry	Insert
Toggle Case	Format
Toggle Looping	File
Toolbar	View
Unassign Keystroke	Tools
Underline	Format
Undo	Edit
Unnest Paragraph	Format
Up	Font

continues

Chapter 35
Customizing Menus and Keyboard Shortcuts

Table 35.1 Continued	Command	Linked menu
	Update Link	Edit
	Uppercase	Format
	Use Short Menu Names	Tools
	Voice Annotation	Insert
	Voice Annotations	View
	White	Format
	Word Count…	Tools
	Word Underline	Format
	Yellow	Format
	Zoom to Fill Screen	Window
	Zoom Window	Window

You can add to menus commands that normally are buried deep within dialog boxes. The Blue command, for example, basically is the option that you see in the Color list box of the Character dialog box.

Many of Word's commands have obvious functions with which you're already familiar, such as Save (File menu); others are new to you or cryptically named. To find out what a mysterious command does, choose Commands from the Tools menu to open the Commands dialog box (see fig. 35.9).

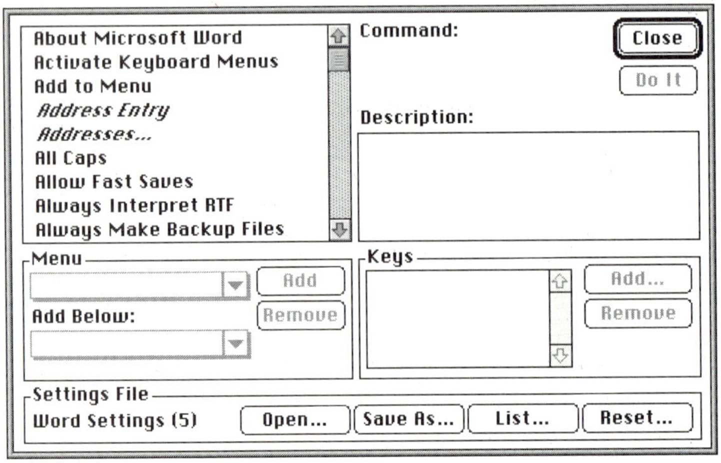

Fig. 35.9
Commands dialog box.

Highlight the name of the command in the list box. A brief description of the command's function appears in the Description box.

CAUTION

Customize the menus as much as you want, but bear in mind that your changes may make your version of Word look unfamiliar to another Word user. You also may find someone else's customized version of Word to be unfamiliar.

Adding Commands to Menus

As Table 35.1 suggests, a wealth of resources lies in Word's Commands command. If you like to choose commands from the pull-down menus, you may want to add one or more commands to menus.

You can customize Word's pull-down menus in two ways:

- *Using the keyboard shortcut.* By far the easier of the two techniques, this technique enables you to add dialog-box, ribbon, and ruler items to menus. Word adds these items to the menus to which the items are linked by default. (You also can remove dialog-box, ribbon, and ruler items.)

- *Using the Commands dialog box.* You can use this dialog box to add commands to the menus to which the commands are linked—and if you want, you can override the default linkage. You even can specify where the command should appear in the menu. (You also can use this dialog box to remove commands from menus.)

The following sections explain both procedures.

Adding Menu Items with the Keyboard

You can use the keyboard to add an item from a submenu or dialog box to the top level of a pull-down menu. You also can use this technique to add to the menus items that you see in the ruler and ribbon.

To add menu items with the keyboard, follow these steps:

1. Display the dialog box or list box that contains the item you want to add.

2. Press ⌘-Option-plus sign (keyboard +). The mouse pointer becomes a plus sign. (To cancel, press Esc or ⌘-period [.].)

3. Activate the option that you want to add. Word adds the item to the appropriate menu.

Chapter 35

Customizing Menus and Keyboard Shortcuts

If you choose a glossary entry, style, or document name, Word creates a new menu called Work and places that menu to the right of the Window menu. (For more information on the Work menu, see "Creating a Work Menu" later in this chapter.)

Removing Menu Items with the Keyboard

To clean up the menus, you can delete items. If you don't plan to create documents with indexes or tables of contents, for example, you can delete the Index Entry and TOC Entry commands from the Insert menu.

Don't worry about adverse consequences of deleting menu items. If you delete an item from a menu, you haven't sent the item off to a computer version of Nowhere—you can retrieve the item by using the Commands dialog box or the keyboard technique.

To delete menu items with the keyboard, follow these steps:

1. Press ⌘-Option-hyphen (-). The mouse pointer becomes a minus sign. (To cancel, press Esc or ⌘-period [.].)

2. In the menu, choose the command that you want to remove. Word deletes the command.

Adding Menu Items with the Commands Dialog Box

The Commands dialog box provides tools for adding items to Word's menus (refer to fig. 35.9). Using this dialog box has two major advantages over the keyboard technique: You can add items that aren't available now in dialog boxes, and you can choose the menus in which Word places the commands. You even can determine where Word places items in menus.

The list box in the Commands dialog box contains every Word command, alphabetized by name. (For a complete list, see Table 35.1.) Look carefully for commands not assigned to menus or keys that may be useful to you in your work.

To add a command to Word's menus with the Commands dialog box, follow these steps:

1. Choose Commands from the Tools menu or press ⌘-Shift-Option-C. The Commands dialog box appears (refer to fig. 35.9).

2. In the list box, select the item you want to add to a menu. The Description box indicates what the command does.

The italicized items refer to Word's plug-in modules (PIMs).

3. If a colon follows the name of the item you want, you must select the item in the drop-down list box below Command at the top of the dialog box. Selecting Apply Style Name in step 2, for example, produces the drop-down list box shown in figure 35.10.

Fig. 35.10
Apply Style Name drop-down list box.

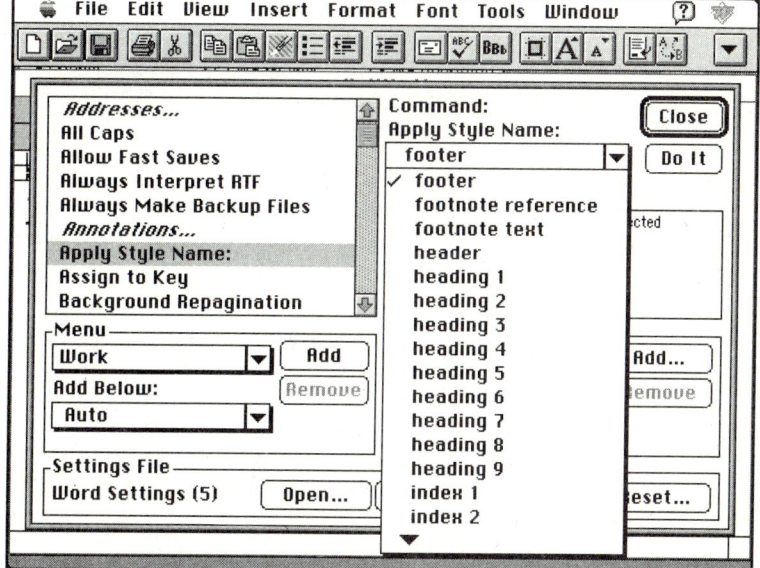

Select the command you want in this drop-down list box so that the correct command name appears above the list box. After you select the command, the Menu section shows the name of the menu to which the command is linked. If the Menu list box is grayed, the command already appears in a menu. If both the Menu and Add Below list boxes are grayed, you cannot add the command to a menu.

4. If you want to change the default menu linkage, drop down the Menu list to see a list of the menu names (see fig. 35.11) and then select the menu to which you want to add the command.

Fig. 35.11
Choosing a menu.

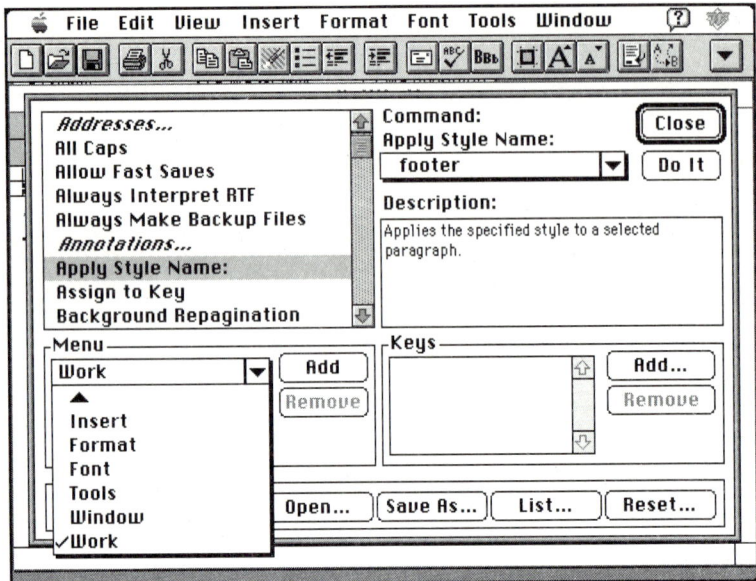

5. If you want to choose where the command appears in the menu you have chosen, drop down the Add Below list box and select the name of the command below which you want the command name to appear. The default setting in this list box is Auto. When the Auto setting is selected, Word uses its default menu location for the command.

6. Click the Add command button to add the selected command to the menu you have chosen.

7. If you want, click Do It to carry out the selected command.

8. Choose Close to return to your document.

Removing Menu Items with the Commands Dialog Box

When you highlight in the Commands dialog box a command that already appears in a menu, Word dims the Menu and Add Below drop-down list boxes. The program also activates the Remove button, which you can click to remove the command from the menu.

To use the Commands dialog box to remove a command from a menu, follow these steps:

1. Choose Commands from the Tools menu or press ⌘-Shift-Option-C. The Commands dialog box appears.

2. Highlight the name of the command you want to remove.

3. Click the Remove button.

4. Choose Close.

Word saves your Commands dialog-box choices when you exit the program. You lose your choices, however, if you cannot quit Word in the normal fashion (by choosing Quit from the File menu) due to a disk crash or power failure. To make sure that you save your Commands changes, click the Save As command button in the Commands dialog box to display the Save dialog box, and then choose Save to overwrite the existing settings file. For more information on settings files, see "Managing Settings Files" later in this chapter.

Customizing Word's Keyboard

If you're a good typist, you may want to assign some additional commands to keyboard shortcuts or to change existing assignments. See Appendix C for a list of keyboard shortcuts. Following is a list of the commands that aren't assigned to keyboard shortcuts.

About Microsoft Word	Change Case…	Cyan
Address Entry	Clear	Date
Addresses…	Collapse Selection	Default Font…
Allow Fast Saves	Collapse Subtext	Delete…
Always Interpret RTF	Columns 1	Delete Cells, Shift Left
Always Make Backup Files	Columns 2	Delete Cells, Shift Up
Annotations…	Columns 3	Delete Columns
Apply Style Name:	Columns 4	Demote Heading
Background Repagination	Command from Key Assignment…	Different First Page
Black	Condensed 1.5 Pt	Drag-and-Drop Text Editing
Blue	Create Envelope…	Drop Cap…
Border…	Create Publisher…	Edit Object…
Bullet		

Even Footer

Even Header

Expand Subtext

Expanded 3 Pt

File...

Files Recently Opened

Find File...

Find Formats

First Footer

First Header

Font Name:

Font Size:

Footer

Footnote Cont. Notice...

Footnote Cont. Notice:
Default

Footnote Cont.
Separator

Footnote Cont. Sep.:
Default

Footnote Separator...

Footnote Separator:
Default

Fractional Widths

Frame (Format)...

Frame (Insert)...

Full Repaginate Now

Glossary Entry

Green

Header

Help...

Include Endnotes in Section

Include Formatted Text
in Clipboard

Index...

Index Entry

Insert Cells Down

Insert Cells Right

Insert Columns

Italic Cursor

Keep Lines Together

Keep with Next Paragraph

Line Numbers by Page

Line Numbers by Section

Line Numbers Continuous

Line Numbers Off

Line Spacing: 1 and 1/2

Line Spacing: Single

Link Options

List All Fonts

List Recently Opened Documents

Lowercase

Magenta

Make Backup Files

Make Body Text

Margin Page Numbers

Measurement Unit: Cm

Measurement Unit: Inches

Measurement Unit: Picas

Measurement Unit: Points

Merge Cells

Move Heading Down

Move Heading Up

Movie...

New Picture

New Window

Normal Character Position

Normal Character Spacing

Object...

Odd Footer

Odd Header

Open Documents in Page View

Open Documents with Ribbon

Open Documents with Ruler

Open File Name:

Open Mail...

Other...

Outline View On/Off

Page Break Before

Page Layout View On/Off

Page Number

Page # Alphabetic Lowercase

Page # Alphabetic Uppercase

Page # Arabic

Page # Roman Lowercase

Page # Roman Uppercase

Palindrome Looping

Paragraph Border:

Paragraph Border…

Paragraph Shading:

Paste Cells

Paste Special…

Picture…

Play Movie…

Preferences…

Print Merge…

Print Merge Helper…

Promote Heading

Prompt for Summary Info

Quick Record Voice Annotation

Red

Redefine Style from Selection

Repaginate Now

Restart Page Numbering at 1

Same as Previous

Save Copy As…

Screen Test

Section Starts on Even Page

Section Starts on New Column

Section Starts on New Page

Section Starts on Odd Page

Section Starts with No Break

Select Window:

Send Mail…

Sentence Case

—Separator—

Set Display Picture

Set Indent Ruler Scale

Set Margin Ruler Scale

Set Table Ruler Scale

Show All Headings

Show Body Text

Show Clipboard

Show Formatting

Show Function Keys on Menus

Show Heading 1

Show Heading 2

Show Heading 3

Show Heading 4

Show Heading 5

Show Heading 6

Show Heading 7

Show Heading 8

Show Heading 9

Show Hidden Text

Show Picture Placeholders

Show Styles on Ruler

Show Table Gridlines

Show Text Boundaries

Side by Side

"Smart" Quotes

Sort

Sort Descending

Space Before ¶: None

Split Cell

Subscribe To…

Summary Info…

Suppress Line # in Paragraph

Symbol…

Table…

Table Cells…

Table Cells Border:

Table Cells Border…

Table Cells Shading:

Table Layout…

Table of Contents…

Table to Text…

Tabs…

Text to Table…

Thesaurus…

Time

Title Case

TOC Entry

Toggle Case

Toggle Looping

Toolbar

Uppercase

Use Short Menu Names

Voice Annotation

Voice Annotations

White

Yellow

Zoom to Fill Screen

You can assign commands to keyboard shortcuts in two ways:

- *Using the keyboard.* Press ⌘-Option-plus sign (keyboard +). The mouse pointer changes to a plus sign. Choose an existing menu option, dialog-box option, or button.

- *Using the Commands dialog box.* You can create keyboard shortcuts for commands that now aren't listed in menus.

As you plan keyboard shortcuts, remember that you must use certain key combinations. You can use no more than four keys in a keyboard shortcut. If you're assigning numeric-keypad keys, make sure that Num Lock mode is off.

If you have an extended keyboard, you can reassign the function keys. You cannot create keyboard shortcuts with the Esc, Tab, Enter, or Return keys, however, and you cannot redefine ⌘-period (.).

You can use the following key combinations:

⌘-character	Control-character
⌘-Control-character	Control-Shift-character
⌘-Shift-character	Control-Shift-Option-character
⌘-Shift-Option-character	Option-keypad character
⌘-Control-Option-character	Shift-keypad character
⌘-Control-Shift-character	Shift-Option-keypad character

Certain ⌘ key combinations distinguish Word's default keyboard assignments, as follows:

- ⌘. Chooses a command, using (as far as possible) the standard Macintosh nomenclature (⌘-X for Cut, ⌘-S for Save, and so on).

- *⌘-Option.* Chooses an editing command, such as scrolling the screen or deleting text.

- *⌘-Shift.* Chooses formatting commands, such as italic, boldface, or right justification.

You can assign more than one keyboard shortcut to a command—and as you discover while you browse through the current keyboard assignments listed in Appendix C, Microsoft already has assigned multiple shortcuts to some commands. (Many commands have two keyboard shortcuts, one shortcut being a function-key shortcut for users of extended keyboards.)

Avoid reassigning any of the ⌘-character shortcuts that are part of Apple's standards for all Macintosh programs, such as ⌘-A (Select All), ⌘-S (Save), and ⌘-X (Cut). If you reassign these keys, you may become confused when you use another program.

Using the Keyboard Technique

To assign a keyboard shortcut with ⌘-Option-plus sign (numeric keypad +), follow these steps:

1. Press ⌘-Option-plus sign (numeric keypad +). The mouse pointer becomes a ⌘ symbol.

   If you see a plus sign instead, you pressed the keyboard plus sign instead of the numeric-keypad plus sign. Press Esc or ⌘-period (.) and try again.

2. Use the ⌘ pointer to choose the menu item you want.

3. When an alert box prompts you for the key combination that you want to assign to the chosen command, press the desired keys. (To assign the command to the key sequence ⌘-Control-B, for example, press these keys as though you were issuing the command at the keyboard.)

   If the key combination already is assigned, an alert box appears, warning that you will erase the existing key definition.

4. To erase the existing assignments, choose OK.

Use caution when erasing current keyboard-shortcut assignments. Creating new shortcuts is better than deleting old ones. Imagine what might happen if another Word user tried your version of Word, only to find that you have reassigned many of the default keyboard shortcuts.

Using the Commands Dialog Box

The Commands dialog box enables you to assign keyboard shortcuts to many commands. You also can delete existing keyboard assignments when you assign new ones.

Chapter 35
Customizing Menus and Keyboard Shortcuts

To assign a command to Word's keyboard by using the Commands dialog box, follow these steps:

1. Choose Commands from the Tools menu or press ⌘-Shift-Option-C. The Commands dialog box appears.

2. Select the command you want to assign to a shortcut.

3. Look at the Keys list box, which lists all keyboard shortcuts already assigned to the chosen command.

   Figure 35.12 shows the current key assignments for the Plain Text command.

Fig. 35.12

Current key assignments for the Plain Text command.

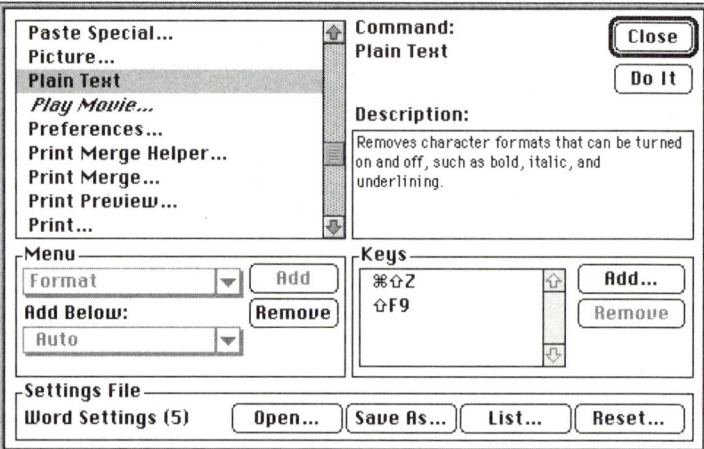

4. Click the Add command button. The dialog box shown in figure 35.13 appears, prompting you to press the key combination you want to use.

5. Press the key combination you want to use as though you were issuing the command. (Press Control-space bar, for example, to assign the command to those keys.)

6. If an alert box appears, warning you that the shortcut keys already are assigned, think twice about reassigning those keys. If you're sure that you want to redefine the shortcut keys, choose OK; otherwise, click Cancel.

7. Choose Close to close the Commands dialog box.

Fig. 35.13

Assigning a command to a key combination.

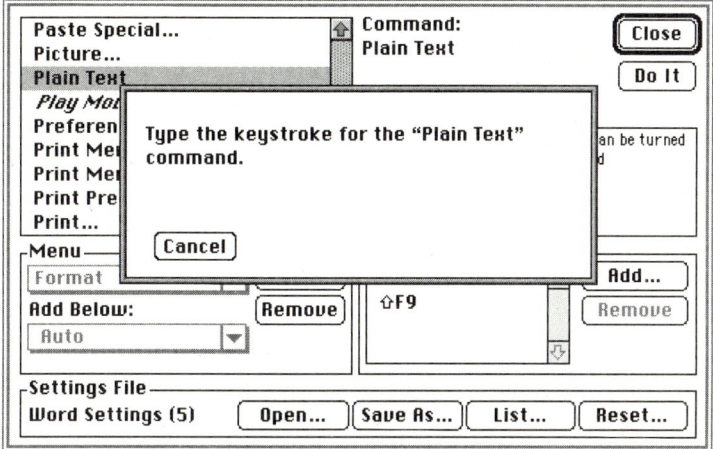

Deleting Keyboard Shortcuts

As mentioned earlier, try to avoid deleting existing keyboard shortcuts. You may want to delete a shortcut, however, if you find yourself continually pressing a key by accident. The key combination ⌘-N (New), for example, is easy to press by accident when you're trying to press ⌘-B (Bold) and inadvertently reach too far. Pressing the former key combination by accident also causes a hassle: Word opens a new document, which you must close before you can return to your work.

To delete an unwanted keyboard shortcut, follow these steps:

1. Choose Commands from the Tools menu or press ⌘-Shift-Option-C. The Commands dialog box appears.

2. Select the command to which the keyboard shortcut is assigned. You see the key assignment in the Keys area.

3. Select the key assignment that you want to delete.

4. Click the Remove button.

5. Choose Close to return to your document.

Assigning Keyboard Shortcuts to Styles

As you already know, you can save the styles you create to the default style sheet or to the document style sheet. (See Chapter 14 for more information on styles.) If you save a style to the default style sheet, the style automatically is available in all the documents you open or create.

Assigning keyboard shortcuts to default styles makes good sense. You also can assign a keyboard shortcut to a document style, but keep in mind that the key works only when you have placed the insertion point in the document containing that style.

To assign keyboard shortcuts to styles, follow these steps:

1. Choose Commands from the Tools menu or press ⌘-Shift-Option-C. The Commands dialog box appears.

2. Select Apply Style Name. The drop-down list box below Command at the top of the dialog box lists the styles available in the current document.

3. Select the style to which you want to assign a keyboard shortcut. Word displays the name of the style you choose in the Apply Style Name list box.

4. Click the Add command button. A dialog box appears, prompting you to press the key combination you want to use for this style.

5. Press the key combination you want to use.

6. Choose Close to return to your document.

Assigning Keyboard Shortcuts to Glossary Entries

If you like to choose options with the keyboard, use this additional time-saving trick: assign glossary entries to keyboard shortcuts.

To assign a glossary entry to a keyboard shortcut, follow these steps:

1. Choose Commands from the Tools menu or press ⌘-Shift-Option-C. The Commands dialog box appears.

2. Select Glossary Entry in the list box. The drop-down list box below Command at the top of the dialog box lists the available glossary entries.

3. Select the entry to which you want to assign a keyboard shortcut. Word displays the name of the entry you choose in the Glossary Entry list box.

4. Click the Add button. A dialog box appears, prompting you to press the key combination you want to use for this glossary entry.

5. Press the key combination you want to use.

6. Choose Close to return to your document.

Creating a Work Menu

In this section, you learn a valuable customization technique: creating a new menu (called Work), which Word positions to the right of the Window menu and to which you can add often-accessed styles, glossary entries, and document names. Figure 35.14, for example, shows a Work menu with two glossary entries added.

Fig. 35.14

A Work menu with two frequently used glossary entries.

Work
date short
print date abbreviated

You can add items to the Work menu easily. Press ⌘-Option-plus sign (keyboard +) so that the mouse pointer changes to a plus sign, and then choose the style, glossary, or document as if you were applying, inserting, or opening that item. Instead of carrying out the command, Word adds the item to the Work menu. If the Work menu doesn't exist, Word creates it the first time you add an item.

To create a Work menu (if it doesn't already exist) and add an item to it, follow these steps:

1. Press ⌘-Option-plus sign (keyboard +). The mouse pointer changes to a plus sign.

2. Choose the name of the glossary entry, style, or document you want to add to the Work menu, using the appropriate command and choosing the option you want as though you were carrying out the command. (If you're adding a document to the menu, for example, use the Open command and select the document's name in the Open dialog box.) Word adds the glossary entry, style, or document to the Work menu.

If you have created stationery documents (described in Chapter 5, "Managing Documents and Files"), add the names of those documents to the Work menu so that you can open them quickly.

Managing Settings Files

When you start Word for the first time, the program creates a file called Word Settings (5), which is stored in your Mac's System Folder (System 6) or in the Preferences folder of the System Folder (System 7). As you redefine the default style sheet, choose preferences, customize the menus, and create new keyboard shortcuts, Word stores your choices in the Word Settings file.

If you know how to save and open settings files, you can create two or more versions of Word, each configured in a different way. By changing settings files, you can change the way Word functions.

Knowing how to change settings files also gives you access to five alternative-settings files, which you can choose to make Word resemble another program. The Settings Files folder (which was created in the Word folder when you installed the program) contains settings files for MacWrite II, Word 4.0, Word for Windows (Version 2), and Short Menus (a simplified version of Word). These settings files cannot change the way Word saves files, handles formatting, or deals with document elements such as headers, footnotes, and page numbers. The files simply rearrange the menus to make Word resemble another program.

If more than one person uses your Macintosh, each user should create a custom settings file and load that file at the start of each session. With this system, each user can customize Word without worrying about confusing other users.

If you're switching to Word from Word 4 or MacWrite II, you can choose one of these settings files to ease the transition, but doing so isn't recommended. Word's menus give you access to Word's features; the other options disguise these features. Because you bought Word for its advanced features, you probably will want to learn Word's menus.

The exception to this suggestion is the Word for Windows (Version 2) option. If you use Word for Windows on another machine, such as a 386 system at your office, you may want to choose the Word for Windows settings file for Word. You then can move effortlessly between your Mac system and the Windows system. Word for Windows (Version 2) closely resembles Word for the Mac, so you don't lose access to Word commands and features by choosing the Word for Windows settings file.

Saving Your Settings File

Before you experiment with different settings files, be sure to save your current settings file. When you save your configuration choices, you can save these choices to the default configuration file or give the settings a new name; the original settings file remains intact.

Unless you want to create different settings files for different purposes—for example, one settings file for letters and another for reports—you probably should save your settings choices to the Word Settings (5) default configuration file. Don't worry about messing up Microsoft's defaults. Later in this chapter, in "Restoring the Defaults," you learn how to remove your changes and restore the settings file to the original defaults.

To save your settings file, follow these steps:

1. Choose Commands from the Tools menu or press ⌘-Shift-Option-C. The Commands dialog box appears.

2. Click the Save As command button. The Save As dialog box appears, displaying a proposed name for the default settings file. Notice that Word automatically selects the Preferences folder.

3. Choose Save to overwrite the default settings file. Alternatively, type a new name in the Save Current Document As text box and then choose Save. The Commands dialog box reappears, displaying the name of the current settings file in the Settings File area.

4. Choose Close to return to your document.

Switching Settings Files

To switch to a new settings file, follow these steps:

1. Choose Commands from the Tools menu or press ⌘-Shift-Option-C. The Commands dialog box appears.

2. Click the Open command button. The Open dialog box appears.

3. Locate the settings file you want to open. You will find several sample settings files in the Settings Files folder, located in Word's folder.

4. Choose Open. You return to the Commands dialog box. Word displays the name of the current settings file in the Settings File area.

5. Choose Close to close the Commands dialog box.

Restoring the Defaults

If you're unhappy with the changes you have made to Word, you can undo those changes quickly by reverting to the last saved version of the configuration file or by restoring Microsoft's defaults.

To undo your configuration choices, follow these steps:

1. Choose Commands from the Tools menu or press ⌘-Shift-Option-C. The Commands dialog box appears.

2. Click the Reset command button. The dialog box shown in figure 35.15 appears.

Fig. 35.15
Choosing reset options.

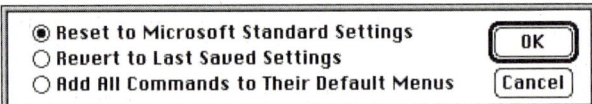

⦿ Reset to Microsoft Standard Settings

○ Revert to Last Saved Settings

○ Add All Commands to Their Default Menus

[OK]

[Cancel]

3. Choose one of the options. You can choose to reset to Microsoft's standard settings, to revert to the last saved settings, or to add all commands to their default menus. (The last option isn't recommended unless you thrive on information overload.)

4. Choose OK.

Listing Key Assignments

As you customize Word's menus and keyboards, you will find that creating a list of key assignments is handy. Word generates an up-to-date list that also shows current menu assignments.

To create a list of key assignments, follow these steps:

1. Choose Commands from the Tools menu or press ⌘-Shift-Option-C. The Commands dialog box appears.

2. Click the List command button. Word creates a table of all Word commands and their key assignments and puts the table in a new Untitled document. You can print and save this document, if you want.

Quick Review

This section summarizes the most useful information in this chapter. Check "Productivity Tips" for a review of high-productivity tips and tricks—the ones that Macintosh and Word pros use every day. Review "Techniques" whenever you need a quick reminder about a specific procedure.

Productivity Tips

- You can customize Word in many ways. If you often change margins or other formats after you create a new document, or if you have to plow through dialog boxes to locate frequently accessed commands, you probably can save time by customizing Word's defaults.

- You can redefine Word's standard styles so that those styles enter the formats you want into your documents. Add to the default style sheet any custom styles that you use in all or most documents.

- You can redefine Section, Document, and Page Setup options by clicking the Use As Default command button in these dialog boxes. With this technique, you can make such changes as turning on page numbering for all new documents, resetting the margins, and choosing a different page size.

- If you're using a slow Macintosh, change the settings in the Preferences dialog box. Turn off Background Repagination, deactivate the Open Documents in Page View option, and activate the Use Picture Placeholders option. If your Macintosh is low on memory, turn off the Include Formatted Text in Clipboard, Always Interpret RTF, and Allow Fast Saves options.

- Add frequently accessed dialog-box options to menus and remove commands that you don't use.

- If you like to use the keyboard to choose commands, assign keyboard shortcuts to frequently accessed dialog-box options, styles, and glossary entries.

- Create a Work menu that contains the names of frequently accessed glossary entries, styles, and documents.

Techniques

This section provides concise summaries of all the procedures introduced in this chapter.

Redefining Styles in the Default Style Sheet

To redefine a default style:

1. Choose Style from the Format menu or press ⌘-T. The Style dialog box appears.

2. In the list box, select the style you want to change. (If necessary, click the All Styles radio button.)

3. Choose the formats you want.

4. Click the Use As Default command button. An alert box appears, asking OK to record style in default style sheet?

5. Choose OK. You return to the Style dialog box.

6. Choose Close.

Changing Formatting Defaults

To change section-formatting defaults:

1. Choose Section from the Format menu or press Option-F14. The Section dialog box appears.

2. Choose the formats you want Word to apply to the current document and to all the new documents you create.

3. Click the Use As Default command button.

4. Choose OK.

To change document-formatting defaults:

1. Choose Document from the Format menu or press ⌘-F14. The Document dialog box appears.

2. Choose the formatting options you want Word to apply to the current document and to all the new documents you create.

3. Click the Use As Default command button.

4. Choose OK.

To change Page Setup defaults:

1. If you haven't done so, choose your printer, using the Chooser desk accessory (Apple menu).

2. Choose Page Setup from the File menu or press Shift-F8. The Page Setup dialog box appears.

3. Click the Use As Default check box.

4. Choose OK.

Choosing Preferences Options

To choose preferences options:

1. Choose Preferences from the Tools menu. The Preferences dialog box appears.

2. To display options other than the General options, click the appropriate icon.

3. Choose the options you want.

4. Click the close box.

Adding a Command to a Menu

To use the keyboard to add a dialog-box or ruler option to a menu:

1. Display the item you want to add.

2. Press ⌘-Option-plus sign (keyboard +). The mouse pointer changes to a plus sign.

3. Select the item you want to add.

To use the Commands dialog box to add a command to a menu:

1. Choose Commands from the Tools menu or press ⌘-Shift-Option-C. The Commands dialog box appears.

2. Select the item you want to add.

3. If a colon follows the name of the item, you must select that item in a drop-down list box. The name of the selected item appears below Command at the top of the dialog box.

4. If you want to change the default menu linkage, drop down the Menu list and select the menu to which you want to add the item.

Chapter 35
Customizing Menus and Keyboard Shortcuts

5. If you want to choose where the item appears in the selected menu, drop down the Add Below list box and select the name of the command below which you want the item to appear.

6. Click the Add command button to add the item to the menu.

7. Choose Close to return to your document.

Removing a Command from a Menu

To use the keyboard to remove a command from a menu:

1. Press ⌘-Option-hyphen (-). The mouse pointer changes to a minus sign.

2. Choose the command you want to remove.

To use the Commands dialog box to remove a command from a menu:

1. Choose Commands from the Tools menu or press ⌘-Shift-Option-C. The Commands dialog box appears.

2. Select the command you want to remove.

3. Click the Remove command button.

4. Choose Close.

Assigning a Keyboard Shortcut to a Command

To use the keyboard to assign a keyboard shortcut:

1. Press ⌘-Option- plus sign (numeric keypad +). The mouse pointer becomes a ⌘ symbol.

2. Choose the menu item you want. An alert box appears, prompting you for the key combination you want to use.

3. Press the desired keys.

4. Choose OK.

To use the Commands dialog box to assign a keyboard shortcut:

1. Choose Commands from the Tools menu or press ⌘-Shift-Option-C. The Commands dialog box appears.

2. Select the command to which you want to assign a shortcut.

3. Look at the Keys list, which lists all keyboard shortcuts already assigned to the chosen command.

4. Click the Add command button.

5. Press the key combination you want to use.

6. If an alert box appears, warning you that the shortcut keys already are assigned, think twice about reassigning those keys. If you're sure that you want to redefine the shortcut keys, choose OK. Otherwise, click Cancel.

7. Choose Close.

Deleting a Keyboard Shortcut

To delete an unwanted keyboard shortcut:

1. Choose Commands from the Tools menu or press ⌘-Shift-Option-C. The Commands dialog box appears.

2. Choose the name of the command to which the keyboard shortcut is assigned.

3. In the Keys area, select the key assignment you want to delete.

4. Click the Remove command button.

5. Choose Close.

Assigning a Keyboard Shortcut to a Style

To assign a keyboard shortcut to a style:

1. Choose Commands from the Tools menu or press ⌘-Shift-Option-C. The Commands dialog box appears.

2. Select Apply Style Name in the drop-down list box below Command at the top of the dialog box.

3. Select the style in the list box.

4. Click the Add command button.

5. Press the key combination you want to use.

6. Choose Close.

Assigning a Keyboard Shortcut to a Glossary Entry

To assign a keyboard shortcut to a glossary entry:

1. Choose Commands from the Tools menu or press ⌘-Shift-Option-C. The Commands dialog box appears.

2. Select Glossary Entry in the drop-down list box below Command at the top of the dialog box.

3. Select the glossary entry to which you want to assign a keyboard shortcut.

4. Click the Add command button.

5. Press the key combination you want to use.

6. Choose Close.

Adding Styles, Glossary Entries, and Document Names to the Work Menu

To add glossary entries, styles, or document names to the Work menu (and create the menu, if it doesn't exist):

1. Press ⌘-Option-plus sign (keyboard +).

2. Choose the name of the glossary entry, style, or document you want to add to the Work menu, using the appropriate command and choosing the option you want as though you were carrying out the command. Word adds the item to the Work menu, creating that menu at the same time, if necessary.

Saving a Settings File

To save a settings file:

1. Choose Commands from the Tools menu or press ⌘-Shift-Option-C. The Commands dialog box appears.

2. Click the Save As command button. The Save As dialog box appears.

3. Choose Save to overwrite the default settings file. Alternatively, type a new name in the Save Current Document As text box and then choose Save. The Commands dialog box reappears.

4. Choose Close.

Switching Between Settings Files

To switch to a different settings file:

1. Choose Commands from the Tools menu or press ⌘-Shift-Option-C. The Commands dialog box appears.

2. Click the Open command button. The Open dialog box appears.

3. Locate the settings file you want to open.

4. Choose Open.

5. Choose Close.

Choosing Preferences Options

To choose preferences options:

1. Choose Preferences from the Tools menu. The Preferences dialog box appears.

2. To display options other than the General options, click the appropriate icon.

3. Choose the options you want.

4. Click the close box.

Customizing Word's Toolbar

U sers of Word 5.1 enjoy a convenient new feature: the *Toolbar*, a row of icons across the top of the screen. You can click the tools to access frequently chosen commands. You already have learned that the number of tools you see depends on the width of your screen, and you probably already have used the tools many times. But you may have concluded that some of the tools aren't useful for you. You probably wish that Word provided tools for other commands—the commands you use repeatedly.

This chapter covers the following topics:

■ *Changing the position of the Toolbar.* You learn how to position the Toolbar on the left or right side of the screen—and how to dispense with it entirely, if you want.

■ *Customizing the tools.* You can assign any of Word's commands to a tool.

■ *Restoring the default.* You learn how to restore Word's default Toolbar if you don't like your changes.

USING
WORD 5.1
FOR THE MAC
SPECIAL EDITION

Changing the Toolbar's Position

Unlike the ribbon and ruler, the Toolbar isn't linked with specific windows. You can turn the ribbon on in one window, for example, and turn it off in another. The Toolbar, however, is either on or off for all windows.

NOTE If you don't like using the Toolbar, learn how to get rid of it. To turn off the Toolbar temporarily, choose Toolbar from the View menu so that the check mark disappears. To turn off the Toolbar permanently, choose Preferences from the Tools menu and then deactivate the View Toolbar option. (Later, you can restore the Toolbar by activating this option, if you want.)

You can control the Toolbar's position. By default, Word places the Toolbar at the top of the screen. You can also position it along the left or right edge of the screen. In figure 36.1, you see what the Toolbar looks like when it is positioned along the left edge.

Fig. 36.1
Toolbar positioned on left side of screen.

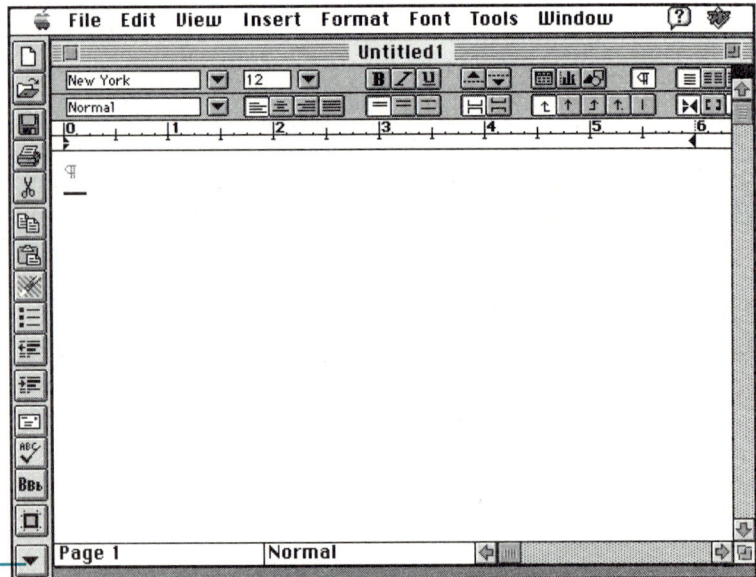

Toolbar tool

NOTE

If you position the Toolbar along the left or right edge of the screen, you see fewer tools, but you see more lines of text in the document window.

To change the position of the Toolbar, follow these steps:

1. Click the Toolbar tool and hold down the mouse button. The Toolbar drop-down menu appears (see fig. 36.2).

Fig. 36.2
Toolbar menu.

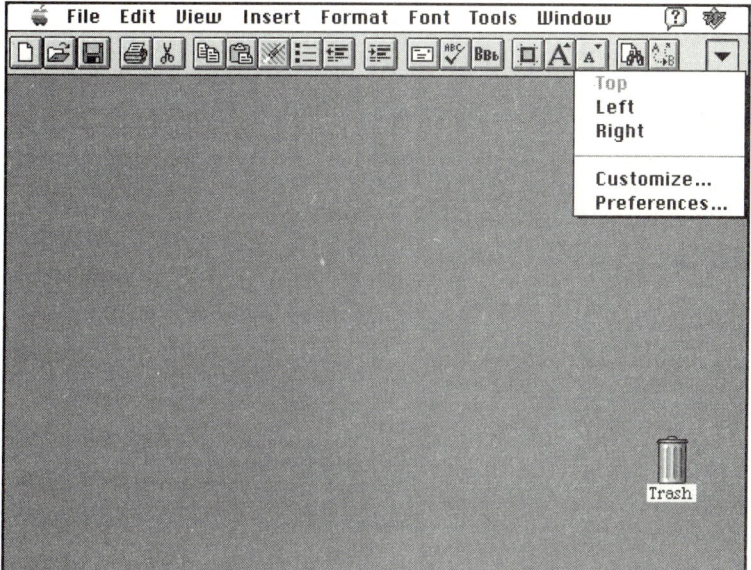

2. Choose the location you want.

You can also choose the Toolbar location by using Toolbar Preferences. To access Toolbar Preferences, follow these steps:

1. Choose Preferences from the Tools menu or choose Preferences from the Toolbar drop-down menu in the Toolbar. The Preferences dialog box appears.

2. In the icons list on the left side of the Preferences dialog box, scroll down until you see the Toolbar icon and then click it. The Toolbar options appear (see fig. 36.3).

Chapter 36

Customizing Word's Toolbar

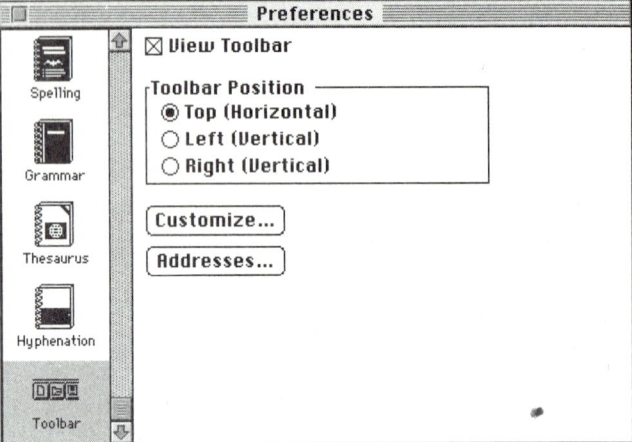

3. In the Toolbar Position area, click the radio button that represents the position you want.

4. Click the close box to confirm your choice and exit the Preferences dialog box.

Customizing the Tools

Word 5.1 offers more than 100 buttons that you can use to customize the Toolbar. The designs of many of these buttons suggest specific functions; the button on which a printer appears, for example, suggests printing. For other buttons, you can use your imagination (one button, for example, is a little yellow happy face wearing sunglasses!). Regardless of design, however, you can assign *any* Word command to *any* buttons.

Figure 36.4 shows all the buttons that are available for use as tools in Word 5.1.

Should you customize the Toolbar? By all means, customize it. The tools you find in the Toolbar are those that Word's designers felt would be useful for most people most of the time, but the tools may not include the commands that you really like using.

As you learned in Chapter 35, Word's design includes an extensive list of named commands that you can access in a variety of ways by using the menus, keyboard, and Toolbar. You can customize the Toolbar so that it contains tools only for the commands that you want to access.

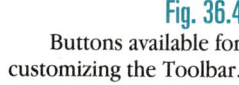
Fig. 36.4
Buttons available for
customizing the Toolbar.

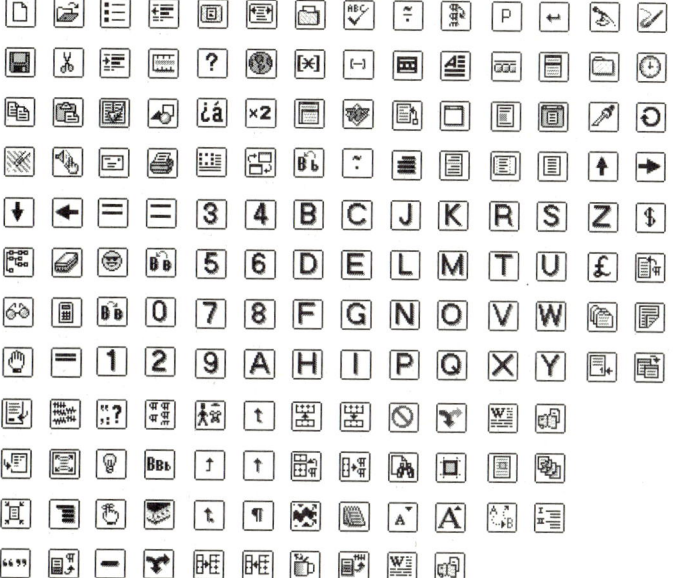

As you think about the commands to which you want to assign tools, try to choose the ones that would require fussing with menus or with the keyboard if you didn't have a tool to click. Suppose that you frequently use the Renumber command to number lists of instructions. To save yourself the trouble of choosing Renumber from the Tools menu, you can add a button to the Toolbar and assign the Renumber command to that tool.

Don't be afraid to experiment with the Toolbar. If you don't like your changes, you can restore the default tool for any given tool location or throw out all your changes and restore Word's defaults. You learn how to restore the defaults later. For now, try some customization.

You can customize the Toolbar in two ways:

- *Replace existing tools with new tools.* You can add buttons to the Toolbar, using those buttons to replace existing tools, and then assign the new tools to different commands.

- *Replace existing tools with blank buttons.* You can use blank buttons to separate groups of tools, if you want.

Both procedures are covered in the following sections.

Chapter 36
Customizing Word's Toolbar

978

Before you start to customize the Toolbar, consider carefully which tools you find convenient. For example, if you like using the keyboard shortcuts for copying, cutting, and pasting (⌘-C, ⌘-X, and ⌘-V, respectively), you may want to dispense with the Copy, Cut, and Paste tools.

Replacing Tools

To customize tools, you use the Customize dialog box (see fig. 36.5).

Fig. 36.5

Customize dialog box.

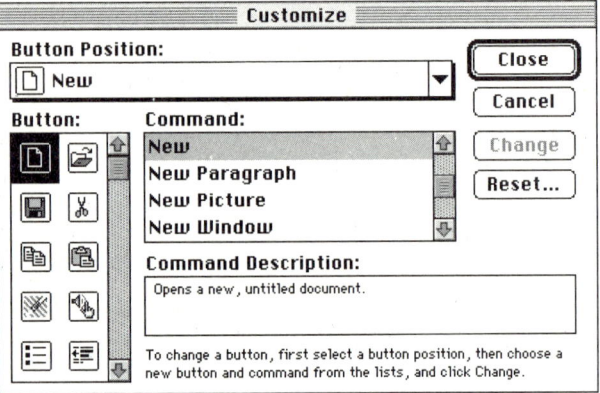

This dialog box has four areas:

Button Position. This drop-down list box shows the current tools. To replace a tool, you first select the position you want to change.

Button. In this list box, you see dozens of buttons among which you can choose. These buttons are not linked to any specific commands; most of them, however, are intended to suggest certain commands.

Command. This list box lists all the commands to which you can assign tools. (For a complete list of Word's commands, see Chapter 35, "Customizing Menus and Keyboard Shortcuts.")

Command Description. In this area, you see a description of the command that currently is selected in the Command list box.

To replace a tool, follow these steps:

1. Click the Toolbar tool and hold down the mouse button. The Toolbar drop-down menu appears.

2. Choose Customize from this drop-down menu. The Customize dialog box appears (refer to fig. 36.5).

3. Drop down the Button Position list and select the position of the tool you want to replace. (To replace the Find File tool, for example, select this tool in the list.)

4. In the Button list box, select the button you want to insert into the Toolbar.

5. In the Command list box, select the command you want to assign to the new tool.

   Figure 36.6, for example, shows the settings you would need to replace the Find File tool with a tool that displays the Footnote dialog box.

Fig. 36.6
Replacing a tool.

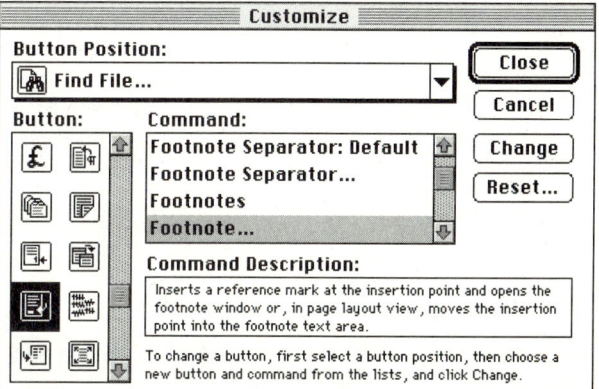

6. Click the Change command button. Word replaces the existing tool with the new tool you specified.

7. To replace more tools, repeat steps 3 through 6.

8. When you finish replacing tools, choose Close to exit the Customize dialog box.

Adding Blank Buttons to the Toolbar

A blank button performs no action. You can add blank buttons to the Toolbar, however, to separate groups of tools, if you want.

To create a blank button, follow these steps:

1. Click the Toolbar tool and hold down the mouse button. The Toolbar drop-down menu appears.

2. Choose Customize from this drop-down menu. The Customize dialog box appears.

3. Drop down the Button Position list and select the position of the tool you want to replace.

4. In the Button list box, select the blank button (the last one).

5. In the Command list box, select Unassigned Button.

6. Click the Change command button. Word replaces the specified tool with a blank button.

7. Choose Close to exit the Customize dialog box.

CAUTION

Word does not save your Toolbar changes until you quit Word by choosing Quit from the File menu (or by pressing ⌘-Q). Don't quit Word by switching off your Mac's power while Word is still on-screen, however; if you do, you lose your Toolbar changes.

Restoring the Toolbar Defaults

If you don't like your Toolbar experiments, you can restore the defaults in three ways:

- *Reset a tool.* You can restore any tool's original setting.

- *Reset to the last-saved Toolbar.* This option resets the Toolbar, restoring the one that was in effect the last time you quit Word. Word saves the Toolbar only when you quit the program. You can use this option to cancel all the Toolbar changes you made during the current operating session.

- *Restore the original Word Toolbar.* You can reset the Toolbar to the Word default Toolbar—the one that was in effect the first time you started the program.

To reset the Toolbar, follow these steps:

1. Click the Toolbar tool and hold down the mouse button. The Toolbar drop-down menu appears.

2. Choose Customize from this drop-down menu. The Customize dialog box appears.

3. If you want to reset a single customized tool to its default setting, select that tool in the Button Position drop-down list box.

4. Click the Reset command button. The Reset To dialog box appears (see fig. 36.7).

Fig. 36.7
Reset to dialog box.

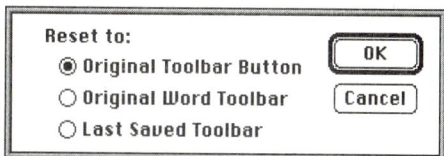

5. Perform one of the following actions:

■ To restore the tool that currently is highlighted in the Button list box, click the Original Toolbar Button radio button.

■ To cancel all the changes you have ever made in the Toolbar, click the Original Word Toolbar radio button.

■ To cancel all the Toolbar changes you have made during the current operating session, click the Last Saved Toolbar radio button.

6. Choose OK. You return to the Customize dialog box.

7. Choose Close.

Quick Review

This section summarizes the most useful information in this chapter. Check "Productivity Tips" for a review of high-productivity tips and tricks—the ones that Macintosh and Word pros use every day. Review "Techniques" whenever you need a quick reminder about a specific procedure.

Productivity Tips

■ If you don't use the Toolbar, hide it permanently by deactivating the View Toolbar option in the Preferences dialog box.

Chapter 36
Customizing Word's Toolbar

- If you use a Mac with a small screen, position the Toolbar on the left or right side of the screen. You see fewer tools, but you see more lines of text on the screen.

- Don't be afraid to customize the Toolbar. If your experiments don't work out, you can restore the default setting for any tool or for the whole Toolbar.

- Keep track of which tools you use—and which ones you don't use. If you frequently choose options that are buried deeply in menus or dialog boxes, you may want to replace some existing tools that you don't use with customized tools that select these options.

- Remember that you can assign any tool to any command. Before you customize the Toolbar, then, review the button designs shown in figure 36.4.

Techniques

This section provides concise summaries of all the procedures introduced in this chapter.

Moving the Toolbar

To move the Toolbar to a different position:

1. Click the Toolbar tool and hold down the mouse button. The Toolbar drop-down menu appears.

2. Choose the location you want.

Customizing Tools

To replace a tool:

1. Click the Toolbar tool and hold down the mouse button. The Toolbar drop-down menu appears.

2. Choose Customize from this menu. The Customize dialog box appears.

3. Drop down the Button Position list box and select the position of the tool you want to replace.

4. In the Button list box, select the button you want to insert into the Toolbar.

Part VII

Customizing Word 5.1

5. In the Command list box, select the command to which you want to assign the new tool.

6. Click the Change command button. Word replaces the existing tool with the new tool you specified.

7. To replace more tools, repeat steps 3 through 6.

8. When you finish replacing tools, choose Close to exit the Customize dialog box.

To create a blank button:

1. Click the Toolbar tool and hold down the mouse button. The Toolbar drop-down menu appears.

2. Choose Customize from this menu. The Customize dialog box appears.

3. Drop down the Button Position list box and select the position of the tool you want to replace.

4. In the Button list box, select the blank button.

5. In the Command list box, select Unassigned Button.

6. Click the Change command button.

7. Choose Close to exit the Customize dialog box.

Resetting the Toolbar

To reset the Toolbar:

1. Click the Toolbar tool and hold down the mouse button. The Toolbar drop-down menu appears.

2. Choose Customize from this menu. The Customize dialog box appears.

3. If you want to restore one customized tool's default setting, select that tool in the Button Position drop-down list box.

4. Click the Reset command button. The Reset To dialog box appears.

   ■ To restore the tool that currently is highlighted in the Button list box, click the Original Toolbar Button radio button.

   ■ To cancel all the changes you have ever made in the Toolbar, click the Original Word Toolbar radio button.

Chapter 36

Customizing Word's Toolbar

 To cancel all the Toolbar changes you have made during the current operating session, click the Last Saved Toolbar radio button.

5. Choose OK. You return to the Customize dialog box.

6. Choose Close.

Appendixes

USING
WORD 5.1
FOR THE MAC
SPECIAL EDITION

Using Word 5.1 with PowerBooks

APPENDIX

With the release of Apple's PowerBook computers, Macintosh users finally have obtained notebook computers that are as powerful, sophisticated, and lightweight as the ones that DOS and Windows users enjoy. To meet the special needs of PowerBook users, Word 5.1 offers two special features:

■ *PowerBook Installation.* This installation option conserves space on your PowerBook's none-too-spacious hard disk.

■ *PowerBook Battery Indicator.* This indicator, which appears on the right edge of the ruler when you install Word 5.1 on PowerBook computers, shows you how much current is flowing from your computer's battery.

Installing Word 5.1 on a PowerBook

When you install Word, you can choose the Easy Install option (see Chapter 1), which installs all of Word's files. PowerBooks, however, have limited disk space. If you want to run other programs on a PowerBook, you may want to choose the PowerBook installation option, which requires only 2.2M of disk space. This installation places the following files on your PowerBook disk:

USING
WORD 5.1
FOR THE MAC
SPECIAL EDITION

- Microsoft Word
- Standard Glossary
- Text Annotations
- Spelling
- Symbol
- Thesaurus
- Toolbar
- Hyphenation
- Command Help

NOTE The PowerBook installation option installs the same number of files as the Minimal Install option, discussed in Chapter 1. You should choose the PowerBook option, however, so that Word installs the version of Word that detects your PowerBook's battery-power level.

If you choose the PowerBook Install option, you will not be able to use certain Word features unless you install them individually later (see "Installing Additional Features" later in this appendix). Following is a brief overview of those features:

- *Microsoft Word Help.* This feature is useful when you're learning your way around Word.

- *Find File.* Using this feature, you can search your disk for files that you can't find manually. (See Chapter 5, "Managing Documents and Files," for information on Find File.)

- *Voice Annotation.* If your PowerBook is equipped with a microphone, you can use this feature to record short vocal comments, which appear in your document as icons. When you click a voice-annotation icon, you can play the annotation.

- *Drop Caps.* You use this feature to create initial drop caps, an attractive formatting feature. (See Chapter 20, "Positioning Text and Graphics," for details.)

- *Picture.* This feature enables you to create drawings and add them to your Word documents.

- *Microsoft Graph.* This accessory program enables you to create charts and add them to Word documents.

Appendix A
Using Word 5.1 with PowerBooks

- *Equation Editor.* This accessory program is a must for anyone who types mathematical equations. (Chapter 25, "Using Math and Typing Equations," introduces Equation Editor.)

- *Grammar.* This accessory program scans your Word documents for many common grammatical and usage errors. (See Chapter 12, "Checking Spelling and Grammar," for information on Grammar.)

- *File and graphics converters.* These converters enable you to exchange your Word documents with people who use other word processing programs. These converters also enable you to import graphics into Word documents. (For information on converters, see Chapter 5.)

If you have more than 2.2M of disk space that you're willing to devote to Word, you can selectively install additional features, such as Equation Editor and Grammar. Begin by installing Word with the PowerBook installation option, as explained in the following section. Then install the additional features, as explained later in this appendix.

Installing the Basic Word 5.1 Program on a PowerBook

Installing Word 5.1 on a PowerBook computer requires 2.2M of disk space. The PowerBook installation option, which installs the version of Word that is designed to run on PowerBook computers, omits many Word features.

To perform a PowerBook installation, follow these steps:

1. Place the Install disk in the disk drive.

2. Double-click the Installer icon. You see an introductory screen that reminds you to register your copy of Word.

3. Click OK.

   If you are installing Word for the first time, a dialog box appears, asking you to type your name and organization. Type your name in the Name text box; optionally, press Tab and type your organization's name. Then click OK.

4. After you click OK, an alert box appears, warning you to stop the installation procedure if you haven't disabled any virus-protection software you may be using.

Appendix A

Using Word 5.1 with PowerBooks

If you have disabled virus-protection software, or if no such software is installed on your Macintosh, click Continue. The Installer dialog box appears (see fig. A.1).

Fig. A.1
Installer dialog box.

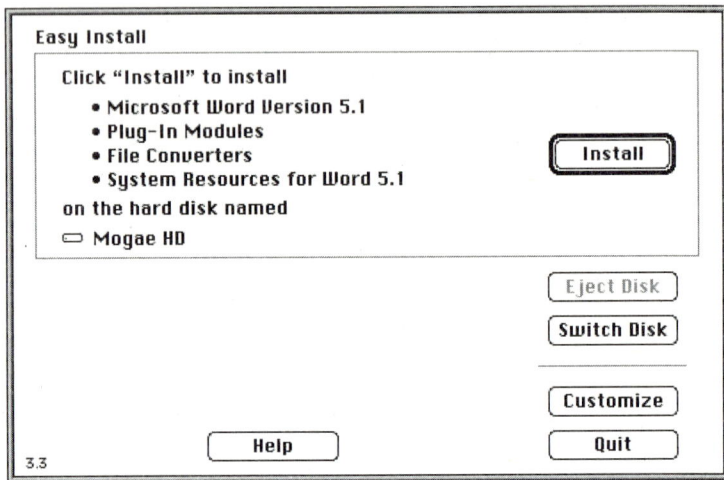

5. Click the Customize button. You see another Installer dialog box (see fig. A.2) that enables you to select the options you want.

Fig. A.2
Custom-installation dialog box.

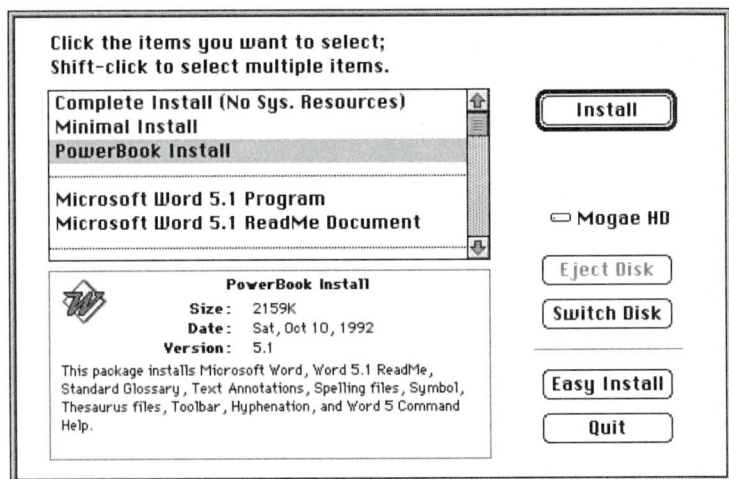

Appendix A

Using Word 5.1 with PowerBooks

6. Click PowerBook Install.

7. Click Install. A dialog box appears, asking you to identify the folder where you want to install Word.

8. Click the New Folder button, and in the dialog box that appears, type **Word 5.1**.

9. Click OK, and then click the Install button.

   You will be prompted to insert the Word disks as Installer does its job. After you insert the last disk, take a break: Word will need to decompress all the files, a procedure that can take a few minutes.

10. When Installer finishes, a dialog box appears, asking you which font and font size you want to use as defaults. Click OK to accept the default font and font size (New York 12), or choose another font and font size and then click OK to confirm your choice.

    A dialog box appears, informing you that the installation was successful. Before you can use Word, however, you must restart your PowerBook.

11. Click Restart to restart your computer.

Installing Additional Features

When you use the PowerBook Install option to install Word, Installer omits many files that support useful Word features. If you have additional room on your disk, you may want to install some of these features.

To install additional features, follow these steps:

1. Place the Install disk in the disk drive.

2. Double-click the Installer icon. You see an introductory screen that reminds you to register your copy of Word.

3. Click OK. An alert box appears, warning you to stop the installation procedure if you haven't disabled virus-protection software.

4. If you have disabled virus-protection software, or if no such software is installed on your Macintosh, click Continue. The Installer dialog box appears.

5. Click the Customize button. You see another Installer dialog box that enables you to select the options you want.

6. Scroll the list box to display the features you want to install. To install more than one feature, hold down the Shift key as you click feature names.

7. Click Install. A dialog box appears, asking you to identify the folder where you want to install Word.

8. Select the Word 5.1 folder and then click OK. You will be prompted to insert the Word disks that contain the files you have requested.

Checking Battery Usage

When you install Word on a PowerBook, you see a battery-power indicator on the right edge of the ruler. This indicator appears only if you install Word on a PowerBook computer.

Depending on the amount of power in your battery, you see one of the following indicators:

 Full power. The battery is fully charged.

 Less than full power. You have used some of the battery's charge.

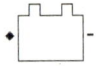 **Almost out of power.** If you see this indicator, *save your work immediately*, quit Word, and recharge your PowerBook.

Because batteries do not discharge at a constant rate, the battery indicator does not tell you how much *time* is left. Your PowerBook's battery maintains its full charge for a very short time, so you see the Less Than Full Power indicator shortly after you turn on your PowerBook and use Word for a few minutes. From that point on, the battery loses power more slowly. When the battery indicator is half full, you have more than half the maximum use time left.

Using PostScript

PostScript is a computer programming language developed by Adobe Systems, Inc. Specifically, PostScript is a *page-description language*, a special-purpose programming language designed to control printers equipped with the necessary decoding circuitry. If you have a PostScript-compatible printer, such as a LaserWriter II NT, you can use PostScript commands to create special effects, such as rotated type, shading, and boxes around text.

Word provides an excellent environment for using PostScript, but if you have never done any computer programming, you're probably thinking that PostScript isn't for you. If so, the good news is that you can use Word's PostScript capabilities without knowing a thing about computer programming. What's more, you don't even need a PostScript printer attached to your system to use PostScript commands in your documents. You can print your document on another system equipped with a PostScript printer, or take your document (on a floppy disk) to a graphics service bureau that specializes in high-quality printing of Macintosh documents.

What's the secret to Word's easy-to-use PostScript capabilities? The secret is the Page Layout Glossary, a Word glossary that you find in the Glossaries folder. This glossary contains many predefined PostScript commands that you can use to add a variety of special effects to your documents.

If you're willing to try your hand at typing PostScript commands yourself, Word also provides special capabilities that make it easy to do so.

Included in Word's standard style is the PostScript style, which does more than just assign the predefined formats that the style includes (including hidden text). Any text formatted with the PostScript style is sent to the printer as a PostScript command. If your printer has the necessary circuitry to decode these commands, you see the special PostScript effects.

This appendix, which briefly introduces the use of PostScript in Word, isn't intended to provide an introduction to PostScript programming. Even if you don't know how to program in PostScript, however, this appendix contains useful information.

Using the Page Layout Glossary

By far the easiest way to use PostScript in Word is to use the Page Layout glossary. In brief, this glossary contains PostScript programs that you can add to your document by inserting them from the glossary. After you add a PostScript program in this way, you can use that program the way Word inserts it, or you can make modifications by carefully retyping some of the settings included in the program instructions.

You don't see the effects of your PostScript programs on-screen. These effects appear only when your document is printed on a PostScript laser printer or on a PostScript-compatible imagesetter.

Looking at the Page Layout Glossary's Contents

Following are descriptions of selected PostScript programs that you can insert from the Page Layout glossary:

- *Crop Marks.* This program creates crop marks in all four corners of your page. (Crop marks signal to a printer where the edge of the page should appear after the document is printed.) You use crop marks to prepare a manuscript that prints at a page size smaller than 8 1/2 by 11 inches.

  By default, this program places the crop marks one inch (72 points) from the top and bottom margins and 1.25 inches (90 points) from the left and right margins. You can change these dimensions by locating the /top, /bottom, /left, and /right commands within the program and retyping the numbers.

Appendix B
Using PostScript

Suppose that you locate the PostScript instruction /top 72. If you carefully retype this instruction as /top 90, your PostScript printer will locate the top crop mark 1.25 inches from the top of the page.

■ *Line Between Columns.* This program is excellent news for newsletter writers, because you can use it to place lines between the columns in a multiple-column format.

■ *Page Border—Landscape.* This program creates a border around an 8 1/2-by-11-inch page printed with landscape orientation. The border appears 1/2 inch from the page's edge.

■ *Page Border—Portrait.* This entry creates a border around an 8 1/2-by-11-inch page printed with portrait orientation. The border appears 1/2 inch from the page's edge.

■ *Word Under Text.* This entry prints a large gray-shaded word, CONFIDENTIAL, diagonally across the page.

To change the font, locate the instruction that says /Times-Bolditalic findfont and then carefully retype the official PostScript font name (for example, /Palatino-Bold findfont prints the text in boldface Palatino. (A list of official PostScript font names for LaserWriter printers appears later in this section.)

To change the font size, locate the instruction that says /FontSize 72 def and then carefully retype the point size. For example, /FontSize 84 def prints the text in 84 point type.

To change the text to be printed, locate the command that says /TextToPrint(CONFIDENTIAL) def and then carefully replace CONFIDENTIAL with the text you want to print. For example, if you type **OUR FIFTEENTH ANNUAL SALE** inside the parentheses, this text will appear when the document is printed.

Following is a list of the PostScript font names you can use with LaserWriter printers:

AvantGarde-Book	Bookman-LightItalic
AvantGarde-BookOblique	Courier
AvantGarde-Demi	Courier-Bold
AvantGarde-DemiOblique	Courier-BoldOblique
Bookman-Demi	Courier-Oblique
Bookman-DemiItalic	Helvetica
Bookman-Light	Helvetica-Bold

Helvetica-BoldOblique	Palatino-BoldItalic
Helvetica-Narrow	Palatino-Italic
Helvetica-Narrow-Bold	Palatino-Roman
Helvetica-Narrow-BoldOblique	Symbol
Helvetica-Narrow-Oblique	Times-Bold
Helvetica-Oblique	Times-BoldItalic
NewCenturySchlbk-Bold	Times-Italic
NewCenturySchlbk-BoldItalic	Times-Roman
NewCenturySchlbk-Italic	ZapfChancery-MediumItalic
NewCenturySchlbk-Roman	ZapfDingbats
Palatino-Bold	

The Page Layout glossary also contains some non-PostScript options that make use of Word styles. These options include Margin Note (adds a note in the margin) and Side Head (adds a heading in the margin).

Opening the Page Layout Glossary

Before you can use the programs provided in the Page Layout glossary, you must open that glossary.

To open the Page Layout glossary, follow these steps:

1. Choose Glossary from the Edit menu. The Glossary dialog box appears (see fig. B.1).

Fig. B.1
Glossary dialog box.

2. Choose Open from the File menu. The Open dialog box appears.

3. In the Glossaries folder, select Page Layout Glossary.

4. Choose Open. Word adds the Page Layout Glossary items to the current glossary.

5. Click Close to return to your document. Word adds the Page Layout glossary entries to those included in the Standard Glossary.

Inserting an Item from the Page Layout Glossary

The PostScript commands you insert into your document affect only the page on which they are inserted. To apply commands to your whole document, you must place the glossary entry in a header on each page.

To insert a glossary entry into a page, follow these steps:

1. Place the insertion point at the beginning of the page you want the command to affect.

2. Choose Glossary from the Edit menu.

3. Click one of the Page Layout Glossary entry names.

4. Click Insert.

To print the effect on every page, follow these steps:

1. Choose Document from the Format menu or press ⌘-F14. The Document dialog box appears.

2. In the Margins area, select Exactly in the drop-down list box adjacent to the Top text box. This option prevents Word from allotting enough room to show the entire PostScript program— which would be pointless, because the PostScript codes will not print anyway.

3. Choose OK to confirm your choice and exit the dialog box.

4. Choose Header from the View menu. The Header window appears.

5. Insert the desired glossary entry as described above.

Introducing PostScript Programming

As you just learned, the Page Layout glossary contains several PostScript programs that you can insert into your documents. When you insert these entries, Word formats them with PostScript style—Normal style, plus boldface and hidden text. This style also sends text to the printer as a PostScript command. If you have a PostScript printer, the printer interprets this command, if possible, and carries it out. (If the command contains an error, the page will not print.) If your printer doesn't recognize PostScript, it ignores the PostScript commands and prints the document anyway.

If you want to experiment with PostScript programming, you can type your own PostScript instructions in a paragraph formatted with the PostScript style, as you learn to do in the following sections.

Understanding Basic PostScript Concepts

Although this isn't the place for a full introduction to PostScript, you will find it helpful to understand a few basic concepts. This section provides an introduction to a few basic concepts of PostScript.

Page Grid. In PostScript, locations on a page are defined by means of an x-y coordinate system that begins (in contravention to normal coordinate practice in mathematics) in the *lower left* corner of the page. For this reason, the coordinates 0,0 are located in the lower left corner.

Coordinates are stated in printer's points (72 per inch). The x axis (horizontal) is stated first; the Y axis (vertical) is stated second. The coordinates 72,72, for example, define the lower left corner of the printed part of the page (assuming that you use 1-inch margins all around); the coordinates 612,792 define the upper right corner of an 8 1/2-by-11-inch page.

Paths. Many PostScript programs begin with a command that tells the printer where to start the effect—where to set its "pen" down on the page, so to speak. This command defines the *path* that the printer should follow. The command 720,72 moveto, for example, tells PostScript to start the following effect in the upper left corner of the printed area (1 inch from the top and left edges of the page).

Operators and operands. PostScript commands are called *operators*. One operator, for example, is moveto. Most PostScript operators are preceded by numbers or other data that provide further information about what the operator is supposed to do. These numbers are called *operands*. The command 720,72 moveto is an example of an operator preceded by an operand.

Appendix B
Using PostScript

Notice that the operator comes last. This arrangement is called *postfix notation*. Some operators, however, don't need an operand.

Comments. PostScript ignores any line preceded by a percentage sign (%). You can use such a line to include comments about what the program does.

Case sensitivity. PostScript is case-sensitive, which means that `Moveto` and `moveto` are different as far as PostScript is concerned. All PostScript commands must be typed in lowercase.

Groups. A PostScript program affects a fixed area called a *drawing rectangle*. A *group* is an operator that tells PostScript what the drawing rectangle should be. Group names have periods before and after (such as `.para.`). The default group is `.page.`. (The groups you can use with Word are listed later in this section.) The `.para.` group is particularly useful; this group defines the drawing rectangle as the next non-PostScript paragraph.

Variables. With Word, you can use variables to insert Word information into your PostScript programs. For example, the variable `wp$page` returns the current page number. A list of the variables you can use with Word appears later in this section.

Table B.1 lists the names of the groups you can use with Word.

Table B.1
Groups

Group	Affects
.page.	Current page
.para.	Following paragraph
.pic.	Following graphic
.cell.	Current cell in a table
.row.	Current row in a table

Table B.2 lists the variables you can use with Word.

Table B.2
Variables

Variable	Returns
Variables for All Groups	
wp$box	Current drawing rectangle
wp$x	Width of the current rectangle

continues

Appendix B
Using PostScript

	Variable	Returns
Table B.2 Continued	wp$y	Height of the current rectangle
	wp$xorig	Left edge of the drawing rectangle
	wp$yorig	Bottom edge of the drawing rectangle
	wp$fpage	Current page number formatted with current page-number format
	wp$page	Current page number
	wp$date	Current date
	wp$time	Current time
	Variables for Pages	
	wp$top	Current top-margin setting
	wp$bottom	Current bottom-margin setting
	wp$left	Current left-margin setting
	wp$right	Current right-margin setting
	wp$col	Current number of columns
	wp$colx	Current column width
	wp$colxb	Current width between columns
	Variables for Paragraphs	
	wp$top	Space before current paragraph
	wp$bottom	Space after current paragraph
	wp$left	Left indent of current paragraph
	wp$right	Right indent of current paragraph
	wp$first	First-line indent of current paragraph
	wp$style	Name of style for current paragraph

Examining a PostScript Program

If you insert the Page Border—Portrait glossary entry into your document, you see the following program (if you don't see it, activate display of hidden text in the Preferences dialog box):

Appendix B
Using PostScript

```
%Page Border - Portrait
.5 setlinewidth
36 36 moveto
0 720 rlineto
540 0 rlineto
0 -720 rlineto
closepath
stroke
```

Following is a brief explanation of this program:

■ The first line is a comment that indicates what the program does.

■ The next line uses the `setlinewidth` operator. This operator sets the width of the line that the program will draw (the operand, `.5`, tells PostScript to draw a line 1/2 inch wide).

■ The next line, `36 36 moveto`, tells PostScript where to start: at a point 1/2 inch from the left margin and 1/2 inch from the bottom margin.

■ The next three lines are commands that draw three sides of an imaginary rectangle.

The first command, `0 720 rlineto`, tells PostScript to draw a line relative to the current point. This line extends from the current point (36 36), and extends 720 points (10 inches) straight up.

The second command, `540 0 rlineto`, draws another imaginary line 540 points to the right of the first line's end (across the top of the page).

The third command, `0 -720 rlineto`, draws the imaginary line down the right side of the page.

■ The `closepath` command tells PostScript to add the last line to create the imaginary box.

■ The last command, `stroke`, tells PostScript to draw actual lines where the imaginary box has been defined.

Typing Simple PostScript Programs into Your Document

You needn't know a lot about PostScript programming to type PostScript programs into a document. Many available books show the instructions you type to create special effects, such as shadowed text, rotated text, and circular text. You can type these programs into your document and use these effects, even if you don't understand all the lines of the PostScript program.

Appendix B

Using PostScript

To learn how to type PostScript programs into your document, try the tutorial in this section. You add a simple PostScript program by using the `.para.` group name, which tells PostScript to apply the instructions to the next Word paragraph.

Because Word formats the PostScript style using hidden text, you must display hidden text in order to work with PostScript. To display hidden text, choose Preferences from the Tools menu to open the Preferences dialog box, click the View icon, and activate the hidden-text option in the Show area. Then click the close box to close the dialog box.

To type a program that applies a very light (2 percent) gray screen to the next paragraph in your document, follow these steps:

1. Position the insertion point at the beginning of the paragraph you want to affect.

2. Type the program, as follows:

   %Grey Screen 2%
   .para.
   .98 setgrey

   Important: At the end of each line, use the New Line command (Shift-Return) to start a new line.

3. Press Return when you finish typing the program.

4. Position the insertion point within the PostScript instructions.

5. Choose Style from the Format menu or press ⌘-T. The Style dialog box appears.

6. Activate the All Styles option, if necessary, and select PostScript in the list box.

7. Choose OK.

When you find PostScript programs that you want to use with Word, bear in mind that Word cannot process all PostScript instructions. The reason is that Word prints on the same page that PostScript does. PostScript commands that reset the printer, therefore, will cause an error, and nothing will print. Avoid using the following commands: banddevice, initmatrix, copypage, nulldevice, framedevice, grestoreall, renderbands, initgraphics, and showpage.

Appendix B
Using PostScript

Printing to a PostScript File

One of the best aspects of PostScript is that many printing machines, including high-resolution printers called *imagesetters*, recognize PostScript instructions. You can save your document as a PostScript file and give it to a graphics service bureau that specializes in high-resolution printing. (A LaserWriter prints at a resolution of 300 dots per inch, but professional equipment can print at resolutions of 1,000 dots per inch or more.)

To print your document as a PostScript file, follow these steps:

1. Choose Print from the File menu, press ⌘-P, or click the Print tool. The Print dialog box appears.

2. In the Destination area, activate the PostScript File option.

3. Choose Print. A Save dialog box appears, asking you to name the file you are creating.

4. Type a file name.

5. Choose Save.

Keyboard Shortcuts

Keyboard Shortcuts (Alphabetized by Command)

Command	Key combination
Activate Keyboard Menus	⌘-Tab
Activate Keyboard Menus	Keypad period (.)
Add to Menu	⌘-Option-equals sign (=)
Add to Menu	⌘-Shift-Option-equals sign (=)
All Caps	⌘-Shift-K
All Caps	Shift-F10
Assign to Key	⌘-Option-keypad plus sign (+)
Assign to Key	⌘-Shift-Option-←
Backspace	Delete
Bold	⌘-B
Bold	⌘-Shift-B
Bold	F10
Calculate	⌘-equals sign (=)
Cancel	Esc
Cancel	⌘-period (.)
Centered	⌘-Shift-C
Change Font	⌘-Shift-E
Change Style	⌘-Shift-S

Command	Key combination
Character...	⌘-D
Character...	F14
Close	⌘-W
Commands...	⌘-Shift-Option-C
Context-Sensitive Help	⌘-/
Copy	⌘-C
Copy	F3
Copy as Picture	⌘-Option-D
Copy Formats	⌘-Option-V
Copy Formats	Shift-F4
Copy Text	⌘-Option-C
Copy Text	Shift-F3
Cut	⌘-X
Cut	F2
Delete Forward	⌘-Option-F
Delete Forward	Delete Forward
Delete Next Word	⌘-Option-G
Delete Previous Word	⌘-Option-Delete
Delete Rows	⌘-Control-X
Document...	⌘-F14
Dotted Underline	⌘-Shift-\
Dotted Underline	Option-F12
Double Space	⌘-Shift-Y
Double Underline	⌘-Shift-[
Double Underline	Shift-F12
Down (one font size)	⌘-Shift-Option-<
Down (one font size)	⌘-[
Edit Link (QuickSwitch)	⌘-,
Edit Link (QuickSwitch)	Option-F2
Extend to Character	⌘-Option-H
Extend to Character	Keypad minus sign (-)

Appendix C
Keyboard Shortcuts

Command	Key combination
Find...	⌘-F
Find Again	⌘-Option-A
Find Again	Keypad equals sign (=)
First Line Indent	⌘-Shift-F
Footnote...	⌘-E
Footnotes	⌘-Shift-Option-S
Glossary...	⌘-K
Go Back	⌘-Option-Z
Go Back	Keypad 0
Go To...	⌘-G
Grammar...	⌘-Shift-G
Hanging Indent	⌘-Shift-T
Hidden Text	⌘-Shift-V
Hidden Text	⌘-Shift-X
Hidden Text	Option-F9
Hyphenation...	Shift-F15
Insert Formula	⌘-Option-\
Insert Glossary Entry	⌘-Delete
Insert Nonbreaking Hyphen	⌘-`
Insert Nonbreaking Space	⌘-space bar
Insert Nonbreaking Space	Option-space bar
Insert Optional Hyphen	⌘-hyphen (-)
Insert ¶ Above Row	⌘-Option-space bar
Insert Rows	⌘-Control-V
Insert Tab	Option-Tab
Insert Tab	Tab
Italic	⌘-I
Italic	⌘-Shift-I
Italic	F11
Justify	⌘-Shift-J
Justify Left	⌘-Shift-L

Appendix C
Keyboard Shortcuts

Command	Key combination
Justify Right	⌘-Shift-R
Larger Font Size	⌘-Shift-period (.)
Line Break	Shift-Return
Move Down One Text Area	⌘-Option-keypad 2
Move Left One Text Area	⌘-Option-keypad 4
Move Right One Text Area	⌘-Option-keypad 6
Move Text	⌘-Option-X
Move Text	Shift-F2
Move to Bottom of Window	End
Move to End of Document	⌘-End
Move to End of Document	⌘-keypad 3
Move to End of Line	Keypad 1
Move to First Text Area	⌘-Option-keypad 7
Move to Last Text Area	⌘-Option-keypad 1
Move to Next Character	⌘-Option-L
Move to Next Character	Keypad 6
Move to Next Character	→
Move to Next Line	⌘-Option-,
Move to Next Line	↓
Move to Next Line	Keypad 2
Move to Next Page	⌘-Page Down
Move to Next Page	Keypad 3
Move to Next Paragraph	⌘-↓
Move to Next Paragraph	⌘-keypad 2
Move to Next Paragraph	⌘-Option-B
Move to Next Sentence	⌘-keypad 1
Move to Next Text Area	⌘-Option-keypad 3
Move to Next Window	⌘-Option-W
Move to Next Word	⌘-keypad 6
Move to Next Word	⌘-Option-;
Move to Next Word	⌘-→

Appendix C
Keyboard Shortcuts

Command	Key combination
Move to Previous Cell	Shift-Tab
Move to Previous Character	⌘-Option-K
Move to Previous Character	Keypad 4
Move to Previous Character	←
Move to Previous Line	Keypad 8
Move to Previous Line	↑
Move to Previous Page	⌘-Page Up
Move to Previous Page	Keypad 9
Move to Previous Paragraph	⌘-keypad 8
Move to Previous Paragraph	⌘-Option-Y
Move to Previous Paragraph	⌘-↑
Move to Previous Sentence	⌘-keypad 7
Move to Previous Text Area	⌘-Option-keypad 9
Move to Previous Word	⌘-keypad 4
Move to Previous Word	⌘-←
Move to Previous Word	⌘-Option-J
Move to Start of Document	⌘-Home
Move to Start of Document	⌘-keypad 9
Move to Start of Line	Keypad 7
Move to Top of Window	⌘-keypad 5
Move to Top of Window	Home
Move Up One Text Area	⌘-Option-keypad 8
Nest Paragraph	⌘-Shift-N
New	⌘-N
New	F5
New Paragraph	Enter
New Paragraph	Return
New ¶ After Ins. Point	⌘-Option-Return
New ¶ with Same Style	⌘-Return
New Window	Shift-F5
No Paragraph Border	⌘-Option-1

Appendix C
Keyboard Shortcuts

Command	Key combination
Normal (View)	⌘-Option-N
Normal Paragraph	⌘-Shift-P
Open…	⌘-O
Open…	F6
Open Any File…	Shift-F6
Open Spacing	⌘-Shift-O
Outline (Format)	Shift-F11
Outline (View)	⌘-Option-O
Outline (View)	Shift-F13
Outline Command Prefix	⌘-Option-T
Outline Character (Format)	⌘-Shift-D
Page Break	Shift-Enter
Page Layout	⌘-Option-P
Page Layout	F13
Page Setup…	Shift-F8
Paragraph…	⌘-M
Paragraph…	Shift-F14
Paste	⌘-V
Paste	F4
Paste Link	Option-F4
Paste Object	⌘-F4
Paste Special Character	⌘-Option-Q
Plain Text	⌘-Shift-Z
Plain Text	Shift-F9
Print…	⌘-P
Print…	F8
Print Preview…	⌘-Option-I
Print Preview…	Option-F13
Quit	⌘-Q
Remove From Menu	⌘-Option-hyphen (-)
Renumber…	⌘-F15

Appendix C
Keyboard Shortcuts

Command	Key combination
Repeat	⌘-Y
Replace…	⌘-H
Revert To Style	⌘-Shift-space bar
Revert To Style	F9
Ribbon	⌘-Option-R
Ruler	⌘-R
Save	⌘-S
Save	F7
Save As…	Shift-F7
Scroll Line Down	⌘-Option-/
Scroll Line Down	Keypad plus sign (+)
Scroll Line Up	⌘-Option-[
Scroll Line Up	Keypad asterisk (*)
Scroll Screen Down	⌘-Option-period (.)
Scroll Screen Down	Page Down
Scroll Screen Up	Page Up
Section…	Option-F14
Section Break	⌘-Enter
Select All	⌘-A
Select All	⌘-Option-M
Shadow	⌘-Shift-W
Shadow	Option-F11
Show/Hide ¶	⌘-J
Small Caps	⌘-Shift-H
Small Caps	Option-F10
Smaller Font Size	⌘-Shift-,
Smaller Font Size	⌘-Shift-<
Spelling…	⌘-L
Spelling…	F15
Split Window	⌘-Option-S
Strikethru	⌘-Shift-/

Appendix C
Keyboard Shortcuts

Command	Key combination
Style...	⌘-T
Subscript 2 pt	⌘-Shift-hyphen (-)
Superscript 3 pt	⌘-Shift-hyphen (=)
Symbol Font	⌘-Shift-Q
Thick Paragraph Border	⌘-Option-2
Unassign Keystroke	⌘-Option-keypad minus sign (-)
Underline	⌘-Shift-U
Underline	⌘-U
Underline	F12
Undo	⌘-Z
Undo	F1
Unnest Paragraph	⌘-Shift-M
Up (one font size)	⌘-Shift-Option-<
Up (one font size)	⌘-]
Update Link	Option-F3
Word Count...	Option-F15
Word Underline	⌘-F12
Word Underline	⌘-Shift-]

Keyboard Shortcuts (Alphabetized by Key Combination)

Key combination	Command
Clear	Cancel
⌘-,	Edit Link (QuickSwitch)
⌘-hyphen (-)	Insert Optional Hyphen
⌘-period (.)	Cancel
⌘-/	Context-Sensitive Help
⌘-equals sign (=)	Calculate
⌘-[	Down

Appendix C
Keyboard Shortcuts

Key combination	Command
⌘-]	Up
⌘-`	Insert Nonbreaking Hyphen
⌘-A	Select All
⌘-B	Bold
⌘-C	Copy
⌘-D	Character…
⌘-Delete	Insert Glossary Entry
⌘-Down	Move to Next Paragraph
⌘-E	Footnote…
⌘-End	Move to End of Document
⌘-Enter	Section Break
⌘-F	Find…
⌘-F4	Paste Object
⌘-F12	Word Underline
⌘-F14	Document…
⌘-F15	Renumber…
⌘-G	Go To…
⌘-H	Replace…
⌘-Home	Move to Start of Document
⌘-I	Italic
⌘-J	Show/Hide ¶
⌘-K	Glossary…
⌘-keypad 1	Move to Next Sentence
⌘-keypad 2	Move to Next Paragraph
⌘-keypad 3	Move to End of Document
⌘-keypad 4	Move to Previous Word
⌘-keypad 5	Move to Top of Window
⌘-keypad 6	Move to Next Word
⌘-keypad 7	Move to Previous Sentence
⌘-keypad 8	Move to Previous Paragraph
⌘-keypad 9	Move to Start of Document

Appendix C
Keyboard Shortcuts

Key combination	Command
⌘-L	Spelling…
⌘-Left	Move to Previous Word
⌘-M	Paragraph…
⌘-N	New
⌘-O	Open…
⌘-Option-'	More Keyboard Prefix
⌘-Option-,	Move to Next Line
⌘-Option-hyphen (-)	Remove From Menu
⌘-Option-period (.)	Scroll Screen Down
⌘-Option-/	Scroll Line Down
⌘-Option-;	Move to Next Word
⌘-Option-equals sign (=)	Add to Menu
⌘-Option-[	Scroll Line Up
⌘-Option-\	Insert Formula
⌘-Option-1	No Paragraph Border
⌘-Option-2	Thick Paragraph Border
⌘-Option-A	Find Again
⌘-Option-B	Move to Next Paragraph
⌘-Option-C	Copy Text
⌘-Option-D	Copy as Picture
⌘-Option-Delete	Delete Previous Word
⌘-Option-F	Delete Forward
⌘-Option-G	Delete Next Word
⌘-Option-H	Extend to Character
⌘-Option-I	Print Preview…
⌘-Option-J	Move to Previous Word
⌘-Option-K	Move to Previous Character
⌘-Option-keypad plus sign (+)	Assign to Key
⌘-Option-keypad minus sign (-)	Unassign Keystroke
⌘-Option-keypad 1	Move to Last Text Area
⌘-Option-keypad 2	Move Down One Text Area

Appendix C
Keyboard Shortcuts

Key combination	Command
⌘-Option-keypad 3	Move to Next Text Area
⌘-Option-keypad 4	Move Left One Text Area
⌘-Option-keypad 6	Move Right One Text Area
⌘-Option-keypad 7	Move to First Text Area
⌘-Option-keypad 8	Move Up One Text Area
⌘-Option-keypad 9	Move to Previous Text Area
⌘-Option-L	Move to Next Character
⌘-Option-M	Select All
⌘-Option-N	Normal (View)
⌘-Option-O	Outline (View)
⌘-Option-P	Page Layout
⌘-Option-Q	Paste Special Character
⌘-Option-R	Ribbon
⌘-Option-Return	New ¶ After Ins. Point
⌘-Option-S	Split Window
⌘-Option-space bar	Insert ¶ Above Row
⌘-Option-T	Outline Command Prefix
⌘-Option-V	Copy Formats
⌘-Option-W	Move to Next Window
⌘-Option-X	Move Text
⌘-Option-Y	Move to Previous Paragraph
⌘-Option-Z	Go Back
⌘-P	Print…
⌘-Page Down	Move to Next Page
⌘-Page Up	Move to Previous Page
⌘-Q	Quit
⌘-R	Ruler
⌘-Return	New ¶ with Same Style
⌘-Right	Move to Next Word
⌘-S	Save
⌘-Shift-,	Smaller Font Size
⌘-Shift- hyphen (-)	Subscript 2 pt

Appendix C
Keyboard Shortcuts

Key combination	Command
⌘-Shift-period (.)	Larger Font Size
⌘-Shift-/	Strikethru
⌘-Shift-<	Smaller Font Size
⌘-Shift-=	Superscript 3 pt
⌘-Shift->	Larger Font Size
⌘-Shift-[	Double Underline
⌘-Shift-\	Dotted Underline
⌘-Shift-]	Word Underline
⌘-Shift-B	Bold
⌘-Shift-C	Centered
⌘-Shift-D	Outline (Format)
⌘-Shift-E	Change Font
⌘-Shift-F	First Line Indent
⌘-Shift-G	Grammar…
⌘-Shift-H	Small Caps
⌘-Shift-I	Italic
⌘-Shift-J	Justified
⌘-Shift-K	All Caps
⌘-Shift-L	Flush Left
⌘-Shift-M	Unnest Paragraph
⌘-Shift-N	Nest Paragraph
⌘-Shift-O	Open Spacing
⌘-Shift-Option-<	Down (one font size)
⌘-Shift-Option-<	Up (one font size)
⌘-Shift-Option-=	Add to Menu
⌘-Shift-Option-C	Commands…
⌘-Shift-Option-Left	Assign to Key
⌘-Shift-Option-S	Footnotes
⌘-Shift-P	Normal Paragraph
⌘-Shift-Q	Symbol Font
⌘-Shift-R	Flush Right
⌘-Shift-S	Change Style

Appendix C
Keyboard Shortcuts

Key combination	Command
⌘-Shift-space bar	Revert To Style
⌘-Shift-T	Hanging Indent
⌘-Shift-U	Underline
⌘-Shift-V	Hidden Text
⌘-Shift-W	Shadow
⌘-Shift-X	Hidden Text
⌘-Shift-Y	Double Space
⌘-Shift-Z	Plain Text
⌘-space bar	Insert Nonbreaking Space
⌘-T	Style…
⌘-Tab	Activate Keyboard Menus
⌘-U	Underline
⌘-Up	Move to Previous Paragraph
⌘-V	Paste
⌘-W	Close
⌘-X	Cut
⌘-Y	Repeat
⌘-Z	Undo
⌘-Control-V	Insert Rows
⌘-Control-X	Delete Rows
Delete	Delete Forward
Delete	Backspace
Down	Move to Next Line
End	Move to Bottom of Window
Enter	New Paragraph
F1	Undo
F2	Cut
F3	Copy
F4	Paste
F5	New
F6	Open…

Appendix C
Keyboard Shortcuts

Key combination	Command
F7	Save
F8	Print…
F9	Revert To Style
F10	Bold
F11	Italic
F12	Underline
F13	Page Layout
F14	Character…
F15	Spelling…
Help	Context-Sensitive Help
Home	Move to Top of Window
Keypad period (.)	Activate Keyboard Menus
Keypad asterisk (*)	Scroll Line Up
Keypad plus sign (+)	Scroll Line Down
Keypad minus sign (-)	Extend to Character
Keypad equals sign (=)	Find Again
Keypad 0	Go Back
Keypad 1	Move to End of Line
Keypad 2	Move to Next Line
Keypad 3	Move to Next Page
Keypad 4	Move to Previous Character
Keypad 6	Move to Next Character
Keypad 7	Move to Start of Line
Keypad 8	Move to Previous Line
Keypad 9	Move to Previous Page
Left	Move to Previous Character
Option-F2	Edit Link (QuickSwitch)
Option-F3	Update Link
Option-F4	Paste Link
Option-F9	Hidden Text
Option-F10	Small Caps

Appendix C
Keyboard Shortcuts

Key combination	Command
Option-F11	Shadow
Option-F12	Dotted Underline
Option-F13	Print Preview…
Option-F14	Section…
Option-F15	Word Count…
Option-space bar	Insert Nonbreaking Space
Option-Tab	Insert Tab in Table
Page Down	Scroll Screen Down
Page Up	Scroll Screen Up
Return	New Paragraph
Right	Move to Next Character
Shift-Enter	Page Break
Shift-F2	Move Text
Shift-F3	Copy Text
Shift-F4	Copy Formats
Shift-F5	New Window
Shift-F6	Open Any File…
Shift-F7	Save As…
Shift-F8	Page Setup…
Shift-F9	Plain Text
Shift-F10	All Caps
Shift-F11	Outline (Format)
Shift-F12	Double Underline
Shift-F13	Outline (View)
Shift-F14	Paragraph…
Shift-F15	Hyphenation…
Shift-Return	Line Break
Shift-Tab	Move to Previous Cell
Tab	Insert Tab
Up	Move to Previous Line

Appendix C

Keyboard Shortcuts

Index

Index

Index

Index

Index

D

Index

Index

Index

G

Index

H

Index

S

Index

Index